Abilities, Motivation, and Methodology

The Minnesota Symposium on Learning and Individual Differences

Abilities, Motivation, and Methodology

The Minnesota Symposium
on Learning and Individual Differences

Edited by

Ruth Kanfer
Phillip L. Ackerman
Robert Cudeck

University of Minnesota

1989

LAWRENCE ERLBAUM ASSOCIATES, PUBLISHERS
Hillsdale, New Jersey   Hove and London

Lawrence Erlbaum Associates, Inc., Publishers
365 Broadway
Hillsdale, New Jersey 07642

848 33281

Library of Congress Cataloging in Publication Data

Minnesota Symposium on Learning and Individual Differences (1988 :
  Minneapolis, Minn.)
    Abilities, motivation,a nd methodology / the Minneapolis Symposium
  on Learning and Individual Differences ; edited by Ruth Kanfer,
  Phillip L. Ackerman, Robert Cudeck.
      p.   cm.
    ISBN 0-8058-0495-1. — ISBN 0-8058-0496-X (pbk.)
    1. Learning, Psychology of—Congresses.   2. Individual
  differences—Congresses.   I. Kanfer, Ruth.   II. Ackerman, Phillip
  Lawrence, 1957–   .   III. Cudeck, Robert.   IV. Title.
  BF318.M56   1988   89-17153
  153.1'5—dc20   CIP

Printed in the United States of America

10   9   8   7   6   5   4   3   2   1

To

Fred and Ruby
(R.K.)

Leonard and Sally Ann
(P.L.A.)

Trisha
(R.C.)

Contents

List of Contributors

Phillip L. Ackerman
Department of Psychology
University of Minnesota

Jack A. Adams
Department of Psychology
University of Illinois at Urbana-
Champaign

K. A. Brookhuis
Institute for Experimental Psychology
University of Groningen

John B. Carroll
Department of Psychology
University of North Carolina at
Chapel Hill

Robert Cudeck
Department of Psychology
University of Minnesota

Jan-Eric Gustafsson
Department of Education
University of Göteborg

Earl B. Hunt
Department of Psychology
University of Washington

James J. Jenkins
Department of Psychology
University of South Florida

Ruth Kanfer
Department of Psychology
University of Minnesota

Uwe Kleinbeck
Department of Psychology
Bergische University

Kristina Kraska
Department of Psychology
University of Osnabrück

Julius Kuhl
Department of Psychology
University of Osnabrück

Patrick C. Kyllonen
Air Force Human Resources
Laboratory
Brooks Air Force Base

David F. Lohman
College of Education
The University of Iowa

J. J. McArdle
Department of Psychology
University of Virginia

William E. Montague
Training Technology Department
Navy Personnel Research &
Development Center

Gijsbertus Mulder
Institute for Experimental Psychology
University of Groningen

L. J. M. Mulder
Institute for Experimental Psychology
University of Groningen

J. Bruce Overmier
Center for Research in Learning,
Perception, and Cognition
University of Minnesota

James W. Pellegrino
Department of Education
University of California, Santa
Barbara

Hans-Henning Quast
Department of Psychology
Bergische University

William Revelle
Department of Psychology
Northwestern University

Ronald Schwarz
Department of Psychology
Bergische University

H. G. O. M. Smid
Institute for Experimental Psychology
University of Groningen

Richard E. Snow
School of Education
Stanford University

A. A. Wijers
Institute for Experimental Psychology
University of Groningen

Dan J. Woltz
Air Force Human Resources
Laboratory
Brooks Air Force Base

Penny Yee
Department of Psychology
University of Washington

Preface

The challenge to the unification of experimental and differential disciplines of psychology is nowhere more salient than in the field of learning and individual differences. Diverse developments in ability research, in motivation research, and in the derivations of new methodological techniques have too often proceeded on parallel courses. In the past 3 years, discussions among the editors of this volume and our discussions with several other concerned scientists gradually led to the notion that communication across domains could be vastly improved through intensive interaction between researchers. With the encouragement of Professor J. Bruce Overmier, the Director of the University of Minnesota Center for Research in Learning, Perception, and Cognition, and the enthusiastic support of Dr. Barbara McDonald at the U.S. Navy Personnel Research and Development Center, plans were made to convene a symposium where researchers with varied perspectives on learning and individual differences could share their respective theories and empirical research in an environment that would foster critically needed cross-fertilization and integration.

On April 14, 1988, 16 distinguished scholars from Europe, Scandinavia, and the United States, serving as participants and discussants, and over 60 local, national, and international observers gathered in Minneapolis, Minnesota for a 2½-day symposium on ability, motivation, and methodology concerns relating to learning and individual differences. Prior to the symposium, the participants had prepared and circulated advance papers that concerned several facets of the topic. The symposium was devoted to the reading and discussion of these papers. Following the conference, the participants were given a chance to finalize their papers for inclusion in this volume. In addition, we compiled and edited transcriptions of the spontaneous discussions among the participants and observers recorded during the conference. This volume represents an amalgamation of these two sources. Each chapter contains the final text produced by the participants and their collaborators, immediately followed by edited discussions concerning each chapter. The resulting product provides a vivid point and counterpoint when paradigms clash, and lively illustrations of how researchers successfully struggle to make needed points of contact across disciplines.

This volume is organized into five parts, each dealing with a major theme of the conference. Part I represents the opening session of the conference. The chapters in this section provide an orientation to the treatment of learning and individual differences from three major perspectives: experimental psychology (Adams), motivational psychology (Kleinbeck), and differential/methodological psychology (Carroll). The panoramic approach taken in these chapters provides the context for consideration of theoretical and empirical developments described in later chapters. Specifically, each chapter, and the discussions following the chapters, highlights controversy and consensus surrounding interdisciplinary approaches to learning and individual differences. These issues reappear throughout the remainder of the chapters.

In chapter 1, Jack Adams reviews several fundamental issues of learning and individual differences. He moves from a description of enduring questions in learning and variability research from the early 1900s to ability-performance research from the 1950s, and concludes with a look at current problems and challenges for integration of experimental and differential psychologies in the 1990s. The discussion following Adams' chapter directly pits the experimental and correlational approaches against one another and sets the stage for several interactions that can be found throughout this volume.

Uwe Kleinbeck and his colleagues Hans-Henning Quast and Ronald Schwarz (chap. 2) discuss motivational and volitional concepts from a dual-task perspective. These authors introduce many information processing concepts and experimental procedures used in the investigation of volitional processes. Kleinbeck and his colleagues illustrate the potential advantages of coordinating motivational and information processing frameworks in the context of empirical studies in cognition and motivation.

In chapter 3, Jack Carroll offers a critical overview of the cognitive/intellectual ability domain from a factor-analytic perspective. In this chapter, Carroll describes the results of an ongoing project aimed at integrating several decades of inquiry into the structure and development of individual differences in abilities. He provides a valuable overview of the corpus of factor analytic ability research, and presents a map of well-defined and well-replicated abilities representing the cumulative accomplishments of ability theory, empirical data, and quantitative methodological advances.

Part II of this volume continues and expands the discussion of quantitative methodology and applications to learning and individual differences. In chapter 4, Jack McArdle presents a mathematical and empirical tour of a multivariate experimental approach and its implications for the study learning and individual differences. Specifically, McArdle describes a unique framework for considering growth functions (for groups, for individuals, and for several different variables) that is based on developments in structural equation modeling.

Another important methodological issue in the design and evaluation of experiments on information processing constructs pertains to the choice of meaningful and appropriate performance measures. In chapter 5, Dave Lohman presents a compelling set of arguments and evidence for a reconsideration of *speed* and *accuracy* constructs as they affect the adequacy of performance measures. In addition, Lohman describes a set of experimental procedures that may be used to efficiently derive speed-accuracy tradeoff functions for information processing tasks. As indicated in Lohman's chapter, this perspective has direct implications for discovering individual differences constructs that pertain to sex differences in spatial abilities and to cognitive style issues.

The section on methodological developments concludes with a commentary by Bob Cudeck (chap. 6). In this chapter, Cudeck presents a factor analytic framework that abstracts the context of the earlier chapters, and draws together a number of related issues raised by Carroll, McArdle, and Lohman.

Part III of this book is devoted primarily to developments in the cognitive ability domain. The first chapter in this section (chap. 7) describes the efforts of Jim Pellegrino, Buz Hunt, and Penny Yee in their search for *information coordination abilities*. Pellegrino and his colleagues focus on dynamic spatial abilities and describe the development of new procedures to assess and model a class of abilities that influence efficient performance of multiple-interrelated tasks. In a notable departure from classic dual-task investigations, these authors demonstrate how the boundaries of contemporary ability theory can be expanded with a transition from classic paper and pencil testing to the use of microcomputer technology.

In chapter 8, Jan-Eric Gustafsson discusses issues involved in integration of hierarchical factor analysis/structural equation techniques with aptitude-treatment interaction (ATI) investigations. Gustafsson describes the results of a series of ATI studies using sophisticated hierarchical factor analytic procedures. His findings indicate that important ATIs can be revealed from educational-instructional manipulations, when attention is accorded to the structure of higher-order intellectual abilities.

Another modern approach, emphasizing the unification of cognitive ability and information-processing perspectives in skill acquisition, is provided by Pat Kyllonen and Dan Woltz (chap. 9). Kyllonen and Woltz propose the use of a four-source framework for determining individual differences in skill and knowledge acquisition. These four sources of general cognitive factors include *knowledge, skills, processing capacity,* and *processing speed.* They describe ongoing investigations on these sources of individual differences at the Air Force Human Resources Laboratory—Learning Abilities Measurement Program. Finally, they indicate how these concepts fit within modern theories of cognitive abilities and theories of skill acquisition.

Part III concludes with commentary by Phil Ackerman (chap. 10). Ackerman discusses the historical context of ability research concerned with individual differences in learning and the points of contact between differential and information processing approaches to common issues. He indicates several ways that contemporary developments in the cognitive ability domain contribute to the interdisciplinary enterprise and identifies promising developments described in previous chapters. In addition, Ackerman relates a number of issues raised in this section to methodological and substantive issues raised elsewhere in this volume.

Part IV addresses the impact of non-cognitive, personal constructs (personality and conation) on learning and performance. In chapter 11, Bill Revelle provides a broad overview of the relations between individual differences in personality, the conative construct of arousal, and information processing components involved in learning. Revelle's conceptual and empirical organization of information processing components and tasks further draws together cognitive and non-cognitive perspectives in a way that suggests when and how conative and personality variables affect learning.

Julius Kuhl and his colleague Kristina Kraska (chap. 12) discuss the structure of self-regulation and individual differences in the development and use of metamotivational strategies. In the model proposed by these authors, volitional processes are described within an information-processing framework that includes affective responses. Kuhl and Kraska report evidence indicating the developmental course of metamotivational knowledge and they discuss the impact of metamotivational knowledge on performance in conflict situations. Their results provide an intriguing opportunity for reconsideration of the relations between metamotivational knowledge and individual differences in cognitive abilities.

Part IV concludes with a commentary by Ruth Kanfer (chap. 13). In this chapter, Kanfer discusses the import of the newer conative approaches in the broader context of motivational psychology, and in the study of individual differences in learning. This commentary attempts to clarify the boundaries of non-cognitive concepts, such as personality, volition, and motivation, as they are applied to the learning domain. Kanfer derives implications of recent advances in the non-cognitive domains that further unify cognitive ability, personality, and motivation streams of research; and she presents a research agenda for research programs aimed at integrating the non-cognitive and cognitive, information processing domains.

Part V contains chapters from the closing session of the conference. The chapters in this section represent both retrospective and forward-looking views of individual differences and learning. One very promising perspective stems from recent developments in psychophysiological research. In chapter 14, Bert Mulder and his colleagues (chap. 14) describe a program of research that concentrates on identification of brain and peripheral psychophysiological correlates of computational processes such as encoding and cognitive resource allocation. Mulder and his colleagues review a program of research concerning the mapping of task information processing demands to corresponding brain and behavioral variables. This approach, fusing advanced electrophysiological techniques with more traditional behavioral measures in an experimental paradigm, provides a wealth of new opportunities for identification and organization of individual difference constructs that affect learning.

In chapter 15, Dick Snow provides an analytical overview of past developments and present trends in research on cognitive-conative aptitude interactions. Adopting an aptitude-treatment interaction perspective, Snow relates previous research on cognitive-aptitude treatment interactions to the cognitive aptitude construct domain. Snow concentrates on the neglected research domain that includes conative-aptitudes as elements of ATIs. He describes several recent studies that provide promising directions for future ATI research. Based on this overview, Snow suggests an integrative ATI framework that coordinates cognitive and conative domains.

In the final chapter of this volume (chap. 16), Jim Jenkins gives closing comments on the conference and addresses several of the larger issues facing researchers (of all perspectives) concerned with the study of learning and individual differences. Jenkins responds to the long-standing concern over the relative efficacy of experimental versus correlational approaches by vividly describing how both approaches are necessary, and neither approach is alone sufficient, for continuing progress in learning and individual differences. Jenkins identifies and illustrates the importance of several specific cautions for each approach, and argues in favor of a more thoughtful delineation of one's objectives in the conduct of both types of research.

The successful completion of a project such as this one is due to the labors of many individuals and organizations. We are grateful for the financial support that allowed The Minnesota Symposium on Learning and Individual Differences to come about. Funds for the symposium were provided by the U.S. Office of Naval Research (ONR) Cognitive Science Program and the Navy Personnel Research and Development Center (NPRDC), and by several organizations at the University of Minnesota, including the Graduate School, College of Liberal Arts, Department of Professional Development, and Continuing Education and Extension. We also want to acknowledge the moral and scientific support provided by the Center for Research in Learning, Perception, and Cognition (CRLPC)—an interdisciplinary unit at the University that provides an ideal environment for scientific interchange across areas. Many individuals in these organizations were especially helpful to the project. We especially wish to acknowledge Dr. Barbara McDonald at NPRDC, Dr. Susan Chipman, the Cognitive Science Program Manager at ONR, Professor J. Bruce Overmier of the

CRLPC, and Ms. Lyn Diaz from the Department of Professional Development. Most of all, we thank the participants in the symposium, who provided thoughtful and incisive discussion throughout the conference, much of which we have recorded in this volume.

Ruth Kanfer
Phillip L. Ackerman
Robert Cudeck

Prolegomenon

J. Bruce Overmier
University of Minnesota

William E. Montague
Navy Personnel Research & Development Center

James J. Jenkins
University of South Florida

A little over 30 years ago Lee Cronbach published a seminal article in which he challenged psychologists to *integrate* the two disjoint disciplines of differential and experimental psychology. Cronbach specifically called for the study of the interactions between individual differences variables (aptitudes) and experimental manipulations (or treatments). Such interactions have become generically known to differential, educational, industrial/organizational, personality, and experimental psychologists as aptitude-treatment interactions. Following the appearance of Cronbach's article, several researchers turned their attention to this area. Some of the most significant discussions emerging from this area have pertained to the study of *individual differences in learning.*

The task at hand has not been an easy one, though. An early conference in 1965 on these issues held at the University of Pittsburgh (R. M. Gagné, Editor, *Learning and Individual Differences.* Columbus, Ohio: Charles E. Merrill) paved the way for later advances in research in this area, and anticipated many subsequent developments in the information processing approach to human abilities. Other conferences have looked specifically at relevant methodological issues, such as the one at the University of Wisconsin in 1962 (C. W. Harris, Editor, *Problems in Measuring Change,* Madison, Wisconsin: University of Wisconsin).

Although there has been substantial growth during the past decade in research concerned with ability, motivation, and methodological approaches to learning and individual differences, much of this research has developed along parallel tracks, with too limited interaction between researchers who investigate related topics. However, guided by contemporary theories of cognition from the mid-1970s, many productive research programs have been initiated in psychology and related fields (namely, experimental-cognitive psychology, differential psychology, curriculum and instruction, organizational behavior, industrial training, and so on). The commonality of underlying theories and the further common ground of methodological tools for assessing individual differences in change and growth, illustrate the potential for bringing these related areas together. Clearly, there are theoretical, methodological, and practical benefits to be gained by studying, discussing, and attempting to integrate these varied developments. The purpose of this book is to move toward realization of these benefits by directing researchers to consider their findings in the larger domain of learning and individual differences.

There has also been increasing recognition of how an integrative focus might benefit those persons involved with instruction and training. An abiding concern among organizational personnel is the development of appropriate instructional technologies for persons of differing ability levels and profiles. Aptitude-treatment interaction frameworks provide a common ground for linking theoretical advances with development of efficient innovations in instructional technologies.

The continuing need for knowledge that can be applied to real-world settings provides basic research efforts with a powerful set of motives and a general sense of the directions and objectives that such research should strive to address. In the U.S. Navy, for example, over 7,000 different courses are taught each year to about 900,000 students. In this setting, theory-based knowledge about the influence of particular types of instruction on individuals of differing abilities is of critical importance. Such knowledge may have far-reaching implications for organizations that build and implement instructional programs affecting large numbers of people. The chapters of this book describe research efforts informed by developments in methodology, and in substantive theories. Particular attention is directed toward the study of interdependencies among ability and motivational aspects of the learning process. The text and interspersed discussions provide promising avenues for understanding and effectively managing aptitude differences in diverse learning environments.

The conference that spawned the chapters and discussion in this volume was enormously intellectually stimulating. The resulting product could not have been accomplished without careful attention to the academic orientation and diverse mixture of participants. In particular, we wish to thank Drs. Ackerman, Kanfer, and Cudeck for bringing these participants and areas of inquiry together, and for providing an ideal setting for the interchange of ideas and data. If we could be assured that every conference would be as well-organized, comfortable, and provocative as this one, we would volunteer to go to conferences all the time.

On a personal note, the conference from which this volume emerged has special meaning for one of us (Jim Jenkins), who spent 34 years on the psychology faculty at the University of Minnesota. The Graduate School's co-sponsorship of this event, held as part of the celebration of the centennial of the Graduate School at the University of Minnesota, reflects a continuing commitment to facilitating and promoting psychological research. The Graduate School at the University of Minnesota is not a passive collection of administrators and it is not simply another organization for pushing paper around. The Graduate School is a dynamic force that plays a very important role in the lives of many graduate students and faculty members at the University. The importance of the Graduate School in furthering research is perhaps best illustrated by Jim's early experience at Minnesota.

Thirty eight years ago, Jim and several other members of the Department of Psychology applied for and received unique support—a grant from a federal agency! This sounds routine now, but at the time few psychology researchers had ever held such a grant. (One must remember that this was in the ancient days before federal grants had such an important role in supporting academic research.) Jim's grant was for basic research on language processes under the Office of Naval Research, which was then laying the groundwork for the National Science Foundation. No one knew quite how to handle this new development. The problem was solved by channeling everything through the Graduate School. The Graduate School did all the paperwork and showed Jim and his colleagues how to manage the grant. Furthermore, the Graduate School supported Jim and several of the younger faculty members in summer sessions so that they could prepare publications and technical reports that would carry the fruits of their research to the field at-large. These efforts finally resulted in the Center for Research in Human Learning (now called the Center for Research in Learning, Perception, and Cognition), which itself was seeded in part by the Graduate School and now by the College of Liberal Arts.

This kind of support does not happen automatically; as faculty from many universities can testify, it is not by any means a simple consequence of having a graduate school. These benefits can only flow from organizations that deeply understand academic values and goals and from those that have the maturity, the resources and the good will towards the graduate students and the faculty that has been true at the University of Minnesota. As the chapters in this volume attest, long-standing commitments by several other organizational units and agencies, in particular, the University of Minnesota College of Liberal Arts and the Center for Research in Learning, Perception, and Cognition, the U.S. Office of Naval Research, and the Navy Personnel Research and Development Center, foster the conditions that make it possible for researchers to develop an integrative and cumulative perspective on topics as central to the field of psychology as learning and individual differences.

I
HISTORICAL PERSPECTIVES

1

Historical Background and Appraisal of Research on Individual Differences in Learning

Jack A. Adams
University of Illinois at Urbana-Champaign

Except for a small band of theoreticians, some of whom are among us, the field of differential psychology is a pragmatic undertaking. The contributions of some other applied areas of psychology are arguable, but not those of differential psychology. A selection test of modest validity will improve the quality of a workforce. Achievement tests in our schools, and tests in the hands of clinicians and counselors, are valued diagnostic instruments. Testing is one of psychology's success stories.

Why should I bother to review individual differences and learning if differential psychology is successful without much attention to it? There are two reasons:

1. As a practical matter, the power of a test to predict a criterion changes with training on the criterion. An aircrew test battery might be validated against success in primary flight school. The predictive power of the battery will not be the same when the criterion is success in advanced flight training. The rank ordering of individuals changes with practice. Psychological testing will be even a bigger success story when learning and individual differences are understood better.

2. In terms of basic science, differential psychology and experimental psychology have long gone their separate ways, to the detriment of both. Boring, in his classic work *A history of experimental psychology,* appears to have been the first to address the separation of the two psychologies (Boring, 1929, pp. 545–549). James McKeen Cattell was a U.S. experimental psychologist who was trained in Europe at the end of the 19th century, when laboratory psychology was beginning. Cattell had turned some of his research with Wundt in Germany toward studies of individual differences, and Cattell had also worked with Galton

in England. When Cattell returned to the United States, the tests of individual differences that he used were simple sensori-motor tests of the kind found in the newly created psychological laboratories, so the study of individual differences and experimental psychology co-existed in the beginning. This effort did not go mainstream in psychology, Boring believed, because of the mistaken belief that simple sensori-motor tests would measure higher mental functions of the kind required in practical situations like schools. Cognitive tests like those developed by Binet came to dominate, and differential psychology and experimental psychology parted. In more recent times, in the 1950s, analysts lamented the parting and have said that a reunion would work to the scientific advancement of both disciplines (Cronbach, 1957; Ferguson, 1954, 1956; Travers, 1954, 1955, 1956). I acknowledge that differential psychology and experimental psychology have gone their own ways, but my historical review will show that there has been an effort in the field of learning over the past 80 years to close the gap.

My frame of reference is the experimental psychology of learning and how variables from differential psychology have been related to it. Glaser (1967) reviewed some of the earlier literature and had the same frame of reference. Learning in school situations is omitted.

To keep things straight, I refer to laboratory situations, such as a learning task, as *tasks,* and psychological tests, such as an arithmetic printed test, as *tests.* The distinction is traditional, not conceptual. Both tests and tasks elicit responses under controlled conditions, but their roles have been different. Tests, for example, have been used as measures of abilities to predict performances in tasks and to infer about the abilities required by them, as I discuss.

LEARNING AND VARIABILITY

Edward L. Thorndike was a dominant figure in the psychology of learning for a long time, and it was he who began systematic research on individual differences and learning. Thorndike went from Harvard University, where William James was a dominant influence on him (Boring & Boring, 1948), to doctoral work at Columbia University under James McKeen Cattell. Thorndike's doctoral dissertation on animal learning (Thorndike, 1898) was directed by James McKeen Cattell, although Thorndike came from Harvard with the plan in hand so Cattell's supervision was only occasional (Jonçich, 1968, p. 121). Thorndike, however, was required to take Cattell's seminar where graduate student research plans were presented for Cattell's commentary, and it was here that the influence of Cattell on him was more frequent and direct (Jonçich, 1968, p. 121). Given his training with Cattell, who was a pioneer of research on individual differences, and given his interest in learning, it is not surprising that Thorndike turned to research on individual differences and learning when he left comparative psychology and shifted to human learning and education.

Thorndike (1908) published a paper that influenced many studies on variability in individual differences during learning, one as recent as 1987 (Ackerman, 1987). The task that Thorndike used was the multiplication of three-place numbers, which shows learning effects in college students. His empirical findings might have been passed over if he had not given them a nature–nurture interpretation. He reasoned that individual differences should decrease with training if differences at the start are differences attributable to pre-experimental training that transfers to the experimental task. If, however, individual differences remain as large as ever with training, then the differences are inherited because training has had no effect on them. Thorndike found that variability increased with training. Nature triumphs over nurture, Thorndike concluded. The implication was that the differences among students with varied backgrounds will not go away with education. Differences among workers will not go away with training on the job. We in the United States like to think that education and training will make us all the same, and we are uncomfortable when we are told that this may not be so. Reed, who was an investigator of this topic, said, "If our great system of public education will have the result of increasing the social, political and economic inequalities between individuals, then it fails in one of its major purposes" (1931, p. 1).

The studies that followed Thorndike's were a mix of tasks and measures, as might be expected, so Kincaid (1925) reanalyzed 24 of them with the same seven methods of analysis. Although the correlations between initial and final performance on learning tasks were found to be positive, the variances decreased, and she concluded that Thorndike was wrong. Reed (1931) was not satisfied with all of Kincaid's seven measures, so he reanalyzed the data of 58–70 experiments with three measures that he found defensible, and he concluded, along with Kincaid, that variability decreases with practice. Within the framework of his theoretical thinking about individual differences and information processing, Ackerman (1987) reanalyzed reaction time data in the 24 studies that were analyzed by Kincaid. He concluded the same: Variability decreases with practice.

So, the opening round for individual differences and learning was lost by Thorndike and won by Kincaid, Reed, and Ackerman. The round was won on points, not a knockout. Individual differences do not disappear with training because the correlation between initial and final scores on a learning task is positive, but the variability of scores does decrease. We tend to become more alike with training, not different. The reason for this is that low-ability subjects are more variable with practice than high-ability subjects. With Reynolds (Adams, 1957; Reynolds & Adams, 1954), I compared subjects on two psychomotor tasks who had been in the top and bottom deciles at the start of training— widely separated by 80% of their peers. Low-ability subjects were more variable than high-ability subjects, with the two distributions overlapping at the end of training. The variance of the group as a whole decreased with training because some of the low-ability subjects came to perform the same as high-ability subjects. The finding is robust. Ackerman (1986, 1987) found the same. If a hope of public education is that some low achievers will benefit disproportionately once given the opportunity to learn, then there is support from experimental data.

INTELLIGENCE AND THE ABILITY TO LEARN

The General Classification Test is a group intelligence test that was used as a selection device by the U.S. military in World War I. The military were assured that the test measured intelligence *and* the ability to learn (Woodrow, 1946). The military were told what we all believe: Bright people learn faster, whatever the situation. To assert otherwise defies our perceptions, and yet investigators have had a hard time demonstrating a positive relationship between intelligence and learning rate.

The main research approach has been to relate measures of acquisition rate in learning tasks to scores on intelligence tests, although other tests might be included also. The hypothesis was not that intelligence tests would predict performance on a learning task; that would be trite because many tests do that to some degree. Rather, the hypotheses were that: (a) intelligence tests would predict learning rate for *all* learning tasks, (b) measures of learning rate would correlate positively across learning tasks, and (c) factor analysis would establish a factor common to the rate measures. Two measures of learning rate were used in the studies: (a) gain, as the difference between initial and final score on a learning task, and (b) value of the rate parameter when a function was fitted to an individual's learning data.

Woodrow was an influential figure who appeared in this field in the 1930s and who anticipated many of the research questions and methods. In one of his studies (Woodrow, 1938a), gain scores were used from seven learning tasks that were each given 6.5 hours of practice. Examples of the tasks were horizontal adding where three- to seven-place numbers for addition were placed in a row, and anagrams; Woodrow's learning tasks were printed tasks, not apparatus tasks. Intelligence tests, along with other tests, were the reference battery. The scores from the reference battery, along with gain scores from the learning tasks and the initial and final scores on which they were based, were all intercorrelated and factor analyzed. Woodrow failed to find a factor common to the seven gain scores; gain scores were poorly related among themselves. Nor did the gain scores correlate appreciably with the intelligence tests. Woodrow had the same negative findings in a similar study in which 3–11 hours of practice were given on four learning tasks (Woodrow, 1939b). Simrall (1947) was a student of Woodrow's, and she drew the same conclusion from her research. Relying mostly on these data, Woodrow wrote a visible article in the *Psychological Review* which said that there was no general ability to learn (Woodrow, 1946).

What is wrong with these studies is that gain scores have two problems. One problem is that gain can be a notoriously unreliable measure (McNemar, 1962, pp. 155–158; Tilton, 1949), and its use is not recommended (Cronbach & Furby, 1970). Unreliability could be the reason for the low correlation of intelligence tests with gain scores. A second problem is the possibility that pre-experimental experience transfers to the experimental task (Woodrow, 1938b, p. 276). Some subjects could perform well because of relevant pre-experimental experience, and they show little gain with practice on the task because increments would be small per unit of practice with negatively accelerated learning curves. Low-performing subjects could have a larger gain score simply because they had less relevant pre-experimental experience and are at an earlier stage of their learning curves where increments are larger. The variability in gain scores introduced by amounts of pertinent pre-experimental experience could obscure any effects of intelligence.

A curve-fitting approach was seen as an alternative to gain scores, and here again Woodrow pioneered (Woodrow, 1940). Using data from two previous studies (Woodrow, 1938a, 1939b), Woodrow fit a curve to the learning data of each subject for each task. The value for the rate parameter was determined for the function. Values for the rate parameter should correlate with intelligence test scores and with each other if there is a general learning ability. The results were negative.

Other major studies using curve fitting were by Allison (1960) and Stake (1961). These experiments had bigger scope than Woodrow's, with a number of learning tasks, a big reference test battery, and factor analysis of it all, but bigger isn't better. The unnoticed problem with both of these studies is that only a few minutes of practice were given on each of the learning tasks, so very little learning could have taken place. It is unlikely that good estimates of the learning rate parameter were possible, and so the findings are questionable. Woodrow, an experimental psychologist with a feel for learning, gave hours of practice.

In summary, some of this research on intelligence and ability to learn is flawed. Some of the findings are negative, with no relationship between intelligence and ability to learn, and maybe this is the correct conclusion. There is an inescapable feeling from this literature, however, that a fresh look at the topic with modern knowledge and know-how would be informative.

FACTOR ANALYSIS AND LEARNING

The research on factor analysis and learning used one or more learning tasks and a reference test battery. The factors, anchored by the test battery, were to explain the abilities of the learning task and how they were affected by practice.

The correlation coefficient was the way that individual differences in a learning task were expressed. Trial scores were intercorrelated, and the intercorrelations became the data. The intercorrelation matrix for trial scores has a special

TABLE 1.1
The Simplex Pattern:
Hypothetical Intercorrelations
of Scores on Five Learning Trials

		Trials				
		1	2	3	4	5
	1		.80	.75	.65	.50
	2			.85	.75	.45
Trials	3				.90	.55
	4					.95
	5					

form that is called the *superdiagonal matrix,* or the *simplex pattern.* Table 1.1 illustrates the simplex with hypothetical correlation coefficients. The orderliness of the simplex suggests an orderliness of individual differences in learning to be explained. The simplex has three empirical characteristics: (a) all correlations are positive, (b) adjacent trials have relatively high correlations, and (c) correlations decrease with remoteness of trials. Learning data are not alone in showing the simplex pattern. Other kinds of data that occur successively over time can show the simplex pattern (Humphreys, 1960). Perl (1933, p. 30) was the first to see the simplex for her data from four simple learning tasks. Perl was aware of Thurstone's early work on factor analysis, and so she used it on her learning data with the hope that it might be useful in explaining individual differences in learning (Perl, 1934). Her work was exploratory, and she did no more with it, but it set the stage for programmatic investigators.

The Research of Woodrow

Perl has explorer status but the land was colonized by Woodrow (1938a, 1938c, 1939a, 1939b). Perl factor analyzed only the intercorrelations of the learning scores, but Woodrow believed that a reference test battery was required to define the abilities whose changes over learning were to be charted. Let me describe, in more detail, the Woodrow experiment (Woodrow, 1938a) already mentioned with respect to his factor analysis that included gain scores. There were 12 measures from 9 printed tests, which were intelligence tests, speed tests, numerical tests, and verbal tests. Initial score, final score, and gain score were used for each of the seven learning tasks. These 33 measures were intercorrelated and factor analyzed. The interpretation of the nine factors that were extracted was not clear, but what stood in relief for Woodrow was that the factor loadings changed with practice, with performance after practice requiring more of an ability or less of it than at the start. This restructuring of abilities, as we rely upon some of our capabilities and then upon others, is how Woodrow explained the learner's progress; it is a theory of learning derived from the analysis of individual differences. These theoretical ideas were drawn from R. H. Seashore (1930, 1939, 1940).

The Research of Fleishman

From the 1950s on, the most visible investigator who factor analyzed learning data has been Fleishman (for overviews of his research, see Fleishman, 1966, 1967, 1972a, 1972b). Fleishman's approach was the same as Woodrow's: A reference test battery and trial scores from a learning task were all intercorrelated and factor analyzed. A difference between Woodrow and Fleishman is that Fleishman used all the trial scores of the learning task rather than initial score, final score, and gain as Woodrow had done in his pursuit of a general learning ability. Fleishman's most frequently cited study was with Hempel (Fleishman & Hempel, 1954), which used the Complex Coordination Test (Melton, 1947) as the learning task (Fig. 1.1). The Complex Coordination Test, as one of the aircrew selection tests of World War II, is a serial, discrete matching test. A

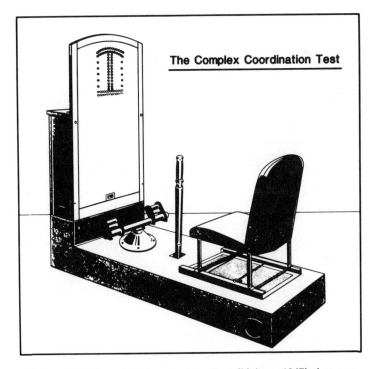

FIG. 1.1. The Complex Coordination Test (Melton, 1947) that was used by Fleishman and Hempel (1954) in their research on individual differences and learning. See text for explanation.

green light appears in each of the three parts of the visual display, and it defines two movements for a two-dimensional stick and one for a rudder bar. Visual feedback about the three movements was from three red lights that moved with control movements, and when the three red lights matched the three green lights a new set of green lights appeared which defined a new response requirement. Score was the number of these matches in a trial. Sixty-four 2-minute trials were given. The reference battery was 12 printed tests that were cognitively and perceptually oriented, three complex motor tests, and three simple motor tests. The motor tests were intended to define factors that were uniquely motor.

The factors derived from the intercorrelation of all these measures are shown in Fig. 1.2, plotted as a function of eight blocks of trials on the Complex Coordination Test. The shaded areas represent the percentage of total variance in performance accounted for by each factor at each stage of practice. Cognitive factors were more heavily weighted early in learning. Motor factors and a specific factor became more influential late in learning. Fleishman's interpretation was the same as Woodrow's: Learning is a matter of giving emphasis to different

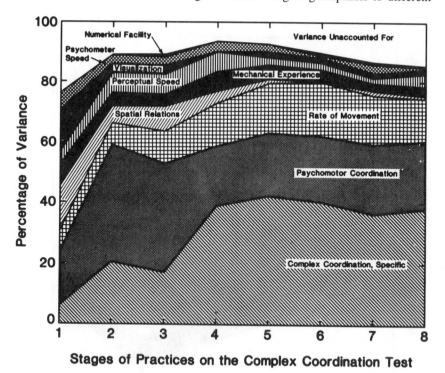

FIG. 1.2. The pictorial presentation that Fleishman and Hempel (1954) used to portray how factor loadings change with practice. The learning task was the Complex Coordination Test (Fig. 1.1). Copyright 1954 by Psychometric Society. Reprinted by permission.

abilities as practice progressed. The data implied evidence for the old idea that there is a shift from conscious, cognitive processes to automatic motor ones with extensive practice (Bain, 1868, pp. 330–332; James, 1890; Spencer, 1881, pp. 450–452). Practically-oriented readers saw a laboratory analogue of how ability requirements can change with training on a job.

Fleishman and Hempel (1955) tested the generalization of their original findings with the same general experimental design but which used the Discrimination Reaction Time Test as the learning task (the Discrimination Reaction Time Test is another aircrew selection test from World War II). The Discrimination Reaction Time Test is a serial choice reaction time task. The results were about the same as before, which was encouraging. The weights of the factors changed with practice. A specific factor for the Discrimination Reaction Time Test developed as training progressed, just as with the Complex Coordination Test.

Pressing the generalization further, which is a good scientific tactic, Fleishman (1960) did about the same experiment again but this time with the Rotary Pursuit Test as the learning task. The Rotary Pursuit Test (another aircrew selection test of World War II) is a pursuit tracking task where the subject tries to keep a stylus on a small target as it spins around on a disk. The generalization did not fare too well. There were only three factors with appreciable loadings on the Rotary Pursuit Test. One was called *control precision,* and the other two were specific factors, one increasing with practice and one decreasing.

A specific factor in these studies is not ascribable to any source of variation other than the learning task itself, and the increase of it with training in all three of the studies is pessimistic for the prediction of behavior in learning situations. When the specific factor becomes large enough and dominates late in practice it implies that only measures from the learning task itself can predict late performance; external measures cannot. If this is so then it should be verifiable in other ways, such as the inability to find tests that predict advanced stages of training. I have pursued this reasoning and have come not to take these specific factors seriously because a good job can be done in predicting performance late in learning. In two multiple correlation studies, I was able to assemble independent tests whose correlation with final performance on the learning task was higher than the zero-order correlation between initial and final performance on the learning task itself (Adams, 1953, 1957). In commenting on these experiments, I said (Adams, 1987, pp. 56–57) that the specificity hypothesis was a doctrine of despair because it implies that, with training, performance on the learning task will increasingly predict only itself, and that external tests will increasingly fail as predictors. My analyses show otherwise and are more encouraging, implying that prediction is a matter of devising tests to measure individual differences at various stages of training.

Fleishman's research has been the target of two criticisms. First, using factors as dependent measures to explain individual differences in learning, with trials as the independent variable, is presenting the data as if they were a *dependency analysis,* where the dependent and independent variables have different conceptual status. Bechtoldt (1962, pp. 323–324), taking the same position as Thurstone had earlier, said in criticism that factor analysis is a technique of *interdependency analysis,* where all variables are treated alike, and so casting the outcome of a factor analysis in dependency form is inappropriate. Thurstone had said, "In multiple correlation it is necessary to designate one of the variables as dependent and all of the others as independent, and the problem is then to predict the one test score from all the rest. In factor analysis there is no problem of prediction of any test scores, and there is no distinction between independence and dependence among the given variables" (1935, p. 54).

Second, Fleishman's factor analyses, as well as Woodrow's, were based on the intercorrelation of all the learning scores and all the scores of reference tests. There was no definition of factors that was independent of learning scores. The factors which were used to explain variation in performance on the learning task were partly derived from it; there is a confounding of the predictor and the predicted. Humphreys (1960, p. 321) recommended that the reference tests be factor analyzed separately from the learning data and vice versa. Ackerman (1987), operationalizing Humphrey's recommendation, re-analyzed the three studies of Fleishman's that I just summarized (Fleishman, 1960; Fleishman & Hempel, 1954, 1955), and obtained different results. A main difference was that specific factors were weaker, which supported the sentiment that I had developed from my straight correlational approach. Ackerman contends that an omnibus factor analysis, which has the simplex derived from learning scores and the reference battery together, leads to spuriously large specific factors (Ackerman, 1986, 1987).

We have not heard the end of these analyses that spin off of Woodrow and Fleishman because Ackerman and his colleagues (Ackerman, 1986, 1987; Ackerman & Schneider, 1985) have now fit this line of research into an information-processing approach. The approach relates such concepts as attentional resources, and automatic and controlled processing, to abilities. The approach is new, without competitors or critics so far. What is refreshing about it is the effort to relate concepts in behavior theory to individual differences. Older approaches related individual differences and learning, but they had minor things to say about learning theory. I have more to say later about modern attempts like these to bring differential psychology and experimental psychology together.

DISCUSSION

Having arrived at the modern era, it is time for appraisal. What do I think of all this? The field of individual differences and learning has been a long-running attempt to join experimental psychology and differential psychology—to bond the two psychologies with learning, and I like it. Good questions were being asked in the research that I reviewed. I am not sure, however, that many of the answers will endure. I say this because I am among those who are discontented with methodology in this field. Critics, often within the tent of differential psychology, have said for decades that something is wrong with the entrenched methods of differential psychology. A case can be made for methodological weaknesses in an approach that is rooted in tests made of items, the correlation coefficient, and factor analysis. I now review some of these criticisms.

Criticisms of Established Methodology in Differential Psychology

The Test Score

Loevinger (1951) once said that the meaning of a test score based on a number of items is unclear. Tests are usually heterogeneous to some degree, with items reflecting different abilities. Two subjects can answer different items and use different abilities and yet get the same score. Similarly, two subjects can invoke different abilities to answer the same item. One subject might use mental imagery to solve a spatial test item and another not, for example.

Differential psychology is wedded to tests made of items that yield a score, meeting the practical requirements of an easy-to-administer, easy-to-score, inexpensive instrument. Practical though tests may be, the method is scientifically shaky because a test can measure different abilities for different subjects. Using different strategies of responding, different abilities can be brought into play, so test scores have a great deal of indecipherable variability at the start. This topic has attracted the research of only a few (e.g., French, 1965; Kyllonen, Lohman, & Snow, 1984; Lohman & Kyllonen, 1983). Not many care about where test scores come from so long as they correlate with something of interest. This pragmatism, this failure to be analytic about the test score, is not praiseworthy.

The Correlation Coefficient

Differential psychology is as committed to the correlation coefficient as it is to the test score. The assumption is made that the correlation between behaviors in two situations means that the two situations have something in common and that these things in common are abilities or traits. Carroll said it clearly:

> Since the time of Spearman and Pearson, it has been assumed that if two measures taken on a given sample are significantly associated, they may be regarded as to some extent measuring "the same thing"; further, that if two acceptably reliable measures are not significantly associated they are measuring "different things." If the observations are taken over a sample of persons, these "same" and "different" things are often assumed to represent attributes, characteristics, or "traits" of the persons. Such an assumption lies at the base of factor-analytic methodology,

which is claimed to permit a detailed analysis of the multiple determination of observed variables by inferred latent traits. (Carroll, 1978, p. 89)

In a later paper, Carroll said:

I still regard correlational analysis as an extremely useful tool in the study of individual differences of cognitive processes, but primarily in a negative sense. When individual differences in two variables are uncorrelated, or appear on two different factors, I think it is an indication that the underlying processes are different, or at least dependent on different stimulus characteristics. I observe much more hesitation in inferring that the underlying processes are the same when the individual differences in two variables show significant relations or appear on the same factor, because the correlations could arise from similar stimulus characteristics, similar experiences, and a host of other things that would not depend on identical or similar cognitive processes. (Carroll, 1981, p. 17)

In other words, a positive correlation could mean the two measures share a common process, *but not necessarily.*

Spence (1944), who was an S-R theorist, called the correlation between two sets of behavior an R-R law, and he considered it a weak law because it only allows the prediction of responses from one situation to another and does not allow for explicit identification and manipulation of controlling stimuli. S-R psychology needs stimuli for its laws, but it is not alone. All psychological theories acknowledge the importance of stimuli; none disparage stimuli even when the emphasis is the cognitive environment. Although it might be contended that differential psychology has control over test-item content, and so has control of the stimulus, the hold is uncertain. Items are heterogeneous in varying degrees. It is seldom clear, for example, how to increase an item's perceptual content and decrease its reasoning requirements.

Factor Analysis

Factor analysis botanizes the data and attempts to specify a taxonomy of underlying behavioral processes in which the subjects vary. The processes are called *abilities* or *traits,* and factor analysis is used to infer about them. Inferences about behavioral processes from correlation coefficients is an uncertain enterprise, as I just discussed. No amount of factor analytic ingenuity can extract what is not solidly there.

All that a factor analyst has is relationships among responses, with no relationships of factors to eliciting stimuli and general behavioral processes like learning, memory, and perception. Carroll, in two interesting attempts to engage this problem, tried to operationalize factors and give them greater scientific credibility by relating them to item characteristics and behavioral processes. In one effort, Carroll (1976) had 48 cognitive tests, 2 for each of 24 factors. Based on an information-processing model of human verbal memory, he devised a coding scheme for items of the tests so that processes of the model could be related to the items. These processes were, in turn, related to factors. In a later study, Carroll (1981) proceeded similarly, except that he worked from cognitive tasks in the experimental literature rather than a model. His analysis of 200 cognitive tasks was reduced to eight paradigms that were seen to involve 10 cognitive processes. For example, reaction time would be a paradigm, but attention would be a cognitive process. Carroll then reviewed 25 factor analyses of cognitive tests and judged the relationship between factors and the paradigms and cognitive processes that he had established.

These Carroll studies are instructive because they get at the heart of the difficulties with factor analysis. The problem is not the indeterminacy of rotation and the need for subjective decision, orthogonal versus oblique solutions, whether there is a general factor or not, whether factor analysis should be used for hypothesis formation or hypothesis testing, whether factors are merely descriptive or are theoretical constructs, or how many factors there might be. Instead, the real problem is brought into focus by Carroll's work: Factors are response-defined, without anchor to stimuli and processes that theory declares as fundamental concepts. Carroll made an effort to provide the anchor. I have the feeling that arguments about factor analysis, and the division between experimental psychology and differential psychology, would fade away if measures of individual differences were related to stimuli and processes, as Carroll tried to do. This brings me to other cognitive psychologists and their efforts to do something about all of this.

Cognitive Psychology and Individual Differences

Cognitive psychology has mostly been concerned with models of general cognitive processes and not individual differences in these processes, as experimental psychology has always done. An exception is Hunt and his colleagues (Hunt, 1978, 1987; Hunt, Frost, & Lunneborg, 1973; Hunt & Lansman, 1975; Hunt, Lunneborg, & Lewis, 1975). Their general approach has been to administer tests with a heavy intellectual component, which might be loosely called intelligence tests, and then also to administer laboratory tasks that have been rationalized by an information-processing model from cognitive psychology. Cognitive psychology is concerned with higher mental processes, and so intelligence tests should correlate positively with performance measures from tasks that are rationalized by cognitive psychology. A fair summary of Hunt's results is that the correlations were low and positive. Sternberg (1977), and Chiang and Atkinson (1976), have done corresponding studies. The findings of these studies are less important than the viewpoint that differential psychology should use measures from laboratory tasks that are not only derived from psychological theory but that allow control of the stimulus and other variables.

The weakness in this research of cognitive psychology is the need to return to psychological tests, as if they are the primary data to be explained. Psychological test scores have been unquestioned as the way of entering individual differences into the scientific structure, and so I understand why cognitive psychologists defer to tests even though test scores, and the correlations and factor analyses based on them, are a weak source of lawfulness, as I discussed. The methodological problems that these instruments and computational methods have can easily get paved over because of the practical success that tests have.

It is time to ask if psychological test scores should be eased out of basic research on individual differences and left to the job of predicting behavior in practical situations. In his most recent paper, Hunt (1987) seems to have moved in this direction, away from his earlier work that interleaved psychological tests and laboratory tasks. As I interpret him, a fresh approach is needed for the basic science, and it should be the laboratory study of individual differences in psychological processes. General experimental research will establish the processes and their determinants, and individual differences among the subjects will then be entered into the structure. Printed tests should stay with practitioners in the everyday world while others work toward a union of the two psychologies without them. I agree with Hunt.

Instead of response-defined test scores, I envision measures of individual differences from the same tasks that experimental psychologists use—tasks whose requirements are rationalized by empirical data and theory in sensory psychology, perception psychology, the psychology of learning, cognitive psychology, and motor behavior. The reliance should be on construct validity, where the tasks are defined by prevailing theory. Any behavioral process worthy of the name will be represented in a number of different situations, so at least two tasks should converge on each process and operationally define it. Chiang and Atkinson (1976), for example, found high correlation between the slopes of functions for memory and for visual search tasks, as well as for the intercepts of the functions. A concept of mental search is given construct validity by securing it in two different ways.

Performances on tasks without concern for individual differences would reflect the processes that define general laws of behavior. Measures from individuals in these same tasks would give human variation in the processes, and this would lead to general laws that include the prediction of individual behavior, which should be the goal of psychology. No longer would abilities and traits of differential psychology be concepts separate from the concepts of experimental psychology. Instead, the differences among individuals would be in terms of the processes themselves—the same focus as experimental psychology. No longer would there be argument about the number of abilities. The number of abilities would always be the same as the number of processes that were credible in psychology at any time. Melton appears to have been saying the same thing when he wrote, ''What is necessary is that we frame our hypotheses about individual differences in terms of the process constructs of contemporary theories of learning and performance'' (1967, p. 239).

Investigators would undoubtedly intercorrelate measures of the various processes to evaluate their relatedness, and so it might be said that the correlation coefficient has surfaced again and we have response-based methodology again. No. This time the response measures that enter the correlations would be anchored to variables that operationally define constructs, and they could be systematically manipulated and fine-tuned. The same class of empirical manipulations that would be made in behalf of the processes of general laws would be made in behalf of individual differences also.

How good would this approach be for a basic understanding of individual differences? No better than the science of psychology at any moment. To the extent that psychology specifies viable theory with constructs that predict behavior, then individual measures in the behavior that represents these constructs will be viable measures of human variation. Because psychology is a comparatively young science, struggling to define its concepts, so will its accounts of individual differences struggle.

How useful would this approach be? Maybe, for a long time, not as useful as the test technology that we now have. But usefulness is seldom a motive that drives basic scientists, and it should not be the issue when new territories are being explored. The issue is the promise for new statements of law and theory that will unify experimental psychology and differential psychology. As the promise is fulfilled, usefulness will follow.

OPEN DISCUSSION

The discussion following Adams' talk highlighted a major theme running throughout the conference—*how* to realize a potentially fruitful unification of experimental and correlational paradigms. In particular, several participants questioned Adams' suggestion that emphasis be placed on experimental psychology methods as the basis for further development and refinement of individual difference constructs in differential psychology.

Pick: You make the argument that the early attempts to use sensory motor tasks to predict important individual differences did not work; that the laboratory people should try to take the lead from the people who were developing differential approaches and look for better processes to base their experimental psychology on.

Adams: I guess I am arguing the other way around—that the differential psychologists should take their lead from experimental psychologists. These recent trends by Hunt strike me as interesting ones which have some long-run ramifications for differential psychology and for the union of correlational psychology and experimental psychology.

Mulder: Most of the problems that Hunt has had concern a difficulty in using measures from real tasks to correlate with laboratory tasks. Therefore his argument was essentially, "I use tests because tests have been predictive (for example, in predicting the successfulness of a lawyer). But it is very difficult for me to measure individual differences among lawyers in their task performance—how do I score that?" I think that was his reason for going back to tests in the first place. So what we need are real indices of real tasks, for example, how good is a driver? We need measures of drivers' behavior to correlate with these type of laboratory tasks. And when we try to do this, we probably then have some problems with some tasks.

Adams: Bert, it seemed to me that when he [Hunt] was studying individual differences he felt a need to enter tests into his relationships with laboratory tasks because tests historically have been the way that individual differences have been represented. And what I think he is suggesting in more recent times is that that may not be necessary. I agree with him; that you can study individual differences in laboratory tasks which represent theoretical processes, and that can be sufficient—these *can* be your representations of individual differences. So the earlier empirical work that Hunt did sort of represents a historical connection to the past which I do not think he sees as necessary anymore, and which I see as unnecessary.

Ackerman: Where does this leave us then in terms of asking the question about the relationship between intelligence and learning? If we cast off the intelligence tests themselves, is it no longer a meaningful question?

Adams: Phil, don't you think that cognitive psychology someday is going to come to a representation of intelligence in its own right, based on constructs derived from their research and their thinking? And, thus, individual differences in those constructs will become the answer to the question about intelligence and learning, and intelligence and other constructs also.

Ackerman: But intelligence has always been, or at least originally was defined, in terms of its practical consequences rather than from a more constructive approach. You're asking for a very different kind of representation.

Adams: Once again you are turning back to practical situations, and I'm suggesting that we ought to separate the practical from the theoretical.

Carroll: I wondered why in your paper you did not consider the very large amount of evidence that has to do with the relation of intelligence and school learning, for example. I know that there are many questions to be raised about it, but nevertheless, I've always felt that this is the prime source of evidence that intelligence has to do with learning rates in school. There is some evidence now that you can do better in measuring learning rates by giving work sample tests, for example, rather than by giving standardized intelligence tests. But you're still measuring individual differences in something that seems to be relevant. So I think that whole area of research has to be considered in thinking about the relation of intelligence and learning. And, also, the lack of discussion of data, for example, on the SAT [Scholastic Aptitude Tests] and college success. Though that has many questions, if you look at it from the standpoint of what it would be if you did not have the restrictions of talent that are involved in so many of the correlations, there would be a large correlation between intelligence and learning.

Adams: Jack, I don't have any excuse. I narrowly concentrated on experimental psychology and individual differences and simply leave that to somebody else. I agree with you, it is pertinent—I didn't touch it.

Carroll: You're forgiven.

REFERENCES

Ackerman, P. L. (1986). Individual differences in information processing: An investigation of intellectual abilities and task performance during practice. *Intelligence, 10,* 101–139.

Ackerman, P. L. (1987). Individual differences in skill learning: An integration of psychometric and information processing perspectives. *Psychological Bulletin, 102,* 3–27.

Ackerman, P. L., & Schneider, W. (1985). Individual differences in automatic and controlled processing. In R. F. Dillon (Ed.), *Individual differences in cognition* (Vol. 2, pp. 35–66). New York: Academic Press.

Adams, J. A. (1953). The prediction of performance at advanced stages of training on a complex psychomotor task. (Res. Bull. No. 53–49). Lackland Air Force Base, TX: Human Resources Research Center.

Adams, J. A. (1957). The relationship between certain measures of ability and the acquisition of a psychomotor criterion response. *Journal of General Psychology, 56,* 121–134.

Adams, J. A. (1987). Historical review and appraisal of research on the learning, retention, and transfer of human motor skills. *Psychological Bulletin, 101,* 41–74.

Allison, R. B., Jr. (1960). *Learning parameters and human abilities.* Princeton, NJ: Educational Testing Service and Princeton University, Technical Report (May).

Bain, A. (1868). *The senses and the intellect* (3rd ed.). London: Longmans, Green.

Bechtoldt, H. P. (1962). Factor analysis and the investigation of hypotheses. *Perceptual & Motor Skills, 14,* 319–342.

Boring, E. G. (1929). *A history of experimental psychology.* New York: D. Appleton-Century.

Boring, M. D., & Boring, E. G. (1948). Master and pupils among the American psychologists. *American Journal of Psychology, 61*, 527–534.

Carroll, J. B. (1976). Psychometric tests as cognitive tasks: A new "structure of intellect." In L. B. Resnick (Ed.), *The nature of intelligence* (pp. 27–56). Hillsdale, NJ: Lawrence Erlbaum Associates.

Carroll, J. B. (1978). How shall we study individual differences in cognitive abilities?—Methodological and theoretical perspectives. *Intelligence, 2*, 87–115.

Carroll, J. B. (1981). Ability and task difficulty in cognitive psychology. *Educational Researcher, 10*, January, 11–21.

Chiang, A., & Atkinson, R. C. (1976). Individual differences and interrelationships among a select set of cognitive skills. *Memory & Cognition, 4*, 661–672.

Cronbach, L. J. (1957). The two disciplines of scientific psychology. *American Psychologist, 12*, 671–684.

Cronbach, L. J., & Furby, L. (1970). How we should measure "change"—Or should we? *Psychological Bulletin, 74*, 68–80.

Ferguson, G. A. (1954). On learning and human ability. *Canadian Journal of Psychology, 8*, 95–112.

Ferguson, G. A. (1956). On transfer and the abilities of man. *Canadian Journal of Psychology, 10*, 121–131.

Fleishman, E. A. (1960). Abilities at different stages of practice in rotary pursuit performance. *Journal of Experimental Psychology, 60*, 162–171.

Fleishman, E. A. (1966). Human abilities and the acquisition of skill: Comments on Professor Jones' paper. In E. A. Bilodeau (Ed.), *Acquisition of skill* (pp. 147–167). New York: Academic Press.

Fleishman, E. A. (1967). Individual differences and motor learning. In R. M. Gagné (Ed.), *Learning and individual differences* (pp. 165–191). Columbus, OH: Merrill.

Fleishman, E. A. (1972a). On the relation between abilities, learning, and individual differences. *American Psychologist, 27*, 1017–1032.

Fleishman, E. A. (1972b). Structure and measurement of psychomotor abilities. In R. N. Singer (Ed.), *The psychomotor domain: Movement behavior* (pp. 78–106). Philadelphia: Lea & Febiger.

Fleishman, E. A., & Hempel, W. E., Jr. (1954). Changes in factor structure of a complex psychomotor test as a function of practice. *Psychometrika, 19*, 239–252.

Fleishman, E. A., & Hempel, W. E., Jr. (1955). The relation between abilities and improvement with practice in a visual reaction time task. *Journal of Experimental Psychology, 49*, 301–312.

French, J. W. (1965). The relationship of problem-solving styles to the factor composition of tests. *Educational and Psychological Measurement, 25*, 9–28.

Glaser, R. (1967). Some implications of previous work on learning and individual differences. In R. M. Gagné (Ed.), *Learning and individual differences* (pp. 1–18). Columbus, OH: Merrill.

Humphreys, L. G. (1960). Investigations of the simplex. *Psychometrika, 25*, 313–323.

Hunt, E. (1978). Mechanics of verbal ability. *Psychological Review, 85*, 109–130.

Hunt, E. (1987). Science, technology, and intelligence. In R. R. Ronning, J. A. Glover, J. C. Conoley, & J. C. Witt (Eds.), *The influence of cognitive psychology on testing* (Vol. 3, pp. 11–40). Hillsdale, NJ: Lawrence Erlbaum Associates.

Hunt, E., Frost, N., & Lunneborg, C. (1973). Individual differences in cognition: A new approach to intelligence. In G. H. Bower (Ed.), *The psychology of learning and motivation* (Vol. 7, pp. 87–122). New York: Academic Press.

Hunt, E., & Lansman, M. (1975). Cognitive theory applied to individual differences. In W. K. Estes (Ed.), *Handbook of learning and cognitive processes* (Vol. 1, pp. 81–110). Hillsdale, NJ: Lawrence Erlbaum Associates.

Hunt, E., Lunneborg, C., & Lewis, J. (1975). What does it mean to be high verbal? *Cognitive Psychology, 7*, 194–227.

James, W. (1890). *The principles of psychology* (Vol. 1). New York: Holt.

Jonçich, G. (1968). *The sane positivist: A biography of Edward L. Thorndike.* Middletown, CT: Wesleyan University Press.

Kincaid, M. (1925). A study of individual differences in learning. *Psychological Review, 32,* 34–53.

Kyllonen, P. C., Lohman, D. F., & Snow, R. E. (1984). Effects of aptitudes, strategy training, and task facets on spatial task performance. *Journal of Educational Psychology, 76,* 130–145.

Loevinger, J. (1951). Intelligence. In H. Helson (Ed.), *Theoretical foundations of psychology* (pp. 557–601). New York: Van Nostrand.

Lohman, D. F., & Kyllonen, P. C. (1983). Individual differences in solution strategy on spatial tasks. In R. F. Dillon & R. R. Schmeck (Eds.), *Individual differences in cognition* (Vol. 1, pp. 105–135). New York: Academic Press.

McNemar, Q. (1962). *Psychological statistics* (3rd ed.). New York: Wiley.

Melton, A. W. (Ed.). (1947). *Apparatus tests: Report No. 4.* Washington, DC: Army Air Forces Aviation Psychology Program Research Reports. Superintendent of Documents, U.S. Government Printing Office.

Melton, A. W. (1967). Individual differences and theoretical process variables: General comments on the conference. In R. M. Gagné (Ed.), *Learning and individual differences* (pp. 238–252). Columbus, OH: Merrill.

Perl, R. E. (1933). The effect of practice upon individual differences. *Archives of Psychology, 24* (Whole No. 159), 1–54.

Perl, R. E. (1934). An application of Thurstone's method of factor analysis to practice series. *Journal of General Psychology, 11,* 209–212.

Reed, H. B. (1931). The influence of training on changes in variability in achievement. *Psychological Monographs, 41,* Whole No. 185.

Reynolds, B., & Adams, J. A. (1954). Psychomotor performance as a function of initial level of ability. *American Journal of Psychology, 67,* 268–277.

Seashore, R. H. (1930). Individual differences in motor skills. *Journal of General Psychology, 3,* 38–65.

Seashore, R. H. (1939). Work methods: An often neglected factor underlying individual differences. *Psychological Review, 46,* 123–141.

Seashore, R. H. (1940). Experimental and theoretical analysis of fine motor skills. *American Journal of Psychology, 53,* 86–98.

Simrall, D. (1947). Intelligence and the ability to learn. *Journal of Psychology, 23,* 27–43.

Spence, K. W. (1944). The nature of theory construction in contemporary psychology. *Psychological Review, 51,* 47–68.

Spencer, H. (1881). *The principles of psychology* (Vol. 1). London: Williams & Norgate.

Stake, R. E. (1961). Learning parameters, aptitudes, and achievements. *Psychometric Monograph, 9,* 1–70.

Sternberg, R. J. (1977). *Intelligence, information processing, and analogical reasoning: The componential analysis of human abilities.* Hillsdale, NJ: Lawrence Erlbaum Associates.

Thorndike, E. L. (1898). Animal intelligence: An experimental study of the associative processes in animals. *Psychological Review, Monograph Supplement, 2,* No. 4, (Whole No. 8).

Thorndike, E. L. (1908). The effect of practice in the case of a purely intellectual function. *American Journal of Psychology, 19,* 374–384.

Thurstone, L. L. (1935). *The vectors of mind.* Chicago: University of Chicago Press.

Tilton, J. W. (1949). Intelligence test scores as indicative of ability to learn. *Educational and Psychological Measurement, 9,* 291–296.

Travers, R. M. W. (1954). *An inquiry into the problem of predicting achievement.* (Res. Bull. No. 54–93). Lackland Air Force Base, TX: Air Force Personnel and Training Research Center.

Travers, R. M. W. (1955). Individual differences. *Annual Review of Psychology, 6,* 137–160.

Travers, R. M. W. (1956). Personnel selection and classification research as a laboratory science. *Educational and Psychological Measurement, 16,* 195–208.

Woodrow, H. (1938a). The relation between abilities and improvement with practice. *Journal of Educational Psychology, 29,* 215–230.

Woodrow, H. (1938b). The effect of practice on groups of different initial ability. *Journal of Educational Psychology, 29,* 268–278.

Woodrow, H. (1938c). The effect of practice on test intercorrelations. *Journal of Educational Psychology, 29,* 561–572.

Woodrow, H. (1939a). The application of factor-analysis to problems of practice. *Journal of General Psychology, 21,* 457–460.

Woodrow, H. (1939b). Factors in improvement with practice. *Journal of Psychology, 7,* 55–70.

Woodrow, H. (1940). Interrelations of measures of learning. *Journal of Psychology, 10,* 49–73.

Woodrow, H. (1946). The ability to learn. *Psychological Review, 53,* 147–158.

2

Volitional Effects on Performance: Conceptual Considerations and Results From Dual-Task Studies

Uwe Kleinbeck
Hans-Henning Quast
Ronald Schwarz
Bergische University, West Germany

Success in school or in the work place requires the use of human resources that contribute to the attainment of goals that persons set for themselves on the task. According to an old tradition in European thinking, the human mind has been viewed as a system composed of a variety of processes, each structurally related to the other but performing separate and distinct functions. In the flow of scientific history this componential theory of the mind has received considerable support, especially from neuroscience (Coltheart, 1985; Kinsbourne & Hicks, 1978). More recently, this viewpoint has become prominent in cognitive psychology and has led to the development of theories of mental functions in which a number of systems are assumed to underlie performance in a particular domain. During task performance, such functional units are supposed to be involved in analyzing task-relevant information and comparing it to memory contents. These units are used to search for action strategies appropriate for mastering the task and for choosing and executing actions according to the demands set by the task goals (see Hacker, 1983; Tulving, 1985; Wickens, 1984).

These examples illustrate some components of an action process that can be conceptualized from different perspectives in psychology; the most important ones are the cognitive and the motivational perspective. The research focus of the cognitive perspective is the development, change, and effectiveness of abilities and skills (e.g., Fleishman & Quaintance, 1984); the motivational perspective focuses on personal goals, which direct action and determine its intensity and persistence (e.g., Atkinson, 1958; Heckhausen, 1980; Locke & Latham, in press). In general, researchers have focused on one of these perspectives exclusively. Only recently have researchers begun to learn that it is difficult to describe the determinants of behavior using only cognitive concepts and neglect-

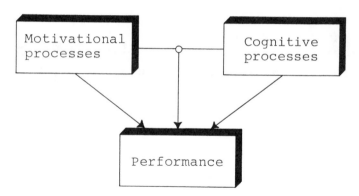

FIG. 2.1. Performance as a result of motivational and cognitive processes.

ing motivational ones. Even more clearly, motivation theorists stated the observation that their explanatory tools cannot describe behavior satisfactorily without taking into account cognitive aspects.

Only detailed knowledge about the motivational as well as the cognitive determinants of action can serve as a basis for understanding performance and learning processes; processes that are characterized by changing features in the structure and function of mental states.

On the basis of the preceding considerations, we believe that progress in performance and learning research can only be made if studies are based on a theory of performance that offers the possibility to integrate motivational and cognitive components under one theoretical heading. Fig. 2.1 depicts this approach.

The aim of this article is to describe concepts, methods, and empirical findings that can be used to develop such a theory of performance. The following sections are concerned with the development of an integrated perspective of motivational and cognitive research concepts. As a consequence of such an integrated perspective, the use of the dual-task paradigm is proposed as a promising method for simultaneous observation of behavioral variations in reaction to experimental manipulations of motivational and cognitive variables. Herein we describe a strategy of using the dual-task paradigm to test assumptions of this integrated perspective.

Furthermore, the experimental paradigm used to test the validity of some concepts in a theory of performance may also be used to gain insight into the dynamics of learning. Toward this objective, we conclude the chapter by suggesting some implications of our experimental results for improving our understanding of performance, learning, and training effects.

THE MOTIVATIONAL PERSPECTIVE:
GOALS AND PERFORMANCE

Motivation psychologists have known for a long time that human behavior and actions are goal directed (Ach, 1935; Lewin, 1926). Therefore, they intensively studied the conditions of goal development (e.g., studies in the framework of the risk-taking model, Atkinson, 1958; Heckhausen, 1980). However, the question of how these goals happen to become part of the actual process of action has been neglected since Ach (1935). Recently, Locke and his co-workers (e.g., Locke, Shaw, Saari, & Latham, 1981) have conducted a number of important studies that again try to answer this question. These researchers rediscovered characteristics of the effects of goals on actions and described these characteristics in new terms, such as *goal specificity* and *goal difficulty*.

Inspired by these studies, my co-workers and I (Kleinbeck, 1985, 1987; Schmidt, 1987; Schmidt, Kleinbeck, & Brockmann, 1984) have conducted a number of studies investigating the impact of goal setting on action. Based on our empirical findings, the findings obtained by Locke and Latham (in press), and Ach's (1935) theoretical conceptualization, we have identified five fundamental ways that goals may influence performance:

1. Goals influence perception processes (e.g., selective attention). This statement describes a selective mechanism that controls the input of action-provoking and controlling stimuli. From the wealth of information available to an individual in his environment, only those aspects of the environment that serve the goal-oriented control of action are registered and processed (Ach, 1935).

2. Goals direct and focus attention according to task requirements. That is, goals help to focus attention on the information that is relevant and important for goal attainment. The information that is obtained through this focusing process can influence the action process more easily than information without such attentional features.

3. Goals organize sequences and/or hierarchies of subgoals; they help to set priorities for action components controlling a behavioral process.

4. Goals aid in the development of new information-processing strategies and support the development of new mental tools that did not exist before as executing components of past actions.

5. Goals are used as memory patterns and action outcomes are compared to these patterns (see Hacker, 1983). In every action process, goals are compared to the action results fed back from the real course of events. In this way, they control a goal-oriented execution of action signaling predictable failure to reach an intended action outcome.

Volitional processes are realized by means of goals. Goal effects on the action process are thus crucial predictors for quantity and quality of human performance. However, it is important to ask whether these conditions are sufficient to explain human performance in psychological terms. We all know that this is not the case, as the mechanisms just described do not include various task-specific cognitive processes (of information processing) that are necessary for executing task-appropriate actions.

THE COGNITIVE PERSPECTIVE:
FUNCTIONAL UNITS
OF INFORMATION PROCESSING

Over the last 20 years, cognitive psychology has contributed to the understanding of human actions in a way that has challenged motivation psychologists interested in the influence of goals on actions. In the tradition of Craik (1948), Broadbent (1958), MacKay (1973), Kahneman (1973), Allport (1980), McLeod and Posner (1984), and others (see, e.g., Smyth, Morris, Levy, & Ellis, 1987, for a summary), the concept of *cognitive functional units* was developed (Shallice, McLeod, & Lewis, 1985). Cognitive psychology assumes that these functional units can be used independently (from each other) to process task-relevant information.

Table 2.1 presents a list of identified functional units based on findings reported by Wickens (1984). The list includes those functional units that have been shown to be independent in a number of experiments (see Wickens, 1984). The functional units indicated in Table 2.1 provide the basis for a series of experiments we describe in the next section.

As different types of tasks require different kinds of information processing, specific investments of different functional units are needed to meet the task demands. This line of reasoning can be illustrated by looking at a vigilance task. Fig. 2.2 presents an analysis of the use of different functional units in the performance of a vigilance task. Of the seven functional units listed in Table 2.1, four are hypothetically needed to do the vigilance task. First, there is the func-

TABLE 2.1
Functional Units as Elements
of Information Processing

Information Input	Central Processing	Information Output
Visual	Symbolic	Manual
Auditive	Spatial	Speech
Tactile		

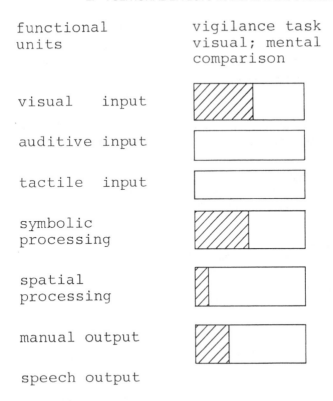

FIG. 2.2.   The use of functional units for performance in a vigilance task.

tional unit responsible for the visual information input. In this example, more than 50% of visual input capacity is needed. Auditive and tactile information inputs are not required, whereas the functional unit responsible for symbolic processing is involved to a large degree. Little is required from the spatial processing functional unit. Furthermore, information output involves manual performance. The corresponding functional unit contributes to a slighter degree, because the motor response asked for in this task is quite simple. In sum, the type of functional units and the extent of their usage are determined by the kind of task that has to be mastered.

However, as motivation psychologists (in particular) among us know, individuals have a certain degree of freedom with respect to their decision to use certain capacities. A substantial part of the variance in actions can be explained by the varying motivationally determined use of functional units' capacity.

Traditional approaches in motivation research have only focused on the relationship between motivation and performance in the achievement process. In contrast, the theoretical concepts proposed here produce a more differentiated perspective. In this framework, the volitional effects of goals on performance capacities and on single elements of information processing—the so-called functional units—can be separately analyzed. Consideration of (cognitive) functional units in psychological research concerning the transformation process from volitional states into action is important for two reasons:

1. The volitional process of goal setting must take into account different functional units according to the specific demands of the task. As a consequence, transformation rules may differ depending on the kind of functional units used in performance.
2. People differ with respect to the availability and capacity of functional units necessary for task performance.

Assuming the validity of these arguments, we may conclude that an individual's goals should be adapted to (a) actual task demands (in a task specific way), and (b) the specific functional unit capacity available to the individual during interactions with tasks.

THE INTEGRATIVE PERSPECTIVE: THE METHODOLOGY OF DUAL TASKS

On the basis of these theoretical considerations, we can now ask: What are the consequences of dividing information processing into cognitive modules or functional units? Can we retain the original plan—investigation of the impact of goals and intentions on performance—in the traditional (cognitively unspecified) form? We do not think so. Adopting an integrative perspective of motivational and cognitive processes requires that we consider whether the intention or plan to act—represented by goals in this case—has a specific impact, depending on which (cognitive) functional units are used in the process of mastering the task. To examine this question, we have developed a research paradigm that helps us: (a) to identify the functional units that are involved in the process of mastering the task, and (b) to analyze the intention- or goal-determined use of capacity given for specific functional units.

The dual-task technique has been successfully used in cognitive psychology to address the problem of identifying (cognitive) functional units. In this technique, experimenters ask their subjects to work simultaneously on two tasks. If there is task interference, that is, if the performance outcome on each of the two tasks in the dual-task situation is lower than performance in the single-task situation, similar or the same functional units are assumed to have been needed. For instance, if the previously mentioned vigilance task is combined with the visual identification task of a spatial object (see Fig. 2.3), we can expect to see task interference in the dual-task situation, because the capacity in the functional units

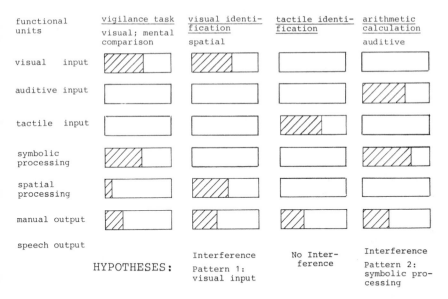

FIG. 2.3.   The use of functional units in different tasks and hypotheses for interference patterns in three dual-task combinations (with vigilance as the primary task).

responsible for information input is not large enough to serve both tasks. In a dual-task experiment of that kind, we should find a performance trade-off. This means that a performance increase in one of the two tasks is accompanied by a performance decrease in the other task (see hypotheses at the bottom of Fig. 2.3).

In contrast, if we combine the vigilance task with a tactile identification task, we would not expect to find task interference when performing both tasks simultaneously. This result is expected because there should be no overtaxing demands on capacity in either the functional units of information input, information processing, or in the functional unit of motor control. Consequently, our experimental analysis should not reveal a substantial performance trade-off in this case (see hypothesis at the bottom of Fig. 2.3).

Finally, if we combine the vigilance task with an arithmetic task, we again expect that we will observe task interference. In this dual-task situation, there is no competition in the area of sensory input (i.e., only the vigilance task requires visual input), but both tasks require symbolic processing resources (e.g., cognitive operations on numbers). The demands of both tasks in the functional unit of symbolic processing are thus predicted to result in an observed performance trade-off (see hypothesis at the bottom of Fig. 2.3).

To examine these hypotheses, we conducted a series of experiments in which we introduced the goal-setting procedure, described by Locke et al. (1981), into the classic dual-task situation. The integration of these two experimental paradigms provides a setting that allows us to observe the effects of goal setting (as a volitional state) on action while also taking into consideration the (cognitive) functional units used for performing the task.

EXPERIMENTAL DESIGN

In arranging an experimental procedure that involves the goal-setting approach (for controlling volitional states) and the dual-task paradigm (indicating cognitive functional units used in task performance), we varied the goal conditions in order to observe motivationally determined changes in performance.

To test the suitability of the dual-task technique for understanding how goals influence behavior, we ran three experiments with three combinations of two tasks. We refer to these tasks as primary and secondary tasks. In our experiments, a vigilance task was used as the primary task. This task was then paired with one of three secondary tasks: (a) a visual identification task (geometric figures), (b) a tactile reaction task (application of a weak mechanical stimulus to the skin of the wrist area), or (c) an arithmetic task with auditive information input.

We assumed that a small performance trade-off should emerge in the combination of the vigilance task with the tactile reaction task, whereas the combination of the vigilance task with the arithmetic task should produce the largest performance trade-off due to the similarity of the central processing involved in both tasks. Because both the vigilance and visual identification tasks required access to the functional unit responsible for visual input, we also expected that a performance trade-off would also occur in the vigilance task–visual identification dual-task condition.

The experiment began with a warm-up phase in which single and dual tasks were performed without setting any goal assignment. After this phase, subjects performed the dual task. Six blocks, with 20 trials in each block, were presented to subjects two times. For each block of trials, subjects were given different goal assignments. These goal assignments consisted of instructions to increase performance in one of the two tasks comprising the dual-task situation. For each trial block, subjects were told to either: (a) do your best, (b) increase your performance on the (target) task by 10%, or (c) increase your performance on the (target) task by 20%. Subjects were also told that they should not lower their performance on the other task while trying to increase their performance on the target task.

The goal assignments given for increasing task performance were anchored individually on the basis of performance during the training period (a day prior to the day of the experimental session). At the end of each block of trials, subjects were given feedback on their performance. Two dependent variables were examined; reaction time and number of errors made.

RESULTS

Effects of Goals in Different Dual-Task Combinations

To identify the effects of various goal assignments on performance and patterns of interference in the different task combinations, we standardized the dependent performance measure with regard to a baseline level of performance, developed on the basis of the day of training. The baseline was given the value 100 and performance in the experimental conditions was calculated as the difference in percentage from the baseline value. Thus, high performance values represent shorter reaction times, taking into account the errors made.

Our results show the predicted pattern of performance in the vigilance–visual reaction dual-task condition. Performance on the visual reaction task increased (i.e., reaction times decreased) when subjects were assigned higher goal standards for this task. At the same time, however, performance on the vigilance task decreased (e.g., reaction time on this task increased (see Fig. 2.4). In contrast, a different pattern of performance outcomes was obtained when subjects were given higher goals in the vigilance task. In this situation, reaction time decreased in the vigilance task and increased in the visual reaction task.

Similar results were obtained for the combination of the vigilance task with the arithmetic task. As shown in Fig. 2.5, higher goal assignments in the arithmetic task resulted in shorter reaction time on this task and longer reaction time on the vigilance task. When subjects were instructed to increase their performance on the vigilance task, reaction time on this component of the dual task

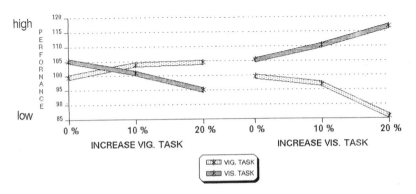

FIG. 2.4. Effects of goal setting on performance when a vigilance and a visual reaction task are combined.

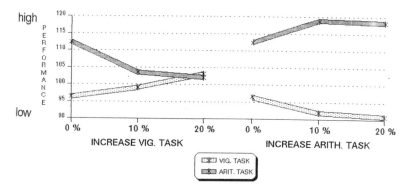

FIG. 2.5. Effects of goal setting on performance when a vigilance and an arithmetic calculation task are combined.

decreased and reaction time on the arithmetic task increased. As can be seen from comparing Fig. 2.4 and 2.5, there is just a small difference between the two pairs of dual-task combinations (i.e., the vigilance–visual task and the vigilance–arithmetic task) with regard to the performance level in the vigilance task.

A quite different picture emerged for the combination of the vigilance and the tactile task. As shown in the right panel of Fig. 2.6, reaction time in the tactile task decreased with the provision of a goal assignment. However, no substantial (significant) performance change was observed in the vigilance task in the tactile goal assignment conditions.

The left panel of Fig. 2.6 presents results obtained when goal assignments were directed toward increasing vigilance task performance. When subjects were instructed to increase their performance on the vigilance task by 10%, reaction time on this task did indeed decrease, but it was not significantly decreased by instructions to improve their performance by another 10% (left part of Fig.2.6).

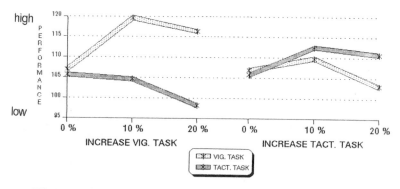

FIG. 2.6. Effects of goal setting on performance when a vigilance and a tactile reaction task are combined.

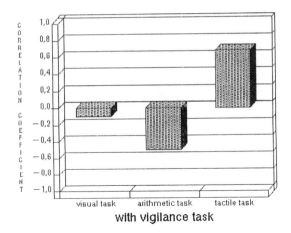

with vigilance task

FIG. 2.7. Correlations between performance indices of two tasks in three dual-task combinations averaged over all goal-setting conditions.

The level of performance in the tactile reaction task was slightly affected by the 20% vigilance task goal assignment, but in a nonsignificant way.

These findings are supported by the analysis of the correlations between the performance outcomes in the two tasks within each type of dual-task combination. Fig. 2.7 displays the correlation coefficients for each dual-task combination averaged over all different goal-setting conditions (i.e., do your best, 10% increase on the secondary task, 10% increase on the primary task, 20% increase on the secondary task, 20% increase on the primary task). A negative correlation was obtained for the combination of the vigilance task with the arithmetic task, a close to zero correlation in the combination of the vigilance task with the visual reaction task, and a positive correlation in the combination of the vigilance and the tactile task. These correlations indicate that there was a substantial performance trade-off in the vigilance–arithmetic dual task and a much smaller trade-off in the vigilance–visual dual task. The positive correlation obtained in the vigilance–tactile dual-task condition indicates that performance changed in the same direction in both tasks.

Another interesting aspect of the relationship between the performance outcomes in the dual tasks can be seen when the differences between the two outcomes are calculated within each type of dual-task combination and goal-setting condition, respectively. As shown in Fig. 2.8, the largest performance difference values (negative signs) are found for the arithmetic task and somewhat smaller difference values are found for the visual reaction task, including fewer values with negative signs. In the vigilance–tactile dual-task combination, almost all difference values obtained were positive. This pattern of findings indicates that the performance discrepancies between the primary (i.e, vigilance) and

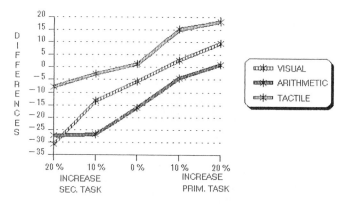

FIG. 2.8. The effect of goal setting on performance differences between primary and secondary tasks.

secondary (i.e., visual, arithmetic, and tactile) tasks were most dramatic in the combination arithmetic–vigilance dual-task combination.

Does this set of findings provide information about the usefulness of the dual-task technique for studying learning processes? One way to approach this question is to consider our results in a historical perspective. The use of the dual-task technique to investigate the effects of training on learning processes may be traced back to the first half of this century (e.g., Mohnkopf, 1933) and the 1950s (Bahrick, Noble, & Fitts, 1954; Bahrick & Shelly, 1958). Bahrick et al. (1954), for example, found that the longer the training period, the less that a simple arithmetic task (a serial reaction task) interfered with a simple primary visual–motor task. These findings were interpreted as an indication of increased automatization in the primary task, resulting in a decreasing performance trade-off over time. Furthermore, these findings are consistent with correlational studies that show a diminishing association between motor performance and a number of other test scores when a high level of training in the motor task had been achieved (Heuer & Wing, 1984).

What is the contribution of our research to this issue? Can changes in interference be observed during the course of training? Does training lead to changes in performance at all? If in fact changes in performance and interference are found, do they go into the same direction in the three dual-task combinations?

Although this series of experiments was not specifically designed to study learning processes, our experimental procedure involved a sequence of tasks presented to the same subjects on two subsequent days (repeated measures). This procedure gave us the opportunity to look at changes in performance and patterns of interference by comparing performance on the first day to performance on the second day.

Comparing total performance (i.e, the sum of performance on both compo-

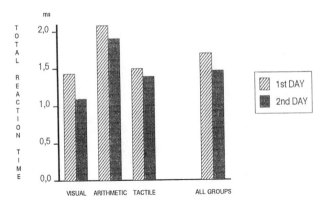

FIG. 2.9. Effects of learning for the sum of reaction times in both primary and secondary tasks.

nents of the dual task) scores averaged over the three types of dual tasks each day shows a significant increase of performance on the second day (see Fig. 2.9). This trend in total performance score was not, in general, affected by goal instructions. Thus, the effects of training could be observed within each dual-task combination. As shown in Fig. 2.9, total reaction time (total performance: the sum of reaction times from both tasks) was shorter in the vigilance–visual and vigilance–tactile dual-task combinations than in the vigilance–arithmetic combination.

If we compare changes in performance in the vigilance task and in the three secondary tasks separately, we find a compatible pattern of performance changes. As shown in Fig. 2.10, the effects of training on the vigilance are

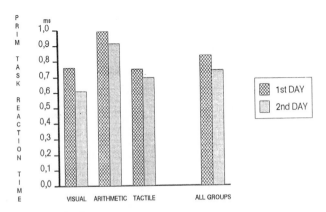

FIG. 2.10. Effects of learning for reaction times in the vigilance task (combined with each of three secondary tasks).

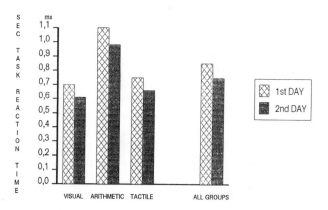

FIG. 2.11. Effects of learning for reaction times in the three secondary tasks (combined with the vigilance task).

significant in the vigilance–visual and vigilance–tactile task conditions but not in the vigilance–arithmetic condition. For the secondary tasks, all training effects proved to be significant (Fig. 2.11).

In addition, the averaged difference scores for all task combinations are lower on the second day than on first day of training (Fig. 2.12). On the first day, the averaged difference score is negative, whereas on the second day, there is almost no difference in the performance level on both parts of the dual tasks (Fig. 2.12). This is due primarily to the changes in performance differences in the vigilance–visual and the vigilance–arithmetic task combinations. No change in performance level differences were observed for the vigilance–tactile dual task. A similar pattern of changes in difference scores within each dual-task pair was reported in the first part of the result section.

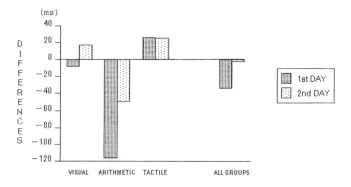

FIG. 2.12. Effects of learning for the differences in reaction times between the vigilance task and the three secondary tasks.

DISCUSSION

After decades, motivation psychologists have again become interested in the volitional aspects of action (Heckhausen, 1987; Kuhl, 1987). Researchers in this area are now concentrating on the question of how intentions or goals are turned into concrete psychological processes responsible for action control. For example, Locke and Latham (1989) have developed one successful approach to validation of concepts pertaining to how volition influences performance. Their findings clearly demonstrate that goals direct action.

Our own findings support the theory of goal setting. Consistently, we have found that task goals, in particular specific goals, influence performance across all tasks and combinations of tasks goals. Using a dual-task procedure that requires subjects to work on two tasks at the same time, we obtain evidence indicating that task goals may induce conflicts or interferences between two lines of information processing.

Conflicting information processing can provide psychological knowledge in two ways. First, it can help in the identification of task-specific functional units that are needed to master the task. Second, such conflicts aid in understanding the effects of goals, specifically with regard to the functional units required by them. Such an approach goes beyond drawing general conclusions concerning the global effects of goals on performance. Although our approach enables us to empirically determine the impact of goals on actions and outcomes in general, it also permits us to simultaneously describe the cognitive processes (in terms of information processing) that comprise elements of the action process.

The reported findings indicate the feasibility of testing theoretical statements about the effects of goals on action in a systematic, empirical fashion. For example, the interference effects obtained in the vigilance–visual reaction task combination indicate that both tasks require capacity within the functional unit responsible for visual information input. The interference effect in the vigilance–arithmetic task combination suggests that both these tasks require capacity within the functional unit responsible for central symbolic processing. However, both visual information input and central symbolic processing were not expected to be involved in the tactile reaction task. As the smallest degree of interference was observed in the vigilance–tactile task combination, we may conclude that no similar or identical functional units were involved. Thus, we can say that two functional units are crucial for the vigilance task: (a) visual information input and (b) symbolic central processing. As we demonstrated for the vigilance task, the dual-task technique provides a tractable method for identifying the functional units involved in task performance.

The dual-task procedure may also be used to examine whether goal effects on performance differ as a consequence of the specific functional units involved in the action process. The results of our correlation analysis support this line of reasoning. It refers to the already mentioned conflict within the functional units;

a conflict that may be intensified by the assignment of more difficult goals. The intensification of conflict was primarily observed in dual tasks that required access to the same functional units, for example, in the overall negative correlation between the vigilance task and the arithmetic task. In the case of low or no conflict between task demands, the overall correlation between both tasks is positive, as can be seen for the combination of the vigilance task and the tactile task. In this situation, an increase in performance in the target task was accompanied by a performance increase in the other task. In summary, our findings suggest that the effect of goals on the action processes depends on the kind and degree of the functional units involved.

The results concerning the effect of goal setting on performance differences between primary and secondary tasks complement this conclusion. The high negative difference scores in the vigilance–arithmetic task combination indicate that the arithmetic task could only be performed at the expense of the vigilance task (in particular, if subjects were instructed to increase performance in the arithmetic task). In contrast, performance in the vigilance task did not suffer from goal assignments focused on improving performance on the tactile task.

There are two competing theoretical notions that can be employed to explain the phenomenon of the trade-off in our dual-task situation (Hirst & Kalmar, 1987). The first concept assumes the existence of capacity-limited functional units. In this view, interferences in dual tasks occur because the total demands of the task exceed the available capacity at some point. The second notion assumes that the organism is unable to share the capacity of the functional unit to serve both tasks separately. In this perspective, mistakes, mismatches, and interferences result from this inability to share functional unit capacity across tasks.

Although our early theorizing was based partly on the assumption of capacity-limited functional units, our findings and the results reported by others (Hirst & Kalmar, 1987; Navon & Miller, 1987) do not exclude the second explanation. Further research is necessary to support or to falsify each of these assumptions.

The dual-task research framework may also be used to investigate the effects of different strategies on learning and training. It is important to note that performance improved for all dual-task conditions with training. However, using the dual-task technique revealed an important phenomenon: Interference processes changed in specific combinations of tasks differently due to training (as indicated by the decrease of the performance differences between primary and secondary tasks). Performance differences clearly decreased with practice in both the vigilance–arithmetic and vigilance–visual reaction task combinations. In contrast, however, no such change was observed in the vigilance–tactile task combination. In some dual-task conditions, learning may be conceptualized as a decrease or reduction in interferences.

Another aspect of learning can be seen by comparing the effects of training on the vigilance task across the three dual-task combinations. A significant training effect on the vigilance task was observed in the vigilance–visual reaction and vigilance–tactile reaction task combinations but not when the vigilance task was combined with the arithmetic task. It may be that the failure to observe the vigilance training effect in the vigilance–arithmetic task combination was due to the fact that the level of symbolic processing demands (imposed by the arithmetic task) interfered with attempts to improve performance on the vigilance task.

In conclusion, our findings underscore the importance of the relationship between motivation and cognitive processes and the potential of the dual-task technique for investigating the impact of these relationships on performance. The use of the dual-task methodology for investigating these relations is still in its infancy. The question of whether it will prove worthwhile remains to be determined by future research.

OPEN DISCUSSION

The discussion focused on three specific issues: (a) the absence of a coordinating process in Kleinbeck's model, (b) the unexpected positive correlation obtained between vigilance performance and tactile task performance, and (c) the extent of an individual's volitional control over resource allocations.

> **Mulder:**   I would like to refer to the figure in which you describe the modules, or functional units of processing [Fig. 2.2]. In this figure you don't indicate a general, coordinating mechanism. Is it that you think you don't need it? Do you think that these modules can work independently and don't need any general resource? Can your effects be partly explained on the use of a general resource (a general coordinating process)?

> **Kleinbeck:**   Well, we didn't need such a coordinating ability to plan the experiments. I also think our results can be explained without such a coordinating ability. That does not mean, however, that it would not be useful to posit such an ability. But we did not posit one and I don't see how such an ability would help us to explain the data better than we can now. I think it is just a question of the broadening of the concept. We certainly can think about that though.

> **Audience:**   I have a question that relates to that. You observe a strong positive correlation between the tactile and vigilance tasks. But in terms of your model, these tasks should have no elements in common. How do you explain that very strong correlation—isn't it the case that they shouldn't be correlated at all?

> **Kleinbeck:**   That is true. Well, the only explanation that I have for this result is that there is some effect such that one task is driving the other. That

is, if you try to perform better at one task it may be a stimulus for improving performance on the second task. Maybe this is the effect that we observe. But I do not know for sure. We will need to do further research to find out if this is really what is happening. It is true, however, that this result is not easily explainable by our theory. The point I wanted to make in showing these correlations is that there is no negative correlation. Our theory is less well equipped to explain why there is a positive correlation.

Ackerman: One of the things that those of us who work with dual tasks have found (for example, work by Wickens and some of his colleagues) is that subjects don't seem to have a lot of control over how much of their resources they devote to one task or another—that there really isn't continuous control in one's volitional adjustments. Can you address that issue at all?

Kleinbeck: Yes. I think that we have no problems with that in this paradigm. We give our subjects concrete goals and subjects learn to handle these goals to get the results that we want them to achieve. If you were to observe our subjects, you would see that after about one hour they can readily translate the goals that we give them into their own goals and into the concrete performances that we demand of them. We do not say, "Please give some attention to this task." Instead, we say, "Please perform this task so that you take 250 milliseconds on the next block of trials." And subjects can learn to perform at that level. It is a fascinating experience. We do observe subjects who are able to control, for example, 30 millisecond changes in their performance. So, I don't think we do encounter this problem of inability to make adjustments when we use this goal-setting methodology.

REFERENCES

Ach, N. (1935). Analyse des Willens [Analysis of volition]. In E. Abderhalden (Ed.), *Handbuch der biologischen Arbeitsmethoden* (Vol. 4) VI. Berlin: Urban & Schwarzenberg.

Allport, D. A. (1980). Patterns and actions: Cognitive mechanisms are content specific. In G. Claxton (Ed.), *New directions in cognitive psychology* (pp. 26–64). London: Routledge & Kegan Paul.

Atkinson, J. W. (1958). *Motives in fantasy, action, and society*. Princeton, NJ: Van Nostrand.

Bahrick, H. P., Noble, M., & Fitts, P. M. (1954). Extra-task performance as a measure of learning a primary task. *Journal of Experimental Psychology, 48,* 298–302.

Bahrick, H. P., & Shelly, C. (1958). Time sharing as an index of automatization. *Journal of Experimental Psychology, 56,* 288–293.

Broadbent, D. E. (1958). *Perception and communication*. London: Pergamon Press.

Coltheart, M. (1985). Cognitive neurology. In M. I. Posner & O. S. M. Marin (Ed.), *Attention and performance* (Vol. 11, pp. 3–37). Hillsdale, NJ: Lawrence Erlbaum Associates.

Craik, K. J. W. (1948). Theory of the human operator in control systems: II. Man as an element in a control system. *British Journal of Psychology, 38,* 142–148.

Fleishman, E. A., & Quaintance, M. K. (1984). *Taxonomies of human performance. The description of human tasks.* New York: Academic Press.

Hacker, W. (1983). Ziele—eine vergessene psychologische Schlüsselvariable? Zur antriebsregulatorischen Tendenz von Tätigkeitsinhalten [Goals—a forgotten psychological variable? Concerning motivational tendencies of task contents]. *Psychologie für die Praxis, 2,* 5–26.

Heckhausen, H. (1980). *Motivation und Handeln* [Motivation and action]. Berlin: Springer Verlag.

Heckhausen, H. (1987). Perspektiven einer Psychologie des Wollens [Perspectives of volitional psychology]. In H. Heckhausen, P. M. Gollwitzer, & F. E. Weinert (Eds.), *Jenseits des Rubikon* (pp. 121–142). Berlin: Springer Verlag.

Heuer, H., & Wing, A. M. (1984). Doing two things at once: Process limitations and interactions. In M. C. Smyth (Ed.), *The psychology of human movement* (pp. 183–213). New York: Academic Press.

Hirst, W., & Kalmar, D. (1987). Characterizing attentional resources. *Journal of Experimental Psychology: General, 116,* 68–81.

Kahneman, D. (1973). *Attention and effort.* Englewood Cliffs, NJ: Prentice-Hall.

Kinsbourne, M., & Hicks, R. E. (1978). Functional cerebral space: A model for overflow, transfer, and interference effects in human performance. In J. Requin (Ed.), *Attention and performance* (Vol. 4, pp. 345–362). Hillsdale, NJ: Lawrence Erlbaum Associates.

Kleinbeck, U. (1985). *Arbeitspsychologische Untersuchungen zur motivationalen Beeinflussung von Bewegungsleistungen* [Work-psychological experiments of the motivational influence on motor performance]. (Reihe 17: Biotechnik Nr. 27). Düsseldorf: VDI Verlag.

Kleinbeck, U. (1987). The effects of motivation on job performance. In F. Halisch & J. Kuhl (Eds.), *Motivation, intention, and volition* (pp. 261–271). Berlin: Springer Verlag.

Kuhl, J. (1987). Motivation und Handlungskontrolle: Ohne guten Willen geht es nicht [Motivation and action control: "Good will" as a necessary condition]. In H. Heckhausen, P. M. Gollwitzer, & F. E. Weinert (Eds.), *Jenseits des Rubikon* (pp. 101–120). Berlin: Springer Verlag.

Lewin, K. (1926). Wille, Vorsatz und Bedürfnis [Volition, intention and needs]. *Psychologische Forschung, 7,* 330–385.

Locke, E. A., & Latham, G. P. (in press). The High Performance Cycle. In U. Kleinbeck, H.-H. Quast, H. Thierry, & H. Häcker (Eds.), *Work motivation.* Hillsdale, NJ: Lawrence Erlbaum Associates.

Locke, E. A., Shaw, K. N., Saari, L. M., & Latham, G. P. (1981). Goal setting and task performance: 1969–1980. *Psychological Bulletin, 90,* 125–152.

MacKay, D. G. (1973). Aspects of the theory of comprehension, memory, and attention. *Quarterly Journal of Experimental Psychology, 25,* 22–40.

McLeod, P., & Posner, M. I. (1984). Privileged loops from percept to act. In H. Bouma & D. G. Bouwhuis (Eds.), *Attention and performance* (pp. 55–66). Hillsdale, NJ: Lawrence Erlbaum Associates.

Mohnkopf, W. (1933). Zur Automatisierung willkürlicher Bewegungen (Zugleich ein Beitrag zur Lehre von der Enge des Bewusstseins) [Automatization of intended motor behavior]. *Zeitschrift für Psychologie, 130,* 235–299.

Navon, D., & Miller, J. (1987). Role of outcome conflict in dual-task interference. *Journal of Experimental Psychology: Human Perception and Performance, 13,* 435–448.

Schmidt, K.-H. (1987). *Motivation, Handlungskontrolle und Leistung in einer Doppelaufgabensituation* [Motivation, action control and performance in a dual task situation]. (Series 17: Biotechnik 39). Düsseldorf: VDI Verlag.

Schmidt, K.-H., Kleinbeck, U., & Brockmann, W. (1984). Motivational control of motor performance by goal setting in a dual task situation. *Psychological Research, 46,* 129–191.

Shallice, T., McLeod, P., & Lewis, K. (1985). Isolating cognitive modules with the dual-task paradigm: Are speech perception and production separate processes? *Quarterly Journal of Experimental Psychology, 37,* 507–532.

Smyth, M. M., Morris, P. E., Levy, P., & Ellis, A. W. (1987). *Cognition in action*. Hillsdale, NJ: Lawrence Erlbaum Associates.
Tulving, E. (1985). How many memory systems are there? *American Psychologist, 40,* 385–398.
Wickens, C. D. (1984). Processing resources in attention. In R. Parasuraman & D. R. Davies (Eds.), *Varieties of attention* (pp. 63–102). New York: Academic Press.

3

Factor Analysis Since Spearman: Where Do We Stand? What Do We Know?

John B. Carroll
University of North Carolina at Chapel Hill

For the past 10 years or so, I have devoted most of my scholarly energies to a critical survey of what the psychological and psychometric research community has accomplished, over the past 60 years, in its efforts to identify cognitive abilities and interpret the results. I have amassed an enormous bibliography—of somewhere near ten thousand items. About 25% of these items concern the methodology of test construction and factor analysis. Another 25%, that is, upwards of 2,500, represent empirical studies of cognitive abilities using factor analysis. Except for a miscellany of items that are hard to classify, the remainder have to do with correlational studies, developmental studies, and studies from experimental cognitive psychology that I consider to be relevant to the interpretation of cognitive abilities. From all this material, with suitable reanalyses of a selected set of empirical factor-analytic studies, I have hoped to assemble, between the covers of a book, a synthesis of present knowledge about cognitive abilities in a number of respects: (a) the identification and characterization of cognitive abilities; (b) the structure and organization of these abilities; (c) the role of cognitive processes in abilities; (d) the development of abilities over the life span; and (e) the sources of variation in abilities as a function of constitutional and environmental variables. Arriving at such a synthesis has turned out to be a formidable enterprise, perhaps eventually beyond my capabilities or indeed beyond the capabilities of any one scholar. Nevertheless, I believe I will be able to accomplish a major part of it.

Such a synthesis, I believe, is essential for addressing many of the questions with which this volume is concerned—in particular, questions pertaining to the development of abilities and their relations with learning.

My focus has been on results from factor-analytic studies, as surveyed and reanalyzed, but not exclusively. I have also looked at a variety of correlational, developmental, and experimental studies. Necessarily, there are limitations imposed by these studies. The studies are limited, generally, to cognitive abilities that can be readily measured by relatively brief psychological tests or in experimental settings; I found few studies in which cognitive abilities were measured as expressed in long-term intellectual, organizational, and creative achievements. One is tempted to ponder whether the available factor-analytic studies are truly adequate to encompass the full range of important cognitive abilities.

The available factor-analytic studies—even those produced by the most reputable investigators—turn out to leave much to be desired in terms of study design and analysis, that is, with respect to selection of variables, selection of samples, procedures of analysis, and reporting of details on all these matters. I have reanalyzed a total of 461 data sets selected from the estimated 2,500 data sets in the factorial literature, involving more than ten thousand variables. A large number of available data sets did not appear to be worth considering, for various reasons. Nevertheless, I selected for reanalysis all or nearly all of the classic studies of Thurstone, Guilford, Cattell, and their followers, as well as many other studies that promised to yield informative results. I even reached back in time to reanalyze some of the studies, inspired by Spearman, that were done in the 1920s and 1930s, as many of these studies (e.g., El Koussy, 1935; Hargreaves, 1927) represent valuable data never heretofore analyzed by currently acceptable methods. In nearly all cases, some reanalysis was desirable and even necessary not only to check published results but also to provide a consistent basis for comparing studies, using hierarchical exploratory factor analysis. Space does not permit detailed description of my methods of analysis; it may suffice to say that I was generally conservative in assessing the number of factors to be analyzed. For example, I find that most of the studies reported by Guilford and Hoepfner (1971) were seriously overfactored. I fail to confirm Guilford's famous Structure-of-Intellect cube. Except in a few cases, I have not used confirmatory factor-analysis techniques such as LISREL; the demands of these techniques were beyond my resources of funds and time, and in any case, I did not regard confirmatory analysis as essential for my purposes. Checking my results by confirmatory techniques can be a task for others, if they care to undertake it.

Looking back on a 60-year history of factor-analytic work, I've been prompted to ask myself to what extent this work represents cumulative science, that is, work that continually builds on prior knowledge, as at least allegedly is the case in the physical sciences, with persistent testing of hypotheses generated from studies as they are completed. The answer is partly positive, but mostly negative. Certainly we know much more about cognitive abilities than was true in Spearman's day. There is a core of knowledge about a certain number of primary factors—mainly those identified by Thurstone and his followers from 1938 to the early 1970s (as reviewed, for example, by Ekstrom, 1979), and about certain higher-order factors identified chiefly by Cattell, Horn, and Hakstian (see, e.g.,

Hakstian & Cattell, 1978). For a period of 20 years (1949–1969), the late J. P. Guilford conducted cumulative science studies in intellectual abilities, in the sense that successive investigations were designed to build upon the results of earlier ones. Unfortunately, the philosophy and methodology of these studies put them out of the mainstream of research, and Guilford's Aptitudes Research Project (Guilford & Hoepfner, 1971) has provided little inspiration to later investigators. (I like to say that Guilford fell victim to "hardening of the categories" about halfway through his project.)

In other factor-analytic research, early Thurstonian results were accepted uncritically and used as the basis for repetitive, largely uninformative studies year after year, even up to the present. The same rather inadequately designed tests were used in study after study; regretfully, some of the tests to which I am referring are those in the kits of factor reference tests issued by Educational Testing Service (e.g., Ekstrom, French, Harman, & Dirmen, 1976). Even when methodological breakthroughs appeared, such as the Schmid–Leiman hierarchical method of analysis (Schmid & Leiman, 1957), such techniques were slow to be accepted and widely used. (As far as I am aware, the Schmid–Leiman technique is not available in any of the commonly used computer program packages such as SPSS, BIMED, and SAS, but I have implemented it in a package for microcomputers.) The *methodology* of factor analysis can possibly be characterized as cumulative science (though it has been exceedingly slow in development), but this feature has not been well transferred to substantive studies.

I can cite many instances in which novel and informative results of early studies have not been taken up and followed in subsequent studies. For example, studies such as those of Davidson and Carroll (1945) and Lord (1956) demonstrated that a distinction between speed and level-of-mastery should be observed in designing factor-analytic studies, but it is a rare study that has done so, with the result that it is difficult to characterize most of the popularly accepted factors in terms of these aspects, as was pointed out by Lohman (1979) in his review of factors in the spatial domain. French (1965) pioneered in showing that problem-solving strategies affect factorial results, but possibly with a few exceptions, no subsequent study has applied his methodology or anything like it.

From these considerations, I have to conclude that the enterprise of the factor analysis of cognitive abilities is a poor exemplar of cumulative science. This is a disgrace, for it could have been otherwise. It would require a good deal of speculation about the sociology and politics of science to discern the reasons for this. Animosities and misunderstandings among schools of thought and the difficult logistics of getting support for and performing good factor-analytic studies may be among those reasons. Currently, some of the difficulties may center in the general disinclination to support or perform research in ability testing because of its putative association with concepts of hereditarianism, racial and ethnic inequalities, and the like.

On the other hand, perhaps my complaint about the noncumulative nature of past factor-analytic research is a Monday-morning quarterback remark, made only from hindsight. I came to make this claim only as a result of my survey, that is, by noticing how defective and unsatisfactory our evidence about cognitive abilities is when that evidence is examined closely.

SOME METHODOLOGICAL
AND THEORETICAL PROBLEMS

Many different methodologies, of varying quality and reliability, have been used in factor-analytic work. In my survey, I attempted to circumvent methodological problems by reanalysis (chiefly of correlation matrices) using certain procedures of exploratory factor analysis that I have described recently in a tutorial on the subject (Carroll, 1985b). Even reanalysis, however, does not override a basic defect that pervades many of the available studies, namely, that of underdefinition of factors, that is, the use of insufficient numbers of variables to define factors, with inadequate variation to permit confident interpretation. This is often true with respect to primary or first-order factors, but it is especially true with respect to the definition and structure of higher-order factors. There are not enough data sets, with a sufficient variety of variables and samples at different age levels, to permit drawing firm conclusions, for example, about the existence, definition, and differentiation of higher-order factors such as *fluid intelligence* and *crystallized intelligence* postulated by Horn and Cattell (1966). Consequently, many of my interpretations of higher-order factors have had to be tentative and speculative. Even at the primary or first-order level, interpretations have been difficult, but at least I can more clearly indicate what problems need to be resolved by further investigation.

I am struck also by the fact that many measures of ability used in the available data sets are not based on adequate conceptions of abilities and of how they might be differentiated. I have already mentioned the general failure to differentiate speed and level-of-mastery aspects of abilities by the persistent use of time-limit tests; this is one of the failures introduced by the wide use, even with the best of intentions, of the Educational Testing Service (ETS) kit tests. Somehow this stems from an inadequate concept of what an ability is and of how one ability might be differentiated from another. It also stems from the failure to assure homogeneity of test content and to scale test variables by item response theory or something like it. Item response theory, of course, is a relatively recent development, but in the future, it should be applied routinely in the construction of variables in batteries designed for factor-analytic investigations.

Also, principles of test design (Embretson, 1985) need to be followed in constructing variables such that item difficulty can be clearly related to particular variations in measurable characteristics of item tasks, and such that, it may be hoped, factor interpretations can relate to these variations in item tasks. This is in line with my claim (Carroll, 1987a) that an ability is a characteristic of individuals that is manifested by the interaction of individuals with tasks of increasing difficulty or complexity in a given domain of behavior, the difficulty or complexity of tasks being indexable in terms of objectively measurable characteristics. Presumably, the latent trait abilities identified in factor analysis refer to interactions of individuals with these task variations, observable through the use of a variety of variables in which similar interactions occur despite the noise possibly produced by irrelevant variations. (For example, a lexical knowledge ability factor appears when a series of variables provide opportunity for individuals to interact with lexical items of varying familiarity or frequency despite variations in format, stimulus modality, etc., that are generally irrelevant to these interactions.) These remarks are intended to suggest a theory of ability that might well underlie future factor-analytic investigations.

Hierarchical factor analysis of data sets is based on the assumption that individuals' standings on variables can be a function of two or more factors, some factors being analyzed at higher orders than others. This assumption is reasonable, and if it is valid, as I believe it to be, then it poses problems for analyzing variables as a function of task characteristics, because it must be shown how the variables are related to two or more linearly independent dimensions of task characteristics. (This will be true, of course, whenever variables are shown to be factorially complex, regardless of the orders of the factors.) The hierarchical analysis implies also that factors differ in generality of application. To a degree, I believe that the Schmid–Leiman procedure, even though it was a breakthrough for its time, constitutes a straitjacket because it assumes that factors at a given order *subsume* factors at a lower order, as indicated by the correlations among those lower-order factors. This assumption may not be correct; the true situation may merely be that factors differ in generality of application, without subsumptions such that a loading on a second-order factor implies a loading on some one of a particular set of first-order factors. One advantage of structural equation models, as represented, for example, in the LISREL program (Jöreskog & Sörbom, 1984), is that they may be able to capture this situation better than exploratory models. As yet, I have not undertaken to pursue this possibility.

Of current interest is the promise that factor-analytic investigations may be able to throw light on the nature and differentiation of cognitive processes. At times, skepticism has been expressed about this (Sternberg, 1977), but as I have pointed out (Carroll, 1988), interpretations of well-accepted factors imply such differentiations. For example, the interpretation of the Flexibility of Closure factor, often measured by the Gottschaldt or embedded figures test, implies that there is such a thing as perceptual closure, differentiated, say, from a visualization process. In approaching this question, I find myself asking how a cognitive process would be defined, or whether, indeed, one would recognize such a process if it presented itself. I can't deal here with this question in any depth, but

I will say that approaches to its solution may lie in several directions: (a) varying tasks in such a way as to control the extent to which hypothesized processes can operate, and (b) breaking tasks into components—in the style of Sternberg's procedures of componential analysis. In each case, the effects on factorial composition of the variables derived from such manipulations would be studied. As far as I am aware, such investigations have not been tried, though I illustrated this possibility with an analysis of some of Sternberg's (1977) data that suggested that components could be aligned with factors in reasonable ways (Carroll, 1980).

Another fundamental problem in the interpretation of factor-analytic results is that of distinguishing between effects of processes involved in the actual performance of tasks and the effects of prior learning. Baron (1987) has pointed to this problem in arguing that factor analysis cannot contribute to the theory of intelligence because it cannot of itself distinguish between different determinants of correlations such as correlated educational opportunities as opposed to common information-processing demands. Certainly many well-accepted factors appear to be strongly influenced by education and prior learning. The well-known verbal factor is one example; performance on vocabulary tests is unlikely to be influenced much, if at all, by individual differences in *processing* conventional multiple-choice vocabulary items. The correlation of the verbal factor with other cognitive factors as reflected in higher-order factors is also likely to be a function of common educational experiences. However, it seems to me possible to detect differences in the influences of individual differences in processes as opposed to those in educational experiences by study designs in which these effects (e.g., amount of education or training) are explicitly measured and taken account of, if not in factor-analytic studies then in path-analytic designs. A prerequisite for such designs, however, would be the availability of precise measurements of factors, constructed through procedures such as those I have mentioned.

Finally, there is the problem of distinguishing process from strategy, or if different processes are associated with different strategies, of distinguishing these different strategies. It is well known, or should be well known, that common factor analysis assumes that the coefficients of factorial equations are identical for all members of a sample that is studied. The idea that strategies of task performance differ over individuals would violate this assumption. If they in fact differ, and are reflected in the factorial coefficients of variables, then these factorial coefficients are in effect averages of the true individual factorial coefficients over the members of a sample. I have mentioned French's (1965) approach to this problem, namely, performing separate factor analyses for groups of individuals reporting different strategies, and I have pointed out that this approach has seldom or ever been used, perhaps because of skepticism about the reliability of strategy reports. Nevertheless, from experimental work (e.g., MacLeod, Hunt, & Mathews, 1978) we now know more about assessing strategies of task performance and I would suggest that renewed work on this problem could be profitable.

THE FINDINGS

The outcomes of my survey are too voluminous to detail here. At this writing I have not completed examining all the data. As yet I have looked closely at only 3 of the 10 domains of ability into which I have organized my data, namely, language abilities, reasoning abilities, and learning and memory abilities. I am postponing detailed consideration of higher-order factor structures until after the first-order domains have been thoroughly analyzed. At this point, therefore, I can render only a progress report.

Perhaps I should explain my general strategy of analysis beyond the initial refactoring of the 461 data sets I had selected. (Actually, I had initially selected 477 data sets, but for various reasons 16 of these proved to be unanalyzable, contrary to the indications in the corresponding published reports.) Using my criteria for the number of factors at each order of analysis, the 461 data sets yielded a total of 2,272 first-order factors, 542 second-order factors, and 36 third-order factors. These counts are of factors considered as tokens rather than as types, in analogy to word-count statistics where a word can be counted either as a token (a particular instance) or a type (a category of words, for example, the word *the*).

But if it is relatively easy to categorize words in terms of their string patterns or dictionary lemmas, it is much more difficult to categorize factors. The prior problem is that of interpreting the factors yielded by a given data set, and as is well known, this presents many difficulties. As each study was analyzed, I made tentative interpretations by considering the nature of the variables having high loadings on each factor, as indicated by their names and what I knew of the nature of these variables and how they had been interpreted in previous literature. One category of interpretation was simply "interpretation postponed."

After all factors were assigned tentative interpretations, they were sorted into what I regarded as domains. This process of assigning factors to domains was difficult, because the boundaries between domains were often unclear, and factors sometimes seemed equally well assignable to any one of two or more domains. Partly, this is due to the inadequacies of study designs, in that specific aspects of ability were not permitted to be differentiated in a particular data set. Once a set of token factors was classified into a particular domain, they were subjected to detailed examination, involving close looks at the variables and their loadings on orthogonalized factors in each data set, with a view to categorizing factors into distinct types within a domain. Occasionally, this examination resulted in reclassifying a factor into a domain different from that into which it had originally been classified. This occurred when closer examination of the variables disclosed that their nature was different from what preliminary information (such as the mere *names* of the variables) had indicated. Because most study reports *at best* give only scanty information on the variables used, examination of these data is often an extremely frustrating process. Superficial descriptions of tests, even with the inclusion of sample items, often fail to yield enough information to draw even tentative conclusions about what ability trait or traits are being tested.

Admittedly, all this sorting and classifying of factors involved much subjectivity of judgment about factor interpretations, but I make no apologies for this, because within the parameters of this type of metasurvey no completely objective procedure seems to be available. In rare instances, when the same set of variables was analyzed in different data sets, it was possible to compute measures of factor congruence, but even in such cases, factor classification could be problematical when congruence coefficients between supposedly similar factors were low. The fact is that factor-analytic data are almost inherently messy, and they will remain messy until carefully worked out study designs resolve questions and inconsistencies. Indeed, one of the purposes of my survey was to identify what those questions and inconsistencies might be, as a guide to future research.

Even in the process of organizing the data for further analysis, however, some general outlines became clear. At least, it became possible to specify a tentative list of factors that appeared to be confirmed in at least two or three data sets, or often, in a substantial number of data sets. Also, some trends appeared in the placement of factors into higher-order domains, although actually, many of the findings in this respect present considerable ambiguity. On several occasions in the past several years, I felt sufficiently secure in my findings tentatively to indicate their general nature by listing a series of factors as classified into higher-order domains (Carroll, 1985a, 1986a, 1986b, 1987b). This list was the basis for a figure published by Snow (1986), and for convenience I reproduce this as Fig. 3.1. I should point out that the only way in which Snow introduced added material was in his depiction of lines (dotted, solid, or doubled, according to the presumed strength of the relation) connecting general intelligence (G) with several of the second-order factors. In all other respects, the figure corresponds to the lists I had published.

From my present perspective, I regard this figure as trustworthy in the main but undoubtedly incorrect or incomplete in many details. Many more factors can be identified than those included in the figure. A much more extensive and elaborate figure, like those often depicting LISREL results, would be required to display all the complexities of a more accurate taxonomy. It should provide, for example, much more information on the degrees of connections between the several orders of factors. (My results suggest that the connections between general intelligence and the last three second-order factors in the figure are not zero, even though they may be smaller than those shown in the figure for the first four

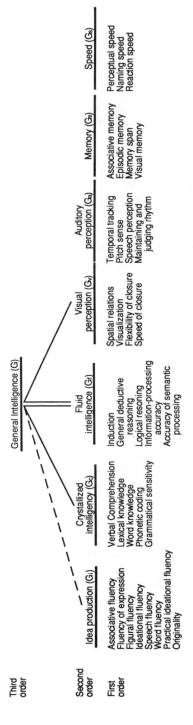

FIG. 3.1. A tentative taxonomy of some cognitive ability factors. (As adapted by Snow [1986] from materials developed by Carroll [1985a].)

51

second-order factors.) Furthermore, the figure should somehow represent the fact that there are cross-connections between factors such that higher-order factors subsume lower-order factors in complex ways. I have already mentioned my notion that the structure of abilities should not be regarded as being governed by strict subsumption relations. Some of the complexity of these relations is probably due to the difficulty of measuring latent traits in a pure form with our presently available measuring instruments and procedures.

To illustrate the kind of detailed examination that I have made of several domains, and that I plan to do for those remaining, I describe tentative conclusions I have reached for two domains, namely, the language domain and the reasoning domain. Roughly, these correspond, respectively, to crystallized intelligence and fluid intelligence. Indeed, Fig. 3.1 suggests that crystallized intelligence subsumes *only* certain language abilities. This is not correct, because various other factors, for example, Numerical Facility (not included in the figure), are frequently found to have loadings on crystallized intelligence.

The language and reasoning domains contrast in a way that illustrates the difficulty of establishing a strict taxonomy. To a large extent, the language domain is characterized by variations in types of acquired content, whereas the reasoning domain is characterized by variations in types of cognitive processes. Both process and content variations occur in both domains, of course, but the contrast in emphasis is still striking.

THE DOMAIN OF LANGUAGE ABILITIES

Initially, more than 350 token factors were assigned to the language ability domain. I should note that this domain was defined to exclude certain kinds of fluencies in producing words and ideas; fluency factors were assigned to the domain of idea production, which I do not discuss here. The language ability domain represents mainly what one may call competence or knowledge in the use of language.

On further examination of the factors assigned to this domain, and the variables defining them, it appeared that the domain could be seen as a cluster of generally correlated factors that represented different aspects or specializations of language development and use. In second- and foreign-language teaching and testing, it has been customary and expedient to define four types of skills: listening, speaking, reading, and writing. These skills can be organized in a two-dimensional scheme in which skills are divided according to whether they are receptive or productive, and whether they are concerned with oral or with written language. Indeed, factor-analytic work in second-language proficiency testing tends to support distinctions among these four skills (Carroll, 1968, 1983). Strangely, factor-analytic work in first-language testing has generally failed to recognize such distinctions in study designs, being largely focused on abilities

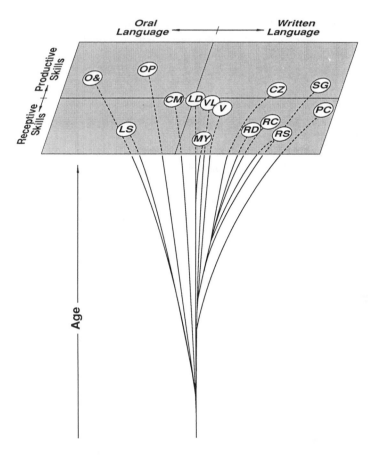

FIG. 3.2. A conceptual representation of factors in the language abil-
ity domain. Symbols for factors: O&, Oral Style; LS, Listening; OP,
Oral Production; CM, Communication; MY, Grammatical Sensitivity;
LD, Language Development; VL, Lexical Knowledge; V, Verbal Com-
prehension; RD, Reading Decoding; RC, Reading Comprehension; CZ,
Cloze Ability; RS, Reading Speed; SG, Spelling; PC, Phonetic Coding.

that can be measured by printed tests requiring reading ability. Nevertheless, I
found this scheme useful in classifying factors in the language domain. Fig. 3.2
depicts a conceptual representation of factors in the language ability domain. The
figure suggests, also, that there is a gradual differentiation of factors with age;
thus, reading ability factors would not become separated from general language
development factors until children start learning to read.

For convenience, I use one- or two-character symbols to identify factors. In
the center of the plane on which the factors are projected in the figure there
appears a factor that I symbolize as LD, representing general language develop-

ment as measured by tests that do not require reading skills, such as vocabulary and sentence comprehension tests that occur in the Stanford–Binet scale. These tests of pure language development were sometimes associated with tests of general or specialized information; partly, this may be due to the tendency of individuals to acquire information along with vocabulary knowledge and to do so in the same way as vocabulary is acquired.

Logical analysis supports the possibility of factorially distinguishing the LD factor from the well-known V or Verbal Comprehension factor as measured by printed tests. In all, I classified 144 token factors into the category of the V factor simply on the basis of the fact that high loadings generally occurred for printed tests of vocabulary, reading comprehension, and the like. In fact, however, in my sample of data sets there was no instance in which LD and V factors were or could be separated. I regard this as attributable to a fatal defect in study designs; a major question to be addressed in future research is whether it is actually possible to distinguish general spoken language development from written language development.

I can only briefly indicate the other factors identified in the language ability domain. The support for distinguishing these factors as linearly independent is erratic but strong enough, in most cases, to suggest distinctions worthy of being further investigated.

The Lexical Knowledge (VL) factor. This represents the extent of an individual's native language vocabulary. There is some evidence that it could be further split into different domains of vocabulary (scientific, literary, sports, etc.).

The Reading Comprehension (RC) factor. This represents the level of difficulty, in terms of the vocabulary and the syntactical and ideational complexity of printed texts, that the individual can comprehend and answer questions about. Recent work (e.g., Frederiksen, 1982) suggests that further linearly independent components can be distinguished within this factor.

The Reading Decoding (RD) factor. This represents the success of individuals, chiefly in earlier stages of reading acquisition, in correctly identifying words from their printed forms in terms of their graphemic characteristics. Frederiksen's work (1982) suggests that this factor, too, can be broken into certain components.

The Reading Speed (RS) factor. There is good factorial evidence for distinguishing reading speed from reading comprehension; that is, individuals can attain equal degrees of comprehension at different speeds. Reading speed appears to be a cardinal variable in reading performance, associated with speed of accessing the memory codes involved in word recognition and sentence comprehension.

Cloze Ability (CZ) factors. There is some suggestion from the factorial literature that measuring reading comprehension by the so-called cloze technique (requiring subjects to restore texts from which selected words have been deleted) calls for slightly different abilities—possibly language production abilities—than those called for in more conventional reading comprehension tests.

Spelling (SG) factors. The ability to spell words in the native language (in our data sets, this could be English, German, or Swedish) is linearly independent of other language abilities. The factorial literature provides disappointingly little information as to other basic cognitive abilities associated with spelling ability. However, it is possibly associated with the next four considered here.

The Phonetic Coding (PC) factor. This appears to represent the ability of the individual to distinguish and encode phonemes in native- or foreign-language words.

The Grammatical Sensitivity (MY) factor. This refers to the ability to distinguish and contrast, on a conscious level, grammatical features of the native or a foreign language.

Communication Ability (CM) factors. These are a series of weakly supported factors having to do with general skills in communication, often involving listening and speech production and interactions with other individuals, with or without involvement of reading and writing.

The Listening Ability (LS) factor. This appears to represent level of vocabulary range and syntactical and ideational complexity that can be attained in comprehension of spoken language. It is probably closely related, if not identical, to the general Language Development (LD) factor.

Oral Production (OP) factors. These are a series of poorly investigated factors measuring ability to communicate ideas in spoken language in different circumstances.

Oral Style (O&) factors. These factors reflect differences (e.g., syntactic complexity, use of personal references, specificity vs. vagueness) in oral language style.

The list just given represents only a very sketchy account of my findings in the language ability domain. The factors differ in many ways: in the degree of empirical support for their existence or for their linear independence from other factors, and in their typical loadings on second-order factors. Much further research would be required to establish and characterize them adequately. Even the brief descriptions I have offered suggest many questions that need to be answered. The domain of language abilities has not received adequate treatment in the factorial literature.

THE DOMAIN OF REASONING ABILITIES

I cannot say that the body of well-supported knowledge is any better in the domain of reasoning abilities. Reasoning abilities are traditionally considered to be at or near the core of what is ordinarily meant by *intelligence*. The initial sorting of token factors in my survey disclosed 241 factors tentatively interpreted as falling in this domain. However, relatively few data sets yielded more than one such factor. This may be due to the fact that few data sets have been addressed to detailed study of the reasoning domain, despite its great importance. Alternatively, it might be concluded that there is only one dominant dimension in the reasoning domain.

Nevertheless, detailed examination of the voluminous data, including consideration of test contents and processes, suggested that reasoning factors could be classified into three types, in at least partial agreement with the suggestions of prior reviewers (e.g., Ekstrom, 1979). These three types are as follows:

1. *Deductive or General Serial Reasoning (RG) factors.* These re factors in which high-loading variables are predominantly measures of deductive .easoning, that is, categorical and linear syllogistic tasks and general verbal reasoning tasks (sometimes including word problems in mathematics). There is often a serial reasoning aspect in that several deductive steps must be taken in order to reach a valid conclusion.

2. *Inductive Reasoning (I) factors.* High-loading variables are predominantly inductive tasks in which the subject is required to inspect a set of materials and from this inspection induce a rule or rules governing the materials, or a particular or common characteristic of two or more stimulus materials, such as a relation, a trend, or a concept. In every case, the subject must demonstrate discovery of the rule or common attribute by applying it in some way; this demonstration inevitably involves what may be called a deductive step, but the primary source of difficulty of the tasks is the discovery of a rule or common attribute. Among the more commonly found subtypes of inductive tasks are: series tasks, multiple exemplars tasks, matrix tasks, odd elements or classification tasks, verbal and nonverbal (figural) analogies tasks, and concept formation tasks.

3. *Quantitative Reasoning (RQ) factors.* Here, the high-loading variables are ones that can emphasize either deductive or inductive processes, but their common characteristic is that they require an appreciation or knowledge of quantitative concepts and relationships, particularly as treated in various branches of mathematics, from simple arithmetic to algebra, geometry, and calculus.

I also recognized a fourth, somewhat subsidiary type: Piagetian Reasoning (RP) factors. Thirteen such factors were found in nine data sets of my corpus. The salient loadings on these factors were measures of Piagetian reasoning such as conservation, class inclusion, and operativity. The available data sets yielded little evidence concerning whether these factors could be cross-identified with any one of the three main types, because the study designs rarely included conventional reasoning tests along with Piagetian tests. Piagetian reasoning factors, however, tend to have substantial loadings on a second-order factor, probably signifying that a considerable portion of their variance is accounted for by a general factor.

Returning to consideration of the three main types of reasoning factors, I found that inspecting the variables having highest salient loadings on 223 token factors allocated to the reasoning domain led to the following classifications: 78 deductive, serial reasoning (RG) factors, 89 inductive (I) factors, and 56 quantitative reasoning (RQ) factors. There were 37 data sets in which two or more of these factors appeared, providing evidence for distinguishing them. This evidence was disappointing in the sense that hardly any data set provided clear support for distinguishing all three. There were substantial numbers of data sets providing evidence for separating each of the three possible *pairs* of factors, however. I conducted certain checks that allowed me to conclude that these results were not wholly an artifact of my initial classifications. Thus, the mass of data available *suggests* the existence and separation of three main factors in the reasoning domain, but the evidence is hardly compelling. Each of the three proposed factors can be found to be strong and well defined in *some* data sets, and all three possible pairs of factors are well separated in *some* data sets.

On the supposition that three main reasoning factors do in fact exist, I believe there are two main reasons why the data failed adequately to support their separation:

1. *Inadequately designed variables.* Many commonly used variables are probably complex in their factorial composition because the item tasks require some combination of deductive, inductive, and quantitative reasoning processes. For example, a number series task can make demands on all three of these processes and in addition can place a demand on numerical facility. An analogies task can require both inductive and deductive processes (respectively, "inference" and "mapping," and "application" and "justification," in terms of Sternberg's [1977] componential analysis). In addition, many verbal analogies tasks have a large vocabulary load, to the extent that they often have high loadings on language domain factors. Nevertheless, I believe that it would be possible to design series, analogies, and other types of reasoning tasks in such a way that they could emphasize either deductive, inductive, or quantitative reasoning processes, minimizing the influence of other factors such as verbal ability and numerical facility. It might also be possible to derive, for a given task, separate scores for inferential and deductive processes.

2. *Inadequate study designs.* Few data sets included, for each factor, adequate numbers of variables that would be expected to measure the factor dis-

tinctively. In saying this I am not criticizing the original investigators, for they often had little adequate basis for decisions about study designs; it is only on the basis of a survey such as mine that it becomes possible to detect the probable reasons for inadequacies of their study designs. However, the general failure of investigators to formulate adequate hypotheses to be tested in successive study designs illustrates the point I made earlier about the mostly noncumulative nature of the factor-analytic enterprise.

CONCLUSION

In two domains of abilities, I have tried to illustrate, on the one hand, how my analyses yielded conclusions about the identification and characterization of cognitive abilities that appear to be supported in a satisfactory way by the available evidence, and on the other hand, how they raise questions for further investigation. In the book which I am preparing I will, of course, deal with other domains of ability and address many other issues, such as the higher-order structure of abilities, the extent to which my data sets and their analysis permit conclusions about the development and modifiability of abilities, and the extent to which abilities can be interpreted in terms of cognitive processes. I hope, in any case, that my remarks can persuade the reader that the metaanalysis of factor-analytic work on cognitive abilities is a useful and productive enterprise, and that there is great need for much more investigation in this field to follow up questions that have arisen in my survey.

OPEN DISCUSSION

The open discussion began with a question about studies that Carroll viewed as particularly noteworthy. The discussion then moved to more general consideration of the advantages and disadvantages of various research approaches and more specific questions about the implications of Carroll's findings.

McArdle: Are there any particular studies you would rate as outstanding?

Carroll: Any outstanding studies? Good ones? There are lots of outstanding studies from one or another point of view, but I won't mention them. Well, some of Thurstone's studies are among the most outstanding studies. They have much better designs than a lot of the subsequent studies. Thurstone's first primary mental abilities study of 1938 was a good one. The Thurstone and Thurstone 1941 study of eighth grade children was good. And Thurstone's study of the perceptual factor is actually a landmark study because it was one of the first and only studies that used laboratory tests. People tend to forget that Thurstone used laboratory tests and that he was very careful about the development of these tests.

Outside of those Thurstone studies, I don't know. I can't say too much about Guilford's studies. Some of those studies were outstanding in their length and complexity, but when you look at the variables that were used, they often seemed very trivial and poorly designed. The tests were very short—2 or 3 minutes—and were designed for some task that I doubt a lot of people understood when they were taking the test.

There have been some other studies that are outstanding. I would have to give a bouquet to Jan-Eric Gustafsson for doing a study using LISREL in which he took a battery of 20 variables and showed that you can set up a nice third-order factor structure. He tries to demonstrate that the fluid intelligence factor is probably very close to a general factor. Actually, I'm afraid that I do not quite approve of the limited number of variables that were used in that study. I think it would have been better if there had been 50 variables. But that just illustrates the difficult logistic problems one encounters in conducting factor-analytic studies.

Snow: Somebody once said that you can concentrate on the doughnut or on the hole. I tend to be criticized by people who too often concentrate on the hole. But aren't you kind of doing the same thing? It is certainly true that there are limits and shortcomings and a lack of cumulative style of research, but can't you also concentrate on the doughnut? Can't you also say there are cumulative consistencies that have grown over the past 60 to 70 years? For example, the hierarchical form and certainly the Verbal–Visual ability split under G, even if it is sometimes difficult to separate fluid and visual?

Carroll: Maybe I have given the wrong impression—that I have been concentrating on the holes in research. Yes, I would say that there is a lot of consistency—I guess it is part of my Minnesota training. When I was in Minnesota as a graduate student, we always participated in a pro-seminar. We would look at the latest material in some area, for example, Henry Murray's personality theory. We would look at the research and tear it apart. And so I have come to be cautionary and to treat data with a certain grain of salt. But I am hoping that when I get all my results, you *will* see some positive material. I have tried to illustrate this with the language domain and the reasoning ability domain. Unfortunately, you can't quite be sure about some aspects of it.

Audience: In your second figure, your second-order factors appear very similar to John Horn's model. John has an SAR [short-term acquisition and retrieval] factor for memory and a TSR [long-term storage and retrieval] factor for memory. Do you consider both of those factors falling within your G_m factor?

Carroll: I do know about John Horn's SAR and TSR and so on. I haven't included these in the list I published 2 or 3 years ago, but I am looking at that now and would tend to agree that there are some second-order factors there. There is also a lot of new material about auditory factors that has not yet been considered.

Revelle: My first question is addressed to all three speakers this morning. It seems that Jack Carroll's factor structure could be mapped onto Kleinbeck's model of what resources are used. That is, Jack Carroll's nice 2 by 2 table of listening, speaking, reading, and writing can be mapped into Kleinbeck's resources model and also gets back to Jack Adams' question about whether we should look at the structure of experimental factors as experimental psychologists or instead focus on exploratory factoring.

I would like to have a discussion between the three of you in terms of your factor structures as they relate to the resources that Kleinbeck talks about and the whole philosophy of science that Adams is suggesting. It seems that your factor structures are very similar to Broadbent's Maltese cross model, which is basically Kleinbeck's seven-resource model. Could the three of you try to integrate the factor structures and the resource structure?

Finally, Kleinbeck mentioned tactile inputs. Do you think you could have factors of a feeling, touching factors and other tactile factors? We know that there are individual differences in acuities for taste and acuities for smell. Would you call these abilities since they are presumably resources?

And one final, final comment. I notice that you did not have any factors in the writing component of your 2 by 2 table. Is that because researchers have not bothered to give tests measuring writing skills, that perhaps these tests are harder to score?

Carroll: Let me answer a couple of the more detailed questions first. You asked about the absence of writing factors in my table. Partly, that is due to the fact that I assigned writing factors to the idea of production domain, which I did not discuss and which I haven't looked at very carefully. There is not very much good evidence about writing factors. Writing is very closely related to general language development in most of the work but it hasn't been looked at adequately.

Second, there certainly are factors of differential sensitivity in different domains and modalities. Nice factor studies were done some years ago on factors of taste, smell, and vision. For example, there is support for a three-factor theory of vision.

Going back to your general question, I think that Jack Adams distinguished between tests and tasks just for convenience. For many years I have been a strong proponent of the idea that the items we put on psychological tests ought to be considered as tasks, and that they can be looked at in the same way that the experimentalist looks at a task that he puts in some experimental paradigm. So, in my mind, there is no principled difference between tasks and tests. It is just a matter of the degree of control you want to exercise—or can exercise.

Kleinbeck: I have one remark related to Bill's question. I think what I called "functional units" is somewhat similar to the term "abilities." However, I think one of the crucial differences is that we have used an experimental procedure to identify these functional units, whereas abilities researchers use correlational data that do not allow you to manipulate things as you can in an experimental procedure. Where does this lead us? Well, if you can manipulate variables, and can conduct experiments specifically planned for special purposes, this may lead further compared to correlational analysis. In other words, the information you can get may be richer in one or the other approach. I don't know, but that seems to be an important distinction.

Adams: Jack Carroll is trying to summarize 50 years of research in factor analysis. I was suggesting that an entirely new tack, that doesn't use the correlational approach or factor analysis at all, would be worthwhile considering for the unification of experimental psychology and correlational psychology. So the approaches are quite different.

Revelle: However, it seems that the results obtained by our English experimentalists and our German experimentalists are very similar; that is, these researchers are coming up with the same seven or so components that come out of both the conceptual and empirical investigations of individual differences. I find that both striking and reassuring.

Carroll: Yes, I also find it reasonable to think that there is a rather finite number of basic dimensions of individual differences. That is one of my complaints about the Guilford structure of intellect, which postulates that there might be as many as 150 or 300 different factors. This doesn't sound quite reasonable, but I do find it reasonable to think that there could be a rather small number of, let's say, broad ability factors—maybe 7, 8, 9, or 10 factors. And subsumed, or somewhere under them, maybe 30 or 40 first-order factors that I can confirm.

Ackerman: I would like to come back to the learning and individual differences issue. This question is related to your depiction of factor differentiation with age. The first part of my question is this: Does this factor differentiation with age occur in any of the other ability domains other than in the language ability domain?

Carroll: Well, not as clearly. One of the surprising things to me is that you find just about the same number of factors over different ages. I have organized all my data on a developmental basis. That is, I have tables that list the mean age of the sample so I can see whether there seems to be much difference. Insofar as I have been able to look at this, I do not find too much evidence for the kind of differentiation of factors that was postulated, for example, by Henry Garrett many years ago. There is also a German researcher who has dealt with this issue very extensively, and researchers at the Max Planck Institute have also looked at this issue. But I don't think there is going to be too much evidence for that kind of factor differentiation.

Ackerman: Let me ask the second part of the question. In the language area, is the breaking out of factors a result of the Schmid–Leiman transformation method? It looks like factors are breaking out; that the higher-order factors have the lower-order factors under them.

Carroll: No, I don't think it has anything to do with that business of orthogonalization.

Kazén-Saad: You mentioned that process and strategies should be distinguished. Is there any way to use factor analysis to reach a decision concerning what may be a process and what may be a strategy?

Carroll: Not by factor analysis itself. I think you have to set up hypotheses about what the strategies and processes are, and then vary the experimental tasks or psychometric tests, whatever they are, in order to capitalize on, or restrict, or interfere with the operation of processes and strategies to see what works. I have not given too much thought to this, but that is my impression.

Jenkins: Jack, you haven't complained about subject selection. I am a little surprised. Not having looked at the literature, I can't be specific. But my impression is that we have oversampled college students and undersampled everything else. Are we doing a psychology of the college student?

Carroll: Well, I have tables that show all kinds of things about the samples. There is a rather heavy representation of the college sophomore, quite true. But there are many other samples as well. John Horn goes out to prisons and selects his subjects that way, although that gives you a male overrepresentation. Guilford used many males and very few females in his samples because most of his subjects were from the military. But at least the military population does give you a wider sampling than the college sophomore. I could say a lot about subject selection procedures. I have always thought it would be nice if we had a Works Progress Administration so that we could go out and test 100,000 subjects and get a really good representative sample with 1,000 tests. But you just have to try to piece things together from the available literature.

Kyllonen: Have you considered the possibility that you have not been able to separate out deductive from inductive reasoning in the reasoning domain has to do with the fact that the distinction is just a *formal* distinction in classical logic but is not really a *psychological* distinction? Perhaps it does not have anything to do with the design of the tasks, per se.

Carroll: Don't misunderstand me. I did say that there is a lot of differentiation between inductive factors and deductive factors. I have dozens of data sets in which those factors are distinguished. My point was that I do not have any data sets that distinguish all three; inductive, deductive, and this quantitative thing.

Kyllonen: So you feel comfortable . . .

Carroll: Yes. I know that there is a group down at the U.S. Civil Service I believe, that has been making a lot of noise about the fact that psychometricians are not logicians, that they [psychometricians] do not understand inductive logic and deductive logic and that sort of thing. But I have more or less left that issue aside and I am comfortable with the idea that you can distinguish inductive and deductive processes in these reasoning tasks. It is done better in some studies than in others.

Bouchard: How do you deal with the broad argument made against factor analysis? That is, the argument that the mind is really just another biological system interacting a little differently with the world than other biological systems. And that all biological systems are really jerry-rigged in very complicated ways. If you look at the development of biological organisms, for example, the lungs, the liver, etc., in an evolutionary sense, it is as though things have been pieced together. They are not neat hierarchies in any manner whatsoever. I don't think you can point to really powerful, successful research schemes in general biology that made their advances by using a hierarchical factor model or some linear, additive model. In fact, those models have never been successful. And therefore, why should we expect differential psychology to be successful in cutting nature at its joints with such a model?

Carroll: Well, are *you* making that accusation or are you just asking me to deal with the hypothetical?

Bouchard: Well, you are one of the few people I have seen get up and discuss all these links going across these factors, which is exactly what I think you would expect from a complex biological function. But I think that kind of data stands in contradiction to the analytic and hierarchical factor schemes that are being used, the linear and additive models.

Carroll: I guess the only defense I would have is that psychologists, myself included, have been trying to do the best they can to analyze things and this is the way it comes out. There are consistencies, more consistencies than you might otherwise think. You do get a consistent set of factors across the studies, and most of them make sense, to me at least, in terms of the logical analysis of types of content. Consider, for example, the mere fact that you have different modalities. We know that there are different sensory modalities, and things come out the way they ought to from that standpoint. So I think we simply have to lay out our wares and see what the public thinks of them.

Overmier: My question comes from a slightly different perspective. It has to do with the concept of learning disability, a concept that has been introduced into the medical practice and educational practice in recent years. Learning disability is a concept that has been introduced as being something that is a state of being; discontinuous with the normal variability in learning capacities. And sometimes, it seems to be portrayed as closely related to minimal brain dysfunction—although no one has found evidence to this effect. But the concept ends up in *DSM-III* and becomes classified as a medical problem nonetheless. It seems to me that what is being done here is moving some class of learning problems out of the domain of this interaction between intelligence, perhaps functional capacities, and so on, that other people have talked about. The assertion is that these people have normal IQs, but have difficulty with some special factor called the "learning factor." I wonder what you have to say about this kind of intrusion of this construct of learning disabilities. Is this a valid way to go or is it simply a misattribution about the consequences of having multiple cognitive functions, each of which has its own normal distribution, and that they interact in producing terminal performance?

Carroll: Well, I have not looked at this in depth, but I would say that you could expect the concept of learning disabilities to develop on the basis of the fact that people do have different profiles. And there are certain factors that are more closely related to learning disabilities in a practical sense; that is, kids who develop in some respects but not in others. For example, consider phonetic coding ability, which I have measured in connection with foreign-language learning. This ability seems also to be related to what is often called dyslexia. That is, there is a class of people who have extreme difficulty, or at least they are at the bottom end of the curve. Usually, the distributions of this ability are negatively skewed. And there are certain people who have a lot of trouble distinguishing phonemes in a sound sense. For example, kids have trouble realizing that *cat* is composed of three phonemes. There seems to be some kind of biological basis for this that we do not yet understand, although we can measure it. So that is one aspect of learning disability you might say.

Overmier: Is it then discontinuous?

Carroll: Well, I won't say that it is discontinuous, but it is certainly a particular profile that does show up.

ACKNOWLEDGMENTS

This material is based upon work supported by the National Science Foundation under Grant No. BNS 82-12486. I wish to acknowledge, with thanks, the devoted and highly capable efforts of Christina M. Gullion and Ann C. Meade, research associates during the years 1983 to 1986, who helped in the reanalysis of data sets and in other project tasks. I am also indebted to the numerous investigators whose published and unpublished factor-analytic studies I have so cavalierly reanalyzed.

REFERENCES

Baron, J. (1987). Tools for studying human intelligence. [Review of D. K. Detterman (Ed.), *Current topics in human intelligence, Vol. 1: Research methodology* (Norwood, NJ: Ablex, 1985)]. *Contemporary Psychology, 32,* 135–136.

Carroll, J. B. (1968). The psychology of language testing. In A. Davies (Ed.), *Language testing symposium: A psycholinguistic approach* (pp. 46–69). London: Oxford University Press.

Carroll, J. B. (1980). Remarks on Sternberg's "Factor theories of intelligence are all right almost." *Educational Researcher, 9*(8), 14–18.

Carroll, J. B. (1983). Psychometric theory and language testing. In J. W. Oller, Jr. (Ed.), *Issues in language testing research* (pp. 80–107). Rowley, MA: Newbury House.

Carroll, J. B. (1985a). *Domains of cognitive ability*. Paper presented at the convention of the American Association for the Advancement of Science, Los Angeles, CA.

Carroll, J. B. (1985b). Exploratory factor analysis: A tutorial. In D. K. Detterman (Ed.), *Current topics in human intelligence, Vol. 1: Research methodology* (pp. 25–58). Norwood, NJ: Ablex.

Carroll, J. B. (1986a). *Dimensions and structures of cognitive abilities: Reanalyses of data sets reported in the literature*. Paper presented at the 21st International Congress of Applied Psychology, Jerusalem, Israel.

Carroll, J. B. (1986b). Psychometric approaches to cognitive abilities and processes. In S. E. Newstead, S. H. Irvine, & P. L. Dann (Eds.), *Human assessment: Cognition and motivation* (pp. 3–15). Dordrecht, Netherlands: M. Nijhoff.

Carroll, J. B. (1987a). New perspectives in the analysis of abilities. In R. R. Ronning, J. A. Glover, J. C. Conoley, & J. C. Witt (Eds.), *The influence of cognitive psychology on testing* (pp. 267–284). Hillsdale, NJ: Lawrence Erlbaum Associates.

Carroll, J. B. (1987b). Psychometric approaches to cognitive abilities and processes. In S. H. Irvine & S. E. Newstead (Eds.), *Intelligence and cognition: Contemporary frames of reference* (pp. 217–251). Dordrecht, Netherlands: M. Nijhoff.

Carroll, J. B. (1988). Editorial: Cognitive abilities, factors, and processes. *Intelligence, 12,* 101–109.

Davidson, W. M., & Carroll, J. B. (1945). Speed and level components in time-limit scores: A factor analysis. *Educational and Psychological Measurement, 5,* 411–427.

Ekstrom, R. B. (1979). Review of cognitive factors. *Multivariate Behavioral Research Monographs,* No. 79-2, 7–56.

Ekstrom, R. B., French, J. W., Harman, H. H., & Dirmen, D. (1976). *Manual for kit of factor-referenced cognitive tests, 1976*. Princeton, NJ: Educational Testing Service.

El Koussy, A. A. H. (1935). The visual perception of space. *British Journal of Psychology Monograph Supplements, 7,* No. 20.

Embretson, S. E. (Ed.). (1985). *Test design: Developments in psychology and psychometrics.* Orlando, FL: Academic Press.

Frederiksen, J. R. (1982). A componential theory of reading skills and their interactions. In R. J. Sternberg (Ed.), *Advances in the psychology of human intelligence* (Vol. 1, pp. 125–180). Hillsdale, NJ: Lawrence Erlbaum Associates.

French, J. W. (1965). The relationship of problem-solving styles to the factor composition of tests. *Educational and Psychological Measurement, 25,* 9–28.

Guilford, J. P., & Hoepfner, R. (1971). *The analysis of intelligence.* New York: McGraw-Hill.

Hakstian, A. R., & Cattell, R. B. (1978). Higher-stratum ability structures on a basis of twenty primary abilities. *Journal of Educational Psychology, 70,* 657–669.

Hargreaves, H. L. (1927). The "faculty" of imagination: An enquiry concerning the existence of a general "faculty," or group factor, of imagination. *British Journal of Psychology Monograph Supplements, 3,* No. 10, 1–74.

Horn, J. L., & Cattell, R. B. (1966). Refinement of the theory of fluid and crystallized intelligences. *Journal of Educational Psychology, 57,* 253–270.

Jöreskog, K. G., & Sörbom, D. (1984). *LISREL VI: Analysis of linear structural relationships by the method of maximum likelihood: User's guide.* Mooresville, IN: Scientific Software.

Lohman, D. F. (1979). *Spatial ability: A review and reanalysis of the correlational literature.* Stanford, CA: Aptitude Research Project, School of Education, Stanford University.

Lord, F. M. (1956). A study of speed factors in tests and academic grades. *Psychometrika, 21,* 31–50.

MacLeod, C. M., Hunt, E. B., & Mathews, N. N. (1978). Individual differences in the verification of sentence–picture relationships. *Journal of Verbal Learning and Verbal Behavior, 17,* 493–507.

Schmid, J., & Leiman, J. M. (1957). The development of hierarchical factor solutions. *Psychometrika, 22,* 53–61.

Snow, R. E. (1986). Individual differences and the design of educational programs. *American Psychologist, 41,* 1029–1039.

Sternberg, R. J. (1977). *Intelligence, information processing, and analogical reasoning: The componential analysis of human abilities.* Hillsdale, NJ: Lawrence Erlbaum Associates.

II
METHODOLOGICAL STRATEGIES

4

A Structural Modeling Experiment with Multiple Growth Functions

J. J. McArdle
University of Virginia

Over three decades ago, Cronbach (1957) pronounced the "Two disciplines of scientific psychology." This provocative article recognized a division between the "experimental" school and the "differential" school of psychology. Cronbach (1957; 1975) called for the merger of these two separate disciplines, and he advocated the "aptitude by treatment interaction" (ATI) methodology as the integrative device. It seems to me that this pronouncement had the unfortunate side effect of providing justifications for the continued separation of these different approaches to the analysis of human behavior. That is, psychological researchers took even more pride in labeling themselves as either an "experimentalist" or a "correlationalist." This question of personal identity is often asked today. This poses some problems for those of us who have attended many schools of psychology and see benefits within and between several approaches. So our task remains—we need to demonstrate the benefits of such a merger for psychology.

A great deal of psychological research has focused on studies of training effects on learning, motivation, and abilities. Some of these studies have taken an experimental focus, with primary emphasis on randomized assignment to treatment followed by an unbiased interpretation of single variable effects. Other studies have taken a correlational focus, with primary emphasis on multiple variable measurement followed by a broad interpretation of multivariable effects. In a few of these studies, strong experimental design has been merged with multivariate measurement to examine concepts of growth and change (e.g., Horn, 1972). In this presentation, contemporary methods of longitudinal structural equation modeling are discussed for multivariate change experiments.

THE MULTIVARIATE
EXPERIMENTAL APPROACH

The analyses to follow use fundamental concepts from factor analysis. However, these analyses require a rather broad view about the nature and goals of factor analysis. First, we need a broad view of experimental modeling:

> an EXPERIMENT is a recording of observations, quantitative or qualitative, made by defined and recorded observations and defined conditions, followed by examination of the data, by appropriate statistical and mathematical rules, for the existence of significant relations. It will be noted that the ambiguous term "controlled", as in, e.g., "under controlled conditions", is deliberately avoided here, as also is the question of whether we are using the relations to create or test an hypotheses.
> . . . By a MODEL, we refer to a theory reduced to some mathematical, physical, or symbolic essentials in which the relations of parts are completely determined by accepted rules.
> . . . The advantage of a model is that it is precise, and clear in its testing implications. Only in some form of model can certain aspects of a theory be sincerely tested. (R. B. Cattell, 1966, pp. 20, 42)

Second, we need a broad view of what is meant by a factor in a model:

> The central concept of the multivariate metatheory is that of *functional unity*, as defined by Cattell. . . . A functional unity is indicated by a configuration—a pattern—of processes which are themselves distinct but are integral parts of more general process. To distinguish a functional unity from a mere collection of distinct processes it is necessary to show that the processes work together—that they rise together, fall together, appear together, disappear together or, in general, covary together. The action of the heart may be taken as an example of a kind of functional unity. The processes which might indicate this function are those recorded by blood pressure measurements taken in various parts of the body, breathing rate, skin moisture and skin temperature. Each of these processes indicated by such measurements is distinct from the other and the intercorrelations among the process measurements will be less than unity even when corrected for unreliability. Yet the several processes work together in a way that gives evidence of the vital function and the function may be indicated by a pattern of covariation among the measurements of the separate processes. Similarly the function of intelligence may be indicated by a pattern of covariance among distinct processes of memory, reasoning, abstracting, etc. . . . A functional unity is thus a rather high level of abstraction. In operational terms it can be defined in a number of ways. One of the simplest such definitions is that furnished by the methods of factor analysis. According to this definition a functional unity is indicated by the set of variables which go together in the sense of correlating in a way that defines a particular factor. (J. L. Horn, 1972, pp. 161–162)

And third, we need to focus on the testable features of factor models:

> The identification of relationships that remain invariant among variables under different conditions and transformations is a major goal of empirical research. . . . Demonstration of factor invariance is one particular realization of a major goal of science—namely the identification of invariant relationships. The invariant relationships involved are those between factors (unobserved or latent variables) and observed variables or, in higher order analyses, other factors. At the first order of analysis, for example, factor invariance signals a kind of constancy of a measurement system and thus the reasonableness of comparing phenomena in quantitative rather than in qualitative terms. . . . From a change-measurement perspective, the emphasis in these models is on structural matters; establishing the properties of the measurement system and the nature of the variables first, then measuring and studying changes in them rather than on modeling and interpreting changes on observed variables directly. As such, factor invariance plays a crucial role in both the assessment of differences and change. (J. R. Nesselroade, 1983, pp. 59, 62–63)

These three statements form the basis of the school of multivariate experimental psychology (see Cattell, 1966; Nesselroade & Cattell, 1988). In presenting these analyses I intend to combine the testable features of experimentation with the testable aspects of multivariate data arrays. The concept of a functional relation between stimulus and response is essential and multiple measures are used for testing construct validity. Randomized assignment to groups is useful as long as ecological validity is retained. In statistical terms, the effects of an experiment may show up in the means, variances, correlations, or other features of the scores, and I try to remain alert to such combinations.

STRUCTURAL EQUATION
MODELING TECHNIQUES

The mathematical and statistical techniques I use here are generically labeled under the heading of "linear structural relations models" (LISREL) (after Jöreskog, 1971; Jöreskog & Sörbom, 1979, 1985) or as "covariance structure analysis" (COSAN) (see McDonald, 1978, 1985). An example of a LISREL model is presented in Fig. 4.1 (from Jöreskog, 1979). This model includes manifest or observed variables y (drawn in squares) and latent or unobserved variables η (drawn as circles). This model also specifies a set of restrictive regressions B_t to estimate the time-forward progression of latent variables over time. These new techniques allow a great deal of statistical precision for the testing of hypotheses about latent variables.

A great deal of activity in this area has come from promises of drawing causal inferences from correlations based on nonrandomized, but longitudinal, data

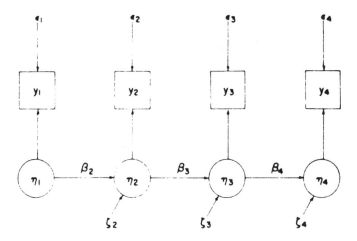

FIG. 4.1. A structural equation model for longitudinal data: The auto-regressive causal model (from Jöreskog, 1979).

structures (see Jöreskog & Sörbom, 1979; Kenny, 1979; Olsson & Bergman, 1977). But some important issues in this literature have focused on the use of a structural model for the improvement of randomized experimental designs (see Alwin & Tessler, 1974; Bagozzi, 1977; Blalock, 1985; Cook & Campbell, 1979). The primary benefits of these structural experiments come because novel experimental hypotheses become testable when multivariate observations are collected (see Nesselroade & Cattell, 1988).

I present my analyses using a slightly different kind of path diagram: Fig. 4.2 is an example of this graphic style (from McArdle & Epstein, 1987). This notation is somewhat unusual but it follows the procedures detailed in other work (Horn & McArdle, 1980; McArdle, 1980; McArdle & Horn, in press). In these diagrams, all variables are drawn as boxes, but the observed variables (r, here) are drawn as closed boxes and the unobserved variables (C and C^* here) are drawn as open boxes. In most models here, a constant 1 will also be needed, and these observed but unmeasured variables will be drawn as a closed triangle. All model parameters are included in the diagram as either one-headed or two-headed arrows. These diagrams can completely take the place of the associated path diagram algebra needed for model specification (see McArdle & McDonald, 1984; McDonald, 1985).

The main differences between the standard graphics of Fig. 4.1 and my unusual graphics of Fig. 4.2 are threefold. First, the notation in Fig. 4.2 places all model parameters in the picture and allows the inclusion of regressions and correlations as well as means and standard deviations. Second, this notation treats all variables, including error variables, as nodes to be included in the picture. These are all included to provide a graphic location for the associated

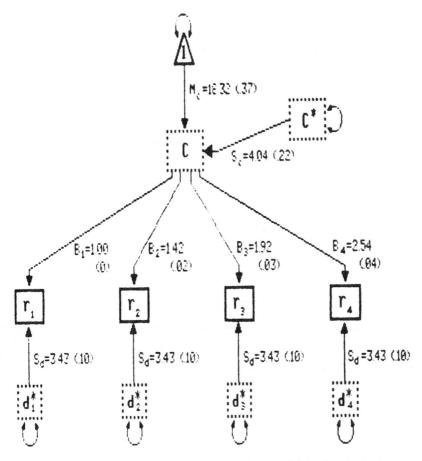

FIG. 4.2. An alternative structural equation model for longitudinal data: The latent growth factor model (from McArdle & Epstein, 1987).

algebraic parameters. These first two features are essential for a complete graphic presentation. Third, the Fig. 4.2 notation uses open boxes to denote latent variables and triangles to denote constants. This third feature is not needed and it can create some confusion for researchers who are used to a separation based on squares, circles, and unlabeled error terms (R. Cudeck, personal communication, 1988). But I have chosen to stick with my new notation here because I think it leads to a graphic description of the interpretation of each variable (e.g., the common factors are not fully closed in, the constant is only half a variable, etc.). Incidentally, the meaning of circles and squares has changed over the last decade, but I think it is relatively easy for anyone to identify the unobserved variables in these new diagrams (see McArdle & Horn, in press; Wright, 1983). I need these graphic features because I want to be technically accurate without extensive algebraic specifications.

The particular models I use here are also unusual—"latent growth models" (LGM) for longitudinal data. This kind of model is depicted in Fig. 4.2, and these LGM are different in several ways. The key feature of any LGM is the resolution of common patterns of change into a common factor. This factor model (a) characterizes change in the means, variances, and correlations, and (b) combines change at the level of the group with change at the level of the individual. Although most applications of confirmatory factor analysis have focused on latent *psychometric* variables, I now use the same techniques to examine latent *chronometric* variables.

The LGMs concepts used here are not at all new. They were originally presented by both Tucker (1958, 1966) and Rao (1958) and have been discussed by many others since (e.g., Hultsch, Nesselroade, & Plemons, 1976; for technical review, see McArdle, 1988). On the other hand, these LGM techniques are not standard or classical structural equation models. The structural equation basis of these models has only recently been introduced by Meredith and Tisak (1984). McArdle (1986, 1988), and McArdle and Epstein (1987) further examined LGMs using the concepts and algorithms of linear structural equation modeling.

All mathematical and statistical aspects of this presentation use the basic LGM ideas. I do not examine any simple causal path models, but I do examine the invariance of features of the factor analysis model (see Alwin & Jackson, 1982; Horn, McArdle, & Mason, 1983; Jöreskog, 1971; Nesselroade, 1983). Basically, I use the principles of factor invariance within the structural equation modeling approach in an unusual way: I examine the invariance of the structure of dynamic processes within different measures and between multiple groups.

OUTLINE

In the next sections, some of the basic data and models are presented as a multivariate experiment—with a Methods, Results, and Discussion section. I do assume some prior experience with the analysis of variance (ANOVA) model, the correlation coefficient, the regression model, and the factor analysis model. This presentation does not offer extensive technical details but uses and interprets some relatively complex analyses (more information on the technical details can be obtained from the author).

The substantive issues examined here are based on real data from an experiment on the short-term effects of cognitive training on ability. This has been a continuing topic of interest in educational, cognitive research, and aging research (e.g., Horn, 1986). In these analyses, we examine groups that have been given different levels of cognitive stimulation and we compare their growth and change on several psychometric measures to test the recent learning and ability predictions made by Horn (1986). These data come from other work reported by McArdle (1988) and McArdle and Epstein (1987), and more complete descriptions of these data can be found therein. These substantive analyses and interpretations are intended to be consistent with the spirit of this symposium. (Readers primarily interested in the substantive results should first compare Tables 4.1 and 4.9).

The main goal of this report is to briefly demonstrate the merger of available structural equation methods with available experimental cognitive data. I try to test out some old ideas about learning, motivation, and ability, but this article is primarily methodological. I use confirmatory factor analysis methods to set up testable hypotheses about functional unities or regularities in longitudinal experimental data.

METHODS

Data Collection

The data of this study were selected from a larger multivariate longitudinal study presented in detail by McArdle (1988). Complete details of the study design are not discussed here but are described in Table 4.1. Briefly, the key features include:

1. About two hundred subjects (Ss) voluntarily participated in a *learning experiment*.
2. Before any measurements were made, these subjects were assigned to one of three experimental groups that varied on the amount of *stimulation* they received; i.e., either G = Low, G = Medium, or G = High.
3. The subjects were all randomly exposed to the same learning materials and they were measured at four preselected times during the *learning trials*— after about 70, 80, 100, and 130 exposures to the stimulus material. (S was allowed to stop the experiment at any time during the experimental procedure, but this attrition was less than 1%.)
4. Two cognitive measures were used: (M = 1) *Verification (V)* measures the factual information in the material presented, and (M = 2) *Persistence (P)* measures how eager the Ss were about continuing with the learning study. (The data analyses reported in McArdle, 1988, consisted of eight cognitive measures repeated at each occasion.)

Data Description

The two measures V and P were obtained at each of four time points, for each of the three groups. The distribution of these scores was plotted to examine the

TABLE 4.1
Experimental Design Summary from a "Learning Experiment"
(McArdle, 1988)

Subjects (S) and Experimenters (E)

Undergraduate college sophomores enrolled in an experimental psychology course signed up for "a learning experiment." Experimenters were assigned to each subject based on convenient meeting times. E were blind to the group assignment (G). Complete records were obtained on $N(S) = 204$ from $N(E) = 17$.

Random Assignment to Groups (G)

(G = 1) No Stimulation—The 15-minute videotape displayed the university logo and played music taped off the university radio station.

(G = 2) Medium Stimulation—The same as G = 1 except for an extra 5-minute section on "Learning and Motivation I," which emphasized the general importance of Task Persistence to Task Accuracy.

(G = 3) High Stimulation—The same as G = 2 except for an extra 5-minute section on "Learning and Motivation II," which demonstrated results on the importance of Task Persistence to Task Accuracy using detailed available evidence from the newspapers and psychological literature.

Stimulus Material and Measurement Trials (T)

Twenty-five items about "statistical reasoning without equations" were derived from the introductory statistics textbook book by Freedman, Pisani, and Purves (1978). These materials were drawn or typed onto slides and randomly presented to the S by an electronic tachistoscope. The exposure time was approximately 19 seconds, with a 1-second delay between slides. The E stopped the t-scope at the following preselected occasions of measurement:

(T = 1) After an average of about 73 exposures to the stimulus material.

(T = 2) After an average of about 83 exposures to the stimulus material.

(T = 3) After an average of about 106 exposures to the stimulus material.

(T = 4) After an average of about 129 exposures to the stimulus material.

Psychometric Measures (M)

(M = 1) Verification (V)—The E asked the S 10 questions to verify the factual information in the material presented. The E simply checked off the factual correctness of each response. All materials presented were randomly ordered, so the latter trials contained the same information content. A "percentage correct" score was obtained for the variable V at each time point by summing these 10 binary items and dividing by 10.

(M = 2) Persistence (P)—The E asked the S 10 questions about how eager they were about continuing with the learning study at this specific time. A "percentage interest" score was obtained for the variable P at each time point by summing these 10 binary items and dividing by 10.

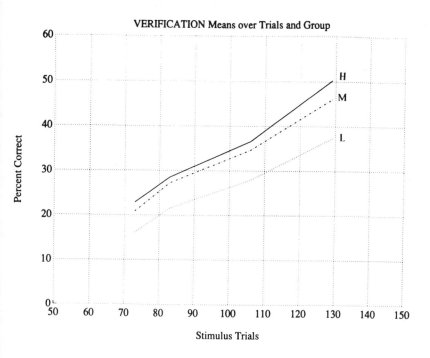

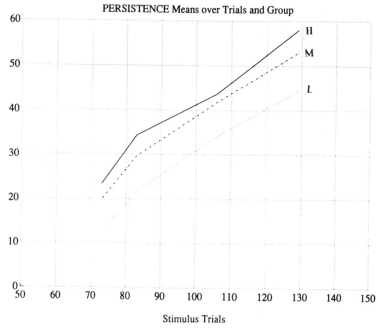

FIG. 4.3. The learning experiment results for the means of two variables.

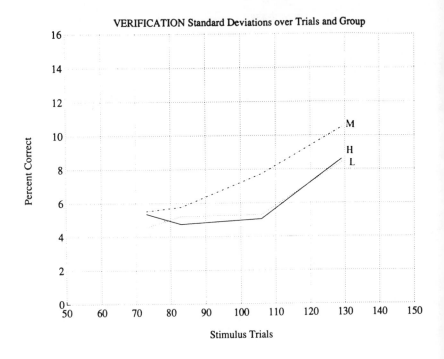

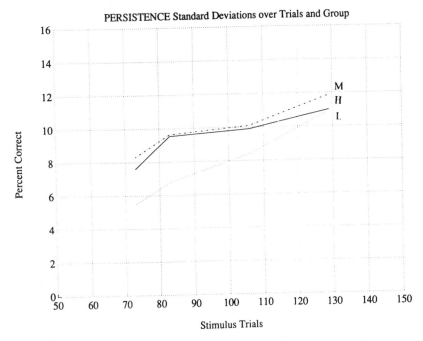

FIG. 4.4. The learning experiment results for the standard deviations of two variables.

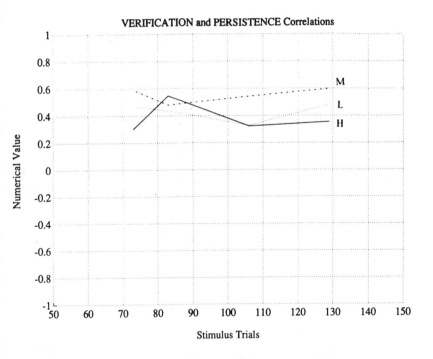

VERIFICATION and PERSISTENCE Correlations

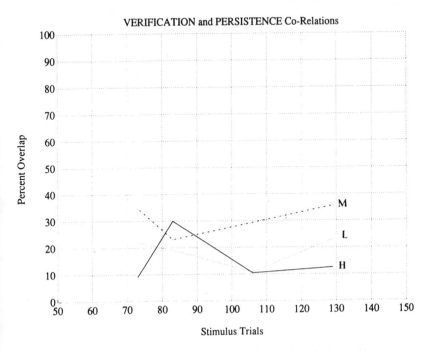

VERIFICATION and PERSISTENCE Co-Relations

FIG. 4.5. The learning experiment results for the correlations of two variables.

TABLE 4.2

Summary Statistics for the Three-Group Learning Experiment

a. Means and Deviations for All Groups Percentages (from Percentage Scores)

Stimulation (N)	Stat.	Verification @ Trials				Persistence @ Trials			
		V@73	V@83	V@106	V@129	P@73	P@83	P@106	P@129
Low (76)	Mean	16.17	21.58	27.92	37.33	12.71	21.57	34.12	44.46
	Sd	(4.56)	(5.21)	(5.31)	(8.42)	(5.48)	(6.78)	(8.41)	(10.91)
	Sem*2	1.05	1.20	1.22	1.93	1.26	1.56	1.93	2.50
Medium (82)	Mean	20.90	27.23	34.69	46.05	19.84	29.63	41.80	52.96
	Sd	(5.52)	(5.76)	(7.73)	(10.50)	(8.30)	(9.64)	(10.10)	(11.87)
	Sem*2	1.22	1.27	1.71	2.32	1.83	2.13	2.23	2.62
High (46)	Mean	22.89	28.52	36.64	50.26	23.35	34.34	43.67	58.01
	Sd	(5.36)	(4.75)	(5.06)	(8.61)	(7.60)	(9.54)	(9.90)	(11.00)
	Sem*2	1.58	1.40	1.49	2.54	2.24	2.81	2.92	3.24
Overall (204)	Mean	19.585	25.415	32.607	43.750	17.977	27.690	39.358	50.932
	Sd	(5.808)	(6.107)	(7.320)	(10.665)	(8.350)	(9.991)	(10.269)	(12.480)
	Sem*2	.81	.86	1.03	1.49	1.17	1.40	1.44	1.75

b. Correlations for Low Stimulation Group

	V@73	V@83	V@106	V@129	P@73	P@83	P@106	P@129
V@73	1.000							
V@83	.581	1.000						
V@106	.534	.632	1.000					
V@129	.400	.566	.711	1.000				
P@73	.470	.364	.384	.292	1.000			
P@83	.268	.437	.337	.348	.610	1.000		
P@106	.301	.361	.328	.395	.613	.677	1.000	
P@129	.351	.315	.355	.480	.526	.597	.774	1.000

c. Correlations for Medium Stimulation Group

	V@73	V@83	V@106	V@129	P@73	P@83	P@106	P@129
	1.000							
	.687	1.000						
	.756	.731	1.000					
	.654	.738	.797	1.000				
	.590	.514	.625	.588	1.000			
	.475	.480	.570	.606	.741	1.000		
	.443	.453	.541	.604	.737	.765	1.000	
	.427	.461	.512	.597	.702	.805	.809	1.000

d. Correlations for High Stimulation Group

	V@73	V@83	V@106	V@129	P@73	P@83	P@106	P@129
	1.000							
	.612	1.000						
	.521	.618	1.000					
	.531	.546	.577	1.000				
	.302	.435	.269	.506	1.000			
	.276	.547	.325	.507	.712	1.000		
	.221	.440	.323	.424	.615	.809	1.000	
	.180	.352	.211	.354	.562	.764	.721	1.000

e. Correlations for Overall Groups

	V@73	V@83	V@106	V@129	P@73	P@83	P@106	P@129
	1.00000							
	.71803	1.00000						
	.72662	.75665	1.00000					
	.65415	.72791	.79746	1.00000				
	.61016	.58517	.62384	.61832	1.00000			
	.51877	.60191	.59239	.63245	.78029	1.00000		
	.46850	.53110	.54574	.59455	.73232	.79304	1.00000	
	.47795	.51214	.53064	.61065	.69584	.78550	.81122	1.00000

distribution shape and to eliminate outliers. The distribution of all eight variables was visibly normal and there were no obvious outliers. The means, standard deviations, standard errors, and correlation matrices for each of the three groups, and also for the overall sample, are presented in Table 4.2.

A plot of the means for each group on both scores is presented in Fig. 4.3. Both plots show the highest means for the High stimulation group, followed by the next highest means for the Medium stimulation group, whereas the lowest means are found for the Low stimulation group. The standard error bars are too small to be included in this plot. The Persistence scores are slightly higher than the Verification scores. These initial results seem consistent with the experimental design.

A plot of the standard deviations for each group on both scores is presented in Fig. 4.4. Here, Verification shows increasing variation over trials, and most variation occurs in the Medium stimulation group. The Persistence scores exhibit increasing variation over trial and the Low stimulation group shows the least variation. A plot of the correlations of Verification and Persistence over trials is presented for each group in Fig. 4.5. This Figure shows all the correlations are positive (and around .5). The group differences are enhanced by the squared correlation plot of [4.2], which shows a mixed pattern of increasing and decreasing correlations for the different groups. For example, the High stimulation group starts lowest, becomes highest, and then tapers off to be lowest again. These initial results are also consistent with the planned experimental design.

A Preliminary MANOVA

Some basic features of these data can be isolated using well-known techniques from the analysis of variance. In these data we have three independent groups of subjects measured on two dependent variables over four sequential testing occasions. The usual questions of interest lead us to examine several alternative analyses of variance models, univariate repeated measures and split-plots analyses as well as multivariate repeated measures or profile analysis (see Bock, 1975, 1979). We can also assume the percentage scores across both variables are in directly comparable form; that is, so raw differences between V and P are informative. This allows us to treat this as a simple problem of a multivariate repeated measures model with one between-groups factor, Group G (with three levels), and two within-groups factors, Occasions T (with four levels) and Measures M (with two levels, V vs. P). Our main questions can now be organized as hierarchical variance components.

For further simplicity of analysis and presentation, all components are transformed into single-degree-of-freedom questions (see Bock, 1975). The Group G effects will be restated as the usual sum components (labeled G_0), a primary group difference between the Low and other groups (G_1), and a secondary question about group differences between the High and Medium groups (G_2).

The Trials effects over the four occasions is restated as orthogonal polynomials representing intercept, linear, quadratic, and cubic single-degree of freedom components (labeled P_i, P_l, P_q, and P_c). The Measures M effects are also restated as the usual sum (M_0) and difference components (M_1).

Table 4.3 presents the basic results from this form of repeated measures MANOVA applied to the experimental data of Table 4.2. This Table lists separate components of variance, F-ratios, p-values for testing of a null hypothesis, and effect sizes (η^2) statistics. All results with a probability less than the 1% level are considered significant, and these effects are interpreted in the last column of Table 4.3.

This preliminary MANOVA analysis is useful because it illustrates some basic features of these data. For example, one main effect shows the Medium and High groups score higher than the Low groups ($\eta^2 = .31$). Another main effect shows the change over trials is largely linear ($\eta^2 = .95$) but also shows significant quadratic ($\eta^2 = .06$) and cubic ($\eta^2 = .30$) changes. One of the significant interactions shows that the Persistence–Verification differences increase over trials ($\eta^2 = .41, .19$). Perhaps the most interesting effect of all is that the Persistence–Verification differences show least change over trials in the Low group (although $\eta^2 = .03$).

This MANOVA is not the focus of our methodology here, but these techniques are widely used for analyzing these kinds of data collections. Under certain restrictive assumptions, the multivariate estimation provides protection against spurious assignment of significant effects. One key assumption here is the equality of covariance matrices of the components over groups. This assumption is needed for standard statistical inference about the mean differences. This kind of assumption is usually palatable when we are mainly interested in the analysis of the means. But, as Figs. 4.4 and 4.5 showed, we might be interested in other features of the data as well. For example, we might be interested in any changes in the correlation of the two measures as a function of training and stimulation. The traditional MANOVA logic needs to be expanded for the substantive needs of this analysis.

Structural Equation Modeling of Latent Growth Curves

The methodology we now use is based on the techniques of linear structural equation modeling. Some basic equations for these analyses are provided in Table 4.4.

By far and away the most popular structural equation model for longitudinal data is the *autoregressive* model listed in equation [4.3a]. This model represents a *time forward* prediction series, where deviations on some variable y^*_t lead to deviations y^*_{t+x} at some later time. This model could be drawn as a path diagram similar to Fig. 4.1 (and LISREL notation could certainly be used here;

TABLE 4.3
A Repeated Measures Multivariate Analysis of Variance Applied
to the Experimental Data of Table 4.1[a]

Effect	Contrast	Dfb	F	P	η^2	Interp. @ .01
0 1 = Constant	$G_0 \times T_0 \times M_0$	1	5408.	.000*	96%	Means > 0
1 G = Between Groups						
Low vs. (Med + High)	$G_1 \times T_0 \times M_0$	1	92.0	.000*	31%	(M + H) >> Low
Medium vs. High	$G_2 \times T_0 \times M_0$	1	7.3	.007*	4%	High > Med
2 M = Between Measures						
V vs. P	$G_0 \times T_0 \times M_1$	1	64.6	.000*	24%	P > V
3 T = Within Trials						
Linear	$G_+ \times T_1 \times M_0$	1	3837.	.000*	95%	Linear >>> 0
Quadratic	$G_+ \times T_2 \times M_0$	1	12.0	.001*	6%	Quad > 0
Cubic	$G_+ \times T_3 \times M_0$	1	86.8	.001*	30%	Cubic >> 0
(4) G × M = Between Groups Within Measures						
	$G_1 \times T_0 \times M_1$	1	4.6	.033	2%	
	$G_2 \times T_0 \times M_1$	1	1.4	.246	1%	
(5) G × T = Between Groups Within Trials						
	$G_1 \times T_1 \times M_0$	1	11.8	.001*	6%	(M + H) > Low on Lin > 0
	$G_1 \times T_2 \times M_0$	1	3.4	.066	2%	
	$G_1 \times T_3 \times M_0$	1	4.3	.034	2%	
	$G_2 \times T_1 \times M_0$	1	1.6	.201	1%	

	df	F	p	%	
$G_2 \times T_2 \times M_0$	1	6.6	.011	3%	
$G_2 \times T_3 \times M_0$	1	2.4	.123	1%	

(6) T × M = Within Trials Within Measures

	df	F	p	%	
$G_0 \times T_1 \times M_1$	1	139.	.000*	41%	Linear > 0 on P > V
$G_0 \times T_2 \times M_1$	1	48.5	.000*	19%	Quad > 0 on P > V
$G_0 \times T_3 \times M_1$	1	2.1	.145	1%	

(7) G × T × M = Between Groups Within Trials Within Measures

	df	F	p	%	
$G_1 \times T_1 \times M_1$	1	6.9	.009*	3%	(M + H) > Low on P > V on T
$G_1 \times T_2 \times M_1$	1	0.0	.967	0%	
$G_1 \times T_3 \times M_1$	1	3.5	.063	2%	
$G_2 \times T_1 \times M_1$	1	1.1	.296	1%	
$G_2 \times T_2 \times M_1$	1	.2	.703	0%	
$G_2 \times T_3 \times M_1$	1	5.1	.025	3%	

(8) Multivariate Trial Effects

	df	F	p	%	
Trials	3	1338.	.000*	95%	Trials > 0
$T \times G_1$	3	5.2	.002*	7%	(M + H) > Low on T > 0
$T \times G_2$	3	3.0	.031	4%	
$T \times M$	3	72.	.000*	52%	P > V on T > 0
$T \times G_1 \times M$	3	3.6	.015	5%	
$T \times G_2 \times M$	3	2.1	.099	3%	

$^a \eta^2 = (F \div dfw) \div (1 + F \div dfw)$ where $dfw = 201$.

All multivariate tests based on Wilk's Lambda approximation in SAS: "proc glm; model V_6 V_7 V_9 V_11 P_6 P_7 P_9 P_11 = low other med_high / nouni int; repeated measures 2, age 4 (73 83 106 129) polynomial / short summary canonical ;"

TABLE 4.4
Mathematical and Statistical Equations for Linear Structural
Growth Models

---

a. Autoregressive Model

$$y_{t,n} = y^*_{t,n} + My_t, \text{ and } y^*_{t,n} = \sum_{q=1}^{Q} A_q\, y^*_{t-q,n} + e_{t,n},$$

where $y_{t,n}$ are the raw scores at time t for subject n, $y^*_{t,n}$ are the mean-deviate scores, My_t is the mean of y at time t, the A_q are autoregressive lag coefficients, the index q represents some specific time lag, and the e_t is an independent error term.

b. The Linear Polynomial Model

$$y_{t,n} = L_n + P_t\, S_n + e_n,$$

where the P_t are time-based coefficients (e.g., trials, times),
the components L are level or intercept scores,
the components S are shape or slope scores, and
the components e are uncorrelated error or disturbance scores.

c. The Latent Growth Model

$$y_{t,n} = L_n + B_t\, S_n + e_n,$$

where the B_t are "basis" coefficients to be estimated from the data, and the components S_n are latent shape or profile scores.

d. Implied Raw Score Mean Expectations

$$E\{y_t,\ 1'\} = M_L + B_t\, M_s,$$

where $E\{.\}$ is the expectation operator, and 1 is the unit constant score.

e. Implied Raw Score Covariance Expectations

$$E\{y^*_t\, y^*_{t+x}{}'\} = V_L + B_t\, V_S\, B_{t+x}{}' + 2\, C_{LS}\, B_{t+x} + V_e,$$

where V_L is the variance of the level scores, V_S is the variance of the shape scores, C_{LS} is the covariance of level and shape scores, and V_e is the variance of the error scores (only when $x = 0$).

f. Implied Cross-Product Expectations

$$E\{y_t\, y_{t+x}{}'\} = [E\{y_t\}\, E\{y_{t+x}\}] + [E\{y^*_t\, y^*_{t+x}{}'\}].$$

g. Likelihood Ratio Criteria for Cross-Products Expectations

$$LRC \approx \sum_{x=0}^{t} \left[[y_t\, y_{t+x}{}'] - E\{y_t\, y_{t+x}{}'\} \right]^2 \Big/ E\{y_t\, y_{t+x}{}'\}$$

$$\approx LRD + LRT + LRM$$

where

$LRD = \ln|\,C\,| - \ln|\,E\{C\}\,| = $ Likelihood Ratio based on Log Determinants,
$LRT = \mathrm{tr}\{C\, E\{C\}^{-1}\} - t = $ Likelihood Ratio based on Matrix Trace,
$LRM = (M - E\{M\})\, E\{C\}^{-1}\, (M - E\{M\})' = $ Likelihood based on Means (T^2).

---

see Jöreskog, 1970; Werts, Linn, & Jöreskog, 1977). But this standard longitudinal model actually has several limitations for our purposes: (a) Model [4.3a] assumes all individuals change according to the same coefficient A_l; (b) Model [4.3a] assumes the *stable* component, $A_l\, y^*_{t-l,n}$, is uncorrelated with the *unstable* component, $e_{l,n}$; (c) Model [4.3a] assumes the raw score means, My, can be removed without loss of generality. These limitations are overcome in the different kind of structural equation models to follow.

To provide a starting point for our further models let us backtrack to the MANOVA model approach. Following the classical traditions (see Bock, 1975), we write the basic polynomial trend model as structural equation model [4.3b]. This model assumes the raw scores $y_{t,n}$ are an explicit function of the fixed coefficients P_t based on the experimental exposure at the time of testing (e.g., 73, 83, 106, 129). The individual differences in this standard model are organized into correlated and uncorrelated components of the time series. The first component, L_n, is a *level* or *intercept* score because we assume a coefficient of unity for each time. The second component, S_n, is a *slope* score since it has a P_t coefficient which varies over time t. The third component, e_n, is an *error* score which will have zero mean and be uncorrelated with any other component within or across time. The means and variances of these individual components are used to define the group growth curves.

This structural equation representation of MANOVA shows how individual differences are organized in the standard linear trend model—individuals are allowed to vary along several common dimensions, these dimensions have a fixed relationship to the original raw scores, and the error terms are independent and random. In these same ways, the autoregressive model of Fig. 4.1 follows conceptually and mathematically from the growth model of Fig. 4.2. (A detailed description of the MANOVA model is presented in Fig. 4.6.)

This standard growth model can now be used and extended in many ways. The most common extension requires the addition of fixed coefficients P_t, each raised to a consecutive power p. Under this structural basis, the components are termed the intercept L_n, linear S_n, quadratic Q_n, and cubic C_n terms. In this repeated measures model, these component scores are correlated and have mean and variances for the overall group.

But other extensions are possible and potentially more revealing. Equation [4.3c] is a model that is exactly the same as the linear trend model except here we assume the coefficients B_t are free to be estimated from the data. In mathematical terms, the B_t are the *bases* of the functional relation between the observed scores on $Y_{t,n}$ and the unobserved scores on S_n. This model also allows component means, standard deviations, and correlations among all common components, and includes error components. This model organizes individual differences over time into a fixed level component L_n as well as an estimable latent component S_n. The a posteriori definition of the basis coefficients B_t means that the S_n scores are latent *slopes* or *patterns of change*. Although these S_n are not directly measurable, the latent model [4.3c] has exactly the same structure as the linear model of [4.3b] (and Figs. 4.2 or 4.6).

The latent growth model is a structural equation form of the model used earlier by Tucker (1958, 1966) to analyze "learning curves" and by Rao (1958) to define a growth curve "metameter." This model was recently revived by

Meredith and Tisak (1984) for the analysis of incomplete data structures, and it has also been used by McArdle (1986) for longitudinal behavior genetics analysis. As pointed out by these authors, several other model restrictions are possible. For example, growth curve models do not require an intercept, and we can make this simple change by dropping the L_n component. This is the single factor model of growth drawn in Fig. 4.2. In general, however, this is a somewhat bold restriction because it implies an absolute metric scaling of means and variances. In this model, results should change with the addition of a constant to all scores, and in many cases this model is undesirable. These restrictions have been explored by McArdle and Epstein (1987) and McArdle (1988).

The two-component latent growth model [4.3c] is later drawn (in Fig. 4.6) and is explored in some other ways here. In one extension, we specify a class of model for the differences between groups in their latent growth patterns. This model allows the bases $B_{g,t}$ to vary over groups and also allows the correlations among the components to vary over groups. Invariance restrictions added to this model will allow the examination of the multiple group growth differences. Another extension will be used to examine differences between measures M in their latent growth patterns. These models allow the bases $B_{m,t}$ to vary over variables and also allow correlations among the components to vary over variables. Invariance restrictions added to this model will allow the examination of the multiple variable growth differences. A final extension will be used to allow differences between both measures and groups on their latent growth patterns. These models allow the bases $B_{g,m,t}$ and the correlations among the components to vary over variables and groups. Invariance restrictions added to these models will allow the simultaneous examination of the multiple variable and multiple group growth properties.

Model Estimation and Goodness-of-Fit

The term *structure* in a structural equation model refers to the fact that some linear models provide restrictive hypothesis about the summary statistics. For the purpose of model fitting, the structural expectations of any latent model need to be rigorously and unambiguously defined. The LGM [4.3c in Table 4.3] assumes the unobserved components are individual scores and this implies the existence of means M_k, standard deviations D_k, and correlations R_k for each of the $k = 1$ to K component scores in [4.3c]. This also leads to an implied structure for the raw score means and raw score covariances, and these are simply listed in [4.3d] and [4.3e]. Because the mean expectations are based on a unit constant (labeled "1"), the mean and covariance expectations can be added together to form expectations for the raw cross-products, as in [4.3f]. These average cross-products are the structural expectations for the latent growth model.

In general, then, the expectations [4.3d], [4.3e], and [4.3f] are identical to the traditional common factor model, except here we fit the model to raw score moments. A most important feature of this model is that the expectations for the means and covariances include the same set of B_t parameters in each equation [4.3d] and [4.3e]. This means the basis B_t should not be separately estimated by either the means or covariances and the latent growth model must be fitted from cross-products. A graphic path-analytic interpretation of this model has been offered by McArdle (1986, 1988) and as a special case of the general latent growth curve models by both Meredith and Tisak (1984) and McArdle (1986).

The nonlinear structural expectations [4.3d] and [4.3e] provide both a way to estimate the model parameters and a way to test a structural hypothesis about the latent construct. It is well known that the likelihood ratio criterion (LRC) statistic can be formed from the scaled sums-of-squared differences between data observations and model expectations (e.g., McArdle, 1986; Sörbom, 1974). In broad terms, the algorithms minimize this discrepancy function and provide approximate maximum-likelihood estimates and standard errors for all free parameters.

A variety of goodness-of-fit indices are available for model evaluation (see Cudeck & Browne, 1983; McArdle, 1986, 1988), but most indices rely in some way on the size of the LRC. Simply stated, if the likelihood of discrepancy is large enough, then the expectations do not match the observations; but if the likelihood of discrepancy is small enough, then the expectations do match the observations. Our goal is to separate those models that clearly do not fit from those models that clearly do fit (for more details, see Cudeck & Browne, 1983; Loehlin, 1987; McDonald, 1985). The use of a combined LRC for the means and the covariances makes this task more complex (as in McArdle, 1986, 1988; Sörbom, 1974).

The practical aspects of fitting a latent growth model require many more details of parameter identification and estimation. These issues are important but they are discussed only as needed here. (For those interested, a copy of the LISREL-VII estimation program for this specific multiple variable and multiple group model can be obtained from the author.)

RESULTS

The application of the structural equation models of Table 4.4 to the cognitive data of Table 4.2 is now presented in some detail. To explain different aspects of the modeling I break up the analysis into subsections and then summarize the results in a final section. I also use structural path diagrams to help explain the overall modeling logic and the possible options that can be used. In these pictures, the observed variables Y_t are drawn as closed boxes and the unobserved variables L, S, and e_t are drawn as open boxes. The deterministic coefficients are drawn as one-way directed "arrows," whereas the stochastic parameters are drawn as two-way undirected "slings." More details on this path notation are presented by McArdle (1980) and McArdle and Horn (in press).

Modeling Growth over Trials

The initial question asked about these data is, "Which growth model is appropriate?" There are many ways to start this kind of an investigation, but here I fitted all models based on the latent growth model of equation [4.3c].

A univariate latent growth model is represented by the path diagram in Fig. 4.6. Here, the observed variables Y_t represent a single measure taken over time (T = 5 in this theoretical diagram, but T = 4 in this experiment). This diagram shows two unobserved common components, L and S, as the outcome of two other unobserved components, L* and S*. The second set of scores, L* and S*, are standardized scores, with fixed unit variance, and these are included so the projections D_L and D_S represent the component standard deviations. In this diagram, the loadings from component L to the observed Y_t are all fixed at unit values, but the loadings from component S to the observed Y_t are listed as B_t. This diagram also includes error variables e_t for each of the observed variables. These error components are uncorrelated with all other components and have a standard deviation of D_e. Since this error is assumed to be random or white noise, the coefficient D_e is presumed to be equal over all occasions.

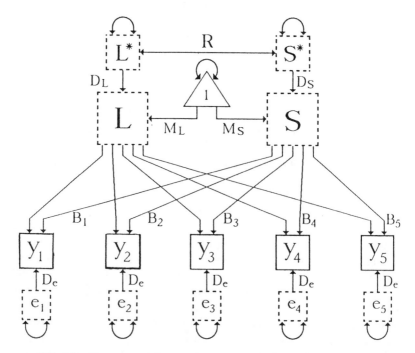

FIG. 4.6. The two-component latent growth curve as a structural equation model: A path diagram of an LGM (using RAM notation from McArdle, 1980).

The L and S components are also an outcome of the unit constant labeled 1 and drawn within a closed triangle. (As always, this constant is observed but not measured.) In this form, the projections M_L and M_S represent means or location parameters. The error components have no relation with the constant, so they have zero means. This inclusion of location parameters within a path diagram is a bit unusual, but these location parameters are needed as a fundamental aspect of the latent growth model restrictions (see equation [4.3d]). It is sufficient now to say that these parameters are essential to the growth curve logic used here (for more details, see Horn & McArdle, 1980; McArdle, 1980, 1986, 1988; McArdle & Epstein, 1987).

The growth model of Fig. 4.6 can now be fitted to the average cross-products of any single-variable time-series in any group. In this experiment, we could fit the model to either variable in any group or to a total score from all groups on the sum of all measures (as in McArdle & Epstein, 1987, Table 1). To retain comparability across models, this single model is now fitted in a slightly more complex fashion. In all models to follow, the latent growth model (Fig. 4.6) is fitted directly to the average cross-products from the three groups on two different measures. This allows different substantive questions to be examined by assuming a subset of parameters are invariant over measures and groups.

Table 4.5 includes the results of several alternative growth models fitted to the same data set (and using a similar program). The numerical results for each model are listed in one column and the corresponding parameter estimates and goodness-of-fit indices are listed in the various rows. The last row offers an interpretation of the model results from an objective statistical and mathematical point of view. Of course, these interpretations may need to be changed based on subjective features of the substantive phenomena.

The first model, labeled #0 in Table 4.5, shows the results obtained from a model fitted without the S variable, so I label it a *No Growth* model. This model includes only one L component that has the same mean M_L = 32.4, common standard deviation D_L = 4.97, and independent error variance D_E = 10.9. The LRC = 2341 on DF = 126 and this can be converted to a normal Z = 39. As the last row of the Table shows, I have interpreted this large likelihood of discrepancy to indicate that there is some growth apparent within these data. This model provides a baseline against which other models can be compared.

The next model, labeled #1 in Table 4.5, is the *Linear* growth model. Here, the coefficients B_t are forced to be equal to the numerical value of the trials index P_t = [73, 83, 106, 129]. This model could easily be fitted with the $B_t = P_t$ and then the L would represent the function at P_0 and the slope would represent a one-trial change in the function. But for estimation purposes I have scaled the distance between trials on a 0 to 1 scale; that is, $B_t = [(P_t - P_q) \div P_q]$, where q is the final occasion of measurement. This scaling results in a fixed B_t = [.000, .179, .589, and 1.000], and these loadings are interpreted as proportions of the overall time scale (e.g., by the second time point, we have reached 17.9% of the

TABLE 4.5
Numerical Results for Basic Latent Growth Models[a]

Model Parameter	#0 No Growth	#1 Linear	#2 Retest	#3 Latent	#4 Partial	#5 Absolute
Factor Loadings						
$L \rightarrow T_1$	1	1	1	1	1	0
$L \rightarrow T_2$	1	1	1	1	1	0
$L \rightarrow T_3$	1	1	1	1	1	0
$L \rightarrow T_4$	1	1	1	1	1	0
$S \rightarrow T_1$: B_1	0	.000	.000	.000	.000	.401*
$S \rightarrow T_2$: B_2	0	.179	.333	.274*	.270*	.565*
$S \rightarrow T_3$: B_3	0	.589	.667	.603*	.589	.760*
$S \rightarrow T_4$: B_4	0	1.000	1.000	1.000	1.000	1.000
Factor Standard Deviations						
$L^* \rightarrow L$: D_L	4.97*	6.17*	5.99*	6.15*	6.16*	.0
$S^* \rightarrow S$: D_S	.0	7.00*	7.31*	7.56*	7.57*	11.5*
$E^* \rightarrow E$: D_E	10.9*	4.34*	4.28*	4.06*	4.07*	4.71*
Factor Correlations						
$S^* \leftrightarrow L^*$: R_{SL}	.0	.378*	.292*	.274*	.278*	.0

Factor Means

	Some Growth	Linear Better	Retest as Good	Latent Better	Partial OK	Intercept Needed
1 → L : M_L	32.4*	20.7*	18.5*	19.4*	19.5*	.0
1 → S : M_S	.0	27.5*	28.6*	28.7*	28.7*	47.5*
Goodness-of-Fit Indices						
Likelihood Ratio	2341	587	559	491	493	620
Degrees of Freedom	126	114	114	112	113	123
Normal Z-Test	39.	17.	16.	14.	14.	17.
Step-Down dLRC	—	1754	1782	96	-2	-129
Step-Down dDF	—	12	12	2	1	9
Step-Down Zd	—	31.	32.	8.2	1.0	9.3
Step-Down dLRC/LRC %	—	+75%	+76%	+84%	-0%	-26%
Interpretation	Some Growth	Linear Better	Retest as Good	Latent Better	Partial OK	Intercept Needed

[a]All parameters estimated from three-group cross-products matrices of Table 4.1 using LISREL program with maximum likelihood fitting function.

All free parameters where $MLE_p > 2*SE_p$ are designated by an asterisk.

All parameters listed assumed invariant over Measures and Groups.

overall time). The intercept mean $M_L = 20.7$ with deviation $D_L = 6.17$ reflects the group features at the first trial. The slope mean $M_S = 27.5$ with deviation $D_S = 7.00$ reflects group features of change over all trials. The correlation among the intercept and slope scores for individuals is $R_{S,L} = .378$. Finally, the independent error deviation is now only 4.34. This *Linear* model fits the experimental data with LRC = 587 on DF = 114, and this is a 75% improvement in fit over the prior *No Growth* model.

At this point we might wish to follow the polynomial model and introduce higher order components with fixed design weights B_t determined by powers of P_t. But instead, we explore a shift of scale with the single growth model. Model #2 is a different linear model, called the *Retest* model. In this model, the scale of the slope scores is reset to reflect the simple change over measurement occasions, $P_t = [1,2,3,4]$, which is rescaled into proportions, $B_t = [.000, .333, .667, 1.000]$. This model is insensitive to the unequal interval between testing occasions. Nevertheless, and somewhat surprisingly, this model fits slightly better than the linear model for trials. In models for single time series with equal measurement points, the effect of testing is confounded with the effects of trials and we will not be able to separate out these effects (but see McArdle, Anderson, & Aber, 1987). Actually, Model #2 is better than the others, but it still does not fit the data very well (with Z = 16).

Model #3 is the first complete *Latent Growth Model*. The main difference here comes because the basis coefficients $B_2 = .274$ and $B_3 = .603$ were allowed to be estimated as model parameters. The parameters of this model can now be directly compared to the *Linear* model parameters. The latent B_2 and B_3 are greater than the linear parameters, and this implies that growth on the latent function B_t is more rapid than on the observed trials P_t. In broad terms, these parameters B_t define a metameter (after Rao, 1958) or learning curve (after Tucker, 1958) or hidden time (after McArdle & Epstein, 1987), which is an optimum structural organization of the individual differences in growth. The means, deviations, and correlations of the components within this model are only slightly different than the *Linear* model counterparts. Nevertheless, this *Latent* model likelihood reflects a 94% improvement over the *Linear* model.

The parameters of Model #3 are often easier to visualize in Cartesian score-based coordinates. Although the latent growth scores L and S are unobserved, we can obtain all necessary features from the model expectations. Fig. 4.7 is a plot of the model parameters of this LGM recast as a set of expectations about the group and individual growth process. The most striking feature of this plot is the fan-shaped expansion of the group and individual growth. This comes from the basic proportional expectations for the means and the deviations defined by the B_t basis coefficients (see table 4.4). The shaded area of the plot designates the 95% confidence boundary for the latent growth scores. This feature of this two-dimensional plot, which is not obvious on first examination, is that the B_t are also reflections of the expectations of the correlations among the scores. Incidentally, this plot does not require estimation of the latent growth curve

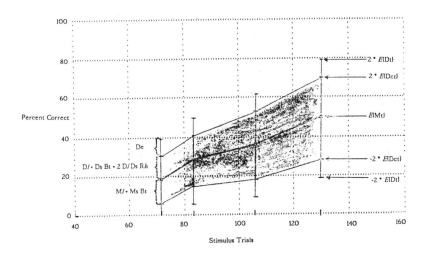

FIG. 4.7. The two-component latent growth curve as a structural equation model: A Cartesian diagram of the LGM expectations (with 95% confidence bands).

scores. All necessary statistical features are generated from the model expectations.

Model #4 of Table 4.5 gives results for a *Partial* LGM, where the $B_2 = .270$ was free to vary but the $B_3 = .589$ from the *Linear* model. This model reflects an interpretation about Fig. 4.7: Change is latent between the first and second trials, but linear thereafter. This model is no different in fit than the full latent model, so it simply provides a precise statistical index of the linearity in Fig. 4.7.

Model #5 is an alternative LGM based on an *Absolute* scale equation (i.e., [4.3c] without L_n, and Fig. 4.2). This model allows the estimation of the latent scale with parameters $B_1 = .401$, $B_2 = .464$, and $B_3 = .760$, and with $B_4 = 1.000$ by definition. This model also eliminates the need for the intercept mean M_L, deviation D_L, and correlation R_{LS}. Thus, the model is a broad simplification of the *Latent Growth* organization, but this simplification does not fit these data very well—the loss of the intercept is a loss of 26% in fit.

These few results suggest the LGM (Model #3) is a relatively good representation of these data. As Fig. 4.7 shows, most of the latent growth occurs between the early occasions of measurement (e.g., Model #3 = Model #4). But the absolute fit of all these models is relatively poor, so we now need to introduce additional variation with respect to groups and measures.

Modeling Growth over Groups

A next question arises: "Are there any differences between the groups on the latent growth?" To answer this question I next present a latent growth model for multiple groups by path diagrams in Fig. 4.8. These diagrams show exactly the

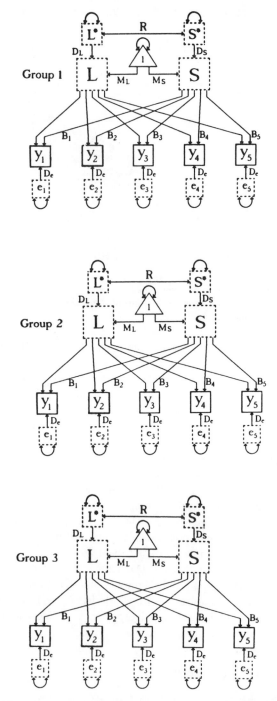

FIG. 4.8. The latent growth model for multiple groups.

same raw score components and relations for each of the groups, but subscripts g = 1 to G are added, which allows these scores and components to vary over groups. This follows the basic structural methods used by Jöreskog (1971) and Sörbom (1974) (also see Jöreskog & Sörbom, 1979). Conceptually I find it most useful to think of this diagram as a single model for a single cross-products matrix (as in McArdle & McDonald, 1984; McDonald, 1985). Of course, the independence of groups is guaranteed by the operations of measurement and these are not individuals under different stimulus conditions. This means the independence of the score components between groups are not testable model hypotheses.

Table 4.6 lists some numerical results for the three-group structural equations. As shown in Table 4.6, Model #6 allows group differences in all the LGM parameters. In this model, however, the basic LGM structure is assumed to be the same, and, because of the way the model was fitted here, the LGMs parameters must also remain the same for both of the two measures (but see next section). The parameters for each group are placed side by side in Table 4.6 and they show very similar patterns of change over groups. The model fits the experimental data with LRC = 369 on DF = 96 with a normal Z = 12.

Model #7, presented in Table 4.6, uses the same basic path structure but requires the shapes of all groups to be identical. This is identical to a structural hypothesis about factorial invariance (see Nesselroade, 1983). The main difference is that here the factors represent latent curves, so here the curves are presumed to be invariant. Notice, however, that this model allows the means and variances of the curves to differ over groups. In this sense, the model organizes growth patterns that reflect the same underlying process in all groups, but the amount and variation in this growth is allowed to be different over groups. This important equality restriction of loading invariance makes only a minor loss of 4% in the goodness of fit in these data. It seems reasonable to say the groups reflect the same growth or learning processes over trials.

As shown in Table 4.6, Model #8 adds the additional requirement that all factor variances (or standard deviations) be identical over groups. Since the growth factors are presumed to be invariant over groups, this represents the variance of the same dynamic construct. In traditional factor analysis we assume that if there is no variability, there is no factor. In this context, we can define this variability as the amplitude or width of the growth. The variance equality hypothesis seems to fit the data relatively well. It seems reasonable to say the stimulation level of the different groups has no effect on the growth process.

Model #9 adds the additional requirement that all factor means be identical over groups. Now since the growth factors are invariant, and since the growth variances are equal, these means reflect the amount or height of growth. The fit of this model of equal group M_L = 19 and M_S = 28 reflects a loss of 20% in relative fit, and this is important here. Although the growth factors have some similar properties, the amount of growth is different for the different groups.

TABLE 4.6
Numerical Results for Multiple Group Latent Growth Models[a]

Model Parameter	#6 Free Growth Lo	Me	Hi	#7 Same Loadings Lo	Me	Hi	#8 Same Variances Lo	Me	Hi	#9 Same Means Lo	Me	Hi
Factor Loadings												
$S \rightarrow T_1$: B_1	.00	.00	.00	.00	.00	.00	.00	.00	.00	.00	.00	.00
$S \rightarrow T_2$: B_2	.27	.28	.27	.27	.27	.27	.27	.27	.27	.27	.27	.27
$S \rightarrow T_3$: B_3	.63	.61	.55	.61	.61	.61	.60	.60	.60	.60	.60	.60
$S \rightarrow T_4$: B_4	1.00	1.00	1.00	1.00	1.00	1.00	1.00	1.00	1.00	1.00	1.00	1.00
Factor Standard Deviations												
$L^* \rightarrow L$: D_L	4.	6.	6.	4.	6.	5.	5.	5.	5.	6.	6.	6.
$S^* \rightarrow S$: D_S	9.	7.	6.	9.	7.	6.	7.	7.	7.	8.	8.	8.
$E^* \rightarrow E$: D_E	4.	4.	4.	4.	4.	4.	4.	4.	4.	4.	4.	4.
Factor Correlations												
$S^* \leftrightarrow L^*$: R_{SL}	−.03	.38	.26	−.03	.38	.31	.04	.37	.18	.17	.37	.33
Factor Means												
$1 \rightarrow L$: M_L	15.	21.	24.	15.	21.	24.	15.	21.	23.	19.	19.	19.
$1 \rightarrow S$: M_S	26.	29.	30.	27.	29.	30.	27.	29.	30.	28.	28.	28.
Goodness-of-Fit Indices												
Likelihood Ratio	369			383			409			492		
Degrees of Freedom	96			100			108			112		
Normal Z-Test	12.			12.			12.			14.		
Step-Down dLRC	—			14			26			83		
Step-Down dDF	—			4			8			4		
Step-Down Zd	—			2.43			3.05			7.65		
Step-Down dLRC/LRC %	—			−4%			−7%			−20%		
Interpretation	Not Invariant over Measures			Invariant Group Loadings			Invariant Group Variances			Not Invariant Group Means		

[a]All parameters listed assumed to be Invariant over Measures.

Looking back on the parameter estimates of Model #8, we see that the Low group has a very low level mean, $M_L = 15$; whereas the other two groups have higher level means, $M_L = 21$ and 23; but the shape means are similar, $M_L = 27$, 29, and 30. The largest discrepancies are coming from the relatively smaller value M_L for the low group.

All of the group differences just discussed could be further broken down into two group comparisons, such as the High and Medium versus Low groups. (And this would match more precisely with the MANOVA model of Table 4.3). Furthermore, there are no regulations about the ordering of the prior hypotheses. The variances could be set equal even if the shapes were different and, even more extreme, the means can be tested without equality of variances and shapes. I have proceeded in this traditional order to retain hypotheses that are used by traditional statistical sampling theorems.

Modeling Growth over Variables

The next question arises: "Are there any differences within the variables on the latent growth?" In response, I present a latent growth model for multiple variables by a path diagram in Fig. 4.9. This diagram shows exactly the same raw score components and relations for each of the two variables, but subscripts m = 1 to M are added, which allows these scores and components to vary over variables. This follows the basic structural methods used by Jöreskog and Sörbom (1977), but here I use the LGM. In contrast to Fig. 4.8, the dependence of variables is important here because this model does have the same individuals under different stimulus conditions. This also means the dependence of the score components, given by the correlations R_{VP}, are available parameters for testing model hypotheses.

Table 4.7 lists some numerical results for the two group structural equations

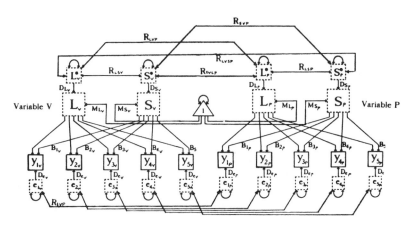

FIG. 4.9. The latent growth model for multiple variables.

TABLE 4.7
Numerical Results for Multiple Variable Latent Growth Models[a]

Model Parameter	#10 Free Growth	#11 Same Loadings	#12 Same Means	#13 Same Scores	#14 Zero Scores
Factor Loadings					
$S_V \rightarrow V_1$: B_{V1}	.000	.000	.000	.000	.000
$S_V \rightarrow V_2$: B_{V2}	.233*	.265*	.263*	.234*	.233*
$S_V \rightarrow V_3$: B_{V3}	.527*	.587*	.583*	.527*	.528*
$S_V \rightarrow V_4$: B_{V4}	1.000	1.000	1.000	1.000	1.000
$S_P \rightarrow P_1$: B_{P1}	.000	.000	.000	.000	.000
$S_P \rightarrow P_2$: B_{P2}	.296*	.265*	.263*	.298*	.295*
$S_P \rightarrow P_3$: B_{P3}	.645*	.587*	.583*	.648*	.645*
$S_P \rightarrow P_4$: B_{P4}	1.000	1.000	1.000	1.000	1.000
Factor Standard Deviations					
$L_V^* \rightarrow {}_{LV}$: D_{LV}	4.57*	4.44*	4.46*	4.56*	4.56*
$S_V^* \rightarrow {}_{SV}$: D_{SV}	7.45*	6.50*	7.69*	6.68*	6.60*
${}_{EV}^* \rightarrow {}_{EV}$: D_{EV}	3.32*	3.45*	3.42*	3.33*	3.30*
$L_P^* \rightarrow {}_{LP}$: D_{LP}	6.74*	7.45*	7.80*	7.16*	7.50*
$S_P^* \rightarrow {}_{SP}$: D_{SP}	6.11*	5.99*	7.69*	3.07*	5.93*
${}_{EP}^* \rightarrow {}_{EP}$: D_{EP}	4.47*	4.60*	4.63*	5.02*	4.50*
Factor Correlations					
$L_V^* \leftrightarrow L_P^*$: R_{L_VP}	.737*	.758*	.733*	.787*	.721*
$S_V^* \leftrightarrow S_P^*$: R_{S_VP}	.378*	.425*	-.055	1.000	.000

102

	Invariant Groups	Not Invar. Loadings	Not Invar. Means	Not Invar. Scores	Independent Processes
$S_V^* \leftrightarrow L_V^*$: R_{SL_V}	.453*	.485*	.425*	.465*	.456*
$S_P^* \leftrightarrow L_P^*$: R_{SL_VP}	.401*	.443*	.148	1.188*	.270
$L_V^* \leftrightarrow S_P^*$: R_{SL_VP}	.137	.118	.071	.261*	.117
$L_P^* \leftrightarrow S_V^*$: R_{LS_PV}	.585*	.592*	.635*	.585*	.619*
$EP \leftrightarrow EV$: C_{E_VP}	1.650*	.830	.840	.680	2.260*
Factor Means					
$1 \rightarrow L_V$: M_{LV}	19.7*	19.2*	19.4*	19.7*	19.7*
$1 \rightarrow S_V$: M_{SV}	24.1*	24.1*	28.1*	24.1*	24.1*
$1 \rightarrow L_P$: M_{LP}	18.0*	18.7*	21.0*	17.9*	18.0*
$1 \rightarrow S_P$: M_{SP}	33.0*	33.1*	28.1*	33.0*	33.0*
Goodness of Fit Indices					
Likelihood Ratio	226	283	400	254	236
Degrees of Freedom	114	116	118	115	115
Normal Z-Test	5.6	8.0	12.	6.9	6.2
Step-Down dLRC	—	-57	-117	-28	10
Step-Down dDF	—	2	4	1	1
Step-Down Zd	—	6.5	9.1	4.8	2.92
Step-Down dLRC/LRC %	—	-25%	-41%	-12%	-4%
Interpretation					

[a]All parameters listed assumed Invariant over Groups.

(including Models #10–#14). In order to estimate these equations I have presumed the parameters listed are invariant over groups (but see the next section). Model #10 starts by allowing free growth parameters between variables. The parameters of most interest here are the intervariable factor correlations (and we turn to these next). This model is not restrictive with regard to these correlations, and it fits these data fairly well with LRC = 226 on DF = 114. The good fit of this model means that all three groups may be fitted with the same overall LGM parameter structure.

Model #11 restricts the two different variables to have the same shape loadings for both measurement variables. This model may be very important in some contexts, but it reflects a loss of 25% in fit; so it probably should not be used again here. Nevertheless, Model #12 again restricts the two different variables to have the same shape loadings, so the variances and means can be tested within the same metric. This model fits poorly, suggesting that the equality of loadings, variances, and means of the two variables are not indicated.

This leads us toward testing hypotheses about the relations between two variables within the individuals given in Model #10. In this free model, the factor level correlation R_{L-VP} = .737 represents individual differences in initial growth level. Likewise, the shape factor correlation R_{S-VP} = .378 represents individual differences in growth over trials. This latter relation between two variables is a key feature of any process study of two or more variables. The last two models, #13 and #14, test two key hypotheses about this coefficient.

Model #13 uses the LGM from #12 but further restricts the two different variables to have a correlation of R = 1.0 between what previously reflected two different shape scores. This implies that the two variables reflect entirely the same dynamic process within the individual. This model represents a loss of 12%, so the R = 1.0 is questionable. Model #14 uses the same logic but goes the other way: Here, we restrict the two different variables to have a correlation of R = 0.0 between the different shape scores. Now the latent growth reflects entirely different processes at the individual level. This model reflects a loss of only 4% in fit, so the model of independent dynamic processes across variables V and P may be retained.

These multiple variable models raise some important controversies. The equality of means and variances and loadings all reflect the typical shape hypotheses that emerge in the study of mean differences. Unfortunately, these are all extrinsic features of the growth of the variables, which are not necessarily reflected in the individuals. Indeed, these kinds of comparisons can be carried out with separate independent groups. In contrast, the latter hypotheses about the size of the correlations of the change components are tests of the intrinsic relations in the growth patterns of the two variables. In many biological growth studies, these correlations of the changes over time are the allometric relations (see Griffiths & Sandland, 1982). In many contexts, these correlations and effects within variables are a key feature of growth analyses.

Modeling Growth over Groups and Variables

A final question arises: "Are there any differences between the groups bound within the measures on the latent growth?" This was a key question of the experimental design, and we are now in a position to answer it. To do so, we present a latent growth model for both multiple groups and multiple variables, presented as a path diagram in Fig. 4.10. This diagram shows exactly the same raw score components and relations for each of the groups and measures, but subscripts for G and M are added. This is a direct combination of the models presented in Figs. 4.8 and 4.9, so the independence and dependence constraints of the score components hold here as well.

Table 4.8 lists some numerical results for some complex mixtures of the three-group, two-variable structural equation models (i.e., Models #15–#18). Model #15 uses the basic structure of a latent growth model with parameters free to vary over groups and measures. To conserve space, only the most crucial parameters are listed. The LRC = 82 on DF = 72 indicates this model fits the data very well. This means the overall LGM structure is an acceptable starting point for further model restrictions.

Model #16 uses the same latent growth basis as before and further restricts the factor loadings to be invariant across groups but not across measures. This group invariance of the extrinsic growth pattern shows a noticeable loss of fit here (22%). But the overall model still fits the data rather well (Z = 1.52), so it seems reasonable to accept this model as only a small loss.

Model #17 again uses the latent growth basis but adds the restriction of the equality of shape correlations R_{S_VP} across the experimental groups. This is a central test of a multivariate hypothesis, which states that the processes are different in the different groups. This model again obviously fits the data well (Z = 1.57). The intrinsic relations among learning or Verification (V) and motivation or Persistence (P) are not different in any of the three groups.

Model #18 again uses this latent growth basis but adds equality of both level and shape correlations, and this model is consistent with these data as well (with Z = 1.55). This result suggests that any group differences are not intrinsic to the individuals. Other intrinsic hypotheses (e.g., R_{S_VP} = 0 or 1) and other extrinsic hypotheses (e.g., $M_{g,L}$ and $V_{g,L}$) can be tested from this new perspective of partial loading invariance. These numerical results are consistent with those we found from the previous models.

In any complete data analysis, numerous models are fit to the same data set and a variety of experimental results emerge. In some cases, it is useful to provide a record of this model fitting, and I now use the graphical comparison of

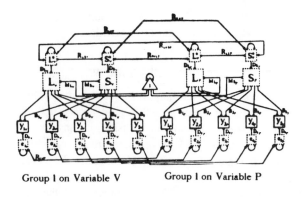

Group 1 on Variable V   Group 1 on Variable P

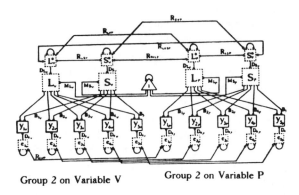

Group 2 on Variable V   Group 2 on Variable P

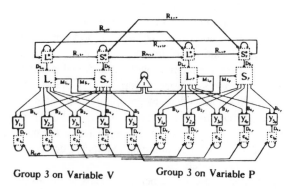

Group 3 on Variable V   Group 3 on Variable P

FIG. 4.10. The latent growth model for multiple groups and multiple variables.

106

TABLE 4.8
Numerical Results for Multiple Group & Multiple Variable Latent Growth Models

Model Parameter	#15 Free Growth			#16 Group Loadings			#17 Shape Corrs.			#18 Level Corrs.		
	Lo	Me	Hi	Lo	Me	Hi	Lo	Me	Hi	Lo	Me	Hi
Factor Loadings												
$S_V \rightarrow V_1$: B_{V1}	.00	.00	.00	.00	.00	.00	.00	.00	.00	.00	.00	.00
$S_V \rightarrow V_2$: B_{V2}	.25	.24	.20	.24	.24	.24	.24	.24	.24	.24	.24	.24
$S_V \rightarrow V_3$: B_{V3}	.54	.54	.49	.53	.53	.53	.53	.53	.53	.53	.53	.53
$S_V \rightarrow V_4$: B_{V4}	1.0	1.0	1.0	1.0	1.0	1.0	1.0	1.0	1.0	1.0	1.0	1.0
$S_P \rightarrow P_1$: B_{P1}	.00	.00	.00	.00	.00	.00	.00	.00	.00	.00	.00	.00
$S_P \rightarrow P_2$: B_{P2}	.27	.30	.32	.29	.29	.29	.29	.29	.29	.29	.29	.29
$S_P \rightarrow P_3$: B_{P3}	.67	.66	.58	.65	.65	.65	.65	.65	.65	.65	.65	.65
$S_P \rightarrow P_4$: B_{P4}	1.0	1.0	1.0	1.0	1.0	1.0	1.0	1.0	1.0	1.0	1.0	1.0
Factor Correlations												
$L_V^* \leftrightarrow L_P^*$: R_{L_VP}	.56	.74	.41	.57	.74	.41	.56	.73	.45	.63	.63	.63
$S_V^* \leftrightarrow S_P^*$: R_{S_VP}	.41	.58	−.13	.41	.57	−.16	.39	.39	.39	.40	.40	.40
$L_V^* \leftrightarrow S_V^*$: R_{L_V}	.03	.58	.19	.05	.52	.30	.05	.52	.30	.05	.52	.30
$S_P^* \leftrightarrow S_P^*$: R_{S_P}	.38	.55	.27	.40	.48	.58	.40	.48	.58	.40	.48	.58

(Continued)

TABLE 4.8
(continued)

Model Parameter	#15 Free Growth			#16 Group Loadings			#17 Shape Corrs.			#18 Level Corrs.		
	Lo	*Me*	*Hi*	*Lo*	*Me*	*Hi*	*Lo*	*Me*	*Hi*	*Lo*	*Me*	*Hi*
Factor Means												
$1 \rightarrow L_V$: M_{LV}	16.	21.	23.	16.	21.	22.	16.	21.	23.	16.	21.	22.
$1 \rightarrow S_V$: M_{SV}	21	25.	27.	21.	25.	28.	21.	25.	27.	21.	25.	28.
$1 \rightarrow L_P$: M_{LP}	13.	20.	23.	13.	20.	23.	13.	20.	23.	13.	20.	23.
$1 \rightarrow S_P$: M_{SP}	32.	33.	35.	32.	33.	34.	32.	33.	35.	32.	33.	34.
Goodness-of-Fit Indices												
Likelihood Ratio	82			100			103			105		
Degrees of Freedom	72			80			82			84		
Normal Z-Test	.85			1.52			1.57			1.55		
Step-Down dLRC	—			18			3			2		
Step-Down dDF	—			8			2			2		
Step-Down Zd	—			2.03			.77			.33		
Step-Down dLRC/LRC %	—			−22%			−3%			−2%		
Interpretation	Good Fit of Latent Model			Invariant Group Loadings			Invariant Shape Corrs.			Invariant Change Corrs.		

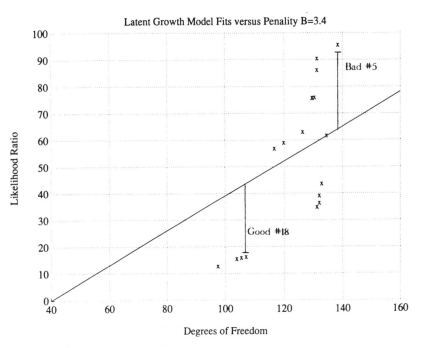

FIG. 4.11. A comparison of alternative latent growth models fit to the experimental data.

Fig. 4.11. Here, I have plotted the likelihood ratio criterion against the degrees of freedom for each of the 18 substantive models fit (I eliminated Model #0 because it was just an initial baseline). Next, I fit a regression line to these indices where the regression was forced through the origin; that is, LRC = 0 when DF = 0. This empirical penalty line has a slope of B = 3.43, which I now use as the expected value of the LRC for each individual DF within these data. Models that are far above this penalty line are very poor models with large discrepancies given their degrees of freedom (or numbers of parameters). Conversely, and more important now, models that are far below this penalty line are very good models with small discrepancies given their degrees of freedom (see McArdle, 1988).

The results that emerge from Fig. 4.11 are not surprising. The poorest fitting models are those listed in Table 4.5, which are presumably invariant across both groups and measures. The worst model overall is the *Absolute* latent growth model with no intercepts. Conversely, the best models are those of Table 4.8, which allow some variation over groups and measures. By this graphical criterion of fit, the best model is the last, Model #18. This final model allows the means to be different over groups, but this is not a critical concern. That is, in stark contrast to the MANOVA model, we may not even be interested in results that only show up in the means. In this model, the change correlations R_{S_VP} are neither zero nor one, but these relational processes are not in any way altered by the stimulation level. Notice that this result is not related to the means, so it is not a usual MANOVA interaction. This final model allows different extrinsic relations of the variables to the time scale and in the means, but the model assumes equal intrinsic relations of the variables within the individuals and groups. The stimulation level affected some extrinsic growth parameters but it did not affect some intrinsic growth parameters.

DISCUSSION

Substantive Verisimilitude

A complete substantive discussion would probably require that even more models be fit and compared. Rather than go into these details now I think it is best to say that the information from Table 4.1 was entirely fictitious and it needs to be replaced by Table 4.9. This latter provides the actual experimental data collection design for the learning experiment just described. These data are actually from a longitudinal study of the Wechsler Intelligence Scale for Children (WISC) originally collected by Osborne and Suddick (1972), and reanalyzed by McArdle and Epstein (1987) and McArdle (1988). In the current transposition: (1) Learning = Testing, (2) Subjects = Young Children, (3) Trials = Months of Age, (4) Verification = Verbal WISC scores, (5) Persistence = Performance WISC scores, and (6) Random Stimulation Groups = Nonrandom Mothers' Education Groups.

These differences in the substantive design are crucial. The latent growth curve is now interpreted as a developmental function (after Wohlwill, 1973) that increases most rapidly during the early school years. This function exhibits extrinsic differences for the Verbal and Performance scales of the WISC, and the intrinsic changes in these two scales is relatively independent in the early school years (ages 6 to 11). In contrast, this developmental function has the same basis for different mothers' education groups and, although the starting points are lower for the educationally disadvantaged, the intrinsic changes are the same for all groups. Furthermore, the lack of random assignment to stimulus groups makes the educational difference effect ambiguous; that is, these groups also differ in other ways that are correlated with mothers' educational level. (but see Stankov, 1986).

In this context we note that McArdle and Epstein (1987) reported different results over groups. We suggested that the educational groups are different on the loadings and means, and we attributed this difference to "catch-up growth in the cognitive domain" (p. 126). This difference of interpretation is due to two different features of the models. First, in McArdle and Epstein (1987) the model

TABLE 4.9
Experimental Design Summary from
the "True Developmental Experiment"
(from Osborne & Suddick, 1972;
see McArdle & Epstein, 1987;
McArdle, 1988)

Subjects (S) and Experimenters (E)

Young school-aged children in several Georgia school districts took in an testing program. Experimenters were school psychologists assigned to various subjects based on convenient meeting times. E were not blind to the group assignment (G). Complete records were obtained on $N(S) = 204$ from $N(E) = 17$.

Nonrandom Assignment to Groups (G)

(G = 1) No Stimulation = Low Mothers' Education—These were children whose mothers' had less than a high school education at the initial testing.

(G = 2) Medium Stimulation = Average Mothers' Education—These were children whose mothers' had obtained a high school education at the initial testing.

(G = 3) High Stimulation = High Mothers' Education—These were children whose mothers' had more than a high school education at the initial testing.

Stimulus Material and Measurement Trials (T)

The Wechsler Intelligence Scale for Children (WISC) was administered to each S individually, and several other intellectual ability tests were administered in group testings. These testings occurred during each of four longitudinal occasions of measurement:

(T = 1) After an average of about 73 months (6 years) of age.

(T = 2) After an average of about 83 months (7 years) of age.

(T = 3) After an average of about 106 months (9 years) of age.

(T = 4) After an average of about 129 months (11 years) of age.

Psychometric Measures (M)

(M = 1) Verbal Ability (V)—The E asked the S numerous questions requiring verbal responses to four WISC scales: Information, Comprehension, Similarities, and Vocabulary. A "percentage correct" score was obtained for each variable individually, and the V at each time point was scored as the average of these percentage correct scores.

(M = 2) Performance Ability (P)—The E asked the S numerous questions requiring active performances to four WISC scales: Picture Completion, Block Design, Picture Arrangement, and Object Assembly. A "percentage correct" score was obtained for each variable individually, and the P at each time point was scored as the average of these percentage correct scores.

was fit to a total scale score. This implies, but does not test, the invariance of pattern and scores over V and P. Second, in McArdle and Epstein (1987) the Absolute scale LGM was used, but here I used the dual component LGM—some differences in group mean level are embedded within the single curve model so the group functions appear different. These substantive differences are due to differences in modeling strategy, and they are limited by the models.

A Triple Blind Experiment

So why did I try to fool you into thinking about this longitudinal data analysis as a cognitive learning experiment? My only purpose in creating and carrying out this charade was to allow the structural methodology to be discussed without the extra surplus meaning attached to either the experimental or differential school of psychology. In the double blind design, neither the subjects nor the experimenters have information about the group assignment. I simply tried to place the data analyst in a triple blind about the nature of the psychological substance. In many cases, these structural models transfer easily from one substantive domain to another, and I wanted to demonstrate this useful flexibility.

I hoped to attract the attention of the experimentalists by offering a randomized design, or true experiment. I then hoped to show some benefits of the more complete examination of multiple variable hypotheses. The main point is that experiments can have effects on the means or on the variances or on the correlations or on combinations of each of these. For various historical reasons, the means are overwhelmingly favored for experimental group comparisons, and covariance differences are presumed to be random. In contrast, group differences in patterns of regression or correlations can provide information about the effects on different processes. This was the methodological goal of the Aptitude by Treatment Interaction. I have carried and extended this logic into dynamic latent variables analysis. Dynamic multivariate experimentation is not a new idea (e.g., Humphreys & Revelle, 1984), but these multivariate models provide a clear and functional organization for testing experimental hypotheses (also see Cattell, 1966; Horn, 1972; Nesselroade, 1983; Nesselroade & Cattell, 1988).

At the same time, I hoped to attract the attention of the correlationalists by using contemporary techniques in confirmatory causal modeling. I then hoped to show some benefits of the examination of factor models for the organization of individual differences in growth patterns. Indeed, the examination of learning curves is a long-standing tradition in experimental research. These classical models represent concepts of change in a different way than do contemporary longitudinal autoregressive models of stability of individual differences (see Rogosa & Willett, 1985; Wohlwill, 1973). I also tried to demonstrate the benefits of randomized assignment to groups. My main point is that we should examine effects on the means or on the variances or on the correlations, but the meaning of such comparisons will always be restricted by the experimental sampling design. As we become clearer about the sources of the group differences, we can more clearly interpret our experimental results.

The multivariate models used here provide a correlational organization for some testable experimental hypotheses. I have suggested several vehicles for the organization and display of the experimental results. I have attempted to take a reasonable approach to model selection (see Leamer, 1983). In addition, I have made many implicit statistical assumptions and I have not discussed all my technical problems. In general, these structural equation models are *not causal* models and they are *not confirmatory* models, but I do hope they are *clear and informative* models.

Latent Growth Extensions

The latent growth model organization used here comes from recent work by Meredith and Tisak (1984). This work initially revived Tuckers' (1958, 1966) approach for use with the LRC in univariate time series data from incomplete groups. A similar example is given by McArdle, Anderson, and Aber (1987). McArdle (1986) revised the LGM for use in the context of longitudinal behavior genetics. McArdle and Epstein (1987) added several features to this model, especially the path analysis interpretations. McArdle (1988) presented several multivariate models based on both changes in factor scores (CUFFS) and factors of change scores (FOCUS) organizations. This presentation used a combination of the full bivariate LGM with multiple groups.

There are many further extensions possible within this LGM logic. For example, these growth models also can be extended to deal with multiple curves, nonlinear relations, and amplitude and phase shifts (see Estes, 1956; Griffiths & Sandland, 1982; compare Keats, 1983; McArdle, 1988). We could also fit an initial model where $R_{SL} = 0$ so the level and shape scores were independent. But here I wanted to conform with some key ideas of multivariate selection (see Meredith's theorems in Horn et al., 1983). Indeed, this factor-analysis-based organization of change allows us to capitalize on well-established theorems of multivariate selection (e.g., Nesselroade, 1983).

There remain many obstacles to an effective and practical latent growth analysis. First and foremost, these new models and computer programs are difficult to use. For example, the MANOVA took only one run and 5 minutes but the LISREL analyses took about 40 runs over 10 hours. I have tried to demonstrate a few theoretical advantages of the LGM. But, at the same time, I have demonstrated many practical advantages of LGM over standard MANOVA. Due to the technical expertise currently required, I think only high quality data and precise theory specifications will warrant these extra efforts. (Perhaps the main result of this experiment really is that theory verification requires methodological persistence!)

As substantive researchers, we are always limited by the available methodological tools. These latent growth structural models provide some useful directions and some untapped potentials. At the same time, these models will not be useful for everyone. There are different schools of psychology and these social organizations have adaptive features for the immediate benefit of the individual. But, especially in a struggling science such as psychology, it seems foolish to ignore the well-developed and selective advantages of any school. I think these multivariate experimental models can bring together the methodological strengths of different schools. I hope they can now be used and extended to produce more reliable psychological substance. These attitudes reflect my school of psychology.

OPEN DISCUSSION

The brief discussion focused on the problem of interpreting findings that indicate a poor fit to the hypothesized model.

> **Kyllonen:** I have a general question. When you looked at the different models, in many cases you found that the models did not fit. However, you drew conclusions based on some of the differences between models despite the fact that neither of the two models you compared fit the data very well. Aren't there some problems associated with doing that? Might there be some radically different model that better represents the true state of affairs?

> **McArdle:** I think that we are stuck with this problem. There is no way out. There are many statistical issues involved and, in fact, there are a number of alternative models that could fit as well. What we are trying to do is to provide an organization that supports the way we work. No model ever fits the data well. When we get a big enough sample size we will be sure to reject any of these hypotheses. This is true of ANOVA and Regression as well. So we are always working within the constraints of inconsistency. I think what needs to be recognized is that we want to be sure to set up a hypothesis that we are really interested in, against an alternative which we are rooting against. I want to give both models a fair chance with the same data. If the models interact with other parameters, then it is not really a fair test. But as long as we have clearly stated what we are doing, then someone can come along, look at the data, and show me that I am incorrect in my prior assertions or something else I have done.

> I also think that much too much is made over small statistical problems. I have seen these kinds of concerns in the literature and have seen researchers get worried. (I think the thing we need to do is to know enough about statistics to not be too worried by statisticians.) We need to press on, get some results out, and produce some practical conclusions or summaries. So

I have been a little less than formal about the issue you mentioned. However, I don't know any other way to do it. I do not trust models that actually fit the data too well, either.

Kyllonen: It is usually studies with small sample sizes that are most worrisome. . . ?

McArdle: Yes, with small sample sizes we have no power to test alternatives. I have not yet found a model that both fits the data very well and that I would want to endorse to other researchers. These are important problems, but they are not new. For example, this is also a problem in analysis of variance. These problems simply become more clear in these structural modeling analyses.

ACKNOWLEDGMENTS

This work is an integration of ideas from various areas of psychology. I was trained in experimental psychology at Franklin & Marshall College; I was trained in repeated measures data analysis at Hofstra University; I was trained in differential psychology at the University of Denver; I now mix up all these ideas at the Jefferson Psychometric Lab at the University of Virginia. I thank all my colleagues then and now for helping me begin and finish this work. I especially thank Bob Cudeck, John Horn, Bill Meredith, John Nesselroade, and Lazar Stankov for their constructive comments on earlier versions of this research.

This research has been supported by grants from the National Institute on Aging (AG02695, AG04704, and AG07137).

REFERENCES

Alwin, D. F., & Jackson, D. J. (1982). Applications of simultaneous factor analysis to issues of factorial invariance. In D. J. Jackson & E. F. Borgatta (Eds.), *Factor analysis and measurement in sociological research 37* (pp. 249–280). Beverly Hills: Sage.

Alwin, D. F., & Tessler, R. C. (1974). Causal models, unobserved variables, and experimental data. *American Journal of Sociology, 80,* 58–86. (Also in Blalock, 1985.)

Bagozzi, R. P. (1977). Structural equation models in experimental research. *Journal of Marketing Research, 14,* 209–226. (Also in Blalock, 1985.)

Blalock, H. M. (Ed.). (1985). *Causal models in panel and experimental designs.* New York: Aldine.

Bock, R. D. (1975). *Multivariate statistical methods in behavioral research.* New York: McGraw-Hill.

Bock, R. D. (1979). Univariate and multivariate analysis of variance in time-structured data. In J. R. Nesselroade & P. B. Baltes (Eds.), *Longitudinal research in the study of behavior and development* (pp. 199–232). New York: Academic Press.

Cattell, R. B. (1966). *Handbook of multivariate experimental psychology.* Chicago: Rand McNally.

Cook, T. D., & Campbell, D. T. (1979). *Quasi-experimentation: Design and analysis issues for field settings.* Chicago: Rand McNally.

Cronbach, L. J. (1957). The two disciplines of scientific psychology. *American Psychologist, 12,* 671–684.

Cronbach, L. J. (1975). Beyond the two disciplines of scientific psychology. *American Psychologist, 30,* 116–127.

Cudeck, R., & Browne, M. W. (1983). Cross-validation of covariance structures. *Multivariate Behavioral Research, 18,* 147–167.

Estes, W. K. (1956). The problem of inference from curves based on group data. *Psychological Bulletin, 53,* 134–140.

Freedman, D., Pisani, R., & Purves, R. (1978). *Statistics.* New York: W. W. Norton.

Griffiths, D. A., & Sandland, R. L. (1982). Allometry and multivariate growth revisited. *Growth, 46,* 1–11.

Horn, J. L. (1972). State, trait, and change dimensions of intelligence. *The British Journal of Educational Psychology, 42,* 159–185.

Horn, J. L. (1986). Intellectual ability concepts. In R. J. Sternberg (Ed.), *Advances in the psychology of human intelligence.* (Vol. 3, pp. 35–77). Hillsdale, NJ: Lawrence Erlbaum Associates.

Horn, J. L., & McArdle, J. J. (1980). Perspectives on mathematical/statistical model building (MASMOB) in research on aging. In L. W. Poon (Ed.), *Aging in the 1980's: Selected contemporary issues in the psychology of aging* (pp. 503–541). Washington, DC: American Psychological Association.

Horn, J. L., McArdle, J. J., & Mason, R. (1983). When is invariance not invariant: A practical scientist's look at the ethereal concept of factor invariance. *The Southern Psychologist, 1,* 179–188.

Hultsch, D. F., Nesselroade, J. R., & Plemons, J. K. (1976). Learning-ability relations in adulthood. *Human Development, 19,* 234–247.

Humphreys, M. S., & Revelle, W. (1984). Personality, motivation, and performance: A theory of the relationship between individual differences and information processing. *Psychological Review, 91,* 153–184.

Jöreskog, K. G. (1970). Estimation and testing of simplex models. *British Journal of Mathematical and Statistical Psychology, 23,* 121–146.

Jöreskog, K. G. (1971). Simultaneous factor analysis in several populations. *Psychometrika, 36,* 409–426. (Reprinted in Jöreskog & Sörbom, 1979.)

Jöreskog, K. G. (1979). Statistical estimation of structural models in longitudinal-developmental investigations. In J. R. Nesselroade & P. B. Baltes (Eds.), *Longitudinal research in the study of behavior and development* (pp. 303–352). New York: Academic Press.

Jöreskog, K. G., & Sörbom, D. (1977). Statistical models and methods for analysis of longitudinal data. In D. J. Aigner & A. S. Goldberger (Eds.), *Latent variables in socio-economic models* (pp. 285–325). Amsterdam: North-Holland.

Jöreskog, K. G., & Sörbom, D. (1979). *Advances in factor analysis and structural equation models.* Cambridge, MA: Abt Books.

Jöreskog, K. G., & Sörbom, D. (1985). *LISREL-VI users guide.* Mooresville, IN: Scientific Software, Inc.

Keats, J. A. (1983). Ability measures and theories of cognitive development. In H. Wainer & S. Messick (Eds.), *Principles of modern psychological measurement* (pp. 81–101). Hillsdale, NJ: Lawrence Erlbaum Associates.

Kenny, D. A. (1979). *Correlation and causality.* New York: Wiley.

Leamer, E. E. (1983). Let's take the con out of econometrics. *The American Economic Review, 73,* 31–43.

Loehlin, J. C. (1987). *Latent variable models: An introduction to factor, path, and structural analysis.* Hillsdale, NJ: Lawrence Erlbaum Associates.

McArdle, J. J. (1980). Causal modeling applied to psychonomic systems simulation. *Behavior Research Methods & Instrumentation, 12,* 193–209.

McArdle, J. J. (1986). Latent growth within behavior genetic models. *Behavior Genetics, 16,* 163–200.

McArdle, J. J. (1988). Dynamic but structural equation modeling of repeated measures data. In J. R. Nesselroade & R. B. Cattell (Eds.), *The handbook of multivariate experimental psychology* (Vol. 2, pp. 561–614). New York: Plenum Press.

McArdle, J. J., Anderson, E., & Aber, M. S. (1987). Convergence hypotheses modeled with linear structural equations. *Proceedings of the Annual Conference of the National Center for Health Statistics* (pp. 351–356). Washington, DC: National Center for Health Statistics.

McArdle, J. J., & Epstein, D. (1987). Latent growth curves within developmental structural equation models. *Child Development, 58,* 110–133.

McArdle, J. J., & Horn, J. L. (in press). An effective graphic model for linear structural equations. *Multivariate Behavioral Research.*

McArdle, J. J., & McDonald, R. P. (1984). Some algebraic properties of the Reticular Action Model for moment structures. *British Journal of Mathematical and Statistical Psychology, 37,* 234–251.

McDonald, R. P. (1978). A simple comprehensive model for the analysis of covariance structures. *British Journal of Mathematical and Statistical Psychology, 31,* 59–72.

McDonald, R. P. (1985). *Factor analysis and related methods.* Hillsdale, NJ: Lawrence Erlbaum Associates.

Meredith, W., & Tisak, J. (1984). *"Tuckerizing"* curves. Paper presented at the Annual Meetings of the Psychometric Society, Santa Barbara, CA.

Nesselroade, J. R. (1983). Temporal selection and factor invariance in the study of development and change. *Life-Span Development & Behavior, 5,* 59–87.

Nesselroade, J. R., & Cattell, R. B. (Eds.). (1988). *The handbook of multivariate experimental psychology, volume 2.* New York: Plenum Press.

Olsson, U., & Bergman, O. (1977). A longitudinal factor model for studying change in abilities. *Multivariate Behavioral Research, 12,* 221–241.

Osborne, R. T., & Suddick, D. E. (1972). A longitudinal investigation of the intellectual differentiation hypothesis. *The Journal of Genetic Psychology, 121,* 83–89.

Rao, C. R. (1958). Some statistical methods for the comparison of growth curves. *Biometrics, 14,* 1–17.

Rogosa, D., & Willett, J. B. (1985). Understanding correlates of change by modeling individual differences in growth. *Psychometrika, 50,* 203–228.

Sörbom, D. (1974). A general method for studying differences in factor means and factor structure between groups. *British Journal of Mathematical and Statistical Psychology, 27,* 229–239.

Stankov, L. (1986). Kvashchev's experiment: Can we boost intelligence? *Intelligence, 10,* 209–230.

Tucker, L. R (1958). Determination of parameters of a functional relation by factor analysis. *Psychometrika, 23,* 19–23.

Tucker, L. R (1966). Learning theory and multivariate experiment: Illustration by determination of parameters of generalized learning curves. In R. B. Cattell (Ed.), *The handbook of multivariate experimental psychology* (pp. 476–501). Chicago: Rand McNally.

Werts, C. E., Linn, R. L., & Jöreskog, K. G. (1977). A simplex model for analyzing academic growth. *Educational and Psychological Measurement, 37,* 745–755.

Wohlwill, J. F. (1973). *The study of behavioral development.* New York: Academic Press.

Wright, S. (1983). On "Path analysis in genetic epidemiology: A critique." *American Journal of Human Genetics, 35,* 757–768.

Estimating Individual Differences in Information Processing Using Speed–Accuracy Models

David F. Lohman
University of Iowa

How can we best represent individual differences in information processing? What should we use as dependent measures? Fig. 5.1 shows one way to think about the dependent measures we might use. Tasks used in psychological research may be located in that figure by their duration, from the simplest reaction-time task at the left, through tasks of intermediate duration and complexity, to complex tasks at the far right that may require minutes or hours to solve. Different dependent measures are most useful at different points along this continuum: eye fixations and latencies for simple tasks, latencies and errors for tasks of intermediate complexity, and think-aloud protocols and retrospective reports for complex tasks. It would seem, then, that one simply chooses the dependent measure that corresponds with the difficulty or duration of the task and gets on with the research at hand. We often look briefly at dependent measures to the left or to the right on the scale, but usually with the aim of dismissing their influence. I have come to believe that we cannot conduct our business in this way, especially when we hope to study individual differences. I am particularly concerned about the way we represent performance for those tasks that are anywhere along the continuum in Fig. 5.1 in which response latencies or response errors

TASK DURATION / COMPLEXITY

FIG. 5.1. Continuum of task duration/complexity and dependent measures commonly used at each region along the continuum.

are taken as the primary dependent measure. I argue that we have often muddied the waters in our efforts to study only one variable—latency or error—while ignoring the other or attempting to dismiss its influence through logical argument or statistical controls. Sometimes this attempt to simplify our research task has led us to accept misleading or false conclusions, and in many ways it has made our task harder than it needed to be.

BACKGROUND

Differences between individual differences in response latencies and response errors is not a minor methodological problem but a pervasive feature of research on individual differences in cognition (Carroll, 1980). I first stumbled across it in my attempts to understand the factor-analytic literature on spatial abilities. Two of the most consistently obtained factors in that literature are called Visualization (*Vz*) or General Visualization (*Gv*) and Speeded Rotation (SR). The question I was attempting to answer was this: What is the psychological basis for the difference between these two factors? After entertaining and rejecting several other hypotheses, I hit upon the notion that the difference might be explained in terms of either task complexity or task speededness. However, complexity is confounded with speededness on most tests, as simple tasks must be speeded in order to generate individual differences in number of items solved. In fact, in my reanalyses of Thurstone's (1938) data, I found a correlation of $r = .75$ between the estimated speededness of a test (average time allotted for each item) and its loading on an unrotated, bipolar *SR–Vz* factor (Lohman, 1979a, p. 24). Thus, tests that defined the *SR* factor were much more speeded than tests that defined the *Vz* factor. Complex, unspeeded tests also had higher loadings on the General (*G*) factor in Thurstone's (1938) data.

This speed-level or complexity dimension can be seen in the correlation matrix for any test battery that contains a wide range of tasks. Simple, speeded tests usually correlate poorly with other tests and fall at the periphery of multidimensional scalings of test correlation matrices or in the lower branches of hierarchical factor models estimated from such correlation matrices. Factors defined by such tests frequently disappear when tests are made less obviously similar. This applies to verbal and numerical tests as well as to spatial tests. For example, the Numerical factor in Thurstone's primary mental abilities (1938) study was defined by speeded computation tests, whereas complex arithmetic achievement tests defined the General Fluid Ability (*Gf*) factor in Marshalek, Lohman, and Snow (1983) and in Werdelin (1961). In the domain of verbal abilities, fluency and reading speed measures define specific factors, whereas vocabulary and verbal reasoning tests often define General Crystallized (*Gc*) ability (Hoffman, Guilford, Hoepfner, & Doherty, 1968; Marshalek et al., 1983). More general speed dimensions appear in some studies, but well-designed studies invariably show speed and level scores on the same task to load on independent factors (Horn, 1985; Kyllonen, 1985). Thus, speed-level and complexity differences are pervasive in the factor-analytic literature on human abilities. The most complex tests cluster together in factors such as *Gc, Gf,* and *Gv* near the top of the hierarchy, whereas the simplest tests define specific factors at the base of the hierarchy. This suggests that individual differences in latencies on error-free tasks would be more likely to define a unique factor near the base of the hierarchy than to load strongly on factors such as *Gc, Gf,* or *Gv* near the top. Further, factors in the lower branches of the hierarchical model are quite sensitive to even minor changes in test format or content. In the extreme, some of these factors are defined by what amounts to a parallel forms reliability coefficient. Factors near the top of the hierarchy are not nearly so sensitive to method variance. Indeed, general ability has historically been defined by a hodgepodge of complex texts (Humphreys, 1985; Thorndike & Lohman, in press). More importantly, speed of solving simple problems in a domain is generally a poor predictor of the difficulty level of problems in that domain one can solve (Lohman, 1979b; Morrison, 1960; Tate, 1948).

The independence of individual differences in speed and level in spatial ability was evident in several different analyses on data from a form-board task I studied several years ago (Lohman, 1979b). For example, in one analysis, solution latencies were regressed on item difficulty (estimated by total errors for all subjects on each item), separately for each subject. Intercepts for each subject in these regressions estimate speed of solving the simplest items. Intercepts showed correlations in the range of $r = -.3$ with a few spatial tests but were not significantly correlated with total number of problems solved correctly. Egan (1976) reported similar results. The implication, of course, is that speed of error-free processing on simple spatial tasks is likely to be quite task-specific and to explain little of the variance in the sort of spatial abilities defined by complex tasks (Lohman, 1979b).

Similar correlations are reported in the literature on mental rotation. Estimated rate of rotating simple alphanumeric stimuli usually shows correlations in the range $r = -.3$ to $-.4$ with number correct on *SR* factor tests (Berg, Hertzog, & Hunt, 1982; Kail, Carter, & Pazak, 1979; Mumaw, Pellegrino, Kail, & Carter, 1984). Correlations with more complex *Vz* factor tests are even lower (Lohman, 1979b).

For the more complex rotation problems studied by Shepard and Metzler (1971), correlations between estimated rate of rotation and reference spatial tests that are not paper-and-pencil versions of the same task have ranged from $r = -.50$ (Lansman, 1981) through $r = -.13$ (McGue, Bouchard, Lykken, & Feuer, 1984), and $r = -.06$ (Egan, 1976) to $r = .20$ (Poltrock & Brown, 1984). The Lansman (1981) correlation may be inflated by nonproportional subject sampling, and the low negative and positive correlations may reflect the fact that only a few items were administered (e.g., Egan, 1976) or that the task was too difficult for many subjects (e.g., Poltrock & Brown, 1984).

Modeling Performance on Complex Tasks

Herein lies one of the most difficult problems in research aimed at developing process theories of ability constructs. Many of the tests that define general abilities are level or power tests. Individual differences are reflected in number of problems of increasing difficulty correctly solved in a liberal but usually fixed time. A problem arises when the investigator attempts to model performance from such tasks, because latencies are ambiguous when a subject responds incorrectly and because errors are ambiguous when time limits vary. The problem has been handled in one or more of the following ways: (a) ignore errors and include all latencies in the analysis; (b) exclude error latencies from the analysis; (c) exclude subjects who make too many errors; (d) simplify the task so that errors are effectively eliminated; (e) repeat error trials later in the experiment with the hope that the subject will respond correctly; (f) ignore latencies and analyze only errors; (g) combine latency and error data in some way, usually in a multivariate analysis; or (h) determine the relationship between accuracy and latency for each subject at each level of trial complexity.

Simplifying a task to eliminate errors may well destroy the validity of the task because simple tasks tend to measure more specific abilities than similar but more difficult tasks. Eliminating subjects who commit errors is not the best way to understand an individual difference construct that is defined by error scores. And modeling either latencies or errors alone can be problematic in several ways, not the least of which is that subjects can trade increases in speed for decreases in accuracy over a substantial range. This is a much greater problem in research on individual differences where subjects are a design facet than in research in which data are averaged over subjects. It is also more of a problem in laboratory experiments in which latencies are recorded for each item than in paper-and-pencil administrations of the same items. Paper-and-pencil tests usually limit total time allotted. In most experiments, however, subjects may examine each item for as long as they wish. The experimenter usually hopes that all subjects follow instructions to respond as rapidly and accurately as possible. This is often an unwarranted assumption in research on individual differences (Lohman, 1979b; 1986).

Modeling Performance on Simple Tasks

Exactly the opposite set of problems confront those who aim to understand individual differences in speeded tasks and the ability constructs they define. Even though average error rates may be low, subjects invariably differ in the number of errors they make. This may in part reflect variation in the speed or accuracy criteria of different subjects. Such errors do not appear particularly meaningful because it would seem that subjects could eliminate them by changing their speed or accuracy emphases. However, I later show that errors on a simple letter comparison task are not all due to variation in speed-accuracy trade-off. Indeed, even when speed-accuracy trade-off has been controlled, errors on simple tasks often show systematic relationships with other variables and thus cannot be dismissed as random events. Some investigators attempt to dismiss errors on simple tasks by showing that they are not correlated with latencies or with the construct the experimental task is presumed to measure. However, we have long known that "rights" and "wrongs" on speeded tests may reflect different abilities (Fruchter, 1953), and so showing that errors on, say, a perceptual speed task are not related to scores on a perceptual speed test does not somehow render them meaningless.

I suggest that one good way to understand individual differences in both complex and simple tasks is to abandon failing attempts to repair incomplete or misleading analyses based on error or latency scores alone and, instead, to determine their joint influence on the performance we hope to understand. Furthermore, I believe that many of the inconsistencies that have surfaced in our attempts to describe individual differences in information processing may be explained by the fact that (a) the relationships among accuracy, latency, and task complexity are nonlinear (see Fig. 5.2), (b) the form of this function is systematically related to ability (see Fig. 5.4), and (c) routine attempts to estimate separate speed scores and level scores usually do not control for individual differences in speed–accuracy tradeoff. The first two points can perhaps be best understood by a brief review of the last point—speed–accuracy trade-off—and methods for studying it.

THE SPEED–ACCURACY PROBLEM

"Speed–accuracy trade-off" refers to the fact that subjects can trade increases in speed for decreases in accuracy and vice versa over a substantial range. Therefore, comparisons of response latencies or errors between subjects or even for the same subject across conditions may be biased by the subject's speed or accuracy emphasis.

Accuracy–Latency Functions

The functional relationship between response accuracy and response latency has been most thoroughly studied in the context of speed–accuracy trade-off (SAT). A typical SAT curve is shown in Fig. 5.2.

Accuracy may be estimated by probability correct, d', or some other measure

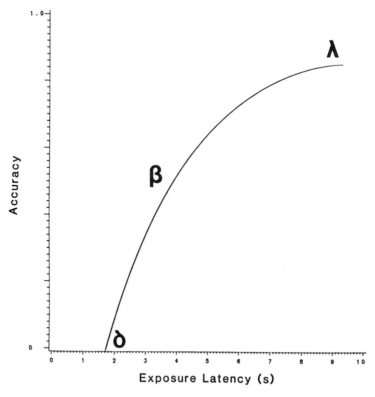

FIG. 5.2.   Hypothetical accuracy–latency curve. δ is the intercept, β is the curvature, and λ is the asymptote. Exposure latency is the sum of presentation latency and response latency.

(see, e.g., Swets, 1986). The abscissa always represents response latency, and so the plot is more properly called a latency–accuracy curve. The curve has three important features. First, there is period of time following stimulus onset during which accuracy remains at the level of random responding. The time at which accuracy begins to rise above this level may be called the intercept (δ) of the function. (In the models described here, the intercept is actually the point at which the curve intersects the abscissa.) Second, accuracy improves monotonically with latency. The rate of improvement in accuracy may be estimated by the curvature of this function (β). Third, the curve approaches an asymptote (λ) that may be considerably less than perfect accuracy. These three characteristics of the speed–accuracy curve may be modeled using different mathematical functions. Probably the most popular function is the exponential equation:

$$AC = (1 - e^{-\beta(t-\delta)}), \ t > 0 \tag{1}$$

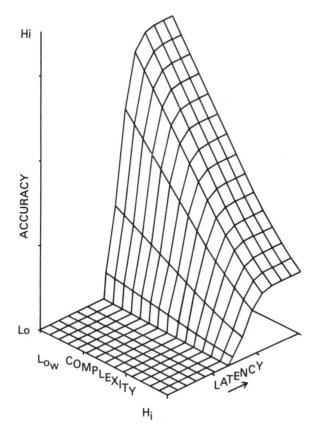

FIG. 5.3. Hypothetical plot of response accuracy by response latency by task complexity.

where AC is the obtained accuracy at processing time t, and δ, β, and λ are the intercept, curvature, and asymptote parameters, respectively (Wickelgren, 1977). Such a function may be used to describe the behavior of a particular subject on a particular type of trial. Note that in the typical experiment in which speed–accuracy curves are not obtained, only one point along this curve is estimated for each subject. Thus, differences between subjects in response latencies may be due in part to the speed or accuracy emphases they adopt, especially when accuracy is near asymptote. If trials differ systematically in complexity, then a response surface like that shown in Fig. 5.3 may be estimated for each subject in an experiment. This surface can be described by a generalization of Equation 1. For example, for three levels of task complexity the model becomes:

$$AC = (\lambda_0 + b_1\lambda1 + b_2\lambda2)\ (1 - e^{-(\beta_0 + b_1\beta_1 + b_2\beta_2)(t - \delta_0 - b_1\delta_1 - b_2\delta2)})\quad (2)$$

The observed scores AC and t, and the parameters λ, β, and δ are defined the same as they are in Equation 1. These parameters are now subscripted according to the number of levels of task complexity in the design. λ_0, β_0, and δ_0 are the average asymptote, curvature, and intercept parameters, respectively. The new coefficients b_1 and b_2 define vectors that distinguish the three λ, β, and δ parameters for each level of processing complexity. Simplified models test the hypothesis that particular parameters are equal to zero. For example, the hypothesis that the intercept remains constant across levels of task complexity may be tested by determining whether δ_1 and δ_2 in Equation 2 are significantly different from zero.

Task complexity can be estimated by observable features of the task, such as the number of task steps and the complexity of the stimulus that must be transformed. However, observables selected to estimate complexity must be chosen on the basis of some information-processing model of the task. This process model also specifies the rule for combining different aspects of complexity into a single index (see, e.g., R. J. Sternberg, 1977). Thus, task complexity cannot be defined without reference to the person performing the task. Even something as seemingly straightforward as the complexity of geometric forms must be defined by how subjects process the stimuli. Like beauty, complexity is in the eye of the beholder.

We escape from an infinite regress by operationalizing complexity in terms of objective (or rated) features of tasks that exert a major influence on processing over a broad class of possible information processing models.

Methods for Obtaining SAT Curves

Three methods have been proposed for obtaining a speed–accuracy trade-off function: (a) post hoc analyses of accuracy and latency scores from a conventional experiment, (b) instructions to respond with varying emphasis on accuracy or speed, or (c) signals to interrupt processing and respond.

Post Hoc Analyses

A simple method for obtaining an SAT function would seem to be to take advantage of the ubiquitous variability in response latencies and to fit some function to the bivariate plots of accuracy versus latency for presumably parallel trials (i.e., within cell of any design imposed on trials) for each subject. Multivariate analyses in which errors (or accuracy) and latencies (or some transformation of latency) are analyzed simultaneously approximate this analysis. A cruder technique, but one that actually produces an SAT curve, is to partition the obtained distribution of latencies into several categories, to average the obtained accuracies within each category, and then to plot average accuracy versus average latency for each category.

There are several problems with these methods. First, it is unlikely that many truly short response latencies will be obtained. For many subjects, the data would then consist primarily of points near the asymptote of the SAT curve. Second, it is unlikely that short latencies represent abbreviated portions of the processing that occurs with long latencies. In other words, short and long latencies may well represent different ways of processing or may reflect nonparallelism of trials. R. Sternberg (1980) has demonstrated such strategy differences for post-hoc partitioning of an obtained distribution of response latencies in a sentence–picture verification task. For these and other reasons, SAT curves obtained from such latencies may be systematically distorted (Wickelgren, 1977; Wood & Jennings, 1976). Pachella (1974) claimed that the SAT function obtained by partitioning latencies may be completely independent of the SAT function obtained by directly manipulating response latency, especially when anything but the simplest tasks are studied (see also Wickelgren, 1977). For these reasons, SAT functions are better constructed through experimental manipulation of subjects' speed–accuracy trade-off than through post hoc analyses of latency and accuracy scores from a conventional experiment. Two general methods have been used to manipulate subjects' speed–accuracy trade-off: instructions and response signals.

Instructions

Four different methods for manipulating speed–accuracy trade-off through instructions have been proposed: (a) general instructions, (b) payoffs, (c) specific deadlines, and (d) time intervals. Subjects may be given *general instructions* to emphasize accuracy or speed across trials or blocks of trials. Or subjects may be induced to vary speed–accuracy trade-offs by systematically manipulating the *payoff* matrix for speed versus accuracy. However, neither of these methods will work for subjects who are excessively cautious or who, in the case of payoffs, do not respond to the payoff scheme. Instructions can be made more specific (or criterion-referenced) by imposing different latency *deadlines* for different trials or blocks of trials. Subjects are then given feedback on how well they are meeting the deadline. Alternatively, subjects may be given both a minimum time and a maximum time for each trial, that is, a time *interval* during which they should attempt to respond. The most important drawback of both time deadlines and time intervals is that subjects must be informed of the deadline or interval in advance of each trial, and thus may adapt their strategies to meet the demands of the deadlines (Reed, 1976; Wickelgren, 1977). This appears to be a legitimate concern on tasks of nontrivial complexity that are amenable to different strategies.

Response Signals

Because of these limitations of response deadlines, most recent studies using the speed–accuracy method (e.g., Dosher, 1982, 1984; Reed, 1973, 1976) have used *response signals* to interrupt processing and signal the subjects that they must respond. Two types of response signals have been used: auxiliary signals and stimulus offset. Schouten and Bekker (1967) introduced the method of auxiliary signals. Subjects in their experiment were shown a visual stimulus and required to make a judgment about the stimulus in coincidence with the third of three, brief auditory signals spaced 75 ms apart. However, the secondary task (attending to the auditory signals) can disrupt performance on the primary task (judging the visual stimulus) (Schouten & Bekker, 1967; Wickelgren, 1977). Because of this potential interference, Reed (1973) argued that a single response signal would be preferable and that the offset of the stimulus itself could be used not only to signal that an immediate response was required, but also to reduce the amount of additional stimulus processing after the signal.

Even though Reed (1976), Wickelgren (1977), and Dosher (1984) argued that using stimulus offset as the signal to respond is preferable to other methods for generating SAT functions, the method is not without its problems. For example, various stimulus exposures (or "lags") are usually randomly ordered, so that subjects are unable to predict how long the stimulus will be exposed until it disappears from view. (If, instead, trials were blocked by length of exposure, then subjects could adjust solution strategy from block to block, as in the method of response deadlines previously discussed.) However, it is still possible that subjects may adopt a different strategy when processing is interrupted than when they are allowed to terminate the trial themselves (i.e, under speeded but self-paced conditions). For example, subjects may adopt a strategy that maximizes their success at the shortest exposures or at the average exposure, both of which might be different than the strategy adopted for longer, self-paced trials. There are two ways to counteract this tendency. First, subjects can be given practice on self-paced trials before response-signal trials are introduced, thereby inducing them to adopt the same strategy for self-paced and response-signal trials. Second, subjects can be instructed to adopt the same strategy for response-signal trials that they used in the self-paced trials and to view the response signal as an interruption of that way of processing.

But one cannot rely on instructions or response sets to equate self-paced and response-signal trials. Therefore, Reed (1976) suggested that investigators conduct two experiments on each subject: a conventional response time (RT) study in which subjects are instructed to respond "as fast and accurately as possible" and an SAT study in which various speed and accuracy emphases are experimentally induced. The SAT curve is then plotted for each subject and the single point from the conventional experiment is plotted in this space. If this data point falls on or near the SAT curve, then it is reasonable to assume that the subject's strategy for self-paced and speed–accuracy conditions did not differ markedly. However, if the data point from the self-paced condition differs significantly from the SAT curve, then processing may differ between the two conditions. Which condition encourages the preferred strategy in this case is an open question.

Reducing the Number of Observations

Estimating even a single speed–accuracy curve at a fixed level of complexity requires many observations. Reed (1976) administered 24,360 trials to each of four subjects to estimate SAT functions and conventional RT results in S. Sternberg's (1969) memory-scanning task. Dosher (1984) administered from 2,352 to 10,240 trials to each subject in each of three experiments on recognition memory for paired associates, more trials being required on those experiments with more conditions. In general, Wickelgren (1977) estimated that speed–accuracy studies require approximately five times as much data as conventional RT experiments. Wickelgren based this estimate on the assumption that the SAT curve would be based on at least five data points, each of which require the same number of observations as the single data point obtained in a conventional experiment. However, such a scheme fails to make use of dependencies between points on an SAT curve or between SAT curves at different levels of task complexity (i.e., curves defined by taking slices through the response surface of Fig. 5.3 at different levels of complexity). Thus, the first way to reduce the number of observations is to use these dependencies by fitting a response surface rather than a series of independent curves. However, the advantages of this method may be offset by the perils of testing even simple nonlinear models.

A second way to reduce the number of observations required for fitting individual SAT curves is through adaptive testing. Individual differences in speed of information processing are typically quite large. A single set of, say, five different stimulus exposures would be inappropriate for many subjects. For slow subjects, too few observations would be obtained near the asymptote, whereas for fast subjects, too few observations would be obtained near the intercept. An adaptive algorithm could be used to help locate the "elbow" of each curve on the response surface so as not to waste observations on the asymptote or the intercept.

We have now used the methodology of the speed–accuracy study in three experiments. In the first study, we investigated individual and sex differences in spatial ability as represented in a complex mental-rotation task. In the second study, we investigated perceptual speed ability using a letter-matching task. And in the third study, we investigated verbal ability using a synonym task. Along the way, we have changed our methods of data collection and analysis.

EXPERIMENT I: MENTAL ROTATION

In the first study, we examined ability and sex differences in speed of mental rotation. Subjects ($N = 83$) attempted 1,200 trials on rotation problems similar to those used by Shepard and Metzler (1971). Stimulus pairs were presented for various fixed durations that were controlled by the experimenter. The subjects' task was to determine if the stimuli could be rotated into congruence. They responded to each trial on a five-point scale with values of (1) *definitely no,* (2) *probably no,* (3) *uncertain,* (4) *probably yes,* (5) *definitely yes.* An accuracy score called P(C) was then defined as the probability of responding *definitely yes* to positive trials or *definitely no* to negative trials, with partial credit for intermediate scale values (see McNichol, 1972).

Trials were administered in blocks of 40. For half of the blocks, subjects were told that they would receive an additional monetary bonus for each trial in that block that they solved correctly, and they were asked to put forth their best effort on these trials. However, subjects were not more accurate on the high-incentive trials than on the low-incentive trials. Either our monetary rewards and instructions did not motivate subjects, or, more likely, motivation exerts a less pronounced influence when trials are experimenter-paced than when subjects control stimulus exposure.

Latency–accuracy curves were then determined by fitting an exponential function of the form: $P(C) = \gamma + \lambda (1 - e^{-\beta t})$, where P(C) is the accuracy score, γ is the intercept of the curve at $t = 0$, λ is the scale factor, β is the rate of increase in accuracy with increases in stimulus exposure, and t is the exposure latency of the stimulus. γ was fixed at .5 in the models reported here, and so the asymptote of each curve is simply $\lambda + .5$. Asymptotes estimate level of performance under liberal time allotment. Curves for each of the five levels of angular separation between stimuli were fit separately for males and females, for subjects high and low in spatial ability, and for individual subjects.

Fig. 5.4 shows latency–accuracy curves for each level of rotation, separately for high- and low-spatial subjects. Dashed lines represent data for high spatials; solid lines represent low spatials. High spatials were here defined as those 28 subjects above the median on both the *SR* composite (sum of standard scores on Thurstone's, 1938, Cards and Figures tests) and the *Vz* composite (sum of standard scores on Ekstrom, French, and Harman's, 1976, Paper Folding and Form Board tests), whereas low spatials were the 28 subjects below the median on both the *SR* and *Vz* composites. Curves for the two off-diagonal groups were intermediate. The most consistent difference between high and low spatials was in the asymptote of the accuracy–latency curves. For all five curves, the asymptote for high spatials was significantly higher than the asymptote for low spatials. Differences in asymptotes between high and low spatials were smallest for 30-degree trials and largest for 150-degree trials. In other words, lows showed significantly greater declines in asymptote than highs with increases in the amount of rotation required. Thus, high spatial ability means, in part, superior accuracy in solving complex rotation problems. Differences between groups in the β parameter were much smaller. Curvatures were greater for high spatials; however the difference was significant only for 90-degree trials. This suggests that low and high spatial subjects differ primarily in the level of performance

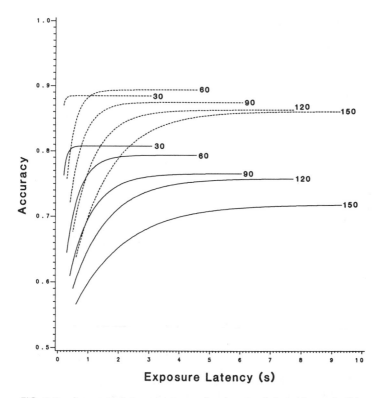

Exposure Latency (s)

FIG. 5.4. Accuracy–latency curves for low-spatial subjects (solid lines) and high-spatial subjects (dashed lines) at each of five levels of angular separation between figures. The length of each curve indicates the range of exposure latencies for trials requiring a given amount of rotation. From "The effect of speed–accuracy trade-off on sex differences in mental rotation" by D. F. Lohman, 1986, *Perception & Psychophysics, 39,* p. 422. Copyright 1986 by The Psychonomic Society, Inc. Reprinted by permission.

they eventually reach (λ) and only secondarily in the rate at which they improve when given additional processing time (β). Further, it is possible that the one significant difference in β at 90 degrees merely reflects the fact that λ and β are correlated in these models (median $r = .68$).

The accuracy–latency curves in Fig. 5.4 can be used to estimate rate of rotation at different levels of accuracy. Rotation latencies for a fixed level of accuracy can be estimated graphically by drawing a horizontal line through the speed–accuracy curves at the chosen accuracy level and then determining the latency that corresponds to each point of intersection. Alternatively, the regression equation can be reversed, and latency estimated from accuracy. Latencies

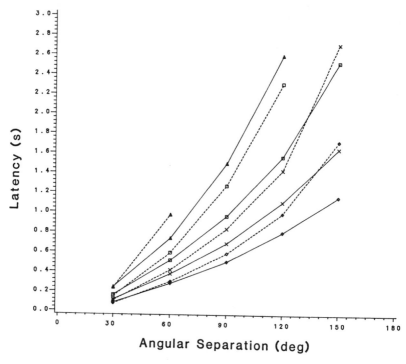

FIG. 5.5.   Rotation latency versus angular separation between stimuli with accuracy {P(C)} fixed at .70 (diamond), .74 (cross), .78 (square), .82 (triangle), and .86 (asterisk). Dashed lines represent data for high-spatial subjects; solid lines, data for low-spatial subjects. Fewer than five points are plotted when accuracy is greater than the asymptote of the corresponding speed-accuracy curve (see Fig. 5.2). From "The effect of speed–accuracy trade-off on sex differences in mental rotation" by D. F. Lohman, 1986, *Perception & Psychophysics, 39,* p. 435. Copyright 1986 by The Psychonomic Society, Inc. Reprinted by permission.

for different levels of accuracy can then be plotted against angular separation between figures, which, according to the Shepard and Metzler (1971) model of this task, estimates rate of rotation.

Fig. 5.5 shows a family of slopes constructed in this manner for five levels of accuracy, separately for high- and low-spatial subjects. Low spatials are solid lines, high spatials are dashed lines. Some lines contain fewer than five points, which occurs when the chosen level of accuracy is greater than the asymptote of the curve, and others show a distinct elevation in the last point plotted, which occurs when the chosen level of accuracy is near the asymptote of the curve. For example, as shown in Fig. 5.5, latencies for 150-degree trials were significantly elevated for low spatials at an accuracy score of .70. On average, lows had great difficulty solving these trials, perhaps making several attempts, or double-checking their answers, or the like, to achieve this level of accuracy.

At higher levels of accuracy, say .74, the accuracy–latency curve for lows did not always intersect the line for fixed accuracy. On average, lows were unable to achieve this level of accuracy on the 150-degree rotation trials, even when allowed 9.5s. Such extreme latencies rarely occur when trials are self-paced rather than experimenter-paced, as in this study. However, when trials are self-paced, subjects impose a deadline and respond, but at the price of an increased error rate (Pellegrino & Kail, 1982). Error rate typically increases with angle of rotation, especially when stimuli are complex (e.g., Lansman, 1981).

For a given level of accuracy, the slope of the line (i.e., estimated rate of rotation) is generally steeper for lows than for highs. However, when accuracy is fixed, lows are always operating at a different point on the accuracy–latency curve than are highs, and so problems are relatively more difficult for lows. On average, asymptotes for highs and lows differed by .11. Thus, lows and highs should be at approximately the same points on their respective latency–accuracy curves if we compare the line for lows at $P(C) = .70$ with the line for highs at $P(C) = .82$. Fig. 5.5 shows these lines to be virtually coincident. The same relationship holds for lows at $P(C) = .74$ and highs at $P(C) = .86$ In both cases the last point plotted is significantly elevated in one group or the other, depending on which curve was approaching asymptote.

Latency–accuracy curves were also estimated for each subject, at each level of angular separation. Plots of these curves revealed that many were not dependable. Therefore, we determined the median λ and median β parameters for each subject, then correlated these parameters with the SR composite (Figures plus Cards) and the Vz composite (Paper Folding plus Form Board). The results are shown in Table 5.1. The SR composite showed the same correlation with both parameters, whereas the Vz composite correlated higher with the λ parameter than with the β parameter. This pattern of correlations is consistent with the hypothesis that Vz tests estimate level or power, whereas SR tests estimate speed of executing the rotation transformation (see Lohman, 1986, for additional details).

Finally, similar analyses in which sex was the grouping factor suggested that the large sex difference often found in rate of rotation (Kail, Carter, & Pellegrino, 1979; Linn & Petersen, 1985; Tapley & Bryden, 1977) may be a predictable consequence of a much smaller sex difference in the asymptotes of latency–accuracy curves for problems requiring the most rotation. These differences are then magnified a second time when response latencies are regressed on angular separation between figures, because trials requiring the most rotation influence the slope of this regression more than trials requiring the average amount of rotation. In other words, much of the observed sex difference in speed of rotation may be an artifact of sex differences in the average error rate on the most complex problems (i.e., level).

TABLE 5.1
Correlations between
Median λ, Median
Normalized β, and
Composite Scores for
the *SR* and *Vz* Spatial
Factors (*N* = 83)

| Composite[a] | Parameter[b] | |
	λ	β
SR	.44**	.43**
Vz	.54**	.29**

[a]*SR* is the sum of standard scores
on the Figures and Cards tests, *Vz* is
the sum of standard scores on the Paper Folding and Form Board Tests (all
tests from Ekstrom et al., 1976).
   [b]βs were first ranked and then normalized (see Lohman, 1986).
   **$p < .01$.

EXPERIMENTS II AND III

Although we were encouraged by the results of this first attempt to use the
methodology of the speed–accuracy study to map a response surface, we were
disappointed that even with 1,200 observations, models for individuals were not
dependable. The problem appeared to be that all subjects received the same 5 (or
10) stimulus exposures. Even though these exposures covered a considerable
range, they were clearly inappropriate for many subjects. Slow subjects had too
few trials near the asymptote of the curve, whereas fast subjects had too few
observations near the intercept. Thus, our first goal was to devise a way to
estimate a latency–accuracy function for each subject that would focus on the
elbow of the curve and would not waste observations on either the intercept or
the asymptote.

Our second goal was to extend our purview beyond the domain of spatial
tasks. Can the sorts of confusions we found in previous attempts to estimate rate
of mental rotation also be found in verbal tasks? And if so, where along the
continuum of task complexity would the speed–accuracy methodology make the
greatest contribution? Would confusions among errors and latencies be greatest
with simple letter-matching tasks, such as the one studied by Neisser (1964) or,
in another form, by Posner and Mitchell (1967)? Or would confusions be greatest
at the other end of the continuum, when subjects must compare the meaning of

words? Or perhaps tasks of intermediate complexity show the greatest confusions when errors and latencies are analyzed separately.

Method

Materials

To this end, we constructed a series of four matching tasks, each assumed to require more complex processing than the previous task. Examples of the trials on each task are shown in Table 5.2. Tasks varied in the type of stimuli presented and in the decision rule subjects were required to use. In all four tasks, subjects saw a target stimulus above two alternatives. The task was to determine which of the two alternative stimuli was the same as the target stimulus. Tasks differed in the decision rule used: same visual features (letter match), same name (name match), same category membership (category match), or same meaning (meaning match).

We began by constructing approximately 1,000 trials of each type. Trials varied systematically in complexity or difficulty. Complexity of the letter-match task was increased by increasing the length of the letter string. Four string lengths were used: 1, 3, 6, or 12 letters. Letters were sampled (with replacement) from the set of 42 upper- and lowercase consonants. Foils were created by randomly changing the case of one letter in the target string. Changes occurred equally often at each ordinal position in the letter string. Complexity of the name-match task was manipulated by increasing the (in)frequency of the homophone; complexity of the category-match task by the abstractness of the category and the typicality of the exemplars; and complexity of the meaning-match task by the (in)frequency and abstractness of the target word, and the similarity between the foil and the correct alternative. For all but the letter-match task, items were subjected to considerable revision before we thought them fit for pilot testing.

Pilot Testing of Stimuli

We then recruited 50 subjects to whom we administered four reference tests: a verbal analogies test (Terman, 1950), a vocabulary test (Marshalek, 1981), a number-comparison test (Ekstrom et al., 1976), and a letter-search test called Finding A's (Ekstrom et al., 1976). A verbal composite was then computed for each subject by combining scores on the verbal analogy and vocabulary tests, and a perceptual speed composite by combining scores on the Finding A's and Number-Comparison tests. Fourteen pairs of subjects with similar scores on these two composites were then identified, such that we represented the entire range of ability on both reference factors. We then randomly assigned one subject to either the letter-match task or to the meaning-match task. Thus, even though we had only 14 subjects assigned to each task, a wide range of verbal and perceptual speed abilities was represented in each sample, and the correlation

TABLE 5.2
Overview of Experimental Tasks

Difficulty	Example Items	Item Construction
	Letter Match	
1	B	Random selection of *n* consonants,
	B b	where *n* = 1, 3, 6, or 12 from the
2	Bqt	set of 42 upper- and lowercase
	BQt Bqt	consonants. Foil is created by
3	BQtNPz	changing one randomly selected
	BqtNPz BQtNPz	consonant in the string to the
4	TgNczYpBrTCG	opposite case.
	TgnczYpBrTCG TgNczYpBrTCG	
	Name Match	
1	B	Simplest items consist of one letter
	b Q	chosen at random from the set of
2	too	52 upper- and lowercase letters.
	tow two	Target is same letter in opposite
3	hear	case. Levels 2 through 4 consist of
	hear hare	homophone of decreasing fre-
4	rain	quency. Foil is a word or pseudo-
	reign ring	word with same letters or similar
		sound as either the stimulus or the
		correct alternative.
	Category Match	
1	apple	Subject must pick alternative in
	orange blue	same category as stem word. Foil
2	Ford	is a randomly selected word from
	Chevrolet Toyota	another category or an associate of
3	chicken	the correct alternative. Complexity
	penguin fish	is increased by increasing the
4	Everest	difference in typicality between the
	McKinley Truman	stem and correct alternative and by
		increasing the abstractness of the
		category.
	Meaning Match	
1	hit	Items represent four levels of
	strike hurt	difficulty, based on pilot testing.
2	cup	More difficult items require subtler
	glass mug	discriminations between meanings.
3	sofa	Foils are associates of target or of
	couch chair	correct alternative.
4	abate	
	case recede	

between these reference abilities was the same in both samples. This procedure was later repeated on another group of 50 subjects, and 14 subjects assigned to either the name-match or category-match tasks. However, we have not yet conducted experiments with the name-match or category-match stimuli, and so I will not discuss these tasks further. I focus, then, on the letter-match task and on the meaning-match task.

For the letter-match task, difficulty was well predicted by string length. The regression of mean latency for each subject for each of the four lengths of strings (1, 3, 6, or 12 consonants) on string length gave an R^2 of .91. For accuracy, the R^2 was .24.

For the meaning-match task, total number correct was moderately correlated with the verbal composite ($r = .47$). An item discrimination coefficient was then computed for each item. Items with low or negative discrimination indices were revised or replaced. Then, the remaining 900 items were divided into four groups of 225 items on the basis of the percentage of subjects who correctly answered the item. Ties were resolved by examining response latencies, such that items with longer response latencies were assigned to the more difficult category.

Subjects

Subjects for Experiments II and III were recruited from an undergraduate psychology course and from newspaper advertisements. Students were offered a choice of course bonus points or money, whereas nonstudents were paid for their participation. In all, 58 students and 17 nonstudents participated in the study. Complete data were obtained from a total of 34 subjects in the letter-match task and from 36 subjects in the meaning-match task.

Procedure

Subjects first attended a group session in which the six reference tests shown in Table 5.3 were administered. Composite scores for verbal ability and perceptual speed were computed for each subject by summing total correct on the respective tests. A bivariate plot of these scores was then used to identify pairs of students with similar scores, one of whom would be randomly assigned to either the meaning-match task or to the letter-match task in the second session. Nonstudents attended only one session. The two perceptual speed and two verbal tests were administered and scored immediately, and subjects assigned to either experimental task. Reasoning tests were not administered to these subjects.

Stimuli consisted of triplets of the words or strings of letters that were previously described. Stimuli were presented in either a *self-paced* condition, in which subjects were given the usual instructions to respond as fast and accurately as possible, or in *fixed-exposure* condition, in which stimuli were exposed for a predetermined amount of time. All subjects began with a set of 10 self-paced

TABLE 5.3
Means and Standard Deviations on Reference Tests and
Composites for Subjects Administered the Letter-Match
and Meaning-Match Tasks

	Letter Match (N = 34)		Meaning Match (N = 36)	
	Mean	S.D.	Mean	S.D.
Verbal Analogies	39.8	5.2	31.6	5.9
Synonyms	28.9	7.8	29.3	6.9
Verbal Total	58.4	11.7	60.9	11.7
Number Comparison	51.9	9.9	54.2	10.8
Finding A's	64.7	18.6	63.9	16.0
Perceptual Speed Total	116.5	24.9	118.1	23.6
Letter Series[a]	11.9	2.0	12.0	1.5
Number Series[a]	19.5	3.8	18.1	4.4
Reasoning Total[a]	31.4	5.1	31.6	5.9

[a]These tests were administered to students only (n = 28 for Letter Match and n = 29 for Meaning Match).

practice items, on which they were given feedback on correctness and latency, and additional assistance and practice if necessary. They then attempted three blocks of 20 self-paced trials. Of these 60 trials, 15 were from each of the four difficulty levels. Each trial began with a warning signal that remained on the screen for a randomly varied interval of from 500 to 1000 ms. The three stimuli appeared immediately after the warning signal and remained in view until subjects pressed a key indicating their choice of the alternative on the left or the right. Interstimulus interval was 1500 ms. Subjects were given feedback on number correct and mean response latency after each of the three blocks of 20 trials.

Subjects were then given new instructions for the fixed exposure trials. They were told that stimuli would appear for a predetermined interval. They were to respond as soon as the stimulus disappeared from the screen. An auditory warning and error message were given if they attempted to respond before the stimuli disappeared. A similar warning was given if they failed to respond within 1000 ms after stimulus offset, and the trial was scored as an error. Subjects first practiced this new procedure on 10 items. Each item was repeated until subjects responded within the 1000 ms window after stimulus offset. They then attempted 42 blocks of 20 trials. Feedback on accuracy and average reaction time (time to respond after stimulus offset) were given after each block. All trials were presented in a different random order to each subject.

Determination of Stimulus Exposures

Exposure durations for stimuli in the fixed-exposure condition were based on the subject's median response times to trials of the same difficulty level in the self-paced condition. Six exposures were determined for the stimuli at each level of difficulty. Pilot work suggested that we make three exposures shorter than this median, one equal to it, and two longer. We first subtracted 400 ms from the median response time at each level of difficulty (to compensate for reaction time). We then divided this time by four. The six exposures were then defined as 1, 2, 3, 4, 5, or 6 times this time. This simple scheme seems to have worked remarkably well. In this way, six different exposure durations were estimated for each of the four levels of difficulty for each subject. Order of presentation of difficulty levels and exposures were randomized anew for each subject.

Results

Letter-Match Task

The results focus on two questions: (a) What happened in the self-paced condition? Presumably this is the sort of data one might ordinarily collect, and so I first present these results. (b) What happened in the fixed-exposure condition? Here, the question concerns what, if anything, the speed–accuracy methodology produced that differed from what was obtained in the self-paced condition.

Self-Paced Condition. Mean accuracies and latencies for each of the four difficulty levels are given in Table 5.4. Correlations between these scores and the Perceptual Speed (*Ps*) and Verbal (*V*) composites are also shown in Table 5.4. Latencies increased substantially and significantly across the four levels of difficulty. Accuracies showed no such trend. Only Level 3 differed significantly from the other three levels (Tukey's, studentized range test). Correlations showed that individual differences at all four levels were highly and approximately equally correlated with the reference *Ps* composite. Neither latency nor accuracy showed a significant correlation with the Verbal composite.

However, correlations are difficult to interpret. Even though average error rates were low, individual error rates ranged from 20% to 0% at Difficulty Levels 1 and 2, and from 27% to 0% at Difficulty Levels 3 and 4. Can latencies for subjects who missed 20% to 27% of the trials be compared with latencies for subjects who missed no trials? Can errors be compared for subjects who differed widely in response latency?

Fixed-Exposure Condition. Mean accuracies averaged over all subjects at each of the six exposure conditions for each of the four difficulty levels are shown in Fig. 5.6. Time scores (on the abscissa) represent exposure time plus

TABLE 5.4
Means, Standard Deviations, and Correlations
of Response Latency and Response Accuracy with
the Perceptual Speed (*Ps*) and Verbal Composites
for Each of Four Difficulty Levels in the Self-Paced
Condition of the Letter-Match Task (*N* = 34)

	Mean	S.D.	Correlation with	
			Ps	Verbal
Latency (ms)				
Difficulty 1	887	170	−.51**	−.13
Difficulty 2	1727	518	−.67**	−.08
Difficulty 3	3056	1235	−.61**	.06
Difficulty 4	5418	1799	−.66**	−.05
Accuracy				
Difficulty 1	.974	.047	.00	.23
Difficulty 2	.966	.053	.18	−.06
Difficulty 3	.927	.068	.02	.31
Difficulty 4	.939	.070	−.06	.10

**p < .01

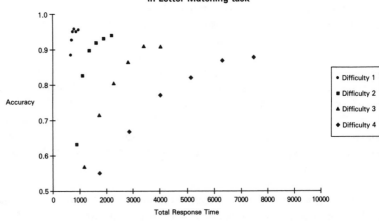

FIG. 5.6. Data for all subjects in the letter-match task plotted in an accuracy by latency response space.

response time. Plots of this sort were made for each subject's data, and most showed good consistency. We then fitted an exponential curve of the form:

$$AC_{ij} = \lambda_i(1 - e^{-\beta_i(T_{ij} - \delta_i)})$$

to each subject's data, separately for each of the four difficulty levels. Here, AC_{ij} is mean accuracy for 35 trials at difficulty level i for stimulus exposure condition j, $T_{i,j}$ is the mean total time (exposure time plus response time) at difficulty level i for stimulus exposure j, and λ_i, β_i, and δ_i are the asymptote, curvature, and intercept parameters of the curve. Distributions of R^2s for individual subjects at each of the four levels of difficulty are shown in Fig. 5.7. Model fits were quite variable for the easiest trials but high for all other trials. The low R-squares at Level 1 partly reflect messiness in the data but are also the result of restricted variability in these scores. Median Root-Mean-Square-Error (RMSE) was .030, .024, .050, and .055 for Levels 1 through 4, respectively.

These 12 parameters (three at each of the four difficulty levels) were then correlated with the Perceptual Speed and Verbal composites, first for all subjects, second excluding those subjects for whom convergence was not achieved or for whom R^2 was nonsignificant, and then a third time excluding all subjects with R^2s less than .50. These correlations are reported in Table 5.5. With one exception (correlation between asymptote and verbal ability at Difficulty 4), correlations were virtually the same across all three analyses. Thus, subjects who were not well fitted by the speed–accuracy models did not differ systematically from other subjects. This is an important result, because ability is often confounded with model fit in analyses based on latency or error alone (e.g., R. Sternberg, 1977).

I see three interesting patterns in the correlations reported in Table 5.5. First, the curvature parameter (β) showed high and significant correlations with Ps for all but the easiest trials. Thus, those who scored higher on the perceptual speed tests showed significantly greater improvements in response accuracy with additional increments in stimulus exposure than did subjects who scored low on such tests. Lack of correlation between β and Ps at Difficulty Level 1 may reflect unreliability in these very steep curves, or that rate of accumulation of information about the visual appearance of individual letters is not related to the construct called *perceptual speed.*

The second finding here is that asymptotic level of accuracy—particularly for three- and six-letter strings—was highly correlated with verbal ability! One explanation for this finding is that specific verbal abilities represent the ability to retain order information on strings of temporally coded events (Snow & Lohman, in press). Letter strings of intermediate length may be processed in such a manner when subjects are given sufficient time.

The third finding here is that the intercept parameter appeared not to be related either to Ps or to V. There is some evidence, however, that it may capture a unique aspect of individual differences. Recall that the 28 students who at-

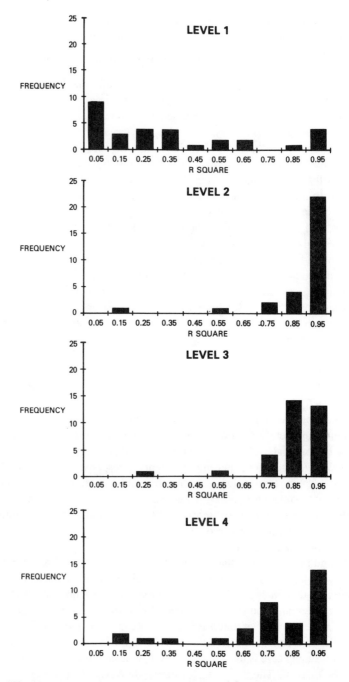

FIG. 5.7. Distributions of R^2s for individual subjects at each of four levels of difficulty in the letter-match task.

TABLE 5.5
Correlations between the Curvature, Intercept, and Asymptote
Parameters and Reference Perceptual Speed (Ps) and Verbal (V)
Composites for the Letter-Match Task (N = 34)

Difficulty Level	N	Curvature (β) Ps	Curvature (β) V	Intercept (δ) Ps	Intercept (δ) V	Asymptote (λ) Ps	Asymptote (λ) V
		All Subjects					
1	34	.20	.08	−.26	.02	.01	.37*
2	34	.52**	−.22	.30	.03	−.04	.52**
3	34	.44**	.03	.20	.26	.06	.46**
4	34	.55**	−.10	.06	.08	−.12	.33*
		Convergence and R^2 Significant					
1	22	.13	.05	−.16	−.03	.13	.45*
2	30	.51**	−.15	.26	.08	−.01	.58**
3	33	.56**	.07	.29	.29	.03	.46**
4	34	.55**	−.10	.06	.08	−.13	.33**
		$R^2 > .50$					
1	9	—	—	—	—	—	—
2	29	.49**	−.25	.22	−.11	−.10	.46**
3	32	.56**	.08	.32	.26	.07	.44**
4	30	.55**	.06	.11	−.07	−.12	−.04

*$p < .05$
**$p < .01$

tempted the letter-match task were also administered two reasoning tests. Correlations between the intercepts and the Reasoning composite were $r = -.44$, $+.47$, $-.06$, and $-.06$ for Difficulty Levels 1 through 4, respectively. For Level 1, those who were fastest—that is, whose curves started to rise above the abscissa sooner—scored higher on the reasoning tests. This is exactly the sort of result Jensen (1982) has obtained in his choice RT studies. It is also about the same magnitude of correlation he has obtained. By Difficulty Level 2, however, the situation had completely reversed. Now those who were a bit slower had higher reasoning scores. This corresponds with the observation that more able subjects spend more time encoding terms on problems of nontrivial difficulty (R. Sternberg, 1985). However, I do not make too much of these correlations. Although correlations with Ps and V should be quite dependable, correlations with Reasoning may be biased by the way subjects were assigned on the basis of their scores on Ps and V. Nevertheless, this is the sort of analysis and theorizing that the speed–accuracy modeling allows.

These same trends are shown graphically in Fig. 5.8, which shows data for groups of subjects with low, medium, or high scores on the Ps composite. Parameters of the models for the curves plotted in Fig. 5.8 are reported in Table 5.6. Note the dramatic difference in curvature parameters between low- and high-Ps groups.

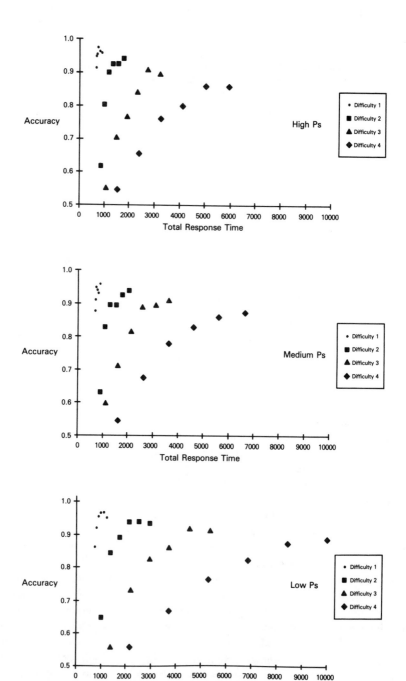

FIG. 5.8. Accuracy by latency plots for subjects of low-, medium-, and high-perceptual speed ability in the letter-match task.

TABLE 5.6
Estimated Curvature, Intercept, and Asymptote
Parameters for Subjects of Low ($n = 11$), Medium
($n = 12$), and High ($n = 11$) Perceptual Speed (Ps)
Ability at Each of the Four Levels of Trial Difficulty on
the Letter-Match Task

	Curvature (β)	Intercept (δ)	Asymptote (λ)
Difficulty 1			
Low *Ps*	14.5	.531	.96
Med *Ps*	85.3	.616	.94
High *Ps*	95.6	.608	.96
Difficulty 2			
Low *Ps*	3.07	.590	.94
Med *Ps*	6.31	.681	.92
High *Ps*	6.34	.646	.94
Difficulty 3			
Low *Ps*	.76	.183	.94
Med *Ps*	1.03	.149	.95
High *Ps*	1.06	.221	.95
Difficulty 4			
Low *Ps*	.40	.00	.89
Med *Ps*	.57	.00	.90
High *Ps*	.61	.00	.89

Meaning-Match Task

Self-Paced Trials.   As in the letter-match task, subjects first attempted 60 self-paced trials, 15 at each of the four levels of difficulty. Basic results for these items are shown in Table 5.7. Latencies showed no significant increase over the first three difficulty levels. The most difficult items (Difficulty 4), however, took longer. Accuracy on these items was also markedly lower than for other items. As expected, accuracy declined almost linearly over the first three difficulty levels.

Correlations of average latency and average accuracy for each subject with the Perceptual Speed and Verbal composites are also shown in Table 5.7. The pattern is typical: Correlations between latency and verbal ability declined as difficulty increased, whereas correlations between accuracy and verbal ability increased as difficulty increased. However, correlations for latencies are difficult to interpret or to defend. Average error rate was 11.7% for the easiest trials, but ranged from 0% to 26.7% for individual subjects on the easiest trials, and increased to 52.8% for the most difficult trials. Even for the easiest trials we cannot compare latencies for the person who missed over one quarter of the trials with latencies for the person who missed none. Perhaps we should use latencies

TABLE 5.7

Means, Standard Deviations, and Correlations
of Response Latency and Response Accuracy with
Perceptual Speed (*Ps*) and Verbal Composites for
Each of Four Difficulty Levels in the Self-Paced
Condition of the Meaning-Match Task (*N* = 36)

	Mean	S.D.	Correlation with	
			Ps	Verbal
Latency (msec)				
Difficulty 1	2160	670	−.26	−.42**
Difficulty 2	2194	718	−.16	−.30
Difficulty 3	2334	821	−.13	−.33*
Difficulty 4	2640	873	−.18	−.15
Accuracy				
Difficulty 1	.883	.075	−.14	.39*
Difficulty 2	.824	.138	.11	.29
Difficulty 3	.707	.121	−.16	.56**
Difficulty 4	.482	.158	−.06	.58**

*$p < .05$
**$p < .01$

only for error-free trials. But then we base our analysis on different trials for different subjects: all of the trials for our best subjects, but only the easier 75% of these trials for our worst performing subject. Or perhaps we should discard subjects who make too many mistakes. But how should we set the cutoff score? And more importantly, how can we interpret our correlations between response latencies and other variables if they represent only a subset of our sample—and a nonrandom subset at that?

Fixed-Exposure Trials.   Fig. 5.9 shows mean probability correct as a function of mean latency (exposure plus response) at each of the four levels of difficulty. The same three-parameter exponential model used in the letter-match task was also fitted to each individual's data. The distributions of R^2 for individuals are shown in Fig. 5.10. Unlike the letter-match task, R^2s were highest for easiest items and lowest for the most difficult items, on which many subjects performed at the level of random responding. Models were also fitted to means for 12 low-, 12 medium-, and 12 high-verbal subjects. Parameters for models fitted to means for the three groups are given in Table 5.8; data are shown graphically in Fig. 5.11. The most dramatic differences among these three groups are in the asymptotes. The correlation between asymptotes for models fitted to each individual's data and verbal ability was significant at all four difficulty levels (see Table 5.9). The three groups appear to differ in curvature parameters, but Table 5.9 shows that this correlation was significant only for the easiest problems. By

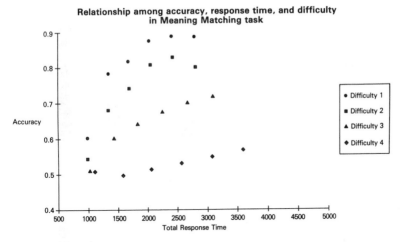

FIG. 5.9.   Data for all subjects in the meaning-match task plotted in an accuracy by latency response space.

Difficulty Level 2, curvature parameters showed significant correlations with Perceptual Speed. Intercepts also increased systematically across groups and showed significant correlations with verbal ability for all but the most difficult problems.

Note that these correlations between intercepts and verbal ability were all positive, which means that more able subjects were slower. I wonder if this reflects something like the fan effect Anderson (1984) has investigated. The idea is that the time taken to accumulate information about a particular concept in an individual's semantic network is inversely related to the number of potential concepts and relationships in that region of the network, because activation spreads down all paths that emanate from a source node. In other words, those who know more should be slower. Larger samples and more precise estimates of trial difficulty are needed to confirm these systematic differences in curvature and intercept parameters for the easiest items. However, differences in curvature and intercept are clearly secondary to the massive differences in asymptote across the groups.

DISCUSSION

What have we learned from all of this? First, we have learned that this sort of study is worthwhile—difficult, but worthwhile. The primary benefit is that it disambiguates otherwise ambiguous data and statistics computed on them. By estimating the parameters of a function that relates response latency to response

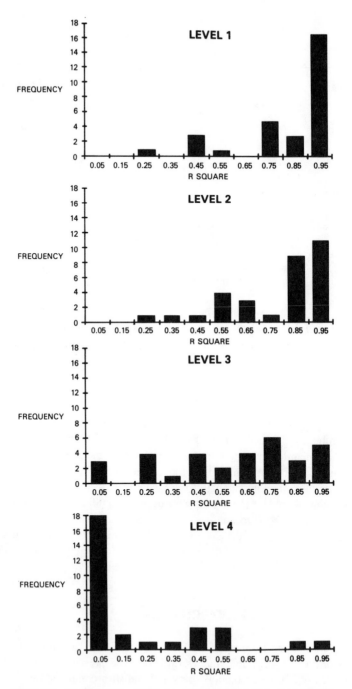

FIG. 5.10. Distributions of R^2s for individual subjects at each of four levels of difficulty in the meaning-match task.

TABLE 5.8
Estimated Curvature, Intercept, and Asymptote
Parameters for Subjects of Low (*n* = 12), Medium (*n*
= 12), and High (*n* = 12) Verbal Ability at Each of
Four Levels of Difficulty in the Meaning-Match Task

	Curvature (β)	Intercept (δ)	Asymptote (λ)
Difficulty 1			
Low *V*	1.40	.198	.88
Med *V*	2.84	.497	.87
High *V*	3.79	.658	.93
Difficulty 2			
Low *V*	1.67	.272	.76
Med *V*	2.01	.417	.84
High *V*	2.55	.597	.88
Difficulty 3			
Low *V*	1.30	.000	.65
Med *V*	1.02	.000	.75
High *V*	4.30	.701	.76
Difficulty 4			
Low *V*	2.07	.000	.49
Med *V*	—	.000	.51
High *V*	1.59	.000	.63

accuracy, one can examine the effects of one variable while the other is held constant, although this turns out to be a bit more difficult than one might have expected. In particular, holding accuracy constant works only if accuracy–latency functions have roughly the same asymptote for each individual. This is highly unlikely for level constructs, such as spatial visualization (*Vz*) or verbal ability (*V*). Indeed, our mental rotation experiment showed that the large sex differences often observed in rate of rotation were a predictable consequence of sex differences in asymptotes of accuracy-latency curves. Even seemingly straightforward ability differences in rate of rotation were found to be not so straightforward when the shapes of the SAT curves were also considered.

Similar and even larger differences in asymptotes were noted for our meaning-match task, even for the simplest trials. This means that subjects would have to be performing at quite different levels of speed or accuracy emphasis if error rates were somehow to be controlled. In the case of verbal ability, differences in asymptotic levels of performance on easy trials also showed some relationship with verbal ability. Asymptotic performance on these trials may also relate other ability constructs, such as memory span, for example.

We also found that individual differences on these level tasks were not simply a matter of differences in asymptote, but also in the rate at which performance improved with additional units of time on easy items (i.e., the curvature of the function) and in the point at which performance rose above random responding

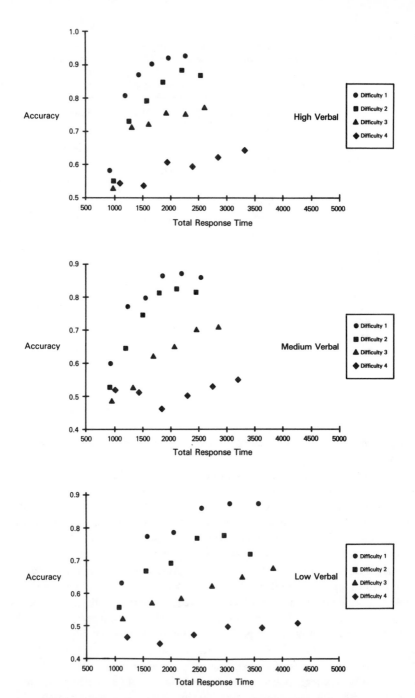

FIG. 5.11. Accuracy by latency plots for subjects of low-, medium-, and high-verbal ability in the meaning-match task.

TABLE 5.9
Correlations between the Curvature, Intercept, and Asymptote
Parameters and Reference Perceptual Speed (*Ps*) and Verbal (*V*)
Composites for the Meaning-Match Task (*N* = 36)

Difficulty Level	N	Curvature (β)		Intercept (δ)		Asymptote (λ)	
		Ps	V	Ps	V	Ps	V
		All Subjects					
1	36	.24	.32	.05	.29	.13	.35*
2	36	.13	.11	.06	.31	−.03	.61**
3	36	−.04	.25	−.03	.45	.29	.59**
4	36	−.19	−.28	.07	−.03	.00	.70**
		Convergence and R² Significant					
1	30	.16	.51**	−.10	.49**	.25	.36*
2	31	.41*	.27	.30	.49**	−.10	.56**
3	31	.03	.34	−.03	.50**	.17	.55**
4	15	−.17	.06	−.09	.28	−.10	.71**
		R² > .50					
1	26	.15	.57**	−.06	.51**	.21	.38**
2	28	.43*	.31	.31	.46**	−.30	.56**
3	20	.10	.35	.08	.30	.31	.47*
4	5	—	—	—	—	—	—

*p < .05
**p < .01

(i.e., the intercept of the function) for all but the most difficult items. However, model fits were poorer here than with the mental rotation and meaning-match tasks, and so inferences must be guarded.

For the letter-match task, both curvatures and asymptotes were dependable and showed strong correlations with other variables. The important finding here was that differences in shape of the accuracy–latency curve—particularly its asymptote—must also be considered when comparing individual differences in latencies on relatively simple perceptual-speed tasks. Further, we found these differences to be systematically related to another ability construct. I think this is a very important finding. We cannot assume that—if given sufficient time—all subjects can compare two strings containing three or six consonants without making mistakes. In our experiment, some continued to make mistakes, even when given much time, and the number of mistakes they made could be predicted from their scores on verbal tests.

Therefore, attempting to hold one variable constant while examining the other may be a bad idea. It would appear far more useful to estimate the function that describes the relationship between accuracy and latency and then to use the parameters of that function to describe the processing characteristics of the individual. I believe the studies summarized here are a start in this direction.

Future Directions

Error and latency are complementary rather than interchangeable aspects of performance. One becomes most interpretable as the other becomes uninterpretable. Complementarity is evident when one attempts to describe performance using a componential or stage analysis of some sort. For example, when components are executed serially, then latencies combine additively, whereas error probabilities combine multiplicatively. In other words, unless a recovery mechanism is postulated, the probability of committing an error when executing a series of operations cannot be less than the probability of error on any one of the components. Attempts to use the same combination rule for both error and latency require that one make strong assumptions about performance. For example, R. Sternberg (1985) justifies an additive combination rule for component difficulties in the following way: "This additive combination rule is based on the assumption that each subject has a limit on processing capacity. . . . Each execution of an operation uses up capacity. Until the limit is exceeded, performance is flawless except for constant sources of error. . . . Once the limit is exceeded, however, performance is at a chance level" (p. 360). Such strong threshold models in which performance drops precipitously from perfect to chance levels are not well supported in studies of recognition memory (Kintsch, 1970) and seem unlikely here as well.

Conversely, Embretson (1985, 1986) has used error probabilities as the dependent measure in her multicomponent latent trait models and, appropriately, a multiplicative combination rule. But she has had to ignore response latencies or has attempted to hold them constant by fixing the exposure latency for item stems. Thus, in one study of verbal analogy performance (Embretson, Schneider, & Roth, 1986), all analogy stems (A : B : C :) were presented for 35 sec. Subjects may have had time for several attempts on the easier problems, and not enough time on the most difficult problems.

Attempts to combine accuracy and latency in the same analysis using canonical variate analysis (R. Sternberg, 1977), sum and difference scores (Lohman, 1979b), or analysis of covariance (Pachella, 1974) all presume a linear relationship between accuracy and latency and presume all subjects adopt the same trade-off between speed and accuracy across all item types. There is much evidence that both of these assumptions are untenable.

The speed–accuracy study provides a possible avenue to reconcile the conflicting demands of latency and error. The simplest solution is to present the entire item on each trial, to vary item exposures in a way that permits estimation of a speed–accuracy trade-off function for each subject, to fit such functions to each subject's data, and then to use parameters of this function as the dependent variables in subsequent analyses. We are about to collect data on a study of numerical analogies using this method.

Alternatively, the functional relationship between accuracy, latency, and complexity can be estimated separately for each component process. Probability of correctly solving the item is then given by the product of the probabilities of executing correctly each of the component processes. Thus, the probability of person p correctly performing component process c is given by:

$$P(X_{pc} = 1) = \lambda_{pc} (1 - e^{(-\beta_{pc}(t_{pc}-\delta_{pc}))}) \qquad (3)$$

The probability that the person correctly solves the full item T is given by:

$$P(X_{pT} = 1) = \Pi_c \, P(X_{pc} = 1) \qquad (4)$$

This model has three person parameters for each component process and no item parameters, as items are assumed to be of uniform difficulty. Item parameters can be added by substituting a variant of Equation 2, that is:

$$P(X_{pck} = 1) = \lambda^*_{pck} (1 - e^{(-\beta^*_{pck} (t_{pck}-\delta^*_{pck}))}) \qquad (5)$$

where:

$$\lambda^*_{pck} = \lambda_{pc} + \Sigma \, b_{ck} \, \lambda_{pck}$$
$$\beta^*_{pck} = \beta_{pc} + \Sigma \, b_{ck} \, \beta_{pck}$$
$$\delta^*_{pck} = \delta_{pc} + \Sigma \, b_{ck} \, \delta_{pck}$$

and:

b_{ck} = a vector that uniquely identifies items of complexity level k on component process c.

When expressed in this way, there are obvious parallels with Embretson's multicomponent latent trait model (MLTM). Two important differences between MLTM and this formulation are (a) MLTM models only one dependent variable, whereas this approach considers latencies as well; (b) person and item parameters are assumed to be independent in MLTM, whereas here they are not.

Some Obstacles and Questions

There are many obstacles to be overcome, and questions that must be addressed. Here are a few that seem important:

1. Better methods to scale difficulty for the complex tasks. We have been most successful when we could manipulate or at least estimate difficulty with some precision, as in the rotation and letter-match tasks, and least successful when we did not have a dependable, unidimensional estimate of difficulty, as in the synonym task. We could do better by administering our 1,000 vocabulary items to large samples. But we have not had the resources to do this. Nor have we found word frequency or other objective indices of difficulty to be good predictors of the difficulty of the item. Much depends on the quality of the foil.

2. Larger samples. This is always desirable, although the number of trials per subject required in a speed–accuracy study makes this an even more difficult task than it ordinarily is in research on individual differences in information process-ing. Our method of matching subjects on two relevant abilities assures us of an equal range of the two abilities in our samples, and equal correlations between the two abilities in these samples. Thus, correlations between scores on the experimental tasks and these reference abilities are much more dependable than sample size suggests. Unfortunately, I know of no easy way to convince readers and reviewers of this fact. Researchers tend to regard a correlation matrix with an *N* of 35 skeptically. But what are the alternatives? Should we relegate all such research to those who can easily assemble 100, 500, or even thousands of cases? I think not. The bandwidth-fidelity dilemma applies to the control one can exercise over subjects in an experiment as much as to the range of tasks admin-istered.

3. More observations per subject. We may need more than 900 or 1,000 trials to estimate accuracy–latency functions for some subjects, particularly those whose performance is erratic, and even when stimulus exposures are adaptively determined for each subject. Here, we stumble once again upon one of the preconceptions we bring as baggage to this meeting ground between correlational and experimental psychology. Correlational psychologists are accustomed to gathering the data in a few minutes. In an hour, one can estimate scores for three or four separate abilities. And although subjects are supposed to be motivated, a considerable range of task engagement can be tolerated with relative impunity. If the sample is large, then many of these differences will cancel—or at least obscure each other. Hence comes the emphasis on large, even gargantuan sam-ples in this tradition.

The experimentalist, on the other hand, aims for a clear and unambiguous understanding of each subject's data. Those who cannot or will not cooperate are eliminated. Conditions are carefully standardized to reduce unwanted variation as much as possible. One, well-practiced, cooperative subject is worth a dozen half-hearted neophytes. After 10 years of research on individual differences, I am gathering increasing sympathy for the experimentalists' views. There is no substitute for careful control and full cooperation of the subject. Parenthetically, I note that we routinely run ourselves as the first subjects in these studies and then attempt to model our own data. This is possible because the methodology is not cognitively penetrable—as Pylyshyn (1984) would put it. But more impor-tantly, it reflects the opinions that those who cannot explain their own behavior on such tasks have little business pretending to explain the behavior of others on the same tasks.

4. More information on models and model-fitting techniques. We spent much time attempting to fit a variant of the three-parameter logistic function used in item-response theory to these data. We wanted to do this in part to show the affinity between these models and the person-characteristic curve Carroll (1987) has recently advocated. The main difference, of course, is that Carroll plots probability correct against difficulty, whereas we include another dimension for response latency, thus examining a response surface defined by accuracy and latency.

However, the logistic model appears less well suited to these data, primarily because of the paucity of scores near the intercept. Matters are further complicated by the fact that the probability of guessing the correct answer cannot be used as the lower asymptote for the function in the synonym task. For these and other reasons I cannot explain here, we have come back to the three-parameter exponential function that Wickelgren (1977) recommended, and we believe it is generally a better choice for data such as these. Nevertheless, there is still much work that remains to be done on the function to be used and the methods for estimating parameters. In its present stage of development, fitting nonlinear functions to such data seems to be as much art as it is science. This is particularly the case for the more complex functions like the one given in Equation 2. Convergence is difficult to achieve if starting values for each parameter differ much from the final value achieved, which means that one must know the results of the model fitting before one can fit the model. Because of this, we have retreated to testing a series of simpler models, one at each level of task difficulty.

5. Robust methods for estimating parameter reliability. Nonlinear models like those we have used in these studies can be difficult to fit when data are not orderly. Therefore, one must worry about the dependability of the parameters obtained from these regressions. One way to approach this task would be randomly to divide each subject's data into two sets, estimate models on each half, and intercorrelate the resulting parameters. But this would require much more data for each subject than we have collected. Instead, we have approached the problem in three other ways: (a) by fitting both two- and three-parameter models to the same data and correlating estimates for parameters shared by the models, (b) by examining intercorrelations of parameters across the four difficulty levels, and (c) by using an index of model fit (e.g., R^2) to screen subjects for inclusion in data analyses.

Our experience has been that the first method gives overly optimistic results, whereas the second gives an overly pessimistic view. Using information on the model fit (i.e., R^2) to make inferences about the dependability of model parameters seems promising but has problems as well, such as establishing a cutoff between good and poor model fits. However, Fig. 5.7 suggests this may not be an intractable problem.

6. Further study of motivation and preferred speed–accuracy trade-off. Our unsuccessful attempt to manipulate motivation in the first experiment may be a more interesting finding than it first seemed. It would be wrong to infer that motivation exerts no influence on performance in the experimenter-paced study. Clearly, subjects must be attentive to the task and try to solve problems in the time allotted. Nevertheless, it may be the case that motivation exerts less of an influence in this paradigm than when subjects control the pacing and exposure of the stimuli. This needs more study.

Perhaps the speed–accuracy study could also be used to investigate the control subjects are able to exert over their own speed–accuracy trade-off. Subjects' performance in the experimenter-paced study could be compared with their performance when instructed to respond as rapidly as possible, or as accurately as possible, or with a specified speed–accuracy emphasis (e.g., 70% or 80% or 90% correct). At least this might provide a way to investigate such motivational and affective variables in ways that are more informative than simply including another individual difference variable in all analyses.

CONCLUSIONS

We are told by those who study differences between expert and novices that novices consistently create mental models that are undercomplicated. Perhaps our models of human performance have been undercomplicated as well. But there is always a trade-off between the complexity of the model and its utility. Complex models—even those that are as elegant as generalizability theory— often wither unused while simpler models that make stronger assumptions (such as classical test theory) continue to enjoy widespread use. The speed–accuracy models proposed here may suffer a similar fate. Nevertheless, the experimental results we have obtained using this approach may encourage others at least to question the assumptions they must make when they measure only one aspect of performance, and may even encourage the development of other ways to estimate the contributions of both accuracy and latency to task performance. There are enough interesting problems here to keep us and many others busy for a long time.

OPEN DISCUSSION

The discussion following Lohman's talk started with comments and controversy regarding measurement issues. Further discussion concerned individual preferences for speed–accuracy trade-offs as a response style issue. The exchange concluded with questions about practice effects and about the techniques Lohman uses for model fitting.

Kyllonen: I have a couple of questions. One is a little question, and one is a bigger question. The little one is this: If you assume that errors are multiplying (and you might assume, for example, that errors even within a component stage are multiplying), then maybe percent correct is not the right measure of accuracy to be looking at in the first place. Maybe you ought to look at something that would reflect the outcome of a multiplicative process. For example, there is a rationale for looking at log errors or for looking a conversion of percent correct to d'. And you might then find something like a linear trade-off between that measure of accuracy and some measure of latency. That would make the goal process of model fitting a lot easier.

Lohman: Let me respond to that and you can then go on to the other question. First, we have tried to get a better measure of response accuracy using signal detection theory. I think, as you might have noted in a footnote to one of the studies we published (Lohman, 1986), it was after we had done several transformations of transformations of scores that one of the reviewers asked why didn't we just stick with probability correct since it was correlated in excess of about .97 (within cell of the design) with our transformation of the transformations that were measures from signal detection theory. Although I have been persuaded by the arguments that I have read in the signal detection literature, it's been a difference I found that didn't make a difference.

The problem with simply transforming the scores and then fitting linear models is that you lose the information you are trying to get here. The main information you need here is the elbow of the curve. You want to find out where the asymptote really begins to form and you want to go back down and find the intercept. If you have transformed that out of your scale someplace, you may indeed find nice linear functions, but you no longer have the parameters that you are really interested in. It is a way to put the data back into a linear system, but I am not sure that it does so at a cost that I am willing to accept.

Kyllonen: I guess the basic funny part about using percent correct is that you are assuming an interval scale. . . .

Lohman: Look at probability correct then, or even just number of errors. . . .

Kyllonen: Probability correct then. You are assuming that the amount of extra cognitive effort it takes to go from 98 percent to 99 percent is the same as the amount of cognitive effort it takes to go from 62 to 63 percent.

Lohman: That's a worthwhile point.

Kyllonen: And then the second point, the bigger question, is that there might be a sense in which a person's speed–accuracy trade-off is part of their signature that they carry around with them. That is, it may influence their performance in any kind of cognitive activity they engage in. So by looking at speed–accuracy trade-off you might be forcing—you're in a sense putting a person's head in a clamp—and you are forcing them to respond in a particular way, when in fact they don't characteristically respond in that way. In an applied setting you might find that these kinds of manipulations would result in a smaller relationship between any kind of parameter estimates you got and some applied learning outcome. Because in the learning situation, they are also going to resort back to their original signature—the way in which they trade off speed and accuracy.

Lohman: Yes, that's a good point. First of all, the reason for doing the speed–accuracy modeling is not so much just to control for speed–accuracy trade-off, but rather to get a defensible way of indexing performance. The purpose is so you don't have problems such as, "How do I compare people who made lots of mistakes with those who did not?" and "How do I compare latencies for these people?" To me, then, the primary contribution of this research is to get defensible dependent measures.

When I started working for Dick Snow years ago, the first data I was asked to reanalyze came from a visual-masking study using film. In this study, a replication of some work by Averbach and Coriell, a bar marker or a circle marker was presented either (approximately) 94 or 170 milliseconds after the appearance of an array. This was done in groups, done with film, done in a large auditorium, and is basically the same sort of thing that we ended up doing in our first study here. But the second issue, which is the reason I refrained from doing this research for a long time, stems from my concern about the possibility of influencing people's strategies and adulterating their behavior in this way. Indeed, the factor that some would call Carefulness is measured by how long you will persist and do these sorts of things.

I think it is really an empirical question as to whether this is something that the person carries around with him/herself or is not. I have found that some persons are quite responsive to explicit requests to go faster or slower in the experiment and some persons are not. If I am trying to estimate something about this person's information processing characteristics, then *that* is the kind of variable I would like to have some control over. It may reduce the correlation with my measures in an applied sense, and that is something to worry about, but I think it cleans them up in an experimental sense. That is, I now have this little trademark of the person under control. So I am not looking at their differences in speed–accuracy trade-off *when I think* I am looking at differences in rate of rotation.

Pellegrino: The kinds of tasks you use typically involve assorted, multiple problems; there are practice effects, accuracy effects, a general speed up, and it varies across components. In estimating your speed–accuracy trade-off functions, you are now presenting lots of trials. Have you looked at the issue of whether or not the parameters of the speed–accuracy trade-off functions change with practice? What I am asking is how stable are those parameters that you are estimating compared with the kind of parameters that you would get when you fit a model to the mean latency data?

Lohman: Yes, we have looked at changes with practice, but not within the context of "Do the parameters of speed–accuracy model change?" because it takes so darn many observations to estimate one of these in the first place. But one of the things we have found most useful there is the notion of what it is that gets automatized. One of the reasons why we were anxious to use the stimuli we got from you for mental rotation was that they vary along a lot of other dimensions. There are four different types of stimuli and there are different axes of rotation and so we weren't re-presenting the same problem again and again. We found that as long as we were just proceduralizing procedures there was a very dramatic improvement, but then it leveled off fairly rapidly. One of the things I hope you noticed, however, is that we created a thousand items for each of these different tasks that differed from one another, so that we weren't re-presenting the same thing. We have found that this substantially reduces practice effects. I think much of the practice effect researchers typically see comes through auto-matization of responding to a particular stimulus set.

Ackerman: I want to follow up on Pat Kyllonen's question. Can you derive speed–accuracy trade-offs for an individual subject under your con-strained condition and then put them in a situation on the task where it is relatively unconstrained, that is, where they can choose whatever trade-off they find comfortable for themselves? Then, do you think it is possible, using these metrics, to derive a score that would essentially be a perpen-dicular line running through their speed–accuracy trade-off to show the distance from what an equal trade-off of accuracy and reaction time would be, and therefore get a more pure measure of carefulness or cognitive style?

Lohman: That's a good idea. One of the things that Reed recommends, and that we did here, is to do both experiments. One of the things we didn't do here was to distribute the self-paced trials throughout the experiment. Rather, we had the self-paced trials up front and then lots of experimenter-paced trials. One of the things you typically do is to plot this speed–accuracy curve within each cell of any design imposed on the trials and then plot the one point you get from the conventional experiment in the same space. The extent to which this one point falls significantly off that curve tells you how different the information is, across the two pacing conditions.

I think which method (self-paced or experimenter-paced) is preferred is a moot question. In much of the speed–accuracy literature it is presumed that the self-paced condition is the preferred data point. Having modeled a lot of self-paced data, I am not so sure. There's lot of noise running around in the way people prefer to do things.

Ackerman: But in order to make it work, must each individual's speed–accuracy trade-off have the same basic function—the same shape to it?

Lohman: Well, no. You could estimate different sorts of functions. But I have not seen dependable data that did not show this same sort of basic exponential form. I think this type of analysis is almost an a priori require-ment for doing anything else with the data. This could be done simul-taneously in perhaps a more complex multivariate system. The way it makes sense to me is to think of it within cell, and then what one does after that. . . .

McArdle: My question may be an old one. Estes, in the 1950s I think, suggested that certain classes of curves could be fit to individuals that would not average over groups. That is, the parameters would not represent the group curve. As I recall, it dealt with the second derivative and it dealt with equations like that—not averaging. How does that fit in here? Is it a problem or is it so close to not being realistic. . . .

Lohman: What it says is that you don't want to just take my evidence when I show you the group data; that you want to know what it looks like for individuals. It is an aggregation problem which indicates that you really want to go back to the level of individual data.

McArdle: Well, is there any reason to push away from that particular model toward a model that does average; where there is dynamic consisten-cy (is this the correct word from Wickelgren?), where there is a consistency in the dynamic at the individual level and at the group level? Is there any movement that should be made in that direction so that there is this parallel relation?

Lohman: I'm not sure. I had enough trouble fitting these curves. I have learned more about nonlinear regression than I ever cared to know after doing this. I have found that it is as much an art as a science. Indeed, one of the problems we have had with the complex models which go across multi-ple levels of complexity is that you basically have to know the results of the modeling in order to do the modeling. You need starting values that are so close to what you are going to get that it is not informative. So we have retreated back in much of our work to testing simpler models of multiple levels of complexity.

McArdle: So you pushed back to the individuals?

Lohman: Yes, that's the only way. I average data (not parameters) over individuals *after* I fit the models to the individuals. That was one of the big steps we were glad to see we could do in going from the first to the second experiment I discussed. In the first experiment on mental rotation the individual data were not that dependable because we used a common set of exposures for all subjects. Once we started doing it adaptively we were able to dependably model most individuals. For those individuals we could not model, I think the problem was related more to motivation or task engagement issues and had nothing to do with their ability on any task or any of the abilities we measured. I think that was a really worthwhile finding.

REFERENCES

Anderson, J. R. (1984). Spreading activation. In J. R. Anderson & S. M. Kosslyn (Eds.), *Tutorials in learning and memory: Essays in honor of Gordon Bower* (pp. 61–90). San Francisco: W. H. Freeman.

Berg, C., Hertzog, C., & Hunt, E. (1982). Age differences in the speed of mental rotation. *Developmental Psychology, 18,* 95–107.

Carroll, J. B. (1980). *Individual differences in psychometric and experimental cognitive tasks* (NR 150-406 ONR Final Report). Chapel Hill, NC: L. L. Thurstone Psychometric Laboratory, University of North Carolina.

Carroll, J. B. (1987). New perspectives in the analysis of abilities. In R. R. Ronning, J. A. Glover, J. C. Conoley, & J. C. Witt (Eds.), *The influence of cognitive psychology on testing: The Buros-Nebraska symposium on measurement and testing* (Vol. 3, pp. 267–284). Hillsdale, NJ: Lawrence Erlbaum Associates.

Dosher, B. A. (1982). The effect of sentence size and network distance on retrieval speed. *Journal of Experimental Psychology: Learning, Memory, and Cognition, 8,* 173–207.

Dosher, B. A. (1984). Degree of learning and retrieval speed: Study time and multiple exposures. *Journal of Experimental Psychology: Learning, Memory, and Cognition, 10,* 541–575.

Egan, D. E. (1976, February). *Accuracy and latency scores as measures of spatial information processing* (NAMRL Rep. No. 1224). Pensacola, FL: Naval Aerospace Medical Research Laboratory.

Ekstrom, R. B., French, J. W., & Harman, H. H. (1976). *Kit of factor-referenced cognitive tests.* Princeton, NJ: Educational Testing Service.

Embretson, S. E. (1985). Multicomponent latent trait models for test design. In S. E. Embretson (Ed.), *Test design: Developments in psychology and psychometrics* (pp. 195–218). New York: Academic Press.

Embretson, S. E. (1986). Intelligence and its measurement: Extending contemporary theory to existing tests. In R. J. Sternberg (Ed.), *Advances in the psychology of human intelligence* (Vol. 3, pp. 335–368). Hillsdale, NJ: Lawrence Erlbaum Associates.

Embretson, S. E., Schneider, L., & Roth, D. (1986). Multiple processing strategies and the construct validity of verbal reasoning tests. *Journal of Educational Measurement, 23,* 13–32.

Fruchter, B. (1953). Differences in factor content of rights and wrongs scores. *Psychometrika, 18,* 257–265.

Hoffman, K. I., Guilford, J. P., Hoepfner, R., & Doherty, W. J. (1968). *A factor analysis of the figure-cognition and figural-evaluation abilities* (Rep. No. 40). Los Angeles: Psychological Laboratory, University of Southern California.

Horn, J. L. (1985). Remodeling old models of intelligence. In B. B. Wolman (Ed.), *Handbook of intelligence* (pp. 267–300). New York: John Wiley & Sons.

Humphreys, L. (1985). General intelligence: An integration of factor, test, and simplex theory. In B. B. Wolman (Ed.), *Handbook of intelligence* (pp. 201–224). New York: Wiley.

Jensen, A. R. (1982). The chronometry of intelligence. In R. J. Sternberg (Ed.), *Advances in the psychology of human intelligence* (Vol. 1, pp. 225–310). Hillsdale, NJ: Lawrence Erlbaum Associates.

Kail, R., Carter, P., & Pazak, B. (1979, November). *Development of individual differences in spatial ability.* Paper presented at the annual meeting of the Psychonomic Society, Phoenix.

Kail, R., Carter, P., & Pellegrino, J. (1979). The locus of sex differences in spatial ability. *Perception and Psychophysics, 26,* 182–186.

Kintsch, W. (1970). *Learning, memory, and conceptual processes.* New York: Wiley.

Kyllonen, P. C. (1985). *Dimensions of information processing speed* (AFHRL-TP-84-56). Brooks AFB, TX: Air Force Human Resources Laboratory, Manpower & Personnel Division.

Lansman, M. (1981). Ability factors and the speed of information processing. In M. P. Friedman, J. P. Das, & N. O'Connor (Eds.), *Intelligence and learning* (pp. 441–457). New York: Plenum Press.

Linn, M. C., & Petersen, A. C. (1985). Emergence and characterization of sex differences in spatial ability: A meta-analysis. *Child Development, 56,* 1479–1498.

Lohman, D. F. (1979a). *Spatial ability: A review and reanalysis of the correlational literature* (Tech. Rep. No. 8). Stanford, CA: Stanford University, Aptitude Research Project, School of Education. (NTIS No. AD-A108-003)

Lohman, D. F. (1979b). *Spatial ability: Individual differences in speed and level* (Tech. Rep. No. 9). Stanford, CA: Stanford University, Aptitude Research Project, School of Education. (NTIS No. AD-A075-973).

Lohman, D. F. (1986). The effect of speed–accuracy tradeoff on sex differences in mental rotation. *Perception & Psychophysics, 39,* 427–436.

Marshalek, B. (1981). *Trait and process aspects of vocabulary knowledge and verbal ability* (Tech. Rep. No. 15). Stanford, CA: Stanford University, Aptitude Research Project, School of Education. (NTIS No. AD-A102-757)

Marshalek, B., Lohman, D. F., & Snow, R. E. (1983). The complexity continuum in the radex and hierarchical models of intelligence. *Intelligence, 7,* 107–128.

McGue, M., Bouchard, T. J., Lykken, D. T., & Feuer, D. (1984). Information processing abilities in twins reared apart. *Intelligence, 8,* 234–258.

McNichol, D. (1972). *A primer of signal detection theory.* London: George Allen & Unwin.

Morrison, E. J. (1960). Effects of time limits on the efficiency and factorial compositions of reasoning measures (Doctoral dissertation, University of Illinois). *Dissertation Abstracts International, 21,* 1638.

Mumaw, R. J., Pellegrino, J. W., Kail, R. V., & Carter, P. (1984). Different slopes for different folks: Process analysis of spatial aptitude. *Memory and Cognition, 12,* 515–521.

Neisser, U. (1964). Visual search. *Scientific American, 210,* 94–102.

Pachella, R. G. (1974). The interpretation of reaction time in information processing research. In B. Kantowitz (Ed.), *Human information processing* (pp. 41–82). Potomac, MD: Lawrence Erlbaum Associates.

Pellegrino, J. W., & Kail, R. (1982). Process analyses of spatial aptitude. In R. J. Sternberg (Ed.),

Advances in the psychology of human intelligence (Vol. 1, pp. 311–366). Hillsdale, NJ: Lawrence Erlbaum Associates.

Poltrock, S. E., & Brown, P. (1984). Individual differences in visual imagery and spatial ability. *Intelligence, 8,* 93–138.

Posner, M. I., & Mitchell, R. F. (1967). Chronometric analysis of classification. *Psychological Review, 74,* 392–409.

Pylyshyn, Z. (1984). *Computation and cognition.* Cambridge, MA: MIT Press.

Reed, A. V. (1973). Speed–accuracy tradeoff in recognition memory. *Science, 181,* 574–576.

Reed, A. V. (1976). List length and the time course of recognition in human memory. *Memory and Cognition, 4,* 16–30.

Schouten, J. F., & Bekker, J. A. M. (1967). Reaction time and accuracy. *Acta Psychologica, 27,* 143–153.

Shepard, R. N., & Metzler, J. (1971). Mental rotation of three-dimensional objects. *Science, 171,* 701–703.

Snow, R. E., & Lohman, D. F. (in press). Implications of cognitive psychology for educational measurement. In R. L. Linn (Ed.), *Educational Measurement* (3rd Ed.). New York: Macmillan.

Sternberg, R. J. (1977). *Intelligence, information processing, and analogical reasoning: The componential analysis of human abilities.* Hillsdale, NJ: Lawrence Erlbaum Associates.

Sternberg, R. J. (1980). A proposed resolution of curious conflicts in the literature on linear syllogisms. In R. S. Nickerson (Ed.), *Attention and performance VIII* (pp. 719–744). Hillsdale, NJ: Lawrence Erlbaum Associates.

Sternberg, R. J. (1985). *Beyond IQ: A triarchic theory of human intelligence.* New York: Cambridge University Press.

Sternberg, S. (1969). Memory-scanning: Mental processes revealed by reaction time experiments. *American Scientist, 4,* 421–457.

Swets, J. A. (1986). Indices of discrimination or diagnostic accuracy: Their ROCs and implied models. *Psychological Bulletin, 99,* 100–117.

Tapley, S. M., & Bryden, M. P. (1977). An investigation of sex differences in spatial ability: Mental rotation of three-dimensional objects. *Canadian Journal of Psychology, 31,* 122–130.

Tate, M. W. (1948). Individual differences in speed of response in mental test materials of varying degrees of difficulty. *Educational and Psychological Measurement, 8,* 353–374.

Terman, L. (1950). *Concept Mastery Test* (Form T). New York: Psychological Corporation.

Thorndike, R. M., & Lohman, D. F. (in press). *A century of ability testing: 1888–1988.* Chicago: Riverside Press.

Thurstone, L. L. (1938). Primary mental abilities. *Psychometric Monographs, 1.*

Werdelin, I. (1961). *Geometrical ability and the space factor.* Lund: Gleerup.

Wickelgren, W. A. (1977). Speed–accuracy tradeoff and information processing dynamics. *Acta Psychologica, 41,* 67–85.

Wood, C. C., & Jennings, J. R. (1976). Speed–accuracy tradeoff functions in choice reaction time: Experimental designs and computational procedures. *Perception & Psychophysics, 19,* 92–101.

6

Simple Solutions
and Complex Problems

Robert Cudeck
University of Minnesota

An old idea in the social sciences, one that in particular can be found in the very beginnings of experimental psychology, is the belief that behavior is regular and predictable (see, for example, a brief overview in Gulliksen, 1959, pp. 178–179). The causes and organization of any realistic facet of behavior are no doubt highly complex, yet humans do behave in predictable, sometimes even lawful, ways. Recurrent themes occur. Regularity characterizes individual as well as group activities. It would be a very unusual typology of behavior that had very many categories with only one member.

I once heard a mathematician say, in a penetrating observation that seemed especially insightful to a layman, that mathematics is the study of patterns. He was referring to the theory of functions, the beautiful body of knowledge that describes the relationships among elements of different sets. Functional relationships are the clearest, most succinct portrayal of patterns that exist. In fact, one might say that if an event is recurrent or predictable, then there is no better way to describe it than with equations.

The connection between this viewpoint and the papers in this section lies in the observation that humans often act surprisingly lawfully. If behavior is regular and occurs in patterns as we often observe, then it should be possible to describe the behavior mathematically. Perhaps the utility of mathematical models of behavior does not need to be emphasized yet again. After all, isn't everyone who studies intellectual performance or individual differences interested in describing the processes that account for their data? But it is still true that most psychological models are not presented as explicit functions of behavioral variables; most models are not easily tested or replicated; and most models are unable to give specific numeric predictions. These are the assets that quantitative models give and that make the enterprise valuable. It is sometimes argued that this approach has the drawback of reducing complex human activity to relatively simple descriptions, and no doubt some richness is lost in the process. Nonetheless, describing behavior with equations has been useful, even though the process sounds unreasonable and unexpected on first hearing. It is gratifying to continue to find distinguished scientists who are pursuing more than a list of variables on which differences are documented between experimental and control groups on learning tasks, who are in addition attempting to develop quantitative models of behavior.

COMMENTS ON DR. GUSTAFSSON'S PAPER

Dr. Gustafsson describes several interesting, even surprising relationships in his study of broad and narrow abilities. Users of modern methods of factor analysis too often are guilty of rather automatically going about the business of fitting models without given due consideration to the processes they study. This has led, in some cases, to unfortunate oversimplifications of complex relationships. Here, by contrast, is an example of creative statistical modeling along with insight into subtle relationships among the constructs.

The major finding is the unexpected interaction between a general hierarchical factor and other specific ability factors. Although the result itself is highly suggestive, I think it should be carefully studied as an example of what surely must happen in many other areas of behavior when quantitative models are applied. There are two parts to the lesson. Gustafsson finds that a pattern of zero-order correlations among observed variables masks a very different pattern of correlations that are revealed in a model that postulates disattenuated factor scores. The second point in the lesson is that the relationships among ability factors can be substantially different in one structure compared to another. Sometimes these differences are small. At other times they can be substantial and, as in this instance, can change the understanding of the underlying relationships altogether. The moral from this work illustrates two statistical artifacts that are well known but perhaps too easily forgotten: (a) measurement error attenuates true score relationships, which biases correlations and regression coefficients (Lawley & Maxwell, 1973; Maxwell, 1975); (b) specification errors (e.g., Costner & Schoenberg, 1973; Rao, 1971; Saris, dePijper & Zegwaart, 1979) hurt—sometimes they hurt a lot. This holds even when the regressions and correlations that we study are based, to the extent that factor analysis permits, on true scores.

In practice, it is easier (relatively) to deal with the problem of measurement error than it is to have great confidence that one's model is correctly specified. All models are wrong, as the cliché goes, but some are more wrong than others. Because it is so difficult to verify that a model is correct, there is too often a tendency to ignore this problem, to simply apply a structure that seems to be more less plausible, and to hope for the best. Sometimes this practice is unavoidable because our experience in an area is limited. In other domains, perhaps especially in the study of human ability, a class of models has emerged after considerable investigation, and researchers can hope that the disastrous effects of misspecification can be minimized. Gustafsson's final model seems plausible. It is certainly provocative. As a textbook case of careful scientific detective work, it is impressive.

COMMENTS ON DR. LOHMAN'S PAPER

Dr. Lohman's paper represents an extremely interesting combination of psychological problem with a creative flurry of model fitting. He begins with a general question about individual difference in information processing, arguing that one aspect of the answer may lie in the characterization of an individual's speed–accuracy trade-off. This conjecture, which appears to be promising for understanding performance on these tasks, led to a major experimental and statistical undertaking to develop a realistic model.

Although it may not be obvious on first glance, it is nonetheless true that Lohman's experimental results have a structure that is broadly related to growth data. A speed–accuracy trade-off (SAT) curve is not identical with individual growth patterns, but the general problem of fitting curves to responses of this kind are related. A comparison of Fig. 5.2 and 5.3 from this paper with Fig. 4.5 from Dr. McArdle's will show the rough correspondence, although McArdle's subjects are probably not yet at their asymptotic performance. There are other psychological processes that share several of these characteristics as well, especially patterns that emerge in learning. The common features are that the behavior exhibits a better-than-chance initial level of performance; the performance improves in a nonlinear fashion; performance reaches a maximum level, after which there is no additional improvement. This maximal level is well below perfect performance. Performance on experimental tasks is sometimes not even consistently monotonic increasingly due to fatigue effects in later trials. Classical learning curves, and especially true growth curves that represent biological growth, do not exhibit this latter inconsistent feature, however. In general then, growth curves constitute a large class of data with many distinctive subgroups.

It would be a pleasure to be able to make a specific suggestion about how such data should be analyzed. Unfortunately, to my knowledge, no completely general model has yet been presented that offers a really satisfactory solution to the problem, although some promising work has begun to appear (Bock & Thissen, 1988; Du Toit, 1979; Lee, 1988; Meredith & Tisak, 1988; Rogosa & Willett, 1985). The models that we will use in the future probably will incorporate several attractive features. There are two aspects that I would be most interested in seeing. Dr. Lohman found it most advantageous to fit individual curves before considering group performance, an approach that was followed partly out of necessity. This method generates valuable information on individuals but only indirectly produces normative data bout group or subgroup performance. No method for treating data of this kind will be satisfactory unless both types of growth can be illuminated. Lohman presents some interesting correlations between parameters of the SAT curve and other variables, in his case tests of spatial ability. The ideal model for data of this kind will allow for the estimation of correlations between curve parameters and other variables in a direct manner.

A general model of this kind will probably be well suited for problems such as Dr. Lohman describes. One can be sympathetic with his unenthusiastic recommendation that more data be collected in order to assist in the model-fitting process of this research. If my hunch is correct about these general procedures for analyzing growth curves, it may soon be possible to estimate the curves in a satisfactory manner without requiring such a large investment in additional subject (and experimenter) labor.

COMMENTS ON DR. MCARDLE'S PAPER

Dr. McArdle presents one of the most comprehensive overviews of the use of structural models to learning data that has appeared. It is fair to say that most researchers who are interested in this technology have limited their attention to cross-sectional designs and only infrequently have considered models in which mean structures are included in the system. Here is a detailed example with a variety of structures that can be used right off the shelf in other problems. I do not mean to minimize the substantive results about developmental change that this work presents, but the review is clearly meant to be read as an example of how one might study data of this kind, and I think this is the major accomplishment of the paper.

In some applications of this technology, one or two carefully developed and defensible models are sometimes tested during the traditional logic for evaluating hypotheses. In unblushingly exploratory studies, on the other hand, or in studies in which the structures are still being built up, it is much more common to fit-and-try models. This latter strategy is so often followed because the method lends itself to this kind of exercise, and because several different models may well be plausible for the data at hand. The danger of considering many alternative structures is that one may never settle on one particular model or class of models that perform adequately in a particular setting. To those who are active users of this methodology, I would encourage some critical model selection beyond the simple listing of many possible alternatives. It may be that several different structures are equally acceptable, but often there are substantive or statistical grounds for narrowing the list of candidates to a small number. This should be done whenever possible. It is tempting with this technology to try many models almost indiscriminately. In the end, we seek an increase in our understanding of some aspect of behavior. It is a mistake to lose sight of this goal. I emphasize that this is not a criticism of McArdle's paper, since his goal was obviously didactic, but rather a reminder that the job of describing behavior is incomplete if one is left with scores of undifferentiated models.

I appreciated the graphical device of plotting values of the test statistic along with the associated degrees of freedom and wish I had thought of it myself. It might be interesting to also include a few of the critical points, at say $\alpha = .10$, for a few selected degrees of freedom. Then, one could also evaluate some of the models in terms of conventional acceptance levels, as well as in terms of their relative performance as the figure now allows. Admittedly, the nominal critical points are more or less meaningless when many models are to be compared, but this information might still be useful as a standard for model evaluation in some cases.

I also have a request for a follow-up paper. In this work, the major activity has been to describe group growth over time. It is sometimes tempting to ignore the very real problem that individuals may exhibit growth that is markedly different from the group norm. It would be a simple matter to estimate individual growth curves from these analyses, most straightforwardly by estimating the associated growth curves using the well-known formulas of factor score estimation. Additional discussion of this point would be useful because models like these will certainly be more common in the future.

SOME GENERAL OBSERVATIONS

Dr. Carroll and Dr. Gustafsson both lament the fact that more comprehensive data sets are not routinely available to investigate very complex structures. There is a limit on the amount of time a subject can be expected to concentrate in a testing session, even a semiconfined subject like a military recruit. This limits the number of tests that can be administered, which in turn limits the number and complexity of primary factors that can be studied. These limitations taken together essentially guarantee that it is difficult to generalize as widely as might be wished. They also ensure that integrating results across different studies is a tricky business that includes many subjective steps in the process. There are two problems here. The first concerns how to gather enough test data to permit very large analyses that are required to identify a wide spectrum of well-determined factors. An analogous problem repeatedly occurs in the literature on item-response theory, where several designs for data collection have been introduced to deal with them (e.g., Vale, 1986). The basic idea is to administer partially overlapping sets of tests to independent samples. For example, Sample 1 might take Tests 1–10, Sample 2 might take Tests 5–15, Sample 3 takes Tests 10–20, and Sample 4 takes Tests 15–20 plus 1–5. Then, an equal number of subjects are

TABLE 6.1
Extensions of Factor Analysis Model to
Multiple Batteries and Multiple Populations

Batteries	Populations	
	One	Two or More
One	Conventional factor analysis	Factor analysis for multiple populations
Two or More	Multiple battery factor analysis	Multiple batteries and populations

available for each test. Muthen, Kaplan, and Hollis (1987) describe methods, using existing computer programs, for treating incomplete data collected in this way.

The second issue concerns the old problem of relating factors across individuals and across tests to ensure that results are truly representative and not simply idiographic descriptions of a sample or battery assembled for the sake of convenience. Some types of generalization of factor analytic results can be improved by taking advantage of methodological work that has been in place for some time. Table 6.1 summarizes two of the ways in which factor analysis can be generalized, using the technology presently available. The obvious ways are extensions across different populations or across different batteries. Virtually all studies have used designs in which one population and one test battery is studied. Obviously, there is nothing wrong with this design. The concern lies in the potential problem that results may not be generally representative.

The classic single-sample, single-battery design was generalized to multiple populations by Jöreskog (1971). Dr. McArdle's paper is an excellent example of this approach. In an analogous fashion, a model for two or more batteries was presented by Browne (1979, 1980). These extensions address the question of factor stability across different groups of tests or groups of subjects. It would be straightforward to develop a comprehensive method that would be appropriate for the composition of both facets simultaneously with a model that combines features of both approaches. I believe that such a hybrid model would be a valuable tool to ensure that the factors that are identified would be truly representative of a broad range of populations and tests.

Many of the papers in this conference mention applications of the factor-analysis model, either tangentially or as a major feature of the research, and I can't resist adding a comment regarding the use of factor analysis in this domain. Factor analysis has a very unusual place in the behavioral sciences. In much multivariate research, it seems to be more or less the only game in town. When a psychologist encounters a matrix of correlations among ability scores, the urge to fit a factor-analysis model seems nearly irresistible. (One is tempted to hypothesize a genetic predisposition toward this behavior.) Recently I have begun to wonder if this interesting model may sometimes be a hindrance to furthering understanding. Most serious efforts to develop models work in a very different manner. Typically, one begins with a conjecture about the process that connects certain independent variables with a response. Then, in cyclic fashion, one evaluates the performance of the model with relevant data, modifies some parts (if it is apparent how this can be done), and begins to evaluate again.

Consider on the other hand the typical use of factor analysis. Whether it is appropriate for a particular domain is hardly discussed. Factor analysis assumes linear regressions. Is that always reasonable? It assumes uncorrelated specific factors. Is that always justifiable? Why is it that we never see studies in which the factor-analysis model is itself tested? In light of a persistent body of work, as Dr. Lohman's and Dr. McArdle's results have illustrated, there are plenty of data to suggest that other functional forms may be preferable. One of the reasons that factor analysis is appealing may be because of its resolution of variables into true score plus error components, or if this strong assumption is not warranted, then into common scores plus uniqueness. It is easy to believe that this decomposition is needed to accurately portray measurements in the behavioral sciences, but why should linear factor analysis always be employed simply because an error structure for observed variables is required?

I hasten to add that I don't have a particular favorite that I would generally recommend as a replacement. Indeed, the point is that insisting on one particular structure for many different behavioral domains is probably a mistake, and it is no doubt most misleading in areas where the process of model development is relatively mature. The study of human ability and the structure of learning in particular are examples of this kind. There are situations where other models can describe our data in a more interesting and useful fashion. The most realistic structure for multitrait–multimethod covariance matrices, for instance, is in many cases a multiplicative relationship between trait and method scores, and is not invariably an additive relationship as is commonly assumed (Campbell & O'Connell, 1967; Cudeck, 1988). Other examples could be cited of plausible structures for a particular domain that are not additive, or if they are additive, they are nonlinear (McDonald, 1983). Behavior is complex, and one might expect that nonlinear models in general may be needed. No doubt there are many cases in which the most satisfying structure will be quite complicated. It seems worth repeating that factor analysis, after all, is a model, and like any other model, its utility for a given data set is a proposition that should be evaluated.

REFERENCES

Bock, R. D., & Thissen, D. (1988). *Statistical problems of fitting growth curves.* Unpublished manuscript, University of Chicago, Chicago, Illinois.

Browne, M. W. (1979). The maximum likelihood solution in inter-battery factor analysis. *British Journal of Mathematical and Statistical Psychology, 32,* 75–86.

Browne, M. W. (1980). Factor analysis of multiple batteries by maximum likelihood. *British Journal of Mathematical and Statistical Psychology, 33,* 184–199.

Campbell, D. T., & O'Connell, E. S. (1967). Method factors in multitrait–multimethod matrices: Multiplicative rather than additive? *Multivariate Behavioral Research, 2,* 409–426.

Costner, H. L., & Schoenberg, R. (1973). Diagnosing indicator ills in multiple indicator models. In A. S. Goldberger & O. D. Duncan (Eds.), *Structural equation models in the social sciences* (pp. 167–199). New York: Seminar.

Cudeck, R. (1988). Multiplicative models and MTMM matrices. *Journal of Educational Statistics, 13,* 131–147.

Du Toit, S. H. C. (1979). *The analysis of growth curves.* Unpublished doctoral dissertation, University of South Africa, Pretoria.

Gulliksen, H. (1959). Mathematical solutions for psychological problems. *American Psychologist, 47,* 178–201.

Jöreskog, K. G. (1971). Simultaneous factor analysis in several populations. *Psychometrika, 36,* 409–426.

Lawley, D. N., & Maxwell, A. E. (1973). Regression and factor analysis. *Biometrika, 60,* 331–338.

Lee, J. C. (1988, February). *Forecasting technological substitutions and the growth curve.* Paper presented at the University of Minnesota School of Statistics Seminar Series, Minneapolis.

Maxwell, A. E. (1975). Limitations on the use of the multiple linear regression model. *British Journal of Mathematical and Statistical Psychology, 28,* 51–62.

McDonald, R. P. (1983). Exploratory and confirmatory nonlinear common factor analysis. In H. Wainer & S. Messick (Eds.), *Principals of modern psychological measurement* (pp. 197–213). Hillsdale, NJ: Lawrence Erlbaum Associates.

Meredith, W., & Tisak, J. (1988). *Latent curve analysis.* Unpublished manuscript, University of California, Berkeley, Department of Psychology.

Muthen, B., Kaplan, D., & Hollis, M. (1987). On the structural equation modeling with data that are not missing completely at random. *Psychometrika, 52,* 431–462.

Rao, P. (1971). Some notes on misspecification in multiple regression. *American Statistician, 25,* 37–39.

Rogosa, D. R., & Willett, J. B. (1985). Understanding correlates of change by modeling individual differences in growth. *Psychometrika, 50,* 203–228.

Saris, W. E., dePijper, W. M., Zegwaart, P. (1979). Detection of specification errors in linear structural equation models. In K. F. Schuessler (Ed.), *Sociological methodology* (pp. 151–171). San Francisco: Jossey-Bass.

Vale, C. D. (1986). Linking item parameters onto a common scale. *Applied Psychological Measurement, 10,* 333–344.

COGNITIVE ABILITIES AND INFORMATION PROCESSING

7

Assessment and Modeling of Information Coordination Abilities

James W. Pellegrino
University of California, Santa Barbara

Earl B. Hunt
Penny Yee
University of Washington

In this chapter we are concerned with the prediction of individual performance in situations requiring people to take action in response to the information in rapidly changing visual-spatial displays. The research attempts to unite two streams of research activity in psychology. One is the study of individual differences in elementary information-processing capabilities and the other is performance on complex cognitive tasks. Most previous research on these two topics can be looked on as an attempt to understand how a person's ability to perform elementary information-processing activities, such as retrieving a word meaning from memory, determines performance on complex, more intellectual tasks, such as those used in a typical intelligence test.

The research described herein addresses a somewhat different question; in many situations, people have to make decisions under extreme time pressure. Aviation, for instance, abounds with examples of such situations. Real-time thinking offers a marked contrast to the sort of thinking that is displayed over minutes, hours, or even days in activities involving academic intelligence. Substantial individual differences in performance are typically observed in real-time tasks. To what extent can these differences be predicted by an evaluation of elementary information-processing capability? How should predictor tests be constructed?

In order to study these question we draw heavily upon a second major research area, the study of time sharing and dual-task activity. In many real-time decision-making situations, people perform several subtasks at once. For example, in aviation pilots talk on the radio as they operate their aircraft. Consequently, the subtasks may involve different modalities. Although dual tasks have been studied extensively in the past few years, only a small proportion of the research has focused on individual differences (Ackerman, Schneider, & Wickens, 1984). A second limitation of dual-task research is that experimenters have focused on a mildly unreal situation in which the subtasks are simultaneous but unrelated, so that they compete for common resources. A good example is a frequently used paradigm in which people are given a memory task and then asked to respond to a simultaneously presented but logically unrelated probe stimulus. We believe that a more realistic paradigm would be one in which the subtasks provide information that must be coordinated in overall problem solving. Consider again the example of the pilot talking on the radio.

More formally, we are interested in characterizing individual differences in real-time, multitask situations that require the coordination of verbal, motor, and visual-spatial information. We shall refer to such situations as *multicomponent coordination tasks*. We wish to establish patterns of individual differences in performance on multicomponent coordination tasks and, if possible, to relate these patterns to the process models now used in cognitive science to explain performance in a variety of problem-solving tasks, including ones with a real-time component (cf. Anderson, 1983; Hunt, 1987a; Hunt & Lansman, 1982; Just & Carpenter, 1985).

Our approach is keyed to the development of a microcomputer-based technology for testing. As we have pointed out elsewhere (Hunt & Pellegrino, 1985), the psychological functions tested by traditional paper and pencil tests are limited by that technology. Computerized testing makes it possible to evaluate individual differences in responding to complex situations under considerable time pressure. However, the appropriate tests and analyses cannot simply be lifted from the experimental psychologist's laboratory, because the paradigms themselves were not developed for individual differences research. What is required is a psychometric model of covariation in performance across tasks that has been derived from process models of the individual tasks, and from process models of how people respond to multicomponent tasks.

The present paper deals with the development and testing of both the process and psychometric models for a variety of multicomponent tasks covering three broad areas of human ability: verbal comprehension, visual-spatial reasoning, and motor responding. These different areas are combined by considering the psychological demands on the operator of an abstract self-propelled machine moving through space. The operator of the vehicle receives information about the outside world through computer controlled video displays units. Although this general description obviously applies to a number of real situations, no attempt has been made to imitate any real machine. The experimental tasks and the paradigms chosen have been designed to pursue general psychological questions rather than to simulate a particular human-machine system.

Why are we interested in individual differences in the coordination of such disparate activities? The topic is clearly worth studying as a topic in basic research. Visual-spatial, verbal-auditory, and motor activities define the chief communication channels through which people deal with the world. A great deal of research activity has been devoted to defining individual differences in the visual-spatial and verbal-auditory domains (see, for instance, Hunt, 1987b; Lohman, Pellegrino, Alderton, & Regian, 1987; Pellegrino & Kail, 1982). Somewhat less has been done in the motor domain, but the absolute amount of research is still impressive (Marteniuk, 1974). In populations of normal adults, performance is generally uncorrelated across these three domains. (The pattern may be somewhat different for the very young, the elderly, and mentally retarded individuals, but these populations are not to be studied here.) Within domains, however, individual differences are determined by a number of correlated traits.

We ask whether or not there is an ability to coordinate information received across these different domains, an ability that is over and above the ability to deal with each domain separately. We note that this is not a trivial question, because coordination essentially implies the ability to prioritize processing of information. It has been suggested that prioritizing and scheduling activities is the primary function of the frontal and prefrontal cortex (Kolb & Whishaw, 1980, chap. 14). Thus, individual differences in interdomain coordination may reflect a basic individual difference in cognitive capacity.

We focus here on tasks that require the coordinate use of information from different channels in order to maximize performance on a single criterion measure. In these coordination tasks, performance depends upon melding the information received on each channel. This sort of task can be contrasted with what is typically referred to in the literature as a dual task. As noted earlier, in dual-task paradigms people simultaneously execute two separate and unrelated tasks, maximizing unrelated criteria. Often one task is defined as being the primary task and thus deserving of more attentional resources. A frequently used example is a situation in which a person simultaneously retains information in memory while performing a signal detection task. Dual-task situations are interesting for theoretical reasons, as they can be used to evaluate the allocation of attention (Kahneman, 1973; Kerr, 1973). In the past, they have also been used to study individual differences in time sharing, with generally negative results (Hawkins, Church, & de Lemos, 1977; Sverko, 1977; see Ackerman, Schneider & Wickens, 1984, for a discussion of possible errors in this work). Although these dual tasks do occur in extralaboratory situations, coordination tasks seem to be more frequent and perhaps more important in gauging human ability.

LOGICAL ANALYSIS OF THE PROBLEM

The logic of our investigation is based on a point about time-sharing abilities that was first made by Ackerman, Schneider, and Wickens (1984) in an analysis of dual-task performance. We follow their general approach, although the details of our statistical treatment are different from theirs. In order to investigate indi-

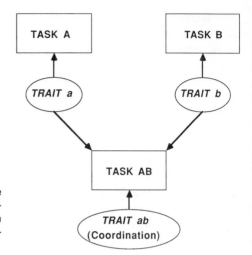

FIG. 7.1. A model for performance on two single domain and one multiple domain task postulating domain specific abilities and a general coordination ability.

vidual differences in the ability to coordinate two activities, it is first necessary to consider a person's ability to do each task singly. Consider two hypothetical tasks, A and B, and a combined task, AB. For concrete reference, let A be a measure of visual-spatial ability, and let B be a measure of verbal ability. Suppose that each task taps an underlying ability (a and b respectively) and that the combined task requires an additional coordinating ability, ab. Fig. 7.1 shows the presumed relationship between abilities (shown in ovals) and observable performance measures (shown in rectangles). Performance on task AB is determined by all three abilities, as indicated by the single-headed arrows.

To translate this reasoning into statistical terms, let $R_{AB.(A,B)}$ be the multiple correlation between task AB and tasks A and B. In order to assert that coordinating trait ab exists it is necessary to show that there is residual variance in AB after performance has been predicted from knowledge of performance in tasks A and B. That is, it has to be shown that the quantity $(1 - R^2_{AB.(A,B)})$ is reliably greater than zero. Unfortunately, this is a necessary but not sufficient condition for asserting the existence of an AB trait, as residual variance could arise in other ways. To consider the most trivial way, suppose that all the tasks had low reliability, but that reliability was not specifically assessed. There would be considerable residual variance in measures of AB after allowing for A and B performance.

There are various ways to avoid mistaking unreliability of measurement for the effect of a coordinating ability. One is to use a repeated measurements approach, in which each individual is tested on two or more occasions. This procedure is preferable to the use of an internal measure of test reliability (e.g., Cronbach's alpha statistic, or split-half reliability measures) because measurement on separate occasions assesses the stability of the trait being measured as well as the reliability of the measurement technique. A possible problem, how-ever, is that practice effects (learning) can affect such reliability estimates given the pattern of declining intersession correlations over multiple sessions with a task (see Ackerman, 1987).

Another approach is to regard A, B, and AB not as single tasks but rather as classes of tasks (e.g., batteries of verbal and visual-spatial tests) and to use an analysis of covariance approach (Bentler, 1980; Jöreskog & Sörbom, 1979). A distinction can then be made between the variance in performance due to class specific traits a, b, and ab (as in Fig. 7.1) and the variance in performance that is specific to a particular task.

The analysis of covariance approach may be used to distinguish between a general ability to control tasks and an ability to coordinate two specific classes of tasks, for example, between a general coordination ability and the ability to coordinate visual-spatial and verbal information. All that is needed is the intro-duction of a third class of measures, C, that evaluate a third ability, c. In our work, this would correspond to the ability to control motor movements. The logic of the approach is illustrated in Figs. 7.2 and 7.3. Fig. 7.2 shows an extension of the model of Fig. 7.1 to encompass measure C and combined task measures AB and BC, where performance is determined by an additional c, and a general coordination ability that applies to all combined tasks. This can be contrasted with Fig. 7.3, where it is assumed that there are separate, although perhaps correlated, abilities to deal with combined tasks based on particular pairs of domains. Several other models may also be contrasted. Note, however, that

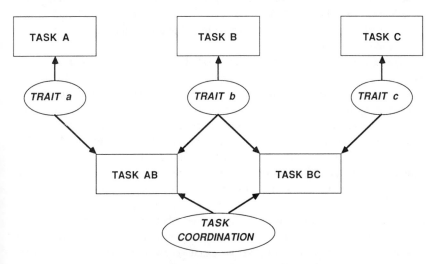

FIG. 7.2. A model for performance on three single domain and two multiple domain tasks postulating domain specific abilities and a gen-eral coordination ability.

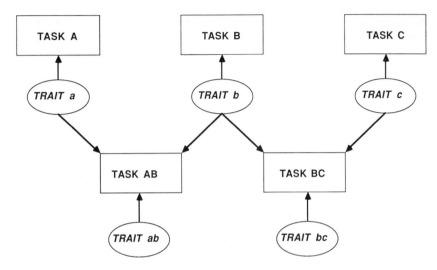

FIG. 7.3. A model for performance on three single domain and two multiple domain tasks postulating domain specific abilities and task specific coordination abilities.

there are some technical problems with applying the analysis of covariance approach. The models shown in Figs. 7.2 and 7.3 are identified in the statistical sense, although the model of Fig. 7.3 has only a single degree of freedom for statistical testing. Therefore, it is essential that the testing be powerful. This is also necessary in order to estimate parameters. For both these reasons, a substantial sample size is required.

A drawback to a large sample approach for analysis of covariance model testing is that repeated testing is frequently not feasible and in general would be an expensive proposition. This means that the large sample method cannot be used to study trait stability or individual differences in stability. Therefore, we have conducted smaller sample size experiments (on the order of 30 to 50 subjects per study) in which performance is observed over several days. The logic of these studies can be illustrated by a reinterpretation of Fig. 7.1. In this reinterpretation, A, B, and AB change from being batteries of different tasks within the same domain to repetitions of single tasks within the appropriate domain; for example, visual-spatial, verbal, and combined visual-spatial and verbal tasks, on different days. The question about the existence of a stable coordination ability can then be answered by a straightforward correlational approach. Let $r(AB_1AB_2 : A,B)$ be the partial correlation between task performance measured at Times 1 and 2, after controlling for performance on tasks A and B, ideally measured at a third time. A necessary and sufficient condition for asserting that there exists an ability to coordinate information across domains A and B is that the partial correlation be reliably greater than zero. More sophisticated models based on this reasoning are possible, but these models begin to approach the complexity and technical requirements of the covariance structure models.

Finally, we ultimately will need to consider a third issue. Suppose that we identify coordinating abilities that are either general and explain multiple pairs of domains, or specific to particular pairs of domains, as illustrated in Figs. 7.2 and 7.3. Can we specify the nature of this ability more precisely? Intuitively, coordinating ability should have something to do with the ability to control attention. In the past 15 years, a substantial number of studies of the ability to control attention have been conducted, using a variety of experimental paradigms. Whereas no single study is definitive, the weight of the evidence is that there is an ability to control attention (see Braune & Wickens, 1986; Gopher, 1982; Gopher & Kahneman, 1971; Hunt, 1987a; Lansman, Poltrock, & Hunt, 1983; and the discussion of Wickens', 1984 text, pp. 305–309). We have planned for the development and testing of an analysis of covariance model to define an ability to control attention. We will then use the key tasks in further research to relate the ability to control attention to the ability to coordinate information received across different domains. This last line of inquiry will not be discussed further in this chapter.

COMPLETED AND IN PROGRESS RESEARCH

In this section, we instantiate the somewhat abstract concepts of the previous section, describing studies that have been conducted thus far on three topics. The first topic is the construction of well-defined within-domain batteries of information-processing tasks. In this area, we briefly consider the verbal and motor domains and spend considerably more time discussing development of tasks for the dynamic visual-spatial domain. The second topic we consider is how information coordination issues can arise in within-domain tasks, again illustrating this for the dynamic visual-spatial-processing domain. The third topic represents our initial attempts to construct and test multiple domain coordination tasks. Evidence in support of a general coordination ability is presented in that context.

The Construction Of Within Domain Task Batteries

The construction of verbal and motor coordination task batteries is fairly straightforward given the extensive amount of experimental and psychometric data available for these domains. Verbal tasks have been extensively studied and, in general, are known to measure the same abilities whether or not computer-controlled presentations are used (Hunt, 1987b; Lansman, 1981). Hunt (1987b) observed that there are three different classes of verbal abilities: those that depend on lexical recognition processes, those that depend on semantic-syntactical processes in which meaning is assigned to a sentence, and pragmatic processes that depend on the total context of the situation. As our focus is on the understanding of the types of messages that would occur in a machinery operating context, we are primarily concerned with the semantic-syntactical processes that operate at the sentence level. These processes are well measured by varieties of the *sentence verification* paradigm first developed by Clark and Chase (1974) and since then studied by several other authors. In this paradigm, information is presented using semantically equivalent sentences that vary in syntactic complexity. The dependent variables are the time and accuracy with which a person can extract meaning from the sentence. The use of sentence verification is illustrated in several of the projects discussed subsequently.

Although the measurement of motor ability in general presents a very difficult task (Marteniuk, 1974), for our purposes we rely on fairly simple manual tracking tasks, as it is an extensively investigated task domain with good face validity and a background of careful research, both in individual differences and in nomothetic studies (see Braune & Wickens, 1986, for a summary of the evidence in support of these statements). Limiting our attention to tracking of necessity limits our conclusions to the area of hand–eye coordination, but this limitation is not severe. By their nature, tracking tasks are also highly suitable for computer-controlled presentation. In this chapter, we do not present any results involving the motor domain, although we have begun investigations in the area.

As noted earlier, our work in the area of visual-spatial ability requires some detailed explanation, particularly because the tasks we have developed and are using differ substantially from both psychometric and information-processing tests of spatial ability. Conventional paper-and-pencil tests of visual-spatial ability present the examinee with a picture and ask him or her to answer some question about it. Examples are the well-known rotations tests, in which pictures of simple line patterns are presented at different orientations, and the examinee must decide if the same pattern is depicted in each picture; and form board tests, in which the examinee is shown several different parts, rather like the parts of a very simple jigsaw puzzle, and asked whether or not the parts can be assembled to display a particular target picture (see e.g., Lohman, et al., 1987; Pellegrino & Kail, 1982).

Research using such tests has identified two correlated spatial ability factors. These are Spatial Relations, the ability to make rapid judgments about the relations between two objects that are distortions of each other, and Visualization, the ability to manipulate and/or piece together the details of a complicated picture (Lohman, 1979; McGee, 1979). Pellegrino and Kail (1982) pointed out that marker tests for Spatial Relations require rapid judgments about simple objects, whereas marker tests for Visualization require reasoning about relatively complex objects. Pellegrino and Kail (1982) reported a number of studies indicating that Spatial Relations tests mapped onto latency measures in computer-controlled tests of visual-spatial reasoning, whereas Visualization tests mapped onto error measures.

In prior research (Hunt, Pellegrino, Frick, & Alderton, 1988; Pellegrino, Hunt, Abate, & Farr, 1987), we developed a battery of computer-controlled visual-spatial tests. One hundred and sixty college students were given the tests as well as a battery of conventional paper-and-pencil psychometric tests. Factor analysis of the conventional tests showed the expected Spatial Relations and Visualization factors. In conformity with Pellegrino and Kail's hypothesis, we found that the computer-based tests and the paper-and-pencil tests defined the same spaces of individual variation, and that, in general, latency and error measures mapped onto the Spatial Relations and Visualization factors, respectively.

In addition to investigating computer-controlled tests of conventional visual-spatial ability, Hunt et al. (1988) examined individual differences in several tasks where examinees had to make judgments about moving objects in the visual field. We found that these tasks defined a dimension of visual-spatial ability that was clearly separate from (although correlated with) the Visualization and Spatial Relations factors. We refer to this as Dynamic visual-spatial ability, to emphasize the point that it can only be tested by using displays that can present a dynamic visual stimulus. We believe that it is particularly important to study the coordination of dynamic visual-spatial reasoning with verbal and motor activities because moving elements are an essential part of the visual display in many real-world tasks.

We found that the two best markers of dynamic visual-spatial reasoning were (a) tasks that required judgments about the relative positions of two moving objects and (b) tasks that required a judgment about the time and point of intersection of the paths of two moving objects. Fig. 7.4 shows an example of a

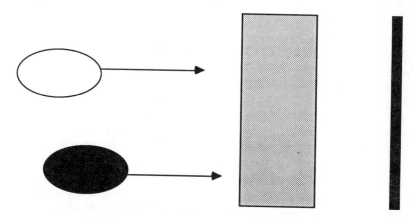

FIG. 7.4.   An illustration of the general stimulus conditions in the two object arrival time comparison task.

relative motion task, which we refer to as an arrival time comparison task. The observer sees two objects moving across the screen, along the direction indicated by the solid line. The objects start from the same vertical positions and proceed at different speeds toward vertical lines at the right of the display. These vertical lines are different distances away from the starting points of the two objects. When the first object reaches an imaginary boundary (indicated by the gray area), both objects disappear. The observer's task is to indicate which object would reach the right-hand vertical line first, on the assumption that both objects continue moving at their current speeds in the observed direction. As is shown subsequently, a variation of this task has been useful in developing tests of coordination ability.

This task of making a comparative judgment about objects moving in space has become the focus of several studies. One set of studies has pursued issues regarding the factors governing task difficulty. If we conduct a logical analysis of this task, it becomes obvious that to make these comparative judgments the individual must take into account two sources of information: (a) distance information—how far each object is from its destination at a given point in time, and (b) speed information—how fast each object is moving relative to the other. Obviously, when the speeds are equal, only distance matters. Therefore, the ability to judge differences in arrival time should be a function of the ability to judge distance alone. However, when the speed ratio of the two objects is other than 1 : 1, the difference in arrival time requires a more complex mental calculation in which both speed and distance information are combined for purposes of the comparative judgment. We have systematically examined how performance in this arrival time comparison task is related to both actual differences in arrival time (from 500 to 1000 msec differences) and differences in speed ratio (1 : 1, 1.5 : 1, and 2 : 1) where the two major variables are orthogonal. Our two objects move on a variety of different path types that are parallel, perpendicular, or oblique to each other. The different variations are shown in Fig. 7.5.

Our results to date have been very clear-cut. Both arrival time difference and speed ratio independently combine to govern judgment accuracy in this task. Fig. 7.6 shows these results very clearly. Within each speed ratio, judgment accuracy is a linear function of the actual difference in arrival time, and this reflects the ability to detect differences in distance. Performance is best under the 1 : 1 speed ratio, where only distance matters. When the speed ratio is 1.5 : 1 or 2 : 1, overall accuracy drops considerably, reflecting the difficulty that individuals have in coordinating both speed and distance information to make proper judgments.

In addition to general performance effects, there was evidence of considerable individual differences in performance, particularly in the 1.5 : 1 and 2 : 1 speed ratio conditions. One illustration of this was evidence of overall sex differences in performance on this arrival time comparison task. Fig. 7.7 shows interactions involving sex and both speed ratio and arrival time difference. The speed ratio interaction, which is shown in the left panel, is quite striking and clearly shows

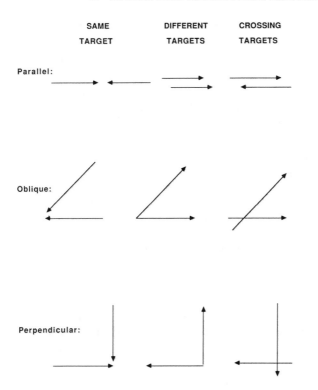

FIG. 7.5. Examples of the different path types and configurations used in the arrival time comparison task.

that there are no sex differences in the 1 : 1 speed ratio situation—the situation where only distance matters. However, when both speed and distance matter— the 1.5 : 1 and 2 : 1 speed ratios—males are considerably more accurate. The sex by arrival time difference interaction, which is shown in the right panel, shows that males were more sensitive to actual differences in arrival time. This increased sensitivity is indicated by the steeper slope of the males' function relating accuracy to actual arrival time difference.

An Illustration of Within-Domain Coordination

Our logical analysis of performance in the arrival time comparison task, coupled with the actual empirical results, provides us with an interesting illustration of the difficulties of within-domain information coordination. It is obvious that individuals have great difficulty in making accurate judgments when the speed ratio relationships are other than 1 : 1, that is, they have great difficulty properly coordinating speed and distance information and often appear to respond solely on the basis of distance rules. In an extension of this research, we therefore

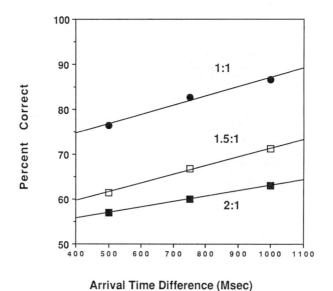

FIG. 7.6. The effects of speed ratio and arrival time difference on judgment accuracy in the arrival time comparison task.

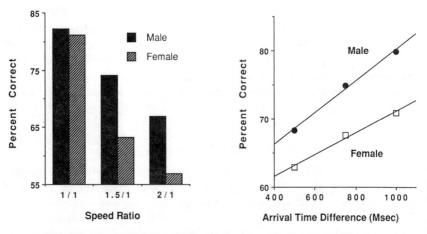

FIG. 7.7. Sex difference effects in the arrival time comparison task: the sex by speed ratio interaction (left panel) and the sex by arrival time difference interaction (right panel).

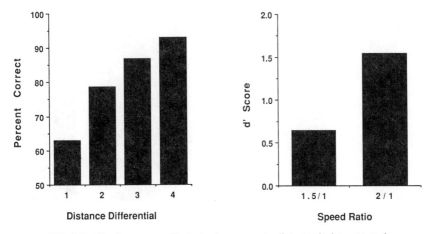

FIG. 7.8. Performance effects in the separate distance judgment and speed judgment tasks: judgment accuracy as a function of the actual difference in distance (left panel) and d' score (right panel) for detection of speed differences as a function of speed ratio condition.

pursued the issue of whether the poor performance of individuals in the nonequivalent speed cases (1.5 : 1 and 2 : 1) could possibly be a function of the inability to detect differences in speed. (We were not really worried that individuals could not detect differences in distance.) Using similar sets of problems, we asked individuals to judge either differences in distance or differences in speed in separate judgment tasks. The subjects also had to perform the overall arrival time comparison task, which involves coordinating and combining both speed and distance information. Our results indicate quite clearly that judging distance is not a problem and, as expected, accuracy is a systematic function of actual differences in distance. This result is shown in the left panel of Fig. 7.8. Our results also indicate quite clearly that subjects can also detect differences in speed and that the d' detection scores are significantly higher for the 2 : 1 than 1.5 : 1 speed ratio case, as shown in the right panel of Fig. 7.8. What is most interesting is that detection of differences in speed is best in the speed ratio condition that leads to the *worst* combined task performance! Clearly, the poor performance exhibited in the combined judgment task for the 2 : 1 speed ratio (see Fig. 7.6) is not due to an inability to detect that the two objects differ in speed. Rather, the poor performance must be due to an inability to adequately combine the speed and distance information about each object to produce a proper judgment of relative arrival time.

We can also look at performance relative to the issue of explaining patterns of individual differences in the combined judgment task. Remember that a sex difference was observed in the overall arrival time comparison task for the nonequivalent speed conditions (see Fig. 7.7). Our separate distance judgment

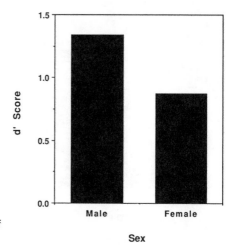

FIG. 7.9. The d' score for detection of
speed differences as a function of sex.

and speed judgment data confirm the lack of a sex difference in the distance judgment task but the presence of a sex difference in the accuracy of detecting speed differences for both the 1.5 : 1 and 2 : 1 speed ratios. The sex difference effect averaged across both speed ratios is shown in Fig. 7.9. At the level of aggregate group data, it appears that the individual speed judgment and distance judgment abilities combine additively to predict performance in the overall arrival time comparison task. This is not true, however, at the level of individuals as we now illustrate.

Fig. 7.10 is a synthesis of most of the correlational relationships among the major performance measures, each of which is represented by a rectangle. (The value in parentheses within each rectangle is the reliability of the performance measure.) First, we need to consider a relationship not shown in Fig. 7.10, that between the two simple performance measures, speed judgment alone and distance judgment alone. These two performance measures are moderately correlated (.54), as well they should be. One's ability to judge speed must be related to one's ability to judge distance, because speed is change in distance per unit time. Next, we need to consider the relationships among the combined task performance measures. As shown in the left panel of Fig. 7.10, performance in the 1 : 1 speed ratio condition has low to moderate relationships with the other speed ratio conditions, which are themselves highly correlated. Thus, it should come as no surprise that the ability to judge distance has a significant correlation only with performance in the 1 : 1 speed ratio condition, the condition where distance alone matters. This is shown in the right panel of Fig. 7.10. Furthermore, the correlation between the ability to judge speed and performance in the 1 : 1 speed ratio condition is totally a function of the relationship between speed judgment and distance judgment ability. This is shown quite readily by the failure of the speed judgment score to contribute anything in a multiple regression predicting performance in the 1 : 1 speed ratio condition.

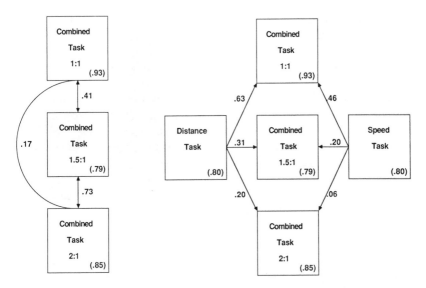

FIG. 7.10.   The correlational relationships among the speed ratio conditions of the combined arrival time comparison task (left panel). The
correlational relationships of the separate distance and speed judgment tasks with the speed ratio conditions of the combined arrival
time comparison task (right panel).

We would argue that our arrival time comparison task provides a simple
within-domain example of the type of model illustrated in Fig. 7.1, particularly
for the nonequivalent speed ratio judgments. What an individual needs to do in
the arrival time comparison task is appropriately combine and coordinate, in real
time, two sources of information, speed and distance, to make a single judgment.
The separate speed and distance judgment abilities fail to individually or in
combination predict performance in the coordination task. What remains to be
explored is why individuals have such great difficulty in combining speed and
distance information and why their judgments are apparently governed by distance information alone. We intend to pursue these effects further, particularly as
they impact our understanding of individual differences in performance in more
complex tasks that involve the coordination of both dynamic visual-spatial and
verbal information sources. Such cross-domain tasks are considered next.

Construction and Testing
of Cross-Domain Coordination Tasks

It would be hopeless to begin studying the general population with coordination
tasks as difficult to manage as airplane piloting. Therefore, we have started by
developing two tasks that we know from our own and others' previous research
to be reliable measures of independent dimensions of human ability. In particu-

lar, we have studied the ability to coordinate verbal information with judgments about visual or auditory displays. We think this captures the essence of the very common situation in which a person observes or listens to something, while another person presents instructions about what is to be observed or reported.

The tasks themselves are depicted in Fig. 7.11. They are based on a modification of the sentence verification paradigm, in which an observer is asked to determine whether or not a statement correctly describes a perceived event. Rather than the typical static event, our events are dynamic and unfold over time. Two such tasks were developed, one requiring judgments about visual events and the other requiring judgments about auditory events.

The visual component of the task was our two-object arrival time comparison task. The multicomponent coordination task was to estimate which ship was going to arrive at its destination first and to answer a question about this judg-

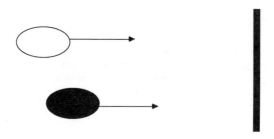

The white ship will not arrive before the black ship

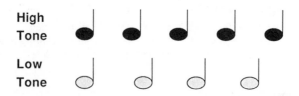

The high tone is repeating slower than the low tone

FIG. 7.11.   Illustrations of the combined visual movement–verbal task (top panel) and the combined auditory–verbal task (bottom panel).

ment. Referring back to Fig. 7.1, it can be seen that the task has A and B components, the person must make a visual judgment about the race, and must comprehend the verbal statement of the question. Insofar as individual differences are concerned, the task can be made one of pure visual judgment by keeping the verbal reasoning statement simple (i.e., "Which ship will arrive first?") while varying the difficulty of the visual task. We have already illustrated that the task can be made more difficult by decreasing the difference in the actual arrival times of the two objects and by varying the speed ratio. The task can be made one of pure verbal judgment by making the visual judgment so simple that there can be virtually no mistake (i.e., one ship would arrive at its endpoint long before the other) and then varying the complexity of the verbal statement. In this condition, a typical statement might be "The black ship will not arrive before the white ship." Performance is then driven by the observer's verbal comprehension ability rather than his or her perceptual ability.

In the combined coordination task, both the visual and verbal tasks vary in difficulty. As the observer can answer only by coordinating the verbal interpretation with the visual observation, the task meets the definition for a combined coordination task. In the terminology of Fig. 7.1, Task A = visual judgment, Task B = verbal comprehension, and Task AB = combining complex visual judgments and verbal comprehension.

The auditory combined task utilized the same basic logic, but the visual judgment was replaced with an auditory judgment. Instead of viewing objects racing across a screen, the observer hears a high and a low tone, cycling at various rates (see Fig. 7.11). For instance, the low tone might cycle at six tones every 5 seconds and the high one at eight tones in 5 seconds. The observer's task is to determine which tone is cycling more rapidly and then to respond to a visually displayed verbal statement about the relation of the cycling rates. The difficulty of the auditory task can be expressed by the ratios of the cycling rates. For instance, a ratio of 1 : 2 indicates that one tone is cycling twice as fast as the other. This is a very easy judgment. By contrast, a 1 : 1 problem would be equivalent to a tie in the visual race task, and a 99 : 100 discrepancy would be virtually impossible to detect. As before, the difficulty of the verbal task can be varied by manipulating the syntactic complexity of the sentence. Returning again to the terminology of Fig. 7.1, Task A = auditory judgment, Task B = verbal comprehension, and Task AB = combined complex auditory judgments and verbal comprehension.

We have conducted three experiments using these combined tasks. In the first experiment, college students performed the visual and verbal tasks, alone, on the first day of the experiment. On the second and third days, the students undertook the combined visual-verbal task. The performance measures of response time and percentage correct reflect the expected patterns for verbal and visual task difficulty, as shown in Figs. 7.12 and 7.13. As shown in Fig. 7.12, as the visual discrimination became more difficult, response latency increased and accuracy

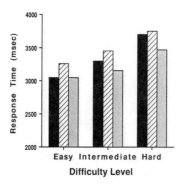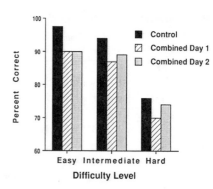

FIG. 7.12.   Visual judgment performance as a function of the expected difficulty level of the judgment and testing context. Response latency results are presented in the left panel and response accuracy results are shown in the right panel.

decreased. This was true for the visual task done alone and for the visual discrimination in the combined task. Combining the visual and verbal components serves to increase overall response latency and reduce the overall level of accuracy, but the pattern across conditions remains the same. As shown in Fig. 7.13, the same can be said about the effects of sentential complexity. As sentential complexity became more difficult, response times and errors increased in a predictable manner in both the verbal alone and combined task conditions.

At the individual subject performance level, correlational analyses were conducted to test the model shown earlier in Fig. 7.1 and the results are summarized in Fig. 7.14. First, a reliability analysis indicated that about 72% of the variance

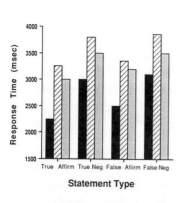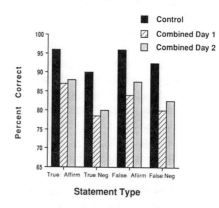

FIG. 7.13.   Verbal judgment performance as a function of the statement type and testing context. Response latency results are presented in the left panel and response accuracy results are shown in the right panel.

DAY 2 VARIANCE PARTITION

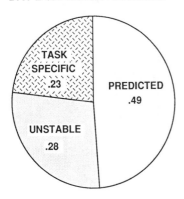

DAY 3 VARIANCE PARTITION

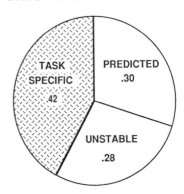

FIG. 7.14. Variance partitioning for performance on the combined visual-verbal task as a function of day of testing.

on the combined task was stable across days. Second, for each day, less than 50% of the combined task variance could be predicted by performance on the individual verbal and visual tasks. Third, and most important with regard to the issue of evidence for a coordination ability, about 30% of the total variance on the combined task appears to be unique to the combination.

Our second experiment with a combined task utilized a slightly altered design to evaluate auditory and verbal combinations. Students performed the auditory task, the verbal task, and the combined task on each of two successive days. We asked to what extent performance on the two combined tasks could be predicted by the individual tasks completed on the same day. To assess the stability of performance on the combined task we attempted to predict performance on one day of the combined task from performance on the other day.

Fig. 7.15 shows that the results were slightly different than those obtained in the study of the combined visual-verbal task. On the first day, stable performance on the combined task was almost completely predicted from the two independent tasks. Further analysis suggested that this is probably because the auditory task was hard to learn, and some subjects may have still been learning it when they attempted to do the combined task. On the second day, however, about 25% of the variance on the combined auditory-verbal task was specific to that task, a result very similar to the results with the combined visual-verbal task. Like the visual-verbal study, the overall performance measures reflect the expected patterns for increasing task difficulty: Reaction times and error percentages increased with increases in the difficulty of the auditory judgment and with sentential complexity.

Although these results were encouraging, we felt that they were weak in two ways. We have argued that coordinating ability exists because we have *failed* to

DAY 1 VARIANCE PARTITION   **DAY 2 VARIANCE PARTITION**

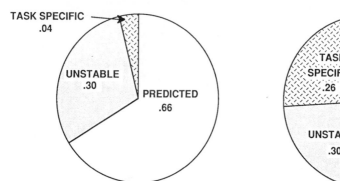
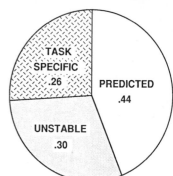

FIG. 7.15. Variance partitioning for performance on the combined auditory-verbal task as a function of day of testing.

predict all reliable variance in a particular task. The argument is rather like one that an intelligence officer might use for the existence of the Stealth bomber; it must be there, because it's not detected on his radar. At least for scientific purposes, we find such arguments unsatisfying. Also we would like to know whether or not there is an ability to coordinate task components that is general across different combined tasks.

Both of these questions could be answered affirmatively if we showed that after we allowed for performance on visual, verbal, and auditory tasks alone, the *residual* variations in ability in the visual-verbal and auditory-verbal combined tasks were correlated with each other. Our third study was designed to do this. The experiment lasted four days. On the first two days, participants performed a visual task, a verbal task, and a combined visual-verbal task. On the third and fourth days, they performed an auditory task, a verbal task, and a combined auditory-verbal task. We could thus repeat analyses reported for Experiments 1 and 2 on the same people and correlate the residual variation.

The results are shown in Fig. 7.16. A statistical technique known as set correlation was used to predict the stable variation (and residual stable variation) on the four different combined tasks. One can think of this as a multivariate extension of the familiar multiple regression technique. The results were quite gratifying. Residual variations were found, and more importantly, they were reliably correlated with each other ($r = .45$). Thus, we have obtained positive evidence that coordinating abilities do exist and that they have some generality.

CONCLUSIONS AND FUTURE DIRECTIONS

We believe that our results to date should be extended in three ways. First, although we have obtained reliable effects, the effects are not large. This may

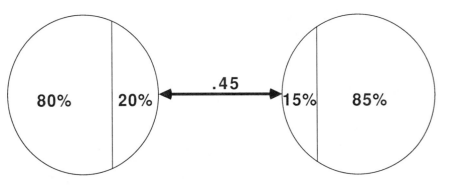

RHYTHM - VERBAL   **MOVE - VERBAL**

FIG. 7.16.   Results of the set correlation analysis of generalized variance across the two combined tasks.

very well be due to the extreme simplicity of the tasks that we have used. In particular, we believe that coordinating ability may be much greater if the task involves a motor response. In other work, we have developed a task that combines visual judgments with motor tracking. In further extensions, verbal comprehension will be added to this task. We wish to conduct further studies along the lines just indicated to see (a) if larger coordinating abilities can be found with more difficult tasks, especially if they involve motor movements, and (b) the extent to which these coordinating abilities are general across different coordination tasks.

The second and third extensions of our work are closely related. Although we have reliable results, a larger and broader sample of the general population would be desirable for accurate parameter estimation. At the same time, we would like to embed our measures of coordinating ability in a larger battery of known tests of spatial, verbal, and perhaps auditory ability, so that we can determine where these abilities fit in the general map of human cognitive capacities. Both these goals necessitate a large sample study. Recruiting very large samples has the additional advantage of extending the range of abilities beyond those present in the college population. This advantage may be more apparent than real. College students are, indeed, selected for verbal ability, but they do approximate the general population in spatial and auditory discriminations. Consequently, the range of scores in the reported experiments may very likely be representative of the general population.

In summary, we have obtained positive evidence that coordination abilities do exist. Performance in the combined visual-verbal and auditory-verbal tasks could not be predicted completely from performance on the visual, verbal, and auditory tasks performed separately. Furthermore, coordinating abilities have some generality across task combinations. After accounting for individual task performance, combinations of these tasks showed significant amounts of common variance. Investigations with more complex tasks with the same methodological framework are currently underway to test further the generality of coordination abilities.

OPEN DISCUSSION

The discussion began with a question about the learning curves associated with the computerized tasks described by Pellegrino. Subsequent questions focused on a variety of issues related to understanding different judgment strategies persons might use in these tasks, and on alternative explanations of the findings.

Adams: In the beginning of complex skill acquisition, you essentially bring the task components together. However, it is normally after a very extensive learning skill that individuals can integrate the components, that is, blend them together. What do the learning curves look like in your tasks?

Pellegrino: I don't have a good answer to that yet. In fact, that is a very important issue. In the single domain situations, at least in the verbal one, we know fairly well what happens with practice. All that happens with practice is that you stabilize some of the parameters. I am not sure about my arrival time task. In fact, it's an interesting issue because in other research we have done on sex differences and spatial ability we observed that a lot of the sex differences go away with practice. I don't know whether the same thing will happen in our movement judgment task. I should indicate, that although there are a lot of trials in these experiments, it is not really extended practice—so I don't have a good handle on the practice functions or how the predictions would change.

I think the same questions apply equally well to the combined task. In fact, some evidence of that may be seen in the data I presented for the auditory combined task. Performance on this task seemed to stabilize on the second day better than on the first day because it was a more difficult coordination task. Now that we have a better understanding of what is happening within each task, those are the kinds of issues that we can now start to look at more closely.

Jenkins: Where do you think the coordinated combined task specific is going to go? In one case it doubles from Day 2 to Day 3, and in the other case it goes up six-fold from Day 2 to Day 3. Where is it going to stop?

Pellegrino: I don't know. Again, I would not make a lot of the size of those parameters. The sample sizes we are looking at in these studies are between 30 and 50 subjects. (I find it amusing that I am apologizing for that.

As an experimental psychologist, 30 to 50 subjects in a within-subjects design would be such that I don't even need to do the analysis of variance. But then I would certainly have to apologize for the correlations.)

We think that, depending on certain kinds of combinations, we may be able to get to the point where we account for perhaps 50 percent of the variance (as task-specific). By task specific, we are talking essentially about management or coordination. I think it is going to vary with the complexity of the coordination task as well. But again, I am not sure of that. That is something that we have to explore more thoroughly. Nonetheless, we are pleased at the moment that we got the evidence we did for the sort of task-specific effects and the correlation across the two domains. Obviously, however, we have a lot more exploration to do, to systematically disentangle that.

Pick: I like the logic of what you are trying to do very much. However, I would like to suggest a different way of interpreting your pattern of results and I would like to focus on the within-domain task that you mentioned. Suppose that you ask people to judge the brightness of spots of light; a dark spot and a light spot. Assume that you found that persons did not do very well on that task or that your pattern of results did not predict when you asked them to judge the relative brightness of the two spots simultaneously. Of course, you wouldn't predict judgments of relative brightness from judgments of absolute brightness of single spots. But it seems to me that judging the relative brightness is not a coordination task, it is detecting a different variable. Further, it seems to me that within-domain tests are particularly susceptible to an explanation that involves some variable (different from the original variable). But it also might be that in some cases cross-domain tasks would also be susceptible to detecting different variables rather than coordinating two separate sources of information. For example, it is easier to see that kind of thing happening in the cross-domain tasks discussed by Uwe Kleinbeck. In your cross-domain tasks, the distance between verbal and spatial tasks may be so great that it would be harder to find the median.

Pellegrino: First of all, in my within-domain example we are not testing absolute judgments; persons must still make relative judgments. Thus, we haven't changed the task characteristic, at least in the sense of judging relative distance and relative speed. I think the reason that relative judgments do not predict may be because the actual differences fit a certain kind of function where you have to be able to more precisely estimate distance-rate-time relationships and differences. So, you need to be able to make more precise judgments. That is a difficult situation and I think that is part of the reason why we cannot predict within the domain.

One thing I did not mention about our cross-domain research is that we do intend to test another kind of model. Specifically, we want to look at the issue of whether or not this evidence for coordination across domains is any different than what happens in sort of a time-sharing ability when you have dual-tasks that are unrelated. That is, are we looking at whether there is some sort of general task management ability which applies to any set of tasks or whether there is something to specific coordination as opposed to simply management of differing loads?

McArdle: My question pertains to the analysis plan. From a structural point of view, your model may be described as a sort of a partial multi-method, multitrait design. But one of the controversies with this design pertains to the differences between additive and multiplicative components. (Bob Cudeck may want to say something about that since he has written a paper on this topic.) The simple combination rule is to multiply these things together; people could be doing such things. Or, another way to say it is that from a simple data analysis point of view, the interaction (as a variable) is easy to represent as a product since you have measured both distance and speed. But you chose not to go that route; you chose not to think of the combination rule in the simple statistical way. Instead, you view it as a new emergent test management component. How come and what is the benefit?

Pellegrino: Are we talking about both situations—the within-domain and across domain?

McArdle: Let me put it another way. When you measure a variable which is a combination of two other things, and you measure both of those things separately, it seems that you might be able to understand the combination simply from the multiplication of the two individual difference scores.

Pellegrino: We have not done it, but it seems perfectly reasonable to test that as an alternative kind of model.

McArdle: I see. So you have nothing against that particular combination?

Pellegrino: No. However, the issue is that although we might find a mathematical solution, I think we will need to provide a psychological explanation. To this point, I had not really thought about the way you are suggesting because we have been focusing more on the process and conceptualization of what this [ability] is.

McArdle: I'm not simply advocating obscure mathematical models, but this is such an obvious one. The interaction component as an individual difference variable still has this possibility and the issue of which mathematical rule we should apply has been frequently raised in the quantitative literature. But are you saying it doesn't have much psychological virtue?

Pellegrino: I'm not sure. As I said, I haven't thought that one through. For example, I know that, from a psychological point of view, the true combination rule in the arrival time judgment task is a multiplicative rule in terms of relating these things. And that is interesting because, if you do an analysis of that rule, what the individual is doing is estimating differences in proportions. Those kinds of rules in the psychological literature are ones that individuals oftentimes have difficulty with, where they have to actually coordinate information of that type and use that kind of a combination rule. Right now we've got the evidence within the task, which I think is intriguing. From my perspective, we have the individual difference data, but we also have a job to do in explaining, from a psychological perspective, why we are getting the results we are getting and what the implications are.

Kazén-Saad: Have you looked at interests or individual differences variables other than sex? For example, imagery differences?

Pellegrino: No, we do not have a large battery of other abilities. I have begun to feel much the same way as Earl Hunt, whom Jack Adams mentioned previously. Why do I have to justify my differences against something else if I understand and have a good model for these differences in my domain? I don't know, for example, what the model is for some of the imagery tests. In fact, some of the imagery tests are notoriously unstable. I want to adopt a strong view, which is that I do not feel obligated, as it were, to correlate against some unknown, poorly understood referent measure. Instead, I am going to stick with what I have designed because I can tell you what is happening in that task. That is what is most important to me. Of course, if you are a journal editor, it may be a different story.

Cudeck: Can you tell me a little more about the sample sizes in that path diagram [Fig. 7.10]?

Pellegrino: That humongous path diagram? Well, in that study we tested subjects at both Santa Barbara and the University of Washington. We had about 170 subjects and they did a mixture of computer-based tests and paper-and-pencil tests over 5 days of testing. In that path diagram, and some other ones which were subtests [of models], the model fit fairly well. We also tried alternative models to subsume the tasks under just the two basic spatial factors. These alternative models did very poorly.

Cudeck: But using 170 subjects sounds like that was really strenuous. Is that the upper limit of what you can expect to get in practice without rebellion among the troops?

Pellegrino: My troops, yes.

Cudeck: Those were Santa Barbara students, right? A good midwestern student could stay with it.

Pellegrino: That's because they have no other diversions!

Lohman: This is partly a question and partly a response to Jack McArdle. When I looked at this race task, it reminded me of baseball and being out in left field, trying to judge where the ball was going to be as soon as it came off the bat. It occurred to me that in a combined task people might be making judgments in a couple of ways. For example, by attending to the distance judgment or by attending primarily to the speed judgment. In either case, you would not expect either of the separate variables to predict the combined performance very well.

Pellegrino: We looked at that. I didn't talk about it but the way that the combined task is designed and structured allows us to look at whether people are using the distance rule. We talk about that in terms of "winner-faster" versus "loser-faster" trials. If you are using a distance rule, then whenever the faster one is the loser, you remain in the race. The one that is moving faster is still going to lose the race; it is way behind in terms of distance. People using the distance rule are highly accurate on those trials and that subgroup of trials is highly correlated with the one-to-one case, which is a distance rule alone.

   In contrast, if you use a distance rule when the winner is the faster one, you're dead in the water. By the time the display goes off, the faster stimulus is still lagging behind. What we find is that individuals using the distance rule in this instance perform worse than chance, at about 30 percent accuracy. Their performance will vary depending on how far behind the faster stimulus is lagging in terms of distance. We have also observed this in another task—an intercept task. It appears that people are driven by distance relationships, *even when we give them speed information* and they know there are speed differences. It is an interesting issue to consider why people can't seem to quite coordinate and relate speed and distance in these tasks.

Lohman: But by using this information couldn't you test the hypothesis that you really didn't have distinguishable subgroups of people; that people were not in some sense shifting their criteria?

Pellegrino: Again, we could test it, but there were variations within that. But what I did not discuss was that if we take the cases where speed matters, and sort them into winner-faster or loser-faster trials, distance predicts the case where distance matters. However, when individuals must use the speed information to counteract distance information, we cannot predict very well. That, in turn, produces the overall low correlation. That is a more complicated explanation involving a more complex design which we can use to look more closely at these issues.

ACKNOWLEDGMENT

The research reported in this chapter was supported by Contract N00014-86-C-0865 from the Office of Naval Research to Earl Hunt and James W. Pellegrino.

REFERENCES

Ackerman, P. L. (1987). Individual differences in skill learning: An integration of psychometric and information processing perspectives. *Psychological Bulletin, 102,* 3–27.

Ackerman, P. L., Schneider, W., & Wickens, C. D. (1984). Deciding the existence of a time-sharing ability: A combined methodological and theoretical approach. *Human Factors, 26,* 71–82.

Anderson, J. R. (1983). *The architecture of cognition.* Cambridge, MA: Harvard University Press.

Bentler, P. M. (1980). Multivariate analysis with latent variables: Causal modeling. *Annual Review of Psychology, 31,* 419–456.

Braune, R., & Wickens, C. D. (1986). *A componential approach to the investigation of individual differences in time sharing* (Technical Report EPL-86-1/NAMRL-86-1). Champaign: University of Illinois, Engineering Research Laboratory.

Clark, H., & Chase, W. (1974). Perceptual coding strategies in the formation and verification of descriptions. *Memory and Cognition, 2,* 101–111.

Gopher, D. (1982). A selective attention test as a predictor of success in flight training. *Human Factors, 24,* 173–183.

Gopher, D., & Kahneman, D. (1971). Individual differences in attention and the prediction of flight criteria. *Perceptual and Motor Skills, 33,* 1335–1342.

Hawkins, H. L., Church, M., & de Lemos, S. (1977). *Time-sharing is not a unitary ability* (Technical Report No. 2). Eugene: University of Oregon, Department of Psychology.

Hunt, E. (1987a). A cognitive model of individual differences, with an application to attention. In S. H. Irvine & S. E. Newstead (Eds.), *Intelligence and cognition: Contemporary frames of reference* (pp. 177–215). Boston: Martinus Nijhoff.

Hunt, E. (1987b). The next word on verbal ability. In P. E. Vernon (Ed.), *Speed of information processing and intelligence. Volume 1* (pp. 205–235). Hillsdale, NJ: Lawrence Erlbaum Associates.

Hunt, E. B., & Lansman, M. (1982). Individual differences in attention. In R. Sternberg (Ed.), *Advances in the psychology of human intelligence. Volume 1* (pp. 207–254). Hillsdale, NJ: Lawrence Erlbaum Associates.

Hunt, E., & Pellegrino, J. W. (1985). Using interactive computing to expand intelligence testing. *Intelligence, 9,* 207–236.

202   PELLEGRINO, HUNT, YEE

Hunt, E., Pellegrino, J. W., Frick, R. W., & Alderton, D. L. (1988). The ability to reason about movement in the visual field. *Intelligence, 12,* 77–100.

Jöreskog, K. G., & Sörbom, D. (1979). *Advances in factor analysis and structural equation models.* Cambridge, MA: Abt Books.

Just, M. A., & Carpenter, P. A. (1985). Cognitive coordinate systems: Accounts of mental rotation and individual differences in spatial ability. *Psychological Review, 92,* 137–172.

Kahneman, D. (1973). *Attention and effort.* Englewood Cliffs, NJ: Prentice-Hall.

Kerr, B. (1973). Processing demands during mental operations. *Memory and Cognition, 1,* 401–412.

Kolb, B., & Whishaw, I. Q. (1980). *Fundamentals of human neuropsychology.* San Francisco: Freeman.

Lansman, M. (1981). Ability factors and the speed of information processing. In M. P. Friedman, J. P. Das, & N. O'Connor (Eds.), *Intelligence and learning* (pp. 441–457). New York: Plenum.

Lansman, M., Poltrock, S. E., & Hunt, E. (1983). Individual differences in the ability to focus and divide attention. *Intelligence, 7*(3), 299–312.

Lohman, D. F. (1979). *Spatial ability: A review and reanalysis of the correlational literature* (Technical Report No. 8). Palo Alto, CA: Stanford University, Aptitude Research Project, School of Education.

Lohman, D. F., Pellegrino, J. W., Alderton, D. L., & Regian, J. W. (1987). Dimensions and components of individual differences in spatial abilities. In S. H. Irvine & S. E. Newstead (Eds.), *Intelligence and cognition: Contemporary frames of reference* (pp. 253–312). Boston: Martinus Nijhoff.

Marteniuk, R. G. (1974). Individual differences in motor performance and learning. In J. H. Willmere (Ed.), *Exercise and sports sciences review.* New York: Academic Press.

McGee, M. G. (1979). Human spatial abilities: Psychometric studies and environmental, genetic, hormonal, and neurological influences. *Psychological Bulletin, 66,* 889–918.

Pellegrino, J. W., Hunt, E. B., Abate, R., & Farr, S. (1987). A computer-based test battery for the assessment of static and dynamic spatial reasoning abilities. *Behavior Research Methods, Instruments, & Computers, 19,* 231–236.

Pellegrino, J. W., & Kail, R. (1982). Process analyses of spatial aptitude. In R. J. Sternberg (Ed.), *Advances in the psychology of human intelligence* (Vol. 1, pp. 311–365). Hillsdale, NJ: Lawrence Erlbaum Associates.

Sverko, B. (1977). *Individual differences in time-sharing abilities* (Technical Report ARL-77-4/AFOSR-77-4). Urbana-Champaign: University of Illinois, Aviation Research Laboratory.

Wickens, C. D. (1984). *Engineering psychology and human performance.* Columbus, OH: Charles E. Merrill.

8

Broad and Narrow Abilities in Research on Learning and Instruction

Jan-Eric Gustafsson
University of Göteborg

Psychometric theory and practice can hardly be accused of an excessive indulgence in fashions. However, even in these fields there have been pendulum swings between opposed positions, which have tended to dominate theories, methods, and modes of practice for longer periods of time. Two such extreme positions are readily identified within the psychometric field. According to one of these, theory and practice are best served if one broad, general, cognitive ability is emphasized; the other position maintains, in contrast, that approaches that allow for a wide array of narrow specialized abilities are necessary.

Spearman (1904), more than anyone else, established the field of psychometry, and he also established the notion that it is possible to identify an ability broad enough to influence performance on any cognitive task. The contributions of Binet and Simon (1905), Terman (1916), and others who developed the first generation of intelligence tests demonstrated that it is possible to measure such a broad cognitive ability by relatively simple means.

As is well known, however, the pendulum relatively soon swung over to the other position, and the single most important force to cause this movement was the contribution by Thurstone (e.g., 1938, 1947). When multiple factor analysis, guided by the principle of simple structure, was applied to large observational materials, overwhelming support was obtained for the position that several narrow abilities are needed to account for individual differences in intellectual performances. Ever since the 1930s, a considerable part of psychometric research has been devoted to demonstrating that even narrower abilities can be identified.

Voices certainly have been raised to argue in favor of broad abilities (e.g., Humphreys, 1962, McNemar, 1964), but it was not until relatively recently that the pendulum moved noticeably from the position of narrow abilities toward the position of broad abilities. One example of such a swing is the growing popularity of the *Gf-Gc* theory of Horn (e.g., 1985, 1986) and Cattell (e.g., 1971). Even though Horn (1986) does not endorse the idea of a single general ability, the dimensions of *Gf* (Fluid Intelligence) and *Gc* (Crystallized Intelligence) are sufficiently broad for this structural framework to be more closely identified with the broad ability position than with the narrow ability position. Horn (1986) said:

> The domain of intellectual abilities can be described at any of several different levels of abstraction. In considering which level is best, objectives should be considered carefully. In some work, rather narrow concepts and measures should be used. In other work broad concepts . . . will be of most value. For the next few years, particularly in developmental psychology, it will be most worthwhile to work with broad concepts. (p. 69)

Dissatisfaction also has been voiced about the lack of gains enjoyed in prediction studies by considering many narrow abilities rather than one broad ability. Thorndike (1985) reanalyzed several studies in which a broad range of job and school performance was predicted from optimally weighted measures of narrow abilities as well as from a general factor. He concluded that: "these data seem clearly to indicate that for job performance, as for training school performance, much of what is predictable from cognitive measures can be predicted from a uniform measure of a general cognitive factor" (Thorndike, 1985, p. 251). The general conclusion of the study was that: "In the context of practical prediction '*g*' appears to be alive and well" (Thorndike, 1985, p. 253).

The research on aptitude-treatment interactions (ATI) is another example of a field in which narrow ability concepts have failed to live up to expectations. In their large review of ATI research, Cronbach and Snow (1977) concluded:

> whereas we had expected specialized abilities rather than general abilities to account for interactions, the abilities that most frequently enter into interactions are general. Even in those programs of research that started with specialized ability measures and found interactions with treatment, the data seem to warrant attributing most effects to a general ability. (pp. 496–497)

These demonstrations of the ubiquitous importance of general ability may be signs that the pendulum now is swinging away from the position of narrow abilities. But before the pendulum comes back to its starting position again there is reason to consider if there may not be some value in the conception of narrow abilities. It would, after all, be quite surprising if concepts and measures developed during several decades of psychometric research would not be of considerable theoretical and practical interest.

The main message of the present chapter is that it is necessary to consider both broad *and* narrow abilities and that any piece of research must do so simultaneously. Tentatively, quite a paradoxical conclusion will be argued, namely that the research on narrow abilities may have failed because due attention has not been paid to broad abilities, and, conversely, that the research on broad abilities has been hampered because the influence of narrow abilities has not been recognized to a sufficient degree.

The structure of the chapter is such that first a very brief review is made of the hierarchical approach to describing the structure of abilities, and, in relation to a concrete example, it is demonstrated how this approach makes it easy to consider broad and narrow abilities simultaneously. In order to illustrate the implications of the hierarchical approach, an ATI study is analyzed both hierarchically and nonhierarchically.

A HIERARCHICAL MODEL OF INTELLIGENCE

The hierarchical approach to the structure on intelligence certainly is not new, and in the British research on intelligence it has been the dominating one. As early as 1927, Spearman claimed to be employing such an approach, but it was not until the contributions by Burt (1949) and Vernon (1950) that more full-grown hierarchical models were presented. The impact of these models on theories and methods in differential psychology has been rather limited, however.

During the 1980s, questions about the structural aspects of intelligence have been reopened in a series of studies (Gustafsson, 1980, 1984, 1988; Gustafsson, Lindström, & Björk-Åkesson, 1981; Undheim, 1981; Undheim & Gustafsson, 1987). In these studies, confirmatory higher-order factor analytic techniques have been used to compare different models of the structure of abilities, with a special emphasis on hierarchical models. This research has resulted in a model that comes close to that proposed by Vernon (1950) but that is also close to the Cattell–Horn model. In brief, the model has the following main components (see Fig. 8.1):

At the lowest level, the model represents as first-order factors abilities similar to the primary mental abilities identified by Thurstone, Guilford (1967), and other researchers working within the multiple factor tradition.

At an intermediate level, the model identifies factors that are easily interpreted as the broad abilities within the Cattell–Horn model. Among the handful of factors identified at this level, three seem to be of particular importance: Fluid Intelligence (Gf), which subsumes primaries such as Induction (I), General Reasoning (R), and Cognition of Figural Relations (CFR); Crystallized Intelligence (Gc), which is most strongly shown in the primary factors Verbal Comprehension (V) and Cognition of Semantic Relations (CMR); and General Visualization (Gv), which is loaded by primary abilities such as Visualization (Vz), Spatial Orientation (SR), and Flexibility of Closure (Cf). It may be noted also that the *Gc* factor is highly similar to the broad group factor that Vernon labels *v : ed* and that the *Gv* factor is highly similar to the *k : m* factor in Vernon's model.

At the highest level, the model includes a factor of general intelligence (g), in which all the broad abilities have loadings. A rather striking result, however, is that the loading of *Gf* on g consistently has been found to be unity, which implies that the g factor is equivalent with fluid intelligence (Gustafsson, 1988; Undheim, 1981). Vernon's model includes a g factor as well, and the kind of tests that Vernon lists as good measures of g come very close to those measuring *Gf*.

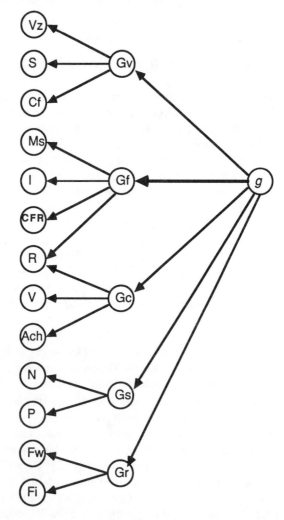

FIG. 8.1.   Hierarchical relations among some well-established dimensions of intelligence.

This hierarchical framework is compatible with most previously presented models of the structure of intelligence, even though these tend to be limited by a focus either on narrow abilities (e.g., Thurstone and Guilford) or on a single broad ability (e.g., Spearman). Among the previous models it seems that only the Vernon model is a full-fledged hierarchical model, with factors ranging in breadth from a completely general factor down to very narrow factors, which account for performance in very limited domains.

It should be pointed out that the hierarchical model sketched here has been obtained by piecing together results obtained in several studies. It must also be stressed that the three-level structure displayed in Fig. 8.1 is quite arbitrary: Depending on how densely or sparsely a domain is sampled, as many or as few levels as is wished may be obtained.

Many researchers seem to agree that some kind of hierarchical structure is the most appropriate type of model to summarize the known facts about the structure of individual differences (e.g., Cronbach, 1984; Sternberg, 1985). However, the hierarchical approach also carries quite far-reaching implications for the measurement and interpretation of individual differences. Some of these implications are highlighted through a concrete example, in which hierarchical models are fitted for a test-battery of limited size.

STUDY 1: HIERARCHICAL MODELS
FOR A BATTERY
OF DIFFERENTIAL APTITUDE TESTS

Hierarchical models require access to scores on a large number of tests, which may be one reason such models are not frequently employed. In confirmatory factor analysis, each latent variable requires two indicators as an absolute minimum, which implies that a model with three second-order factors necessitates administration of at least 12 well-chosen tests. Thus, in almost every study we have to live with quite incomplete hierarchies, but it seems that even incomplete hierarchical models are better than nonhierarchical models.

The specification of hierarchical models is illustrated with a rather small, and a rather typical, battery of tests. The data to be analyzed here were collected by Härnqvist (1960) in an investigation of the development of intraindividual differences. In the study, a battery of 12 tests was administered to approximately 500 pupils in each of Grades 4 to 8, and a subset of the battery was readministered 1 year later. The present reanalysis only serves the purpose of illustrating different methods of modeling, so the analysis will be restricted to the scores on 8 tests from the first administration for boys in Grade 6 ($N = 207$). These tests (see Table 8.1) were constructed to measure four primary factors, and exploratory factor analyses presented by Härnqvist (1978) strongly support the hypothesized factor structure.

In the present analysis the specification of hierarchical models is illustrated

TABLE 8.1
Tests Used in the Hierarchical Model

Test	No. Items	Primary Factor
Synonyms (SY)	40	Verbal Comprehension (*V*)
Opposites (Op)	40	Verbal Comprehension (*V*)
Letter Grouping (LG)	30	Induction (*I*)
Figure Series (FS)	30	Induction (*I*)
Metal Folding (MF)	30	Spatial Visualization (*Vz*)
Block Counting (BC)	40	Spatial Visualization (*Vz*)
Additions (AD)	2 × 48	Numerical (*N*)
Multiplications (Mu)	2 × 48	Numerical (*N*)

with two different approaches: a higher-order model, in which first-order factors are related to observed variables, second-order factors are related to first-order factors, and so on; and a variance-component model with latent variables that span a varying number of observed variables.

Higher-Order Models

Among the tests in the battery, six are essentially unspeeded power tests, while two (Additions [Ad] and Multiplications [Mu]) are rather highly speeded. In the unspeeded tests, odd and even items were scored separately, so that 12 half-test scores were obtained (Synonyms [Sy]-Odd, Sy-Even, Opposites [Op]-Odd, . . .). The speeded tests were administered as two separately timed halves (Ad-1, Ad-2, Mu-1, and Mu-2). These 16 half-tests will be used as observed variables, as this design makes it possible to differentiate test-specific components from random error components. The matrix of covariances among the 16 half-tests is shown in Appendix 8A.

The fitting of higher-order models has proceeded in a sequence of steps, in which successively more constrained confirmatory maximum likelihood factor models have been fitted to data (the LISREL VI program by Jöreskog & Sörbom, 1986, has been used for estimation and testing of models throughout the studies reported in this chapter). The statistical results from these models are presented in Table 8.2.

Model 1 is an oblique factor model with 8 first-order factors, each of which is related to a pair of half-tests. These latent variables thus represent the tests purged from error of measurement. In Model 2, the assumption is introduced that the half-tests are parallel (i.e., that they have equal true score variances and equal error variances). As may be seen from the significant increase in the value of the test-statistic relative to the degrees of freedom gained, the assumption of parallelity is not quite tenable, but because the absolute level of fit still is very good, this model will be accepted without further modification. The fit could, however,

TABLE 8.2
Summary of Statistical Tests of Higher-Order Models

Model	χ^2	df	p	GFI
1. 8 first-order factors	56.83	76	.95	.968
2. As 1, with parallel half-tests	94.40	92	.41	.948
3. As 2, with 4 second-order factors	114.56	106	.27	.937
4. As 3, with 1 general factor	122.77	108	.16	.933
5. As 4, with no residual in I	123.68	109	.16	.932

easily have been brought back to the level of Model 1 by relaxation of the parallelity assumption for the half-tests for Block Counting (BC) and Mu.

In Model 3, the four primary factors hypothesized in Table 8.1 are introduced as four correlated second-order factors. This causes a somewhat poorer fit of the model to the data, but the overall fit of the model still is excellent. It may thus be concluded that the hypothesized primary factor structure of the test battery is supported by these data. In Model 4, a third-order factor (g) is introduced. The significantly worse fit of this model indicates that the general factor is not quite able to account for the interrelations among the four second-order factors. The major reason for the misfit is a covariance between the residuals of Mu and the Vz factor. However, the deviation between Model 4 and data is so slight that the unmodified model will be retained.

In the very last step of the analysis it was investigated if the $Gf = g$ relation holds true even in this very limited test battery, in which the I factor is the only Gf representative. In Model 5, the residual in I is constrained to be zero and the fit of this model is not significantly worse than the fit of Model 4, as may be expected from the fact that the estimated standardized relation between g and the I factor is 1.05 in Model 4.

The third-order model is shown graphically in Fig. 8.2, along with standardized estimates of all parameters.

The model shown in Fig. 8.2 is similar in structure to the models fitted for larger batteries (Gustafsson, 1984, 1988; Undheim & Gustafsson, 1987), except that the limited number of primary factors here prevents identification of the broad abilities Gc and Gv. However, the previous studies have shown that Vz is so highly related to Gv and that V is so highly related to Gc that these labels may be used more or less interchangeably. The same may be said for the relation between I and Gf, which is also strongly supported by the empirical result reported earlier.

Higher-order models have the advantage of being very parsimonious, while at the same time they contribute a considerable amount of information. Thus, for the model shown in Fig. 8.2 only 28 parameters need to be estimated; for the considerably less informative first-order model, 44 parameters are estimated.

When higher-order models are depicted as is done in Fig. 8.2, one may gain

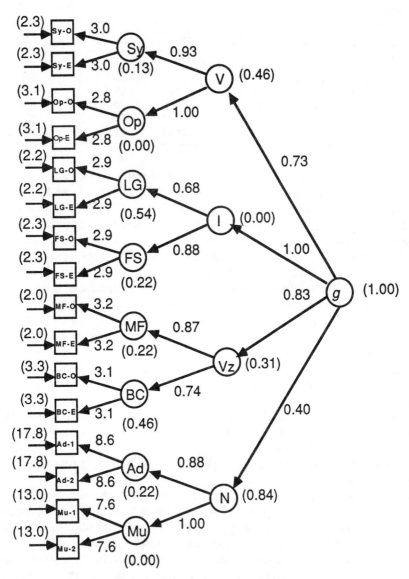

FIG. 8.2.   The higher-order model for half-tests.

the impression that the factors at higher levels in the hierarchy are more removed from the level of concrete observation and that they are more artificial and difficult to interpret than are the low-order factors. It would, however, be easy to compute from the estimated parameter values in Fig. 8.2 the proportion of variance in the observed variables accounted for by the factors at the different levels. This corresponds to the Schmid and Leiman (1957) transformation in exploratory factor analysis, and such a decomposition of the observed score variances produces a pattern in which the g factor accounts for variance in all the observed variables, and factors at lower levels in the hierarchy account for variance in successively smaller classes of observed variables (see Gustafsson, 1988, pp. 56–57). This transformation thus makes it clear that higher-order factors are not at a larger distance from the observed variables than are lower-order factors; the level at which a factor appears is a function of how broad a domain of performance the factor influences. This reasoning suggests that there may be a conceptual and practical advantage in formulating hierarchical models in such a way that there are latent variables at one level only, which have relations with smaller and larger groups of observed variables.

Variance-Component Models

In principle, it is easy to specify a hierarchical confirmatory model with a set of orthogonal factors, some of which are related to many observed variables, and some of which are related to few observed variables. Unless further constraints are imposed, however, models that treat one latent variable as embedded within (or as a subset of) another latent variable are not fully identified. Suitable constraints can rather easily be added, however, by requiring relations (i.e., factor loadings) to be equal or standing in a fixed relation to one another.

The approach used here is to impose very strong constraints on the relations between latent and observed variables: Not only is the number of latent variables and the pattern of their relations with observed variables determined in advance, but also the (relative) size of these relations. In essence, the variance-component modeling approach introduced by Bock (1960) and Bock and Bargmann (1966) thus is used (cf. Jöreskog, 1978).

Table 8.3 presents the matrix of hypothesized relations between observed and latent variables. The design matrix includes 13 factors (along with 8 error factors, one for each pair of half-tests) that are assumed to account for the variances and covariances among the 16 observed variables. One of these factors (g) is assumed to affect every observed variable, with the strength of the relation hypothesized to be proportional to the number of items in the test (i.e., number of items/10). This amounts to an assumption that performance on each and every item in the test battery is equally determined by the general factor. Such an assumption certainly is wrong but it may be useful as an approximate starting point.

The design matrix also hypothesizes four latent variables ($V, I, Vz,$ and N [Numerical]), each of which affects performance on four observed variables. Here too the size of the relationship is assumed to be proportional to the number of items in the observed variable. The last eight latent variables in the design matrix each are related to two half-tests, and these factors account for test-specific variance.

The test-statistic for this model, in which all latent variables are assumed to be

TABLE 8.3
Hypothesized Relations Between Observed and Latent Variables in
the Variance-Component Model

Test	g	V	I	Vz	N	Sy	Op	LG	FS	MF	BC	Ad	Mu
Sy-Odd	2.0	2.0				2.0							
Sy-Even	2.0	2.0				2.0							
Op-Odd	2.0	2.0					2.0						
Op-Even	2.0	2.0					2.0						
LG-Odd	1.5		1.5					1.5					
LG-Even	1.5		1.5					1.5					
FS-Odd	1.5		1.5						1.5				
FS-Even	1.5		1.5						1.5				
MF-Odd	1.5			1.5						1.5			
MF-Even	1.5			1.5						1.5			
BC-Odd	2.0			2.0							2.0		
BC-Even	2.0			2.0							2.0		
Ad-1	4.8				4.8							4.8	
Ad-2	4.8				4.8							4.8	
Mu-1	4.8				4.8								4.8
Mu-2	4.8				4.8								4.8

Key: g = General Intelligence factor   LG = Letter Grouping test
      V = Verbal Comprehension factor   FS = Figure Series test
      I = Induction factor   MF = Metal Folding test
      Vz = Spatial Visualization factor   BC = Block Counting test
      N = Numerical factor   Ad = Additions test
      Sy = Synonyms test   Mu = Multiplications test
      Op = Opposites test

uncorrelated, is highly significant ($\chi^2 = 181.15$, $df = 115$, $p < .00$). The descriptive goodness-of-fit index (*GFI*) is .903, however, which indicates that even this extremely highly constrained model reproduces the observed covariance matrix with some accuracy.

The diagnostic measures indicate that there are unexplained covariances between the *g* factor on the one hand, and *I*, *N,* and Metal Folding (*MF*) on the other. The model thus was modified in such a way that the loadings of the observed variables defining *I, N,* and *MF* were specified as free parameters to be estimated from the data. Within each of these three groups of variables, however, constraints of equality of the parameters were imposed. The modified model, which has three degrees of freedom less than the original model, has a nonsignificant test statistic ($\chi^2 = 128.88$, $df = 112$, $p < .131$, $GFI = .930$). It may also be noted that the *p* value for this model is about the same as that obtained for the final higher-order model (see Table 8.2). Table 8.4 presents the estimates obtained in the variance component model.

If the parameter estimates in Table 8.4 are compared with the hypothesized values in Table 8.3, it may be noted that for the *I* tests and *MF* the relations with *g* are higher than hypothesized, and for the *N* tests the relations are lower. These

TABLE 8.4
Estimated Parameters in the Variance-Component Model

Test	g	V	I	Vz	N	Sy	Op	LG	FS	MF	BC	Ad	Mu
Sy-Odd	2.0	2.0			2.0								
Sy-Even	2.0	2.0			2.0								
Op-Odd	2.0	2.0					2.0						
Op-Even	2.0	2.0					2.0						
LG-Odd	2.4*		1.5					1.5					
LG-Even	2.4*		1.5					1.5					
FS-Odd	2.4*		1.5						1.5				
FS-Even	2.4*		1.5						1.5				
MF-Odd	2.3*			1.5						1.5			
MF-Even	2.3*			1.5						1.5			
BC-Odd	2.0			2.0							2.0		
BC-Even	2.0			2.0							2.0		
Ad-1	3.1*			4.8								4.8	
Ad-2	3.1*			4.8								4.8	
Mu-1	3.1*			4.8									4.8
Mu-2	3.1*			4.8									4.8
Variance	1.0	1.0	−0.3	0.7	2.1	0.3	−0.1	1.9	1.1	1.5	0.8	0.7	−0.0
t-value	5.9	7.0	−1.4	3.4	8.5	2.7	−1.4	6.5	4.7	5.5	4.0	4.2	−0.3

Note: * indicates estimates of free parameters constrained to be equal within groups of tests.

Key: g = General Intelligence factor   LG = Letter Grouping test
      V = Verbal Comprehension factor   FS = Figure Series test
      I = Induction factor   MF = Metal Folding test
      Vz = Spatial Visualization factor   BC = Block Counting test
      N = Numerical factor   Ad = Additions test
      Sy = Synonyms test   Mu = Multiplications test
      Op = Opposites test

results closely correspond with the estimates in the higher-order model. It is also interesting to note that the estimate of the variance for the I factor is (nonsignificantly) negative. Thus, when the g variance is partialled out, the I (or Gf) factor ceases to exist. Most of the other variance components are highly significant, the two exceptions being the test-specific components in Op and Mu.

The results presented in Table 8.4 indicate that the variance-component approach rather straightforwardly can be employed to decompose the observed score variance into different components. The relative contribution from each source of variance is not so easily seen in Table 8.4, however, thus in Table 8.5 the results are presented in terms of proportions of observed score variance.

Results are presented for one half-test only, because under the present model the results are identical for the half-tests. In all tests, except for the N tests, the g factor is the most important source of variance. It may also be noted that the test-specific factors are strong in the I and Vz tests.

The results presented in Table 8.5 apply to half-tests, but from the estimates

TABLE 8.5
Proportions of Variance Accounted for in the Observed
Variables by the Latent Variables

Test	g	V	Vz	N	Test-spec	Error
Sy-Odd	0.35	0.36			0.09	0.20
Op-Odd	0.36	0.37			0.00	0.27
LG-Odd	0.46				0.35	0.18
FS-Odd	0.54				0.24	0.22
MF-Odd	0.44		0.13		0.27	0.16
BC-Odd	0.30		0.21		0.24	0.25
Ad-1	0.10			0.53	0.18	0.19
Mu-1	0.13			0.68	0.00	0.18

Key: g = General Intelligence factor   LG = Letter Grouping test
      V = Verbal Comprehension factor   FS = Figure Series test
      Vz = Spatial Visualization factor   MF = Metal Folding test
      N = Numerical factor   BC = Block Counting test
      Sy = Synonyms test   Ad = Additions test
      Op = Opposites test   Mu = Multiplications test

of parameters in the model, it is easy to compute the measurement characteristics for lengthened tests and for tests that are composites of different item types. Even though it would carry too far to present such algebraic exercises in the present context, it may be noted that when tests are lengthened, the amount of variance contributed by all the systematic sources increases, while the effect of the error component decreases (e.g., Cronbach, 1951). Composites of different types of tests will be strongly influenced by the general factor and weakly influenced by all other systematic sources of variance, because the general factor is present among all tests but all the other factors only influence subsets of items.

Discussion

It must be stressed that the factor-analytic approach used here is but one of several useful methods to identify the dimensions underlying cognitive performances. Marshalek, Lohman, and Snow (1983; see also Snow, Kyllonen, & Marshalek, 1984) showed that nonmetric multidimensional scaling of intercorrelations among large sets of tests almost invariably yields one dimension reflecting the complexity of the tests and another dimension representing type of content (e.g., verbal, figural, and numerical) in the test items. They also pointed out that the complexity dimension coincides with the g (or Gf) dimension in hierarchical factor solutions and that the content dimension easily can be translated into factors at levels below g in the hierarchical model.

One common characteristic of the radex (Guttman, 1954) type of models, that Marshalek et al. (1983) took as a starting point, and the hierarchical models is that both these types of models identify several sources of variance in each test score. This is quite a trivial observation, but it has nontrivial implications for measurement theory and practice.

As was pointed out by Humphreys (1985), current psychometric theory is guided by ideals of homogeneity of test items and unidimensionality of test scores. These ideals can be approximated by reducing the number of facets allowed to vary among the items in a measurement instrument. However, when tests are constructed from similar items chosen to represent selected facets, we will have a test that is: "psychologically complex although statistically homogeneous" (Humphreys, 1985, p. 206).

The inherent complexity of the observed score variance is clearly seen in the results in Table 8.5, and the results also show that no single test may be taken as a pure measure of any underlying variable. In the BC half-test, for example, g accounts for 30% of the variance; Vz (or Gv) for 21%, and some kind of specific block-counting ability for 24% of the variance. If this test is correlated with another variable (an outcome variable in an ATI study, for example), any obtained correlation may have multiple interpretations, as may differences in the correlations among different treatment groups. It is also easy to imagine quite severe implications of the complexity of our measures: Suppose that the g factor is involved in an interaction with a treatment variable (a steeper regression on g in a verbal than in a figural treatment, say), and the Gv factor is involved in another interaction (a steeper regression on Gv in a figural than in a verbal treatment, say). However, if any typical spatial test is used as an aptitude variable, these effects will cancel out, and both effects will remain undetected.

In the remainder of this chapter, an empirical study is briefly reported, in which the empirical consequences of the fact that our tests simultaneously measure broad and narrow abilities are investigated.

STUDY 2: INTERACTIVE EFFECTS
BETWEEN MODALITY OF PRESENTATION
AND GENERAL AND SPECIALIZED APTITUDES

The theoretical background of the study is derived from a series of studies conducted by Brooks (1967, 1968) on suppression of visualization in reading. In laboratory experiments, Brooks showed that subjects made fewer errors in learning messages describing spatial relations when listening than they did when both listening and reading, while the reverse pattern of results was found for nonspatial messages. These results, which have been replicated and extended in other studies (e.g., Peterson, Thomas, & Johnson, 1977), may be interpreted to indicate that reading interferes with the generation of an internal representation of spatial relations.

If, however, processes of visualization are more difficult to perform under visual presentation of verbal information than under auditive presentation, there may also be a differential effect of modality of presentation as a function of visualization ability: Under visual presentation, visualization ability should have a low relation with outcomes reflecting acquisition of spatial content, as the possibilities for engaging in visualization are poor. Under auditive presentation, in contrast, a higher relationship between visualization ability and learning of spatial content would be expected, as no restrictions are imposed on the possibilities for using visualization processes.

Subjects, Treatment, and Materials

The study was conducted as an ATI experiment with four treatments, only two of which are considered here:

The VISU Treatment (N = 125). Subjects read a mimeographed copy of the instructional material (discussed later), which did not contain any illustrations. The subjects were instructed to read the material twice, and almost all subjects read the material at least twice.

The AUDI Treatment (N = 109). Subjects listened to a presentation via tape recorder of the same material as was read in the VISU treatment. The tape was played twice, with a pause of about 30 seconds between presentations.

Each treatment was administered to seven sixth grade classes. The treatments were administered within regular classes by project personnel.

The instructional material was divided into two parts. After a short orientation about the purpose of the project, Part 1 was given at the beginning of a regular class, which required approximately 20 minutes. Then the subjects were given a questionnaire with completely unrelated items, after which there was a break of 10 to 20 minutes. After the break, the subjects studied Part 2 of the instructional materials (20 minutes) and were then immediately given two posttests (discussed later).

The instructional materials, which were entitled "About weather," dealt with basic concepts within meteorology and physics.

In Part 1 of the instructional materials, which consist of 1,177 words, some basic phenomena and concepts are introduced. A description first is made of the atmosphere, and the concept of air pressure is introduced. In the next step, the sun's heating of the earth is introduced, along with the consequences that at the equator there is always a low air pressure and wind blowing toward the equator. However, because the earth rotates from west to east at a faster pace, the closer you are to the equator these winds have a westward orientation at the equator. At this point, rather lengthy explanations are given, where the turning of the wind is viewed both from the perspective of the wind and from a position above the equator. Then the topic of condensation is introduced and there is an explanation how clouds are formed.

Part 2, which consists of 948 words, starts with a description of masses of air that is either cold and dry or warm and moist. The terms *cold front* and *warm front* are also introduced, along with a description of the notation for these on weather maps. The remainder of the material is devoted to a rather detailed description of how low pressure systems are formed over the North Atlantic, which exert strong influence on the weather conditions in Scandinavia.

Immediately after the instruction, the subjects were given two posttests, one verbal and one pictorial. Two weeks later, these tests were readministered as retention tests.

The items in both posttests were constructed to assess knowledge of verbal content and of the understanding of the spatial and structural relations that are involved in the meteorological processes. The items in the posttests thus can be classified into four groups according to the two facets *test format* and *content type:*

Verbal Posttest/Verbal Content (VERB-VERB). The 12 items in this group are all verbally formulated and require a written response. Most items ask about terms and names, but a few require numbers in response.

Verbal Posttest/Structural Content (VERB-STRUCT). This category contains 16 items, which are all verbally formulated and require a written response. Most of the items ask in which direction different winds blow. A few items also ask for more elaborate descriptions of processes.

Pictorial Posttest/Verbal Content (PICT-VERB). The 10 items in this category all present an illustration and ask a question that requires a written response, typically a name or a term.

Pictorial Posttest/Structural Content (PICT-STRUCT). There are 23 items of this kind, all of which present an illustration and a question that typically is answered through completing the illustration with a drawing. As in the VERB-STRUCT items, several items ask about directions of winds. In addition, several items ask the subjects to complete a drawing describing a process.

A few weeks before the learning experiment took place, the pupils were given a rather large test battery, comprising 13 tests of cognitive ability (cf. Gustafsson, 1984; Gustafsson, Lindström, & Björck-Åkesson, 1981). For the present study, a selection has been made of tests from this battery so as to be able to represent the ability factors Fluid Intelligence (*Gf* or *g*), General Visualization (*Gv*), and Crystallized Intelligence (*Gc*). As the tests are described in detail elsewhere, and as many of them are very similar to those used in Study 1, the aptitude variables are described very briefly.

Two tests were selected to measure the *Gv* factor: Metal Folding (MF), in which transformations are made from two-dimensional to three-dimensional representations; and Group Embedded Figures (EF), in which the task is to find a simple figure within a more complex figure.

To measure *Gf,* three tests were selected: The Raven Progressive Matrices Test (Ra), sections B–D; Number Series II (NS), where the task is to complete a series of eight numbers, six of which are given; and Letter Grouping II (LG), which is similar to the LG test in Study 1 but with only 20 items.

To represent *Gc,* three tests were selected: Opposites (Op), where antonyms of words are asked for; Standardized Achievement Test in Swedish (SA), which consists of six subtests with a total of 116 items; and Standardized Achievement Test in English (EA), which has 145 items, divided among four subtests.

The within-treatment covariance matrices for the aptitude and outcome variables are presented in Appendix 8B.

Results

In the first step of the analysis of the data, we consider only one of the outcome variables, for the sake of simplicity, and only the descriptive pattern of results is attended to. The zero-order correlations between the aptitude variables and the PICT-STRUCT achievement variable within treatments are presented in Table 8.6.

If the hypothesis about suppression of visualization by reading is true, we would expect higher relations between the *Gv* tests (MF and EF) and achievement in the AUDI treatment than in the VISU treatment for this particular outcome variable. The pattern of correlations does not, however, provide any support for the hypothesis, as the correlations with the spatial tests are virtually identical in the two treatments. To the extent that there are any differences for the other variables, the correlations tend to be higher within VISU than within AUDI. Thus, the correlations with NS and SA both are higher in the VISU group than in the AUDI group.

From this pattern of differences between the correlations it seems safe to predict that results from an analysis of the homogeneity of the within-treatment regressions on observed variables would not support any hypothesis about interactions with spatial ability. Quite possibly, however, such an analysis would

TABLE 8.6
Correlations Between Aptitudes and the PICT-STRUCT Achievement
Variable Within Treatments

Test	MF	EF	Ra	NS	LG	Op	SA	EA
VISU	.38	.41	.28	.46	.34	.44	.52	.41
AUDI	.37	.43	.26	.29	.34	.43	.34	.35

Key: *MF* = Metal Folding Test   *Op* = Opposites test
     EF = Group Embedded Figures test *SA* = Standardized Achievement test
     Ra = Raven Progressive Matrices test   in Swedish
     NS = Number Series II test   *EA* = Standardized Achievement
     LG = Letter Grouping II test   test in English

provide evidence that a general factor is of greater importance for achievement in the VISU. The results from the present study thus would fit well into the general pattern of findings in ATI research.

However, the aptitude variables in the present study have been selected to fit a factor model, and an analysis of within-treatment regressions on latent aptitude variables is to be preferred for at least the following two reasons: (a) the bias in estimates of within-treatment regressions caused by errors of measurement in the observed variables is avoided, and (b) such analyses are more powerful and provide more parsimonious results.

With the present selection of tests, it is reasonable to assume three first-order factors (i.e., Gv, Gf, and Gc) and onto these latent variables the observed PICT-STRUCT outcome variable can be regressed within treatments. Fig. 8.3 presents such a LISREL model, estimated from the within-treatment covariance matrices.

In this model, all parameters in the measurement model for the aptitude variables are constrained to be equal in the two treatment groups, but the within-treatment regression coefficients are free parameters. This model fits the data quite well ($\chi^2 = 72.78$, $df = 60$, $p < .13$).

The estimated parameters are presented in the Figure, and it may be seen that there is a higher coefficient for the relation between Gc and outcome in the VISU treatment, and a higher coefficient for the relation between Gv and outcome in the AUDI treatment. Within neither of the treatments is there a significant relationship between Gf and outcome.

The LISREL analysis with a nonhierarchical model for the aptitude variables thus gives a pattern of results that is dramatically different from the impressions gained from the correlations with the observed variables. The results obtained here do indeed support the hypothesis that Gv (or spatial ability) is of greater importance under auditive than under visual presentation, and the results also indicate that Gc (or verbal ability) is more highly related to achievement when the information is read than when the pupils listen.

It is also interesting to note that whereas the correlations suggested that a general factor may be of greater importance in the visual than in the auditive treatment, there is no sign of such an effect in the LISREL analysis.

This latter result, however, can be challenged on the grounds that the model shown in Fig. 8.3 does not include any general factor, so even if there are interactions with g, they will not be detected. This is clearly seen when the nonhierarchical model in Fig. 8.3 is transformed into a hierarchical model, through addition of a g factor. In the hierarchical model, there is no residual in the first-order Gf factor, but there are residuals in Gv and Gc, which are referred to as Gv' and Gc', respectively. This model is shown in Fig. 8.4, along with the estimated parameters.

Again, a rather dramatically different pattern of results is obtained: The estimates of within-treatment regressions on Gv' and Gc' closely correspond with those obtained in the flat model, but in the hierarchical model there is a much

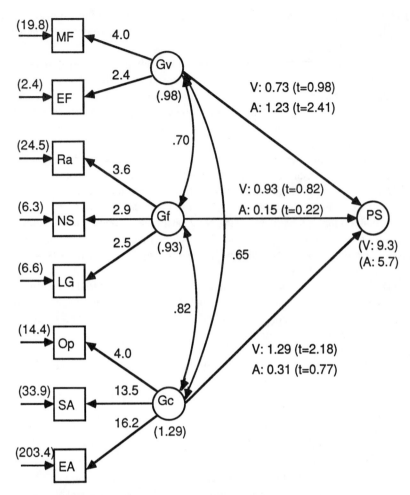

FIG. 8.3. Nonhierarchical LISREL model for the relations among the aptitude variables and the PICT-STRUCT outcome variable.

higher relation between *g* and outcome in the VISU group than in the AUDI group. Furthermore, within both treatments the relations with *g* are highly significant, whereas in the flat model the relations with *Gf* do not reach significance.

It is quite easy to see why the flat model gives the same estimates for the narrow abilities as does the hierarchical model and also why the models disagree on the estimates for *Gf*. The regression coefficients express the expected increase in the outcome variable with an increase of one unit in the latent aptitude variable, with the other latent aptitude variables kept constant. Thus, the regression on *Gv* is correctly estimated because *Gf* and *Gc* control for the general variance in *Gv,* and in the estimate of the *Gc* regression, *Gf* and *Gv* partial out the

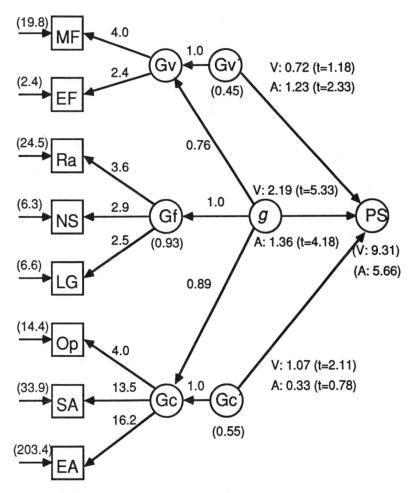

FIG. 8.4. Hierarchical LISREL model for the relations among the aptitude variables and the PICT-STRUCT outcome variable.

general variance in *Gc*. However, the regression on *Gf* is estimated in such a way that *Gv* and *Gc* partial out a large share of the *g* variance in *Gf*, and thereby they destroy the predictive power of *Gf*.

The results obtained in the hierarchical model also explain why the correlations between observed aptitude variables and outcome do not exhibit a clear-cut pattern of differences between the treatment groups. The observed score variance is influenced by both broad and narrow abilities, and because there are different patterns of interaction for *g*, *Gv'*, and *Gc'* the effects more or less cancel out.

The illustrative example just considered is restricted to the PICT-STRUCT achievement variable, and the results do indicate some support for the hypothesis under investigation. However, until it is made clear that the higher relationship with Gv' in the AUDI treatment is restricted to acquisition of spatial content, this result should not be interpreted in terms of suppression of visualization by reading.

As was already explained, the posttests are constructed according to a faceted design, involving the two facets testtype (verbal vs. pictorial) and content type (verbal vs. structural). Analyses of sources of variation of observed scores on such faceted tests are quite complicated, however, because it is necessary to take into account the fact that any one of the observed variables contains variance from every facet. One possible way to solve this problem is to use a latent-variable approach, in which the variance associated with each facet is extracted and used as dependent variables in structural equation models.

With only four outcome variables, it is necessary to use a very highly constrained model in order to be able to identify the latent sources of variation. Using an approach similar to the one applied in the variance-component models in Study 1, it has been assumed that each of the facets contribute variance in proportion to the number of items in the posttests. The design matrix is shown in Table 8.7.

The design, which was applied separately to the achievement and the retention tests, assumes that there are three latent sources of variance in the posttests: a Total component, representing the common level of achievement on all four tests; a Format component, representing the contrast between verbal and pictorial types of items; and a Content component, representing the contrast between items referring to verbal and structural types of content. For each of the components, it is assumed that it contributes to the observed variance in proportion to the number of items in the observed outcome variable. The models for the achievement and retention tests were combined in such a way that relations were allowed between corresponding latent variables at the two occasions, and covariances between the unique parts of corresponding observed variables were also allowed over the two occasions. The latent variables were not constrained to be orthogonal for the achievement tests, but the covariances among the residuals in the retention tests were constrained to be zero.

TABLE 8.7
Hypothesized Relations Between the
Observed Outcome Variables and
Design Facets of the Posttests

Test	Total	Format	Content
PICT-STRUCT	2.3	2.3	2.3
PICT-VERB	1.0	1.0	−1.0
VERB-STRUCT	1.6	−1.6	1.6
VERB-VERB	1.2	−1.2	−1.2

TABLE 8.8
Obtained Estimates of Parameters
in the Model for the Outcome Variables
Within Treatments

	Total		Format		Content	
	est.	t	est.	t	est.	t
Variance achievement						
VISU	2.09	7.06	0.26	3.96	0.31	4.35
AUDI	0.98	5.72	0.15	2.41	0.14	2.23
Correlation achievement-retention						
VISU	0.91	16.02	0.44	2.41	0.81	4.78
AUDI	0.87	9.20	0.80	3.67	0.86	4.58

The model was estimated from the within-treatment matrices of moments around zero, with parameters included in the model to represent the means of the latent variables (see Jöreskog & Sörbom, 1986). No constraints of equality over treatments were imposed, however. The goodness-of-fit test indicates a very good fit of the model to the data ($\chi^2 = 34.39$, $df = 34$, $p < .45$, $GFI = .972$). Table 8.8 presents the within-treatment estimates of a subset of the parameters in the model.

Within all treatments, the Total component contributes the largest amount of variance to the achievement variables, but the contrast components are statistically significant as well. The Table also presents the standardized correlation coefficients between the latent achievement and retention variables. For the Total component in particular, these coefficients are high, indicating that there are very little individual differences in the changes in level of performance at the two occasions of measurement. For the facet components, the stability coefficients are quite high as well, with the exception of the Format facet in the VISU treatment.

The model for the outcome variables may be used to study treatment main effects. In these analyses, constraints on the treatment means and intercepts have been introduced to obtain an overall test of the treatment main effects. This test is highly significant ($\chi^2 = 15.55$, $df = 6$, $p < .00$), which indicates that the level of performance on one or more of the latent variables differs between treatments. Separate tests of each latent variable show, however, that the entire effect is accounted for by a significant difference in favor of the VISU treatment on the Total achievement variable ($t = 2.79$, $p < .00$).

A variance-component model was applied for the aptitude variables as well, as such a model was found to have practical advantages in the process of estimation. The hypothesized design matrix for the aptitude variables included a general factor (g) with relations to all observed variables; a Gv factor with relations to MF and EF; and a Gc factor with relations to Op, SA, and EA. The strength of each relationship was hypothesized to be proportional to the number of items in the test.

The model was estimated from the covariance matrices for the two treatment groups with every parameter constrained to be equal in the two groups. The fit of this model is not very good, and analyses of the reasons for mis-fit indicate two sources of deviation between model and data: (a) for some variables (EF, NS, LG, and Op), the relations with the g factor do not conform to the hypothesized ones; and (b) for some pairs of variables (MF and Ra, MF and Op, and EF and EA), the covariances among the specific parts are not zero as was hypothesized in the initial model. When the model is modified to take these deviations into account, a good fit between model and data is obtained ($\chi^2 = 66.11$, $df = 53$, $p < .11$, $GFI = .929$). There is little reason to show the parameter estimates of this model, because the results are similar to those obtained in Study 1.

In the analyses of ATI effects, the latent outcome variables have been regressed onto the latent aptitude variables within treatments. In these analyses, relations with the three aptitude variables g, Gc', and Gv' on the one hand, and the three achievement components, on the other, have been studied. As in no case is there a significant relationship between the aptitude variables and the latent retention variables, these relations have not been included in the model.

The unconstrained model, in which the relations between latent aptitude variables and latent outcome variables were allowed to vary within treatments, has a very good fit ($\chi^2 = 196.67$, $df = 195$, $p < .45$, $GFI = .907$). The difference between this test statistic and the test statistic for a model in which all relations are constrained to be equal over treatments gives an overall test of ATI effects. This test is significant ($\chi^2 = 19.73$, $df = 9$, $p < .02$), which indicates that it is meaningful to study interaction effects for different combinations of aptitudes and outcomes. Table 8.9 presents a summary of the results of the statistical tests performed.

As may be seen in the Table, there are significant differences among the treatments for the regression of the Total achievement score on g and for the regression of the Format facet on Gv'. Chi-square values that are significant at

TABLE 8.9
Results of Statistical Tests of Differences
Between Within-Treatment Regressions
for Combinations of Latent Aptitude
and Latent Achievement Variables
(*Chi-Square Values with 1 df*)

	Total	Format	Content
g	7.97*	0.05	3.36
Gv'	.92	4.10*	2.65
Gc'	1.05	0.02	0.00

*$p < .05$

TABLE 8.10
Estimates of Within-Treatment Relations Between Latent Aptitude
and Latent Achievement Variables

		Total		Format		Content	
		est.	t	est.	t	est.	t
Unstandardized							
g:	VISU	1.12	9.73	.01	.14	−.25	−3.44
	AUDI	.70	7.14	−.01	−.20	−.06	−.89
Gv':	VISU	.08	.83	.03	.44	−.03	−.49
	AUDI	−.05	−.51	.22	3.23	.12	1.82
Gc':	VISU	.74	4.28	−.15	−1.33	−.25	−2.23
	AUDI	.51	3.44	−.13	−1.29	−.24	−2.24
Standardized							
g:	VISU	.86		.02		−.49	
	AUDI	.53		−.03		−.12	
Gv':	VISU	.08		.08		−.08	
	AUDI	−.05		.60		.30	
Gc':	VISU	.45		−.26		−.39	
	AUDI	.31		−.22		−.37	

the 10% level are also obtained for the regression of the Content component on Gv' and g. Unstandardized and standardized estimates of within-treatment regression coefficients are presented in Table 8.10.

The regression of Total on g is steeper in the VISU treatment than in the AUDI treatment. Furthermore, pupils high on g achieve relatively better on verbal content than on structural content in the VISU treatment, whereas in the AUDI treatment there is no relationship between the g factor and the Content facet. In the AUDI treatment, the Gv' factor is associated with good performance on the pictorial type of posttests, and to a certain (but nonsignificant) extent also to a better performance on structural than verbal content.

In addition to these differential patterns of relationships it is interesting to note that within both treatments the Gc' factor is negatively related to both the Format and Content components, implying that pupils high on Gc' performed better on verbal than on pictorial posttest items and that their performance is better on verbal content than on spatial content.

Discussion

It is interesting to compare the results obtained in the analysis of the single PICT-STRUCT achievement variable with the results obtained when a hierarchical model is fitted for the outcome variables as well. Such a comparison indicates that the relation between Gv' and PICT-STRUCT in the AUDI treatment to the largest extent is accounted for by the pictorial item type used in these items, and also, but to a smaller extent, by the spatial content asked about in these items. The relation between Gc' and PICT-STRUCT in the VISU treatment, however, is completely accounted for by the Total component. Thus, it seems that quite different sources of variance in PICT-STRUCT are responsible for the interactions with Gv' and Gc'.

It would carry too far to discuss the substantive findings in detail here, so just a few brief comments are offered.

The results show overall performance to be more highly related to g and Gc when the pupils read than when they listen. As the mean on the Total variable is higher in the VISU treatment, this interaction may well be ordinal, implying that the high-g/high-Gc pupils in particular perform better when they read than when they listen. Reading skills are a fundamental component of Gc, so it would seem that the steeper regression on Gc in the VISU group is not in need of more elaborate explanations. The higher relationship with g in this group is not self-evident, however. One possible explanation is that the process of reading in itself poses higher demands on attention and other cognitive processes and that these demands cause the relations with g to increase (cf. Ackerman, 1986). Another difference between the treatments is that when the pupils read on their own, they are themselves responsible for organizing their learning activities, including decisions of how much time should be spent on different sections, what parts should be reviewed, and so on. According to Cronbach and Snow (1977; see also Snow & Yalow, 1982) several studies indicate that when the pupils have to (or can) organize their own learning, the relation between general cognitive ability and achievement tends to be higher. With the present data, there is no possibility, however, to test the validity of these different explanations.

The results also show Gv' to be more highly related to proficiency on the pictorial type of items and to acquisition of spatial content when the pupils listen then when they read. Because there are no differences in level of performance on the Format and Content, these interactions are disordinal. These results do support the hypothesis that the possibilities for using visualization processes are better when verbal information is presented auditively than when it is presented visually. However, only pupils high in Gv' gain from these increased possibilities, and the positive effects are restricted to specific outcomes. It may also be noted that in the VISU treatment the high-g pupils perform relatively better on verbal content than on spatial content, which is not the case in the AUDI treatment. This finding may also be interpreted in such a way that the VISU treatment causes the pupils to process the information in a more purely verbal form than does the AUDI treatment.

It should be stressed, finally, that the present results are restricted to printed posttests. Such tests are visual in the same way that the VISU treatment is visual and answering them may of course also cause interference with processes of visualization (cf. Brooks, 1968).

CONCLUSION

The results of the studies presented here indicate that the conflict between those who argue that individual differences are best described in terms of a single general ability and those who claim that individual differences should be studied in terms of a larger number of narrow abilities is futile, because the existence of both broad and narrow abilities is so easily demonstrated. However, not only is there truth in both positions, but it also seems that neglect of narrow abilities when broad abilities are the focus of interest may lead to biased results, just as neglect of broad abilities may cause uninterpretable or erroneous results when narrow abilities are studied.

Narrow abilities present great problems whenever a measure of general intelligence is sought. The results presented in Study 1 (see also Gustafsson, 1988, p. 56) indicate that in any single measure of the Gf type the g factor accounts for considerably less than 100% of the true variance. Most of the remaining variance is caused by very narrow test-specific factors, which easily can be transformed into primary factors if sufficiently similar tests are constructed (Humphreys, 1962, 1985). In any study which uses a single homogeneous test, such as the Raven Progressive Matrices Test or Embedded Figures Test, as a measure of the general factor, these test-specific factors will attenuate relations, and they may well systematically bias estimates of relations with the g factor.

The heterogenous collections of items assembled to measure IQ in tests such as the Stanford-Binet are less influenced by narrow test-specific factors. However, tests of this type have generally been developed with a close look at the predictive validities of the items against scholastic criteria, which has caused the tests to be biased towards Gc. Relative to the g factor, Gc' is a narrow ability; so in these tests too a more narrow ability may cause bias.

In every task used to measure cognitive ability there is specific content, the task is presented in a particular format, and a particular type of response is required. Most of these, and numerous other, facets are unavoidable sources of variance in test scores. When measures of general abilities are sought, these sources of variance must, however, be counterbalanced in such a way that no particular source of variance influences the scores. In previous research this has not been done to any large extent, so most results attributed to the general intellectual factor are more or less contaminated by effects due to more narrow abilities.

The results of Study 2 demonstrate the rather intricate problems involved in identifying relations between narrow abilities and learning outcomes. In this study, there seems to be one pattern of relations with the g factor and a different pattern of relations with the (more) narrow abilities Gv and Gc. However, as the Gv tests measure both g and Gv, neither of these effects will be found if the analysis is restricted to one test at a time. A multiple regression analysis of several tests could, in principle, detect the relations with the narrow abilities, but this requires that all the general variance in the *Gv* test is properly partialed out. However, even such a trivial and well-known problem as random errors of measurement in the tests prevents correct estimates of the partial regression coefficients to be obtained, let alone the considerably more difficult problems of systematic bias introduced by narrow factors.

With the latent variable approach used here, these measurement problems are avoided; and in the nonhierarchical model, the within-treatment relations with the narrow abilities are correctly estimated. It must be stressed, however, that unless the model includes a latent variable dominated by *g* variance, the partial regression coefficients will not be correctly estimated.

The nonhierarchical model, however, fails to bring out the relations with the general factor, and only with a hierarchical model is it possible to find the relations with the broad as well as the narrow abilities. Thus, the present findings suggest the rather ironic paradox that a major reason for the failure of narrow abilities to demonstrate their theoretical importance and practical worth is that due consideration has not been paid to the more general factors and that the research on the general factor has been hampered because the measurement devices have included variance from narrow abilities!

The hierarchical approach implies that measurement is conceived of as a multivariate enterprise (cf. Humphreys, 1985), which in turn implies considerably higher demands on selection and administration of variables in empirical studies. It is interesting to note, however, that the recommendations given by Cronbach and Snow (1977) on selection of aptitude variables in ATI research may be quoted as advice on how to select aptitude variables for hierarchical models: "Even when especially interested in one characteristic of the learner, the investigator should measure additional aptitudes. If chiefly concerned with a specialized ability, he nonetheless should include one or more general measures" (p. 511). As this piece of advice has been followed in the design of more than one study, a relatively inexpensive way to investigate the utility of hierarchical models would be to reanalyze already collected data.

It should be stressed, finally, that so far the empirical basis is much too limited to allow any claims of a general superiority of hierarchical approaches over nonhierarchical in studies of relations between abilities and learning. However, the results presented here do seem encouraging enough to warrant the suggestion that the hierarchical approach should be tried on a wide array of problems, in theoretical as well as applied research.

OPEN DISCUSSION

Discussion following Gustafsson's talk concentrated on methodological issues in the modeling of ability factors and learning outcome variables. Additional discussion was devoted to the model-based distinctions between g (general intelligence) and Gf (fluid intelligence).

Kyllonen: If I understand correctly, you partialed out the effect of the general factor so that you could look at the relationship between the second-order factors and the learning outcome variable. Why didn't you do the same process at the next lower step; why didn't you look at the relationship between the primaries and learning outcome?

Gustafsson: Well, because I didn't have any primaries. I had too few tests to identify the primaries. I would have liked to do that, but with only eight variables, it wasn't possible to do it. I agree that it could be done. However, you need to be careful that you don't proceed with this analysis using a normal LISREL setup. What you must do is to extract the residual factors and put them into the model as latent variables on their own. Otherwise, the specification is faulty. But that is a technical issue.

Snow: You should go into the business of reanalyzing aptitude-treatment interaction studies. There are thousands of studies that would be shaped up by what you have done.

Gustafsson: Considering the blood, sweat, tears, and huge amounts of computer money associated with this analysis, I would appreciate some help!

Carroll: In reference to my earlier comment, I just wanted to set the record straight. In my earlier statement, I did not mean to criticize your 20-variable study. In fact, I think it is one of the landmark studies. My concern relates to establishing adequate hierarchical models. In order to do this, it will be necessary in the future to use more variables and to develop much better measures of the underlying factors, particularly the primary factors.

Gustafsson: Yes, I agree.

McArdle: My question concerns your path diagram figure [Fig. 8.4]. Is the g in this figure actually needed as an additional latent variable?

Gustafsson: Yes, it is.

McArdle: Couldn't you write the same relationships as effects back from Gf, and eliminate g altogether?

Gustafsson: No.

McArdle: Fair enough! If one could, which in a three-variable factor model I believe is true, I think it would represent something else in this particular case. Thus, if *Gf* were the same as *g*, with no residual, then that would represent a slightly different concept than a hierarchy. I understand that you have it correctly specified here, but in other researcher's minds, there might not be a *g* if *Gf* was *g*. And since you are saying that *Gf* is *g*, it might be useful to write diagrams representing that kind of concept. I recognize the principle, but my point is that this was also part of Cattell's theory, the triadic theory of growth. So, in effect, you have actually demonstrated an important principle in the development of abilities. That is, as Cattell suggested, *Gf* would proceed and lead to these other variables. I think that is a nice demonstration. These pictures had *Gf* leading to these other things, but it is the same basic idea.

Gustafsson: Yes. What still remains to be demonstrated, however, is that Cattell's investment theory is correct. I have some data which seems to support it, but the details are not yet worked out. This is the kind of analysis one needs to show that empirically.

ACKNOWLEDGMENT

The research reported in this paper has been supported financially by the Swedish Council for Research in the Humanities and Social Sciences and by the National Board of Education in Sweden.

REFERENCES

Ackerman, P. L. (1986). Individual differences in information processing: An investigation of intellectual abilities and task performance during practice. *Intelligence, 10,* 101–139.

Binet, A., & Simon, T. (1905). Méthodes nouvelles pour le diagnostic du niveau intellectuel des anormaux [New methods for diagnosing the intellectual level of non normals]. *L'Anné Psychologique, 11,* 191–244.

Bock, R. D. (1960). Components of variance analysis as a structural and discriminal analysis for psychological tests. *British Journal of Statistical Psychology, 13,* 151–163.

Bock, R. D., & Bargmann, R. E. (1966). Analysis of covariance structures. *Psychometrika, 31,* 507–534.

Brooks, L. R. (1967). The suppression of visualization by reading. *Quarterly Journal of Experimental Psychology, 19,* 289–299.

Brooks, L. R. (1968). Spatial and verbal components of the act of recall. *Canadian Journal of Psychology, 22,* 349–368.

Burt, C. L. (1949). The structure of the mind: A review of the results of factor analysis. *British Journal of Educational Psychology, 19,* 100–111, 176–199.

Cattell, R. B. (1971). *Abilities: Their structure, growth, and action.* Boston: Houghton-Mifflin.

Cronbach, L. J. (1951). Coefficient alpha and the internal structure of tests. *Psychometrika, 16*, 297–334.

Cronbach, L. J. (1984). *Essentials of psychological testing* (4th ed.). New York: Harper & Row.

Cronbach, L. J., & Snow, R. E. (1977). *Aptitudes and instructional methods.* New York: Irvington.

Guilford, J. P. (1967). *The nature of human intelligence.* New York: McGraw-Hill.

Gustafsson, J. -E. (1980). *Testing hierarchical models of ability organization through covariance models.* Paper presented at the annual meeting of the American Educational Research Association, Boston.

Gustafsson, J. -E. (1984). A unifying model for the structure of intellectual abilities. *Intelligence, 8*, 179–203.

Gustafsson, J. -E. (1988). Hierarchical models of individual differences in cognitive abilities. In R. J. Sternberg (Ed.), *Advances in the psychology of human intelligence* (Vol. 4, pp. 35–71). Hillsdale, NJ: Lawrence Erlbaum Associates.

Gustafsson, J. -E., Lindström, B., & Björck-Åkesson, E. (1981). *A general model for the organization of cognitive abilities.* Report from the Department of Education, University of Göteborg, Sweden.

Guttman, L. (1954). A new approach to factor analysis: The radex. In P. F. Lazarsfelt (Ed.), *Mathematical thinking in the social sciences* (pp. 216–257). Glencoe, IL: The Free Press.

Härnqvist, K. H. (1960). *Individuella differenser och skoldifferentiering* [Individual differences and school differentiation]. Stockholm: SOU no. 13.

Härnqvist, K. H. (1978). Primary mental abilities at collective and individual levels. *Journal of Educational Psychology, 70*, 706–716.

Horn, J. L. (1985). Remodeling old models of intelligence. In B. B. Wolman (Ed.), *Handbook of intelligence. Theories, measurements, and applications* (pp. 267–300). New York: John Wiley & Sons.

Horn, J. L. (1986). Intellectual ability concepts. In R. J. Sternberg (Ed.), *Advances in the psychology of human intelligence* (Vol. 3, pp. 35–78). Hillsdale, NJ: Lawrence Erlbaum Associates.

Humphreys, L. G. (1962). The organization of human abilities. *American Psychologist, 17*, 475–483.

Humphreys, L. G. (1985). General intelligence. An integration of factor, test, and simplex theory. In B. B. Wolman (Ed.), *Handbook of intelligence. Theories, measurements, and applications* (pp. 201–224). New York: Wiley.

Jöreskog, K. G. (1978). Structural analysis of covariance and correlation matrices. *Psychometrika, 43*, 443–477.

Jöreskog, K. G., & Sörbom, D. (1986). *LISREL VI. Analysis of linear structural relationships by maximum likelihood and least squares methods.* Mooresville, IN: Scientific Software, Inc.

Marshalek, B., Lohman, D. F., & Snow, R. E. (1983). The complexity continuum in the radex and hierarchical models of intelligence. *Intelligence, 7*, 107–128.

McNemar, Q. (1964). Lost: Our intelligence? Why? *American Psychologist, 19*, 871–882.

Peterson, M. J., Thomas, J. E., & Johnson, H. (1977). Imagery, rehearsal, and compatibility of input-output tasks. *Memory and Cognition, 5*, 415–422.

Schmid, J., & Leiman, J. M. (1957). The development of hierarchical factor solutions. *Psychometrika, 22*, 53–61.

Snow, R. E., Kyllonen, P. C., & Marshalek, B. (1984). The topography of ability and learning correlations. In R. J. Sternberg (Ed.), *Advances in the psychology of human intelligence* Vol. 2, Hillsdale, NJ: Lawrence Erlbaum Associates.

Snow, R. E., & Yalow, E. (1982). Education and intelligence. In R. J. Sternberg (Ed.), *Handbook of intelligence* (pp. 493–585). Cambridge, England: Cambridge University Press.

Spearman, C. (1904). General intelligence objectively determined and measured. *American Journal of Psychology, 15*, 210–293.

Spearman, C. (1927). *The abilities of man*. London: Macmillan.

Sternberg, R. J. (1985). *Beyond IQ. A triarchic theory of human intelligence*. Cambridge, England: Cambridge University Press.

Terman, L. M. (1916). *The measurement of intelligence*. Boston: Houghton-Mifflin.

Thorndike, R. L. (1985). The central role of general ability in prediction. *Multivariate Behavioral Research, 20,* 241–254.

Thurstone, L. L. (1938). Primary mental abilities. *Psychometric Monographs, No. 1.*

Thurstone, L. L. (1947). *Multiple factor analysis*. Chicago: University of Chicago Press.

Undheim, J. O. (1981). On intelligence IV: Toward a restoration of general intelligence. *Scandinavian Journal of Psychology, 22,* 251–265(d).

Undheim J. O., & Gustafsson, J. -E. (1987). The hierarchical organization of cognitive abilities: Restoring general intelligence through the use of linear structural relations. *Multivariate Behavioral Research, 22,* 149–171.

Vernon, P. E. (1950). *The structure of human abilities*. London: Methuen.

APPENDIX 8A
COVARIANCE MATRIX FOR THE VARIABLES IN STUDY 1

	Sy-Odd	Sy-Even	Op-Odd	Op-Even	LG-Odd	LG-Even
Sy-Odd	11.181					
Sy-Even	9.237	12.008				
Op-Odd	8.467	9.071	11.173			
Op-Even	7.751	8.324	8.096	11.208		
LG-Odd	3.997	3.517	4.580	4.304	10.818	
LG-Even	3.756	3.532	3.838	4.419	8.131	9.842
FS-Odd	5.150	5.413	5.167	4.875	4.851	4.391
FS-Even	5.568	5.739	5.720	5.728	5.207	4.530
MF-Odd	4.691	4.573	5.005	5.075	4.420	3.642
MF-Even	4.988	4.738	5.144	5.585	5.433	4.785
BC-Odd	3.600	3.794	4.103	4.240	4.272	3.803
BC-Even	3.359	3.437	4.080	3.943	3.871	3.872
Ad-1	5.072	4.893	5.946	6.751	8.515	8.376
Ad-2	6.249	5.751	6.970	7.876	8.137	7.139
Mu-1	7.073	7.156	7.426	8.505	8.184	7.083
Mu-2	8.284	8.355	8.406	10.036	9.079	8.246

	FS-Odd	FS-Even	MF-Odd	MF-Even	BC-Odd	BC-Even
FS-Odd	10.282					
FS-Even	8.136	10.575				
MF-Odd	5.625	6.700	12.824			
MF-Even	5.835	6.793	10.529	12.221		
BC-Odd	5.440	5.096	6.707	6.727	14.841	
BC-Even	4.448	4.714	6.509	6.510	9.809	11.428
Ad-1	6.866	6.651	3.473	6.431	6.885	5.274
Ad-2	8.434	7.448	5.623	7.995	7.315	6.143
Mu-1	6.846	7.096	3.154	5.597	4.807	3.050
Mu-2	7.141	7.618	3.902	6.250	4.324	2.607

	Ad-1	Ad-2	Mu-1	Mu-2
Ad-1	88.985			
Ad-2	74.679	96.065		
Mu-1	50.874	54.729	61.981	
Mu-2	61.581	65.315	57.199	78.415

Key: Sy = Synonyms test   MF = Metal Folding test
Op = Opposites test   BC = Block Counting test
LG = Letter Grouping test   Ad = Additions test
FS = Figure Series test   Mu = Multiplications test

APPENDIX 8B
COVARIANCE MATRIX FOR THE VISU GROUP IN STUDY 2

	P-STRUCT1	P-VERB1	V-STRUCT1	V-VERB1	P-STRUCT2	P-VERB2
P-STRUCT1	14.626					
P-VERB1	4.429	5.184				
V-STRUCT1	4.986	1.834	5.665			
V-VERB1	5.053	3.759	4.323	7.120		
P-STRUCT2	9.969	2.971	4.608	4.880	12.884	
P-VERB2	3.457	2.262	2.003	2.701	3.313	4.211
V-STRUCT2	4.201	1.745	3.620	3.707	4.536	1.926
V-VERB2	4.791	2.972	3.162	4.546	4.243	2.749
MF	8.813	4.489	4.473	6.368	8.643	3.294
EF	4.648	2.542	2.659	3.590	3.937	1.385
Ra	6.040	3.989	3.540	4.556	5.525	2.164
NS	6.822	3.860	4.280	5.282	6.857	2.958
LG	4.103	3.016	2.407	3.134	3.935	1.444
Op	10.425	5.598	7.116	10.273	9.369	5.411
SA	31.727	19.317	20.687	27.616	29.415	16.306
EA	34.473	16.367	26.921	30.854	39.612	15.299

	V-STRUCT2	V-VERB2	MF	EF	Ra	NS
V-STRUCT2	5.381					
V-VERB2	3.128	5.498				
MF	3.205	4.389	37.383			
EF	1.835	2.167	10.867	8.732		
Ra	3.235	3.240	18.299	8.072	32.270	
NS	3.321	3.917	10.162	5.882	10.143	14.897
LG	2.086	1.957	6.336	3.149	7.428	6.617
Op	6.470	8.045	13.923	8.091	10.658	11.798
SA	18.099	23.119	41.972	20.193	36.671	33.720
EA	21.805	24.322	51.197	26.546	34.309	36.465

	LG	Op	SA	EA
LG	9.885			
Op	7.077	39.244		
SA	21.982	72.943	258.618	
EA	22.178	88.912	250.628	482.193

(Continued)

APPENDIX 8B
(continued)
COVARIANCE MATRIX FOR THE AUDI GROUP IN STUDY 2

	P-STRUCT1	P-VERB1	V-STRUCT1	V-VERB1	P-STRUCT2	P-VERB2
P-STRUCT1	7.978					
P-VERB1	1.792	3.021				
V-STRUCT1	2.107	1.651	4.731			
V-VERB1	0.969	1.634	2.291	4.854		
P-STRUCT2	5.309	1.502	1.559	0.654	7.882	
P-VERB2	1.569	1.830	1.315	1.283	2.321	3.305
V-STRUCT2	2.567	1.344	2.163	1.970	2.862	1.873
V-VERB2	1.006	1.062	1.352	2.754	1.191	0.945
MF	6.088	2.534	1.264	0.324	4.742	1.421
EF	3.206	1.242	1.369	0.502	3.192	1.205
Ra	4.791	2.382	3.480	2.547	3.479	2.400
NS	2.996	2.103	2.902	2.399	3.004	2.209
LG	3.815	1.324	2.222	2.972	3.528	1.426
Op	6.612	4.031	4.425	5.399	5.438	3.139
SA	16.097	11.201	15.090	19.311	12.933	9.910
EA	24.110	13.871	15.476	24.111	14.855	13.866

	V-STRUCT2	V-VERB2	MF	EF	Ra	NS
V-STRUCT2	4.922					
V-VERB2	1.901	3.131				
MF	0.957	0.630	34.674			
EF	1.658	0.616	8.665	7.214		
Ra	1.362	2.608	14.717	5.597	41.268	
NS	2.537	2.095	4.013	4.098	7.873	13.586
LG	2.944	2.426	7.380	4.630	10.491	7.296
Op	4.868	3.918	11.959	7.145	9.535	8.249
SA	14.897	12.994	23.883	18.332	41.414	31.258
EA	13.436	14.698	44.250	31.166	69.006	39.176

	LG	Op	SA	EA
LG	15.519			
Op	10.556	30.252		
SA	35.834	64.728	276.910	
EA	40.862	75.120	319.258	610.515

Key: P-STRUCT = Pictorial posttest/structural content
P-VERB = Pictorial posttest/verbal content
V-STRUCT = Verbal posttest/structural content
V-VERB = Verbal posttest/verbal content
MF = Metal Folding test
EF = Group Embedded Figures test
Ra = Raven Progressive Matrices test
NS = Number Series II test
LG = Letter Grouping II test
Op = Opposites test
SA = Standardized Achievement test in Swedish
EA = Standardized Achievement test in English

9

Role of Cognitive Factors in the Acquisition of Cognitive Skill

Patrick C. Kyllonen
University of Georgia and Air Force Human Resources Laboratory

Dan J. Woltz
Air Force Human Resources Laboratory

Facility in acquiring cognitive skills, such as those associated with programming computers or troubleshooting electronics equipment, is popularly regarded as an indication of general intellectual proficiency. At least part of the reason for this is that learning new skills is intellectually demanding and thereby discriminating. We generally avoid learning new skills when the old ones are adequate, even barely adequate, because skill learning is such an intellectually excruciating process. And mathematics, physics, and computer science classes, which can be characterized as emphasizing the acquisition of novel cognitive skills, as opposed to the accumulation of domain facts, are generally regarded as the most difficult in the college curriculum.

In recent years, cognitive psychology has begun to consider the processes by which students come to acquire new cognitive skills. It is appropriate, we think, to view this research as having the goal of identifying the underlying mechanisms and capacities that enable and mediate skill acquisition and development. The primary focus of this work has been on cataloging the kinds of errors students make when learning new skills (e.g., Anderson, Greeno, Kline, & Neves, 1981; Brown & Burton, 1978) and on developing sophisticated formal models, primarily computer simulations, of the skill acquisition process (Neches, Langley, & Klahr, 1987). These models provide computationally plausible explanations for how skill can develop in light of the kinds of errors students typically make. But interestingly, a potentially powerful methodology for the analysis of skill acquisition, that of comparing those who acquire skill easily with those who do not, in terms of other differentiating cognitive factors, has only infrequently been employed. Although there have been some studies comparing domain experts with novices (Chi, Feltovich, & Glaser, 1981), systematic individual differences analyses of cognitive skill acquisition per se have only very recently begun to appear in the literature (Kanfer & Ackerman, in press) and have not enjoyed anything like the popularity of individual differences analyses of performance on intelligence tests, as exemplified in the work of Sternberg (1977) or Hunt (1978). This is especially surprising given the historical association of intelligence and learning in the individual differences literature.

In this chapter we review a number of recently completed and in-progress studies we have conducted that have employed an individual differences approach to the analysis of cognitive skill acquisition. Much of the earlier research on individual differences in skill acquisition focussed on the development of perceptual motor skills (e.g., Fleishman, 1972). Our focus is on the development of cognitive skills in which procedures for transforming information are more critical than perceptual and motor operations. In studying cognitive skills, our primary interest is in the role of working memory capacity. But this reflects as much an anticipation of conclusions as it does an initial intention. Over many studies, we simply have not found any other cognitive factor that plays as critical a role in governing success in cognitive skill acquisition as that played by working memory capacity.

DEFINITION OF COGNITIVE SKILL

Our work has been guided by the notion that much of cognitive skill can be characterized as the possession of two kinds of knowledge: (a) knowledge of how domain operators work, that is, knowledge of what output is produced by an operator as a function of input; and (b) knowledge of when to select particular operators to achieve particular problem-solving goals.

For example, in learning a programming language, such as LISP, the operators initially learned are the predefined functions, such as CAR, CDR, CONS, LIST, APPEND, and so forth, which operate on the data structures of the language, atoms and lists, to build new atoms and lists. In geometry, the operators are the postulates and theorems that transform a statement into a new conjecture. In learning logic gates, the operators are the gates—AND, OR, INVERT, NAND, NOR, XOR, and so on—that transform incoming signals to an outgoing signal.

In all these domains, the successful student must first learn how the operators work, that is, learn how statements, signals, or other kinds of data are transformed by the domain operators. Next, usually through experience, the student must learn when, and in what order, to apply the various operators. In some contexts, knowing when to apply operators is a creative process: consider the task of writing computer programs, solving geometry proofs, or designing circuits. In some contexts, learning when to apply operators is a matter of learning a sequence of steps to follow: for example, knowing emergency procedures for dealing with system failures. In any event, true cognitive skill is achieved when the student knows the domain operators and knows when to use them.

Our claim is not that this is all there is to acquiring cognitive skill. For one thing, these forms of knowledge do not seem to capture the essence of creativity or insight-based problem solving. Certainly, an important cognitive skill involves not merely the memorization of how given operators work, but the development of new operators that perform "interesting new actions" (Neches, Langley, & Klahr, 1987). We also are not claiming that these two kinds of knowledge are necessarily explicit. There is evidence that people can learn to employ an operator successfully without explicitly knowing how it works (Berry & Broadbent, 1988; Lewicki, Czyzewska, & Hoffman, 1987; Nissen & Bullemer, 1987). Rather, our claim is that much of cognitive skill can be understood as knowing how operators work and when to use them and that an analysis of how students come to acquire this kind of knowledge can be an important first step in understanding how students acquire more complex cognitive skills.

Cognitive skill characterized as simply knowledge of operators and when to use them suggests that skill learning is just a special case of fact learning, where the facts are operators and the conditions associated with their proper use. But in keeping with contemporary views on the matter, we believe it is useful to distinguish *declarative* (factual) knowledge from *procedural* skill.

A current learning theory that employs the declarative–procedural distinction is Anderson's (1987) Adaptive Control of Thought (ACT*) theory. This theory also serves as the foundation for much of our thinking about the role of cognitive factors in acquiring cognitive skill, and thus we briefly review that theory here. Following Fitts (1963), Anderson has proposed that acquiring cognitive skill involves three distinct learning phases. We illustrate these in Fig. 9.1, along with an example drawn from learning logic gates.

Knowledge Acquisition Phase

The learner first commits to memory a declarative representation (propositions and relations) of the rules regarding how domain operators work. In learning logic gates from text, for example, the learner encodes the relation between the spatial description and the name of the AND gate (i.e., "the AND gate looks like D"). The learner also encodes the assertion, found perhaps in an instructional text, that "the AND gate outputs a high signal if all inputs are high, but it outputs a low signal otherwise." Although this is a single sentence, it is a fairly complex single sentence in terms of what the learner has to encode. For example, we informally broke this sentence down into the following propositions:

P1: AND (gate)
P2: high (signal)
P3: outputs (P1, P2)

MODEL OF THE DEVELOPMENT OF COGNITIVE SKILL

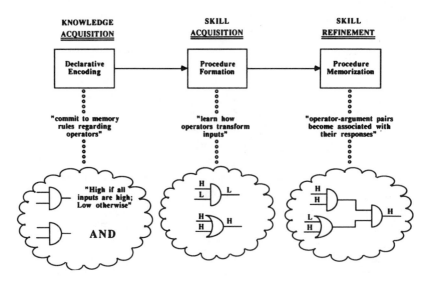

FIG. 9.1. Three-phase model of cognitive skill acquisition (following Anderson, 1987), applied to the learning of logic gates. Descriptions of logic-gate rules are assumed to undergo initial declarative encoding, then transformed into executable procedural rules, then refined and memorized as automatically executable procedural rules.

P4: all (inputs)
P5: high (P4)
P6: if-then (P5, P3)
P7: low (signal)
P8: outputs (P1, P7)
P9: not (P5)
P10: if-then (P9, P7)

After reading the gate definition, and encoding these 10 propositions, the learner could be said to possess declarative but not procedural knowledge regarding the AND gate. (There is some controversy on this point. Kieras and Bovair, 1986, suggest that learners can encode if-then rules directly as procedures.) Applying this declarative knowledge in problem solving, to predict the output of an AND gate given the input "High, Low," for example, would be slow and error-prone. The learner would have to keep the 10 propositions encoding the AND description active in working memory, which is a considerable memory load, while simultaneously having to evaluate the actual gate presented in the problem, determine its state, and determine whether P5 or P9 were true in this particular problem. Encoding the problem itself would involve encoding at least the following three propositions:

P11: gate-type-is (AND-gate)
P12: high (line-1)
P13: low (line-2)

along with a proposition representing the goal of problem solving:

P14: goal (determine-output-value)

Knowledge in this form is not sufficient for solving problems. Rather the learner has to have general problem-solving knowledge that guides the process of applying this propositional knowledge to the task of determining the answer to the presented problem. For example, the learner has to know that if the goal is to determine an output value, and the output is dependent on input values, then look at what those input values are. The reason problem solving at this point is so difficult is that there is a considerable memory load and there is a need to make a sequence of decisions involving the propositional information. Mistakes made anywhere along the way may result in errors in the subject's decision about whether a high or low signal will be output.

Skill Acquisition Phase

Following declarative encoding, the learner advances toward bona fide cognitive skill in a couple of different ways. First, by a process of *proceduralization,* the learner begins to develop a procedural understanding of how the various operators work as a result of solving problems. An example of the kind of procedure (i.e., if-then or production rule) acquired in learning logic gates is the following:

IF   (a) there is an AND gate, and
        (b) line-1 (one of the inputs) is HIGH, and
        (c) line-2 (the other input) is LOW,
THEN   the output is LOW

Having this and similar production rules reduces working memory burden, as follows. When a problem involving the AND gate is presented, it is now no longer necessary to activate all 10 propositions that encode the AND rule, because the knowledge of how AND works is stored in long-term memory in the form of these production rules. Rather, only three propositions have to be active; specifically, those that encode the state of the illustrated logic gate (i.e., what kind of gate it is, what the value of one incoming line is, and what the value of the other incoming line is; see P11, P12, and P13) and the goal (see P14). In other words, having proceduralized knowledge of the AND gate amounts to having a production rule, or set of production rules, that encode that knowledge. Because these production rules are assumed to be stored permanently in long-term memory, having these rules results in a reduction of the load on working memory and leads to speedier and more accurate problem solving.

Intuitively, this idea of a declarative to procedural transition seems right: It is possible to know a skill on a declarative-factual level yet not be capable of procedural execution of that skill. For example, we might be able to dictate the steps necessary to land an aircraft on a runway, yet not be able to actually do it. A demonstration in a more purely cognitive realm comes from a dissertation by Schmalhofer (1982). He had computer science and psychology students read a chapter from a programming textbook teaching the language LISP, with which neither group had any prior familiarity. An immediately following posttest demonstrated that both groups developed an adequate declarative knowledge base of the material presented in the chapter. The psychology students remembered as much of the propositional content as did the computer science students. However, for the psychology students, this knowledge was strictly declarative. They were unable to apply this knowledge to problem solving (verifying and debugging LISP programs). In contrast, the computer science students apparently went beyond a strictly declarative understanding and were able to proceduralize some of the knowledge taught in the text, as indicated by their ability to verify and debug LISP programs. This study nicely demonstrates that prior knowledge may determine the degree to which new incoming knowledge about a skill will become proceduralized.

A second way, besides proceduralization, in which learners attain cognitive skill, is *composition*. By this method, long chains or sequences of production rules (which can be thought of in this context as mental steps) are collapsed into single production rules. Composition thus represents one way in which the learner comes to know when to apply particular operators. An example, from logic gates, is a problem consisting of a series of logic gates linked together in a circuit, where the output of one gate serves as the input to another. The novice problem solver undoubtedly solves circuit problems sequentially, one gate at a time. In contrast, there may be experts who have composed sequences of single gate problems, who can evaluate entire multiple-gate circuits in a single step, simultaneously.

Skill Refinement Phase

Once knowledge is proceduralized and composed, it continues to undergo further refinement. In a third and final learning stage, cognitive skill is tuned or automatized, as the learner develops increasingly specialized production rules to handle any of the possible problem types likely to be faced. That is, the learner essentially comes to memorize correct responses to particular stimulus configurations. These more specialized production rules can be seen as straightforward stimulus–response pairs, where the stimulus is the operator (e.g., AND gate) and the arguments (e.g., high and low incoming signal). With practice, these more specialized rules grow in strength to the point where they ultimately require minimal conscious attention for their application. Problem solving becomes rapid, and relatively error-free, and can even be accomplished while the solver is engaged in other cognitive activity. This might characterize experts who can trace signals through logic gates while simultaneously conversing with fellow troubleshooters, for example.

It is useful to consider how the Anderson–Fitts three-phase model intersects with our ideas about the two kinds of knowledge (*how* domain operators work and *when* to apply them). One way of thinking about the relationships is that phase and knowledge type are independent dimensions. Operator knowledge of either type (how or when) can be in declarative, procedural, or automatic form. In the normal course of cognitive skill development (though, as we pointed out earlier, not necessarily in all cases), operator knowledge originates in declarative, how-it-works form, as the result of lecture or textbook instruction. Then, with problem-solving experience, the learner becomes increasingly proficient in two ways. First, the knowledge of how operators work becomes increasingly proceduralized and automatized, along the lines of the Anderson–Fitts model. Second, knowledge of when to apply the operators is acquired, usually tacitly. Conventional instruction typically fails to explicate the conditions under which operators should be used, leaving it up to the student to infer when those operators are relevant (Lewis & Anderson, 1985). Presumably, this type of knowledge, of when operators should be applied, also undergoes proceduralization and automatization with experience.

DETERMINANTS OF SUCCESS
IN ACQUIRING COGNITIVE SKILL:
THE FOUR-SOURCE FRAMEWORK

Given this model of cognitive skill acquisition, it is useful to consider what determines success at each stage. For example, we might expect that prior knowledge will facilitate the declarative to procedural transition of new material, as Schmalhofer (1982) demonstrated. As another example, we might expect that working memory capacity will play an important role in early stages of skill development, when working memory demands are high; but other cognitive factors, such as the speed with which items can be retrieved from long-term memory, will play an important role relatively late in the process, after the rules are well practiced. There is support for this prediction as well. A number of studies (Ackerman, 1987; Fleishman, 1972) have shown that measures of general cognitive ability, which presumably stress working memory capacity (a point we return to in a later section), are especially highly correlated with performance on initial trials of various learning tasks. Conversely, more specifically speeded tests become better predictors of performance on later trials, after the subject becomes familiar with the task. Interestingly, if subjects somehow can be prevented from proceduralizing their task knowledge, then working memory demands will be kept high, and working memory capacity (or general cognitive ability) therefore will remain a strong determinant of task success regardless of how much practice subjects have (Ackerman, 1986).

In our own work, we have been guided by what we have called the *four-source framework* (Kyllonen & Christal, 1989). According to this general proposal, illustrated in Fig. 9.2, performance in each of the three learning phases (knowledge acquisition, skill acquisition, and skill refinement) is presumed to be determined by (a) *prior learning factors* representing the degree of completeness of the prior learning phase, and (b) four categories of *general cognitive factors:*

Knowledge—general and domain-specific;

Skills—general and domain-specific;

Processing capacity (i.e., working memory capacity); and

Processing speed (e.g., retrieval speed, decision speed)

As an illustration of how this framework can be applied, consider a model for predicting the acquisition of procedural skill in some domain, say logic gates. Suppose that an individual had already been given declarative instruction on the rules governing the workings of logic gates and was now engaged in applying those rules to solving gate problems. An individual's success at this phase of skill acquisition would be presumed to be predictable from (a) the level of general world knowledge possessed by the individual (e.g., as indicated by performance on a general knowledge survey); (b) the level of domain-specific knowledge (e.g., the degree of prior declarative knowledge of logic gates); (c) the amount of general skill or strategic knowledge available (e.g., the degree of knowledge of good problem-solving strategies, such as those found in Wickelgren, 1974, or Hayes, 1981); (d) the amount of specific procedural skill (e.g., experience with logic gates or logical operators in other contexts, such as a formal logic course); (e) working memory capacity (e.g., as indicated by performance on something like the Daneman–Carpenter [1980] reading span test; (f) processing speed (as indicated by performance on retrieval speed tests such as physical-name-semantic matching tasks used by Jackson and McClelland, 1979); and (g) degree of prior learning, that is the degree of success experienced during the declarative portion of the task, or more abstractly, the strength of the declarative knowledge that serves as the foundation for procedural skill development.

We cannot claim that these factors are *sufficient* for determining learning

FOUR - SOURCES FRAMEWORK

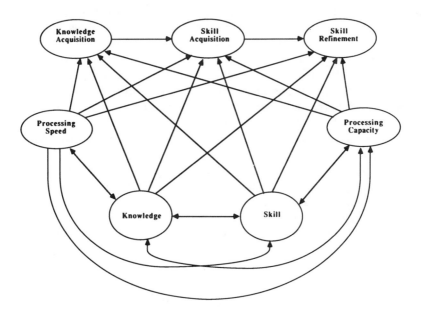

FIG. 9.2. Four-source framework for modeling the determinants of
learning success in each of the three phases of learning. At each
phase, learning success is presumed to be determined by the success
of prior learning and by proficiency in four facets of cognition: (a)
processing speed, (b) knowledge, (c) procedural skill, and (d) working
memory or processing capacity.

success, but we now have evidence over a number of studies on declarative
learning that these factors are *necessary* for determining learning success, insofar
as each can be shown to predict declarative learning uniquely. We now briefly
consider that evidence before launching into studies of the relationship between
cognitive factors and cognitive skill learning.

ROLE OF THE FOUR SOURCES
IN DECLARATIVE LEARNING

Knowledge

When we speak of the role of existing knowledge in acquiring new knowledge,
potentially we are referring to the depth, breadth, accessibility, and organization
of the knowledge possessed by an individual. In Kyllonen and Christal (1989),
we provided a detailed rationale for how each of these attributes of general

knowledge could be considered important in learning. However, in actual empirical research to date, we have investigated only the breadth attribute.

In a series of experiments (Kyllonen & Tirre, in press; Kyllonen, Tirre, & Christal, in press) with over 2,500 subjects, we have repeatedly found that breadth of knowledge is an important predictor (with correlations ranging from .23 to .54) of the success an individual experiences in acquiring new arbitrary facts. We have measured breadth of knowledge in a variety of ways: by performance on tests of (a) vocabulary, (b) general world facts (such as "Ostrich is the name of the bird that cannot fly and is the largest bird on earth, true or false?" after Nelson & Narens, 1980), and (c) general science facts (such as "Water is an example of a gas, solid, liquid, or crystal?"). Scores on these kinds of tests are typically highly intercorrelated and thus define a general knowledge factor. The learning criterion is typically some indicator of learning speed on a paired-associates or free-recall learning task.

This finding of a relationship between knowledge and learning speed seems to be particularly robust. It seems not to depend on study time (Kyllonen et al., in press), on whether the learning task consists of arbitrary pairs or whole sentences, or on whether the test is of a recognition, multiple-choice, or recall nature (Kyllonen & Tirre, in press; Kyllonen et al., in press). However, the finding thus far is limited to learning verbal (or at least pronounceable alphanumeric) stimuli.

There are a variety of ways to think about why general knowledge should predict success in acquiring new declarative facts. One is that learning paired-associates involves establishing relations between pair terms through a process of elaboration (Kyllonen et al., in press). The success of the relation establishment process depends on the amount of material, especially distinct material, available for forming elaborations. High-knowledge individuals, by definition, have more material and more distinct material available, that is, a richer network of facts and associations into which new facts and associations might be interwoven. This seems rather obvious, and might even be dismissed as trivial except for the fact that others (e.g., Underwood, Boruch, & Malmi, 1978) have failed to find a relationship between general, semantic knowledge and episodic learning success.

Skills

Skills refer to the general and domain-specific problem-solving skills, strategies, and metacognitive approaches students bring to the learning situation. In procedural learning, these may be general heuristics (e.g., if the first method fails, try a new one) and general problem-solving strategies (e.g., means–ends analysis, working backward, hill-climbing, depth- and breadth-first search through the problem space). Or they may be specific skills (strategies and heuristics) for solving specific problems, such as how to trace a complex circuit. In declarative learning, problem-solving skill is primarily knowledge of how to learn, such as mnemonic strategies.

We have not conducted an extensive investigation of the role of general skills, partly because it is not entirely obvious how to measure them directly in a context-free way. In most cases, we can only infer the possession of an extensive repository of general problem-solving procedures in an individual indirectly—by his or her performance on a novel task that requires the invocation of such procedures. But tasks with these characteristics, such as progressive matrices (Raven, 1960) or letter series, inevitably are considered primarily to reflect general intelligence. Then there is an interpretation problem: Should we attribute performance on these tasks to procedural skill proficiency or to general intelligence?

We do have evidence that some kinds of general skills are important in declarative learning. In a series of studies (Kyllonen et al., in press; Tirre, in preparation), we demonstrated the importance of a form of strategic knowledge (or procedural skill)—knowledge of mnemonics—by showing that a 5-minute lesson on elaboration boosted paired-associates learning scores by roughly 20% ($N = 500$). However, the most interesting feature of these studies was that such strategy provision actually served to increase the relationship between general knowledge and learning performance (from $r = .28$ to $r = .49$). That is, it seems that in declarative learning at least, knowledge of mnemonics is primarily a noise factor: When everyone is given the same strategic knowledge, learning's dependency on general declarative knowledge actually increases (Hughes, 1983, found a similar result). It is interesting that Anderson and Bower (1972) suggested that strategic knowledge might have been an important factor determining individual differences in associative learning. Wang (1983) apparently found evidence for the Anderson–Bower view, in that fast learners were demonstrated to naturally use more sophisticated mnemonics than slow learners. Our research suggests that although individual differences in mnemonics knowledge are important in one sense (they affect performance), they are unimportant in another—namely in that they are relatively unstable and can easily be changed with a short instructional intervention. It is obviously much more difficult to change an individual's breadth of general knowledge.

Processing Speed

A considerable literature has formed around identifying processing speed relationships with learning, particularly learning through reading text. This line of research began with Hunt and colleagues' (Hunt, Lunneborg, & Lewis, 1975) somewhat surprising finding of a correlation between lexical access time and scores on standard tests of verbal ability, such as vocabulary and paragraph comprehension. This relationship has been demonstrated in declarative learning by Jackson and McClelland (1979), who showed that reading speed (a composite of reading time and comprehension accuracy) could be almost completely accounted for by two factors: general comprehension ability and lexical access. In this and myriad replications, lexical access time is typically estimated by subjects' reaction time to recognize opposite-case letters (*A a*) or words (*CAT cat*) as matches, minus their time to recognize same-case, "physically-identical" letters (*A A*) or words (*CAT CAT*) as matches. According to the popular interpretation, only on the opposite-case task is it necessary for subjects to access long-term memory; in the physically identical case, perceptual information is sufficient for reaching a matching judgment. Thus, a subject's difference in reaction time between the name-identical and physical-identical conditions can be taken as an uncontaminated measure of long-term memory retrieval time. As long-term memory accesses are repeatedly executed during reading, those who spend less time on it have a major advantage over those who linger, not only in terms of how long it takes to get through the text, but also in terms of how much attentional resources are available for higher-level comprehension processes (Perfetti & Lesgold, 1979).

Based on our own more recent research, and that of colleagues collecting data at the LAMP facility, it seems that the role of processing speed in learning needs to be qualified somewhat. In one extensive study ($N = 240$), Tirre and Rancourt (1986) separated out the reading speed and comprehension factors that Jackson and McClelland collapsed over, and found that semantic access time (time to judge two words to be synonyms) predicted reading speed but did not uniquely contribute to reading comprehension. In Kyllonen et al. (in press), we found that semantic access time was a significant predictor of the probability of remembering a pair of words, but only when study time was short (0.5 s to 2 s per pair). Further, we were unable to replicate the finding with lexical access time. Over a number of studies, we have found that lexical access time does not uniquely contribute to a learning criterion when a semantic access time score is also included in the model (Kyllonen et al., in press). Thus, it would seem that processing speed may be an important determinant of declarative learning, but subject to at least two qualifications. First, the processing speed measure must reflect time to search long-term memory for semantic as opposed to lexical information. Second, there must either be study time stress or the criterion must be of a processing-time (e.g., reading time) nature for the relationship to emerge.

Processing Capacity

Our use of the construct of processing capacity primarily follows Baddeley (1986), who defines working memory as "the temporary storage of information that is being processed in any range of cognitive tasks" (p. 34). The key feature of this definition, as opposed to the classic definition of short-term store, has to do with the implication that performance, on any of a range of tasks involving "different processing codes and different input modalities," even those without a short-term memory component (e.g., retrieval from long-term memory), will deteriorate if the limited working memory capacity is used by a supplementary task. The implication is that we can measure working memory capacity by requiring a subject simultaneously to process and store new information.

For example, in the reading span test (Daneman & Carpenter, 1980), subjects read (i.e., process) a series of sentences and simultaneously attempt to remember (i.e., store) the last word in each one. The subject's score is the number of successive sentences that can be read (and comprehended) before the subject is no longer able to recall all the final words (typically, this is three to five sentences). Engle (1988) has generalized this method, so that the primary task can be arithmetic operations rather than reading sentences, and the secondary task can be remembering digits or words presented separately after the end of each sentence or arithmetic expression, rather than being words included in the primary sentence, as in the Daneman–Carpenter version. Engle's variants are all highly intercorrelated, suggesting the existence of a general working memory factor.

The importance of this factor in declarative learning is demonstrated in studies that show that high-scoring subjects (i.e., those with high working memory capacity) tend to comprehend text better (Daneman & Carpenter, 1980; Engle, 1988; Tirre & Rancourt, 1986), resolve ambiguous words and inconsistencies in prose passages more accurately (Daneman & Carpenter, 1983), and learn novel words set in a paragraph context more reliably (Daneman & Green, 1986). In contrast, simple memory span scores typically correlate only modestly with indicators of declarative learning success, such as reading comprehension scores.[1]

A noteworthy discovery we have made about the working memory construct over the last year or so is that it seems to be closely related to the construct of general reasoning ability. Christal and Kyllonen (in preparation) prepared a series of working memory tasks that conformed to Baddeley's definition in that they required working memory resources to be split between concurrent processing and storage of information. They also constructed a set of tasks, such as letter series, letter sets, and other measures adapted from the Educational Testing Service Kit of Reference Tests for Cognitive Factors (French, Ekstrom, & Price, 1963) that have historically been treated in the differential literature as measures of general reasoning ability. Over four independent studies, using different subjects and different measures of the working memory capacity and reasoning factors, a consistent finding was that a single-factor model could account for the interrelationships of all the measures.

There are numerous studies in the literature reporting a relationship between

---

[1]However, Engle's (1988) research has shown that simple word span predicts comprehension almost as highly as does reading span, as long as subjects are required to recall words in serial order.

reasoning ability and declarative learning (e.g., Allison, 1960; Kyllonen & Tirre, in press; Snow, Kyllonen, & Marshalek, 1984; Stake, 1961; Thurstone, 1938). The Christal–Kyllonen result, equating reasoning ability with working memory capacity, suggests that it may be working memory capacity that governs the efficiency of declarative learning.

ROLE OF THE FOUR SOURCES
IN COGNITIVE SKILL LEARNING

We have presented evidence concerning the role of the four sources—declarative knowledge, procedural skills, processing speed, and processing capacity—in declarative learning. We now consider in somewhat more detail some recently completed work on the role of the four sources in cognitive skill learning. Insofar as the first phase of skill learning is essentially declarative learning, according to the model shown in Fig. 9.1, we should expect to replicate the findings reported earlier of the role of each of the four sources. But we are mainly concerned in this section with how each of the four sources predicts the subject's ability to transform declarative knowledge to effective procedural skills that can be used in problem solving. Thus, in both of the investigations to be reported, we observe a subject in extended learning—usually from 30 to 90 minutes. We begin by teaching domain facts, such as the rules guiding the operators in the domain. Then we have the subject solve problems with these rules.

STUDY 1:
DISTINGUISHING ATTENTION CAPACITY
FROM ACTIVATION CAPACITY

The first investigation in this series was concerned primarily with the role of working memory at different stages in cognitive skill acquisition. In the discussion of declarative learning earlier, we defined the working memory construct in the sense used by Baddeley. Specifically, working memory was assumed to be severely limited (three to seven chunks) and responsible for performance deterioration when a subject is required simultaneously to store and actively process information. Woltz (1988a) refers to this as the *controlled attention capacity* conceptualization of working memory, as both the storage and processing require controlled attention operations. Woltz pointed out that there is a second definition of working memory in the psychological literature that pertains to the limitations of automatic spreading activation and decay of that activation over time. As conceptualized in this manner, working memory is assumed to be larger (20 chunks may be activated simultaneously, at least to some degree) and is limited by automatic rather than controlled cognitive operations.

To test the degree to which these two theoretical definitions match up empirically, Woltz (1988a) estimated attention capacity and activation capacity in subjects by their performance on various tasks, then correlated the two sets of measures. Two attention capacity measures were administered. In one, which he called *Digit Order,* subjects were required to remember either three (e.g., *2 8 5*) or six digits (e.g., *9 4 8 2 1 3*), then verify sentences concerning the order of the digits (e.g., "8 does not come before 2, true or false?"), then recall the digits by pressing number keys on a keyboard. Consistent with findings on similar tasks by Baddeley and Hitch (1975), Woltz found that substantial performance deterioration on the sentence verification task occurred in the 6-digit load condition, indicating consistency between the original Baddeley–Hitch definition of working memory and Woltz's operationalization of the construct.

In a second test, *ABCD Order,* subjects were required to construct an ordering of the letters *A, B, C,* and *D,* consistent with three statements constraining their order. A typical item would begin with the assertion "B follows A," followed by the statement that "Set 1 [i.e., the letters A and B] precedes Set 2 [i.e., the letters C and D]," followed by the statement that "D precedes C." The subject then would be expected to recognize the order of the four letters as "ABCD." Woltz found that performance on these two tests was highly correlated ($r = .63$).

Woltz estimated subjects' activation capacity by observing latency savings on repeated trials (i.e., time on Trial 1 minus time on Trial 2, where Trial 2 occurs 1 to 8 trials after Trial 1) of a semantic identity task requiring subjects to determine whether two words (e.g., *big, large*) were synonyms. The rationale was that latency savings reflect the degree to which activation of semantic elements is maintained over time. Consistent with this general rational, subjects did respond faster to repeated trials, and the amount of savings decreased with the number of trials intervening. Savings scores were thus considered measures of an individual's capacity to maintain activation over time. Correlations of this measure with the attention working memory measures described in the previous paragraph were zero, suggesting that activation and attention capacities represent independent working memory limitations.

Capacity Limits in Learning Sequenced, Cognitive Procedures

Given two kinds of working memory capacity, an obvious question is which one is predictive of cognitive skill acquisition? A follow-up study (Woltz, 1988b) addressed this question. The idea was to develop a task that resembled a typical operator's task in which actions are based on a series of condition evaluations. For example, the operator of a complex system, such as a power plant, has to evaluate many conditions prior to taking an action. In Woltz's version of the generic operator's task, subjects ($N = 701$) made a sequence of judgments about a number presented on a computer screen. Subjects had to determine whether the

WOLTZ' PROCEDURAL SEQUENCE TASK

(a)

If a new number is presented, determine if it is odd or even.
If the number is a odd, determine if it is big or small.
If the number is big, determine if it is at the bottom.
If the number is at the bottom, press L, else press D
If the number is small, determine if it is at the top.
If the number is at the top, press L, else press D.
If the number is even, determine if it is a digit or word.
If the number is a digit, determine if it is at the bottom.
If the number is at the bottom, press L, else press D.
If the number is a word, determine if it is at the top.
If the number is at the top, press L, else press D.

(b)

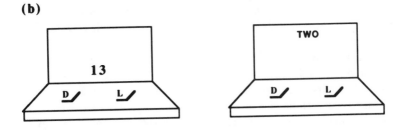

11 blocks @ 64 trials per block

FIG. 9.3. Woltz's procedural sequence task. Subjects were presented with screen displays such as those shown in (b) and were required to evaluate the presented stimulus according to the rules shown in (a).

number was big (11–20) or small (1–10), even or odd, alphabetic or numeric, and whether it appeared at the top or the bottom of the screen, and then respond according to rules such as those listed in Fig. 9.3a. Fig. 9.3b illustrates a typical trial.

With respect to our model of skill learning, this task requires that subjects learn how the operators *big, even, position,* and *alphanumeric-type* worked, in the sense of (a) learning how to determine whether a number is big, even, etc., and (b) learning which judgment to make about a number next, given that a judgment regarding one of its properties has just been made. We assume that subjects come to the experimental session with at least a declarative understanding of the operators—that is, they know what it means for a number to be even or big or written in alpha or numeric form. Proceduralizing this knowledge is probably fairly trivial, amounting to simply a slight modification of already well-known concepts to suit the demands of this experiment (e.g., to proceduralize the fact that in this experiment *big* means greater than 10). We assume that much of this proceduralization takes place during the early learning trials.

Perhaps the more important learning skill tapped by this task, and one that becomes particularly important on the later trials, is composition. Subjects learn which order operators are applied, then these sequences are composed into larger production rules. Subjects learn to apply the evenness operator followed by the alpha operator and the bigness operator, for example. Composition efficiency is thus what will primarily be reflected in various measures of performance over trials, particularly later trials after proceduralization is more or less complete.

Cognitive Proficiency Measures

Subjects were also administered four sets of tasks designed to tap different cognitive proficiencies. *Verbal knowledge* was indicated by performance on a standard vocabulary test. *Attention capacity* was measured with two tasks: (a) the *ABCD Order* task used in the previous study, and (b) an *Alphabet Recoding* task, which required subjects to memorize a three-letter string (e.g., *M F Q*) then transform the string by adding or subtracting a value to each of the letter's alphabetical ordinal value to obtain a new set of letters, for example, *M F Q + 3 = P I T*. *Activation capacity* was measured as latency savings on repeated trials of semantic-identity judgments, as in the previous study. A fourth construct, *component efficiency*, was indicated by response time to one-operator judgments about numbers (e.g., Big–12, true or false; Even–10, true or false).

Results and Discussion

Over the 11 trial blocks (64 trials each), subjects made the number judgments with increasing speed and accuracy, and both log latency and log errors were linearly related to log trial number, consistent with the power law of practice (Newell & Rosenbloom, 1981). This was an important finding in that production composition is assumed to be responsible for power law improvement (Lewis, 1978). Thus, it can be claimed that the data from this task were consistent with what would be expected if composition were taking place. (See Woltz, 1988b, for a detailed explanation of the likely nature of composition on the number judgment task.)

More importantly, for the present discussion, is the pattern of changing relationships between the cognitive proficiency measures and performance on the successive trial blocks, which are shown in Table 9.1 for the condition in which subjects become most proficient in the skill ($N = 330$). Consider first the results for the accuracy measure. Accuracy in early trials was determined jointly by verbal knowledge ($r = .25$) and attention capacity ($r = .44$), but the dependency of performance on these two factors diminished with experience on the task (to $r = .10$ and $r = .22$, respectively). Neither component efficiency nor activation capacity predicted task accuracy at any point in learning. Results for latency provide a different picture. The dependency of task latency on component effi-

TABLE 9.1
Aptitude–Learning Correlations by Trial Block (N = 330)

Aptitude	Trial Block										
	1	2	3	4	5	6	7	8	9	10	11
	Learning Task Accuracy										
Verbal Knowledge	.25	.21	.15	.18	.21	.19	.15	.12	.15	.17	.10
Component Efficiency	-.09	-.14	-.10	-.08	-.06	-.04	-.03	.00	-.03	-.03	.01
Attention Capacity	.44	.41	.37	.39	.37	.36	.34	.29	.29	.29	.22
Activation Capacity	-.03	-.09	-.03	-.05	.01	.04	-.03	-.03	-.03	.01	-.02
	Learning Task Latency										
Verbal Knowledge	-.04	-.18	-.18	-.15	-.14	-.14	-.13	-.13	-.11	-.10	-.11
Component Efficiency	.23	.22	.36	.39	.40	.46	.48	.46	.50	.47	.55
Attention Capacity	-.01	-.14	-.19	-.21	-.26	-.25	-.21	-.22	-.23	-.24	-.18
Activation Capacity	.05	.08	.15	.19	.17	.15	.17	.19	.21	.21	.27

Note. Correlations were significant at $r > .13$ ($p < .05$, 2-tailed).
Source: Woltz, 1988b.

256

ciency and on activation capacity steadily increases from the early trial blocks (r = .23 for component efficiency; r = .05 for activation capacity) to the later ones (r = .55; r = .27, respectively). Attention capacity and verbal knowledge, on the other hand, play their most important role during the middle blocks.

These findings are consistent with the idea that attention capacity and verbal knowledge are what govern the rate at which initial declarative rule acquisition and proceduralization occur. During these initial stages of learning, performance requires active maintenance and processing of declarative knowledge of the sequential steps. Later performance, dominated by production composition, depends more on component procedure efficiency and activation capacity. Here, performance no longer requires the interpretation of declarative knowledge; rather, it depends on the availability or activation of many large, composed productions.

This differential pattern points up the importance of the distinction between attention and activation capacity, which are separable working memory capacity limits. The attention capacity limit pertains to the amount of information that can simultaneously be processed or attended to. This limit apparently governs success in proceduralizing new knowledge. The second limit, activation capacity, corresponds to the temporal nature of the process of automatic spread and decay of activation. Individual differences in this limit, which are reflected in how long one can keep material active in working memory without rehearsal, determine relative success in composing and strengthening new rules.[2]

At one level, Woltz's (1988b) findings are consistent with those of Fleishman and Hempel (1954) and Ackerman (1987), who found that general cognitive abilities are most important in early skill acquisition. Ackerman (1987, 1988) interpreted these patterns in terms of a learning model that suggests that early learning should depend on general abilities and that later learning should be less dependent on general abilities and more dependent on perceptual and motor skills. But Woltz's results diverge from those of these other investigators in that activation capacity, which should be seen as a general cognitive ability in that it affects performance on a wide range of tasks, had increasing relations to performance as practice continued.

STUDY 2:
ACQUISITION OF SKILL: LOGIC GATES

The Woltz (1988b) study was intriguing in showing an apparent dissociation between attention and activation capacity in predicting early versus later success

---

[2]An alternative explanation is that Woltz's activation capacity measure is a measure of strength accrued by a memory trace from a single retrieval. Woltz (1989) has evidence that this may be correct.

in acquiring a cognitive skill. Our goals for the second investigation (Kyllonen, Stephens, & Woltz, 1988) were two-fold. First, we wished to investigate skill acquisition on a learning task where proceduralization is an important learning process, that is, one in which subjects are taught rules for operators they have not been exposed to prior to the experiment. This provides somewhat of a contrast to Woltz's learning task in which proceduralization is mostly complete after some initial trials and in which composition is probably therefore the main learning skill being called upon. Second, we wished to include additional measures of cognitive proficiency drawn from the four-source framework, so that we could more precisely evaluate the importance of working memory (activation and attention capacity) as opposed to other cognitive factors in determining skill acquisition success.

Fortunately, a study recently conducted by Gitomer (1984) suggested an ideal learning task for our purposes: the logic-gates task. In Gitomer's paper-and-pencil version of this task, subjects determine how various logic gates (such as AND, OR, etc.) transform incoming signals (e.g., High and Low) to an outgoing value (High or Low). Gitomer administered this task along with a battery of other tests designed to probe other facets of troubleshooting skill, such as tests of electronics component knowledge and retrieval efficiency, to a group of experienced U.S. Air Force electronics equipment troubleshooters. Although the study was rather small-scale ($N = 13$), performance on the logic-gates task was shown to be significantly related to troubleshooting proficiency as indicated by supervisor ratings. Further, no other task administered by Gitomer was as discriminating in its relationship to rated expertise. This encouraged us that logic gates was an ecologically valid performance task and that an analysis of the determinants of success in learning logic gates might yield insights into an important class of learning.

Fig. 9.4 illustrates the sequence of events undergone by the $N = 200$ subjects participating in the Kyllonen et al. (1988) study, along with descriptive statistics for each event.[3] First, subjects were given a paired-associates learning task (the *associative pretest*), in which they learned to associate gate names (e.g., AND, OR XOR, INVERT) with pictures of the gates. After achieving a criterion of three successive successful responses, subjects were given 10 to 15 minutes of instruction on how the logic gates worked, that is, the rules by which incoming signals were transformed to an outgoing signal. Fig. 9.5 presents a synopsis of the instructions we provided in the form of a cheat sheet subjects were allowed to use during the instruction period.

Following instructions, subjects were given a *declarative matching test,* in which they were shown either a name-symbol, name-function, or symbol-function pair (exactly as shown on the cheat sheet) and were required to indicate

---

[3]In this chapter, we are reviewing data from only one of four studies reported in Kyllonen et al. (1988). due to space limitations.

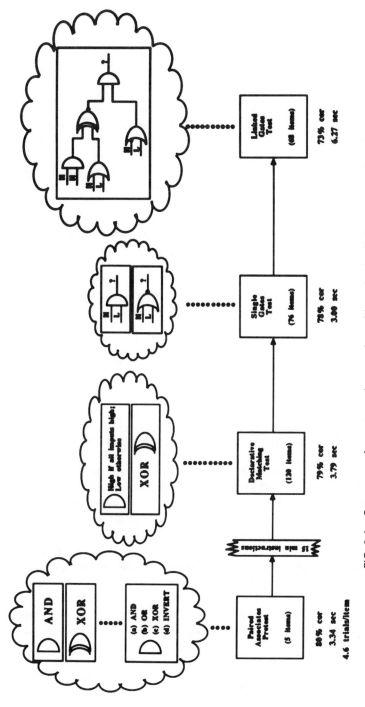

FIG. 9.4. Sequence of events undergone by subjects in the Kyllonen et al. (1988) study. Sample items are presented in the cloud. Descriptive statistics are presented below the test-name box.

259

LOGIC GATES

SYMBOL	NAME	FUNCTION
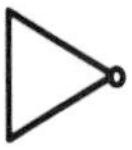 ▷o	INVERT	High if incoming signal is low; Low if incoming signal is high.
 D	AND	High if all incoming signals are high; Low otherwise.
 D)	OR	High if at least one incoming signal is high; Low otherwise.
 D)	XOR	High if only one incoming signal is high; Low otherwise.
o	CHANGE	Changes high to low; and low to high.

FIG. 9.5. Cheat sheet given to subjects during the instruction phase of the Kyllonen et al. (1988) study. Symbols, names, and function descriptions were also used in the paired-associates pretest and the declarative matching test in various combinations as test stimuli.

whether the two paired entities referred to the same logic gate. Following this declarative test, subjects were given a *single-gate procedural test,* in which they were shown signals coming into logic gates (e.g., a High and Low signal coming into an AND gate) and were required to indicate the value (either high or low) of the resulting outgoing signal. Following this, subjects were given a *whole-circuit* or *linked-gates test,* which required them to evaluate a sequence of linked gates. Then subjects were administered a symbol-name matching test. We assumed that by this point, given all the practice they had received, subjects would have known the symbol-name relationships quite well, and thus response time would reflect the degree to which memory strength for these pairs had accrued automatically as a function of practice.

Cognitive Proficiency Measures

We administered five sets of tests to measure five cognitive factors: general knowledge, processing speed, working memory attention capacity, activation capacity, and proceduralization efficiency. *General knowledge* measures were a standard vocabulary test, a survey of general science facts (e.g., "The chief nutrient in lean meat is [a] fat, [b] starch, [c] protein, or [d] carbohydrates?") taken from the Armed Services Vocational Aptitude Battery, and a survey of general world knowledge (e.g., "Photosynthesis is the process by which plants make food from sunlight, true or false?") adapted from Nelson and Narens (1980).

Processing speed measures were (a) a choice reaction time task, (b) a synonym-matching task, in which each word used was determined in a pilot study to be such that 95% of the sample could properly identify its synonym, and (c) a word string (e.g., triangle square circle) and picture string (e.g., pictures of triangles, squares, and circles) matching task adapted from Santa (1977).

We administered two *working memory attention capacity* measures. The first was a computerized adaptation of Daneman and Carpenter's (1980) *reading span test*. Subjects read a set of unrelated, successively presented 10–15-word sentences. The number of sentences in a set ranged from two to six. After completing the set, subjects typed in the first letter (so as to minimize the importance of typing ability) of the last word in each sentence. To ensure semantic processing of the sentences as they were presented, subjects were required to verify whether the sentences presented were true or not. Half the sentences were declarative versions of the Nelson–Narens general world knowledge questions, and half were falsified versions of those sentences (e.g., "Stockholm is the capital of Norway, true or false?"). In fact, these sentences were the same as those used to produce a measure of general knowledge (see earlier discussion). The subject's working memory score was simply the proportion of last word-first letters correctly typed in.

The second working memory capacity measure was *ABC assignment*, which had been found to produce reliable scores in a previous study (Christal, 1987). In this task, subjects are presented a series of frames in which either numerical values or simple equations are assigned to the letters *A, B,* and *C*. A typical item might present the following frames one at a time (subjects were not allowed to move backwards): "A = B/2" "C = B + A" "B = 4" "B = ?" "A = ?" "C = ?" This task stresses working memory in that subjects must simultaneously remember the assignments of previous frames and process the current frame. In addition to these two working memory capacity measures, which tap the attention capacity attribute of working memory, we also administered Woltz's (1988a, 1988b) latency savings task to measure activation capacity.

We also administered two *procedural skill* tests, designed to measure the efficiency with which subjects were able to transform simple declarative rules into problem-solving procedures. The first task, based on Thurstone and Thurstone's (1941) *ABC task*, required subjects to transform a five-letter string consisting only of the letters *A, B,* and *C* (e.g., *ABACC*) according to two rules. The first rule is that successive same letters evaluate to the same letter (e.g., *AA = A; BB = B*). The second rule is that successive different letters evaluate to the third letter (e.g., $AB = C; CB = A$). Working from left to right, one evaluates the first pair, then takes the result as the first letter of the second pair until a final letter is determined.

The second task, adapted from Harvey (1984) and dubbed the *HI-LO* task, required subjects to match a cue letter (either X or O), with a spatial position probe (either the word *HI* or the word *LO*). The cue letter appeared on the left side of the display screen, either toward the top ("high") or the bottom ("low"). The probe appeared on the right side of the display screen, either toward the top or the bottom. The cue signaled the rule by which subjects were to make the cue-probe matching judgment. If the cue letter were X, then subjects were to "match by position." That is, an X in the top position, flanked by either probe in the top position, was considered a match; but an X in the top position flanked by either probe in the bottom position was considered a mismatch. An X in the bottom position was considered to match either probe appearing in the bottom position. The cue letter O, on the other hand, signaled subjects to "match by meaning." That is, an O in the top position matched the word *HI* regardless of whether it appeared in the top or bottom position. An O in the bottom position matched the word *LO* regardless of whether it appeared in the top or bottom position. (The letter-rule mappings were reversed for half the subjects.) Although Harvey was able to train subjects to the point where they made few errors, we found in pilot work that considerable variance in accuracy occurred over the 100 trials administered.

Results

We constructed a number of latent variable path models representing various hypotheses regarding the relationships among the variables and the hypothetical factors measured in this study. In all the models, dependent variables were accuracy measures from the various phases of the learning task, the (a) associative pretest, (b) the declarative matching test, (c) the single-gates test, and (d) the whole-circuit test. Independent variables were both (a) factors reflecting performance on the cognitive proficiency measures, and (b) accuracy scores from the previously completed learning phase(s). Models were tested against the variance-covariance matrix of all learning and cognitive task scores (from a reduced sample, $N = 144$, which had scores on all measures) using Bentler's (1985) EQS computer program. This program fits latent variable path models using full information maximum likelihood procedures to estimate model parameters.

Three issues deserve brief mention before considering results. First, accuracy measures on both learning and cognitive proficiency tasks were typically d′ either computed as z (Hit)−z (False Alarm) or by the Hacker–Ratcliff (1981) forced-choice conversion tables. Although in Kyllonen et al. (1988) we provide a theoretical rationale for why d′ is the preferred measure, for present purposes it is useful simply to point out that for most of our tasks, d′ is usually normally distributed (even on the choice-reaction time task, which averages 95% accuracy), whereas percentage correct usually is not. Second, log latency was typically the latency measure we used. This simply represents a transformation of convenience (log latency is more normally distributed than latency, almost always), without a theoretical rationale. Finally, a reparameterization of accuracy and latency scores from the information-processing speed tasks was accomplished as an attempt to deal with speed–accuracy trade-off problems. (In none of these tasks did accuracy correlate significantly with speed over subjects.) A processing efficiency score was the difference between standardized (0, 1) d' and standardized log latency for each task. A processing carefulness score was the sum of the standardized d' and standardized log latency. This reparameterization was shown in a factor analysis to result in more interpretable processing speed factors. Third, percentage correct was chosen as the learning measure on the paired-associates pretest because it is known to be a good estimator of memory strength as indicated by probability of passing on a hypothetical next trial (Underwood, 1964).

Fig. 9.6 shows the best-fitting model and its associated parameter estimates. In this model, the four learning phase scores, from the associative pretest through the whole-circuit test, are ordered as a simplex, reflecting their temporal relationship and reflecting the hypothesis that performance in each learning phase serves as a determinant of subsequent learning success. In the model, these four learning scores are treated as observed, dependent (i.e., endogenous) variables (EQS allows free mixing of observed and latent variables in models). The four scores, in turn, are each regressed on the preceding learning event (except for the associative pretest, which was the first learning event) and four cognitive factors—general knowledge, working memory attention capacity, processing speed, and proceduralization skill. The activation capacity factor is not shown in the Figure, because it was found to be uncorrelated with any of the learning variables, and including it in the model resulted in poorer model fits.

Considering first results from the paired-associates pretest, the cognitive proficiency factors accounted for 26% of the variance on this measure, which is roughly consistent with results we have obtained with other paired-associates tasks (Kyllonen et al., in press; Kyllonen & Tirre, in press). The fact that working memory capacity was the factor predicting associative learning success is consistent with previous work and is consistent with our claim earlier in the context of Woltz's study, that the initial declarative phase of cognitive skill learning is dependent on attention capacity. However, contrary to past research, no other cognitive measure contributed to the prediction of associative learning success. In previous work (Kyllonen et al., in press; Kyllonen & Tirre, in press), breadth of general knowledge added to the working memory factor in predicting declarative learning. It is informative to consider the difference between that previous work and the current study. In this study, the items paired were a name and a symbol: This pairing may have tapped nonsemantic spatial encoding mechanisms and thereby reduced the dependence on semantic knowledge. Had we

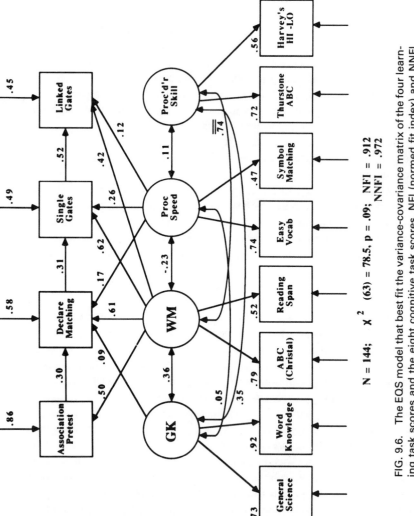

FIG. 9.6. The EQS model that best fit the variance-covariance matrix of the four learning task scores and the eight cognitive task scores. NFI (normed fit index) and NNFI (nonnormed fit index) are goodness-of-fit statistics produced by the program. Bentler suggests that values greater than .90 represent "adequate" fits.

$N = 144; \quad \chi^2 \ (63) = 78.5, \ p = .09; \quad NFI = .912$
$NNFI = .972$

264

administered a test of spatial declarative knowledge (if such a factor could be defined), we might have expected such a factor to predict success in the kind of associative learning task we administered in this study.

The declarative matching task was designed to reflect the strength (d' accuracy) of subjects' declarative knowledge following study. Subjects performed considerably less than perfectly on this task ($M = 21\%$ errors), reflecting the fact that subjects exited text instruction with only partial declarative knowledge of the gates. Fig. 9.6 shows that 66% of individual differences variance in that knowledge ($1-.582$) was accounted for by all factors combined, with accuracy on the immediately preceding paired-associates task accounting uniquely for 9% of the variance. This latter correlation reflects the role of domain-specific knowledge gained as a result of the initial exposure to the symbol-name relationships. Controlling for that domain-specific knowledge, other general cognitive factors contributed to the prediction of how well subjects learned from instruction after they had received initial exposure to the pairs. Specifically, general knowledge ($r = .09$), working memory capacity ($r = .61$), and processing speed ($r = .17$) each uniquely contributed to the prediction of accuracy in declarative matching. Thus, each of these cognitive factors is a partial determinant of the declarative knowledge a subject acquires as a result of studying a short lesson in a text. It is probably theoretically significant that more cognitive factors are relevant in determining learning of actual text than in determining learning of arbitrary associated pairs. It is also noteworthy that of all the factors, working memory capacity again played the most important role in determining learning.

After declarative matching, the single-gate task was administered prior to the whole-circuit task and was the first chance subjects had to demonstrate procedural skill in tracing signals over logic gates. Mean error rate on this task was 22% (chance was 50%). As can be seen in Fig. 9.6, 76% of the variance in accuracy on the single gates test was predicted by the factors in the model. Of that, 10% was due to the strength of individuals' declarative knowledge going into the procedural test, and the remaining 66% was due to the general cognitive factors, holding declarative knowledge constant. Thus, there was an excellent accounting of performance on this task, and the cognitive proficiency measures alone accounted for an overwhelming share of the variance in signal tracing performance. Further, the single factor of working memory capacity ($r = .62$) was responsible for most of the prediction. The single order correlations are informative. The correlation between signal-tracing accuracy and accuracy on the ABC Assignment task, for example was .69, a remarkably high correlation between a general cognitive measure and a learning outcome measure.

Following the single-gate task, subjects were administered the whole-circuit task, which differed only in that each item required a series of responses rather than a single response (subjects were given feedback after each response so that there was no response dependency within an item). As shown in Fig. 9.6, 80% of the variance in accuracy on the whole-circuit task was accounted for by all the cognitive factors. Of these, the most important factor was accuracy on the single-gate task, which accounted for 27% of the variance (the single-order correlation suggested an even stronger relationship between the two tasks, $r = .84$). Given this strong relationship, it is somewhat interesting that what uniqueness the whole-circuit task possessed was related to, again, working memory capacity ($r = .42$) and processing speed ($r = .12$). That is, controlling for the strength of procedural gate knowledge, as indicated by performance on the single-gate task, working memory, in particular, still was an important determinant of success in the whole-circuit task. The whole-circuit task probably places more working memory demands on the subject than does the single-gate task, in that subjects must additionally keep track of where they are on the circuit. Thus, performance on the whole-circuit task, controlling for procedural gate knowledge, reflects the subject's ability to deal with that extra load.

Finally, it is worth inspecting the intercorrelations among the factors. For the most part, correlations are in the modest range, but there are two that stand out. One is the negative correlation between processing speed and working memory capacity ($r = -.22$). Processing speed is the inverse of latency, and so we expected the correlation to be positive. We have administered these measures in other studies and generally do find a positive correlation between these two factors, and so we might dismiss this result as anomalous.

A more striking finding is the high correlation between working memory and proceduralization skill ($r = .74$). Recall that we designed the proceduralization factor to reflect the breadth of general procedural skills a subject brings to the testing or learning situation. Because we cannot measure procedural skill directly, we do so indirectly by having the subject learn new rules and apply those rules in problem solving. Put another way, the proceduralization factor reflects proceduralization skill directly (i.e., the ability to proceduralize novel declarative rules) and the breadth of procedural knowledge indirectly. That this factor correlates highly with working memory capacity can be interpreted in at least two ways. First, working memory capacity may largely be a function of the sophistication of the central executive, in Baddeley's (1986) model. Subjects with a good store of general-purpose procedural skills have an advantage in monitoring and controlling working memory resources and therefore do well both on the proceduralization tests and on tests of working memory capacity. Another interpretation is that the success of the proceduralization process, which is indicated by performance on the proceduralization factor tests, depends on one's working memory capacity. This interpretation is consistent with our discussion of Woltz's (1988b) finding that working memory capacity governs proceduralization success.

Summary and Discussion

The results just presented appear at first glance rather complicated, and so it is useful to step back and consider the major findings. First, perhaps the most consistent and striking finding is the role played by working memory capacity (in the attention capacity sense) in determining all phases of learning success. Working memory capacity was shown to predict performance in the initial declarative stages following study of the pairs and study of the text. Following this, controlling for how well subjects acquired that initially taught declarative knowledge, working memory capacity played an additional role in determining a subject's success in transforming that knowledge into effective problem-solving procedures that could be applied to the task of tracing signals over logic gates. Beyond this, working memory capacity predicted the success of the transfer of procedural knowledge from the single-gate to the whole-circuit problems.

Second, activation capacity did not exert the same kind of influence on performance as it did in the Woltz (1988b) study. In various models we tested, model fit was always improved by leaving the activation capacity factor out of the model. This suggests that the role of activation capacity might be confined to composition as we suggested earlier.

Finally, the data suggest that acquiring skill on a task like the logic-gates task is not appropriately characterized as a continuous process of knowledge incrementing. If it had been, we would have found two results that did not materialize. First, we would have found that performance on one phase of the task was highly predictive of performance on the next phase. This clearly did not happen, as can be seen by comparing the magnitude of the contribution of prior test performance with the contribution of the general cognitive factors. In no instance did prior performance account for even half the total variance accounted for, suggesting a discontinuity in learning. Second, we would not have found the changing pattern of relationships between cognitive proficiency measures and learning performance variables actually observed. Specifically, although working memory capacity affected learning at all phases, declarative knowledge only influenced learning of the text, and processing speed modestly affected learning during all but the initial stage of learning. Together, the pattern of changing relationships with cognitive variables over learning phases, and the discontinuities in phase-to-phase performance, reinforce the view that cognitive skill learning has a multidimensional character (cf. Cronbach & Snow, 1977).

CONCLUSIONS

It is useful at this point to reflect on what we have learned about the acquisition of cognitive skill. First, perhaps a rather obvious point is that cognitive skill learning is not the same as declarative learning. Much of our work over the last several years has been concerned with identifying determinants of declarative learning as evidenced by the extensive data we cited in motivating the four-sources framework. But the limitations of this focus are particularly clear when we see that despite the fact that declarative learning can be a necessary first step in establishing the foundation for learning a procedure, success in the declarative portion of a skill-learning task is not highly predictive of success in subsequent procedural portions of that task.

A second point is that working memory capacity, in the attention capacity sense, plays a key role in governing the success of skill acquisition at virtually all phases of skill acquisition. This was certainly true in the Kyllonen et al. (1988) study, but even on Woltz's (1988b) procedural task, the relationship between working memory capacity and performance, while declining over trial blocks, still was substantial toward the end of session. One may reach the point in learning where working memory capacity plays only a minimal role, but our data suggest that that point, if reached at all, occurs well into learning, after subjects stop making errors. Our individual differences analyses of the critical role of working memory capacity in cognitive skill acquisition can be seen as validating conclusions drawn by others who have used alternative methodologies (e.g., Anderson & Jeffries, 1985).

Third, beyond the role of working memory generally, Woltz's (1988a, b) proposal for two kinds of working memory limits allows a more refined statement regarding the role of working memory in cognitive skill acquisition. The main finding in Kyllonen et al. (1988) was that one of those limits, attention capacity, predicted learning success in all phases of learning, and the other limit, activation capacity, was unrelated to learning. In contrast, Woltz (1988b) concluded that attention capacity was most important early in learning and that activation capacity was increasingly important with practice.

A reason for this discrepancy may be that the two studies tapped different kinds of learning. We claimed that Woltz's (1988b) sequenced-cognitive-procedures task, although it required some proceduralization initially as subjects first learned the categorization rules, primarily entailed composition, especially during the later phases of learning. Composition, which combines temporally contiguous productions, is a learning process governed by the temporal flow of information through working memory. Thus, it makes sense that a variable that reflects how long items stay active in working memory, namely, Woltz's activation capacity measure, predicts the success of this process. In contrast, the logic-gates task used in the Kyllonen et al. (1988) study was claimed to involve primarily the proceduralization of initially declarative rules. There may not have been any opportunity for composition (though see footnote 2).

To summarize, attention capacity refers to how much information can be held in working memory at one time; activation capacity refers to how long activation can be maintained. The success of learning by proceduralization therefore depends on *how much* information one can hold in working memory at a time; the success of learning by composition depends on *how long* one can maintain an item in working memory.

At the beginning of this chapter, we proposed that acquiring cognitive skill involved learning how operators worked and learning when to apply them. From this standpoint, the Kyllonen et al. study was concerned primarily with analyzing the cognitive abilities associated with learning how operators worked. It is likely that many of the problems students have with acquiring cognitive skills begin with a failure to understand how the basic operators in the skill domain actually work, and thus we believe there is a significant payoff simply to analyze this part of the skill acquisition process. As evidence, consider that Gitomer (1984) found wide differences among electronics equipment specialists in basic understanding of logic gates, despite the fact that these individuals had been servicing electronics equipment out in the field for at least a year.

But perhaps learning how to select operators in solving problems is an even more important cognitive skill. The difficulty of selecting operators is certainly what makes tasks such as solving geometry proof problems, writing computer programs, designing electrical circuits, and solving physics problems so demanding, especially compared to the parallel tasks of recognizing a good proof, double-checking an already written program, and tracing a signal through an already designed circuit. The Woltz (1988b) study can be seen as an initial attempt to understand this part of cognitive skill acquisition. But there might be fundamental differences between learning when to apply operators (a) in the sense of learning a sequence of procedures as in the Woltz task versus (b) in the context of these more complex operator selection tasks, such as geometry proof construction. Analysis of skill acquisition in these tasks is an obvious next step in our research programs.

Finally, it is useful to consider the merits of the four-sources framework that has guided our research in cognitive task selection. The four-source framework is meant to serve as a first-cut approximation to a fundamental factor model of the cognitive ability space. That is, we believe that individuals differ fundamentally in processing speed, working memory capacity (attention and activation capacity), declarative knowledge, and procedural skills. Although fine-grained distinctions may be made within each of these categories, it is useful to see how far this approach can carry us in predicting success in a variety of learning tasks. We have demonstrated that these sources make independent contributions in determining a variety of learning outcomes, and together account for much of the individual variability in learning success. The challenge now is to determine whether other sources not currently included in the framework might make important contributions to important classes of learning.

OPEN DISCUSSION

The discussion following Kyllonen's talk covered many issues. Several methodological and substantive observations were offered concerning the path diagrams shown during the talk. Further discussion concerned the nature of the logic-gates task, the nature of score distributions and transformations, and the nature and operationalization of the working memory construct. Finally, the participants discussed the separation of inductive and deductive reasoning components, and the relationship between working memory and reasoning.

Gustafsson: If your conclusions about the relations between working memory and *Gf* are correct, which I think they are, does that imply that your path models are not correct? That is, should working memory be lifted above the other latent variables? Doing this suggests that you would obtain stronger coefficients relating to your learning measures.

Kyllonen: Yes, I agree with you entirely. That is why I was so excited about reading your paper, because I want to redo these analyses. One of the surprising things in our data is that this procedural skill variable [see Fig. 9.6] did not have any sort of predictive relationship to any task measures. It may be that the procedural skill component is highly correlated with working memory capacity. Your approach would help me resolve the problem that procedural skill is not as correlated with any of these other measures as is working memory capacity. By doing the Gustafsson hierarchical decomposition, I think we may be able to see some of those kinds of relationships. I think that would be a very good idea. And now that you have given your paper, I think I know how to do it.

Kazén-Saad: What is the relationship between general knowledge and processing speed?

Kyllonen: General knowledge and processing speed, $r = .05$.

Kazén-Saad: Anderson suggests that it takes longer to search a richer semantic network. Should we expect that the correlations become different? Maybe the lack of relationship in your study . . .

Kyllonen: Actually, this is the positive correlation of a processing speed. I should have said this is a latency factor. The more knowledge you have, the longer you search through the network. It is true, however, that is it not much of a relationship.

Kazén-Saad: That is what I am asking.

Kyllonen: Let's put it this way—it's not inconsistent with that idea. Actually, we did investigate that directly in one study, although I did not go into details of the study here. It's one of the studies I showed when we looked at long-term memory retrieval time and knowledge. Maybe we should talk about that later because it gets a little involved.

Sager: You indicated that performance on the paired-associate tasks had to do with how many facts the individual had available in long-term memory. Would that imply some correlation between crystallized intelligence and performance on those tasks even when the symbols you are associating are very simple (i.e., it wouldn't take very much crystallized intelligence to understand what they were)?

Kyllonen: Are you referring to the fact that we do not find a relationship here?

Sager: Yes.

Kyllonen: Well, I agree that it is troubling.

Sager: To support your argument, I think you would have to show that.

Kyllonen: Right. But I think what we are measuring with this general knowledge [test] is really knowledge of verbal facts—general science and word knowledge is the way we did it here. It is not really general knowledge—it is general verbal knowledge. It would be interesting to think of a way to get at how much spatial knowledge an individual has available. I don't know what you could do. Perhaps you could show people diagrams or something and ask them to compare it.

Sager: Well, to make your argument strong, I think you would need to find some variable that loads very highly on crystallized intelligence, but at the same time is strongly correlated with performance on the paired-associates tasks.

Kyllonen: Well, that happens frequently. We have lots of studies that show that performance on these kinds of tasks is highly predictive of performance on a lot of different associative memory tasks.

Sager: Even when the elements are very simple ones?

Kyllonen: When there are consonant-vowel-consonant trigrams paired with words or when there are surnames paired with two-digit numbers, we find a strong relationship between amount of general knowledge and how well one does in that kind of situation. But I think that the characteristics of that situation (i.e., memorizing consonant-vowel-consonant trigrams and word pairs) are such that success is dependent on the individual's ability to create interesting elaborations of those two things being hooked up. However, I do not think that is true in the logic-gates paired-associates task. Success in doing the logic-gates paired-associates task is a matter of determining, or parsing, the picture (i.e., the spatial gate). For example, the individual needs to say, "this is a vertical line with a curved line next to it." I think that represents a very different sort of skill than the elaboration skill involved in verbal learning.

[*Editor's note: The following discussion concerned Fig. 9.6 in the Kyllonen and Woltz chapter.*]

Cudeck: The way you have superimposed the factor analysis on the bottom and the simplex on the top presents an interesting solution for how to handle those two kinds of data. I like the way you have done that . . .

Kyllonen: Thank you.

Cudeck: That's okay. I also have a more substantive question. The simplex part may be viewed as a kind of causal model. Do you think the association between the simplex part and the factor part would be different if you had considered that as a multivariate regression with four dependent variables without a structure?

Kyllonen: Yes, sure.

Cudeck: Then I wonder, do you consider that simplex part a highly causal structure, is it a regression structure, or what?

Kyllonen: That is a very good question. I don't like how I have done this. What I did was to estimate the whole model with full information maximum likelihood. What I should have done, and actually did do, but it changes things around a bit, was to fit this model [the learning tasks] first, *then* fix those loadings, and maybe then do the factor model, and then fix those loadings, and then look at the relationship.

Cudeck: I don't know what I would recommend you do differently than you have done. I just think it is very interesting. I just wondered how you considered the simplex part because, as you can tell by the coefficients, it is a beautifully fitted simplex that does everything the textbooks want for the simplex. But, do you consider the associations among those four dependent variables as highly causal or just more or less predictive . . .

Kyllonen: Yes, highly causal. That is a major part of the argument that performance on the single-gates task (i.e., this procedural component) is dependent on your performance on the declarative knowledge portion (the Declarative Matching pretest). An interesting thing in this regard comes from comparing my study with a study Ray Christal did a few weeks ago. In his study, he gave subjects 9 blocks or 11 blocks of 70 items each. He found that people asymptoted at 78 percent. But it took them four blocks to get there—four blocks of practicing these things. In my study, I gave 72 simple items and subjects got 78 percent correct. It appears that by giving subjects declarative knowledge, I am teaching them the procedural component by giving them the declarative component. In contrast, Ray had subjects get the procedural component on their own. I think that by comparing my study with Ray's there is strong evidence that subjects would not have done as well if that would have been the first time they performed those items; this fits closely with the causal notions I mentioned.

Cudeck: I have one other question. With respect to your four-variable simplex, are those observed score distributions slightly skewed?

Kyllonen: Are they skewed? Do you mean the observed score distributions? No. What I have done, in all cases, is to find a transformation that will give me a symmetric distribution. This may be cheating, but I do try to come up with a theoretical rationale for the transformation.

Cudeck: That's OK. This is not a confessional. But if you had not transformed the data, would they have been skewed compared to the paper-and-pencil test data which may not have been skewed?

Kylloyen: This one [the Declarative Matching pretest] will not be. It is normally distributed with percent correct. But these three [Paired Associates, Single Gates, and Complex Circuits] are skewed.

Mulder: How sure are you that there is a single good measure of working memory capacity? Or do you think that all of these measures still have some domain-specific content?

Kyllonen: Yes, I do think the measures still have some domain-specific content. For example, take the reading span measure, which is an adaptation of the Daneman–Carpenter measure. Again, I think I could improve the model fit slightly by allowing this a loading on the general knowledge factor. That is why I really do not like this measure—it is not a good, clean measure of working memory capacity. This is fairly obvious by looking at the measure. If you are reading through some text and you have lots of general knowledge that enables you to read the text easily, you are not exerting much cognitive effort. Then you have plenty of cognitive capacity available for remembering the last word. So it is a contaminated measure. In contrast, the ABC task is not.

[*Editor's note: The following discussion concerned a Figure that does not appear in the final version of the Kyllonen and Woltz chapter. The figure has been reproduced here in light of the discussion about these data.*]

van den Broek: I have a question on the finding of the year [see Fig. 9.7].

Kyllonen: Yes, that is the finding of the year.

van den Broek: Yes, I see it hasn't changed since you presented it. My question pertains to the ABC task. It seems to me that the three tasks used to operationalize working memory are actually very similar to the four tasks used for reasoning in the sense that both groups need working memory as well as reasoning. Are those seven measures highly interrelated? If so, I do not think it is fair to say they measure working memory exclusively.

Kyllonen: Yes, I agree with you. The only thing is that I did test a model in which I reduced the factors (working memory and reasoning) to one factor. Then scores on all seven tests loaded on the one factor. That model did not fit the data as well as the presented model. I think that provides evidence for the two factors. The fact that they are highly intercorrelated suggests that they are not really that different.

As to which (i.e., reasoning or working memory) has prior status, I think that historically I should be saying that I am talking basically about reasoning phenomena. But in terms of the process model I displayed, and the fact that I think we have a better understanding of working memory capacity (at least from a Baddeley perspective), I think that what we ought to be studying, decomposing, and understanding more thoroughly is working memory capacity. In this view, reasoning tasks are just particular tasks that require a lot of working memory capacity. I think that is a nice way to understand reasoning. You could develop an alternative theoretical framework that would make reasoning the primary factor. I couldn't really argue with that except on the basis of which approach has a better heuristic value.

Pellegrino: I would like to quibble with you about this issue. As I understand, you want to emphasize working memory. As you were talking, however, I was thinking about what Jack Adams said yesterday about the distinction between inductive and deductive reasoning. If you look at process models for performing those kinds of [reasoning] tasks, what you find is that the models are going to be very dependent on assumptions about storing information in working memory. If working memory is *primary,* then you

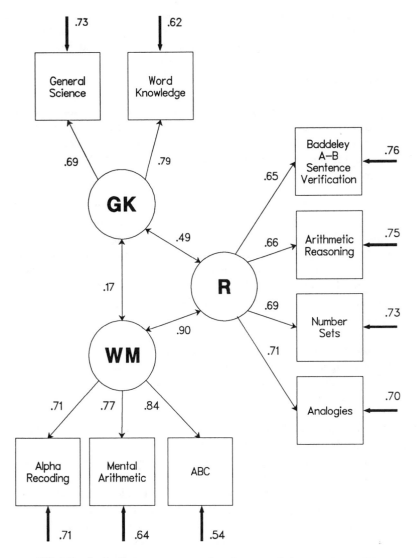

FIG. 9.7. Path diagram representing intercorrelations among GK (General Knowledge), WM (Working Memory), and R (Reasoning) factors, and associated indicators (from Christal & Kyllonen, 1989). N = 400, χ^2 (24) = 47, p = .003, *NFI* = .965, *NNFI* = .974; Residuals: M = .023; *Max* = .079.

would expect the reasoning factors to fall out and cluster together because working memory is the critical thing. But there has got to be something else there to explain why you get the separation of induction and deduction and yet they may hang together only because of the issue of sharing working memory capacity.

Kyllonen: I'm in full agreement with you—that the reason they hang together is because both these kinds of measures stress working memory capacity. The question you raise about why induction and deduction tests load on different factors is not addressed in this work at all. But I think that is certainly an interesting topic to pursue.

Carroll: I think the deductive reasoning tests probably put a larger demand on working memory, particularly when they are sequential in nature. I think we have to develop better measures of reasoning ability; measures in which we can control the amount of working memory and the amount of sequential memory required. I should also comment that my studies look at the primary factor only. As I recall, they are all fairly highly loaded with the general factor; the general factor may be the working memory part of it. I don't know.

Kyllonen: Yes, I like that sort of thinking about the issue. Again, I think that we might use Jan-Eric's methods to start teasing apart what might be specific to deductive and inductive reasoning tasks compared to what they have in common. Next year's work!

McGue: It is apparent from looking at the seven variable loadings on those two factors that they are all highly intercorrelated. Because of that you get this high correlation between these two factors. Another way to account for that fact is to say that the tasks are themselves factorially complex. In particular, it is a little hard to reconstruct the correlations here, but it looks to me as if arithmetic reasoning correlates higher with mental arithmetic (which is not unreasonable) than with other variables in its set. Have you considered a multifactor model of these variables?

Kyllonen: Can you explain how you get that?

McGue: How I am reconstructing the correlations? Well, I am assuming the correlations between arithmetic reasoning and mental arithmetic is .66 by .9 by .77.

Kyllonen: Right. But I thought you made the statement that arithmetic reasoning has something in common with mental arithmetic but not with the other two measures.

McGue: No. Arithmetic reasoning correlates higher with mental arithmetic than it does with the Baddeley AB sentence-verification task. Does this suggest there is an arithmetic factor? That these are not pure measurements but instead are factorially complex?

Kyllonen: Yes, I think that is likely to be the case. But the problem is that I do not have enough data points in this study to be able to tease that apart. I would speculate, not based on any good evidence, that such a finding would not change anything around as far as reasoning and working memory. If you were able to extract these so-called content factors, I do not think that would change the relationship between working memory and reasoning. I could be wrong though. It may be that what these factors have in common is the fact that there is a little bit of arithmetic in one test in the working memory group (the mental arithmetic test) and in one test in the reasoning group (arithmetic reasoning test).

Fletcher: In complex information processing tasks, you cannot keep all the information in working memory. Thus, it becomes important to decide what you want to focus your attention on. Maybe that is what reasoning is all about. Perhaps it is separate from working memory per se. . . .

Kyllonen: Yes, it could be. Although when Baddeley talks about working memory capacity, he does also talk about the importance of the central executive in making those kinds of attention allocation decisions. And he does admit that there has not been much work on this topic. But he also thinks that we will need to do more work on this topic in order to get a better handle on exactly what the working memory system is all about.

REFERENCES

Ackerman, P. L. (1986). Individual differences in information processing: An investigation of intellectual abilities and task performance during practice. *Intelligence, 10,* 101–139.

Ackerman, P. L. (1987). Individual differences in skill learning: An integration of psychometric and information processing perspectives. *Psychological Bulletin, 102,* 3–27.

Ackerman, P. L. (1988). Determinants of individual differences during skill acquisition: Cognitive abilities and information processing perspectives. *Journal of Experimental Psychology: General, 117,* 288–318.

Allison, R. B., Jr. (1960). *Learning parameters and human abilities.* Unpublished doctoral dissertation, Educational Testing Service and Princeton University.

Anderson, J. R. (1987). Skill acquisition: Compilation of weak-method problem solutions. *Psychological Review, 94,* 192–210.

Anderson, J. R., & Bower, G. H. (1972). *Human associative memory.* Hillsdale, NJ: Lawrence Erlbaum Associates.

Anderson, J. R., Greeno, J. G., Kline, P. J., & Neves, D. M. (1981). Acquisition of problem solving skill. In J. R. Anderson (Ed.), *Cognitive skills and their acquisition* (pp. 191–230). Hillsdale, NJ: Lawrence Erlbaum Associates.

Anderson, J. R., & Jeffries, R. (1985). Novice LISP errors: Undetected losses of information from working memory. *Human-Computer Interaction, 1,* 107–131.

Baddeley, A. D., & Hitch, G. (1974). Working memory. In G. H. Bower (Ed.), *The psychology of learning and motivation* (Vol. 8). New York: Academic Press.

Baddeley, A. (1986). *Working memory.* Oxford: Clarendon Press.

Bentler, P. M. (1985). *Theory and implementation of EQS: A structural equations program (manual for version 2.0).* Los Angeles: BMDP Statistical Software, Inc.

Berry, D. C., & Broadbent, D. E. (1988). On the relations between task performance and associated verbalizable knowledge. *Quarterly Journal of Experimental Psychology, 36A,* 209–231.

Brown, J. S., & Burton, R. (1978). Diagnostic models for procedural bugs in basic mathematical skills. *Cognitive Science, 2,* 155–192.

Chi, M. T. H., Feltovich, P. J., & Glaser, R. (1981). Categorization and representation of physics problems by experts and novices. *Cognitive Science, 5,* 121–152.

Christal, R. E. (1987). [Correlation matrices and factor analysis results from two working memory test batteries]. Unpublished raw data.

Christal, R. E., & Kyllonen, P. C. (1989). *Reasoning ability is (little more than) working memory capacity.* Unpublished manuscript.

Cronbach, L. J., & Snow, R. E. (1977). *Aptitudes and instructional methods: A handbook for research on interactions.* New York: Irvington.

Daneman, M., & Carpenter, P. A. (1980). Individual differences in working memory and reading. *Journal of Verbal Learning and Verbal Behavior, 19,* 450–466.

Daneman, M., & Carpenter, P. A. (1983). Individual differences in integrating information between and within sentences. *Journal of Experimental Psychology: Learning, Memory, and Cognition, 9,* 561–584.

Daneman, M., & Green, I. (1986). Individual differences in comprehending and producing words in context. *Journal of Memory and Language, 25,* 1–18.

Engle, R. W. (1988). *Working memory: An individual differences approach* (Tech Rep. No. 1) Columbia, SC: Department of Psychology, University of South Carolina.

Fitts, P. M. (1963). Perceptual-motor skill learning. In A. W. Melton (Ed.), *Categories of Human Learning* (pp. 244–285). New York: Academic Press.

Fleishman, E. A. (1972). On the relation between abilities, learning, and human performance. *American Psychologist, 27,* 1017–1032.

Fleishman, E. A., & Hempel, W. E. (1954). Changes in the factor structure of a complex psychomotor test as a function of practice. *Psychometrika, 19,* 239–252.

French, J. W., Ekstrom, R. B., & Price, L. A. (1963). *Kit of reference tests for cognitive factors.* Princeton, NJ: Educational Testing Service.

Gitomer, D. (1984). *A cognitive analysis of a complex troubleshooting task.* Unpublished doctoral dissertation, University of Pittsburgh.

Hacker, M. J., & Ratcliff, R. (1981). A revised table of d' for M-alternative forced choice. *Perception and Psychophysics, 26,* 168–170.

Harvey, N. (1984). The Stroop effect: Failure to focus attention or failure to maintain focusing? *Quarterly Journal of Experimental Psychology: Human Experimental Psychology, 36,* 89–115.

Hayes, J. R. (1981). *The complete problem solver.* Philadelphia: Franklin Institute.

Hughes, O. L. (1983). A comparison of error based and time based learning measures as predictors of general intelligence. *Intelligence, 7,* 9–26.

Hunt, E. (1978). The mechanics of verbal ability. *Psychological Review, 85,* 109–130.

Hunt, E., Lunneborg, C., & Lewis, J. (1975). What does it mean to be high verbal? *Cognitive Psychology, 7,* 194–227.

Jackson, M. D., & McClelland, J. J. (1979). Processing determinants of reading speed. *Journal of Experimental Psychology: General, 108,* 151–181.

Kanfer, R., & Ackerman, P. L. (in press). Dynamics of skill acquisition: Building a bridge between abilities and motivation. In R. J. Sternberg (Ed.), *Advances in the psychology of human intelligence* (Vol. 5). Hillsdale, NJ: Lawrence Erlbaum Associates.

Kieras, D. E., & Bovair, S. (1986). The acquisition of procedures from text: A production system analysis of transfer of training. *Journal of Memory and Language, 25,* 507–524.

Kyllonen, P. C., & Christal, R. E. (1989). Cognitive modeling of learning abilities: A status report of LAMP. In R. Dillon & J. W. Pellegrino (Eds.), *Testing: Theoretical and applied issues.* New York: Freeman. (Also Tech. Paper No. AFHRL-TP-87-66, Brooks AFB, TX: Manpower and Personnel Division, Air Force Human Resources Laboratory, 1988.)

Kyllonen, P. C., Stephens, D., & Woltz, D. J. (1988). *The role of working memory and accretive learning processes in learning logic gates.* Unpublished manuscript.

Kyllonen, P. C., & Tirre, W. C. (in press). Individual differences in associative learning and forgetting. *Intelligence.*

Kyllonen, P. C., Tirre, W. C., & Christal, R. E. (in press). *Knowledge and processing speed as determinants of associative learning* (Tech. Paper No. AFHRL-TP-87-68). Brooks AFB, TX: Manpower and Personnel Division, Air Force Human Resources Laboratory.

Lewicki, P., Czyzewska, M., & Hoffman, H. (1987). Unconscious acquisition of complex procedural knowledge. *Journal of Experimental Psychology: Learning, Memory, and Cognition, 13,* 523–530.

Lewis, C. H. (1978). Production system models of practice effects (Doctoral dissertation, University of Michigan, 1978). *Dissertation Abstracts International, 39,* 5105B. (University Microfilms No. 79-07, 120)

Lewis, M., & Anderson, J. R. (1985). Discrimination of operator schemata in problem solving: Learning from examples. *Cognitive Psychology, 17,* 26–65.

Neches, R., Langley, P., & Klahr, D. (1987). Learning, development, and production systems. In D. Klahr, P. Langley, & R. Neches (Eds.), *Production system models of learning and development* (pp. 1–54). Cambridge, MA: MIT Press.

Nelson, T. O., & Narens, L. (1980). Norms of 300 general-information questions: Accuracy of recall, latency of recall, and feeling-of-knowing ratings. *Journal of Verbal Learning and Verbal Behavior, 19,* 338–368.

Newell, A., & Rosenbloom, P. S. (1981). Mechanisms of skill acquisition and the law of practice. In J. R. Anderson (Ed.), *Cognitive skills and their acquisition* (pp. 1–55). Hillsdale, NJ: Lawrence Erlbaum Associates.

Nissen, M. J., & Bullemer, P. (1987). Attentional requirements of learning: Evidence from performance measures. *Cognitive Psychology, 19,* 1–32.

Perfetti, C. A., & Lesgold, A. M. (1979). Coding and comprehension in skilled reading and implications for reading instruction. In L. B. Resnick & P. A. Weaver (Eds.), *Theory and practice of early reading* (Vol. 1, pp. 57–84). Hillsdale, NJ: Lawrence Erlbaum Associates.

Raven, J. C. (1960). *Guide to the standard progressive matrices.* London: H. K. Lewis & Company.

Santa, J. L. (1977). Spatial transformations of words and pictures. *Journal of Experimental Psychology: Human Learning and Memory, 3,* 418–427.

Schmalhofer, F. (1982). Comprehension of a technical text as a function of expertise. (Doctoral dissertation, University of Colorado, 1982). *Dissertation Abstracts International, 44,* 293B.

Snow, R. E., Kyllonen, P. C., & Marshalek, B. (1984). The topography of learning and ability correlations. In R. J. Sternberg (Ed.), *Advances in the psychology of human intelligence* (Vol. 2, pp. 47–103). Hillsdale, NJ: Lawrence Erlbaum Associates.

Stake, R. E. (1961). Learning parameters, aptitudes, and achievement. *Psychometric Monographs, No. 9.* Chicago: University of Chicago Press.

Sternberg, R. J. (1977). *Intelligence, information processing, and analogical reasoning: The componential analysis of human abilities.* Hillsdale, NJ: Lawrence Erlbaum Associates.

Thurstone, L. L. (1938). Primary mental abilities. *Psychometric Monographs, No. 1.* Chicago: University of Chicago Press.

Thurstone, L. L., & Thurstone, T. G. (1941). Factorial studies of intelligence. *Psychometric Monographs No. 2.* Chicago: University of Chicago Press.

Tirre, W. C. (in preparation). *Knowledge and ability factors underlying meaningful associative learning.* Unpublished manuscript.

Tirre, W. C., & Rancourt, C. R. (1986). *Individual differences in learning by accretion: It all begins with comprehension.* Paper presented at the annual meeting of the American Educational Research Association, San Francisco, CA.

Underwood, B. J. (1964). Degree of learning and the measurement of forgetting. *Journal of Verbal Learning and Verbal Behavior, 3,* 112–129.

Underwood, B. J., Boruch, R. F., & Malmi, R. A. (1978). Composition of episodic memory. *Journal of Experimental Psychology: General, 107,* 393–419.

Wang, A. Y. (1983). Individual differences in learning speed. *Journal of Experimental Psychology: Learning, Memory, and Cognition, 9,* 300–311.

Wickelgren, W. A. (1974). *How to solve problems.* San Francisco: Freeman.

Woltz, D. J. (1988a). *Activation and decay of semantic memory: An individual differences investigation of working memory.* Unpublished manuscript.

Woltz, D. J. (1988b). An investigation of the role of working memory in procedural skill acquisition. *Journal of Experimental Psychology: General, 117,* 319–331.

Woltz, D. J. (1989, March). *The strengthening of memory traces with use: A study of learner differences.* Paper presented at the annual meeting of the American Educational Research Association, San Francisco, CA.

Abilities, Elementary Information Processes, and Other Sights to See at the Zoo

Phillip L. Ackerman
University of Minnesota

As has been mentioned elsewhere in this book (e.g., see chapter by Adams), there is a long history to the literature on learning and individual differences. From the perspective of ability theorists, this work goes back at least to Thorndike (1908), though discussion of many of the same issues can be found in recent journal articles as well (e.g., Ackerman, 1988; Adams, 1987; Woltz, 1988). There have, of course, been many changes over the years. For example, ability theories have developed in ways that take into account general notions of intelligence (Spearman, 1904), specific ability notions of intelligence (e.g., Guilford, 1985; Thurstone, 1938), and more recently, information processing notions of intellectual abilities (e.g., Sternberg, 1985).

When constructs concerning intelligence (or intellectual abilities) are discussed, the constructs of individual differences in learning are rarely far removed (whether the mapping between constructs is explicit or implicit). Many ability theorists have tried to map intellectual abilities onto learning constructs in ways that unify these two generally disparate scientific inquiries (e.g., see Cronbach, 1957; Underwood, 1975). For historical discussions, the reader might consult a number of sources, for example, Glaser (1967), Gagné (1989), and Snow (1989). This chapter, though, focuses on the basis for, and nature of, recent developments in relating ability, information processing, and learning constructs.

NATURE OF INQUIRY

Modern psychological investigation into the relations between intellectual abilities and individual differences in learning has changed much over the past 80 years. At first, most researchers *assumed* that intelligence and individual differences in learning were inextricably connected. For example, one theorist (Buckingham, 1921) suggested simply that intelligence "is the ability to learn." Developments in ability theory during the 1930s and 1940s brought about a reconsideration of the unitary notion of intellectual ability (e.g., Thurstone, 1938); a change in perspective that implied learning ability was not unitary, either, but rather domain specific (Simrall, 1946). Later developments in ability theory carried this approach to often impractical dimensions (viz. the 150 ability cube proposed by Guilford, 1985). If these models of *independent* abilities were to be adopted, there might be a unique learning ability associated with each ability upon which individuals differed. Although recent years have brought about more interrelated ability models (e.g., Humphreys, 1982; Vernon, 1961), few of these theorists have directly addressed the structure of learning abilities.

The older learning literature (e.g., Thorndike, 1908) also considered learning as a general phenomenon. In developments somewhat analogous to the demarcation of different abilities, experimental psychologists sought to catalogue the knowledge, memory, and attentional mechanisms that determine the nature of learning and skill acquisition (e.g., see Lachman, Lachman, & Butterfield, 1979). In recent years, the field has determined that learning is not unitary, any more than intelligence is unitary. One particularly striking distinction of knowledge and skill acquisition, proposed by Anderson (1983), concerns *declarative* knowledge (knowledge about things) and *procedural* knowledge (knowledge of how to do things).

From each of these two research fields, the basic learning field and the ability theory field, we have come to a generally accepted view of learning and individual differences that is fundamentally different from the early considerations. Specifically:

1. We no longer believe that intelligence is unitary, but rather is multifaceted. It is therefore unlikely that a single learning ability exists.
2. We no longer consider all types of learning to be alike. In particular, acquisition of declarative knowledge (such as that of an historian) is fundamentally different from the acquisition of procedural knowledge (such as involved in flying an airplane).
3. We no longer assume that intelligence and learning are different names for the same construct. There are multiple determinants and manifestations of both intelligence and learning that may overlap, but are not identical.

These three statements underscore contemporary approaches to learning and individual differences. The inquiry has become decidedly more complex than earlier approaches. The complexity derives from new considerations of the range of abilities and from considerations of the building blocks of information processing, the so-called elementary information processes. However, such complex approaches allow for the science to discriminate along several dimensions of abilities and information processes, such as between global and narrow conceptions of learning (e.g., school learning vs. the acquisition of videogame skills), and global and narrow conceptions of abilities (e.g., reasoning vs. perceptual speed).

THE ZOO ANALOGY

The analogy of the zoo adopted in this chapter is meant to imply that research in this domain involves many characteristics found in a person's first trip to the (human abilities) zoo. The activities discussed here range from the discovery of new and different types of abilities; to the understanding of the differences between big (broad) and small (narrow) abilities; and to the hybridization, or genetic engineering, of ability measures. At this stage of development, the research to be described has the flavor of constructing a human abilities zoo; some scientists are searching far and wide for new abilities, others seek to categorize abilities already found, and still others are in the process of discovering the behavioral repertoire of these abilities, namely, how abilities affect different types of learning.

SPECIFIC COMMENTS ON OTHER CHAPTERS

One purpose for this chapter is to provide direct commentary on four chapters: those by Pellegrino, Hunt, and Yee; Kyllonen and Woltz; Gustafsson; and Lohman. Each of these chapters is briefly discussed in turn.

Pellegrino, Hunt, and Yee

Pellegrino et al. and Kyllonen and Woltz have taken on the task of filling in some missing cells in our human abilities zoo. The work that Pellegrino et al. are doing, that is, the study of information integration abilities, we can perhaps liken to the search for Bigfoot or the Loch Ness Monster. That is, they are pursuing some of the larger animals that the zoologists may have missed in their initial survey of the field. Not only does the availability of computer technology make such research logistically feasible, the prevalence of such technology has the side effect of making the search for such abilities pragmatically more important. For example, human factors researchers have been telling us for some time that more automation in the workplace often reduces the load on human muscles, but in turn, increases the load on the person's complex monitoring skills. In the modern nuclear power plant, for example, operators must be able to sort out a multitude of lights, meters, sirens, klaxons, bells, and so on, that indicate everything from a need to replace computer paper in a high-speed line printer to a potential meltdown situation. Even a task as simple as driving a car to the airport in a new city can involve such integrative abilities (or skills), for example, when one is faced with remembering instructions from a friend and reading a map, while integrating these sources of information with the visual field ahead.

Clearly, individuals are faced with situations where information integration is an essential task component. Is there an identifiable ability to integrate information? It seems that there is. Pellegrino et al. have demonstrated that there is something that determines performance in these integration tasks, that also exists outside the standard component task-content abilities. Clearly, there is much promising work ahead of them in this area.

My own orientation, though, would be to pursue a few questions that are related to those asked by Pellegrino et al. First of all, I would ask how general intelligence relates to performance of such information integration tasks. For the sake of argument, lets consider Godfrey Thomson's (1919) theory of overlapping bonds. To paraphrase, without doing too much damage to his more elegant theorizing, Thompson's hypothesis was that g (the general intelligence factor) is a resultant of the fact that ability tests represent samples of behaviors, knowledge, and thinking that overlap to varying degrees. The broader the sample of processes, the greater the saturation with g. Given that the information integration tests sample across domains (including more executive processes of attentional control), it seems that such an ability is greatly saturated with general intelligence. The addition of information integration requirements should increase the g saturation above and beyond the rather impressive saturations one sees with more standard dual-task scenarios.

Second, it would be interesting to understand the *mechanisms* underlying information integration. For example, if one were to create a set of task pairings that differed along a dimension of task integrality/separability, is the integration ability (or abilities) most prevalent when the tasks are only moderately integral? That is, with complete integrality, we have a single, complex task—with extreme task separability, that is, independence, we might get the elusive time-sharing ability.

Is information integration a malleable skill or a result of less plastic information-processing mechanisms? It is typical to find rather poor task performance in dual-task experiments, even among subjects who are exhaustively trained on individual task components (e.g., Fisk & Schneider, 1983). Does size of short-term or working memory limit performance in these situations, or is the issue one of attentional control, as Pellegrino suggests? From a skill-acquisition perspective (such as the one taken by Kyllonen & Woltz), perhaps the range of individual differences is the result of the load on working memory; memory that is necessary for a reproceduralization of component task-specific productions that must be integrated. To address this issue, subjects could be placed directly in the dual-task information-integration situation from the start (rather than give them training on the individual component tasks first). Perhaps this alternative approach will have different ability correlates than the procedure used by Pellegrino et al. Again, from a pragmatic perspective, this is an important issue; it pertains to both instructional and training program design disciplines. For example, when decisions need to be made about part-task training versus full-task training, it would be critical to know how the ability-learning parameter correlates change as a function of each training method.

Kyllonen and Woltz

After this brief consideration of the larger animals that might perhaps be seen in the human abilities zoo (of the future), let's discuss some smaller quarry, that are, it appears, just as difficult to capture. Kyllonen and Woltz offer us a view of several, apparently fundamental, aspects of information processing that may underlie broad abilities and that most certainly are related to individual differences in learning. Back in the dim dark past for research concerned with individual differences in information processing (namely the 1970s), investigators, such as Hunt and his colleagues, started off with off-the-shelf information-processing tasks (sort of like visiting a zoo of cats and dogs). Much of the work in this area in the last 15 years has been concerned with such standard information-processing tasks. The tasks created by Pellegrino et al., though, break away from this tradition. The research that Kyllonen, Woltz, and their colleagues have recently undertaken is also at the forefront of this domain. Without beating the zoo metaphor into the ground, we might say that Kyllonen and Woltz are engaged in a bit of genetic engineering. We see some mighty strange animals (i.e., tasks), such as the ABC Assignment and ABCD Order tasks they describe in their chapter.

Psychologists, and especially those of us involved in the investigation of individual differences, have historically behaved much like the person who loses car keys at night and is found looking for them under the streetlight. When asked if this is the location where the keys are likely to be found, the person answers "No, but it is much more convenient to look under the light, than in the darkened street." Too often we have been content with taking ability tests, and more recently information-processing tasks, off the shelf because they have been convenient, rather than for clearly scientific reasons. For example, Carroll (1983) has repeatedly admonished us not to be cavalier about such tests (e.g., the ETS Kit of Factor-Referenced Tests), but few of us are willing to expend the resources to develop more appropriate batteries for our domains of interest.

However, it is clear that the innovative approach taken by Kyllonen and Woltz provides important building blocks for the evaluation of learning abilities. They have pointed out that individual differences in working memory capacity may play an important role in separating those individuals who acquire skills from those who do not. Other important components were also identified and measured within their paradigm: namely, knowledge, skills, and processing speed. At this early stage of investigation, it is too soon to evaluate the success of their theoretical viewpoints, but the current data are impressive; even if they only have a few thousand cases on which to base their conclusions!

One important issue about the skill acquisition and learning domain, though, is to make a distinction between two types of learning, one type (like learning how to drive a car) that my colleague Ruth Kanfer and I call closed-ended skills (Kanfer & Ackerman, in press). As one learns how to drive a car, the task starts out quite difficult; one must keep in mind all of the components of the task (such as the speedometer, the rear view mirror, the turn signals, the fuel gauge, and so on). After sufficient practice, say a few weeks or months, these component skills become automatic. Once the skill is automatic, the majority of learning has taken place. In my own work, I have found that for simple, consistent skills, general intellectual abilities no longer play an important role in determining individual differences in task performance after extended practice. More often, individual differences in skilled performance are determined by perceptual speed and especially psychomotor abilities (e.g., see Ackerman, 1988; Kanfer & Ackerman, in press).

In contrast to closed-ended skills, Kanfer and I call the other type of skills open-ended skills. When one learns to play chess, or say, learns to become a research methodologist, lower-order skill learning leads of necessity to the engagement of higher-order learning. For example, in acquiring research methodology skills, after one learns about the *t*-test or the Pearson product-moment correlation coefficient, one ordinarily confronts a more difficult or involving set of skills to learn (e.g., ANOVA or factor analysis). The learning process then continues (ad infinitum, if desired). Although the individual component skills may become automatic, and indeed we often see terminal skills for *t*-tests in our undergraduate students, the patterns of relations between intellectual abilities and performance are likely to be divergent. That is, whereas development of closed-ended skills reveals a diminished dependence on general intelligence, the continuing process of developing more and more complex open-ended skills appears to increasingly involve general intelligence.

The theoretical inference, then, is that there is an important relationship between general intelligence (or other broad abilities) and the facility with which an individual transfers from one skill to a new skill. This point was made some years ago by George Ferguson (1954, 1956), and later, by Arthur Sullivan (1964; see also Skanes, Sullivan, Rowe, & Shannon, 1974); and it seems critical to our understanding of how learning and intellectual abilities go hand in hand. Sullivan (1964), for example, showed that as transfer-of-training becomes more distant, (i.e., less similarity between initial instruction and the new skill to be learned), intellectual abilities become increasingly more important determinants of individual differences in transfer performance. There are inferences from this research to notions about the developmental differentiation of abilities, something that Carroll mentions in his chapter.

Gustafsson

In a rather oblique fashion, this observation leads to a discussion of Gustafsson's chapter. A learning and transfer approach, or more abstractly a developmental approach to ability acquisition and expression, involves the complex interactions between both higher-order (i.e., general) abilities and lower-order abilities. As Ferguson pointed out, for all but the neonate, transfer of training is the basis for any new learning. On the one hand, acquisition of new skills or facts often requires broad strategies for learning (e.g., the type of abilities that load highly on a general intelligence factor). On the other hand, an individual's knowledge repertoire, including both declarative and procedural types of knowledge (many of which surely represent lower-order abilities), also appears to play a role in transfer.

Gustafsson's work in modeling the hierarchical structure of intellectual abilities provides a framework that allows linkages between various different views of intelligence. By demonstrating the relations between broad abilities (e.g., so-called crystallized and fluid intelligences) and general intelligence, along with their lower-order constituents, he has provided a powerful rubric for simultaneously considering abilities of all types in the context of learning (big and small animals in our human abilities zoo, if you will). The arguments about aptitude-treatment interactions at various levels in the ability hierarchy are compelling, even though he admits to a certain post hoc theorizing about the particulars of any given sample.

Lohman

The chapter by Lohman is important to the domain of learning and individual differences in several respects. Whereas many researchers are content to glibly operationalize their constructs in whatever manner leads to easy-to-use dependent variables, Lohman makes us confront our choices of dependent variables by the use of an *enlightened* information-processing and psychometric perspectives. From the human abilities zoo analogy, we can imagine that the same ruler is differentially effective for measuring the size of elephants and insects. Lohman's chapter is especially effective in showing us that a choice among measurement procedures must be made and that some procedures are clearly preferred when we wish to describe particular abilities.

For the typical information-processing psychologist, explicit integrative treatment of speed and accuracy variables has always been a source of discomfort. As Lohman and others have pointed out, the source of this discomfort usually pertains the exponential increase in requirements on the data collection end of the process (e.g., see Pachella, 1974; Wickelgren, 1977). The information-processing domain's response to this issue by instructing subjects to "respond as quickly and as accurately to the stimulus" is clearly insufficient, in that speed and accuracy are negatively interrelated.

For the differential psychologist, the speed–accuracy issue is also a thorny one, partly because of the historical dependence on paper-and-pencil testing. Before computers became prevalent tools for the collection of ability data, differential psychology inquiry was limited to collecting aggregate information (number of items correct, number of items wrong, number of items attempted, etc.). Even explicit treatment of number correct and number wrong within a single test has been an uncommon method of analysis in the literature, although early analyses were instrumental in discovering particular aspects of cognitive style (e.g., the Carefulness factor in the study by Davis, 1947). Other attempts to modify the nature of the testing-time requirements were similarly promising (e.g., Lord, 1956) but have not been followed up in a systematic manner. The ability test creator's response to the issue by attempting to equalize speed (timed tests), allow infinite time (power or level tests), or attempt an explicit trade-off ("your score will be a total of items correct minus a fraction for each item wrong") is lacking in a fashion similar to the approach taken in many information-processing experiments. In each case, a band-aid is applied to a patient with a serious disease.

Lohman has described a series of experiments that accomplish the desire to get a more complete, unconfounded measurement of subjects' performance on information-processing tasks, while *also* generating measures that can be compared to the more traditional ability-test repertoire of the differential psychologist. This approach is very much in the spirit of Cronbach's (1957) call for the unification of experimental and correlational psychology disciplines. In the case of spatial abilities, for example, this research has yielded data that offer an important step toward localizing the information-processing determinants of sex differences in mental rotation (Lohman, 1986).

Still, there remain several concerns that prevent such forms of analysis from enjoying popular usage, despite the promise demonstrated by Lohman. One issue has to do with the evaluation of task (or item) complexity. Lohman claims that "complexity is in the eye of the beholder," but this critical dimension cannot be overlooked or merely operationalized away. Although we can acknowledge that few, if any, information-processing models of task complexity currently predict *how* individual subjects will process a particular test item, it is not so clear that this is an impossible task for psychology. If the number of solution strategies is finite (preferably small in number), it should be possible to work out a particular surface of speed–accuracy trade-off curves for each type of strategy and each ability or knowledge level. Such an interaction of strategy and individual level of ability might be tractable if tasks are created that yield different speed–accuracy trade-off curves for different strategies and ability levels. In fact, the speed–

accuracy methodology described by Lohman might be the very technique that can determine such strategy–ability interactions. These interactions, then, might be used for diagnosing individual differences in capacities, limitations, and cognitive styles.

In the context of other chapters in this book, Lohman's work offers promise to other sources of inquiry and may derive benefits from other methodological approaches to human performance. The promise of the speed–accuracy methodology lies in the possibility of delineating the particular information-processing effects of arousal-inducing manipulations (as in Revelle's work), in delineating the information-processing determinants of ability test scores (e.g., Kyllonen & Woltz's work and Pellegrino et al.'s work), and in determining the nature of volitional control of attention (as in Kuhl & Kraska's work). The notion of speed–accuracy trade-off might be tied to both dispositional and transitory notions of motivation (e.g., n-ach, mastery orientation, action vs. state orientation, etc.). It may be that persons with an action orientation (as described by Kuhl & Kraska) differ mainly in their preference for increased activity (perhaps speed emphasis rather than accuracy emphasis), whereas those persons who maintain a state orientation have shifted to a more careful, accuracy emphasis. To the degree that these orientations are more stable dispositions, persons may have a signature speed–accuracy trade-off (as Kyllonen suggested in the discussion of Lohman's presentation). However, if action-state orientation can be induced (as Kuhl & Kraska have shown), speed–accuracy methodology might provide a signal contribution to the discovery of such changes. This methodology might also be illustrative in showing the extent of malleability possible for particular individuals.

In terms of benefits *to* the speed–accuracy methodology, the approach of Mulder et al. seems especially promising. That is, an evoked-potentials perspective would view the speed–accuracy trade-off function as determined by the accretion of information (perhaps reflected by the P300 component). Rather than plotting a macro-oriented speed–accuracy trade-off function, one might rather estimate the *rate* of information accretion in conjunction with changes in the information threshold an individual uses for determining when a response to the stimulus is to be made.

For the macro approach described by Lohman, individuals who cannot always correctly answer even the easiest trials prove to be problematic for derivation of speed–accuracy functions (see Lohman's chapter). The evoked-potentials methods described by Mulder et al. might be used to estimate the specific information-processing limitations of these particular individuals. For example, such an approach might show that some individuals accrete information in a fashion different from other individuals, so that information is not maintained long enough to result in crossing a decision threshold. Using this type of procedure may remove the apparent incommensurability between certain classes of individuals found in the macro-based analysis.

The set of technical procedures developed and described by Lohman for derivation of speed–accuracy trade-offs is especially promising for the field in general. The adaptive procedure he described may bring speed–accuracy trade-off methods within the range of feasibility for both differential and experimental psychologists. In particular, the adaptive framework reduces the testing requirements so as to make the method accessible to the many correlational/experimental psychology researchers using desktop computers for data collection. With additional research, this method may reach a point where Monte Carlo techniques may be used in conjunction with real data collection to derive important aptitude-treatment interaction information.

CLOSING COMMENTS

Despite this demonstrated progress, it seems that we are still in dire need of a more functional (rather than strictly psychometric) framework for intellectual abilities, both broad and narrow. As has been pointed out, the hierarchical arrangement of ability factors is rather general, a researcher can derive an ability hierarchy with many or only a few levels. From a psychometric viewpoint, the number of levels to the hierarchy is purposely left undetermined. This being the case, we may be left with an infinite regress in the search for aptitude-treatment interactions, *unless* we have a framework that sets out the functional relations between higher-order abilities (e.g., general intelligence) and the lower-order abilities (e.g., specific types of information-processing capacities).

To derive functional-relation specifications, perhaps we need an adequate taxonomy of human intellectual functioning. Do we have one at this point? Apparently not, given the examples of new abilities described by Pellegrino et al. Can we generate one? Possibly. Ability theorists have been relatively mute when it comes to specification of quantitative parameters associated with structures of intellectual abilities. For example, we can take the Cattell and Horn theory of intelligence. . . . Do we even have a good estimate of the correlation between fluid and crystallized intelligence, in the population at large? There have been a few studies in this area (including some analyses by Gustafsson, 1984), but the quantitative parameters are generally missing from even the well-specified theories of intelligence.

Thus, we end up with conceptual frameworks with which to work, but predictions (quantitative or even qualitative) are difficult to make from these conceptual frameworks. As a result, when abilities are used as aptitudes, we often can only make broad inferences for the shape of aptitude-treatment interactions. To capitalize on the methods that Gustafsson has suggested, it is clear that we need to concentrate on fleshing out the structure of intelligence (as was suggested by Carroll). I believe that it is also critical for us to speak about *functional* relations among abilities and among abilities and information processes; some initial examples of which are provided by Kyllonen and Woltz. A continued over-reliance on the correlation coefficient to describe relations between abilities and information processes will probably limit the utility of our approaches, especially with respect to discovering the determinants of individual differences in learning. I see the task before us as follows:

1. Find the determinants of *initial performance* (what ability, information-processing, knowledge, strategy, conative, and other environmental factors predict how well individuals do when they begin a learning task).
2. Find the factors that determine *asyptotic,* or postinstruction/postpractice performance level (e.g., information-processing capacities, strategies).
3. And finally, determine the factors that relate to the path (or *speed*) of moving from point (1) to point (2). That is, what personal and situational constraints determine who benefits from instruction/practice; what types of instruction go with what types of personal attributes, etc.

The data from experiments such as the ones Kyllonen and Woltz describe are quite rich; in a single experiment, one derives (a) a battery of standard ability measures, (b) some information-processing measures (often, both speed and accuracy), and (c) a series of leaning measures; either on one task or even on a variety of tasks. From these data, one can examine correlations between the abilities, or information-processing variables (as predictors) and task performance over practice. With this information, one can state the degree of association between these variables and performance at various stages of practice. One can look further at how treatment variables (such as strategy instructions) change these correlations between abilities and performance.

On the other hand, one might wish to look at the learning curves themselves and study the paths that various subgroups or individual subjects take from initial, novice performance, to skilled, expert performance. The correlational analyses just mentioned tend to obscure these sources of information. We can predict initial and final performance individual differences by correlational methods. However, procedures are not yet adequate for describing how individual differences in abilities affect the more fundamental aspects of *how* individuals learn. That is, we can state that if an individual has higher general intelligence (or more background knowledge), he or she will likely start a new task at an advantage, but we cannot yet predict the specific path or timing of development of insight, contingent on such abilities or knowledge. It is the ability to predict these important aspects of individual differences in learning that awaits us.

The chapters discussed here appear to move us in the right directions. But there is much interesting work that remains to be done. From what we have heard at this conference, I think that we may rise to the task. My crystal ball indicates that we will see a more varied set of exhibits in the human abilities zoo of the future. Hopefully, by then, we will know what new abilities are related to the traditional abilities, and the precise nature of their relationships. Maybe, even, we will have an understanding of the origin of species, or how such different abilities come about. For example, we may begin to understand the complex relations between abilities and individual differences in learning. Finally, it is important to note that constructs other than abilities relate to learning. Such constructs as volition or motivation must moderate the relations between abilities and learning both in the short term (for example, in a simple skill-acquisition paradigm), but also from a broader perspective (for example, in the development and expression of the abilities themselves). The chapters by Revelle, Kleinbeck, and Kuhl address the very important determinants of motivated performance and the mechanisms of the volitional systems as well.

REFERENCES

Ackerman, P. L. (1988). Determinants of individual differences during skill acquisition: Cognitive abilities and information processing. *Journal of Experimental Psychology: General, 117,* 288–318.

Adams, J. A. (1987). Historical review and appraisal of research on the learning, retention, and transfer of human motor skills. *Psychological Bulletin, 101,* 41–74.

Anderson, J. R. (1983). *The architecture of cognition.* Cambridge, MA: Harvard University Press.

Buckingham, B. R. (1921). Intelligence and its measurement: A symposium. *Journal of Educational Psychology, 12,* 271–275.

Carroll, J. B. (1983). Studying individual differences in cognitive abilities: Through and beyond factor analysis. In R. F. Dillon & R. R. Schmeck (Eds.), *Individual differences in cognition* (Vol. 1, pp. 1–33). New York: Academic Press.

Cronbach, L. J. (1957). The two disciplines of scientific psychology. *American Psychologist, 12,* 671–684.

Davis, P.C. (1947). Measures of specific traits of temperament. In J. P. Guilford & J. I. Lacey (Eds.), *Army Air Forces Aviation Psychology Program Research Reports: Printed Classification Tests. Report No. 5* (pp. 673–720). Washington, DC: U.S. Government Printing Office.

Ferguson, G. A. (1954). On learning and human ability. *Canadian Journal of Psychology, 8,* 95–112.

Ferguson, G. A. (1956). On transfer and the abilities of man. *Canadian Journal of Psychology, 10,* 121–131.

Fisk, A. D., & Schneider, W. (1983). Category and word search: Generalizing search principles to complex processing. *Journal of Experimental Psychology: Learning, Memory, & Cognition, 10,* 177–195.

Gagné, R. M. (1989). Some reflections on learning and individual differences. In P. L. Ackerman, R. J. Sternberg, & R. Glaser (Eds.), *Learning and individual differences: Advances in theory and research* (pp. 1–11). New York: W. H. Freeman.

Glaser, R. (1967). Some implications of previous work on learning and individual differences. In R. M. Gagné (Ed.), *Learning and individual differences* (pp. 1–18). Columbus, OH: Charles Merrill.

Guilford, J. P. (1985). The structure-of-intellect model. In B. B. Wolman (Ed.), *Handbook of intelligence* (pp. 225–266). New York: Wiley.

Gustafsson, J. (1984). A unifying model for the structure of intellectual abilities. *Intelligence, 8,* 179–203.

Humphreys, L. G. (1982). The hierarchical factor model and general intelligence. In N. Hirschberg & L. G. Humphreys (Eds.), *Multivariate applications in the social sciences* (pp. 223–239). Hillsdale, NJ: Lawrence Erlbaum Associates.

Kanfer, R., & Ackerman, P. L. (in press). Motivation and cognitive abilities: An integrative/aptitude-treatment interaction approach to skill acquisition. *Journal of Applied Psychology.*

Lachman, R., Lachman, J. L., & Butterfield, E. C. (1979). *Cognitive psychology and information processing.* Hillsdale, NJ: Lawrence Erlbaum Associates.

Lohman, D. (1986). The effect of speed–accuracy tradeoff on sex differences in mental rotation. *Perception & Psychophysics, 39,* 427–436.

Lord, F. M. (1956). A study of speed factors in tests and academic grades. *Psychometrika, 21,* 31–50.

Pachella, R. G. (1974). The interpretation of reaction-time in information processing research. In B. Kantowitz (Ed.), *Human information processing: Tutorials in performance and cognition* (pp. 41–82). Hillsdale, NJ: Lawrence Erlbaum Associates.

Simrall, D. V. (1946). *The effects of practice on the factorial equations for perceptual and visual-spatial tests.* Unpublished doctoral dissertation, University of Illinois, Urbana.

Skanes, G. R., Sullivan, A. M., Rowe, E. J., & Shannon, E. (1974). Intelligence and transfer: Aptitude by treatment interactions. *Journal of Educational Psychology, 66,* 563–568.

Snow, R. E. (1989). Aptitude-treatment interaction as a framework for research on individual differences in learning. In P. L. Ackerman, R. J. Sternberg, & R. Glaser (Eds.), *Learning and individual differences: Advances in theory and research* (pp. 13–58). New York: W. H. Freeman.

Spearman, C. (1904). "General intelligence," objectively determined and measured. *American Journal of Psychology, 15,* 201–293.

Sternberg, R. J. (1985). *Beyond IQ: A triarchic theory of human intelligence.* Cambridge: Cambridge University Press.

Sullivan, A. M. (1964). *The relation between intelligence and transfer.* Unpublished doctoral dissertation, McGill University, Montreal.

Thomson, G. (1919). On the cause of hierarchical order among correlation coefficients. *Proceedings of the Royal Society, A, 95,* 400–408.

Thorndike, E. L. (1908). The effect of practice in the case of a purely intellectual function. *American Journal of Psychology, 19,* 374–384.

Thurstone, L. L. (1938). Primary mental abilities, *Psychometric Monographs, 1.*

Underwood, B. J. (1975). Individual differences as a crucible in theory construction. *American Psychologist, 30,* 128–134.

Vernon, P. E. (1961). *The structure of human abilities.* New York: Wiley.

Wickelgren, W. A. (1977). Speed–accuracy tradeoff and information processing dynamics. *Acta Psychologica, 41,* 67–85.

Woltz, D. J. (1988). An investigation of the role of working memory in procedural skill acquisition. *Journal of Experimental Psychology: General, 117,* 319–331.

IV

MOTIVATIONAL AND VOLITIONAL PROCESSES

Personality, Motivation, and Cognitive Performance

William Revelle
Northwestern University

A classic problem in the study of behavior is the relationship between what we know and what we do (see Woodworth & Schlosberg, 1954). Perhaps the most important aspect of the study of motivation is this distinction between competence (knowing) and performance (doing). This is particularly the case when studying individual differences in learning and motivation. Indeed, folk wisdom attributes poor performance on the part of some students not to an inability to learn, but rather to a lack of effort or motivation. Many are the poor students told by a teacher that if only they would try harder they would do better. However, as is true of much of contradictory folk wisdom, we are also told that people can get too motivated or too excited to do well. Many students, after a particularly bad performance on an exam will explain to their professor that they knew the material but while taking the test their mind just went blank because of test anxiety.

For psychologists, the competence–performance distinction was well shown in Blodgett's (1929) prototypic demonstration that learning could occur for hungry rats even when not rewarded, but that this learning was masked by a lack of an incentive to perform when food was not available in the goal box. When food was available, rats who had previously shown no evidence of learning were suddenly able to solve mazes with the same alacrity shown by their previously rewarded companions. Tolman and Honzik (1930) extended this study with the demonstration that the performance of previously rewarded rats will revert to the unrewarded level when reward is removed just as previously unrewarded rats will perform as well (or even better) than previously rewarded rats when reward is introduced. The Blodgett (1929) and Tolman and Honzik (1930) studies are important to motivational theorists because they made clear that performance was a function of prior learning as well as the motivational conditions present at the time of performance.

Even earlier evidence showing a relationship between situational manipulations affecting motivation and subsequent learning was reported by Yerkes and Dodson (1908). They showed that increasing levels of foot shock facilitated learning in an easy visual discrimination task but had a curvilinear (inverted U) effect for moderate and difficult discrimination tasks. Maximal performance was associated with moderate levels of foot shock and the peak of the function was at lower levels of foot shock for more complex tasks. Although Yerkes and Dodson interpreted this as an effect on learning, their study is frequently cited as an example of complex motivational effects upon performance.

It is this belief that a failure in performance for an otherwise competent individual reflects a *lack* or an *excess* of motivation that I address in this chapter. Presumably noncognitive individual differences in personality systematically affect learning and performance as a function of motivational state. Some of these effects are upon the development of competence in that they affect rates of learning and retention; other effects are on performance in that they affect how well previously learned material can be manipulated and processed. Furthermore, although certain motivational manipulations can facilitate learning for some individuals, these same manipulations can actually hurt both the learning and the performance of others.

Before starting, I review some basic theoretical concepts from current research in personality. I then discuss some recent research that shows how differences in personality interact with situational and task manipulations to have strong effects upon learning. These effects are upon the learning and retrieval of material that is to be retained for periods ranging from a few seconds to one week. These same personality differences interact with similar manipulations to affect complex performance tasks. Some of these tasks are quite similar to those used to assess verbal and abstract reasoning ability in standardized ability tests. Others are more similar to the simple memory, attention, and abstract reasoning problems so popular among experimental psychologists. I conclude with a plea for the detailed analyses of personality, situational, and task variables that are required if we are to understand how individual differences relate to learning and motivation.

PERSONALITY TYPOLOGIES; EYSENCK'S AND GRAY'S BIOLOGICAL PERSPECTIVES

Although most American researchers are familiar with the trait theoretic approach of Raymond Cattell (1947, 1957, 1973) and some of the typological work associated with the adequate taxonomy project (e.g., Allport & Odbert, 1936; Cattell, 1957; Digman & Takemoto-Chock, 1981; Goldberg, 1982; McCrae & Costa, 1987; Norman, 1963, 1969; Tupes & Christal, 1961; Wiggins, 1979), many are less familiar with the biological taxonomy developed in Europe by Hans Eysenck (H. J. Eysenck, 1947, 1952, 1967, 1981, 1987; H. J. Eysenck & M. W. Eysenck, 1985) and his associates (Gray, 1972, 1981, 1982, 1987; Strelau, 1983, 1985). It is, however, this biologically based theory of Eysenck that is most relevant to the understanding of efficient and inefficient cognitive performance.

Over the past 40 years, Hans Eysenck has studied four dimensions of individual differences: introversion–extraversion, neuroticism–stability, psychoticism, and intelligence. In this time, he has developed a broad and compelling theoretical explanation of how differences in a genetic-biological substrate can lead to differences in sensitivity to the environment, to conditioning, to the development of conscience, and to most aspects of human behavior. Although his theories are extremely wide ranging and often controversial, he is perhaps best known for his extensive analysis of the biological basis of introversion–extraversion and its behavioral correlates.

In brief, Eysenck hypothesizes that introverts are more cortically aroused than are extraverts and that these differences in arousal are reflected in a greater conditionability in introverts than in extraverts.[1] This greater ease of conditioning is thought to lead to the development of a stronger conscience on the part of introverts and thus to their subsequently more moral behavior. With the twin assumptions that extraverts are less aroused than introverts and that intermediate levels of arousal are most preferred, Eysenck explains extraverts' greater stimulation-seeking behavior, higher rate of sexual activity, and tendency to engage in dangerous or illegal activities as an attempt to compensate for lower internal levels of arousal with higher external levels.

Arousal is taken here as a theoretical construct asociated with the state of being alert, wide awake, and energized. Arousal is seen as a nonspecific energization in response to stimulation (Duffy, 1972). It is increased by changes in the environment or by the processing demands placed upon the subject. It can also be thought of as the inverse probability of falling asleep (Corcoran, 1965, 1972). Arousal is meant to summarize the common behavioral effects of stimulant drugs, time on task, diurnal variations in alertness, and moderate exercise. Indices of arousal include EEG amplitude and frequency, heart rate (HR), pupillary dilation, skin conductance (SC), body temperature, and self-report. It should be realized, however, that these separate indices also reflect activity in specific systems and have unique as well as common sources of variance. In addition each of these indices has different temporal parameters, with different delays and sampling rates, so that these different indices reflect arousal averaged over different lengths of time and with different delays (e.g., EEG activation will

---

[1]At least under appropriate conditions (H. J. Eysenck & Levey, 1972). It is also likely that impulsivity rather than extraversion is the important dimension in conditioning (Frcka & Martin, 1987).

occur within milliseconds of a stimulus onset, SC changes after several seconds, self-reports of activity and energy reflect arousal sampled over a longer period than either EEG or SC, and body temperature seems to indicate average activity over a period of minutes to hours). Finally, it is important to note that although these indices tend to covary within individuals, they do not necessarily covary between individuals; some individuals will respond to stimuli with greater changes in HR than in SC, whereas others will have large increases in SC but only small increases in HR. Within subjects, changes in SC and HR can correlate positively even though there is zero or a negative correlation between subjects.

Although there are serious problems with H. J. Eysenck's hypothesis that introverts seek less stimulation *because* they are more aroused, there is a modest amount of evidence to suggest that, in fact, introverts are more aroused more of the time than are extraverts (Davis & Cowles, 1988; Gale, 1986). Furthermore, introverts seem to prefer lower levels of sensory stimulation than do extraverts (Elliot, 1971; Ludvigh & Happ, 1974), and these differences change in response to stimulant and depressant drugs (Bartol, 1975). Simply put, extraverts given a stimulant drug are like introverts, or alternatively, introverts given alcohol or a barbiturate are like extraverts (Bartol, 1975; Gupta, 1974).

One difficulty in explaining stimulation-seeking behavior as a consequence of these arousal differences is that arousal has a pronounced diurnal rhythm (Blake, 1967a, 1967b). That is, most people are more aroused in the afternoon and evening, when they seem to be seeking stimulation, than they are in the morning, when most people tend to avoid going to lively parties. According to naive arousal models, extraverts should prefer sex origies early in the morning (in order to achieve a higher level of arousal) and prefer to study in the evening (in order to reduce an already high level of arousal). Although I know of no data directly testing this hypothesis, it does not seem intuitively compelling.

An important modification of H. J. Eysenck's theory has been proposed by Jeffrey Gray (1972, 1981), who suggested that the appropriate basis of analysis of the two-dimensional space made up of introversion–extraversion and neuroticism–stability are the dimensions of anxiety and impulsivity. It had long been known that the dimension of extraversion could be decomposed into the subscales of impulsivity and sociability (Carrigan, 1960; H. J. Eysenck, 1977b; Guilford, 1975, 1977). Similarly, anxiety is a major component of most concepts of neuroticism. Integrating this psychometric work with behavioral responses to antianxiety drugs, Gray (1972, 1981, 1982) suggested that anxiety reflects a sensitivity to cues for punishment and impulsivity reflects sensitivity to cues for rewards. Gray suggested that anxiety plus impulsivity can be equated with Eysenck's dimension of neuroticism (i.e., neurotics are highly sensitive to both cues for reward and for punishment). Furthermore, Gray proposed that introversion–extraversion reflects the balance between sensitivity to cues for reward (impulsivity) and cues for punishment (anxiety). To the extent that one is more sensitive to cues for reward than for cues to punishment, one is more extraverted.

To the extent that one is more sensitive to cues for punishment than to cues for reward, one is more introverted. Thus, Gray equates extraversion with impulsivity minus anxiety.

Although Gray's theory is flawed on psychometric grounds (neither anxiety nor impulsivity is a 45 degree rotation away from neuroticism and extraversion; Rocklin & Revelle, 1981), the concept of differential sensitivity to cues for rewards and punishments is very important to understanding individual differences in rates of learning. Furthermore, by emphasizing the role of *impulsivity* rather than extraversion, Gray has made an important modification to Eysenck's theory. As my colleagues and I have argued extensively (Revelle, Humphreys, Simon, & Gilliland, 1980; Revelle, Anderson, & Humphreys, 1987), it seems as if the dimension of impulsivity is more related to arousal than is sociability or the higher-order dimension of extraversion. (See also Campbell, 1983, and Revelle, 1987, as well as the counterargument by H. J. Eysenck, 1987.)

Even though I review the evidence for this point much more thoroughly in the subsequent sections, let me say now that it seems as if high impulsives are much less aroused in the morning than are low impulsives, equally aroused by midday, and somewhat more aroused by evening.[2] Furthermore, it seems as if high impulsives are more sensitive to cues for reward than are low impulsives and that highly anxious individuals are more sensitive to cues for punishment than are less anxious individuals.

PERSONALITY, MOTIVATION, AND LEARNING

When studying any difference in learning or performance, it is important to be sensitive to the possibility of other, extraneous differences. This is particularly important when one proposes to study noncognitive differences on cognitive tasks. To show that one group learns more rapidly than another is not very compelling evidence for a motivational difference, because the difference could just as easily be one of ability. For this reason, we have followed the path of searching for manipulations that have disordinal interactions with our personality variables in order to show that any presumed ability difference cannot account for our effects.

That is, we try to show that a particular manipulation (say, caffeine) will facilitate the performance of one group (say, high impulsives) while it hinders the performance of another (say, low impulsives). That these are not ability effects is shown by the rough equality of the mean performance of high and low

---

[2]The evidence for the morning differences in arousal between high and low impulsives is consistent with much of the Eysenckian literature. The evidence for the reversal in the evening is more tenuous and requires assumptions about the relationships between arousal and performance. Some of these assumptions are discussed later.

impulsives when averaged across conditions. Furthermore, as the results are disordinal (crossover) interactions, it is impossible to dismiss them as being due to mere scaling artifacts (Maxwell & Delaney, 1985; Revelle & Anderson, in press). Finally, in order to show that the effects are lawfully related to different aspects of cognitive processing, we try to include measures presumed to differ along relevant dimensions of cognitive requirements.

In our prototypic study, we cross one or two personality variables with one or two situational variables and with one or two task variables. To exclude as many competing hypotheses as possible, we frequently design studies that predict two- to four-way interactions. Typically, our studies are designed such that different patterns of interactions or main effects will be predicted by different motivational theories (e.g., Anderson, 1981; Leon & Revelle, 1985; Zinbarg & Revelle, in press). Although I have said why we chose to conduct studies predicting high level interactions, I should also suggest why one should not. Perhaps the most compelling reason *not* to search for such interactions is that they are extremely hard to communicate to others. Without presenting several two- and three-panel graphs, some of our results are quite hard to understand.[3] To ease the difficulty of communication, we typically have taken an effect found in another aspect of the arousal, cognition, or performance literature and done a conceptual replication and extension by including an additional personality, motivational, or task variable. Thus, we explore how individual differences and situational manipulations affect the boundary conditions of more classic cognitive effects. Equally important, we examine how situational or cognitive variables allow for theoretical refinements of our models of personality. Finally, in order to make sure that our results are robust, we have preferred to conceptually replicte our own studies several times in order to look for the consistent patterns across studies.

Perhaps to compensate for our complex data, we have also searched for theoretical explanations that are particularly simple. Thus, to account for a variety of motivational manipulations we have argued that only two basic concepts are needed: effort and arousal. To organize a wide range of performance tasks, we have suggested that only three cognitive constructs need to be considered: the amount of resources needed for Sustained Information Transfer, Short-Term and Long-Term Memory. Finally, to describe the process of learning, I consider only three separate stages: the initial acquisition and encoding of the stimuli, the organization and storage of the information, and the subsequent retrieval of the to-be-remembered material. In all of our theorizing we have recognized that these assumptions are oversimplifications and that careful research can and does indicate many specific sources of variance in each task and each experimental manipulation. However, we believe that as a way of organizing large bodies of data, a limited set of constructs is a useful and appropriate first approximation.

---

[3]One colleague at a doctoral oral examination asked, perhaps seriously, whether psychology is really ready for three-way interactions. The answer was a strong yes!

In the following section, I review evidence that impulsivity and stimulant drugs affect the acquisition of new information by modifying the rate at which information is detected and transformed; that impulsivity and anxiety affect the encoding of information by modifying the salience of positively and negatively valenced information; and that impulsivity and time of day affect the storage of information in different ways for short and extended periods of time. I also report a lack of evidence supporting state-specific effects on recall.

Personality and the Acquisition of Information

The first stage in most models of learning requires detection and encoding of the to-be-learned material (see Broadbent, 1984, for a particularly appealing organization of the cognitive processes involved in learning and performance). There have been many studies showing how various cognitive factors affect this stage of processing. For example, expectations can affect the allocation of attention to various parts of the perceptual field (Posner, 1978), and familiarity with the material to be learned allows for more efficient chunking of complex displays. Characteristics of the stimuli can also affect the perceptual process. With extensive practice, it is possible to detect stimulus features that do not vary across trials much more rapidly and accurately than those stimuli that have features varying from trial to trial (Shiffrin & Schneider, 1977). More relevant for our concerns in this chapter, however, are those studies that have demonstrated how differences in personality can affect even this earliest stage of learning.

Impulsivity and Sustained Information Transfer

The first requirement in learning is to detect and encode the material to be learned. Although obvious, it is important to remember that a subject who is too bored, sleepy, or otherwise inattentive is less likely to learn new material than is one who is paying attention to the learning task. Although we have mainly examined other, later processes in learning, Paul Bowyer, Michael Humphreys, and I have pointed out that individual differences in impulsivity also reflect the ability to stay alert while learning new material (Bowyer, Humphreys, & Revelle, 1983).

Humphreys and I have described certain tasks that we believe require resources for Sustained Information Transfer (SIT; Humphreys & Revelle, 1984; Humphreys, Revelle, Simon, & Gilliland, 1980). Information transfer (IT) tasks are ones in which a subject must rapidly make an arbitrary response to a simple stimulus input. Typical experimental examples include simple and choice reaction time, letter scanning, and simple arithmetic problems. An additional set of IT tasks are those requiring sustained performance over periods lasting minutes to hours. Excellent applied examples of tasks requiring SIT resources are vigilance tasks such as driving a truck or a train for long periods of time, operating a sonar detector trying to locate submarines, or monitoring vital signs during an extended medical operation. A shared characteristic of these tasks is that they require detection and response to low probability stimuli that occur at irregular intervals. Even with skilled subjects, performance on vigilance tasks rapidly deteriorates as a function of time but is sustained by manipulations that increase alertness or arousal (Gale, 1977; Mackie, 1977).[4]

Extraverts and high impulsive subjects exhibit strong vigilance decrements (Bakan, Belton, & Toth, 1963; Thackray, Jones, & Touchstone, 1974). In fact, it was the similarity of the characteristic decline of performance during vigilance tasks for extraverts and sleepy or tired subjects that led Claridge (1967), Corcoran (1965), and H. J. Eysenck (1967) to first suggest that perhaps extraverts were less aroused than introverts.

A similar decline in performance over trials had been found in verbal learning by Underwood (1978), who suggested that decay of attention might be involved in the performance decrement over trials. Underwood had presented subjects with four lists of words and examined the decline in accuracy across these four lists. We conceptually replicated the Underwood study with the addition of a personality variable (impulsivity) and an arousal manipulation (caffeine). Across trial blocks of 24, 80, 80, and 24 words (replicating Underwood), we found that for high impulsives the number of correct forced-choice recognitions for the last 20 words in each block deteriorated from .97 to .84, whereas for the low impulsives recognition went from .92 to .88. With the addition of 4 mg of caffeine per kilogram body weight, however, the performance of the high impulsives showed markedly less deterioration (from .96 to .91; see Fig. 11.1; Bowyer, Humphreys, & Revelle, 1983).

Our results show a remarkable similarity to those of a more standard vigilance task. The obvious message from this study is that subjects who are unable to sustain the resources necessary for information transfer are also less likely to detect and encode material in a learning task. Our least aroused subjects (high impulsives without caffeine) increased their error rates on this simple recognition memory task by a factor of 5 in the space of only a few minutes. The administration of caffeine reduced this decrement by a factor of two.

Impulsivity, Anxiety, and Cue Valence

Once a stimulus is detected, it needs to be encoded. Individual differences enter at this stage by interacting with the valence of the stimulus. In a set of four studies, Richard Zinbarg and I have shown that impulsivity and anxiety interact with cue valence (reward or punishment) to affect learning a simple discrimination task. Our task involved learning to press (Go) or not to press (No-Go) the button on the mouse of a microcomputer. On each trial, a pair of letters made up

---

[4]There are, of course, many other determinants of the vigilance decrement. Interested readers should consult the volumes by Mackie (1977) and by Davies and Parasuraman (1982) for discussions of how presentation rate, signal-to-noise ratio, and type of processing demands affect the vigilance decrement.

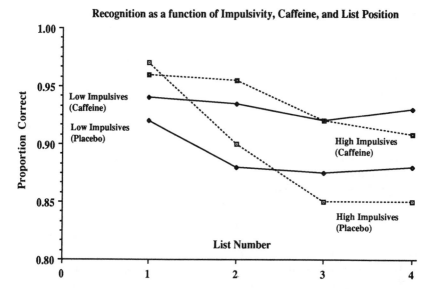

FIG. 11.1.   Accuracy in forced-choice recognition as a function of time on task (trial blocks), impulsivity, and caffeine (adapted from Bowyer et al., 1983).

of one discriminative and one distractor cue was presented on the screen of a Macintosh. These letters were drawn from a set of 16 letters, 8 of which were distractors and 8 of which were cues for pressing or not pressing the mouse button. Of the discriminative letters, two were asociated with reward for pressing the button (*Active Approach* or *Ap*), two were associated with reward being presented for not pressing the button (*Omission* or *Om*), two were cues for punishment following not pressing (*Active Avoidance* or *AA*), and two were cues for punishment following pressing (*Passive Avoidance* or *PA*). In his frustration = punishment and lack of punishment = reward hypothesis, Jeffrey Gray has suggested that high impulsives are more sensitive to those cues that signal reward (Ap) or lack of punishment (AA) than are low impulsives, whereas high anxious subjects are more sensitive to the cues that signal punishment (PA) or lack of reward (Om). Thus, in our experiment, half of the cues were signals to respond for rewards or to avoid punishments (Ap and AA), while the other half were cues for not responding in order to get a reward or to avoid being punished (Om and PA).

In each of four studies, we found a triple interaction of impulsivity, anxiety, and cue type (Zinbarg & Revelle, in press).[5] For trials where making a response led to a reward or avoided punishment (Ap and AA), anxiety inhibited learning

---

[5]In two of the four studies, this effect was significant. The other two studies (with smaller *N*s) showed the same interaction, but the effects were not significant.

among the high impulsives. However, for trials where not making a response led to a reward or avoided punishment (Om and Pa), high anxiety facilitated learning for the low impulsives. That is, the high impulsive subjects were best able to learn to make a response, unless they were also highly anxious. The highly anxious subjects were best able to learn to not make a response, if they were also less impulsive (Fig. 11.2). Impulsivity and anxiety seemed to have had mutually inhibitory effects on the encoding of the to-be-learned material.

The implication of these four studies is that individual differences in personality interact with the valence of the stimulus material to affect learning. The particular pattern of results could not be explained by Spence's theory of anxiety and conditioning (Spence & Spence, 1966), by Eysenck's theory of extraversion and conditioning (H. J. Eysenck, 1965, 1977a), by Gray's hypotheses concerning conditioning in terms of extraversion or in terms of impulsivity (Gray, 1972, 1981, 1982), or by Newman's theory of extraversion and conditioning (Newman, Widom, & Nathan, 1985; Patterson, Kosson, & Newman, 1987). We have suggested that it is necessary to consider how impulsivity and anxiety interact in forming expectations of the to-be-learned material in order to explain our results (Zinbarg & Revelle, in press). It seems that high impulsives are more likely to form expectations that an action will lead to a reward than are low impulsives, and that the highly anxious are more likely to expect that an action will lead to punishment than are the less anxious. In addition, a bias toward expecting rewards can be thought of as inhibiting the development of an expectation about punishment.

Personality and the Storage of Information

Once stimuli are acquired and encoded, it is then necessary to store them for later retrieval. Although much of experimental psychology has been devoted to determining the environmental and situational conditions that facilitate learning, there has been less concern with the personality and motivational effects on storage. One interesting effect that we can now interpret in terms of arousal theory is the effect of time of day at study on subsequent recall. Ebbinghaus (1883/1964) found systematic effects of time of day on the ease of learning nonsense syllables in a well-practiced subject (himself). Learning was an inverted-U function of the time of day. In a later series of studies of the effect of time of day on learning, Gates (1916) recommended that serious academic material should be offered in the morning, as "learning" was greater then than later in the day. These studies did not, however, examine individual differences, but rather set the stage for later studies.

Arousal Theory and Short-Term versus Long-Term Retention

More recent research on the effect of time of day and learning has been interpreted in terms of diurnal rhythms in arousal (Blake, 1967a, 1967b; Folkard,

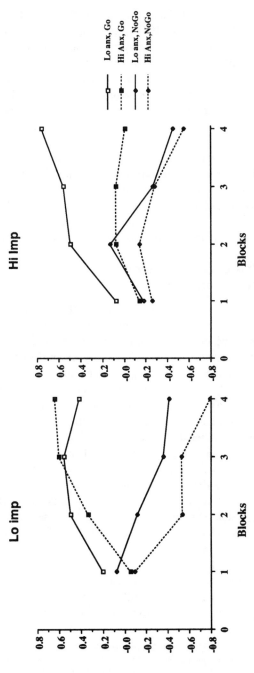

FIG. 11.2. Standardized response rate as a function of impulsivity, anxiety, and cue type (*Go* versus *No-Go*) (adapted from Zinbarg & Revelle, in press).

1975; Folkard & Monk, 1980; Folkard, Monk, Bradbury, & Rosenthal, 1977; Oakhill, 1986, 1988). Folkard et al. (1977) found that time of day interacted with retention interval (immediate vs. one-week delay) and explained their results in terms of a beneficial effect of arousal on long-term memory but a detrimental effect on short-term memory. This explanation was partly based upon the early reports of Galvanic Skin Response (GSR) arousal interacting with the length of the retention interval (Kleinsmith & Kaplan, 1963). In those earlier studies, subjects were to learn associations between digits and words. GSR arousal to each word was correlated with subsequent cued recall of the word-digit pair. High arousal to a word at study time led to poor immediate recall but better recall after 45 minutes. These results were explained in terms of Walker's consolidation hypothesis that arousal increased consolidation of the memory trace but that the trace was unavailable during the process of consolidation (Walker, 1958; Walker & Tate, 1963). Although there have been subsequent replications of this effect, the consolidation hypothesis has not received much acceptance.

Impulsivity, Time of Day, and Short-Term versus Long-Term Retention

If high and low impulsives differ in the phase of their diurnal rhythm as we have suggested (Revelle et al., 1980), then impulsivity should moderate the relationship between time of day and short- versus long-term retention. Mark Puchalski and I have recently completed a study examining this hypothesis (Puchalski, 1988; Puchalski & Revelle, in preparation). We replicated the Folkard et al. (1977) study with the addition of impulsivity as a subject variable.

Ninth grade students in a local school listened to a 12-min tape recording of a 2,000-word passage. One half of the students were then given an immediate test of their comprehension and recall of material from the story, whereas the other half were given a one-week delay interval before being asked about the story. One half of the subjects were run at 8 a.m., the other half at 2 p.m. Of the subjects tested with a week delay, one half were tested at the same time of day as the original story, the other half were tested at the other time. Finally, impulsivity and extraversion were assessed by using the Eysenck Personality Inventory (EPI; H. J. Eysenck & S. B. G. Eysenck, 1964).[6] The results are striking (Fig. 11.3).

For material learned in the morning, high impulsives were far superior to low impulsives in their immediate recall, whereas they were inferior to low impulsives in their delayed recall. These results were reversed for material learned in the afternoon. For these subjects, low impulsives were able to recall more

---

[6]Because we are more interested in assessing impulsivity than extraversion, we use the EPI rather than the more recent Eysenck Personality Questionnaire (EPQ; S. B. G. Eysenck & H. J. Eysenck, 1975). As we have argued elsewhere (Revelle et al., 1980; Rocklin & Revelle, 1981), extraversion as assessed by these two tests is not the same construct. We have found empirically that the impulsivity scale of the EPI is more related to arousal differences than are the scales of the EPQ.

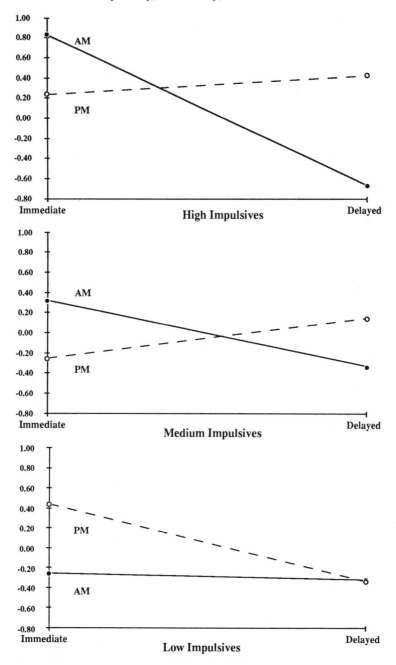

FIG. 11.3. Standardized number of problems correct on a recall-comprehension test as a function of delay (immediate vs. one week), time of day (8 am vs. 2 pm), and impulsivity (adapted from Puchalski & Revelle, in preparation).

material immediately than the high impulsives, but the high impulsives were superior after the one-week retention period. Perhaps most striking is the absolute increase from short-term to long-term recall on the part of the high impulsives in the afternoon: For material learned in the afternoon, the high impulsives remembered more about the story after a delay of one week than they did immediately after the story. There were no reliable effects of state dependence (i.e., better morning recall for material studied in the morning than in the afternoon).

One way to understand the magnitude of the effects of individual differences in learning is to consider the additional variance accounted for as various classes of variables are added. Relevant variables for our listening comprehension/recall task include the task variable of short- versus long-delay interval, the situational variable of morning versus afternoon, individual differences in reading ability, and finally, individual differences in impulsivity. The effect of the delay interval accounted for 4% of the variance of recall. Time of day and the interaction of time of day and delay accounted for an additional 3%. Adding reading ability accounted for an additional 11%. Finally, adding the interaction of impulsivity, time of day, and length of delay added an additional 7%, which accounted for a total amount of variance of 25%.[7]

PERSONALITY, MOTIVATION, AND PERFORMANCE

In the preceding sections I have shown how personality variables can affect the development of competence (i.e., learning). The personality dimensions of impulsivity and anxiety, in combination with situational manipulations of arousal, affect the initial detection of material, how that material is encoded, and how well that material can be stored for later retrieval. These same variables also affect performance of well-learned skills. Inspired by the personality theories of H. J. Eysenck (1967) and Gray (1972, 1982) and the performance theories of the experimental psychologists Donald Broadbent (1971), Simon Folkard (1975), and Robert Hockey (1979), my colleagues and I have been examining how personality combines with situational and task variables to affect performance on simple and complex cognitive tasks. We have been able to show a consistent pattern of effects in which the personality dimensions of impulsivity and anxiety interact with situational manipulations such as time of day, stimulant drugs, or time on task and with task variables such as the amount of resources required for Sustained Information Transfer or for Short- versus Long-Term Memory to affect performance on many types of tasks.

---

[7]The model tested was in fact the full model. These stepwise multiple Rs are reported merely to give an estimate of the relative importance of each class (task, situational, ability, personality) of variable.

Personality, Stress, and Performance

Our earliest demonstrations of the importance of considering personality variables in combination with situational manipulations were studies investigating how introversion–extraversion combined with various situational stressors or arousers[8] to affect performance. In the first of this series (Revelle, 1973), several ad hoc performance tasks were used, including anagrams, digit-symbol substitution, and maze performance. In addition to the personality variables of introversion–extraversion and neuroticism, individual differences in arousal were indexed by Skin Conductance (SC). Within each type of task, there were three levels of difficulty. Stress was manipulated by combining the presumed stressors of group size, incentive motivation, and noise using an additive design.[9] The expected finding was to show that performance fit the pattern predicted by the Yerkes–Dodson law and that these results were an interactive effect of personality and stress. Thus, a difficulty by stress by introversion interaction was predicted. Furthermore, it was predicted that the use of SC would allow for a clear ordering of the effects and therefore a SC by task difficulty effect was expected. However, as is often the case in naively ambitious dissertations, this was not to be the case: Across all six stress levels, there was no indication of an interaction between personality and stress or personality and arousal. When these situational manipulations were held constant, however, there was a reliable interaction between arousal as indexed by SC and introversion–extraversion: Performance was a monotonically decreasing function of increases in SC for introverts but a curvilinear function (an inverted U) for extraverts. That is, introverts performed best if they had low skin conductance, but extraverts performed best with moderate levels of skin conductance. The lack of interactions of personality and arousal when incentives were varied and the presence of an

---

[8]Our earliest work did not distinguish between these two concepts. It was only when the pattern of results indicated that arousal and effort manipulations needed to be considered separately that a more clear-cut distinction was made.

[9]For a more complete treatment of the types of designs used in these and similar studies, see Revelle and Anderson (in press). The most common between-subjects designs used to test arousal are the factorial, the additive, and the multiple-level design. In factorial designs, two or more presumed sources of arousal are crossed in the typical N-way analysis of variance. Unfortunately, as a means of testing for inverted-U relationships, such designs make up for the simplicity of the statistical analysis with a complexity of interpretability. It is easier to use these designs to show that different variables do not affect the same underlying construct (arousal) than it is to show that they do (Craig, Humphreys, Rocklin, & Revelle, 1979; Revelle, 1973).

In the additive design, the independent variables are not fully crossed but merely added onto each other. Although this makes for a more efficient allocation of subjects to conditions that may be unambiguously ordered, additive designs suffer from a lack of explicitness in determining whether the variables all add to the same underlying construct.

Multiple-level designs allow for unambiguous ordering of conditions by varying a treatment such as drug dosage. There are few situational variables other than drug dosage that yield so easily to such a design, however.

interaction when incentives were held constant was interpreted as indicating the importance of considering effort and arousal as separate constructs rather than as one unified motivational term.

In a follow-up study (Revelle, Amaral, & Turriff, 1976), performance on items from a practice Graduate Record Examination (GRE) was an interactive function of introversion–extraversion and situational stress. Stress was manipulated by increasing time pressure and administrating caffeine. In a within-subjects additive design, subjects were given 60 GRE items under instructions to take as long as they needed (relaxed) or to do them in 10 minutes with or without caffeine (timed-placebo vs. timed-caffeine). The amount of caffeine (200 mg) was roughly equivalent to that consumed in two–three cups of coffee. The results were strikingly clear-cut: Compared to the relaxed condition, time pressure and caffeine hindered the performance of introverts by .6 standard deviations, while the same manipulations facilitated the performance of the extraverts by .45 standard deviations (Fig. 11.4).

In an early replication and extension of this study, Kirby Gilliland (1976, 1980) found that these effects were strongest for the impulsivity component of introversion–extraversion rather than for the whole scale. Using a between-subjects multiple-level design with three levels of caffeine (0, 2, and 4 mg per kilogram body weight) and comparing predrug with postdrug performance on practice GREs, Gilliland found that the performance of the high impulsives was a monotonically increasing function of caffeine, and the performance of the low impulsives was a curvilinear (inverted-U) function of caffeine.

Working independently, Gupta (1977) used a between-subjects, multiple-level design to examine the interaction of amphetamine dosage and introversion–extraversion on an IQ test. Dosages of 0, 5, 10, and 15 mg were given to extreme introverts and extraverts.[10] For the introverts, performance deteriorated across all levels of amphetamine. For the extraverts, on the other hand, performance first increased (from 0 to 5 to 10 mg) and then decreased (at 15 mg). Thus, there was a negative monotonic function of amphetamine dosage for introverted subjects, but a curvilinear function for extraverted subjects.

In a further series of five experiments extending the Revelle et al. (1976) and Gilliland (1976) experiments, we found that the personality dimension that most reliably interacted with caffeine was not introversion–extraversion, but rather one of its components, impulsivity (Revelle et al., 1980). Including the Gilliland (1976) experiment, each of the five studies conducted in the morning showed the same effect: The performance of high impulsives was facilitated by caffeine, and the performance of low impulsives was impaired by caffeine. The median improvement was .55 standard deviations for the high impulsives, and the median decrement was .22 standard deviations for the low impulsives. In addition, we

---

[10]By using this extreme-groups design, Gupta was unable to distinguish between the impulsivity and sociability components of introversion–extraversion. This is an excellent demonstration of the advantages and disadvantages of using extreme groups: The statistical power is increased, but the possibility of reanalysis of the personality scale is lost,

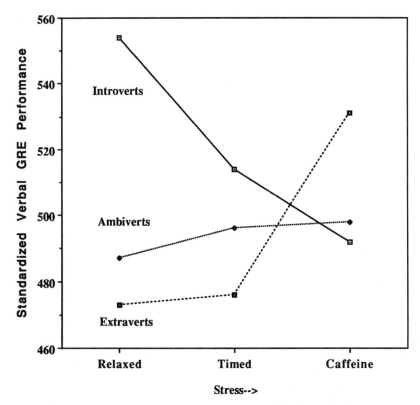

FIG. 11.4.   Standardized performance on a practice Graduate Record Exam as a function of stress (relaxed, time pressure, time pressure + caffeine) and introversion–extraversion (adapted from Revelle, Amaral, & Turriff, 1976).

discovered that this interaction was reversed in those studies conducted in the evening. In three of four studies conducted in the evening, the performance of the low impulsives was improved with caffeine, whereas in all four studies the performance of the high impulsives was impaired. The median improvement for the low impulsives was .27 standard deviations, and the median decrease was .15 standard deviations for the high impulsives (Fig. 11.5). In addition to these interactions with time of day, there were interactions with day of study (Day 1 vs. Day 2) that are difficult to understand or to explain.[11]

---

[11]However, consider the discussion by Gale (1977) and Davis and Cowles (1988) about the effects of multiple days upon arousal. It is possible that the interactions of days with time of day and impulsivity might be due to a differential adaptation to the laboratory (Davis & Cowles, 1988) for high and low impulsives. In a new situation (i.e., a caffeine study), high impulsives are fairly alert in the evening of the first day, while the low impulsives are tired from being aroused all day. By the second or third day, however, this initial excitement has passed for the high impulsives, and they become less aroused than the low impulsives.

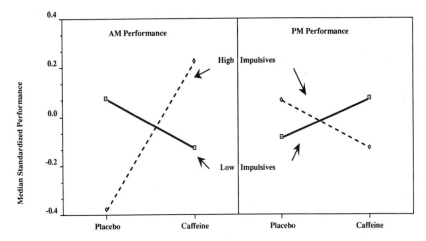

FIG. 11.5. Standardized performance on seven ability measures as a function of impulsivity, caffeine, impulsivity, and time of day (adapted from Revelle et al., 1980).

We have interpreted these time of day results as showing that impulsivity relates not to absolute arousal level but rather to the phase of the diurnal arousal rhythm. The arousal level of high impulsives seems to lag behind that of low impulsives by several hours. Similar diurnal differences have been reported for introversion–extraversion (Blake, 1967b, 1971) and for impulsivity (M. W. Eysenck & Folkard, 1980).

Although having only two levels of situationally induced arousal (placebo vs. caffeine), we interpreted our data as providing evidence for the inverted-U effect (e.g., Hebb, 1955; Yerkes & Dodson, 1908). For the studies in the morning, we assumed that high impulsives were less aroused than were low impulsives and that increases in performance with caffeine were due to increases in arousal. The decrease in performance on the part of the low impulsives we explained in terms of an initially higher level of arousal and a subsequent overarousal leading to inefficient performance. In the evening, the explanation was reversed: High impulsives were now seen as optimally aroused without caffeine and overaroused with caffeine; low impulsives were underaroused and improved their performance when given caffeine (Revelle et al., 1980). Unfortunately, these studies provided no evidence for curvilinearity per se. Gilliland (1976, 1980) and Gupta (1977) had shown curvilinearity, but using between groups designs that do not provide unequivocal evidence for inverted Us. It is possible that some subjects get better as arousal increases and others get worse; curvilinearity at the aggregate level could merely reflect changing proportions of these two types of subjects.

In an elegant demonstration of the importance of examining data at the aggregated, group level as well as the unaggregated, subject level, Kristen Anderson (1988) has found that GRE performance is in fact a inverted-U function of increasing dosages of caffeine for low impulsive subjects, but is a monotonically increasing function for high impulsives. In a within-subjects multiple-level study using five levels of caffeine (0, 1, 2, 3, and 4 mg per kilogram body weight) and two performance tasks, caffeine facilitated the performance of both high and low impulsives on a letter-scanning task but had an inverted-U relationship for the performance of low impulsive subjects on a GRE task. For the high impulsives, GRE performance monotonically increased with increasing dosages of caffeine. That these curvilinear relationships were not an artifact of aggregation was shown when the data were examined at the individual level: A reliable number of subjects showed the pattern predicted by the Yerkes–Dodson law (Anderson, 1988). These data supply convincing evidence that the Yerkes–Dodson effect is not some statistical artifact but is rather a powerful phenomenon that needs to be explained.

Personality, Motivation, and Task Components

All of these studies indicated the importance of considering individual differences and situational manipulations when examining efficient performance, but they did nothing for explaining the effect. The statement that performance is a curvilinear function of arousal is a description, not an explanation. In an effort to go beyond merely describing our results, we have proposed a model that organizes a variety of personality and situational manipulations along two dimensions of motivation: effort and arousal. In addition, we explain the curvilinear relationship between arousal and performance in terms of two monotonic relationships, one increasing and one decreasing (Fig. 11.6; Humphreys & Revelle, 1984).

Personality and Motivation

It is possible to categorize several different dimensions of personality as well as the effect of a variety of situational manipulations in terms of two motivational constructs: on-task effort and arousal. In everyday terms, effort can be associated with trying harder, arousal can be associated with alertness. In somewhat more formal terms, effort is an indication of the direction of action and arousal is an indication of the intensity of action.

The dimension of impulsivity, as well as situational manipulations such as time of day, stimulant drugs, or time on task, are related to arousal level. High impulsives are less aroused than low impulsives in the morning, equally aroused in the early afternoon, and more aroused in the evening. Stimulant drugs increase arousal, as do moderate increases in noise or light.[12]

---

[12]Noise has contradictory effects, partly because moderate levels of white noise can mask other distracting stimuli. It is also likely that prolonged exposure to high levels of noise leads to fatigue. See Broadbent (1978) and Poulton (1978, 1979) for a more thorough treatment of the issues involved with noise.

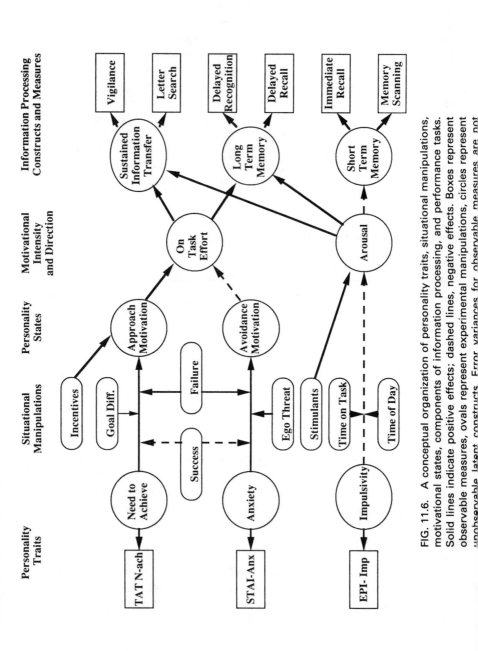

FIG. 11.6. A conceptual organization of personality traits, situational manipulations, motivational states, components of information processing, and performance tasks. Solid lines indicate positive effects; dashed lines, negative effects. Boxes represent observable measures, ovals represent experimental manipulations, circles represent unobservable latent constructs. Error variances for observable measures are not

The personality dimension of achievement motivation may be associated with on-task effort. High achievement motivated subjects will spend more time, engage more frequently, and persist longer in tasks that require effort and reflect ability (Atkinson, 1957, 1964; Atkinson & Birch, 1978). Incentives such as money or other rewards as well as higher task demands (Locke, 1968) will also increase on-task effort. Success or failure feedback interacts with achievement motivation to affect on-task effort. For high achievement oriented subjects, failure feedback leads to an increase in effort, success feedback leads to a decrease in effort. Effort is typically assessed in the achievement domain by amount of time spent on task or by the frequency and persistence of choosing a task. Shifts in performance or preference for task difficulty over time can be interpreted as supporting the belief that failure leads to an increase in effort for high achievers (Revelle & Michaels, 1976) or for all individuals with a more rapid shift for high achievers (Kuhl & Blankenship, 1979).

Individual differences in anxiety are associated with both effort and arousal. High levels of anxiety can be associated with high levels of arousal. However, at least among college students, the effects of anxiety can most easily be interpreted in terms of a reduction of on-task effort. Failure feedback and ego-involving instructions increase state anxiety and reduce performance for trait anxious individuals. Success feedback, on the other hand, reduces anxiety and improves performance for highly anxious subjects. Many earlier demonstrations of the effect of anxiety on learning (e.g., Spence, Farber, & McFann, 1956) confounded task difficulty with feedback manipulations. (By their very nature, difficult tasks lead to more failure experiences than do easy tasks.) When feedback and difficulty are deliberately crossed (Weiner & Schneider, 1971), the effects of feedback account for the previously observed difficulty effects: Success feedback facilitates the performance of highly anxious subjects but hinders the performance of less anxious ones. Failure feedback, on the other hand, reduces the performance of high anxious subjects but improves the performance of the less anxious ones. These effects can be interpreted as showing that anxiety inhibits on-going behavior (Atkinson & Birch, 1970, 1978; Gray, 1982) or initiates inappropriate responses (Sarason, 1975; Wine, 1971).

Motivation and Performance

If personality and situations combine to affect two different motivational components, effort and arousal, then how are these components related to performance? To answer this question requires considering at least two different dimensions along which tasks can differ: Tasks can vary in the amount of resources they require for Sustained Information Transfer (SIT), as well as the amount of resources required for retaining information in an available state for short periods of time (Short-Term Memory—STM). Some tasks have a low STM load but require substantial amounts of SIT resources. Other tasks have a high STM load but require only moderate levels of SIT resources. Finally, some (complex) tasks require both large amounts of SIT and STM resources.[13]

Increases in either effort or arousal improve performance on SIT tasks. Both trying harder and being more alert facilitate performance on simple and choice reaction time tasks, letter scanning, vigilance, and simple proofreading. The pattern of results found by Bowyer et al. (1983) is typical for SIT tasks. The performance of high impulsives starts off at roughly the same level as that of low impulsives but then shows a pronounced drop within a few minutes of starting the task. The administration of caffeine inhibits this decay. Caffeine or diurnally induced arousal also facilitates the speed at which simple repetitive tasks can be performed. Anderson (1988) has shown that across five levels of caffeine and for both high and low impulsive subjects, letter scanning improved as a monotonic effect of caffeine. Blake (1967a) found that on tasks we would characterize as having a large SIT component, performance improved from morning to midafternoon. Folkard, Knauth, Monk, & Rutenfranz (1976) found that performance on a simple scanning task was positively correlated with the body temperature of (both of) their subjects when the subjects were on a cycle of rapidly rotating shift work.

In striking contrast to the effect of effort and arousal on SIT tasks is the effect of arousal on tasks that require the availability of material presented a few seconds earlier. A demonstration of this was the finding by Folkard et al. (1976) that when the memory load of a letter-scanning task was increased, the correlation with body temperature went from positive (low memory load) to negative (high memory load). High arousal, as indexed by body temperature, was associated with poor performance. In a conceptual replication and extension of Folkard et al., we found that caffeine facilitated performance on the low memory task but hindered performance on the high memory load version (Anderson & Revelle, 1983a). We have also shown that impulsivity and caffeine interact with memory load in a proofreading task (Anderson & Revelle, 1983b). The results of that study suggested that tasks with a higher memory load are more sensitive to arousal-induced decrements than are tasks with a lower memory load.

I have already discussed Folkard's study showing that the immediate availability of aurally presented material is hindered by high arousal. When discussing our replication and extension of this effect (Puchalski, 1988; Puchalski & Revelle, in preparation), I suggested that this effect is a demonstration of how personality affects the learning and storage of new material. It is the case, however, that this study can also be seen as supporting our hypothesis that arousal has a detrimental effect on some aspect of short-term or working memory. Subjects thought to be most aroused (low impulsives in the morning, high impulsives in the afternoon) made more errors than those who were thought to be

---

[13]There are, of course, many ways to index complexity. Degrading the stimulus in a signal-detection task will make it more difficult to detect, but the task is still not complex. I am defining complex as requiring both SIT and STM resources.

less aroused (low impulsives in the afternoon, high impulsives in the morning). We have recently been exploring tasks that show how increases in arousal can have facilitatory effects on one information-processing component of the task and detrimental effects upon other components. In the first of these (Anderson, Revelle, & Lynch, in press), we examined how caffeine and impulsivity affected the ability to do a modified Sternberg memory-search task (Sternberg, 1969). Extending an earlier study by M. W. Eysenck and M. C. Eysenck (1979) that had examined the effects of personality on memory scanning, we varied impulsivity level, caffeine, and category match versus physical match (Burrows & Okada, 1976). The primary result of interest was that caffeine reduced the intercept but increased the slope of reaction time as a function of memory load. Intercept in such memory-scanning tasks is viewed as the time it takes to prepare to respond, whereas slope is seen as the amount of time it takes to process each item in short-term memory. We interpret our findings as lending support for the Humphreys and Revelle (1984) model and not supporting Easterbrook's hypothesis that arousal narrows the range of cue utilization (Anderson, 1981; Easterbrook, 1959).

The second study that compared performance on different task components made use of geometric analogies similar to those used by Mulholland, Pellegrino, and Glaser (1980). Our multiple-choice analogies are presented on a computer screen and response times and accuracies are taken for each problem (Onken & Revelle, 1984; Fig. 11.7). Problems can vary in the number of elements per term as well as the transformations per element.[14] Mulholland et al. (1980) suggested that transformations reflect memory load and affect accuracy, whereas elements merely affect solution time.

Using our computerized version of this task, Melissa Benzuly (1985) crossed 0 and 4 mg per kilogram body weight of caffeine with high and low impulsivity between subjects and varied the number of elements and transformations within subjects. Caffeine interacted with transformations but not with elements: Performance on low memory load problems was facilitated with caffeine, performance on high memory load problems was not (Fig. 11.8). In that the number of elements reflects the Information Transfer load of the task, and that transformations are related to the short-term memory load, these results are consistent with our two-factor model of performance.

In an earlier study using this same task, Margie Leon and I found that high anxiety led to slower and less accurate performance when subjects were under low time pressure but to faster and still less accurate performance under high time pressure (Leon & Revelle, 1985). We failed to detect the interaction of anxiety with transformations (i.e., memory load) predicted by M. W. Eysenck's (1979, 1981) hypothesis that anxiety reduces working memory capacity. We interpreted our results as supporting the Humphreys–Revelle interpretation of

---

[14]Mulholland et al. (1980) categorize their problems in terms of the total number of transformations, which will be simply the number per element times the number of elements.

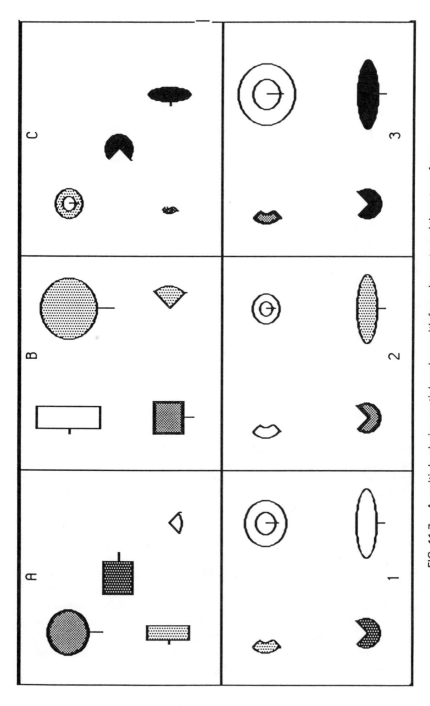

FIG. 11.7. A multiple-choice spatial analogy with four elements and three transformations per element. Problems can vary in the number of elements and the number of transformations.

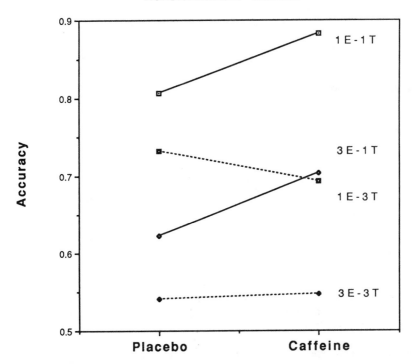

FIG. 11.8.   Geometric analogy performance as a function of number of Elements (SIT load), number of Transformations (STM load), impulsivity, and caffeine. Task complexity is a combination of the number of Elements and number of Transformations: e.g., 1 E–1 T is a one element, one transformation per element problem (from Benzuly, 1985).

Sarason (1975) and Wine (1971) that anxiety reduces the amount of effort applied to the task.

In a recent review of many of these studies (Revelle, Anderson, & Humphreys, 1987) we have shown how caffeine has a facilitatory effect on those tasks that have a low memory load for all subjects. We have also shown that caffeine has either a detrimental effect or interacts with impulsivity to help low aroused subjects (high impulsives in the morning) but to hurt high aroused subjects (low impulsives in the morning).

To explain the results that have cross-over interactions (caffeine helps high impulsives but hurts low impulsives) and to explain rather than describe inverted-U relationships, we have argued that one must consider the combination of two monotonic functions. One of these is a monotonically increasing relationship

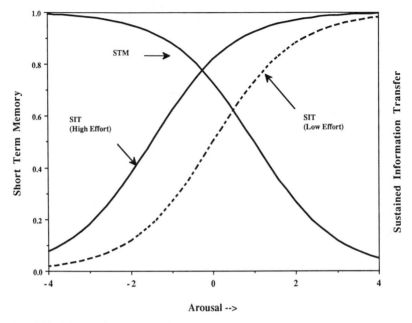

FIG. 11.9. Hypothetical relationship between arousal, effort, sustained information transfer (SIT), short-term memory (STM), and complex performance (adapted from Humphreys & Revelle, 1984).

between arousal and resources available for SIT. The other is a monotonically decreasing relationship between arousal and availability of working or short-term memory resources. A simple combination of these two functions can produce curvilinearity and furthermore can predict peak performance at lower levels of arousal for tasks with high degrees of memory load (Fig. 11.9). At low levels of arousal, performance is limited by a lack of resources for sustained information transfer. Response speed is slow and the probability of detecting new stimuli is low. Immediate availability of recently detected stimuli is high, but unhelpful, given the lack of SIT resources. As arousal increases, SIT resources increase with a decrease in availability of recently presented material. Performance improves until the decrease in immediate or short-term memory resources is greater than the gain in SIT resources. Performance at high arousal levels is memory limited, and improvements in speed or accuracy of stimulus detection do not compensate for the lack of availability in immediate memory. Increases in on-task effort increase SIT resources but have no effect upon resources available for working memory (Humphreys & Revelle, 1984; Revelle et al., 1987).[15]

---

[15]It is, of course, difficult to impossible to have a pure STM task. In that effort increases SIT resources available for detecting and encoding stimuli, effort can have a positive effect on immediate memory *tasks* even though we claim that effort does not affect the availability of information that has been encoded but is no longer attended to.

Multiple Levels of Analysis and Resource Trade-Offs

One important finding from much of our work is that the effects of various sources of motivation do not show similar effects, even though they are presumed to affect the same system. For example, Anderson (1988) found that increasing levels of caffeine facilitated letter cancellation, but that the presumably less aroused high impulsive subjects cancelled more letters than did the more aroused low impulsives. Puchalski and Revelle (in preparation), using the identical letter-cancellation task, found that although high impulsives cancelled fewer letters in the morning than in the afternoon (when they were presumably more aroused), the high impulsives also cancelled more letters than did the low impulsives (who were assumed to be more aroused). The lack of parallelism of impulsivity and either the caffeine or the time of day manipulations forces one to wonder why we claim that all are arousal related.

Multiple Levels of Analysis

The answer to this question is to realize that behavior is multiply determined and that performance on any one task will have several sources of variance. One source is arousal. Other sources that also affect performance are a *strategic* preference for speed versus accuracy and a *directional* tendency to engage in a task versus devoting time elsewhere. Yet another source of variability is *stylistic* differences in task choice and preference. Each of these sources of variance accounts for behavior at different levels of temporal aggregation.

Theories that explain behavior at one level do not necessarily explain it at another level. Stable personality dimensions such as anxiety and impulsivity can affect behavior at each of these levels in different ways. At one level, impulsivity combines with time of day to affect arousal. Arousal in turn affects the relative amount of resources available for SIT and for STM processes. At a broader level, impulsivity leads to a bias toward responding rapidly rather than accurately (Dickman & Meyer, 1988; H. J. Eysenck & M. W. Eysenck, 1985). This is probably due to a greater sensitivity to rewards and a tendency to respond on the part of the high impulsives. At this same level, anxiety leads to a bias to respond carefully, avoiding mistakes (Sabates, 1986). At an even broader level, anxiety increases the number of off-task thoughts, thereby reducing the SIT resources applied to the experimenter-defined task. And, at yet an even broader level, impulsivity and anxiety affect task choice. High impulsives prefer to engage in tasks that require rapid responding or have deadlines, low impulsives avoid such tasks. Highly anxious students will avoid classes in their major and devote more time to work on other projects (Atkinson & Birch, 1978; Atkinson & Raynor, 1974). It is possible that the effects at this level are also due to differential sensitivity to rewards, or alternatively, to learning from past experience. Highly impulsive students might wait until the last night to finish a term paper because they know that they work well under deadline pressure and are able to stay up until late at night working on the paper. Low impulsive students, on the other

Types of Resource Tradeoffs	Mechanism/ Measure	Personality Dimensions Impulsivity	Anxiety
Level I: Automatic SIT/STM	Arousal: facilitates SIT impairs STM	Caffeine on complex tasks: facilitates high Imps hinders low Imps	
Level II: Strategic Speed/ Accuracy	Sensitivity to reward Sensitivity to punishment	High Imps fast Lows Imps accurate	Low Anx fast High Anx accurate
Level III: Directional Effort	Allocation of effort to on task or off task thoughts		Low Anx on task High Anx off task
Level IV: Temporal/ Stylistic Choice, Frequency	Latency to initiate task Persistence on task Act frequency	Low Imps slow to initiate but persistent High Imps fast but not persistent	Low Anx choose challenging tasks High Anx avoid possibility of failure

FIG. 11.10. Multiple levels of trade-offs related to impulsivity and anxiety (adapted from Revelle, 1987).

hand, might learn that they do not function well under time pressure nor can they work all night. As a consequence, they will learn to better budget their time and start the work well ahead of time.

These distinctions between different levels of analysis can be used to organize some of the effects of individual differences upon performance. At each level, different trade-offs are involved, and different mechanisms are presumed to operate. The personality dimensions of impulsivity and anxiety have effects at several of these levels, but the causes for the effects can be quite different. These levels of analysis may be organized figurally with trade-offs arranged in increasing order of the temporal breadth of the effects (Fig. 11.10).

Given the concept of levels of analysis, it is easy to see why a manipulation that interacts with a personality trait at one level does not necessarily have the same effect at another level.[16] Caffeine interacts with impulsivity to affect performance by increasing arousal and changing the relative amount of resources

[16]Another form of levels of analysis is to consider data at the subject level versus the aggregate level (Anderson, 1988). All of the analyses discussed here are at the group level, where data are aggregated across subjects. The underlying assumption here is, of course, that such aggregation preserves the relationships that exist at the subject level.

available for immediate or delayed processing. It is unrealistic to expect caffeine to change the speed–accuracy trade-off strategy of a subject or to turn a procrastinating high impulsive into a conscientious low impulsive. Similarly, changing the payoffs for speed versus accuracy will change performance strategies but affect neither SIT nor STM resources.

Performance Efficiency and Resource Trade-offs

An important question to ask once again is why should performance not be maximal? Why should performance not demonstrate level of competence? To Blodgett or Tolman and Honzik, the answer was easy. Without food as an incentive, the rats did not need to perform; the rats had better ways to use a scarce resource: their time or their energy. Why run down a maze if there is nothing in the goal box? Why not just spend the same amount of time strolling through the maze looking for other ways to get out?

In more formal terms, performance of several tasks with shared or partly shared and limited resources will involve trade-offs between those resources. If multiple resources are required for each task, and if these resources are limited to some extent, then performance along one dimension may reduce the resources available for the other dimension. To the extent that resources are limited, maximal performance along one dimension will typically result in submaximal performance along the other dimension. The analysis of performance along both of these dimensions will result in an performance operating characteristic (POC) curve showing the degree of trade-off between them.

In our work, the differential effect of arousal upon SIT, STM, and LTM (long-term memory) resources can be analyzed in terms of such trade-offs. High arousal facilitates the ability to respond rapidly, but at a cost of reducing the availability in memory of recently occurring events. This trade-off is beneficial in a situation where a premium is upon rapid responding without much processing of what has led up to the situation. An additional benefit of high arousal is that even though there is a temporary unavailability, events are remembered better later. When one is required to work rapidly *and* process stimuli that are no longer present (i.e., use working memory) increases in arousal lead to increases in net performance if one is initially not very aroused, but to decrements if one is already aroused.

Trade-offs also occur at the strategic level. Impulsives typically make use of a strategy that puts a premium on speed rather than accuracy. It is possible to change this strategy by instructions and make low impulsives respond more rapidly or to make high impulsives respond more slowly. There are indications, however, that each group performs best when using their normal strategy (Dickman & Meyer, 1988). Anxiety is also related to this strategic trade-off of speed for accuracy (Geen & Kaiser, 1985). For instance, Angela Sabates found that a self-report measure of test-taking strategies involving a preference for accuracy rather than speed correlates very highly (.5–.7) with various anxiety scales (Sabates, 1986). Other trade-offs occur between doing the experimenter-defined task versus doing the subject-defined task (such as maintaining self-esteem) or between choosing to do one task versus another. Trade-offs are particularly important at these broader levels and involve a consideration of the various ways of measuring preference. We follow the logic of Atkinson and Birch (1970, 1978) in proposing that preference can be measured by choice (choosing to do A versus B), latency (delay in initiating B when doing A), persistence (in a two-task situation, persistence of A is the same as the latency of B), frequency (how often is A done), or total time spent (frequency of A times average persistence). Although frequently correlated, these measures are not identical in any dynamic system (Atkinson & Birch, 1970, 1978; Revelle, 1986).

Cumulative Performance

Finally, when discussing cognitive competence and performance, it is important to note that performance over the short run is not the same as cumulative performance summed over a long period of time (e.g., 4 years of academic performance as measured by grade point average (GPA) for an undergraduate, or a lifetime of productivity as measured by the total number of patents issued for an inventor). Cumulative performance is the sum of many separate acts that themselves are a function of individual differences in ability and moment-to-moment fluctuations in efficiency of performance. Issues of concern for the study of cumulative performance include all the variables relevant to momentary performance as well as determinants of total time spent engaging in the relevant activities. Even a very able student's GPA, for instance, will not be very high unless he or she spends considerable time in academic rather than social activities. Thus, the study of cumulative performance is concerned with the broader stylistic issues of task choice, frequency, and persistence, as well as the narrower issues of moment-to-moment efficiency. (For a more detailed consideration of cumulative performance, see Atkinson, 1974, and Revelle, 1986.)

Personality, Cognition, and the Psychological Spectrum

As a way of relating these multiple levels of trade-offs to fundamental issues in personality and cognition, it is useful to organize psychological phenomena in terms of their average duration (Fig. 11.11). At this conference we have heard reports of measures that range over 12 orders of magnitude: from discussions of neural firing rates lasting a millisecond (10^{-3} seconds) to cumulative performance over a lifespan representing 95 years (3×10^9 seconds). To some extent, psychological theorists tend to specialize at different parts of the spectrum: Psychophysiologists examine high frequency–short duration events (e.g., rates of neural transmission, frequency of resting EEG alpha activity, heart and

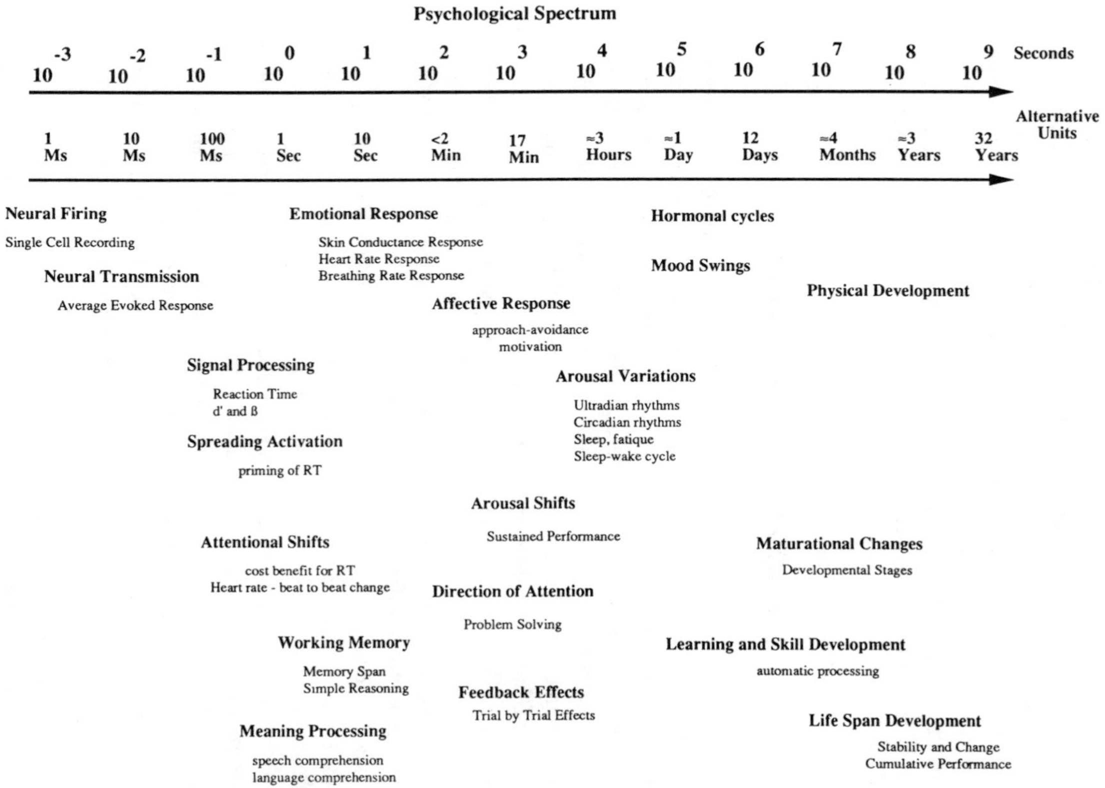

Psychological Spectrum

10^-3	10^-2	10^-1	10^0	10^1	10^2	10^3	10^4	10^5	10^6	10^7	10^8	10^9 Seconds
1 Ms	10 Ms	100 Ms	1 Sec	10 Sec	<2 Min	17 Min	≈3 Hours	≈1 Day	12 Days	≈4 Months	≈3 Years	32 Years

Alternative Units

Neural Firing
Single Cell Recording

Neural Transmission
Average Evoked Response

Signal Processing
Reaction Time
d' and β

Spreading Activation
priming of RT

Emotional Response
Skin Conductance Response
Heart Rate Response
Breathing Rate Response

Affective Response
approach-avoidance motivation

Arousal Variations
Ultradian rhythms
Circadian rhythms
Sleep, fatigue
Sleep-wake cycle

Hormonal cycles

Mood Swings

Physical Development

Attentional Shifts
cost benefit for RT
Heart rate - beat to beat change

Working Memory
Memory Span
Simple Reasoning

Meaning Processing
speech comprehension
language comprehension

Arousal Shifts
Sustained Performance

Direction of Attention
Problem Solving

Feedback Effects
Trial by Trial Effects

Maturational Changes
Developmental Stages

Learning and Skill Development
automatic processing

Life Span Development
Stability and Change
Cumulative Performance

FIG. 11.11. The Psychological Spectrum: An organization of psychological phenomena across 12 orders of magnitude.

327

breathing rates, and skin conductance responses); cognitive psychologists tend to specialize in events ranging in duration from 100 milliseconds (e.g., priming effects in reaction time) to 10 seconds (e.g., limits of working memory); theorists of affect examine emotional-affective responses that are seen as lasting for periods ranging from a few seconds (emotions) to a few hours (moods); developmental psychologists examine growth and change indexed in months (3×10^6 seconds) to life spans (3×10^9 seconds). Individual differences occur at all parts of this Psychological Spectrum. It is only in conferences such as this that the full range of the psychological spectrum can be examined and the degree of relationship of individual differences across this range of temporal frequencies can be studied.

SUMMARY AND PROSPECTS

In this chapter, I have reviewed how an understanding of personality allows for a clearer distinction between competence and performance. The stable personality dimensions of impulsivity and anxiety, in combination with situational stressors such as time pressure, feedback, or particularly time of day and caffeine, have systematic, although complex relationships to performance. Without a proper theoretical framework, these results make it seem as if there is no consistency in the effects of individual differences in personality on performance. That is, I hope, an error. Consistency in results exists, but one needs to consider individual differences at multiple levels (physiological, directional, strategic, stylistic) as well as to consider how different components of tasks (SIT, STM, LTM) will respond differently to different motivational states.

We need to consider at least seven classes of variables: (a) individual differences in stable predispositions; (b) manipulations such as stimulant or depressant drugs, time of day, or time on task that change physiological state; (c) cognitive/affective manipulations such as feedback, incentives, or threat; (d) the resulting motivational states of arousal and effort that reflect a combination of stable traits, physiological manipulations, and cognitive/affective manipulations; (e) stylistic and strategic components of task performance that include preferences for speed over accuracy or a sensitivity for reward versus a sensitivity to punishment; (f) the differences in task components and requirements such as the demands for sustained information transfer and retrieval of recently or not-recently presented information; (g) and finally, the many ways in which we can measure outcomes such as accuracy, speed, persistence, frequency, or latency. When these seven classes of variables are considered, consistent patterns emerge. Moreover, when one does not pay attention to the complexities involved, there seems to be a hopeless confusion of results. Sophisticated methodologies, as have been proposed at this conference, will only be of use when applied to appropriate data to test adequate theories.

OPEN DISCUSSION

Discussion following Revelle's talk started with a clarification of the meaning of the effort construct. Further discussion focused on the relations between impulsivity, learning, and intelligence. Additional questions were devoted to the variance-accounted-for in Revelle's higher-order interactions, to the tactics of aptitude-treatment interaction studies, and to strategies for the experimental manipulation of effort and arousal.

Mulder: What are the psychological mechanisms underlying effort in your model? What does effort do?

Revelle: I think of effort as the volitional focusing of attention, that is, the focusing of an individual's resources. Atkinson, for example, has suggested that effort refers to the subjective feeling of trying hard and feeling more alert. The important theoretical question is whether there is a path between increases in effort and increases in arousal. For instance, it is the case that you cannot will yourself to be awake via effort. If you try driving a long distance, or sitting in a long colloquium, you often cannot keep yourself awake no matter how hard you try. So I am not sure how effort is going to change the amount of resources available, but it may change the allocation of those resources. I think of effort as changing the allocation of resources to the experimenter or to the salient task. Effort is what most people think of as motivation. In fact, I try to add the word arousal to our motivational constructs. I think it is an unfortunate tendency to just think of effort when we say that a person is motivated. We mean that the person is trying hard, but there is also more involved—the intensity or arousal component. In a historical sense, we have rediscovered the D and K components of drive theories. I am quite willing to map arousal fairly closely into D. With respect to incentives and motivation, I would relate those to K. Spence's K component. As you can see, there are not that many new concepts being developed. We are just relabeling them and trying to change our terminology.

Kleinbeck: I have no problems with your simple models, but could you please help me understand the interactions between impulsivity, arousal, and time of day? Specifically, I don't recall you saying that you had controlled for effort in these experiments. If you did not, perhaps effort is a variable that affects your data. Thus, could effort be viewed as a kind of confounding variable?

Revelle: We did not control for effort. What makes me think that it [effort] is not a confounding variable, though, is that we have looked at anxiety manipulations, which we think relate to effort (i.e., trait anxiety, state anxiety) in all of these studies. Routinely, we do not find the same pattern of interactions. That is, the pattern of interactions we get with caffeine or time of day manipulations almost never interact with our anxiety or incentive manipulations. And the things that anxiety or incentive manipulation variables affect almost never produce patterns of results similar to those we obtain with the caffeine manipulations. So what we are really getting from our results are two different patterns of effects.

As I indicate in [Fig. 11.6], there are different categories of variables that we need to look at; for example, the set of personality variables, such as impulsivity, anxiety, achievement motivation, if you will. And then there are physiological manipulations, such as time of day, caffeine, how long you have been working at the task. The effects of the physiological manipulations are very different from the effects of our cognitive manipulations, such as feedback, threat, and incentives. They are a different category of variables. Subjectively, one can feel that they are trying very hard when they are aroused. But you can be aroused yet feel that you are not trying very hard. I think you need to look at each one of these sets of variables as having different types of effects.

And yet another type of variable pertains to the type of measure you take. This was discussed yesterday by Dave Lohman. Although theoretically related, accuracy, speed, persistence, frequency, and latency give different patterns of results.

In summary, I don't think that effort differences here present a problem, although we have not controlled for it. When we do look at the effect of anxiety, it is always different from arousal effects; anxiety variables just do not have these interactions with memory load or caffeine or time of day, for example. We always look for it, but we don't find it.

Ackerman: Let's consider impulsivity and learning. If I understand your figures correctly, you would expect that a high impulsive student who is sitting through the classroom lecture would have a very difficult time learning; his/her performance at the end of the day should be less than the low impulsive student?

Revelle: During the morning.

Ackerman: But not so in the afternoon?

Revelle: Yes. If we look at our time of day by learning study.

Ackerman: Given that school runs from 8 o'clock in the morning to 3 o'clock in the afternoon, does it average out so that low impulsives and high impulsives have the same intelligence?

Revelle: The high impulsives have been discriminated against. In 1912 Gates did a study suggesting that we should teach complex topics in the morning and schedule gym and art in the afternoon. I take pity upon the poor high impulsive student who has an 8 o'clock a.m. math class. This student may be really good in the class and have no recollection of it the next day. The one thing that is in their favor, however, is that when they take the stressful exam at the end of the quarter, they may perform well because they are not peaked out—they are not overaroused.

Jenkins: But homework comes at night. So would that be to the high impulsive student's advantage?

Revelle: Maybe—if they can remember to do their homework! The problem with our high impulsives is that they are not very conscientious. They are not going to be doing their homework. But the time of day by learning interaction obtained in our research was done in the school setting. And the conclusion of this study is quite clear. You are being misled if you think that your high impulsive students remember the material right after it has been taught. Teachers often say, "Oh, this kid is not trying hard. He knew it in the classroom but he didn't remember it the next day." In my view, it is not a matter of trying hard—the poor kid was asleep! If I were to give recommendations to educational personnel, I would say that they should have these high impulsive students take their classes later in the day. Have them take gym early in the morning. The first class for a high impulsive student should be something to get them going—something like gym.

Ackerman: But it seems that the cards are stacked against the high impulsive student in today's society. One hypothesis, for example, would be that high impulsives have lower intelligence, as measured at adulthood, than low impulsives.

Revelle: I am not going to respond to that immediately. However, I will point out one interesting finding in that regard. Students in our high school sample were much more impulsive than students who had gone on to Northwestern University. So there does appear to be some weeding out of out high impulsives by the time of college. And perhaps it is the low impulsives who are doing the conscientious schoolwork. But I won't say that the high impulsive is less intelligent. With caffeine, for example, a high impulsive can outscore a low impulsive by 100 SAT points.

Ackerman: So we should give coffee to our high impulsive children before they go to school in the morning?

Revelle: We do—it's called Ritalin. That is what is given to hyperactive children. And the alternative is that you don't give them Ritalin but instead have them wait a couple of hours before taking the complex topic classes. Instead, give them gym first thing in the morning.

Cudeck: Do you remember the approximate size of your three- and four-way interactions? Your designs are quite complicated and I wonder if the interactions are big or discardable interactions, like some of the two-way interactions you obtained in the simpler experiments.

Revelle: Let's go back to the time of day data and talk about variance accounted for in those interactions. In that study [see Fig. 11.3, Puchalski & Revelle, in preparation], when we used ability as a covariate, straight ability measures predicted reading comprehension and accounted for about 11 percent of the variance. When we added short-term versus long-term retention, that added about another 4 percent of the variance. When we added retention interval, time of day, and the interaction of retention interval and time of day, that added another 4 percent of the variance. When we added impulsivity, and all the two-way interactions with impulsivity (none of which were significant), and the triple interaction of impulsivity, time of day, and length of retention, we got up to a total of 25 percent of the variance. So it is about 7 percent on that one triple interaction. And the important thing to point out here is that this is really an extra 12 percent over and above the ability component.

Cudeck: Right, and that indicates that your interactions are not just down to the level of noise because you still have a lot of power. That is, these interactions still describe stable, replicable phenomena that the average individual differences psychologist should consider.

Revelle: Yes, the interactions are not trivial effects. For instance, we report our findings in standard score units so that one gets a fair feeling of the effects. For example, we have standardized the total recall score and these are one standard deviation effect sizes.

Cudeck: OK. Now on to a harder question. Your data suggest some major rethinking in the area. How would you design a series of experiments to investigate intellectual performance, individual differences, and your personality and arousal variables? How can one account for so many possible influences?

Revelle: With good theory. One of the arguments made against looking at interactions is that there are all kinds of possible interactions. For example, think of all the possible triple interactions. That is why we have used simple theories as a way of conceptually organizing the data.

With respect to future research, I would suggest that researchers with access to thousands of subjects routinely include marker variables for some of these personality traits.

Cudeck: But would it be practical to include so many measures? Which specific measures would you suggest be included?

Revelle: Well, obviously measures of impulsivity and anxiety. Those two variables work pretty well. In terms of the personality taxonomy projects in the United States, a structure of three to five dimensions of personality seems to do a good job. For example, my concept of impulsivity maps fairly well with Norman's conscientiousness factor; anxiety and emotional stability factors are clearly the same.

I would tend to use at least three of the "big five" factors as marker variables. And I would tend to use the ones that adopt the biological perspective put forth by those in England. The problem with the big five factors as developed in the United States is that the rotations are arbitrary and depend on the simple structure rotation criterion the researcher likes to use. In contrast, the Europeans tend to rotate to simple structure of tasks, to rotate their personality factors to task simple structures. Impulsivity is a terrible variable in terms of the unreliability of measurement. But it does relate to a lot of performance tasks.

In addition, I would look at some measure of achievement motivation and I would avoid, if possible, the Thematic Apperception Test (TAT) versions of the achievement motivation construct. And I would include some measure of self-reported effort and willingness to engage in challenging tasks. Those measures also tend to do fairly well.

Cudeck: One final question. Do you think that by using designs that include these individual differences variables, researchers will show that the relationships reported are too low—that by studying them in this fashion the effects will be disattenuated?

Revelle: I think that the result will be that motivational components will disattenuate the relationships between ability measures and performance measures. That is the clear implication of our regression model. We find 12 percent of the variance accounted for by ability and another 13 percent accounted for by these motivational manipulations interacting with the situation. Researchers should be looking at personality and motivation, as well as cognition.

Ackerman: When you do include ability measures, are there any interactions or is it just a . . .

Revelle: Ruth Kanfer asked me about that earlier. Unfortunately, I have not yet looked at any interactions of ability by the personality variables. I suspect, however, that I will not get that kind of aptitude-treatment interaction. I don't know why I never bothered to do that quadruple interaction.

Ackerman: In concert with Pat Kyllonen's discussion about working memory, it seems that it is not just a matter of increasing working memory or decreasing working memory that has to with these other interactions. If you have a threshold of working memory, then it ought to be sufficient for doing the task whether you are very much awake or not very awake.

Revelle: In that sense, there should be a ability by task by motivational state interaction because we are setting a ceiling of resource limitation. However, it probably will not be a disordinal interaction. I prefer disordinal interactions because I like to make sure the effects are not due to scaling artifacts. Many kinds of interactions that we might obtain would just be ordinal interactions.

Kyllonen: Since these variables you have discussed are so important, I am interested in learning more details about the methodology one should use. First of all, am I correct to assume that you typically do not manipulate effort?

Revelle: We have manipulated effort in a couple of studies, primarily in our caffeine studies. In those studies we tell people to try harder and we have attempted to sweep out speed–accuracy trade-offs by telling people to go slowly and accurately.

Kyllonen: But for the most part, then, you just get self-report measures of effort. With respect to arousal, however, you do manipulate arousal by amphetamines or caffeine, or whatever. Are there any other manipulations that you can think of? Also, what do you use as a manipulation check, other than performance on a task?

Revelle: Self-reports of arousal do, in fact, go up with caffeine. We have avoided doing physiological manipulation checks mostly because we don't have the time to simultaneously measure physiology as well as our other variables. Enough other people have shown, however, that caffeine is a stimulant. So I don't bother to show in every study that caffeine does indeed stimulate the individual. We run our studies as double blind studies, using a placebo for caffeine. So that subjects can't taste the difference, we put the caffeine in Tang and cut it with quinine water. It tastes terrible. Some people claim that they can taste the difference but I do not think they can do it reliably. Subjects just know that they are getting an evil concoction.

Kyllonen: Well, I guess it is pretty clear with caffeine. But what about other ways to manipulate arousal?

Revelle: Well, a brisk walk around the building, or standing up at one's seat. Bob Thayer has used exercise as a manipulation. But a lot of people use standing up versus sitting down. This manipulation gives you differences in heart rate and body temperature. Thayer has looked at a lot of self-report measures of alertness, peppiness, activeness, and vigorousness. In fact, these measures do track the pattern that I have been arguing for. The advantage of caffeine is that it is a fairly simple manipulation. The disadvantage of anxiety manipulations is that it is really difficult to convince subjects that they should be frightened, or differentially frightened. They are terrified when they see these geometric analogies—that's bad enough. But I find that it takes more acting ability to do the anxiety manipulations; I far prefer the caffeine manipulations. It also depends partly on my graduate students— whether they like caffeine or anxiety manipulations.

Jenkins: Is there any other way to alter arousal?

Revelle: Alcohol. But the problem is that the predictions are dull. The nice thing about caffeine manipulations is that you predict crossover interactions. With alcohol, you predict that everybody will get worse. That's no big deal. Also, you get a lot of drunks in your lab if you use an alcohol manipulation.

There is also Valium. Research on the effects of Valium on short- and long-term memory gives some interesting results. Things that are learned under Valium result in poor recall for those events. This is why dentists use Valium for surgery—you don't remember that you were in pain when you come out. Valium has that effect and amphetamines have the opposite effect. Some nice Dutch studies investigating the effects of amphetamines on long-term memory provide a very clean pattern of results.

Kazén-Saad: One of the classic definitions for Eysenck was motor reminiscence, that is, improvement in motor performance after a break. I think a modern equivalent to that notion is this phenomenon of hypermnesia, that following an initial level of learning, there is increased memory performance after repeated attempts. I wonder whether the classical distinction between learning and performance has something to do with this phenomenon. Perhaps high impulsives can recall better and then demonstrate a decline in performance without being exposed to the material again? Have you considered that possibility?

Revelle: Actually, no. One of the things that we are thinking about doing is to sweep out the time of day effect. What you are suggesting is that we sweep out over the delay effect. We have not done that yet.

Let's go have some caffeine.

ACKNOWLEDGMENTS

I would like to thank Kristen Anderson, Ruth Kanfer, Steven Sutton, and Richard Zinbarg for their comments and suggestions on this manuscript. Many of the ideas expressed here have come from long hours of pleasant debate with them.

REFERENCES

Allport, G., & Odbert, H. S. (1936). Trait names: A psycholexical study. *Psychological Monographs, 47* (No. 211), 1–171.

Anderson, K. J. (1981). *The current status of the Easterbrook hypothesis.* Unpublished manuscript, Northwestern University, Evanston, IL.

Anderson, K. J. (1988). *Impulsivity, caffeine, and task difficulty: A within-subjects test of the Yerkes–Dodson Law.* Unpublished manuscript, Colgate University, Hamilton.

Anderson, K. J., & Revelle, W. (1983a). Impulsivity, caffeine, and proofreading: A test of the Easterbrook hypothesis. *Journal of Experimental Psychology: Human Perception and Performance, 8,* 614–624.

Anderson, K. J., & Revelle, W. (1983b). The interactive effects of caffeine, impulsivity, and task demands on a visual search task. *Personality and Individual Differences, 4,* 127–134.

Anderson, K. J., Revelle, W., & Lynch, M. J. (in press). Arousal and memory scanning: A comparison of two explanations for the Yerkes-Dodson effect. *Motivation and Emotion.*

Atkinson, J. W. (1957). Motivational determinants of risk-taking behavior. *Psychological Review, 64,* 359–372.

Atkinson, J. W. (1964). *An introduction to motivation.* New York: D. Van Nostrand.

Atkinson, J. W. (1974). Strength of motivation and efficiency of performance. In J. W. Atkinson & J. O. Raynor (Eds.), *Motivation and achievement* (pp. 117–142). New York: V. W. Winston.

Atkinson, J. W., & Birch, D. (1970). *The dynamics of action.* New York: Wiley.

Atkinson, J. W., & Birch, D. (1978). *Introduction to motivation.* New York: D. Van Nostrand.

Atkinson, J. W., & Raynor, J. O. (Eds.) (1974). *Motivation and achievement.* New York: V. W. Winston.

Bakan, P., Belton, J., & Toth, J. (1963) Extraversion–introversion and decrement in an auditory vigilance task. In D. N. Buckner & J. J. McGrath (Eds.), *Vigilance: A symposium* (pp. 22–33). New York: McGraw-Hill.

Bartol, C. R. (1975). The effects of chlorpromazine and dextroamphetamine sulfate on the visual stimulation preference of extraverts and introverts. *Psychophysiology, 12,* 25–29.

Benzuly, M. (1985). *Caffeine and memory load: Their effect on analogical reasoning*. Unpublished honor's thesis, Northwestern University, Evanston, IL.

Blake, M. J. F. (1967a). Time of day effects on performance in a range of tasks. *Psychonomic Science, 9*, 349–350.

Blake, M. J. F. (1967b). Relationship between circadian rhythm of body temperature and introversion–extraversion. *Nature, 215*, 896–897.

Blake, M. J. F. (1971). Temperament and time of day. In W. P. Colquhoun (Ed.), *Biological rhythms and human performance* (pp. 108–148). London: Academic Press.

Blodgett, H. C. (1929). The effect of the introduction of reward upon the maze performance of rats. *California University Publications in Psychology, 4*, 113–114.

Bowyer, P., Humphreys, M. S., & Revelle, W. (1983). Arousal and recognition memory: The effects of impulsivity, caffeine, and time on task. *Personality and Individual Differences, 3*, 41–49.

Broadbent, D. E. (1971). *Decision and stress*. London: Academic Press.

Broadbent, D. E. (1978). The current state of noise research: A reply to Poulton. *Psychological Bulletin, 85*, 1052–1067.

Broadbent, D. E. (1984). The Maltese Cross: A new simplistic model for memory. *Behavioral and Brain Sciences, 7*, 55–68.

Burrows, D., & Okada, R. (1976). Parallel scanning of physical and category information. *Memory and Cognition, 4*, 31–35.

Campbell J. B. (1983). Differential relationships of extraversion, impulsivity, and sociability to study habits. *Journal of Research in Personality, 17*, 308–314.

Carrigan, P. M. (1960). Extraversion–introversion as a dimension of personality: A reappraisal. *Psychological Bulletin, 57*, 329–360.

Cattell, R. B. (1947). Confirmation and clarification of primary personality factors. *Psychometrika, 12*, 197–220.

Cattell, R. B. (1957). *Personality and motivation: Structure and measurement*. Yonkers on Hudson, NY: World Book.

Cattell, R. B. (1973). *Personality and mood by questionnaire*. San Francisco: Jossey-Bass.

Claridge, G. (1967). *Personality and arousal*. Oxford: Pergamon.

Corcoran, D. W. J. (1965). Personality and the inverted-U relation. *British Journal of Psychology, 56*, 267–273.

Corcoran, D. W. J. (1972) Studies of individual differences at the applied psychology unit. In V. D. Nebylitsyn & J. A. Gray (Eds.), *Biological bases of individual behavior* (pp. 269–290). New York: Academic Press.

Craig, M. J., Humphreys, M. S., Rocklin, T., & Revelle, W. (1979). Impulsivity, neuroticism, and caffeine: Do they have additive effects on arousal? *Journal of Research in Personality, 13*, 404–419.

Davies, D. R., & Parasuraman, R. (1982). *The psychology of vigilance*. London: Academic Press.

Davis, C., & Cowles, M. (1988). A laboratory study of temperament and arousal: A test of Gale's hypothesis. *Journal of Research in Personality, 22*, 101–116.

Dickman, S. J., & Meyer, D. E. (1988). Impulsivity and speed–accuracy trade-offs in information processing. *Journal of Personality and Social Psychology, 54*, 274–290.

Digman, J. M., & Takemoto-Chock, N. K. (1981). Factors in the natural language of personality: Reanalysis, comparison, and interpretation of six major studies. *Multivariate Behavioral Research, 16*, 149–170.

Duffy, E. (1972). Activation. In N. S. Greenfield R. A. Sternbach (Eds.), *Handbook of psychophysiology* (pp. 577–622). New York: Holt, Rinehart & Winston.

Easterbrook, J. A. (1959). The effect of emotion on cue utilization and the organization of behavior. *Psychological Review, 66*, 183–201.

Ebbinghaus, H. (1964). *Memory: A contribution to experimental psychology*. Republished in translation. New York: Dover. (Originally published 1883)

Elliot, C. D. (1971). Noise tolerance and extraversion in children. *British Journal of Psychology, 62*, 375–380.

Eysenck, H. J. (1947). *Dimensions of personality*. New York: Praeger.

Eysenck, H. J. (1952). *The scientific study of personality*. London: Routledge & Kegan Paul.

Eysenck, H. J. (1965). Extraversion and the acquisition of eyeblink and GSR conditioned responses. *Psychological Bulletin, 63*, 258–270.

Eysenck, H. J. (1967). *The biological basis of personality*. Springfield: Thomas.

Eysenck, H. J. (1977a). *Crime and personality*. London: Metheum.

Eysenck, H. J. (1977b). Personality and factor analysis: A reply to Guilford. *Psychological Bulletin, 84*, 405–411.

Eysenck, H. J. (Ed.). (1981). *A model for personality*. New York: Springer-Verlag.

Eysenck, H. J. (1987). The place of anxiety and impulsivity in a dimensional framework. *Journal of Research in Personality, 21*, 489–493.

Eysenck, H. J., & Eysenck, M. W. (1985). *Personality and individual differences: A natural science approach*. New York: Plenum Press.

Eysenck, H. J., & Eysenck, S. B. G. (1964). *Eysenck Personality Inventory*. San Diego: Educational and Industrial Testing Service.

Eysenck, H. J., & Levey, A. (1972). Conditioning, introversion–extraversion, and the strength of the nervous system. In V. D. Nebylitsyn & J. A. Gray (Eds.), *Biological bases of individual behavior* (pp. 206–220). New York: Academic Press.

Eysenck, M. W. (1979). Anxiety, learning, and memory: A reconceptualization. *Journal of Research in Personality, 13*, 363–385.

Eysenck, M. W. (1981). Learning, memory and personality. In H. J. Eysenck (Ed.), *A model for personality* (pp. 169–209). Berlin: Springer-Verlag.

Eysenck, M. W., & Eysenck, M. C. (1979). Memory scanning, introversion–extraversion, and levels of processing. *Journal of Research in Personality, 13*, 305–315.

Eysenck, M. W., & Folkard, S. (1980). Personality, time of day, and caffeine: Some theoretical and conceptual problems in Revelle et al. *Journal of Experimental Psychology: General, 109*, 32–41.

Eysenck, S. B. G., & Eysenck, H. J. (1975). *Manual of the EPQ (Eysenck Personality Questionnaire)*. London: Hodder & Stoughton.

Folkard, S. (1975). Diurnal variation in logical reasoning. *British Journal of Psychology, 66*, 1–8.

Folkard, S., Knauth, P., Monk, T. H., & Rutenfranz, J. (1976). The effect of memory load on the circadian variation in performance efficiency under a rapidly rotating shift system. *Ergonomics, 19*, 479–488.

Folkard, S., & Monk, T. H. (1980). Circadian rhythms in human memory. *British Journal of Psychology, 71*, 295–307.

Folkard, S., Monk, T. H., Bradbury, R., & Rosenthal, J. (1977). Time of day effects in school children's immediate and delayed recall of meaningful material. *British Journal of Psychology, 58*, 45–50.

Frcka, G., & Martin, I. (1987). Is there—or is there not—an influence of impulsiveness on classical eyelid conditioning? *Personality and Individual Differences, 8*, 241–252.

Gale, A. (1977). Some EEG correlates of sustained attention. In R. R. Mackie (Ed.), *Vigilance* (pp. 263–283). New York: Plenum Press.

Gale, A. (1986). Extraversion–introversion and spontaneous rhythms of the brain: Retrospect and prospect. In J. Strelau, F. H. Farley, & A. Gale (Eds.), *The biological bases of personality and behavior: Psychophysiology, performance, and application* (Vol. 2, pp. 25–42). Washington, DC: Hemisphere.

Gates, A. (1916). Variations in efficiency during the day. *University of California Publications, 2,* 1–156.

Geen, R., & Kaiser, M. (1985). *Test anxiety and performance on the Stroop color word task.* Unpublished manuscript, University of Missouri, Columbia.

Gilliland, K. (1976). *The interactive effect of introversion–extraversion with caffeine-induced arousal on verbal performance.* Unpublished doctoral dissertation, Northwestern University.

Gilliland, K. (1980). The interactive effect of introversion–extraversion with caffeine-induced arousal on verbal performance. *Journal of Research in Personality, 14,* 482–492.

Goldberg, L. R. (1982). From ace to zombie: Some explorations in the language of personality. In C. D. Spielberger & J. N. Butcher (Eds.), *Advances in personality assessment* (Vol. 1, pp. 203–234). Hillsdale, NJ: Lawrence Erlbaum Associates.

Gray, J. A. (1972). The psychophysiological basis of introversion–extraversion: A modification of Eysenck's theory. In V. D. Nebylitsyn & J. A. Gray (Eds.), *The biological basis of individual behavior* (pp. 182–205). New York: Academic Press.

Gray, J. A. (1981). A critique of Eysenck's theory of personality. In H. J. Eysenck (Ed.), *A model for personality* (pp. 246–276). Berlin: Springer-Verlag.

Gray, J. A. (1982). *Neuropsychological theory of anxiety: An investigation of the septal-hippocampal system.* Cambridge: Cambridge University Press.

Gray, J. A. (1987). Perspectives on anxiety and impulsivity: A commentary. *Journal of Research in Personality, 21,* 493–510.

Guilford, J. P. (1975). Factors and factors of personality. *Psychological Bulletin, 82,* 802–814.

Guilford, J. P. (1977). Will the real factor of extraversion please stand up? A reply to Eysenck. *Psychological Bulletin, 84,* 412–416.

Gupta, B. S. (1974). Stimulant and depressant drugs on Kinaesthetic Figural After-Effects. *Psychopharmacologia, 36,* 275–280.

Gupta, B. S. (1977). Dextroamphetamine and measures of intelligence. *Intelligence, 1,* 274–280.

Hebb, D. O. (1955). Drives and the C. N. S. (conceptual nervous system). *Psychological Review, 62,* 243–254.

Hockey, R. (1979). Stress and cognitive components of skilled performance. In V. Hamilton & D. M. Warburton (Eds.), *Human stress and cognition* (pp. 141–178). Chichester, England: Wiley.

Humphreys, M. S., & Revelle, W. (1984). Personality, motivation, and performance: A theory of the relationship between individual differences and information processing. *Psychological Review, 91,* 153–184.

Humphreys, M. S., Revelle, W., Simon, L., & Gilliland, K. (1980). Individual differences in diurnal rhythms and multiple activation states: A reply to M. W. Eysenck and Folkard. *Journal of Experimental Psychology: General, 109,* 42–48.

Kleinsmith, L. J., & Kaplan, S. L. (1963). Paired associate learning as a function of arousal and interpolated interval. *Journal of Experimental Psychology, 65,* 190–193.

Kuhl, J., & Blankenship, V. (1979). The dynamic theory of achievement motivation: From episodic to dynamic thinking. *Psychological Review, 85,* 239–248.

Leon, M. R., & Revelle, W. (1985). The effects of anxiety on analogical reasoning: A test of three theoretical models. *Journal of Personality and Social Psychology, 49,* 1302–1315.

Locke, E. A. (1968). Toward a theory of task motivation and incentives. *Organizational Behavior and Human Performance, 3,* 157–189.

Ludvigh, E. J., & Happ, D. (1974). Extraversion and preferred level of sensory stimulation. *British Journal of Psychology, 65,* 359–365.

Mackie, R. R. (Ed.). (1977). *Vigilance.* New York: Plenum Press.

Maxwell, S. E., & Delaney, H. D. (1985). Measurement and statistics: An examination of construct validity. *Psychological Bulletin, 97,* 85–93.

McCrae, R. R., & Costa, P. T. (1987). Validation of the 5-factor model of personality across instruments and observers. *Journal of Personality and Social Psychology, 52,* 81–90.

Mulholland, T. M., Pellegrino, J. W., & Glaser, R. (1980). Components of geometric analogy solution. *Cognitive Psychology, 12*, 252–284.

Newman, J. P., Widom, C. S., & Nathan, S. (1985). Passive avoidance in syndromes of disinhibition: Psychopathy and extraversion. *Journal of Personality & Social Psychology, 48*, 1316–1327.

Norman, W. T. (1963). Toward an adequate taxonomy of personality attributes: Replicated factor structure in peer nomination personality ratings. *Journal of Abnormal and Social Psychology, 66*, 574–583.

Norman, W. T. (1969). "To see oursels as ithers see us!" Relations among self-perceptions, peer perceptions, and expected peer-perceptions of personality attributes. *Multivariate Behavioral Research, 4*, 417–443.

Oakhill, J. (1986). Effects of time of day and information importance on adults' memory for a short story. *Quarterly Journal of Experimental Psychology, Section A—Human Experimental Psychology, 38*, 419–430.

Oakhill, J. (1988). Text memory and integration at different times of day. *Applied Cognitive Psychology, 2*, 203–212.

Onken, J., & Revelle, W. (1984). ANATEST: A program to generate geometric analogy problems varying in number of elements and number of transformations. *Behavior Research Methods Instruments and Computers, 16*, 333–334.

Patterson, C. M., Kosson, D. S., & Newman, J. P. (1987). Reaction to punishment, reflectivity, and passive avoidance learning in extraverts. *Journal of Personality and Social Psychology, 52*, 565–575.

Posner, M. I. (1978). *Chronometric explorations of mind: The third Paul M. Fitts Lectures.* Hillsdale, NJ: Lawrence Erlbaum Associates.

Poulton, E. C. (1978). Continuous intense noise masks auditory feedback and inner speech. *Psychological Bulletin, 85*, 1068–1079.

Poulton, E. C. (1979). Composite model for human performance in continuous noise. *Psychological Review, 80*, 90–92.

Puchalski, M. (1988). *Impulsivity, time of day, and retention interval: the effect on cognitive performance.* Unpublished doctoral dissertation, Northwestern University.

Puchalski, M., & Revelle, W. (in preparation). *Impulsivity, time of day, and retention interval: The effect on cognitive performance.* Unpublished manuscript.

Revelle, W. (1973). *Introversion/extraversion, skin conductance, and performance under stress.* Unpublished doctoral dissertation, University of Michigan, Ann Arbor.

Revelle, W. (1986). Motivation and efficiency of cognitive performance. In D. R. Brown & J. Veroff (Eds.), *Frontiers of motivational psychology: Essays in honor of John W. Atkinson* (pp. 107–131). Berlin: Springer-Verlag.

Revelle, W. (1987). Personality and motivation: Sources of inefficiency in cognitive performance. *Journal of Research in Personality, 21*, 436–452.

Revelle, W., Amaral, P., & Turriff, S. (1976). Introversion–extraversion, time stress, and caffeine: The effect on verbal performance. *Science, 192*, 149–150.

Revelle, W., & Anderson, K. J. (in press). Models for the testing of theory. In A. Gale & M. W. Eysenck (Eds.), *Handbook of individual differences: Biological perspectives.* Chichester, England: Wiley.

Revelle, W., Anderson, K. J., & Humphreys, M. S. (1987). Empirical tests and theoretical extensions of arousal based theories of personality. In J. Strelau & H. J. Eysenck (Eds.), *Personality dimensions and arousal* (pp. 17–36). London: Plenum Press.

Revelle, W., Humphreys, M. S., Simon, L., & Gilliland, K. (1980). The interactive effect of personality, time of day, and caffeine: A test of the arousal model. *Journal of Experimental Psychology: General, 109*, 1–31.

Revelle, W., & Michaels, E. J. (1976). The theory of achievement motivation revisited: The implications of inertial tendencies. *Psychological Review, 83,* 394–404.

Rocklin, T., & Revelle, W. (1981). The measurement of extraversion: A comparison of the Eysenck Personality Inventory and the Eysenck Personality Questionnaire. *British Journal of Social Psychology, 20,* 279–284.

Sabates, A. (1986). *Anxiety and speed–accuracy trade-offs.* Unpublished masters thesis, Northwestern University.

Sarason, I. G. (1975). Anxiety and self-preoccupation. In I. G. Sarason & C. D. Spielberger (Eds.), *Anxiety and stress* (Vol. 2, pp. 27–44). Washington, DC: Hemisphere.

Shiffrin, R. M., & Schneider, W. (1977). Controlled and automatic human information processing: II. Perceptual learning, automatic attending, and a general theory. *Psychological Review, 84,* 127–190.

Spence, J. T., & Spence, K. W. (1966). The motivational components of manifest anxiety: Drive and drive stimuli. In C. D. Spielberger (Ed.), *Anxiety and behavior* (pp. 291–326). New York: Academic Press.

Spence, K. W., Farber, I. E., & McFann, H. H. (1956). The relation of anxiety (drive) level to performance in competitional and non-competitional paired-associates learning. *Journal of Experimental Psychology, 52,* 296–305.

Sternberg, S. (1969). The discovery of processing stages: Extensions of Donders' method. In W. G. Koster (Ed.), *Attention and performance* (Vol. 2, pp. 276–315). Amsterdam: North-Holland.

Strelau, J. (1983). *Temperament–personality–activity.* London: Academic Press.

Strelau, J. (1985). Temperament and personality: Pavlov and beyond. In J. Strelau, F. H. Farley, & A. Gale (Eds.), *The biological bases of personality and behavior: Psychophysiology, performance, and application* (Vol. 1, pp 25–43). Washington, DC: Hemisphere.

Thackray, R. I., Jones, K. N., & Touchstone, R. M. (1974). Personality and physiological correlates of performance decrement on a monotonous task requiring sustained attention. *British Journal of Psychology, 65,* 351–358.

Tolman, E. C., & Honzik, C. H. (1930). Degrees of hunger, reward and non-reward, and maze learning in rats. *California University Publications in Psychology, 4,* 241–275.

Tupes, E. C., & Christal, R. E. (1961). *Recurrent personality factors based on trait ratings.* USAF ASD Technical Report, No. 61-97.

Underwood, B. J. (1978). Recognition memory as a function of length of study list. *Bulletin of the Psychonomic Society, 12,* 89–91.

Walker, E. L. (1958). Action decrement and its relation to learning. *Psychological Review, 65,* 129–142.

Walker E., & Tate, R. (1963). Memory storage as a function of time. *Journal of Verbal Learning, 2,* 13–119.

Weiner, B., & Schneider, K. (1971). Drive versus cognitive theory: A reply to Boor and Harmon. *Journal of Experimental Psychology, 52,* 296–305.

Wiggins, J. S. (1979). A psychological taxonomy of trait terms: The interpersonal domain. *Journal of Personality and Social Psychology, 37,* 395–412.

Wine, J. (1971). Test anxiety and direction of attention. *Psychological Bulletin, 76,* 92–104.

Woodworth, R. S., & Schlosberg, H. (1954). *Experimental psychology.* New York: Holt, Rinehart & Winston.

Yerkes, R. M., & Dodson, J. D. (1908). The relation of strength of stimuli to rapidity of habit-information. *Journal of Comparative Neurology and Psychology, 18,* 459–482.

Zinbarg, R., & Revelle, W. (in press). Personality and conditioning: A test of four models. *Journal of Personality and Social Psychology.*

Self-Regulation and Metamotivation: Computational Mechanisms, Development, and Assessment

Julius Kuhl
Kristina Kraska
University of Osnabrück, West Germany

For several decades, psychological research on learning has focused on cognitive abilities and motivational factors as the two fundamental types of determinants of performance. In recent years, a third class of variables has been studied intensively. These variables refer to metacognitive processes that coordinate the cognitive skills involved in memory, reading, text comprehension, and so on (Brown, 1978; Flavell & Wellman, 1977; Weinert & Kluwe, 1987). For example, after children have acquired some metacognitive knowledge about the functional characteristics of memory, they start using this knowledge to improve memory performance (e.g., by testing their performance level, rehearsing the material when necessary). Compared to the extensive metacognitive research performed in recent years, higher-level skills controlling *motivational* processes have been neglected in research on learning. In this chapter, we would like to summarize some of our work related to metamotivation.

Young children's motivation is a function of their needs, their expectations, and the incentives provided by the immediate environment. Later in childhood, they develop executive skills that enable them to control their motivational states, increasing or decreasing them when necessary, or keeping them stable even in an environment with changing incentives. These skills are based on metamotivational knowledge, that is, knowledge regarding one's own motivational functioning (e.g., what thoughts produce an increase or decrease in motivation, what environments contain effective personal incentives, etc.). Mischel's experiments on self-regulation have provided interesting insights concerning the development of strategies children use to control their own motivation (Mischel, 1974; Mischel & Mischel, 1983). This research was confined, however, to two experimental paradigms (i.e., delay of gratification and resistance to temptation) that focused on molar behavior rather than information-processing mechanisms mediating cognitive performance. The important role self-regulatory (metamotivational) processes play for learning and cognitive functioning has been underestimated until now.

Controlling one's molar behavior (e.g., working at a task despite tempting distractors in the environment) is a necessary requirement for cognitive efficiency. In addition, metamotivational processes are needed on a more molecular level of processing. For example, when children learn to read and comprehend a text, they must develop strategies that support the maintenance of various goals, for example, the goal to understand the gist of a paragraph even when an interesting, but irrelevant piece of information distracts from the main idea. Although similar strategies have occasionally been studied in connection with metacognitive strategies (Kluwe, 1986), the theoretical analysis of the similarities and differences between metamotivational and metacognitive processes has been neglected.

Previous research on self-regulation in children has lacked three important things. First, there has been no comprehensive theory of the psychological mechanisms mediating self-control functions. Second, a psychological theory specifying functional requirements and developmental precursors of self-regulation was missing. Third, no standardized tests that avoid typical confoundings (e.g., confounding self-regulatory deficits and motivational change) are available for the assessment of self-regulatory efficiency and metamotivational knowledge. In this chapter, we address these three issues. In the first part, we analyze the distinctive features of metamotivational processes on the basis of a theory of action control (Kuhl, 1983, 1984, 1985; Kuhl & Kazén-Saad, 1988) and provide a model that specifies several computational mechanisms underlying *action control,* a term we use to refer to our definition of self-regulation. In the second part, we outline a theory of the development of action control and discuss two instruments we developed to assess developmental precursors of action control and metamotivational knowledge. Results from several studies exploring the reliability and validity of these instruments are presented. In addition, we interpret the personality construct *action versus state orientation* in terms of our model and provide a reinterpretation of *learned helplessness* that has important implications for the prevention and therapy of underachievement.

THE THEORY OF ACTION CONTROL

In this section, we use a typical self-regulatory problem (how to enact the intention to work despite the temptation to play) to explain the theory of action control (Kuhl & Kazén-Saad, 1988). In this theory, *action control* (or volition) is defined as the ability to maintain and enact an action tendency the organism is committed to despite the impulsive nature of competing action tendencies. In contrast to many classical theories of volition (or willpower), our theory provides functional definitions of theoretical terms such as *commitment, impulsivity,* and *volitional efficiency* (strength of will) rather than relying on their ambiguous commonsense connotations.

Defining Cognition, Emotion, and Motivation

The difficulties concerning the concept of volition in the history of psychology are partly attributable to conceptual confusions regarding the definition of the basic terms *cognition, emotion,* and *motivation.* Therefore, we take some time to elaborate our definitions of these terms. The term *cognition* has become more and more ambiguous in psychology. In its narrow and best defined sense, it refers to a specific type of representation of objects and facts (i.e., propositional representations). In a broader sense, *cognition* refers to *any* representation of incoming information, including all sorts of multidimensional representations (e.g., spatial imagery). Even *emotions* could be subsumed under this definition of cognition because they can be interpreted as multidimensional encodings of positive or negative discrepancies between behavioral consequences and organismic standards (Norman, 1980; Ortony, Clore, & Collins, 1988). In this chapter, we use quotation marks when referring to "*cognition*" in this broader sense (see Fig. 12.1).

The exciting advances made in cognitive research during the past two decades has prompted many cognitive psychologists to use the term *cognition* in an even broader sense that encompasses virtually all mental structures or processes, except for biological generalizations that define the functional architecture (e.g., physical changes caused by maturation or damage; Pylyshyn, 1984). We do not consider this inflated concept of cognition useful. Specifically, we believe that the all-encompassing concept of cognition conceals the fact that very little is known about the processing of *outgoing* information, that is, information related to preference values associated with action alternatives. According to an earlier analysis (Heckhausen & Kuhl, 1985), the way from wishful consideration of action alternatives to the formation and maintenance of intentions is longer than one might expect on the basis of cognitivistic models of action (Anderson, 1983). We show in this chapter that the neglect of the distinction between cognitive and motivational processes impedes the development of an adequate theory of volition.

The term *motivation* in its broadest sense refers to the processing of outgoing information regarding future action alternatives, that is, to all processing stages from the wishful consideration of pleasurable actions (i.e., emotional preferences) to the formation of a cognitive representation of an intention that may or may not be compatible with the currently dominant emotional preference. The term *motivation* is frequently used in a narrow sense referring to emotional preference, that is, to a cumulative encoding of emotions experienced in associa-

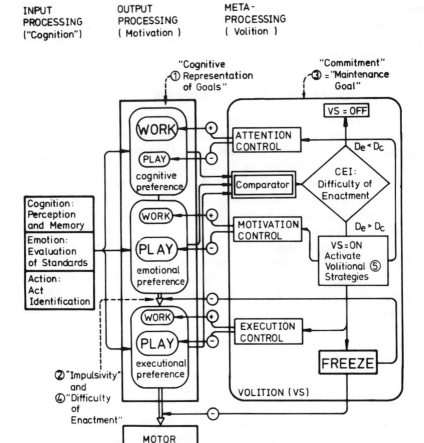

FIG. 12.1. A model of the basic mechanisms underlying a theory of action control.

tion with an action in the past. We use the term *motivation* in this sense to refer to those emotional processes that are closely connected with preferred actions (cf. Frijda, 1986). We will confine the term *emotion* to a category of processes that mediate the evaluation of *incoming* information on the basis of organismic standards. Again, we will use quotation marks when we refer to the broader definition of *"motivation"* encompassing the processing of all outgoing (i.e., action-related) information, including action plans and cognitive representations of intentional states (see Fig. 12.1).

At first glance, *"motivational"* processing may appear similar to problem solving because both concepts imply anticipation and evaluation of future consequences of various action alternatives (Dörner, 1985). However, *"motivation"* is the more general of the two terms because it is not confined to situations in which it is difficult to find a way to reach the desired goal. In addition, whereas problem-solving approaches predict selection of action alternatives on the basis of their instrumentalities for reaching a goal, motivational approaches include intrinsic values and emotional qualities associated both with action alternatives and goals. These motivational variables are the most important predictors of human behavior in a variety of everyday situations in which the only problem consists of choosing one goal among many alternative goals, each of which could be achieved *without* solving any problem. Motivational psychologists are interested in individual differences in the selection of goals and actions that remain even if individual differences in perception, attention and memory are controlled (Atkinson & Birch, 1970).

Whereas many cognitive theories of action suggest a unitarian model of the human mind, our theory is based on a segmentary conception of the mind that entails the assumption that cognitive, emotional, and executional processing occurs in closely interacting, but separate subsystems (Kuhl, 1986). Specifically, we believe that the traditional distinction between cognition, emotion, and action is important because it refers to three subsystems that are functionally different and neurophysiologically separable (Arnold, 1984). This segmentary assumption implies a distinction between the terms *"cognition"* and *information processing.* The latter is more general than the former. It encompasses processing within the motivational and executional systems in addition to *"cognitive"* information processing (Kuhl, 1986). Although many cognitive psychologists prefer unitarian theories (Anderson, 1983), there are good reasons for a segmentary approach even when the analysis is restricted to *"cognitive"* information processing (Fodor, 1983; Sherry & Schacter, 1987). We prefer the term *segmentary* to the term *modular* for developing a process model of self-regulation because we need not make as strict assumptions as implied by the latter term (Fodor, 1983). For example, we need not exclude the existence of a common data base that can be accessed by the cognitive, emotional, and motivational subsystems. The most important characteristic of our segmentary conception of cognition, emotion, and motivation is the assumption that conflicting or discrepant pieces of information can coexist without interference in these three subsystems. For example, the system can simultaneously have an emotional preference for playing and a cognitive preference for working (see Fig. 12.1). We show in the following sections why the analysis of action control requires this segmentary approach.

Three Types of Preference

An important aspect of the model is that *executional preference* values (i.e., the relative strengths of action schemas) have separate realizations from cognitive and emotional preferences. The commonsense concept of preference confounds these three meanings of the term *preference* (or *motivation*). In most psychological theories, *preference* is defined on the basis of an individual's manifest choices. We believe that the theoretical difficulties in accounting for volition have been caused by the failure to distinguish among the three types of preference. A similar problem impeded early cognitive research regarding perceptual defense. Classical studies supposedly demonstrating increased perceptual thresholds for fear-arousing stimuli (McGinnies, 1949) were criticized by pointing to the paradox that one cannot identify a stimulus as fear arousing without perceiving it. This problem has been solved by replacing the one-level definition of perception by a multilevel definition. According to the more recent definition, incoming information passes several levels of processing (Craik & Lockhard, 1972): A stimulus can be identified as fear arousing on an early level of processing and its representation can be attenuated on higher levels, thus preventing it from reaching conscious representation (Blum & Barbour, 1979).

The distinction between the three types of preference is based on a generalization of the levels-of-processing idea to the *motivational* (i.e., efferent) part of mental systems: A cognitive preference represented on a high level of processing may be modified when passing lower levels on its way toward the executive system as a result of facilitating or inhibiting influences affecting them. For example, the cognitive preference (commitment) for finishing one's work rather than indulging in some more pleasurable play activity may be reversed on an emotional level of processing (i.e., when the aversive experience of working comes into play) and be reversed again before it reaches the executive system as a result of an attention-control strategy that restores the original (cognitive) preference on the level of action schemas corresponding to the competing response alternatives. The paradoxical sentence that a child decides to finish her homework although she prefers to go out playing becomes meaningful if we mean cognitive preference in the first part and emotional preference in the second part of the sentence.

The Process of Action Control

Fig. 12.1 illustrates the basic assumptions of the model. The three subsystems that constitute the efferent or "*motivational*" part of cognition, emotion, and action systems contain units of information that refer to a typical volitional problem, that is, a conflict between cognitive and executional preference. The interactions within and among the three subsystems are described by single arrows indicating effects of normal strength or double arrows indicating strong effects. The assumption of *impulsivity* describes an important aspect concerning the interaction between two subsystems. It says that emotional processes have a greater impact on the action system than cognitive processes.

The relative activational strength of the information concerning the two action alternatives in our example (i.e., work and play) are indicated by small and big circles, respectively, within each subsystem. Fig. 12.1 illustrates the case in which a child has a strong emotional preference for playing, that is, on an emotional level, past experiences with playing are activated that are more pleasant than those associated with working. This emotional preference for playing is entirely congruent with an executional preference for playing; that is, the action schema for playing is more strongly activated than the one for working. The executional preference for playing may be a combined result of the strong impact of the emotional preference for playing on the executional system and the acquisition of a strong habit to play in the situation at hand. In general, habit formation directly affects the relative strengths of action schemas, whereas emotional preferences are affected by the quality and intensity of past emotional consequences of performing the activity in question.

During early childhood, congruence between emotional and executional preferences is the rule rather than the exception. In a subsequent section, we relate children's intrinsic playfulness to the congruence between emotional and executional preferences. Later in childhood, children develop the ability to generate cognitive representations of their own intentional states. As we point out in greater detail later, the development of cognitive representations of one's intentions is the basis for new abilities and new problems. One new ability is self-regulatory maintenance of a cognitive preference (i.e., the cognitive representation of an intention) even if it is incongruent with emotional and executional preferences. This case is illustrated in Fig. 12.1: The child has a cognitive preference for working, whereas her emotional and executional preference is in favor of playing. The cognitive preference for working may be based on a past decision to finish homework before going out to play with friends. Note that at the time when this decision was made, cognitive and emotional preferences may have been congruent. That is, when considering the various consequences of playing versus working, she formed the intention to work and felt emotionally better about it than about playing. Later, while working, the incongruence between cognitive and emotional preferences depicted in Fig. 12.1 may have developed as a result of unpleasant experiences associated with working, while the cognitive preference (i.e., the commitment) remained unchanged or was less affected than the emotional preference.

According to the impulsivity assumption, emotional preference has a stronger effect on the generation of action schemas in the executional system than cognitive preference. As a result, the model predicts behavior that is congruent with the current emotional rather than with the cognitive preference unless additional assumptions are made. These additional assumptions are provided by the theory of action control. In young children, the cognitive representation of preference values is likely to change quickly when emotional preferences change. When they develop an emotional preference for escaping the unpleasant experience of working, their cognitive representation of preference values changes accordingly. Young children's smooth and conflict-free transitions from one activity to the next one may result from this congruence between cognitive and emotional preferences. In older children and adults, a cognitive preference developed in an earlier decision-making process may be maintained even when emotional preference changes. According to the theory of action control, this happens if, after making a decision, the organism anticipates a change of emotional preference in a future situation that will render the maintenance of the decision difficult. The anticipation of a difficulty of enactment (cf. Fig. 12.1) is based on metamotivational knowledge regarding the impulsive nature of conflicting emotional preferences. The anticipation of a difficulty of enactment prompts the organism to generate a commitment to maintain the cognitive preference despite this expected change in emotional preference.

Commitment can be defined in terms of a superordinate goal directed at the maintenance of a decision. The cognitive encoding of the fact that a commitment has been made can be described in terms of a commitment marker that is associated with the cognitive representation of an intention. The generation of a commitment marker is closely associated with relevant aspects of the self-concept. People are presumably more likely to commit themselves to a cognitive preference and maintain it if it relates to a relevant aspect of their perceived self-identity. For example, smokers are more likely to commit themselves to quit if being healthy is a salient aspect of their self-concept. In our example, a commitment marker is associated with the cognitive preference for working (Fig. 12.1). The commitment marker encodes the fact that a decision has been made to maintain the cognitive preference for working despite the anticipated difficulty of enactment. According to the model, volitional support for the maintenance of the intention (i.e., the cognitive preference for working) is initiated when a comparison among the three subsystems results in a discrepancy between cognitive and emotional or between cognitive and executional preferences (cf. Fig. 12.1: CEI = Cognition-Execution Incongruence, that is, a conflict between cognitive preference and the dominant action schema). This incongruence constitutes what we call a difficulty of enactment.

Although young children may learn to activate volitional support for an intention if *any* degree of cognitive-executional or cognitive-emotional incongruence is encountered, a more parsimonious strategy may be developed in later years. This strategy is based on a finer-grained appraisal of the degree of the difficulty of enactment. Specifically, difficulty of enactment (d_e) can be estimated in terms of the relative strength (T_c) of the action schema that corresponds to the cognitive preference compared to the sum of the strengths of all competing action schemas (T_i), that is, $d_e = T_c/\Sigma_i T_i$). At this stage of development, the volitional maintenance of the current intention is activated only if the difficulty of enactment exceeds a critical value (Fig. 12.1). When the critical value is exceeded, the child may recall the commitment and generate a maintenance goal. This goal can activate volitional strategies that support the maintenance of the cognitive preference.

When a child emotionally prefers playing to working and the action schema for playing is dominant, a cognitive preference for working would have no chance to be enacted unless she has the capacity to inhibit the dominant action schema from being performed. Because the operation of volitional strategies requires time, the executional system has to be frozen until the action schema corresponding to the current intention (i.e., the intention to work) has been made dominant. Freezing is the first step of a volitional intervention cycle. It creates a time window for the operation of volitional strategies.

The facilitating and inhibiting effects of these strategies on the activational strengths of cognitive, emotional, and executional preferences is illustrated in Fig. 12.1. The strategy of *attention control* (Kuhl, 1983, 1985) enhances the cognitive preference for working and inhibits the cognitive representation of playing by channeling attentional resources accordingly (see Norman & Shallice, 1985, for a theory of volition based on a similar mechanism). The second strategy illustrates *motivation control,* which enhances the activation of the emotional preference for working and reduces the emotional attractiveness of playing. This can be achieved by focusing on positive incentives of being able to maintain an intention in general or of being able to enjoy the good feeling of having finished one's work. Experimental evidence for the facilitation of decision making and enactment through the use of a motivation-control strategy has been obtained (Beckmann & Kuhl, 1984). Both attention control and motivation control increase the probability that the individual eventually succeeds in performing the cognitively preferred (i.e., the intended) action despite the initial emotional and executional preference for an alternative action.

The third strategy, *execution control,* directly affects the strengths of action schemas. This mechanism strengthens the action schema corresponding to the current intention either through an automatic facilitation process or through complex strategies such as the deliberate development of a habit to perform the intended action in a specified situation at a particular time (e.g., doing homework right after lunch). Execution control is similar to Norman and Shallice's (1985) Supervisory Attentional System. In contrast to their model, however, our model postulates additional volitional mechanisms that affect the strengths of action schemas *indirectly* through their impact on the cognitive representation of action schemas (i.e., attention control, in our terminology) or on emotional preferences. *Volitional efficiency,* that is, the probability that the intended action (i.e., working) is initiated and maintained until goal attainment, is a function of the relative strength of: (a) the initial strength of the incongruent emotional and executional preference (for playing), (b) the relative strength of the freezing mechanism (determining the length of the time window for volitional intervention), and (c) the impact volitional strategies have on the three subsystems involved. We are currently running computer simulations of the model to develop a more precise way of describing its implications.

The model we have outlined can help avoid traditional confusions concerning the concept of volition. The term *volition* has been used in at least three different meanings. Its first meaning, which is accepted by many cognitive psychologists, refers to the currently intended (willed) action (cf. executional preference in Fig. 12.1), that is, to the currently dominant action schema. According to this definition, terms like *volitional efficiency* or *weakness of will* are meaningless because the organism always performs the volitionally intended action by definition (provided it has the necessary skills and opportunity to do so). We do not find this concept very useful because it excludes the concept of volitional control (self-regulation) by definition rather than by experimental evidence. The second meaning of *volition* refers to what we call cognitive preference, that is, a deliberate (frequently conscious) intention based on a cognitive representation of an action plan (cf. Neumann & Prinz, 1987). In our terminology, we have reserved the term *intention* for this meaning of the term *volition*. Note that we distinguish between an active (dominant) action schema and an intention. The latter term is reserved for the case in which a cognitive representation of an action schema has been formed. According to our terminology, an intention in this sense is not to be identified with, although it may be considered a prerequisite for, volitional control.

In sum, we use the term *volition* in its third meaning, which refers to a set of mechanisms that mediate the maintenance of an intention (i.e., the second meaning of *volition*), especially when it is incongruent with the currently active action schema (i.e., the first meaning of volition). These mechanisms include: (a) freezing; (b) the generation of a superordinate maintenance goal (commitment), which may be mediated by similar processes as the generation of any other goal; and (c) volitional strategies that directly or indirectly modify the strengths of action schemas until they are congruent with the current cognitive preference. Cognitive, emotional, and executional preferences can be incongruent despite their close interactions because each of them depends, at least in part, on a unique set of determinants (i.e., cognitive anticipation of future consequences, past emotional experiences, and frequency of past performance [habit formation], respectively). Although volitional control may be mediated by fundamental computational mechanisms such as selective attention, strategic-serial (vs. automatic-parallel) processing, and/or consciousness, it is not identical with any of them. Volitional control requires the development of a particular set of metagoals that is focused on the detection and resolution of conflicts between cognitive and emotional/executional preferences. The three computational mechanisms may be utilized to achieve volitional control, just as they are utilized for many other purposes.

THE DEVELOPMENT OF METAMOTIVATION AND ACTION CONTROL

Although the theory of action control does not make any explicit developmental assumptions, it has several interesting implications regarding the functions that children have to acquire before they can develop self-regulatory skills. In this section, we sketch a theory of the development of action control suggested by the model outlined in Fig. 12.1. Action control has six functional requirements that define corresponding developmental stages. Although we do not assume a fixed developmental sequence of these stages, we discuss a prototypical course of development. The first four stages refer to developmental precursors of self-regulation, whereas Stages 5 and 6 comprise the two essential aspects of self-regulation. The functional requirements for action control refer to the cognitive representation of the following factors: (a) *the ongoing action tendency and the current goal,* (b) *the concept of impulsivity* (i.e., metamotivational knowledge concerning the impulsive nature of emotionally supported action tendencies), (c) *self-congruent commitment* to an action alternative (i.e., cognitive preference for an action alternative on the basis of a perceived congruence between the *self* and that action alternative even if it is in conflict with an emotionally preferred action alternative), (d) *difficulty of enactment* (i.e., estimation of the risk that an impulsive [emotionally preferred] action tendency will interfere with the enactment of an intended [cognitively preferred] action), (e) *volitional strategies* (i.e., metamotivational knowledge concerning ways to increase the strength of a cognitively preferred action tendency or inhibit an emotionally preferred action tendency). The final stage in the development of action control is characterized by (f) *strategies of integration,* which remove discrepancies between emotional preference and commitment by achieving emotional preference for actions one is committed to. When emotional and cognitive preferences are integrated, the maintenance and enactment of a commitment does not require volitional mediation any longer. In the following paragraphs, we discuss these six stages in the development of action control in more detail.

Developmental Precursors of Self-Regulation

Representation of Ongoing Action Tendencies

Early in infancy, children have many action tendencies and goals, but they do not have cognitive representations of them. Nonetheless, they are able to maintain a goal and shield it against distractors. However, this goal maintenance is probably mediated by automatic processes, which do not require effort or claim central processing capacity (Posner & Snyder, 1975). We know from animal studies that goal maintenance is even mediated by certain subcortical mechanisms (Stamm, 1955). Automatic maintenance of whichever goal is currently supported by the strongest action tendency gives the stream of behavior its flowing characteristic that is based on smooth and conflict-free transitions from one activity to the next (cf. the concepts of flow experience and intrinsic motivation; Cziksentmihalyi, 1975; Deci, 1975). During play, young children can be totally immersed in their activities without being affected by distractors in the environment. However, whenever any cue does elicit an emotional preference for a different activity, a conflict-free change of behavior takes place (Atkinson

& Birch, 1970). Our model explains the paradoxical coexistence of low distractibility and smooth transitions from one activity to the next in intrinsically motivated behavior: As long as a given behavioral schema is dominant, it is supported by the automatic attentional maintenance mechanism. When another schema becomes dominant, the maintenance mechanism supports the new activity.

In contrast, when maintenance and change are mediated by volitional control, transitions between successive activities should be characterized by interruptions of variable length caused by volitional mechanisms such as freezing and strategic change of the dominance relations in the emotional and executional subsystems (Fig. 12.1). The acquisition of semantic representations of action tendencies provides the first step toward the development of cognitive preferences and a qualitatively different type of goal maintenance (Astington, 1986). The ability to form a cognitive representation of one's current goal is the first prerequisite for the transition from automatic to strategic goal maintenance. Having the representation "I want to work" is associated with a new type of goal maintenance because a representation of this kind can persist even when the system is not executing the intended action. Strictly speaking, an *intention* is a *metarepresentation* because it refers to an action schema that is a representation of behavior. A metarepresentation such as "I believe this is a cup" can be maintained independent of the truth of the primary representation it refers to, that is, even if the object it refers to is not a cup. As the satisfying condition for an intentional proposition is execution or goal attainment rather than truth (Searle, 1983), we can say that a metarepresentation of an intention can be maintained even if the intention it refers to is not being performed. In fact, one can argue that a decoupling between cognition and action is the prerequisite (if not the mediating process) for forming any metarepresentation (Leslie, 1987).

The decoupling between cognition and action helps explain a paradox that has rendered the analysis of volitional processes very difficult: In order to achieve a higher-order ability of maintaining and enacting difficult intentions, the organism develops a mechanism that first produces the opposite of what is intended. That is, decoupling the representation of an intention from its performance reduces the probability of its immediate execution. The long-term advantage of this procrastination is that an intention can be maintained even if its performance has to be postponed until a better opportunity arises. To obtain this advantage, however, the organism has to develop additional mechanisms or (volitional) strategies that undo the decoupling. The freezing mechanism postulated in our model may be closely related to the decoupling function discussed here (Fig. 12.1). In a later section, we discuss the concept of *state orientation,* which can be defined as a disposition toward prolonged decouplings between intention and action. If, for any reason, the organism develops a decoupling mechanism that is so strong that it cannot be counteracted by the existing volitional strategies (i.e., if the organism is state-oriented), volitional efficiency (that is, the proportion of intentions that are actually enacted) is reduced, whereas volitional maintenance of the intention can be so high that we can speak of an inability to disengage from unattainable goals.

Generating a superordinate maintenance goal may be a further developmental consequence of having a cognitive (meta-) representation of the current intention. Having a separate representation of the current intention sets the stage for a new type of conflict. The congruence between the cognitive representation of the current goal and the emotional preference for this goal is disrupted when emotional preference changes (e.g., a new object in the environment is emotionally preferred), whereas the cognitive representation of the original goal perseverates. We expect two types of observable signs of this type of cognition-emotion conflict: (a) An increased persistence in pursuing a goal even when the instrumental activity becomes unpleasant or when strong competing response tendencies are elicited by cues in the environment, (b) disruptions in the flow of behavior, that is, hesitating or oscillating behavior at the junctures between successive actions.

At the first glance, these two characteristics may not seem to be unique indicators of volitional control because high perseverance and disruptions characterize the behavior of frontal-lobe patients that suffer from a *lack* of volitional control (Fuster, 1980; Luria, 1966; Milner, 1964; Norman & Shallice, 1985). A more careful analysis reveals, however, that the frontal-lobe syndrome differs from volitional control with regard to the eliciting conditions of perseverance and disruption. Whereas the disruptions in the behavior of frontal-lobe patients are associated with a behavioral change elicited by external cues (distractors), the disruptions associated with volitional control do not involve a behavioral change and they are elicited by an internal conflict rather than by external distractors. Moreover, the perseverance mediated by volitional control differs from the symptoms of perseverance displayed by frontal-lobe patients in that volitional perseverance occurs despite the presence of strong distractors, whereas perseverance in frontal-lobe patients requires the absence of distractors.

In addition to the two indicators of volitional control mentioned until now, an incongruence between cognitive and emotional preference can produce a reduction of intrinsic motivation for the ongoing activity. The ability to become totally immersed in an activity is impaired and children become less playful. At this stage of development, children sometimes experience an incongruence between cognitive and emotional preference, but they do not have the concept of commitment (i.e., they do not have intentions in our terminology) or self-regulatory skills needed for maintaining and enacting a cognitive preference against a strong emotional preference for an alternative activity.

The Concept of Impulsivity

Once they have developed cognitive representations of current goals and preferences, children sometimes experience interruptions of their ongoing activities when new incentives change emotional preference. Gradually, they learn to distinguish between distractors in the environment that do not interrupt an ongoing activity and distractors that have a strong emotional impact. Children cannot anticipate the need for volitional maintenance of a cognitive preference unless they have acquired some knowledge concerning the impulsive nature of emotional preferences. This metamotivational knowledge enables children to anticipate the motivational impact of emotional preferences on their behavior and to have a rudimentary concept of the difficulty of enactment associated with certain goals.

Self-Congruent Commitment

As a result of repeatedly experiencing interruptions of cognitively initiated activities by emotionally powerful distractors, children gradually realize that yielding to impulsive tendencies to obtain short-term gratifications renders the attainment of some goals difficult. The anticipation of conflicts between currently preferred goals and future temptations prompts them to commit themselves to some goals. Thus, anticipation of a difficulty of enactment is closely associated with the concept of commitment (Fig. 12.1). Being committed to a goal means that one has decided to maintain this goal even when, on a future occasion, an attractive distractor occurs. The ability to recall this decision in a situation in which maintenance of the goal is difficult (i.e., retrieving a commitment marker in this situation) is a prerequisite for generating a maintenance goal. We use the term *intention* to refer to an action alternative an individual is committed to. Commitment is also closely associated with the child's conception of the self, that is the beliefs concerning attitudes and goals that define her or his own identity. For example, if a child's self-concept contains the belief "I am a good student," she is likely to generate the commitment to finish homework if she anticipates that some attractive alternative will come up.

Difficulty of Enactment

Although the concepts of impulsivity and commitment imply a rudimentary concept of difficulty of enactment, the ability to generate a more precise estimate of it presumably develops at a later age. During this stage, children learn to base their estimate of the difficulty of enactment on the number and strengths of action alternatives that are likely to compete with an intention on a future occasion. This estimate serves as a basis for anticipating the amount of volitional effort necessary to protect the intention whenever those competing action tendencies are aroused. As a result, children are able to invest as much volitional effort as necessary to resist temptation and maintain their intention without wasting too much of their processing resources. In accordance with Ach's (1935) difficulty law of motivation, we assume that this positive relationship between difficulty of enactment and volitional strength is mediated by an automatic process that normally does not become conscious.

Self-Regulatory Skills

Volitional Strategies

When a child has decided that a cognitive preference should be maintained and enacted (i.e., when she or he has generated a commitment), a shift in emotional preference resulting from a tempting alternative requires strategies that support the commitment and the corresponding action schema (see Fig. 12.1). We have already mentioned three such strategies, namely, attention control, motivation control, and execution control. Attention control is the most fundamental of these strategies. In fact, selective attention may be the mechanism that forms the basis for all additional strategies that develop later. The term *attention control* refers to the utilization of attentional resources for strengthening the cognitive representation of one's current intention. It can be a fast and efficient process mediating resistance to temptation. Motivation control is tantamount to creating or strengthening an emotional preference that serves as a motivational basis for the intended action schema (e.g., thinking of the positive aspects of one's work). Although motivation control may be mediated by an attentional mechanism, it requires the development of a metagoal that is directed at the improvement of the system's motivational support for the current intention. As the motivational effects of various thoughts are often more delayed and less obvious than the effects of changes of attentional focus, motivation control probably develops later than attention control. However, motivation control has the advantage that it can have a stronger and longer-lasting effect because it capitalizes on the impulsivity of the emotional system.

In our research with children, we studied additional strategies that can be interpreted as special cases of motivation control. *Coping with failure* is a motivation control strategy. It is difficult to acquire because failure can have either positive or negative effects on subsequent performance (Atkinson, 1974; Wortman & Brehm, 1975). Thinking of a past failure can facilitate a new effort or it can reduce motivation and produce feelings of helplessness. Children gradually learn to recognize when failure-related thoughts are useful and when they can be harmful. One criterion is expectation of control. When a future effort is likely to re-establish control, reminding oneself of a past failure to stick to a commitment is likely to increase one's effort to try harder. When expectation of control has diminished after many futile attempts, failure-related thoughts have a paralyzing effect (Kuhl, 1981).

Another specific strategy related to motivation control is emotion control. This strategy is based on knowledge regarding the effect of various mood states on self-regulatory efficiency. Thinking of something sad can reduce one's ability to maintain an intention, whereas having happy thoughts can facilitate maintenance (Mischel, 1974). Emotion control consists of using that knowledge for modifying one's own mood state in situations that require volitional maintenance of a difficult intention.

As the research reported in the remainder of this chapter was confined to these four strategies (i.e., attention control, motivation control, coping with failure, and emotion control), we do not discuss other strategies postulated in the theory of action control (i.e., execution control, encoding control, and parsimony of decision making, cf. Kuhl, 1985).

Volition-Emotion Integration

The final stage in the development of action control is characterized by the complete removal of the conflict between commitment and emotional preference. Volitional mediation of action is not adaptive in the long run because it requires effort and because it is based on a continuous conflict. Conflict-free enactment of an important commitment can be achieved by developing an emotional preference for actions one is committed to. Maintaining the commitment to quit smoking becomes easy when the emotional preference for smoking disappears. In a delay of gratification situation, this volition-emotion integration requires a modification of the emotional response to the waiting experience. When waiting becomes a normal or even relaxing rather than a frustrating experience, delay of gratification can be achieved without volitional mediation. A deficit in this ability to develop emotion-commitment congruence can cause serious disorders. Chronic alienation (i.e., incongruence between behavior and emotional preference) and depression can result from an overload of commitment-emotion conflicts that exhaust volitional resources (Kuhl & Eisenbeiser, 1986; Kuhl & Helle, 1986; Kuhl & Kazén-Saad, 1988).

THE ASSESSMENT OF ACTION CONTROL

Mischel & Mischel (1983) investigated knowledge about self-regulatory strategies in children ranging in age from 3 to 8 years. In these studies, children were to imagine a delay-of-gratification situation and were asked to decide which of two phrases would help them to wait for the more attractive reward (marshmallows). Children from Grades 3 and 6 showed a significant preference for task-oriented (e.g., "I am waiting for the marshmallows") compared to consummatory ideation (e.g., "The marshmallows are yummy and chewy"). The usefulness of abstract ideation (e.g., "The marshmallows are puffy like clouds") was acknowledged by sixth graders only. In addition, third and sixth graders showed a preference for covering (vs. exposing) the rewards, whereas preschoolers did not show this preference.

On the basis of our model of action control, we can draw some interesting conclusions from these results concerning the development of various components of action control. The preference for task-oriented compared to consummatory ideation can mean two different things. First, it can mean that the children who showed this preference had acquired the concept of impulsivity (i.e., realizing that consummatory ideation strengthens the emotional preference for escaping the frustration). Second, having a preference for task-oriented compared to consummatory ideation can mean that a child has acquired the concept of commitment and knows that rehearsing the commitment helps maintain it. In our research, we made an attempt to assess these two and other developmental precursors separately. In addition, we developed a scale assessing children's metamotivational knowledge and a computer-assisted test procedure for assessing actual self-regulatory efficiency. We focused on the age range between 6 and 10 years because self-regulatory skills presumably develop during this period.

Assessing Developmental Precursors of Action Control

Before studying metamotivational knowledge and self-regulatory efficiency, we were interested in finding out to what extent elementary school children have acquired the prerequisites for action control as spelled out in our developmental theory. We presented 41 children (Grades 1 to 4) with several scenarios describing a conflict between maintaining a commitment and yielding to a temptation. For example, in one scenario the subjects were introduced to a doll, Petra (or Peter if the subject was male), who asked her friend (Karin or Bernd) to tell her (him) a secret. Petra promised that she would not tell the secret to anyone else. Subsequently, Petra meets Sonja, who tries to persuade Petra to tell her the secret by offering a series of increasingly more intensive incentives (from offering some sweets to announcing the end of their friendship). The subjects played the role of Petra (or Peter). During and after the game, subjects were asked several questions to assess whether they understood Petra's commitment and whether they had a concept of impulsivity, that is, whether they had a global understanding of the difficulty of enactment (i.e., of keeping the promise). In addition, we included one item from a pool constructed by Astington (1986) to test semantic representation of an intentional state. This item consists of two drawings, one showing a child sitting on a swing, the other showing the child going to the swing. As can be seen from Table 12.1, the majority of the children in all grades seem to have acquired the developmental prerequisites for action control that we tested.

Virtually all children can identify the picture on which the actor may have an intention. We interpret the ability to identify situations in which someone may have a certain intention as an indication that, when they enter elementary school, children have developed a concept of an intention and are able to generate semantic representations of their own intentions. This conclusion is consistent with the results reported by Astington (1986). The second developmental step concerns the concept of impulsivity. We assume that a global concept of the difficulty of enactment is a first indication that children know about the im-

TABLE 12.1
Percentages of Subjects Who Gave Correct Answers to Questions
Assessing Developmental Prerequisites of Action Control

Developmental Prerequisite	Grades (N = 41)			
	1	2	3	4
Semantic Representation of Intentional States	100	88	100	100
Concept of Impulsivity	78	89	90	85
	(90)[a]	(95)	(85)	(100)
Initial Commitment	100	100	100	100
Actual Maintenance	44	56	80	93
Maintained Commitment	78	100	100	93

[a]Figures in parentheses are from a study with 80 children from grades 1 to 4.

pulsive nature of emotionally supported temptations. In our roleplay, we asked children, after confronting them with the series of increasingly more tempting incentives, whether it was easy or hard for Petra (Peter) to keep her (his) promise. The vast majority of the children said it was hard. This result was confirmed in another study with 80 children (Grades 1–4). Until now, we did not examine the degree to which children within this age group have acquired the more sophisticated concept of difficulty of enactment requiring a quantitative grading of that difficulty as a function of the number and strengths of tempting action alternatives (cf. Fig. 12.1). We assume that this quantitative concept of difficulty develops considerably later than the global difficulty concept. We are planning to test this assumption in a future study.

Table 12.1 also shows the percentage of children who did not tell the secret ("Actual Maintenance") throughout the seven tempting episodes. Obviously, these percentages do not indicate actual maintenance in a real-life situation. However, even in this fictitious situation, about half of the first and second graders yielded to the temptation at some point. Interestingly, a measure computed to estimate "Maintained Commitment" suggests that virtually all children older than 7 years maintained their commitment throughout the seven tempting episodes. This measure combines the number of children that kept the secret and the number of children that expressed regret after telling the secret. Note that it was not our intention to measure the actual ability to maintain a commitment but to assess the extent to which children are able to understand the *concept* of commitment. For this purpose, the use of a fictitious situation is appropriate. Our results seem to indicate that virtually all children beyond the age of 7 have developed the concept of commitment. In the next two sections, we report some results obtained with two instruments developed to assess actual self-regulatory efficiency and metamotivational knowledge.

Assessing the Efficiency of Action Control

The experimental paradigms developed by Mischel (1974) and his associates have been very useful for investigating the effects of various self-regulatory strategies. Unfortunately, they are not very practical for diagnostic purposes. Therefore, we made an attempt to develop a computer-assisted test for assessing self-regulatory efficiency that should satisfy the following requirements: (a) induction of a conflict between commitment and emotional preference, (b) fine-grained assessment of failures to maintain the commitment (e.g., measuring even short [< 1 sec] attentional shifts toward the distractor even without any overt contact with the distractor), and (c) avoidance of the usual confounding of self-regulatory deficits and motivational change.

Our test consists of a main task and a distractor. A static copy of the stimulus screen is presented in Fig. 12.2. As shown in the Figure, the task-relevant information is displayed in the lower left quarter of the computer screen, whereas the distractor is shown in the upper right quarter. The task consists of a random sequence of the letters X and O forming the outline of a rectangle. Subjects are

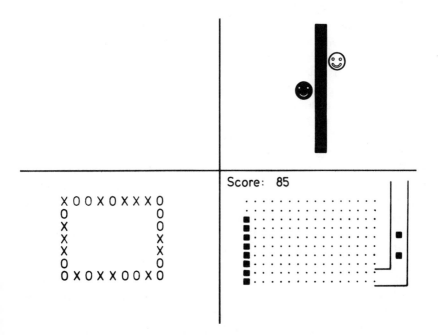

FIG. 12.2.   An illustration of the self-regulatory efficiency test for children. The Figure is a static representation of the test display. See text for a description of task elements.

instructed to push the X key when an X is flashing and push the O key when an O is flashing. After each correct response, the next letter in the sequence starts flashing. For each correct response, the subject's score, which is displayed in the lower right quarter of the screen, is increased by one. After completing 10 correct responses, a dime is added to the subject's account, which is also displayed in the lower right quarter of the screen. The subject is told that she or he will be able to buy little toys with the money accumulated during the experiment. After each period of 20 sec, the distractor episode starts in the upper right quarter of the screen. During this episode, two little smilies, a dark one and a white one have a tree-climbing competition. When the white smiley reaches the top first, it jumps down, takes a tube, and sucks a variable number of dimes from the subject's account. When the dark smiley wins, it jumps down, takes the tube, and blows a variable number of dimes into the subject's account. Subjects are instructed that they cannot influence the outcome of the competition and that watching it reduces the amount of dimes they can accumulate.

After understanding the contingencies involved, children readily form a commitment to concentrate on the task. Maintaining this commitment is difficult during the distractor episodes because the children are curious to find out who wins the competition and how many dimes are added to or subtracted from their account. Looking at the competition or thinking about it normally leads to a decrease in the speed and/or accuracy of performance as measured by inter-response times and number of errors. Results from a pilot study with this instrument ($N = 49$) did not show the expected decrease in speed and accuracy of performance during the distractor episodes. The most obvious reason for this finding is that our distractor was not attractive enough to beat the strong task-oriented commitment the children had formed.

This interpretation is inconsistent, however, with our observation that many children looked at the distractor frequently. An examination of individual plots of the time course of interresponse times revealed that about one third of the subjects had a substantially increased variance of interresponse times during distractor episodes compared to nondistractor episodes. Closer inspection of the data showed that these subjects frequently showed sudden increases in inter-response time followed by very short interresponse times. Apparently, they slowed down when looking at the distractor and tried to make up for the delay by increasing speed subsequently.

Although it would be premature to draw any firm conclusions regarding the validity of the variance measure, we believe that it may help solve one of the most difficult problems involved in the measurement of self-regulatory efficiency. The common performance measure (e.g., decrease in performance from nondistractor to distractor episodes) confounds impaired action control and motivational change. A behavioral shift to the distractor may indicate a failure to stick to one's commitment or it may indicate disengagement from the commitment. A shift to the distractor is an unequivocal sign of volitional inefficiency only if the task-oriented commitment still exists during and after the contact with the distractor. The most obvious behavioral indications of the continuous existence of a commitment are signs of conflict. Increased variance of interresponse times may be a combined indicator of yielding to a temptation and still being committed to the task. Children who yield to the temptation (i.e., watch the competition) without feeling committed to the task any longer do not have any reason to make up for the performance deficit caused by the behavioral shift to the distractor. This interpretation of the variance measure is supported by the results from our pilot study. Within Grades 2 to 4, correlations between the variance measure and teachers' ratings of various behavioral correlates of self-regulation (attentiveness in class, concentration on task, independence) ranged from − .22 to − .72. Children having a higher variance of interresponse times during the distractor episodes compared to episodes without distractors were rated rather low by their teachers with regard to the behavioral indicators of self-regulatory efficiency. Although these correlations cannot be taken as conclusive evidence for the validity of the variance measure, they encourage us to further explore this measure in future studies.

The Assessment of Metamotivational Knowledge

Our study into the developmental precursors of self-regulation revealed that, beyond the age of 7, most children have acquired semantic representations of intentional states, the concept of impulsivity (including a global concept of difficulty of enactment), and the concept of commitment. According to earlier findings, metamotivational strategies develop during elementary school years (Mischel & Mischel, 1983). In our research, we have focused on the development of a standardized test of strategy knowledge. The first version of this test contained 16 scenarios illustrated by a drawing and described verbally. Each scenario described a situation in which it is difficult to maintain an intention. For example, one scenario describes a classroom situation in which two children have committed themselves to listening to the teacher and resist listening to the boy sitting in between them trying to tell them something interesting. One child thinks ''I think he wants to tell me something funny,'' while the second child thinks ''I'm not going to look at him.'' Subjects are asked which of the two children cannot maintain the intention to listen to the teacher.

Four scenarios were constructed for each of the following four strategies: (a) attention control (focusing attention on information related to the active intention), (b) motivation control (enhancing one's motivation to maintain the intention, e.g., by thinking of its attractive consequences), (c) coping with failure (ignoring uncontrollable failures and using controllable failures for self-motivational purposes), and (d) emotion control (e.g., avoiding emotions that reduce self-regulatory efficiency).

This instrument was administered to 60 German children from Grades 1 to 4 (Kuhl & Mlynek, 1986). In this study, attention control and motivation control showed an almost linear increase from Grade 1 to Grade 4, whereas scores in emotion control and coping with failure are rather low in Grades 1 to 3 and show a sudden increase in Grade 4. Similar results were obtained in a sample of 120 Mexican school children from Grades 1 to 6 (Guevara, 1987).

In the German sample, several measures were obtained to estimate convergent and discriminant validity of the test. Significant relationships were found between strategy knowledge and criterion variables (i.e., a resistance-to-temptation measure and teachers' ratings of attentiveness in class, frequency of finishing homework, and independence). No significant relationships were found between strategy knowledge and variables not related to self-regulation (motivation for learning and fear of failure).

We are currently investigating the usefulness of a new instrument, the Metamotivational Knowledge Test for Children (MKTC). This test is based on three scenarios that describe three everyday situations in great detail. We reduced the number of scenarios because we observed that many children had difficulties maintaining attention when confronted with 16 different scenarios. The three-scenario version has the advantage that each scenario can be described in greater detail, which helps children to get involved in the story and identify with its hero. Another new feature of the MKTC is the fact that only one scenario depicts a school-related setting (trying to finish one's homework while friends are playing outside in front of the window). The other two scenarios refer to everyday situations that children interviewed in a pilot study mentioned as examples for situations in which it is difficult to maintain an intention (saving money to buy a toy, not telling a secret). Eight questions are asked in each scenario (two questions per strategy), yielding a total of 24 items. The three-scenario version of the MKTC replicates the developmental trends obtained with the 16-scenario test for three of the four strategies investigated.

As can be seen from Fig. 12.3, we did not find any significant increase in emotion-control scores from Grades 1 to 4. We are currently investigating the hypothesis that this finding may be attributable to high variability of facilitating emotions. Whereas sadness may, in fact, reduce volitional efficiency in some children, it may have a facilitating effect for other children. If this were the case, we could not score correct or wrong answers in the MKTC without testing the actual effect of various mood states on self-regulatory efficiency for each individual child. According to an alternative interpretation of the lack of a developmental trend for emotion-control scores, the acquisition of emotion control is more difficult and develops later in childhood. We found some support for this interpretation in a sample of adults who were administered the MKTC ($n = 31$).

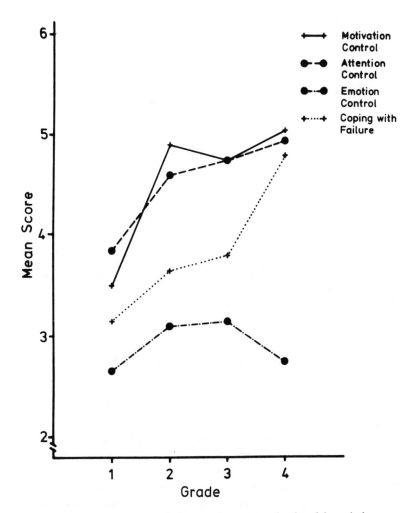

FIG. 12.3. Developmental changes in metamotivational knowledge for four action-control strategies (mean Metamotivational Knowledge Test for Children [MKTC] scores).

We found 74%–87% consensus as to which of the two emotion-control strategies to be compared was more useful for maintaining self-regulatory efficiency. When eliminating the emotion control scale, the current version of the MKTC has sufficient internal consistency (Cronbach's alpha = .72).

A conjoint validation of the MKTC and the volitional efficiency test was obtained when the variance of interresponse times during nondistractor and distractor episodes was computed separately for children having low versus high MKTC scores (median-split). A 2 × 2 (nondistractor vs. distractor × MKTC

TABLE 12.2
Mean Variance of Interresponse Times
as a Function of Metamotivational
Knowledge (Median-Split of MKTC Scores)
and Presence of an Attractive Distractor
("Smiley Competition")

Metamotivational Knowledge	Distractor	
	Off	On
Low	.25	1.04
High	.24	.38

group) ANOVA revealed a significant interaction, $F(1,23) = 5.84, p < .05$). As can be seen from Table 12.2, this interaction was attributable to the fact that children having high strategy-knowledge scores did not show any significant difference between nondistractor and distractor episodes in the variance of interresponse times, whereas children having low strategy knowledge showed about four times as much variance during distractor episodes compared to nondistractor episodes.

ACTION VERSUS STATE ORIENTATION

The theory of action control has been applied in research on various phenomena related to learning deficits such as learned helplessness and loss of intrinsic motivation. This research has been based on an aspect of the model (Fig. 12.1) that we explain in this section. The adaptiveness of the volitional maintenance functions described in Fig. 12.1 depends on the situational appropriateness of the intention that benefits from volitional support. Maintenance of an intention that has to be postponed or that turns out to be unrealistic is maladaptive because it interferes with the formation and execution of situationally appropriate new intentions. Overmaintenance of unrealistic goals can lead to a fixation on past, present, or future states, for example, on a past failure to attain a goal, on the present emotional consequences of that failure, or on the desired goal state itself. In earlier papers, *state orientation* has been defined in terms of these behavioral and phenomenal consequences of overmaintenance (Kuhl, 1981, 1984). The opposite mode of control, *action orientation,* is characterized by an attentional focus on a situationally appropriate action plan. Earlier research has shown considerable individual differences in subjects' ability to disengage from unattainable goals. A questionnaire assessing a disposition toward action versus state orientation has been constructed. This questionnaire has good internal consistency and has been used to make interesting predictions ranging from performance deficits observed following failure experiences to short-term memory deficits in depressed patients following interruption of a routine activity.

According to the results of one study, state orientation seems to develop early during childhood as a result of socialization practices characterized by an increased frequency of interruptions of childrens' activities by their mothers (Humbert, 1981). Other developmental determinants of the disposition toward state orientation are parents' rubbing in of failures to meet moral or academic standards and a heavy emphasis on behavioral consistency, for example, keeping one's promises, emphasizing duties and responsibilities, and inducing self-blame after failures (Kästele, 1988). According to the experimental findings obtained, subjects having a disposition toward state orientation have more problems than action-oriented ones when disengagement from an unrealistic goal is necessary to make processing resources available for a new (realistic) task (Brunstein & Olbrich, 1985; Kuhl, 1981; Kuhl & Helle, 1986; Kuhl & Weiss, in press).

A Reinterpretation of Learned Helplessness

Repeated exposures to uncontrollable outcomes can produce considerable learning and performance deficits. This has been demonstrated both in laboratory experiments on learned helplessness (Hiroto & Seligman, 1975) as well as in educational settings (Dweck & Repucci, 1973; Diener & Dweck, 1978). The theory of action control provides an alternative interpretation of performance deficits observed following exposure to uncontrollable failure (Kuhl, 1981, 1984). When subjects are given a solvable task after having been exposed to a helplessness treatment (i.e., obtaining noncontingent feedback while working on an unsolvable task), some subjects show performance decrements even when the solvable task differs substantially from the unsolvable one. This result has been attributed to a generalized expectancy of lost control that undermines task motivation (Hiroto & Seligman, 1975). However, our experiments have shown that performance deficits caused by a failure experience often occur even when subjects do not generalize their expectancy of lost control. It could be shown that state-oriented subjects suffer from performance deficits because they are unable to disengage from the goal to solve the first task even when they are trying hard to focus all their attentional resources on a second task and are confident that they can solve it.

The ability of humans to pursue important goals despite repeated failures sometimes has the negative side effect of rendering the deactivation of unrealistic intentions very difficult. State-oriented subjects have more problems than action-oriented ones to deactivate context-inadequate intentions. After having made many futile attempts at an unsolvable task, state-oriented subjects cannot deactivate the intention to solve that task even when they are confronted with a new solvable task. As a result, they experience intrusive thoughts related to the first task while they are trying hard to focus on the new task (Brunstein & Olbrich, 1985; Kuhl, 1981; Kuhl & Weiss, in press). The most important educational implication of these results is that learned helplessness is not always mediated by expectancies of lost control and by motivational deficits. Our results show that failure experiences can produce performance deficits even when expectancy of control and motivation is still intact. Our state-oriented subjects were not able to concentrate fully on the new task although they were highly motivated to do so and had no expectancy deficits. Their problem was a self-regulatory one: They were trapped in the state-oriented cycle of volitional maintenance of an unrealistic intention (i.e., to solve the original task) and were unable to switch to the action-oriented cycle (i.e., disengaging from the old task and concentrating volitional resources on the new task).

When underachieving students' learning deficit is caused by state orientation rather than perceived helplessness, psychological intervention should focus on the training of self-regulatory skills rather than inducing unwarranted concepts of intact control or external and specific attributions of failure (cf. Peterson & Seligman, 1987). Specifically, our model suggests to teach them how to discover context-inadequate intentions and how to disengage from them. In one study, we found that making state-oriented subjects expect that they will not meet their high standards of excellence in a certain task domain helps them to disengage from an unsolvable task and removes all helplessness effects on a subsequent task (Kuhl & Weiss, in press).

In our current research, we are investigating another target for intervention. In a recent study, we hypothesized that a global search schema screening long-term memory for commitments (e.g., "Is there any intention I do not have completed yet?") is more often activated in state-oriented than in action-oriented subjects. On the basis of this hypothesis, we expected and found that state-oriented subjects can think of more long-term goals than action-oriented subjects (Kuhl & Kazén-Saad, in press). Frequent use of the global commitment-search schema can increase the difficulty to disengage from context-inadequate intentions. In a new experimental paradigm, we found strong evidence for the assumption that state-oriented subjects have greater difficulties in deactivating uncompleted intentions that cannot be carried out in the current situation. Using recognition latencies as measures for activational strength of words related to uncompleted, context-inadequate intentions, we found that state-oriented subjects maintained an induced intention active in memory even in a situation in which they could not carry it out (Goschke & Kuhl, in preparation; Kuhl & Goschke, in press). We assume that this overmaintenance of context-inadequate intentions can be reduced by teaching state-oriented individuals to stop searching for commitments too frequently. According to our model, activating the commitment-search schema less frequently helps avoid an overly frequent activation of the volitional system. In addition, teaching state-oriented individuals how to develop context-specific rather than global intentions and how to perform context-adequacy checks frequently will help them deactivate context-inadequate and focus on context-adequate intentions.

It should be noted that the maladaptive consequences of state orientation are associated with its context-blind, intrusive properties. State-oriented activities can be very useful, however, provided the individual is able to interrupt them when they impede the attainment of an important goal. Rehearsing uncompleted intentions, analyzing the causes of past failures, focusing on one's current emotional state, and many other state-oriented activities can be adaptive as long as they can be terminated or interrupted when an important and realistic goal requires all processing resources for immediate action. Thoughts about the causes of a past plane crash are not helpful when they intrude into a pilot's consciousness while he or she is trying to handle a different emergency situation.

CONCLUSION

At the beginning of this chapter, we mentioned three unresolved problems of past research on self-regulation: the lack of a theory that provides functional definitions of the mechanisms underlying self-regulation, the lack of a theory specifying developmental precursors of self-regulatory functions, and the lack of diagnostic techniques that provide unconfounded measures of self-regulatory efficiency. We have described our attempts to take a few steps toward solving these three problems. The difficulties we encountered in developing better assessment techniques convinced us that advances in the measurement of self-regulation cannot be made unless we have a theory that solves some of the difficult problems concerning the identification of self-regulatory mechanisms (e.g., distinguishing between self-regulatory deficits and motivational change, separating emotional and cognitive preferences, etc.). Our experiments on learned helplessness in which we successfully separated motivational from self-regulatory deficits illustrate the practical significance of this separation: Self-regulatory and motivational deficits require totally different kinds of psychological intervention.

OPEN DISCUSSION

During the discussion, Kuhl distinguished between research directed toward measurement of self-regulatory efficiency and studies aimed at remediation of self-regulatory deficits. Additional questions pertained to the application and implications of Kuhl's model for adult behaviors, the possible relationship between self-regulatory processes and intellectual abilities, and the concept of disengagement.

Adams: In your model, you allow the socialization processes to perform the self-regulatory behaviors. Then you move in at various points of time and measure and evaluate them. What steps would you take to have more or less of a particular regulatory process? Suppose you were a therapist and you have to advise a parent and child how to increase or decrease one of these processes? I suppose I am asking about the operationalizing of the self-regulatory processes.

Kuhl: Well, operationalizing has two sides: (1) measuring what is there and (2) focusing on the influence of an intervention. I think your question deals with the intervention. The research I reported focuses on the first side—measurement. Our second step will be to find out how we can influence self-regulatory strategies. We don't know how stable these strategies are, nor how much we can influence them. We plan to try to use, for instance, Meichenbaum's self-instructional techniques to influence these strategies. We are now preparing video scenes in which children can observe various behaviors of successful and unsuccessful children in order to determine how much this modeling will influence self-regulatory processes. My guess is that self-regulatory strategies will operate like an individual difference variable. Some children may be easy to influence while other children may be very resistant to change.

Kyllonen: Except for your discussion about learned helplessness work with adults, the studies you have talked about were concerned with children. How important are self-regulatory processes for understanding behavior of high school students, college students, and adults?

Kuhl: The only adult data we have at this point concerns the ability to disengage from unattainable goals. In this research, we find strong and consistent effects. With regard to all the other mechanisms, we need to do further research.

Kyllonen: Are you interested in following this up?

Kuhl: Yes, very much. We have already been thinking about developing an instrument for adults that measures self-regulatory efficiency. We have thought of using a stock market situation, but that may be too specific. We think some game situations of that type may tap the same aspect.

Among adults, we have very strong data demonstrating that certain identifiable people—we call them state-oriented subjects—showed responses that allow for the inference that these people have high memory maintenance of concepts related to unattainable, unrealistic goals. What we did in that experiment was to first induce an intention. Then we took the subject out of the situation in which they could enact the intention and told them that they could enact their intention later. For example, we might induce an intention to set a table and provide all the materials needed to enact that intention: tablecloth, glasses, candles, etc. Then we move the person to a different situation in which they performed a word-recognition task on a computer screen. In this new task, subjects got words that referred to their previous intention or to other scripts that related to intentions that were not to carry out in the first phase of the experiment.

Our general finding from these types of studies is very clear and has been replicated in several experiments: State-oriented subjects are faster in recognizing words related to uncompleted intentions. It seems that these subjects don't disengage from the intention and keep related words active in memory even when they are in a situation where they cannot do anything about it. Action-oriented subjects, on the other hand, seem to clear their system and deactivate concepts that are related to context-inadequate prospective intentions (i.e., intentions that they cannot carry out at the moment). I think this difference between persons helps to explain the differential effects of failure on adult performance.

Pellegrino: In terms of your developmental progression, you seem to be looking at children's understanding of various strategies for goal attainment and things like that. In the story comprehension, story production literature there have been some nice developmental data collected which shows a progression in terms of the strategies that children recognize as ways to either meet goals or get around goals. I think these data are consistent with some of your measurement devices.

Kuhl: I think that is true. It will be interesting to find out how highly these various measures are related. Our first step in this research program was to design a specific instrument. Our next step will be to relate our instrument to other developmental phenomena. One hypothesis is that there is some general factor that develops. I think that is a very plausible assumption.

Sager: To what extent would your measure of metamotivational knowledge overlap or correlate with g? Also, to what extent do you think you would find the same relationships between measures of g and this ability to put goals out of your mind when it is appropriate?

Kuhl: Ruth asked me similar interesting questions prior to my talk. One possibility is that self-regulation may just be an ability component, for instance, a g factor. If self-regulation is represented in general intelligence, then perhaps you might think of general intelligence as simply a summary concept for a lot of different things where one of those things is self-regulatory efficiency. However, to know the components may be especially helpful for intervention purposes. It is an issue that we plan to address.

Tellegen: When you talk about disengagement, do you mean suspension?

Kuhl: That is a theoretically very important question. when I speak about disengagement, I mean deactivation in memory, that is, inhibition or reducing the activational strength of related memory structures. It is not to be confounded with disengagement in behavior. Although a person may stop performing goal-directed actions, that does not mean that the person has deactivated the intention in the system.

Tellegen: So your state-oriented persons might be the ones least likely to resume activities later on?

Kuhl: Yes, exactly. That is one of the funny things that may happen. We have some data indicating that already. Behaviorally, these persons stop fairly early, but cognitively they keep perseverating; that is, they don't deactivate the intention.

REFERENCES

Ach, N. (1935). Analyse des Willens. [Analysis of the Will]. In E. Abderhalden (Ed.), *Handbuch der biologischen Arbeitsmethoden, [Handbook of biological research methods]*. Bd. VI. Berlin: Urban & Schwarzenberg.

Anderson, J. R. (1983). *The architecture of cognition*. Cambridge: Cambridge University Press.

Arnold, M. B. (1984). *Memory and the brain*. Hillsdale, NJ: Lawrence Erlbaum Associates.

Astington, J. W. (1986). Children's comprehension of intention. *British Journal of Developmental Psychology, 4*, 43–49.

Atkinson, J. W. (1974). Strength of motivation and efficiency of performance. In J. W. Atkinson & J. O. Raynor (Eds.), *Motivation and achievement* (pp. 193–218). Washington DC: Winston.

Atkinson, J. W., & Birch, D. (1970). *The dynamics of action*. New York: John Wiley & Sons.

Beckmann, J., & Kuhl, J. (1984). Altering information to gain action control: Functional aspects of human information processing in decision-making. *Journal of Research in Personality, 18*, 223–237.

Blum, G. S., & Barbour, J. S. (1979). Selective inattention to anxiety-linked stimuli. *Journal of Experimental Psychology: General, 108*, 182–224.

Brown, A. (1978). Knowing when, where, and how to remember: A problem of metacognition. In R. Glaser (Ed.), *Advances in instructional psychology* (pp. 77–165). Hillsdale, NJ: Lawrence Erlbaum Associates.

Brunstein, J. C., & Olbrich, E. (1985). Personal helplessness and action control: An analysis of achievement-related cognitions, self-assessments, and performance. *Journal of Personality and Social Psychology, 48*, 1540–1551.

Craik, F. J. M., & Lockhard, R. S. (1972). Levels of processing: A framework for memory research. *Journal of Verbal Learning and Verbal Behavior, 11*, 671–684.

Cziksentmihalyi, M. (1975). *Beyond boredom and anxiety*. San Francisco: Jossey-Bass.

Deci, E. L., (1975). *Intrinsic motivation*. New York: Plenum Press.

Diener, C. J., & Dweck, C. S. (1978). An analysis of learned helplessness: Continuous changes in performance, strategy, and achievement cognitions following failure. *Journal of Personality and Social Psychology, 36*, 451–462.

Dörner, D. (1985). Thinking and the organization of action. In J. Kuhl & J. Beckmann (Eds.), *Action control: From cognition to behavior* (pp. 219–235). Heidelberg and New York: Springer-Verlag.

Dweck, C. S., & Repucci, N. D. (1973). Learned helplessness and reinforcement responsibility in children. *Journal of Personality and Social Psychology, 25,* 109–116.

Flavell, J. H., & Wellman, H. (1977). Metamemory. In R. V. Kail & J. W. Hagen (Eds.), *Perspectives on the development of memory and cognition* (pp. 3–33). Hillsdale, NJ: Lawrence Erlbaum Associates.

Fodor, J. A. (1983). *The modularity of mind.* Cambridge, MA: MIT Press.

Frijda, N. H. (1986). *The emotions.* New York: Cambridge University Press.

Fuster, J. M. (1980). *The prefrontal cortex.* New York: Raven.

Goschke, T., & Kuhl, J. (in preparation). Memory for intention-related knowledge: Task-irrelevant activation of future goals. Manuscript submitted for publication.

Guevara, M. L. (1987). *Desarollo de estratégias de autocontrol.* [The development of self-control strategies]. Tésis Inédita, México, D.F.: Universidad Nacionál Autónoma de México.

Heckhausen, H., & Kuhl, J. (1985). From wishes to action: The dead ends and short-cuts on the long way to action. In M. Frese & J. Sabini (Eds.), *Goal directed behavior: Psychological theory and research on action* (pp. 134–159). Hillsdale, NJ: Lawrence Erlbaum Associates.

Hiroto, D. S., & Seligman, M. E. P. (1975). Generality of learned helplessness in man. *Journal of Psychology, 31,* 311–327.

Humbert, C. (1981). *Schwierigkeitswahl und Leistung nach Erfolg und Misserfolg als Funktion von Lageorientierung und Standardsetzung* [Risk-taking and performance following success and failure as a function of state orientation and standard-setting]. Unpublished thesis, Ruhr University Bochum, West Germany.

Kästele, G. (1988). *Anlage-und umweltbedingte Determinanten der Handlungs- und Lageorientierung nach Mißerfolg im Vergleich zu anderen Persönlichkeitseigenschaften: Eine emprirische Untersuchung an 22 ein- und zweieiigen Zwillingspaaren* [Hereditary and environmental determinants of action and state orientations]. Unpublished doctoral dissertation, University of Osnabrück, West Germany.

Kluwe, R. H. (1987). Executive decisions and regulation of problem solving behavior. In F. E. Weinert & R. Kluwe (Eds.), *Metacognition, motivation, and understanding* (pp. 31–64). Hillsdale, NJ: Lawrence Erlbaum Associates.

Kuhl, J. (1981). Motivational and functional helplessness: The moderating effect of state versus action orientation. *Journal of Personality and Social Psychology, 40,* 155–170.

Kuhl, J. (1983). *Motivation, Konflikt und Handlungskontrolle. [Motivation, conflict, and action control].* Heidelberg and New York: Springer-Verlag.

Kuhl, J. (1984). Volitional aspects of achievement motivation and learned helplessness: Towards a comprehensive theory of action control. In B. A. Maher (Ed.), *Progress in experimental personality research.* (Vol. 13, pp. 99–171). New York: Academic Press.

Kuhl, J. (1985). Volitional mediators of cognition-behavior consistency: Self-regulatory processes and action versus state orientation. In J. Kuhl & J. Beckmann (Eds.), *Action control: From cognition to behavior* (pp. 101–128). Heidelberg and New York: Springer-Verlag.

Kuhl, J. (1986). Motivation and information processing: A new look at decision-making, dynamic conflict, and action control. In R. N. Sorrentino & E. T. Higgins (Eds.), *The handbook of motivation and cognition: Foundations of social behavior* (pp. 404–434). New York: Guilford.

Kuhl, J. & Kazén-Saad, M. (in press). Motivational and volitional aspects of depression: The role of state orientation. In J. Kuhl & J. Beckmann (Eds.), *Volition and personality: Action- and state-oriented modes of control.* Heidelberg and Toronto: Hogrefe.

Kuhl, J., & Eisenbeiser, T. (1986). Mediating vs. meditating cognitions in human motivation: Action control, inertial motivation, and the alienation effect. In J. Kuhl & J. W. Atkinson (Eds.), *Motivation, thought, and action* (pp. 288–306). New York: Praeger.

Kuhl, J., & Goschke, T. (in press). A computational analysis of action vs. state orientation: Maintenance of intention-related memory representations. In J. Kuhl & J. Beckmann (Eds.), *Volition and personality: Action- and state-oriented modes of control.* Heidelberg and Toronto: Hogrefe.

Kuhl, J., & Helle, L. (1986). Motivational and volitional determinants of depression: The degenerated intention hypothesis. *Journal of Abnormal Psychology, 95*, 247–251.

Kuhl, J., & Kazén-Saad, M. (1988). A motivational approach to volition: Activation and deactivation of memory representations related to uncompleted intentions. In V. Hamilton, G. H. Bower, & N. H. Frijda (Eds.), *Cognitive perspectives on emotion and motivation* (pp. 63–85). Dordrecht, The Netherlands: Martinus Nijhoff.

Kuhl, J., & Mlynek, H. (1986). *Metakognitive Handlungskontrollstrategien und Ablenkungsresistenz: Validierung zweier Tests an Grundschulkindern.* [Metacognitive strategies of self-regulation: Validity of two tests for elementary-school children]. Unpublished manuscript.

Kuhl, J., & Weiss, M. (in press). Performance deficits following uncontrollable failure: Impaired action control or generalized expectancy deficits. In J. Kuhl & J. Beckmann (Eds.), *Volition and personality: Action- and state-oriented modes of control.* Göttingen and Toronto: Hogrefe.

Leslie, A. M. (1987). Pretense and representation: The origins of "theory of mind." *Psychological Review, 94*, 412–426.

Luria, A. R. (1966). *Higher cortical functions in man.* London: Tavistock.

McGinnies, E. (1949). Emotionality and perceptual defense. *Psychological Review, 56*, 244–251.

Milner, B. (1964). Some effects of frontal lobectomy in man. In J. M. Warren & K. Akert (Eds.), *The frontal granular cortex and behavior* (pp. 313–334). New York: McGraw-Hill.

Mischel, W. (1974). Processes in delay of gratification. In L. Berkowitz (Ed.), *Advances in experimental social psychology* (Vol. 7, pp. 249–292). New York: Academic Press.

Mischel, H. N., & Mischel, W. (1983). The development of children's knowledge of self-control strategies. *Child Development, 54*, 603–619.

Neumann, O., & Prinz, W. (1987). Kognitive Antezedentien von Willkürhandlungen [Cognitive antecedents of volitional action]. In H. Heckhausen, P. M. Gollwitzer, & F. E. Weinert (Eds.), *Jenseits des Rubikon: Der Wille in den Humanwissenschaften* (pp. 195–215). Berlin: Springer.

Norman, D. A. (1980). Twelve issues for cognitive science. *Cognitive Science, 4*, 1–32.

Norman, D. A., & Shallice, T. (1985). Attention to action: Willed and automatic control of behavior. In R. J. Davidson, G. E. Schwartz, & D. Shapiro (Eds.), *Consciousness and self-regulation: Advances in research* (Vol. 4). New York: Plenum Press.

Ortony, A., Clore, G. L., & Collins, A. (1988). *The cognitive structure of emotions.* Cambridge: Cambridge University Press.

Peterson, C., & Seligman, M. E. P. (1987). Helplessness and attributional style in depression. In F. E. Weinert & R. Kluwe (Eds.), *Metacognition, motivation, and understanding* (pp. 185–215). Hillsdale, NJ: Lawrence Erlbaum Associates.

Posner, M. I., & Snyder C. R. R. (1975). Facilitation and inhibition in the processing of signals. In P. M. A. Rabbitt & S. Dornic (Eds.), *Attention and performance* (Vol. 5). New York: Academic Press.

Pylyshyn, Z. W. (1984). *Computation and cognition. Towards a foundation for cognitive science.* Cambridge, MA: MIT Press.

Searle, J. (1983). *Intentionality: An essay in the philosophy of mind.* New York: Cambridge University Press.

Sherry, D. F., & Schacter, D. L. (1987). The evolution of multiple memory systems. *Psychological Review, 94*, 439–454.

Stamm, J. S. (1955). The function of the median cerebral cortex in maternal behavior of rats. *Journal of Comparative and Physiological Psychology, 48*, 77–88.

Weinert, F. E., & Kluwe, R. H. (1987). *Metacognition, motivation, and understanding.* Hillsdale, NJ: Lawrence Erlbaum Associates.

Wortman, C. B., & Brehm, J. W. (1975). Responses to uncontrollable outcomes: An integration of reactance theory and the learned helplessness model. In L. Berkowitz (Ed.), *Advances in experimental social psychology* (Vol. 8, pp. 277–336). New York: Academic Press.

Conative Processes, Dispositions, and Behavior: Connecting the Dots Within and Across Paradigms

Ruth Kanfer
University of Minnesota

Individual differences in learning and performance cannot be explained solely by individual differences in cognitive abilities. In addition to abilities, the learning process requires individuals to deliberately focus attentional effort and to persist, despite initial failures and difficulties. In recognition of this fact, some researchers seeking a more complete account of individual differences in learning and performance have turned their attention to the role of conative mechanisms. At a theoretical level, the inclusion of conative concepts (such as motivation, effort, arousal, and volition) raises several new questions about how these non-cognitive process may affect cognitive processing during learning. Pragmatically, the integration of ability and motivation approaches to learning provides a tractable framework for understanding the all-too-common situation in which individuals with sufficient cognitive abilities sometimes demonstrate poor learning.

The recent attention to motivational processes in learning comes at a time when there has also been substantial new activity in the field of motivational psychology. For the past two decades, no grand theory has dominated the study of motivation. Theories of motivation, such as Atkinson's (1957, 1964) achievement motivation formulation, Weiner's (1985, 1986) attributional model of motivation and emotion, Locke's (1968; Locke, Shaw, Saari, & Latham, 1981) goal-setting model, Kanfer's (1977; Kanfer & Hagerman, 1987) self-regulation model, and Bandura's (1977, 1986) social learning approach and Kuhl's (1984, 1986) action control framework have resulted in overlapping but *disparate* programs of research. On the one hand, each of these research programs has made substantial contributions to the field. On the other, the lack of coherence across programs has also made the task of incorporating conative contructs and processes into learning and abilities research even more difficult. All too often, the choice of which noncognitive constructs to consider seems to depend more on a researcher's specific notion of what *motivation* means rather than on a shared and integrated view of the conative domain. As a consequence, evidence regarding the role of conative mechanisms in the context of information processing and abilities tends to be noncumulative, making it difficult to draw conclusions across studies.

During the past decade, however, there have been several attempts to coordinate different theoretical perspectives in motivational psychology (e.g., Bandura, 1988; Heckhausen & Kuhl, 1985; Humphreys & Revelle, 1984; Hyland, 1988; F. Kanfer & Stevenson, 1985; R. Kanfer, 1987, in press; Kuhl, 1982, 1986; Naylor, Pritchard, & Ilgen, 1980; Schmidt, Kleinbeck, & Brockmann, 1984; Weiner, 1985, 1986). A key feature of these attempts has been the recasting of conative processes into information-processing terms. In Kleinbeck's work, for example, motivation is defined in terms of the individual's allocation of attentional resources across tasks. In Revelle's perspective, individual differences in personality are posited to affect performance via their effects on arousal and information processing. In Kuhl's paradigm, the information-processing perspective is used to describe the dynamic processes by which cognition, affect, and behavior are integrated. Although these newer perspectives differ in their emphases, the trend toward adoption of an information-processing framework in motivational psychology is unmistakable.

One important benefit of this trend is the opportunity it presents for unification of the field. Contemporary approaches demand a reexamination of our conative constructs—that we take a closer look at the motivation/volition domain, and that we direct more of our attention toward understanding the relations among various noncognitive traits and conative processes. As Revelle and Kuhl and Kraska point out, consensus has yet to be reached about the constructs that comprise the nomological network for motivation. Reminiscent of earlier learning-based theories emphasizing drive, Revelle asserts that we must preserve the arousal construct in the conative domain and differentiate this construct from the effort construct. In a different vein, Kuhl (e.g., Kuhl, 1984) contends that we must differentiate motivational constructs pertaining to the establishment of cognitive preferences (motivation in his terms) from volitional constructs pertaining to will and effort. The emerging picture of the conative domain is that multiple constructs influence, and are influenced, by one another.

In addition to issues related to construct differentiation within the conative domain, additional complexity is introduced when considering the effects of individual differences in personality on conative processes. Empirical findings indicate, for example, that different noncognitive traits may affect performance via arousal (Revelle), choice (motivation, see e.g., Feather, 1982), and/or volition (Kuhl & Kraska). The information-processing framework provides a valuable context for examination of the relations among dispositional, conative, and self-regulatory processes. These new directions in the study of motivation also have potential implications for an even broader integration of motivation and cognitive ability determinants of learning and performance.

The objectives of this chapter are twofold: (a) to highlight advances and issues in conation associated with work discussed in the chapters by Revelle and by Kuhl and Kraska; and (b) to relate these advances to the broader quest for an integrated ability–motivation perspective—a perspective in which learning and performance are determined by the dynamic and interactive effects of abilities and conation. As implied by the title of this chapter, the task of coordinating recent developments within motivational psychology and across motivation and abilities domains is analogous to drawing a scene by connecting the dots. Like the child who engages in such activities, one does not recognize the picture from the dots alone. Unlike the child, however, the placement of the dots that ultimately fill in the sketch depends in part on us—where and how we place the dots to help fill out the picture.

Programs of research described in the chapters by Revelle and by Kuhl and Kraska provide an outline for a tractable conceptual foundation linking individual differences in cognitive abilities, conation, and personality. After discussing this work, I conclude by suggesting several directions for future research aimed toward development of a unified framework for individual differences in learning and performance.

ADVANCES IN MOTIVATIONAL PSYCHOLOGY

A Short Overview

In the historical context of motivational psychology in the United States, the terms *effort* and *arousal* represent the two fundamental constructs in the study of conation. The effort construct refers to changes in the direction, intensity, and persistence of attentional effort. In the past two decades, cognitive-type theories of motivation have stressed the choice dimension of effort—an individual's desire to exert effort in a particular direction or of a particular intensity. Changes in effort of this type are often measured by self-report of choice outcomes and/or observable changes in the direction and intensity of behavior over time.

A second, related conceptualization of effort emphasizes volition, or the individual's willful allocation of attentional, cognitive resources to a particular goal. Similar to choice indices of changes in effort, changes in volition are often readily recognized by the learner. With experience, the learner may develop a declarative knowledge representation of how various events influence volitional processes (e.g., "When the test is timed, I increase my effort") as well as how changes in his or her effort influence events (e.g., "If I work harder now, I will finish earlier and can go to a movie"). Kuhl and Kraska refer to the learning and use of such metacognitive knowledge for the purpose of attaining desired goals as *metamotivational*.

Arousal, referring to the mobilization of the individual's nonspecific attentional resources, represents the second major motivational construct (Humphreys & Revelle, 1984; Revelle, 1986). Although learners may recognize changes in arousal, and come to anticipate the factors that bring about such changes, arousal is usually considered to be less amenable to conscious control than choice or cognitive effort. Changes in effort and/or arousal, in turn, influence learning, action, and task performance.

In extant theories of motivation, changes in effort and arousal are brought about by the interaction of individual differences in dispositional tendencies and situational variables. The list of conative aptitudes and situational variables that may influence arousal and effort is extensive. Revelle's work notwithstanding, during the past two decades there has been far greater attention given to the mapping of conative aptitude-situation interaction effects with respect to effort than to arousal.

Despite numerous studies demonstrating motivational effects of arousal and effort on performance, relatively little is known about the mechanisms that determine how these constructs exert their effects. Two problems arise in this regard. First, prior research has focused primarily on cumulative measures of learning and performance, such as number correct in a test situation. Substantially less attention has been given to determining the influence of conative processes on the information-processing components that comprise efficient task performance (e.g., in the type of analyses suggested by Lohman [Chapter 5] and by G. Mulder, Wijers, Smid, Brookhuis, & L. Mulder [Chapter 14]).

Second, cognitively oriented motivation theories do not account for the processes that sustain effort. In these theories, learners who sustain effort over time would need to engage in continuous choice activity. Alternative conceptualizations of how learners sustain effort stem from theory and research on volitional processes. In U.S. psychology, two streams of research are relevant to this issue. Cybernetic control theories, such as Carver and Scheier's (1981) model, emphasize the organization of a learner's goals and the mechanisms by which such structures affect information processing and action. In this approach, higher-order goals, such as need for achievement, may trigger conative processes that influence information processing and learning.

Self-regulation theories and empirical research (e.g., Bandura, 1982; F. Kanfer, 1977; R. Kanfer & Ackerman, in press) provide another framework. Similar to the distinction made by Kuhl and his colleagues (e.g., Heckhausen & Kuhl, 1985), this framework asserts that mechanisms underlying goal-directed effort differ from mechanisms influencing goal choice. In U.S. perspectives, mechanisms such as self-monitoring, self-evaluation, and self-reactions form the basis for a conative system where learners manage cognition and affect in ways that promote execution of goal-directed behaviors. As Kuhl and Kraska point out, however, early theories of self-regulation are difficult to coordinate with recent developments in cognitive, information-processing psychology. Furthermore, such theories have, until recently, neglected individual differences in self-regulatory functioning and efficiency.

Overall, four features characterize the theoretical and empirical environment out of which contemporary developments in motivation are emerging. First, the prevalence of cognitive-type theories of motivation has channeled attention toward understanding the processes involved in choice. The emphasis on choice processes has been accompanied by the relative neglect of other aspects of conation, such as volition and arousal. Second, a large body of empirical evidence supports the notion of interactive effects of personality and situations on effort and behavior. Third, most approaches tend to view individual differences in cognitive abilities as conditioning variables or as determinants of the content of expectations (which influence choice). Finally, virtually all approaches to motivation have been concerned with problems of measurement; in particular, the distinction among an individual's intentions, behavior, and performance. To date, however, much recent research has been directed toward identifying the antecedents and processes underlying choice and behavioral intentions. A few formulations have examined the dynamic processes affecting the linkage between choice and performance (e.g., Atkinson & Birch, 1970). The advantage of dynamic approaches lies in their potential for unifying the field of motivational psychology; again, however, such approaches tend to neglect differences in cognitive abilities and the effects of motivation on learning processes per se.

Revelle: Personality, Arousal, and Performance

The arousal concept played a major role in Hullian theories of motivation and learning during the 1930s. As interest in these approaches declined during the 1950s, so did motivational research involving arousal. By linking arousal to individual differences in personality variables, situational factors, and modern approaches to learning, Revelle and his colleagues (e.g., Humphreys & Revelle, 1984; Revelle, 1986) have renewed interest in arousal. Revelle's framework integrates concepts from many areas. For simplicity, it is helpful to decompose Revelle's conceptualization into four interlocking segments. First, Revelle begins by using Eysenck's typology of personality to coordinate three personality dimensions (extraversion, impulsivity, and anxiety) with individual differences in arousal. Next, Revelle adopts an aptitude-treatment interaction approach to demonstrate the interactive effects of individual differences in personality (aptitudes) and situational variables (motivational treatments) on global measures of performance.

The third segment of Revelle's conceptualization focuses on the consequence side of affective and conative processes. Specifically, Revelle proposes that information processing can be decomposed into three stages: encoding, organization and storage, and retrieval of information. The unique effects of personality–situation interactions obtained by Revelle and his colleagues on each of these information-processing components provides a potentially very valuable nomological network for abilities researchers concerned about the influence of affect and conation on specific information-processing components of learning.

Finally, Revelle addresses the abiding problems associated with delineating the effects of affect and conation upon a wide spectrum of tasks. To organize this wide range of performances, Revelle uses an information-processing rubric to classify performances as requiring sustained information transfer, short-term memory, and/or long-term memory. The effects of personality and conative factors are then related to cumulative performances in diverse tasks via their effects on broader mediating variables, such as stylistic preferences in speed–accuracy trade-offs.

Revelle has built his case for the influence of personality and motivation on learning and performance very carefully. The essence of his approach is to continuously move back and forth between the perspectives that drive his conceptualization (e.g., personality psychology, information processing) and motivational psychology. This strategy has the unique advantage of providing validity checks for both the source perspective and his own conceptualization. A good example of this methodology is illustrated in the studies that examine the interactive effects of personality and physiological manipulations of arousal. The demonstration of disordinal interaction effects on performance not only informs personality formulations and strengthens the case for inclusion of an arousal construct, but also suggests how noncognitive determinants of performance may go undetected when situational variables are not taken into account.

In a broader sense, Revelle's approach demonstrates the advantage of converging on conative constructs from traditionally nonoverlapping perspectives. Revelle uses physiological manipulations (e.g., caffeine) as well as psychological manipulations (e.g., time pressure). The consistent body of results obtained with these manipulations strengthens construct validity by reducing concerns associated with mode-of-manipulation confounds. Unification of physiological and psychological perspectives on arousal concerns raises several intriguing questions, such as the extent to which learning deficits may be ameliorated by more careful matching of environmental demands and patterns of arousal, as indexed by individual differences in personality.

Revelle's formulation also extends the domain of noncognitive aptitudes posited to affect conation, learning, and performance. Previous theorizing has emphasized noncognitive traits in higher-order motives, such as need for achievement, need for affiliation and fear of failure. Revelle focuses on traits more closely linked to classic views of the fundamental dimensions of personality. The marriage of these noncognitive differences and arousal moves us closer to a reunification of cognitive and behavioral theories of learning. For example, Revelle notes that his approach also provides an account for how individual differences in personality and arousal may affect effort. Going one step further, we might think about Revelle's approach in light of the wish–action framework developed by Heckhausen and Kuhl (1985). From this perspective, we might further speculate that individual differences in personality (such as impulsivity) or changes in arousal also affect the parameters that govern transformation of wants into intentions, and/or intentions into actions.

Kuhl and Kraska: Individual Differences, Volition, and Behavior

This research focuses on individual differences determinants of efficient self-regulation. As Kuhl and his colleagues suggest (e.g., Heckhausen & Kuhl, 1985; Kuhl, 1982, 1984), self-regulation represents part of the neglected area of volition in motivational psychology. Whereas effort often has been thought of as trying hard, self-regulatory perspectives propose that effort during learning involves higher-order or executive processes to protect, sustain, and guide attention to the task. Individual differences in the supply and use of such knowledge represents a relatively unexplored but potentially powerful determinant of learning success. For example, many college students seem to know that the amount of schoolwork that one gets done on a Friday evening is often not just a matter of one's cognitive ability or trying hard but instead a consequence of one's self-regulatory efficiency. More simply put, learning is not just a matter of good intentions.

To understand how individual differences in metamotivational knowledge and dispositional tendencies affect performance, Kuhl and Kraska have proposed a model that depicts the volitional mechanisms and the process of self-regulation. Adopting an information-processing framework, Kuhl and Kraska propose that the essence of self-regulation is the effective resolution of discrepancies among cognitive, affective, and executional preferences. In the context of learning, volition refers to bringing discordant affective and executional preferences in line with one's task goals. A unique feature of this model is the notion of changes in the strength of various action tendencies over time as cognitive preferences come into contact with incompatible affective preferences.

With experience and maturation, persons learn strategies for resolving conflicts between the different preference components of the model. That is, individuals develop a repertoire of metamotivational strategies for sustaining goal-directed effort in the face of distractions, boredom, initial task failure, and/or frustration. Although it is not yet clear what determines the development of the repertoire or the use of strategies, individual differences in metamotivational knowledge are likely to involve both conative and cognitive aptitudes. Thus, we may conceive of these differences as comprising another type of noncognitive individual difference constructs.

In their chapter, Kuhl and Kraska focus on individual differences in action–state orientation as a dispositional tendency of particular import in the functioning of the volitional system. Action–state orientation refers to stable predispositions in attentional focus. Persons maintaining an action orientation are posited to focus attention on task elements. In contrast, individuals with a state orientation attend more frequently to nontask elements, such as the goal. As with other dispositional tendencies, situational factors may interact with action–state orientation to yield different levels of performance. Previous research by Kuhl and his colleagues (see, e.g., Kuhl, 1986) provides empirical evidence indicating that individual differences in action–state orientation do affect certain types of task performance. The advantages of an action or state orientation on performance, however, appear to depend in part on the demands of the task. During the initial stages of complex skill acquisition, when the task demands a large proportion of a learner's resources, individuals with action orientations demonstrate higher levels of performance than individuals with state orientations (e.g., Kuhl & Koch, 1984; R. Kanfer & Ackerman, in press). It would be interesting to explore whether the advantages of an action orientation are maintained across later stages of skill acquisition, when there are decreases in attentional demands imposed by the task.

Kuhl and Kraska also present empirical data pertaining to the development of metamotivational knowledge among children. The adoption of a developmental approach to volitional mechanisms differs from previous notions of self-regulation. Previous notions implicitly assumed that volitional deficits were independent of cognitive aptitudes. The developmental nature of metamotivational knowledge suggests how cognitive aptitudes and volition may interact as well as points to several potential sources of deficits in self-regulatory functioning. From a more molecular perspective, the differential pattern of response latencies obtained from children in the smiley face experiment suggests that individual differences in metamotivational skill among older subjects may affect learning via differences in the pattern of activity that is adopted during skill acquisition.

The developmental perspective raises several other new questions with potential implications for adult functioning. One of the most interesting issues concerns the plasticity and attributes of such skills. For example, how is metamotivational knowledge encoded, what mechanisms are involved in the acquisition of metamotivational skill, are such skills automatized, how are such skills accessed, and what mechanisms facilitate skill transfer across settings?

COMPLEMENTARY PERSPECTIVES OR FURTHER FRAGMENTATION?

As I stated at the beginning of this chapter, fragmentation of the conative domain has made attempts to integrate motivation and cognitive abilities research an arduous task. A reasonable question one may ask, then, is whether the Revelle and the Kuhl and Kraska frameworks represent fundamentally complementary·or contrasting perspectives on conation.

Adopting the viewpoint of a researcher concerned primarily with conative processes, one notes two basic distinctions between the two approaches. The first obvious difference between Revelle's and Kuhl and Kraska's formulations pertains to the conative mechanisms under investigation and the conceptual proximity of these mechanisms to overt action. Revelle concentrates on determinants of arousal and emphasizes what I would call *distal* determinants of performance, as arousal affects intermediate constructs (e.g., sustained information transfer) important in the path to performance. On the other hand, Kuhl and Kraska focus on volition and what may be termed *proximal* determinants of action: the computational mechanisms involved in sustaining and self-promoting learning activities.

Second, Revelle's investigations involve prediction of performance in testlike and often conflict-free task environments. In contrast, Kuhl and Kraska are concerned with performance in unstructured environments fraught with conflicts between accomplishing cognized goals and doing something that is more enjoyable.

Although these distinctions have import for researchers focused on further understanding of conative processing, such differences pale when one adopts a broader perspective concerned with cognitive and noncognitive individual differences, as well as conation. In the context of the quest for an integrated framework, taking the position of complementarity seems more productive for producing a coherent picture. In the following section, I identify several of the unique and joint contributions these approaches are likely to have for a contemporary perspective on learning and individual differences.

A common dissatisfaction with many theories in motivational psychology is that they are too imprecise to be used for predicting specific task performance. For example, we may know that persons high in achievement motivation will generally set higher goals and exert more effort in achievement contexts. But we cannot readily say how and when such effort will yield higher levels of performance.

Revelle's framework largely overcomes this difficulty by decomposing dispositional tendencies and task demands using an information-processing, performance-resource framework. With this framework, we may ultimately be able to identify dispositional tendency-task type combinations that optimize learning and performance.

Similar to Revelle, Kuhl and Kraska also seek to enhance the precision of prediction by identifying the conative mechanisms involved in performance. In terms of individual differences in learning, Kuhl and Kraska's model suggest that inefficiencies in the volitional system may mask an individual's capabilities and/or disrupt information-processing activities involved in cognitive skill development. For researchers interested in the conative-cognitive interface, an important question to be answered in future research concerns the relationship between metamotivational abilities and information-coordination abilities such as those described by Pellegrino, Hunt, and Yee (Chapter 7). The emphasis on individual differences in attentional control in both these research efforts have theoretically important implications for bridging the gulf between motivation and ability domains.

Kuhl and Kraska specify many of the processing operations involved in self-regulation of action but do not specifically address how these processes may interact with information-processing demands imposed by the task. It would be helpful to know whether the effects found by Kuhl and his colleagues can be found across task types, as distinguished by Revelle. Investigations of this sort may help further clarify the centrality of metamotivational skills for learning and the potential costs of self-regulation in a learning environment.

On the criterion side, Revelle and Kuhl and Kraska note that research on motivation and volition requires careful attention to the criterion. The criterion framework presented by Revelle provides a useful heuristic for understanding how and when conative processes may affect learning. The criteria used in many of the studies reported by Revelle involve discrete performance scores on tests. Effects of noncognitive traits and arousal on these criteria are related to information-processing activities that presumably exert a direct effect on the performance outcome. In contrast, Kuhl and Kraska focus on the pattern of activity over time in the face of distractions and conflict. Effects of metamotivational mechanisms are posited to mediate the fidelity of information-processing activities and performance outcomes. Clearly, the Revelle and Kuhl and Kraska approaches complement each other, as neither type of criteria alone is likely to be sufficient for predicting individual differences in complex skill acquisition.

CONATION IN LEARNING: A LOOK AHEAD

Motivational psychologists have generally not been concerned with individual differences in cognitive abilities (though see Vroom, 1964, for an exception). In part, this may be due to the complexities and difficulties involved in dealing with conative constructs alone. As the previous chapters indicate, however, the motivation area is becoming more cohesive and the rubric that is emerging offers many opportunities for greater consideration of motivation–ability interactions.

It has been efficient, and often sufficient, for ability researchers to view motivation (effort) as a unitary construct that can usually be assumed to be monotonically related to performance. However, the previous chapters indicate the multiplicity of processes involved in conation. Furthermore, the assumption of a monotonic relation is likely to become increasingly problematic as research on cognitive abilities and skill acquisition moves toward understanding the effects of attentional control.

Traditional methods used to control motivational variables, such as providing instructions to "exert effort," are not likely to be sufficient given what we now know about conative processes and the influence of noncognitive traits on these processes. Revelle's work, for example, indicates that manipulations of arousal (via personality–situation interactions) have selective effects on different aspects of cognitive processing—different effects than those obtained when manipulating intentional effort. Kleinbeck et al.'s findings (Chapter 2) indicate that the effects of explicit goal setting on performance may help or hurt task performance depending on the cognitive demands imposed by the task (also see R. Kanfer & Ackerman, in press). And as Kuhl and Kraska suggest, the effects of motivational manipulations depend in part on the individual's metamotivational knowledge. Taken together, these research programs challenge the frequent working assumption that the effects of conative processes may be minimized simply through incentives or instructions. Instead, recent research suggests that we view conative mechanisms and processes as a complex system that produces varying effects on learning depending on its interaction with the cognitive system.

As a next step, we may also ask what specific advantages a conative system approach offers for understanding learning and individual differences. First, thinking in terms of such a system may help us better understand the often inconsistent effects of various motivation-oriented instructional practices on learning. For example, data presented by Kleinbeck et al., Revelle, and Kuhl and Kraska indicate that performance may be substantially affected by mechanisms and processes that occur outside the realm of an individual's conscious intentions and goals. Both the chapters by Revelle and by Kuhl and Kraska advocate more careful consideration of the influence of noncognitive individual difference characteristics on conative processing and performance. Further research is needed to assess whether person–situation interaction effects on learning are similar across persons with differing levels of ability or with differing ability profiles.

Second, empirical research demonstrating conative effects on performance serves as a strong reminder of the potential dangers involved in conducting research that conceptually divorces the cognitive system from the individual. Affect and self-regulation play a critical role in determining the fidelity of cognitive processing–performance relations. An individual's metamotivational knowledge (i.e., knowledge about cognitive–affective conflicts) and skill in using this knowledge represents another potentially critical type of aptitude. From an experimental perspective, failure to take these mechanisms into account may yield uninterpretable data. From an abilities perspective, Kuhl and Kraska's model, for example, provides an alternative theoretically based framework for understanding the executive abilities involved in the management of cognitive processes.

A basic research agenda for persons interested in understanding the role of noncognitive individual differences and conative processes in learning and individual differences might include the following questions:

1. What are the relations between metamotivational knowledge and various cognitive abilities?

2. Are metamotivational skills trainable across the ability spectrum? Or do different metamotivational skills have different threshold requirements on working memory?

3. Are conative aptitudes (such as impulsivity as defined by Revelle) related to deficits in the volitional system as well? That is, can and do impulsive students who take math in the morning engage in the same volitional activities as nonimpulsive students?

4. If one function of metamotivational activities is to freeze action, how should we account for that in terms of Lohman's speed–accuracy trade-off paradigm? Are speed–accuracy signatures a reflection of volitional processing, cognitive processing, or both?

5. How do changes in one part of the conative system (e.g., arousal) affect the instantiation and/or operation of other parts of the conative system (e.g., volitional processes)?

For persons interested in the implications of these processes in applied settings, we might derive the following research agenda:

1. As Kleinbeck et al.'s data indicate, there are some instances in which explicit goal assignments directed toward the primary task facilitate performance on the secondary task. These data suggest that persons are able to improve their cognitive efficiency when the full task demands it. What motivational/volitional mechanisms underlie this phenomenon? Is this responsiveness to task demands mediated by individual differences in cognitive abilities, conative aptitudes, or personality?

2. As Kyllonen and Woltz (Chapter 9) have noted, difficulties have been encountered when attempting to use computerized tutor systems with persons of lower general intellectual ability. One explanation for these difficulties may be that these persons do not develop specific cognitive preferences or the goals necessary for the initiation of self-regulatory processes. Goal setting research (e.g., see Locke et al., 1981) demonstrates that persons with specific goal assignments generally perform better than persons with vague, global goals. What cognitive abilities are required for the formation of a personal goal? How does the active construction of task goals influence processing of errors and speed–accuracy functions? Are individual differences in learning attenuated or exacerbated by provision of explicit goals?

These questions represent only a sampling of the issues raised when we focus on the cognitive–conative interface. Advances in quantitative methodology and cognitive, information-processing psychology provide a cross-paradigm foundation for developing an integrated account of learning. As the previous chapters indicate, such advances have substantially affected contemporary research in motivational psychology. The growing attention to individual differences constructs from theories of motivation and volition, the long-standing emphasis on environmental determinants and normative processes, and the integration of the conative domain itself provides an attractive and unique opportunity for research on the interactive effects of cognitive and noncognitive determinants of learning.

REFERENCES

Atkinson, J. W. (1957). Motivational determinants of risk-taking behavior. *Psychological Review, 64*, 359–372.

Atkinson, J. W. (1964). *An introduction to motivation.* Princeton, NJ: Van Nostrand.

Atkinson, J. W., & Birch, D. (1970). *The dynamics of action.* New York: Wiley.

Bandura, A. (1977). *Social learning theory.* Englewood Cliffs, NJ: Prentice-Hall.

Bandura, A. (1982). The self and mechanisms of agency. In J. Suls (Ed.), *Psychological perspectives on the self* (Vol. 1, pp. 3–40). Hillsdale, NJ: Lawrence Erlbaum Associates.

Bandura, A. (1986). *Social foundations of thought and action. A social cognitive theory.* Englewood Cliffs, NJ: Prentice-Hall.

Bandura, A. (1988). Self-regulation of motivation and action through goal systems. In V. Hamilton, G. H. Bower, & N. H. Fryda (Eds.), *Cognition, motivation, and affect: A cognitive science view* (pp. 31–67). Dordrecht, The Netherlands: Martinus Nijhoff.

Carver, C. S., & Scheier, M. F. (1981). *Attention and self-regulation: A control theory approach to human behavior.* New York: Springer-Verlag.

Feather, N. T. (Ed.). (1982). *Expectations and actions: Expectancy-value models in psychology.* Hillsdale: NJ: Lawrence Erlbaum Associates.

Heckhausen, H., & Kuhl, J. (1985). From wishes to action: The dead-ends and shortcuts on the long way to action. In M. Frese & J. Sabini (Eds.), *Goal-directed behavior: The concept of action in psychology* (pp. 134–160). Hillsdale, NJ: Lawrence Erlbaum Associates.

Humphreys, M. S., & Revelle, W. (1984). Personality, motivation, and performance: A theory of the relationship between individual differences and information processing. *Psychological Review, 91*, 153–184.

Hyland, M. E. (1988). Motivational control theory: An integrative framework. *Journal of Personality and Social Psychology, 55*, 642–651.

Kanfer, F. H. (1977). The many faces of self-control, or behavior modification changes its focus. In R. B. Stuart (Ed.), *Behavioral self-management* (pp. 1–48). New York: Brunner/Mazel.

Kanfer, F. H., & Hagerman, S. (1987). A model of self-regulation (pp. 293–307). In F. Halisch & J. Kuhl (Eds.), *Motivation, intention, and volition.* New York: Springer-Verlag.

Kanfer, F. H., & Stevenson, M. K. (1985). The effects of self-regulation on concurrent cognitive processing. *Cognitive Therapy and Research, 9*, 667–684.

Kanfer, R. (1987). Task-specific motivation: An integrative approach to issues of measurement, mechanisms, processes, and determinants. *Journal of Social and Clinical Psychology, 5*, 237–264.

Kanfer, R. (in press). Motivation theory and industrial/organizational psychology. In M. D. Dunnette (Ed.), *Handbook of industrial and organizational psychology. Vol. I: Theory in industrial and organizational psychology.* Palo Alto, CA: Consulting Psychologists Press.

Kanfer, R., & Ackerman, P. L. (in press). Motivational and cognitive abilities: An integrative/aptitude-treatment interaction approach to skill acquisition. *Journal of Applied Psychology - Monograph.*

Kuhl, J. (1982). The expectancy-value approach within the theory of social motivation: Elaborations, extensions, and critique. In N. T. Feather (Ed.), *Expectations and actions: Expectancy-value models in psychology* (pp. 125–160). Hillsdale, NJ: Lawrence Erlbaum Associates.

Kuhl, J. (1984). Volitional aspects of achievement motivation and learned helplessness: Toward a comprehensive theory of action control. In B. A. Maher (Ed.), *Progress in experimental personality research* (Vol. 13, pp. 99–171). New York: Academic Press.

Kuhl, J. (1986). Integrating cognitive and dynamic approaches: A prospectus for a unified motivational psychology. In J. Kuhl & J. W. Atkinson (Eds.), *Motivation, thought, and action* (pp. 307–336). New York: Praeger.

Kuhl, J., & Koch, B. (1984). Motivational determinants of motor performance: The hidden second task. *Psychological Research, 46,* 143–153.

Locke, E. A. (1968). Toward a theory of task motivation and incentives. *Organizational Behavior and Human Performance, 3,* 157–189.

Locke, E. A., Shaw, K. N., Saari, L. M., & Latham, G. P. (1981). Goal setting and task performance: 1969–1980. *Psychological Bulletin, 90,* 125–152.

Naylor, J. C., Pritchard, R. D., & Ilgen, D. R. (1980). *A theory of behavior in organizations.* New York: Academic Press.

Revelle, W. (1986). Motivation and efficiency of cognitive performance. In D. R. Brown & J. Veroff (Eds.), *Frontiers of motivational psychology* (pp. 107–131). New York: Springer-Verlag.

Schmidt, K-H., Kleinbeck, U., & Brockmann, W. (1984). Motivational control of motor performance by goal setting in a dual-task situation. *Psychological Research, 46,* 129–141.

Vroom, V. H. (1964). *Work and motivation.* Malabar, FL: Krieger Press.

Weiner, B. (1985). An attributional theory of achievement motivation and emotion. *Psychological Review, 92,* 548–573.

Weiner, B. (1986). *An attributional theory of achievement motivation and emotion.* New York: Springer-Verlag.

V
PARADIGMS IN TRANSITION

14

Individual Differences in Computational Mechanisms: A Psychophysiological Analysis

Gijsbertus Mulder
Albertus Wijers
Henderikus Smid
Karel Brookhuis
Lambertus Mulder
University of Groningen, The Netherlands

Individual differences in task performance may arise either from individual differences in the effectiveness or competence of computational mechanisms and/or from energetical or state controlling mechanisms determining the gain or signal-to-noise ratio of computational mechanisms. In this chapter, we concentrate on individual differences in computational mechanisms as revealed by both response time (RT), response accuracy, and Event-Related Brain Potentials (ERPs).

The study of human information processing can be divided into broad areas. Fast process research deals with tasks usually performed on the order of milliseconds, or at most a few seconds. In such tasks, introspective analysis would be of little use, as subjects are usually unaware of how they proceeded. Fast process research has made heavy use of RT and mathematical modeling as methods of studying behavior. In general, fast process research aims at the discovery of elementary information processes (the mechanics of thought; Hunt, 1978). The additive factor method (S. Sternberg, 1969) and the subtraction method (Donders, 1969) are still widely used in this area of human information processing. The methods used in fast process research have been successfully applied to the analysis of mental operations underlying cognitive activity in verification tasks, semantic memory search, quantification tasks, mental rotation, short memory and display search, selective attention, and so forth.

In contrast, slow process research involves tasks usually performed over minutes and hours—tasks that are somewhat accessible by introspection. From introspective protocols, one may derive a set of rules that describe how a person solves a problem. These production rules can be formalized by writing a computer program that expresses our ideas about what a person is doing inside his or her head. Such programs can be run on a digital computer, and the correspondence between the logic of the program and the logic of mental symbol processing can be examined. In general, slow process research is concerned with the general plan of human information processing in cognitive tasks.

Individual differences in cognitive ability, usually measured with tests, probably arise from three different sources: (a) mechanistic capacities for encoding, storing, retrieving, transformation, programing, and so on (i.e., differences in elementary information processes); (b) strategic aspects of thought; in order to solve a problem, the mechanistic capacities must be applied in a particular and possibly highly flexible order (the program); and (c) knowledge aspects of thought; every activity that we consider intelligent presumes some coordination between the present situation and the problem solver's previously acquired knowledge.

The information-processing approach of individual differences can be divided into two approaches: the cognitive correlates and the cognitive components approach. The cognitive correlates approach uses aptitude tests as criterion measures and seeks to identify the more elementary mechanistic processes that are correlated with the test criterion (Hunt, 1978). In contrast, the cognitive components approach uses tests as tasks to be analyzed in a search for the component processes (elementary processes, called components) of test performance itself (R. Sternberg, 1977).

In this chapter, we focus mainly on fast process research. We argue that fast process research can benefit from the study of Event-Related Brain Potentials (ERPs), that is, from the study of electrical (and in the near future also of magnetic) brain activity that occurs during task performance, as well as from studies using regional changes in average cerebral blood flow and glucose utilization (Petersen, Fox, Posner, Mintum, & Raichle, 1988).

In addition, individual differences may not only be related to individual differences in computational processes, as revealed by slow and fast process research, but also to individual differences in energetical or motivational states. In this respect, the efficiency of human information processing is of particular relevance. When the actual state of an individual's information-processing system differs from the required state, individuals may differ in the amount of effort they must exert (see Hockey, Gaillard, & Coles, 1986, and G. Mulder, 1986, for a detailed discussion of this determinant).

FAST PROCESS RESEARCH
AND COGNITIVE PSYCHOPHYSIOLOGY

The Study of Computational Processes
Using Response Time (RT)

Response Time (RT) has been and remains a favorite dependent variable of cognitive psychologists. In particular, the RT method is often used in fast process research. Either explicitly or implicitly, many studies have used the additive factor method. This method requires finding task variables that affect one stage of processing and not the others. Consequently, the appropriate test is to look at interactions in the analysis of variance. Experimental separation of stages is considered successful if one observes main effects but no interactions.

In many of the more functional models that have been developed out of this type of research it is possible to distinguish between more perceptual and cognitive stages, such as feature extraction, identification, serial comparison, binary decision; and motor stages, such as response choice, response programing, organization, and so on. It would be highly desirable to know how much of the total RT is explained by nonmotor stages, such as preprocessing, encoding or identification, serial comparison, and binary decision; and how much is explained by motor stages, such as response choice, motor programming, motor initiation, and motor adjustment.

Cognitive psychologists have come to recognize the possibility that motor processes may considerably affect RT. As a result, these researchers often use binary classification tasks. A binary classification task is one in which a decision rule partitions a set of stimuli into exhaustive and mutually exclusive classes or categories, such as targets (e.g., members of a memory set) versus nontargets, or relevant versus irrelevent (e.g., red targets and nontargets are relevant and blue targets and nontargets are irrelevant). The binary classification tasks are popular because of the belief that it is possible to manipulate the perceptual or cognitive demands of the situation while keeping the motor components simple and constant. By using only two responses, the motor component is not only kept constant and simple but also represents a sufficient small fraction of the total processing time.

To illustrate the approach, we focus our discussion on the selective attention paradigm. In the divided attention mode, the subject's task is to search for target(s) in a visual display and respond to the presence or absence of these target(s). In the focused attention mode, a (visual) cue (e.g., color, spatial location, size, or a conjunction of cues) is used to separate relevant from irrelevant information. The subject is required to search for the presence of a target in the relevant channel and react only to the presence of a target with a motor response.

The approach discussed in this chapter can be generalized to other mental tasks using response time as the major dependent variable. A specific problem in analyzing response times with the additive factor method is that if no interactions are found, one cannot conclude that an additive stage model is correct. However, a model that assumes that stages are overlapping or nonindependent may be used (McClelland, 1979; Miller, 1982; Taylor, 1976).

Recently, there has been increased interest in continuous models of information processing. These models assume that the results of a component process accumulate gradually and feed continuously into subsequent processes. Thus, a process may have already started based on the availability of partial information from an earlier process that is still in progress. Continuous models, therefore, allow elementary processors to operate in parallel (Eriksen & Schultz, 1979; Grice, Nullmeyer, & Spiker, 1982; McClelland, 1979; Meyer, Yantis, Osman, & Smith, 1986).

However, it has proven difficult to test discrete versus continuous models with RT alone, and only a few procedures have been developed that seem promising in this respect. One of these promising procedures is the noise/compatibility procedure—a selective attention paradigm developed by Eriksen and Eriksen (B. Eriksen & C. Eriksen, 1974; C. Eriksen & B. Eriksen, 1979). In this procedure, target letters are presented at a predefined location, either (or not) flanked by different types of distractors, either compatible or incompatible. The flankers are placed at irrelevant display positions and should be ignored (focused attention). Compatible arrays are associated with faster RTs than incompatible arrays. The effects of the irrelevant flankers on performance constitutes a "focused attention deficit" (Shiffrin & Schneider, 1977).

In order to understand what happens in these types of situations, two independent systems are assumed to be operating: (a) a stimulus evaluation system and (b) a response activation system. Both incompatible and compatible arrays are believed to activate response preparation in parallel with stimulus evaluation. However, in the first case, an incorrect response is first activated followed by correct response activation. Perceptual variables may therefore activate response processes in parallel with stimulus evaluation and may lead to either response facilitation or response competition. This type of experimental data suggests that the motor component is not a simple, constant, and final part of the information-processing flow, but rather a complex, variable contributor to the total processing time reflected in RT. Thus, it is not just highly desirable but necessary that we unravel the contributions of perceptual, cognitive and motor processes to final task performance. Brain-evoked potentials may be of some help in this enterprise.

The Study of Computational Processes Using ERPs

ERPs are obtained from the ongoing EEG by means of an averaging procedure. This procedure consists of adding together the set of recorded EEG activity patterns associated with a particular event, for example, the presentation of a target, the presentation of a nontarget at an irrelevant display location, the presentation of an array containing incompatible noise, and so forth. The addition can be initiated by a timing signal or may be placed under the control of a program. As the common signal waveform is synchronized with the event, while unrelated activity is supposed to be sufficiently irregular, the signal waveform will sum in direct proportion to the number of events used, whereas unrelated activity will increase less rapidly due to cancellation effects. When completed, the sum of waveforms is divided by the number of stimuli delivered. This normalizes the result to the average response.

Fig. 14.1 depicts an idealized waveform. In this waveform, a number of components can be distinguished based on their dominant derivation (e.g., central, occipital, parietal), their latency, and amplitude.

A distinction can be made between exogenous and endogenous components. Exogenous components are mainly stimulus or data driven. Endogenous components only appear if a certain psychological process is present. Subtracting ERPs associated with a certain cognitive process (e.g., memory search) from a ERP in which this process is present to a lesser extent or not present at all emphasizes the endogenous components. It is assumed that the exogenous components are minimally affected by the presence or absence of a certain psychological process. These components signal the registration of information in the central nervous system, but not their use.

The sensitivity of endogenous components, in terms of either latency and/or amplitude, to the cognitive demands of mental tasks is the topic of much current research of cognitive psychophysiology. The latency of a number of components, especially the P300 component, can be determined from trial-to-trial using an adaptive averaging technique (Brookhuis et al., 1981; L. Mulder, Brookhuis, van Arkel, & G. Mulder, 1980). In this way it is possible to compare trial-to-trial variations in latency with trial-to-trial variations in RT. Table 14.1 presents a summary of a number of exogenous and endogenous components found in selective attention tasks and their associated psychological processes.

THE ELECTROPHYSIOLOGY
OF COGNITIVE PROCESSES

In their well-known article, Hillyard and Kutas (1983) discuss the relationship between endogenous ERPs and cognitive processing. The experiments they review investigate the effects of task variables (believed to affect the nature and duration of perceptual and cognitive processes) on the latency and amplitude of the endogenous components for the purpose of determining the psychological processes with which these components are associated.

Converging evidence from different laboratories and from neurophysiological studies gradually increase the confidence one may have in the usefulness of the components in signaling the presence or absence of a particular process and its timing. The advantages of ERPs are threefold. First, they continuously reflect brain activity. Second, ERPs can also be evoked in the absence of overt behavior. And third, ERPs can help to identify information-processing modules, their relative timing and connections, and brain systems that participate in specific cognitive activities. This potential benefit of studying ERPs thus helps contribute to further exchange of the computer metaphor of human cognition with the brain metaphor. ERPs have been found to be associated with early selection, multidimensional stimulus selection, properties of attentional channels, resource allocation, detection and recognition, mental chronometry, and language processing.

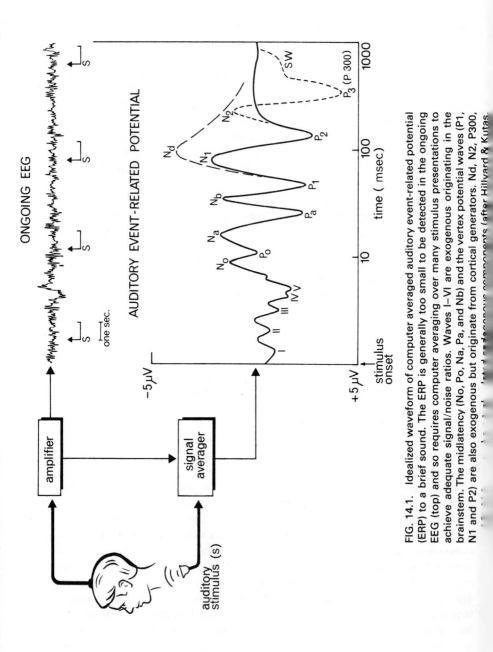

FIG. 14.1. Idealized waveform of computer averaged auditory event-related potential (ERP) to a brief sound. The ERP is generally too small to be detected in the ongoing EEG (top) and so requires computer averaging over many stimulus presentations to achieve adequate signal/noise ratios. Waves I–VI are exogenous originating in the brainstem. The midlatency (No, Po, Na, Pa, and Nb) and the vertex potential waves (P1, N1 and P2) are also exogenous but originate from cortical generators. Nd, N2, P300, ~~and endogenous components (after Hillyard & Kutas~~

396

TABLE 14.1
Summary of the Relevant ERP Components in the Study
of Selective Attention

Component	Peak or Onset Latency	Nature	Psychological Process
Occipital N200	160 ms	Exogenous	Pattern Recognition; pre-attentive
Selection Negativity	Cue dependent 100–200 ms	Endogenous	Contingent with early early selection; obtained by subtracting irrelevant from relevant ERPs
N2b central-frontal	200–250 ms	Endogenous	Allocation of attention; obtained by subtracting irrelevant from relevant ERPs
Search Negativity central-frontal	250–300 ms	Endogenous	Controlled search; obtained by subtracting ERPs associated with lower memory load from ERPs associated with higher memory load
P300 parietal	300–400 ms	Endogenous	Contingent with stimulus evaluation and independent of motor selection and execution
CMA central	120–200 ms	Endogenous	Indexes the start of selective motor activation; obtained by double subtraction RH (C3′ − C4′) − LH (C3′ − C4′)

Selective Attention and Memory: The Stimulus Evaluation System

The latency and amplitude of the P300 has been investigated in both divided and focused selective attention tasks. The P300 component appears to be very sensitive to changes in perceptual and cognitive processes, but is unaffected by response-related processes (Coles, Gratton, Bashore, Eriksen, & Donchin, 1985; Duncan-Johnson, 1981; Magliero, Bashore, Coles, & Donchin, 1984; G. Mulder, Gloerich, Brookhuis, van Dellen, & L. Mulder, 1984).

In divided attention tasks, the subject is first presented with a memory set containing one or more letters, followed by a visual display also containing one or more letters. The number of characters (letters or numbers) in the memory set is called the memory load. The number of characters in the display set is called the display load. The subjects' task is to indicate the presence or absence of a target (i.e., a memory-set item) as soon as possible by pressing one of two buttons on the visual display (see Fig. 14.2). In varied mapping (VM) conditions, responses change across trials; in consistent mapping (CM) conditions, the subject makes the same overt or covert response each time the stimulus occurs. Findings by Shiffrin and Schneider (1977) and Schneider and Shiffrin (1977)

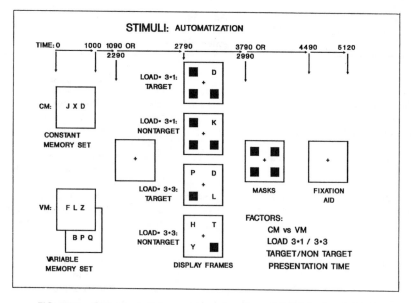

FIG. 14.2.   Sequence of frames (as a function of time) in the divided attention and automatization experiments (for explanation, see text).

suggest that CM-training leads (after extended practice) to automatic detection, whereas subjects in VM conditions engage in controlled search, that is, a slow, capacity-limited effortful process.

Studies by Brookhuis et al. (1981) and Brookhuis, G. Mulder, L. Mulder, & Gloerich (1983) indicate that the latency of the P300 increases and its amplitude decreases as a function of both memory and display load in VM conditions. The latency of the P300 is longer and its amplitude smaller for target absent (negatives) than for target present (positive) trials. However, whereas the functions relating P300 latency to load for both types of trials suggest exhaustive search, the RT data suggest terminating search (see Fig. 14.3). As shown in Fig. 14.3, the slope of the CRT is nearly halved when P300 latency is plotted. This discrepancy indicates that the well-known 39-msec./letter slope of the RT function in fact reflects contributions of both the memory search process and response-related processes that are affected by increasing memory search.

Until now, we considered the divided mode of selective attention. However, we have also conducted a number of studies using a focused attention paradigm. In this paradigm subjects are required to attend to one stimulus category (the relevant input channel) and to ignore another stimulus category (the irrelevant input channel). The relevant and irrelevant stimulus categories are discriminable on the basis of simple physical stimulus characteristics. Before each block of trials, the subject is presented with a memory set consisting of a variable set of letters. The subject's task is to detect the occurrence of target letters within the

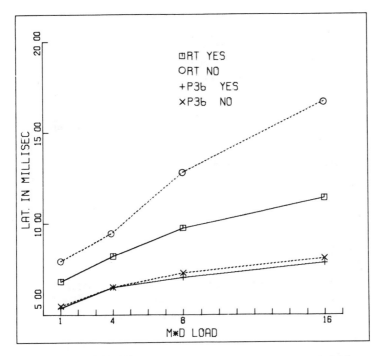

FIG. 14.3. RT and P300 latency as a function of memory and display load (Brookhuis et al., 1981).

attended input category and to respond as quickly as possible to the attended targets only (go/no-go task).

Okita, Wijers, G. Mulder, and L. Mulder (1985) presented subjects with a memory set of either one, two, or four letters. This set constituted the target set for a block of 200 trials. Stimulus displays were arranged in a square around a central fixation dot. Subjects had to attend to one diagonal of this display and ignore the other. Fig. 14.4 presents an illustration and explanation of the task display.

On each trial, two letters were presented, either on the attended or on the ignored diagonal. Thus, relevant (attended) and irrelevant (unattended) stimuli were presented successively. Half of the trials were relevant, the other half irrelevant. Thirty percent of both relevant and irrelevant displays contained a target letter. Subjects were required to attended targets only. Fig. 14.5a and 14.5b display the ERPs elicited at different derivations for nontarget and target stimuli, respectively.

The major findings of this study can be summarized as follows: The difference potential obtained by subtracting ERPs to unattended diagonal stimuli from ERPs to attended diagonal stimuli showed a negative-positive biphasic

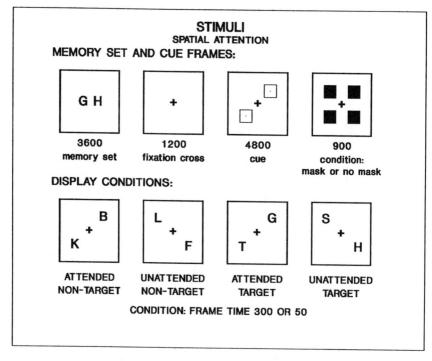

FIG. 14.4.   Sequence of frames in the focused attention experiments (for explanation, see text).

pattern, starting at 210 ms with a maximum amplitude at Cz (see Fig. 14.6).

This negative-positive (N2b-P3a) complex is thought to reflect covert orienting of attention towards relevant information (Näätänen & Gaillard, 1983). A negative shift appears in the higher memory load conditions as compared to the lower loads only in the ERPs to attended stimuli (see Fig. 14.7).

This central-frontal search-negativity has an onset latency of about 300 ms and lasts several hundred milliseconds. This negativity is found in ERPs to targets and nontargets and is believed to be contingent with a controlled search process within the attended input category. A P300 was elicited only by attended targets. In agreement with earlier studies, the latency of this component is delayed in the higher load conditions and its amplitude decreased as a function of load. The P300 component is thought to be contingent with at least three stimulus evaluation operations: orienting, search, and target detection and decision. ERPs to unattended targets do not differ from ERPs to unattended nontargets. These ERPs do not contain a N2b-P3a complex, search-related negativity, or a P300 component. Consequently, this result indicates that for these frames, at an early stage of processing, evidence must have been available that the presented infor-

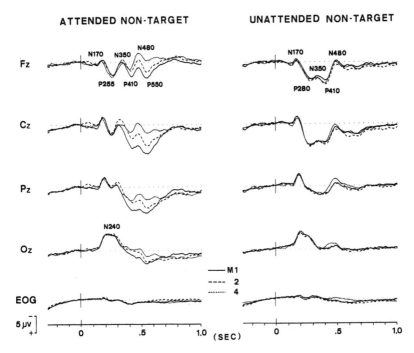

FIG. 14.5a.   Grand-average ERPs to nontarget frames. In the left column, ERPs to attended frames are depicted; in the right column, ERPs to unattended frames. ERPs are depicted for four electrode-sites: Fz, Cz, Pz, and Oz. The ERPs for the different memory-set size conditions (M1, M2, and M4) are superimposed. The average EOG is also depicted. The most prominent deflections are labeled with their polarity and mean latency (Okita et al., 1985). Note that subjects do not emit an overt response to nontargets.

mation is irrelevant and that, as a consequence, orienting, search, and decision should be avoided.

In summary, we found that the effects of our task manipulations on onset latencies suggest three successive stages of processing; namely, *orienting, controlled search,* and *target detection and decision.* Controlled search and target detection and decision are selectively confined to the attended input signal.

In subsequent research, we have investigated other selection cues, such as color (Wijers, G. Mulder, Okita, L. Mulder, & Scheffers, 1988), location (Scheffers, Wijers, G. Mulder, & L. Mulder, in preparation), size, and the conjunction of color and size (Wijers, G. Mulder, Okita, & L. Mulder, in press). In each of these experiments, we replicated the basic findings just described. Irrespective of the selection cue, attended stimuli evoked a N2b-P3a complex, confirming the feature-unspecific interpretation (orienting) of this component. In

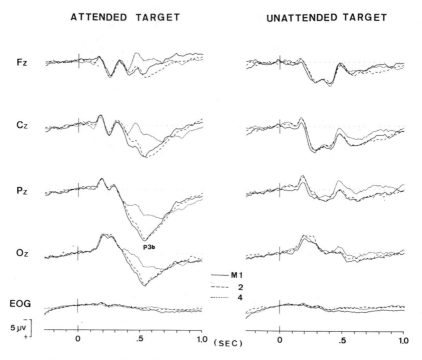

ATTENDED TARGET   UNATTENDED TARGET

FIG. 14.5b. Grand-average to target frames. See also Fig. 14.5a.
(Okita et al., 1985).

addition, earlier effects of attention (preceding the N2b-P3a complex) were
found as well. When attention is directed toward one location on the visual
display, an early negativity (onset about 120 ms), preceding the N2b-P3a complex, appears. This finding suggests that attending to one location is qualitatively
different from attending to two spatially separated locations (such as in the case
of attending to a diagonal); apparently, the spotlight of attention influences early
stages of processing but cannot be directed to more than one location (see also
Posner, Snyder, & Davidson, 1980). When attention is directed to a particular
color, an early positivity can be found at the anterior electrodes (Fz, Cz, and Pz)
and an early negativity at Oz (onset latency about 150 ms), again preceding the
N2b-P3a component. Finally, when attention is directed to letter size, the effects
of attention are similar to those observed when the diagonal is the selective cue:
The relatively late N2b-P3a complex is the first sign of selective attention.

    These findings suggest that elementary features such as color and location are
selectively processed in an early stage of processing (i.e., before attention is
oriented to the relevant input). Furthermore, there seems to be a priority system,
with location first, followed by color, and followed finally by size and diagonal.
If relevant stimuli are defined in terms of a conjunction of features, for example,

A.   **ERPs**

         Att.−Unatt.

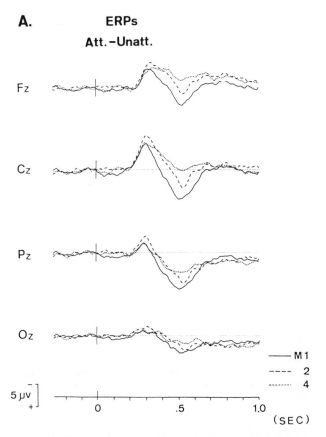

FIG. 14.6.   Difference waves obtained by subtracting the grand-average ERPs from unattended nontargets from the grand-average ERPs for attended nontargets (Fig. 14.5a). The difference waves are depicted for the four electrode-sites Fz, Cz, Pz, and Oz. For each electrode-site the difference waves for the three memory load conditions (M1, M2, and M4) are superimposed (Okita et al., 1985).

color and size, color and location, there appears to be a self-terminating selection process. For example, if the location of a stimulus is irrelevant, then its color will no longer be tested (Hillyard & Münte, 1984); that is, color selection is hierarchically dependent on location selection. In the same vein, Wijers et al. (in press) found that, early in processing, size was dependently processed based on the earlier processing of color. In the later stage of processing, indexed by the N2b, however, both attributes appeared to be processed independently; there was an enhanced N2b when one of the attributes (either color or size) was relevant and the other irrelevant.

Most recently, we have further explored the resource-specificity of search-

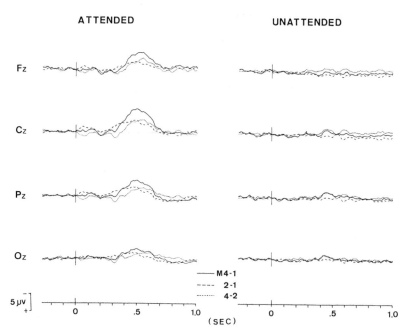

FIG. 14.7. Difference waves resulting from subtracting the grand-average ERP in the lower memory load condition from the ERPs obtained in the higher memory load conditions (nontargets). Note that no memory load effects were observed for unattended stimuli (Okita et al., 1985).

negativity and the P300. Veltman, G. Mulder, & L. Mulder (in preparation) used a focused visual selective attention task (selection cue color) and required subjects in some conditions to keep a running mental account of the number of times a certain target was presented. Thus, this task required subjects to select the relevant information, search within the relevant input channel, decide about the presence of a target, and (if a letter was a target) increase the appropriate mental counter by one. It is clear that these operations place a heavy load on working memory because the operations of updating the values of the counters and rehearsing them must be time-shared with the operations mentioned previously.

Aasman, G. Mulder, L. Mulder, and Wijers (1987) have shown that in comparable counting conditions, heart-rate variability systematically decreased as a function of memory load. A decrease of heart-rate variability most probably reflects increased operator effort (G. Mulder, 1980; Vicente, Thornton, & Moray, 1987). However, although heart-rate variability is probably a sensitive index of effort, it is not resource-specific (Wickens, 1984). A decrease has been observed in quite different types of mental tasks. Veltman et al.'s data showed that search-negativity and P300 latency and amplitude were affected by memory load but were not affected by the requirement to count. On the other hand, the requirement to count was visible in a frontal-positive slow wave. Our conclusion, therefore, is that the different resources needed to perform the task are reflected in different endogenous components.

In a related experiment, we examined the relation between selective attention, memory search, and mental rotation (Wijers, Feenstra, Otten & Mulder, L., 1989). The stimuli which we used are shown in Fig. 14.8. We used a focused search task (selection cue color) with a memory load of either one or four. Stimuli consisted of single colored letters. Within each stimulus category (attended targets, attended nontargets, unattended targets, and unattended nontargets), the letters were presented in either their normal upright position or

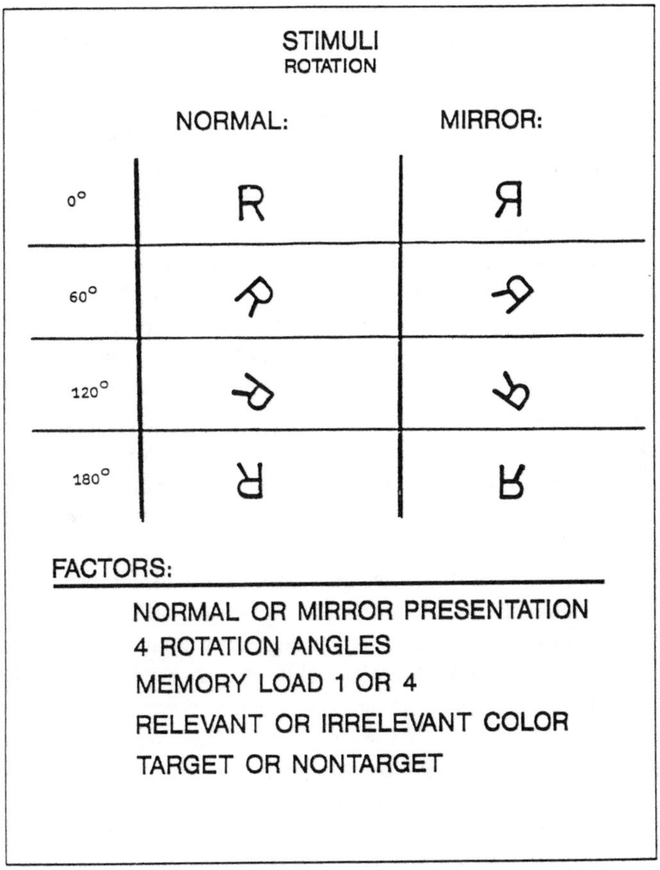

FIG. 14.8.   Stimuli used in the mental rotation experiment (for explanation, see text).

rotated to the left over 60, 120, or 180 degrees. In addition, each letter could either be presented normally or in mirror image.

The subject's task was to attend to letters in the relevant color, determine whether a letter target was presented in the attended color, and if so, respond with the right hand if the letter was normal and with the left hand if the letter was in mirror image. This task was modeled after Cooper and Shepard (1973), who assume at least four stages of processing. The first stage of processing (encoding) involves the representation of the stimulus (i.e., establishing its identify and orientation and storing this information in working memory). The second phase involves rotation of the mental representation of the nonvertical stimulus to bring it into congruence with the vertical stimulus. This is followed by a third stage, in which the subject compares the stimulus representations to determine if they are identical. Finally, in the last stage of processing, the outcome of the comparison leads to a positive or negative response.

Our reaction time data closely resemble the findings obtained by Cooper and Shepard (1973); (a) RT increases as a function of angular disparity of the stimulus letters, and (b) RTs are longer for reversed letters than for normal letters. In addition, we found that RTs were affected by memory load. The effects of orientation, memory load, and normal/mirror were virtually independent, suggesting different stages of processing (S. Sternberg, 1969). The ERPs showed that the expected effects of attention, memory load, and presence or absence of a target stimulus were unaffected by the rotation requirement.

Angular disparity had two different effects. The first effect consisted of an occipital positivity of the 60 and 120 rotated letters compared to the 0 and 180 rotated letters in the 200–300 ms range. This effect is found both for attended and unattended stimuli and both for targets and nontargets. This early effect most probably reflects the operation of the early encoding stage hypothesized by Cooper and Shepard. Apparently, this stage is preattentive.

The second effect of angular disparity is a parietal negativity, which increases as a function of the angle over which stimulus letters have to be rotated (see Fig. 14.9).

This negativity is only found in the ERPs to attended target stimuli. It is unaffected by memory load and it has a different scalp-distribution than search negativity. The onset latency of rotation negativity is about 400 ms and lasts several hundred milliseconds. Most probably, this negativity reflects the operation of Cooper and Shepard's second stage (rotate comparison stimulus). The effects of memory load precede the effects of mental rotation, suggesting that letter identification and memory search precede rotation. As memory search and mental rotation have different electrophysiological correlates, it is quite conceivable that the associated psychological processes take place in different subsystems of working memory (Baddeley, 1983). Again, the latency of the P300 showed resource specificity; that is, its latency increased as a function of memo-

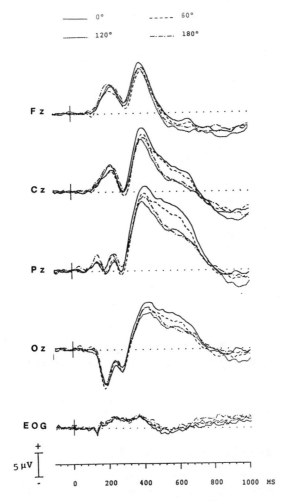

FIG. 14.9. The effects of rotation on the ERP (for explanation, see text).

ry load but not as a function of angular disparity. P300 latency is apparently contingent with the duration of symbolic operations.

In summary, the following operations appear to take place in the following order in this task: (a) selective processing of color, (b) encoding of the stimulus, (c) orienting of attention, (d) controlled search, (e) target detection and decision, and (f) mental rotation and response selection and execution. The ordering and occurrence of these operations is displayed graphically in Fig. 14.10. In this conceptualization, encoding is represented as a preattentive, automatic process,

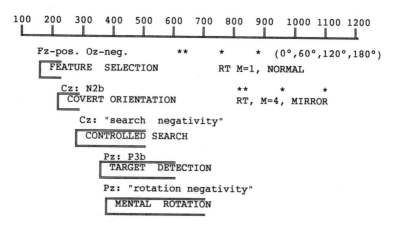

FIG. 14.10. Onset latencies of different endogenous components in selective attention paradigms.

whereas search and mental rotation are controlled and selective applied to the attended input change and to attended targets.

INDIVIDUAL DIFFERENCES
IN SELECTIVE ATTENTION AND MEMORY

In this section, we discuss differences between subjects in the rate of automatization and the relation between ERP components and performance.

ERP Correlates of Practice in Visual Search

In a study by van Dellen, Brookhuis, G. Mulder, Okita, & L. Mulder (1985), eight subjects participated in an experiment in which they were first trained in VM sessions, followed by four CM sessions, and finally followed again by a VM condition. The experimental design schedule for this study is presented in Table 14.2 (see van Dellen et al., 1985 for further details).

The display consisted of one or three consonants arranged in a square around the central fixation point. The memory set consisted of three elements (see also Fig. 14.2). In CM conditions, the memory set consisted of the consonants [J, X, D], whereas nontargets were always chosen from the set [B, D, F, G, H, K, L, N, P, R, S, T, V, W, Y]. In VM conditions, the memory set, and nontargets were randomly chosen from the set [B, D, F, G, H, K, L, M, N, P, Q, R, S, T, V, W, Y, X, Z] for each trial. On the final day of the experiment, the consonants [J, X, Z] were not used as VM distractors. The number of letters in the display is called display load, with the levels '3*1' (memory set three, display set one) and

TABLE 14.2
Schedule of Experimental Sessions

Session	VM/CM[a]	Trial nrs	Trial with EEG registration	Name
1.	VM	1–1000	—	—
2.	VM	1001–1800	1501–1800	VM1
3.	CM	1801–2800	1901–2200	CM1
4.	CM	2801–3900		—
5.	CM	3901–5000		—
6.	CM	5001–5300	5001–5300	CM2
7.	VM	5301–5700	5401–5700	VM2

[a] VM = Varied mapping conditions; CM = Consistent mapping conditions

'3*3'(memory set three, display set three). ERP recordings were made at VM1 and CM1 and CM2 and VM2 (see Tables 14.2).

The comparison between VM2 and VM1 mainly reflects the effects of practice; the comparison between CM2 and CM1 reflects the effects of practice and the effects of mapping. We focus our discussion on the effect of load, response type, practice, mapping on CRT, the N200, and the P300.

As can be seen in Fig. 14.11a and 14.11b, RT is affected by practice, mapping, response type, and load. Practice decreased response type and display load effects.

The difference in RT between targets and nontargets increased with display load, especially in the VM conditions. Both display load and response type effects were smaller in CM conditions. Taken together, these findings suggest a serial, self-terminating search in VM conditions and a trend toward parallel, exhaustive search after CM practice.

P300 amplitude is decreased as a function of load, is smaller for nontargets, and tends to increase as a function of practice. P300 latency is still affected by load; only nontarget P300s tend to decrease after CM mapping. N200 latency shows a small but consistent decrease as a function of practice. This occipital component is related to early data-driven visual encoding operations. That is, its amplitude increases with the number of elements in the visual display (Brookhuis et al., 1981), an effect independent of attention. In addition, its amplitude decreases, its latency increases with masking (Okita et al., 1985), and its latency decreases and amplitude increases with letter size (Wijers, G. Mulder, Okita, & L. Mulder, in press).

If the ERPs of targets are subtracted from the ERPs of nontargets, it appears that the difference between target and nontarget ERPs occurs earlier during CM training (around 100 ms!) than during VM training (around 371 ms). Together, these results seem to indicate that training, especially under CM conditions,

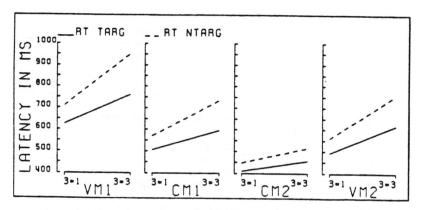

FIG. 14.11a. Mean RTs in VM1, CM1, CM2, and VM2. TARG = target trial; NTARG = nontarget trial (van Dellen et al., 1985).

accelerates the buildup of evidence. However, since P300 amplitudes are not significantly reduced, one is tempted to conclude that automatic processing is still a capacity limited process. Similar conclusions were reached by Hoffman, Nelson, and Houck (1983) and Hoffman, Simons, and Houck (1983).

Let us now consider individual differences. A hierarchical cluster analysis, based on RTs from sessions 2 to 6, identified two clusters (each of four subjects). The cluster factor was included in the ANOVA design as a between-subject factor. The two groups, which we shall call Fast and Slow, respectively, differed in mean RT. In addition, there was a Cluster × Response Type interaction and a Cluster × Response Type * Display Load interaction. These interactions indicate that search rate was different for the two groups. In Table 14.3, the intercepts of

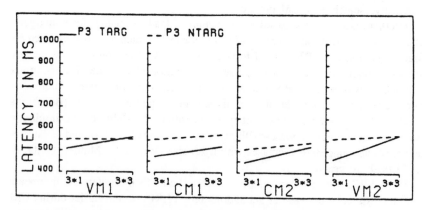

FIG. 14.11b. Mean P300 latencies in VM1, CM1, CM2, and VN2. TARG = target trial; NTARG = nontarget trial (van Dellen et al., 1985).

TABLE 14.3
Intercepts of CRT-Set Size Functions,
Separately for the Fast and
Slow Subjects

Group	VM1[a]	CM1[a]	CM2	VM2
Fast	550	447	390	430
Slow	555	462	397	442

[a]VM = Varied mapping conditions; CM = Consistent mapping conditions

the regression equation relating RT to the number of comparisons as predicted by a serial, self-terminating search model are depicted. Clearly, intercepts of the Fast and Slow subjects are very similar. However, a different pattern can be observed in the slopes (see Table 14.4). As can be seen in Table 14.4, Slow subjects needed about 50% more time per item in the comparison process.

The ERPs of the Fast subjects appear to be more negative at Oz and Pz. On the other hand, after about 350 ms, the ERPs showed more positivity for the Fast subjects. The negative shift, especially at Oz, might indicate a better preparation of perceptual mechanisms at the moment of stimulus presentation. In addition, we examined cluster effects on the P300 and N200. As shown in Fig. 14.12, P300 amplitudes of the Slow subjects (Fig. 14.12b) were more affected by display load than those of the Fast subjects (Fig. 14.12a).

These results suggest that the Fast subjects used a faster and more efficient comparison process. The large slope of the RT-set size function and the larger effect of display load and response type on P300 amplitudes among Slow subjects suggest that these subjects continued to rely heavily on a serial comparison process. The large effects of display load and response type on the P300 (i.e., the P300 shows a stronger decrease as a function of load and is smaller for negative responses) probably indicate a larger overlapping controlled search related negativity in the Slow subjects.

TABLE 14.4
Slopes of RT-Set Size Functions,
Separately for the Fast and
Slow Subjects

Group	VM1[a]	CM1[a]	CM2	VM2
Fast	36	20	10	29
Slow	52	42	17	42

[a]VM = Varied mapping conditions; CM = Consistent mapping conditions

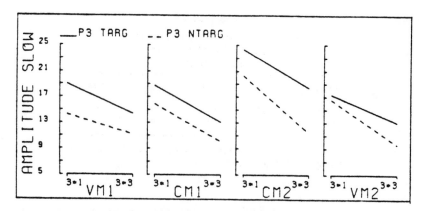

FIG. 14.12a.   P300 amplitudes in the different conditions for the Fast subjects (van Dellen et al., 1985).

A recent study by Strayer (1987) is relevant to these findings. Strayer examined the development of automaticity among young and elderly subjects. Both young and elderly persons improved with practice, as manifested in decreases in RT and increases in response accuracy. Elderly subjects, however, appeared to respond more slowly and more accurately than younger subjects following practice. Reductions in the slope function relating RT and memory set size were apparent for both age groups. But reductions in the slope relating P300 latency and memory set size were apparent only for the young subjects. This result suggests that the stimulus evaluation process becomes more efficient for the young, but not for the elderly. The improvement of their RT has to be attributed to response-related processing. In fact, the improvements in performance of the elderly are not the result of more automatic processing but are due to a reduction

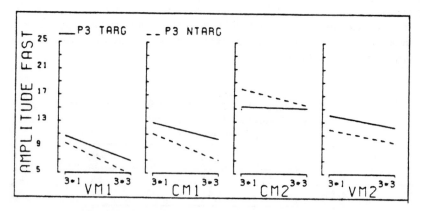

FIG. 14.12b.   P300 amplitudes in the different conditions for the Slow subjects (van Dellen et al., 1985).

in post stimulus evaluation processes (see later discussion on the response activation system).

Component Relations
and Component-Task Performance Relations

A metaanalysis across different focused attention experiments supports our emerging view that individual differences in endogenous components are related to individual differences in performance or to individual differences in other endogenous components. It appears that the amount of search negativity is positively related to the slope of the RT function (the correlations in the different experiments range from +.24 to +.49). In addition, the results obtained in some studies indicate that larger search negativity is accompanied by less false alarms (i.e., a negative correlation between search negativity and number of misses and false alarms—in the experiments with color and color and size as selection cues the correlation ranges from −.49 to −.63). This result suggests that a more thorough evaluation process is a determinant of relatively error-free performance.

A very interesting observation is that a large early frontal positivity as the result of altering the stimulus color is associated with less search negativity in the irrelevant channel. This finding suggests that frontal positivity is likely to be a reflection of an attention controlling mechanism involved in the selectivity of attention. Another interesting feature of this frontal positivity is its relationship with RT. The larger frontal positivity, the faster the RT (overall correlations range from −.26 to −.78).

Finally, a high N2b, indicating active orienting toward task-relevant information, was found to be associated with large attention demanding, controlled search related negativity. Correlations of this relation range from .29 to −.72 (overall −.54).

Overall, the findings suggest that the competent information processor is in general characterized by a larger N200, more frontal positivity, a larger N2b, much search negativity and a relatively fast P300.

ELECTROPHYSIOLOGY OF MOTOR PROCESSES:
THE RESPONSE ACTIVATION SYSTEM

It is common practice for many experimental psychologists to define responses only as a mechanical event (e.g., switch closures) that is recorded by the experimenter (Gratton, Coles, Sirevaag, Eriksen, & Donchin, 1988). In fact, however, a quite complicated mechanism is involved. The response process consists of different levels. In this vein, Gratton et al. (1988) introduce the notion of *response channels*. They use this term as a heuristic device to refer to that complex of structures whose activities are more or less directly related to the mechanical event that is defined as the overt response.

Response channels constitute the response activation system. This system is thought to be activated by the stimulus evaluation system and indexed by the ERP components discussed in the preceding section, either after complete stimulus evaluation or with partial information. However, other factors may also play an important role, such as response priming, bias, facilitation, and competition (Coles et al., 1985; de Jong, Wierda, G. Mulder, & L. Mulder, 1988; Eriksen, Coles, Morris, & O'Hara, 1985; Gratton et al., 1988; Smid, G. Mulder, & L. Mulder, 1987; Smid, G. Mulder, & L. Mulder, 1989).

The activation of response channels can be studied at two different levels: (a) at the level of the overt response in conjunction with EMG activity or (b) at the cortical level, using a component of the ERP known as the Readiness Potential. The Readiness Potential component of the ERP was first described by Kornhuber and Deecke (1965). These researchers observed a negative, ramplike potential, starting at about 800 ms prior to the execution of a voluntary movement. This slow premovement negativity, called the Bereidschafts or Readiness Potential, is initially of equal amplitude over both hemispheres but begins to increase asymmetrically at 400 ms or more prior to movement onset, with larger amplitudes over the hemisphere contralateral to the responding side. This lateralization is strongest for potentials recorded at scalp locations above the motor cortex.

A similar negative-going potential, known as the terminal Contingent Negative Variation (CNV), is obtained in the interval between the warning and the imperative stimulus in the forewarned reaction time paradigm (Rohrbaugh & Gaillard, 1983). A contralateral predominance for the terminal CNV is also found if the warning stimulus specifies the hand with which to respond to the imperative stimulus (Syndulko & Lindsley, 1977).

From evidence like this it is reasonable to assume that premovement lateralized negativities reflect the differential involvement of the left and right motor cortex in preparing to execute unimanual motor acts (Kutas & Donchin, 1980). As a consequence, the *onset* latency of such motor asymmetries can be assumed to reflect the time at which response preparation processes start to become *specific* with respect to response hand.

Motor asymmetries may be overlapped by a variety of asymmetries related to other differences between hemispheres, either functional or structural. To address this issue, de Jong et al. (1988) developed an index of motor asymmetry called Corrected Motor Asymmetry (CMA), defined as CMA = Right Hand (C3'-C4') − Left Hand (C3'-C4'). C3' and C4' are scalp regions close to the brain motor areas. De Jong et al.'s equation assumes that the processing preceding a left- or right-hand response would be essentially similar except for its specifically response-related part. In such cases, the motor asymmetry can be obtained simply by subtracting the total asymmetry obtained for the left hand from that for the right hand. CMA can be monitored almost continuously as are

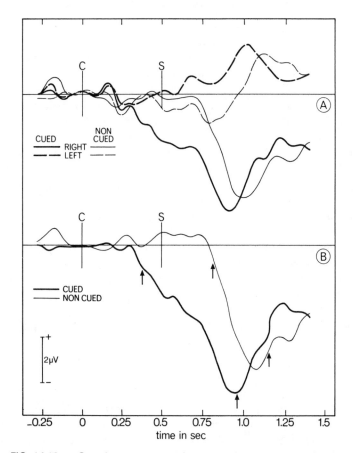

FIG. 14.13.a Grand-average waveforms depicting the voltage difference between the scalp electrodes located above the left and right motor cortex (C3' and C4') for the left- and right-hand responses and for both precue conditions (cued, noncued). C and S correspond to the onset of the precue and the imperative stimulus respectively (de Jong et al., in press).

FIG. 14.13b. CMA waveforms for the two precue conditions. These waveforms were obtained by subtracting the waveform for the left-hand responses in Fig. 14.13a from the corresponding waveforms for right-hand responses. The arrows correspond to CMA onset latency as determined by a statistical procedure described in van Dellen et al. (1985) and to mean RT, respectively (de Jong et al., in press).

other endogenous components (see preceding section). Fig. 14.13 (a and b) provides illustrative results from a recent experiment by de Jong et al. (1988).

In this experiment, we employed the response precueing technique, developed by Rosenbaum (1980), to investigate whether CMA reflects the response priming process that is assumed to operate when response hand is specified in advance. Two types of precue were used; informative and neutral. The informative precue specified response hand, whereas the neutral precue served as control and did not provide specific response information.

The precue was presented at the center of the display. The precue consisted of one of three letters: The letters L and R, indicating left or right hand, respectively, or the letter U, leaving response hand unspecified. The imperative stimulus consisted of two letters that were located $0.7°$ to the left and right of the fixation point. The left letter indicated response hand L for left and R for right hand. The right letter indicated response finger: I for index and M for middle finger. Mean correct RT for neutral precues, measured from the onset of the imperative stimulus and averaged across index and middle fingers, were 687 and 642 ms for left- and right-hand responses, respectively.

Averaged C3'-C4' difference potentials for left- and right-hand responses and for both precue types are shown in Fig. 14.13a. Corresponding CMA waveforms for the two precue types are shown in Fig. 14.13b. As shown in Fib. 14.13b, CMA for informative precues started well before the onset of the imperative stimulus, CMA started only after onset of the imperative stimulus in the neutral precue condition. Obviously, the large difference in waveform for cued and noncued responses must be attributed to the advance preparation of the two responses on the precued hand. Most importantly, however, the results of this experiment clearly show that CMA can serve as a useful index of advance preparation for a subset of responses on the same hand.

Selective motor preparation before the imperative stimulus (i.e., prestimulus motor asymmetry—termed PREMA) reflects response bias. If PREMA is high, the mere presentation of the stimulus may be sufficient for raising the activation level above threshold and producing a so-called fast guess. Instructional sets (e.g., instructions emphasizing speed, priming, or warning stimuli; manipulations of response probability) may increase PREMA. Related to these findings, Gratton et al. (1988) introduce the variable baseline hypothesis.

Selective motor preparation after the imperative stimulus (i.e., poststimulus motor asymmetry—termed POSTMA) refers to the activation of the response channels that occurs as a consequence of processing of the imperative stimulus. Some theorists assume that preliminary analysis of stimulus information could have already primed motor channels, a priming that would be further increased by complete stimulus evaluation or that could be inhibited if more stimulus information indicates that another response should be given (e.g., Eriksen & Schultz, 1979; Miller, 1982).

The second approach used to study the motor system is at the peripheral level of EMG activation. At this level, response activation can be interrupted or further increased (Coles et al., 1985; Smid et al., 1987; Smid, G. Mulder, & L. Mulder, 1989). By monitoring EMG activity in the different response channels (e.g., hands), it is possible to define four different activity patterns, described as follows:

1. *No-Error category.* EMG activity precedes overt responding in the correct hand; there is no EMG activity in the incorrect channel.
2. *Incorrect-Correct (IC) category.* Incorrect EMG activity precedes correct EMG activity. This kind of error is related to errors in response selection and requires central attentional processes to be corrected (Schmidt, 1982).
3. *Correct-Incorrect (CI) category.* Correct EMG activity precedes incorrect EMG activity, which is then followed again by correct EMG. This type of error is related to errors in response execution and requires low level reflexive processes to be corrected (Schmidt, 1982).
4. *Error.* Trials in which an incorrect overt response was emitted. Note that error categories 2 and 3 do not finally result in a wrong response.

Having a separate measure for the start of peripheral responding enables us to study the duration of response execution as defined by the interval between EMG onset and switch closure of the button press in the correct response channel. Furthermore, the duration of response execution may be related to response preparation in the following way. Several lines of research suggest that response preparation has a pretuning or permissive effect on the duration of response execution (i.e., longer preparation results in faster and more accurate execution of a response—see Marteniuk & Mackenzie, 1980; Requin, 1985; Smid et al., 1987; Smid et al., 1989; Turvey, 1977).

Motor Bias, Priming, and Response Execution

In this section, we focus on two experiments: one in which instructional set was manipulated and the other which used the noise/compatibility paradigm (B. Eriksen & C. Eriksen, 1974; C. Eriksen & B. Eriksen, 1979). Our emphasis in discussion of both of these experiments is on the differences in how subjects approached these two tasks.

Individual Differences and the Effects of Response Bias

In the divided attention tasks, as we have discussed them in the preceding section, the probability of a target is $p = .50$. A recent study by G. Mulder, Gloerich, Brookhuis, van Dellen, and L. Mulder (1984) varied response probability (i.e., the probability that the display would contain a target). The memory set contained either one or two consonants. The imperative signal consisted of four consonants that were displayed in a square around a central fixation dot. In other words, display load was always four.

G. Mulder et al. (1984) used a VM procedure. In the control condition, there was a probability of $p = .50$ that the display contained a memory set item. In the experimental condition, this probability was $p = .25$. We hypothesized that the effects of response probability would affect only the response activation system and would not affect the stimulus evaluation system. As a consequence, we predicted that RT, but not the P300 latency, would be affected by relative response frequency.

Subjects were trained in both conditions before participating in the experiment. Subjects were instructed to make positive responses with the preferred finger of the dominant hand and negative responses with the preferred finger of the nondominant hand. Subjects were also informed about the probability of responses. In the experimental condition, subjects were explicitly instructed to *prepare* for the frequent, negative response.

The results obtained in the pilot phase of this experiment indicated that not all subjects were able to adopt a response strategy that resulted in faster negative and slower positive responses in the experimental condition compared with the control condition. As a consequence, we divided the subjects in each condition into two groups on the basis of the RT for negative responses obtained in each trial. We placed subjects who showed a significant difference between the control and the experimental condition in the expected direction into the Well group, and subjects who did not show such a difference into the Poor group.

We then examined behavioral data (RT and errors) as well as physiological data (late CNV as an index of motor bias, and P300 as an index of the relative duration of the stimulus evaluation process). As can be seen in Fig. 14.14a, the RT data showed that response probability did not affect search rate but did affect the binary decision stage (i.e., the time needed to decide for a positive or negative response).

As expected, the two groups labeled Well and Poor were not equally sensitive to the effect of response probability. The Well group showed the expected bias for negative responses, as evidenced by a highly significant interaction between response probability and response mode. The Poor group was not much affected by the probability manipulation, and as a consequence there was no significant interaction between response mode and response probability. The number of errors for both groups can be found in Table 14.5.

From this Table, it is evident that the subjects in the Well group committed more errors in the positive responses: Apparently, these subjects had developed more of a bias for negative responses than had subjects in the Poor group. Consequently, subjects in the Well group tended to emit a negative response even in the presence of a target.

Let us now consider the P300 component, as shown in Fib. 14.14b. Similar to RT findings, the P300 latencies also indicate that relative response frequency did

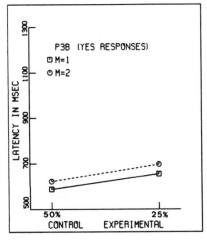 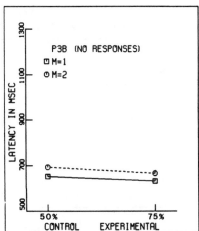

FIG. 14.14a. The effects of relative response frequency on RT for targets (left panel) and in RT for nontargets (right panel) (G. Mulder et al., 1984).

not affect search rate but did affect the time needed to decide about making a positive or negative cognitive response. In contrast to the performance data, however, analysis of variance on the P300 latencies of the two groups separately did not show differential effects of relative response probability. In both the Well and the Poor groups, response probability interacted significantly with response mode.

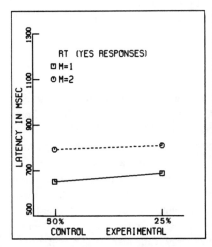 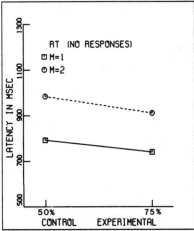

FIG. 14.14b. The effects of relative response frequency on P300 latency for targets (left panel) and on P300 latency for nontargets (right panel (G. Mulder et al., 1984).

TABLE 14.5
Percentage of Errors Under Different Conditions

Probability	Load	Response	Group Well	Group Poor
	M = 1	Yes	5.8	4.6
Control		No	1.3	4.6
50%–50%	M = 2	Yes	7.1	5.8
		No	3.1	4.2
	M = 1	Yes	9.2	7.1
Experimental	M = 2	No	3.8	11.7
25%–75%	M = 1	Yes	19.6	11.3
	M = 2	No	2.1	13.3

On the one hand, these data indicate that the stimulus evaluation process was affected by relative response frequency in both groups. That is, negative displays were evaluated faster than positive displays. On the other hand, this effect was manifested in behavior only among subjects in the Well group. Why was this the case? It may be that the Well group selectively biased their motor system. In order to check this possibility we computed the late CNV (in this experiment it was not possible to compute CMA). Fig. 14.15 presents the grand averages across all conditions for the Well and Poor groups separately.

As can be seen in Fig. 14.15, the Poor group did not show a late CNV compared to the Well group. In other words, the Well group prepared their motor system. It would be very interesting to see if preparation was also selective, that is, if the preparation was in the direction of the negative response.

Individual Differences in Motor Priming and Response Execution

Table 14.6 depicts the conditions used in the noise/compatibility paradigm (Eriksen & Eriksen, 1974; 1979; Smid, G. Mulder, & L. Mulder 1989). Four types of trials are presented in the mixed condition. The subject's task is to react only to the central stimulus and ignore the noise stimuli. One of the important findings in this paradigm is that the presence of incompatible noise increases RT.

At least two processes operate in these tasks: identity analysis (or letter form analysis) and location analysis. The subject must locate and identify the central letter in order to determine the response: D requires responding with one hand and H with the other hand. Letter identity analysis is initially feature driven in that it uses the dominant features of the entire array. Consider the INC condition. Initially, the dominant features of the array call for the response associated with the noise stimuli. However, over time, location analysis narrows letter identity analysis to the central target letter, which is associated with another response,

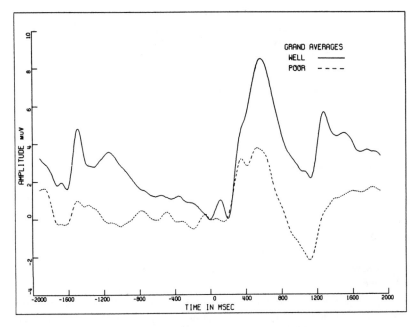

FIG. 14.15.   Grand average ERP of subjects sensitive (Well) and insensitive (Poor) to the relative response frequency manipulation. Note that in the Well group, there is a negative-going ERP shift (CNV) before the presentation of the display set at 0 ms. (G. Mulder et al., 1984).

TABLE 14.6
Conditions in the Noise/Compatibility
Paradigm[a]

Conditions		Stimuli	
Blocked	no noise(BNO)	D	H
		^	^
Mixed	no noise(MNO)	D	H
		^	^
	compatible noise(COM)	DDDDDDD	HHHHHHH
		^	^
	neutral noise(NEU)	XXXDXXX	XXXHXXX
		^	^
	incompatible noise(INC)	HHHDHHH	DDDHDDD
		^	^

[a] ^ denotes target position

TABLE 14.7
Identity and Location Analysis in the Different Conditions
of the Noise/Compatibility Paradigm

	Mixed No Noise MNO	Compatible Noise (COM)	Neutral Noise (NEU)	Incompatible Noise (INC)
Identity Analysis	+	+	+	+
Location Analysis		+	+	+

that is, the correct one. Thus, it may be that the wrong channel is activated first (because information processing is initially feature driven, but, as a function of time, the correct motor channel is activated because letter identity analysis of the central target dominates at that moment (see Table 14.7 and Fig. 14.16).

In this experiment, we monitored the information-processing system at four different levels. We used P300 latency as an index of stimulus evaluation time, CMA as an index of central motor activation, EMG from both forearms to monitor peripheral motor activation, and, finally, RT as an index of the final motor response. Table 14.8 provides a brief summary of our findings. In Fig. 14.17, we indicate the type of EMG errors that were made in the different conditions.

Our data indicate that RT is less sensitive than P300 latency. We found that stimulus evaluation time becomes increasingly delayed as the compatibility between targets and flankers decrease. Evaluation time is shortest if there are no

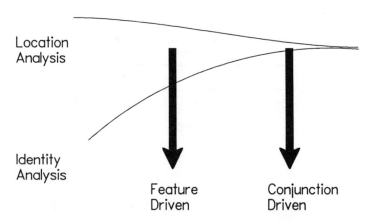

FIG. 14.16.   Location and letter form analysis as a function of time in the noise/compatibility paradigm.

TABLE 14.8
CRT and Latency of P300 in the
Noise/Compatibility Paradigm (Correct
Trials Only)

CRT	P300
compatible = no noise	compatible > no noise
compatible < neutral	compatible < neutral
incompatible > neutral	incompatible > neutral
	neutral > no noise

flankers at all. The number of overt errors (i.e., wrong responses) also increases as compatibility decreases. If we look at EMG errors, we see that the number of ICs (i.e., incorrect EMG activity followed by correct EMG activity) steadily increases. It seems as if the motor system is fooled by the nature of the irrelevant flankers. Motor execution time (i.e., the time between onset of correct EMG activity and the overt response) is also affected—in the case of CI errors, motor execution time is 155 ms (on average) compared to 114 ms in the case of no errors. In general, response execution time is longer on incompatible trials than neutral trials and shorter on compatible trials compared with no noise trials. In

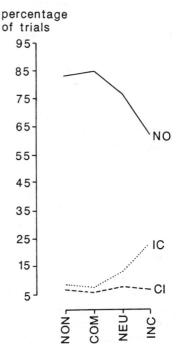

FIG. 14.17. Frequency of trials in the three EMG error categories in the four stimulus conditions used (NON = No noise, COM = Compatible noise, NEU = Neutral noise, INC = Incompatible noise). NO, CI, and IC are correct response trials associated with no incorrect EMG (NO), correct followed by incorrect EMG (CI), and correct EMG followed by incorrect EMG (CI). (Smid et al., 1987; 1989).

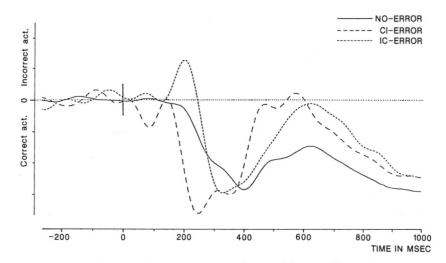

FIG. 14.18.   Grand average waveform of CMA in the three EMG error categories. Ascending activity represents activation of the wrong response channel, whereas descending activity represents activation of the correct response channel (Smid et al., 1989).

other words, there appears to be facilitation and inhibition at different levels of the information-processing system: inhibition at the level of the stimulus evaluation process and facilitation (in the case of compatible trials) at the level of response execution.

Let us now consider the CMA findings in more detail. Fig. 14.18 shows CMA as a function of EMG error type. For IC errors, we see that CMA first goes in the wrong direction and is then followed by CMA in the correct direction. Note that IC errors occur mostly during the incompatible trials. In other words, very early partial stimulus information (i.e., information at the feature level) has already started to drive the motor channels (around 120 ms!). Depending on the type of information, this motor activation may be in the correct or in the incorrect direction. If more information becomes available, the system "changes mind." Additionally, our data indicate that stimulus evaluation and response activation can occur in parallel. More details and confirming evidence can be found in Smid et al. (1987, 1989) and Gratton et al. (1988).

Let us now return to the original design. As indicated previously, we ran both a blocked and a mixed condition. Previous research has found that if conditions are mixed, CRT is longer in all conditions than if the different conditions are blocked (C. Eriksen & B. Eriksen, 1979; C. Eriksen & Schultz, 1979). Such results suggest that subjects process the information faster if they know in advance what type of trials will be presented. In other words, subjects may *prepare* their information-processing system. Note that the stimulus array presented is completely identical in both conditions. If targets are presented alone, subjects do not have to use location analysis but instead only use identity analysis. If targets are presented together with flankers, both location analysis (visual search) and identity analysis are required. Preparation may occur at either or both the stimulus evaluation level and the response execution level.

Where are the differences between the blocked and the mixed condition localized? We use P300 latency as an index of stimulus evaluation. If the P300 latency is shorter in the blocked conditions, it is reasonable to conclude that part of the preparation process is localized in the stimulus evaluation system. However, it is equally possible that the subject prepares his or her motor system—a preparation that would be evidenced in shorter response execution. Advance perceptual preparation for targets alone in the blocked condition may consist of presetting the letter identity processor. In contrast, the subject in the mixed condition should also preset location analysis. Preparation of an extra processor may drain resources, an effect which would be demonstrated in less accurate and/or slower stimulus evaluation or response execution. Furthermore, there may be individual differences among subjects in their preparation strategy.

To examine this issue, we compared the blocked-target-alone condition with the mixed-target-alone condition using data averaged across all six subjects, and for each subject separately. In the blocked-target-alone condition, button press RT and EMG RT in the correct response channel were shorter than in the mixed-target-alone condition. Incorrect button presses were slightly more frequent in the blocked condition (5.2%) than in the mixed condition (1.7%). On average, the P300 peak latency was not affected by the blocked mixed manipulation. These results suggest that only response-related processes are affected (i.e., the processes that occur after stimulus evaluation is finished) *if* subjects know in advance what kind of processing will be required. Another noteworthy finding is the small decrease in response execution obtained in the blocked condition. Taken together, these results appear to be consistent with a speed–accuracy trade-off explanation. The function of accumulation of evidence in the perceptual system seems to be identical in both conditions, but responses are initiated and executed earlier in response to it. This shift in the response criterion results in a slight enhancement of the number of incorrect button presses.

If we examine the data of the individual subjects, a very different picture emerges. In these analyses, we see a consistent pattern of effects across subjects. Fig. 14.19 presents the P300 peak latency, EMG RT, button press RT, and percentage of trials containing respectively incorrect EMG responses and incorrect button presses data for each of the six subjects. All latency data were collected from the trials in which no incorrect EMG activity occurred. For each subject, both button press RT and EMG RT are shorter in the blocked condition. The P300 latency data, however, differ substantially across subjects. Subjects 2 and 3 show a clear effect of perceptual preparation (i.e., the duration of the stimulus evaluation process is shorter in the blocked condition as a result of

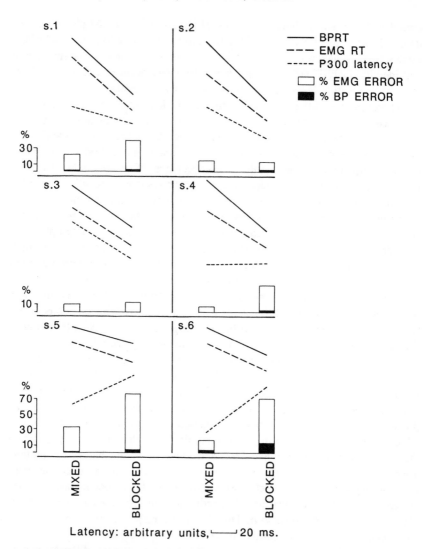

FIG. 14.19. Individual differences in the mixed and blocked conditions of the noise/compatibility paradigm (for explanation, see text).

knowing in advance that only letter identity analysis and not location analysis
were required in evaluating the stimulus). Subjects 1 and 4 do not seem to use
this advance knowledge to prepare their perceptual system. Subjects 5 and 6 have
an even longer P300 latency in the blocked condition; a finding which indicates
that they had not prepared their perceptual system as well as in the mixed
condition.

Response execution duration also differed across subjects. Subjects 1 through
4 executed their responses faster in the blocked condition, whereas Subjects 5

and 6 executed their responses in the blocked condition more slowly. It seems, then, that Subjects 2 and 3 prepared both their stimulus evaluation and motor activation system better in the blocked condition, that Subjects 1 and 4 only prepared their response activation system better in the blocked condition, and that Subjects 5 and 6 prepared both systems worse in the blocked condition.

By relating individual differences in preparatory activities to individual accuracy data we can now specify the overall speed–accuracy effect in more detail. Our findings indicate a clear relationship between the accuracy of the responses given and the relationship between the slopes of the EMG RT and P300 latencies. If the slopes of these latency measures are about equal, we observe no decrement in accuracy in the blocked condition (Subjects 2 and 3). However, as the difference between the slopes becomes larger, so does the difference in accuracy between the blocked and mixed conditions (Subject 1: 17%; Subject 4: 27%; Subject 5: 43%; and Subject 6: 53%; see Table 14.9). Subjects 5 and 6 have extreme error rates of 76% and 69%, which for the most part consist of response selection errors (IC).

Our results can be interpreted as arising from three different preparatory strategies. Remember that in the mixed condition it was necessary to be prepared for carrying out letter identity and location analysis. In the blocked no noise condition however, only identity analysis was required. Accordingly, an efficient preparatory strategy was to prepare for identity analysis only. As a result, accumulation of stimulus evidence may proceed faster. In this strategy, it was also useful to lower the response criterion. In the mixed condition, the criterion consisted of location and identity information about the target. In the blocked condition, however, it could be reduced to identity information only. This strategy then, should result in faster performance at both the perceptual and RT level

TABLE 14.9
Summary of Results for Each Subject on Blocked and Mixed
Condition Experiment[a]

Subject	Condition	P300	EMG	Resp.	ED	% EMG ER	% BP ER
1	B	403	229	329	100	40	4.1
	M	424	298	401	103	23	1.1
2	B	392	296	391	95	12	3.8
	M	434	356	466	110	14	1.7
3	B	389	285	379	94	12	3.2
	M	436	335	433	98	9	0.7
4	B	443	293	383	89	34	2.0
	M	442	341	449	108	7	0.1
5	B	389	197	340	143	76	5.0
	M	353	223	362	139	33	1.3
6	B	426	256	377	121	69	12.8
	M	368	292	412	119	16	5.2

[a]BP = Button press; ED = Execution duration; EMG ER = EMG errors (BP errors included); BP ER = Button press errors

(with equal accuracy) than in the mixed, no noise condition. In our data, only Subjects 2 and 3 seemed to have used this strategy.

A second strategy was demonstrated in the data obtained for Subject 1 and 4. These subjects did not prepare their perceptual system differently but did lower their response criterion. Although they reacted faster in the blocked condition, their stimulus evaluation speed remained the same, resulting in a large increase of EMG errors.

Subjects 5 and 6 performed on the basis of a third, very inefficient strategy. The fact that their P300 latency was larger and their response execution took longer in the blocked condition indicates that these subjects prepared their perceptual and motor systems in the blocked condition even more poorly than in the mixed condition. As might be expected, this strategy yielded the smallest profit in reaction speed among all subjects and a dramatic increase in errors. It appears that, in about 65% of the trials, these subjects set their response criterion very low and initiated both responses in reaction to very little available stimulus information. Nonetheless, all of these error trials led to a correct button press. This is because more stimulus evidence became available during response execution—evidence that enabled central processes to interrupt ongoing incorrect response activation and to execute the correct response up to the button press level. Note that this kind of corrective performance is only detectable with the aid of the EMG measure.

From these results, we can conclude that preparation of information-processing substructures is optional in nature. Some subjects use advance knowledge of events to do better than others. On the basis of P300 latency and response execution duration data, we were able to distinguish between subjects who did or did not prepare their perceptual and/or motor systems in advance of stimulus presentation. The most efficient preparation strategy consisted of preparing both systems for processes that the subject could expect to have to carry out for accurate task performance. Subjects who used this strategy were able to improve their reaction speed substantially and still maintain their accuracy at the same high level (about 90% at the EMG level, see Table 14.1 for exact figures).

A less efficient strategy consisted of preparing only the response system in accordance with the requirements of the task, but not the perceptual system. This strategy yielded the same profit in RT but was associated with a drop in accuracy to approximately 65%. This type of strategy provides a classic example of the speed–accuracy trade-off in performance. The difference between this strategy and the more efficient strategy, described previously, appears to be due entirely to differences in preparation of the perceptual system. In both strategies, one observes lowering of the response criterion. But in the less efficient strategy, such lowering was also accompanied by slower accumulation of stimulus evidence, in turn resulting in premature initiation of responses.

The poorest strategy observed involved a relative lack of preparation in both the perceptual and the motor system. Whereas the two previous strategies entailed better or no different preparation in the blocked conditions, the poorest strategy was characterized by *worse* preparation in both systems. Such a strategy resulted in an accuracy level of no higher than 35% at the EMG level and a rather small RT profit. Remarkably, at the button press level, accuracy was still higher than 90%, although this accuracy level was still lowest of all strategies we observed. The reason that this strategy is so poor is likely to be that it relies too much on corrective effort during response execution (based on central attentional mechanisms).

CONCLUSIONS

Task variables are believed to affect the nature and/or duration of hypothesized mental operations such as encoding, comparison, rotation, and motor preparation. Studies using both behavioral measures and ERPs provide reliable evidence indicating that hypothesized computational processes such as automatic encoding, feature specific attention, the allocation of attentional resources, memory search, binary decision, mental rotation, and premotor and motor activation have distinct correlates in brain and peripheral activity. By using ERP measures, we can follow these processes more precisely in real time. The combination of behavioral indices, such as RT and errors, and ERP indices enables us to discern whether the effects of task variables act on operations in the stimulus evaluation system, in the response activation system, or in both systems.

Overt behavior is not required for observation of brain activities associated with hypothesized mental operations. Individual differences in performance can be understood in terms of the efficiency and timing of the operations within the stimulus evaluation and the response activation system and in terms of the information-processing strategy (see previous discussion). However, the use of both behavioral and ERP indices is likely to greatly aid our understanding of mental operations. Future research efforts should focus more on quantitative patterns of RT distributions *in combination* with quantitative patterns of ERP components to examine the effects of aging and changes in psychophysiological state on the efficiency, timing, and processing strategy used, and on the cerebral localization of the sources from which this endogenous brain activity associated with computational processes arises.

OPEN DISCUSSION

The discussion following Mulder's talk began with a question about Mulder's rationale for viewing automatic processing as capacity-limited. Subsequent questions addressed the methodology used in Mulder's experiments, Mulder's current work, and potentially fruitful avenues for future research.

Kuhl: I think I missed something. Can you explain again on what basis you infer that so-called automatic processes are capacity-limited?

Mulder: The P300 is a brain event potential component which is largely affected by the amount of resources a subject uses. So if you do experiments in which you have dual tasks, you will see the amplitude of the P300 increase or decrease in association with the amount of perceptual resources the subject has to use. So the P300 is very sensitive to, let us say, capacity demands. Now, we have also observed that the amplitude of the P300 is still affected by memory load after consistent-mapping training. So the system is apparently still using resources. Using behavioral evidence, Hoffman has found a similar thing. Specifically, he found that even after training (automatic processing) subjects still had problems with time-sharing tasks. So it appears that the system is still in use. We think, then, that's what automatic processing is. That is, the motor system can use early features already on the stimulus display and can start motor preparation. But at the same time, controlled processing is going on. So you have two simultaneous lines of processing. Therefore, the subject knows very early, "Oh, I have made an error." He has pressed the button already, but his automatic system says well, there was still a member of the memory set on the display. So, in summary, I think there are two processes going on in parallel.

Revelle: How many trials does it take to get such clean data?

Mulder: I think clean data means that you first have to use a good filtering technique; that is, put your electrodes in the right place and have no noise in the environment. In most of these cases we used 120 trials; 60 positive and 60 negative. That appears to be enough. That's approximately the same number of trials you use in normal performance experiments.

Pick: Have you combined your paradigm with stimulus-response compatibility? I would think they would amplify the kinds of effects you were talking about.

Mulder: Yes, exactly. We have done that experiment. I don't have the data here with me, but we found that this does not affect the P300. Only the motor system was affected by it.

Kuhl: Did you ever look at the correlations you were talking about in individual differences within these different components of cognitive processing abilities? An interesting question, of course, would be whether they are correlated and at which stages they are correlated. Specifically, I would be interested in the size of the correlations between similar things going on in the input versus the output side, such as stimulus competition versus response competition. Did you use something like the Stroop test, for instance?

Mulder: Well, Eriksen's task is a kind of Stroop test because its conflicting evidence is coming out. We recently did an experiment with irrelevant colors on the computer display. But the problem with this type of task is that I usually use 10 subjects, because I am an experimental psychologist. And that means that 10 subjects should be enough! But your point is very interesting. What we are trying now to do is to establish these correlations across experiments. We have now completed a large number of experiments and so it is now possible to have more subjects and to do a kind of metacorrelational analysis. That is what we are currently doing.

Kyllonen: If you wanted to do large-scale individual differences studies, you could show how certain experimental paradigms would allow you to estimate certain aspects of these components through experimental manipulations. For example, one thing that strikes me about your findings is that simply subtracting out a reaction time component in order to estimate some component that presumably occurs later, such as a decision component, would be a funny thing to do, because you are finding that there is a preparation of the motor response that occurs prior to any other cognitive activity. It would be interesting to look for other ways in which some of the things you are showing could constrain the sorts of statistical and experimental models that would be based just on reaction time.

Mulder: That is a very interesting question. We are currently doing are some experiments based on Miller's work. Specifically, we are looking at the following possibility: When you look at overt responding, you find the kind of curves typically associated with exponential distributions. Well, a number of experimental psychologists have always said that this type of curve, which you get on the response side, is a convolution of two types of curves: a normally distributed process and an exponentially distributed process. We are now doing research to see if this so-called hypothetical, normal process is in this region in the information-processing system and if the onset of the motor system follows this, so that we can predict from these two things the overt things.

Kyllonen: That is very nice because, as far as I know, that sort of work has only been done on reaction-time data, and not tied to evoked potentials.

REFERENCES

Aasman, J., Mulder, G., & Mulder, L. J. M. (1987). Operator effort and the measurement of heart-rate variability. *Human Factors, 29,* 161–170.

Baddeley, A. D. (1983). Working memory. *Philosophical Transactions of the Royal Society London, 302,* 311–324.

Brookhuis, K. A., Mulder, G., Mulder, L. J. M. & Gloerich, A. B. M. (1983). The P3 complex as an index of information processing: The effects of response probability. *Biological Psychology, 17,* 277–296.

Brookhuis, K. A., Mulder, G., Mulder, L. J. M., Gloerich, A. B. M., van Dellen, J. H., & van der Meere, J. J. (1981). Late positive components and stimulus evaluation time. *Biological Psychology, 13,* 107–123.

Coles, M. G. H., Gratton, G., Bashore, T. R., Eriksen, C. W., & Donchin, E. (1985). A psychophysiological investigation of the continuous flow model of human information. *Journal of Experimental Psychology: Human Perception and Performance, 11,* 529–553.

Cooper, L. A., & Shepard, R. N. (1973). Chronometric studies of the rotation of mental images. In W. G. Chase (Ed.), *Visual information processing* (pp. 75–176). New York: Academic Press.

de Jong, R., Wierda, M., Mulder, G., & Mulder, L. J. M. (1988). The use of partial information in response processing. *Journal of Experimental Psychology: Human Perception and Performance, 14,* 682–692.

Donders, F. C. (1969). On the speed of mental processes. (W. G. Koster, Trans.) In W. G. Koster (Ed.), *Attention and Performance II* (pp. 421–431). Amsterdam: North-Holland.

Duncan-Johnson, C. C. (1981). P300 latency: A new metric of information processing. *Psychophysiology, 18,* 207–215.

Eriksen, B. A., & Eriksen, C. W. (1974). Effects of noise letters upon the identification of a target letter in a nonsearch task. *Perception and Psychophysics, 16,* 143–149.

Eriksen, C. W., Coles, M. G. H., Morris, L. R., & O'Hara, W. P. (1985). Electromyographic examination of response competition. *Bulletin of the Psychonomic Society, 23,* 165–168.

Eriksen, C. W., & Eriksen, B. A. (1979). Target redundancy in visual search: Do repetitions of the target within the display impair processing? *Perception and Psychophysics, 26,* 195–205.

Eriksen, C. W., & Schultz, D. W. (1979). Information processing in visual search: A continuous flow conception and experimental results. *Perception and Psychophysics, 25,* 249–263.

Gratton, G., Coles, M. G. H., Sirevaag, E., Eriksen, C. W., & Donchin, E. (1988). Pre- and post-stimulus activation of response channels: A psychophysiological investigation. *Journal of Experimental Psychology: Human Perception and Performance, 13,* 331–344.

Grice, G. R., Nullmeyer, R., & Spiker, V. A. (1982). Human reaction times: Toward a general theory. *Journal of Experimental Psychology: General, 111,* 135–153.

Hillyard, S. A., & Kutas, M. (1983). Electrophysiology of cognitive processing. *Annual Review of Psychology, 34,* 33–61.

Hillyard, S. A., & Münte, T. F. (1984) Selective attention to color and location: An analysis with event-related brain potential. *Perception and Psychophysics, 36,* 185–198.

Hockey, G. R. J., Gaillard, A. W. K., & Coles, M. G. H. (1986). *Energetics and human information processing.* Dordrecht, The Netherlands: Martinus Nijhoff.

Hoffman, J. E., Nelson, B., & Houck, M. R. (1983). The role of attentional resources in automatic detection. *Cognitive Psychology, 51,* 379–410.

Hoffman, J. E., Simons, R. F., & Houck, M. R. (1983). Event-related potentials during controlled and automatic targets detection. *Psychophysiology, 20,* 625–632.

Hunt, E. (1978). Mechanics of verbal ability. *Psychological Review, 85,* 237–259.

Kornhuber, H. H., & Deecke, L. (1965). Hirnpotentialänderungen bei Willkürbewegungen und passiven Bewegungen des Menschen: Bereitschaftpotential und reafferente Potentiale [Brain potential changes associated with human voluntary movements: Readiness potential and re-afferent potentials.] *Pflügers Archiv fr die gesamte Physiologie, 284*, 1–17.

Kutas, M., & Donchin, E. (1980). Preparation to respond as manifested by movement-related brain potentials. *Brain Research, 202*, 95–115.

Magliero, A., Bashore, T. R., Coles, M. G. H., & Donchin, E. (1984). On the dependence of P300 latency on stimulus evaluation processes. *Psychophysiology, 21*, 171–186.

Marteniuk, R. G., & MacKenzie, C. L. (1980). A preliminary theory of two hand coordinated control. In G. E. Stelmach & J. Requin (Eds.), *Tutorials in motor behavior* (pp. 185–197). Amsterdam: North-Holland.

McClelland, J. (1979). On the time relations of mental processes: A framework for analyzing processes in cascade. *Psychological Review, 86*, 287–330.

Meyer, D. E., Yantis, S., Osman, A. M., & Smith, J. K. (1986). Temporal properties of human information processing: Tests of discrete versus continuous models. *Cognitive Psychology, 17*, 445–518.

Miller, J. (1982). Discrete versus continuous models of human information processing: In search of partial output. *Journal of Experimental Psychology: Human Perception and Performance, 8*, 273–296.

Mulder, G. (1980). *The heart of mental effort.* Unpublished doctoral dissertation, University of Groningen, The Netherlands.

Mulder, G. (1986). The concept of mental effort. In G. R. J. Hockey, A. W. K. Gaillard, & M. G. H. Coles (Eds.), *Energetics and human information processing* (pp. 175–198). Dordrecht, The Netherlands: Martinus Nijhoff.

Mulder, G., Gloerich, A. B. M., Brookhuis, K. A., van Dellen, H. J., & Mulder, L. J. M. (1984). Stage analysis of the reaction process using brain-evoked potentials and reaction time. *Psychological Research, 46*, 15–32.

Mulder, L. J. M., Brookhuis, K. A., van Arkel, A. E., & Mulder, G. (1980). Detection of variable latency components in EEG-evoked potentials. In *Proceedings of the Digital Equipment Computer Users Society, 7*, no. 1. Amsterdam.

Näätänen, R., & Gaillard, A. W. K. (1983). The orienting reflex and the N2 deflection of the event-related potential (ERP). In A. W. K. Gaillard & W. Ritter (Eds.), *Tutorials in event-related potential research: Endogenous components* (pp. 119–141). Amsterdam: North-Holland.

Okita, T., Wijers, A. A., Mulder, G., & Mulder, L. J. M. (1985). Memory search and visual spatial attention: An event-related brain potential analysis. *Acta Psychologica, 60*, 263–292.

Petersen, S. E., Fox, P. T., Posner, M. I., Mintum, M., & Raichle, M. E. (1988). Positron emission tomographic studies of the cortical anatomy of single-word processing. *Nature, 331*, 585–589.

Posner, M. I., Snyder, C. R. R., & Davidson, B. J. (198). Attention and the detection of signals. *Journal of Experimental Psychology: General, 109*, 160–174.

Requin, J. (1985). Looking forward to moving soon: Ante factum selective processes in motor control. In M. I. Posner (Ed.), *Attention and performance XII* (pp. 147–166). Hillsdale, NJ: Lawrence Erlbaum Associates.

Rohrbaugh, J. W., & Gaillard, A. W. K. (1983). Sensory and motor aspects of the contingent negative variation. In A. W. K. Gaillard & W. Ritter (Eds.), *Tutorials in event-related potential research: Endogenous components* (pp. 269–310). Amsterdam: North-Holland.

Rosenbaum, D. A. (1980. Human movement initiation: Specification of arm, direction, and extent. *Journal of Experimental Psychology: General, 109*, 444–474.

Scheffers, M. K., Wijers, A. A., Mulder, G., & Mulder, L. J. M. (in preparation). An ERP-analysis of memory search and spatial attention during variable and constant cueing conditions. Unpublished manuscript.

Schmidt, R. (1982). More on motor programs. In J. A. Scott Kelso (Ed.), *Human motor behavior: An introduction* (pp. 189–217). Hillsdale, NJ: Lawrence Erlbaum Associates.

Schneider, W., & Shiffrin, R. M. (1977). Controlled and automatic human information processing. I: Detection, search and attention. *Psychological Review, 84,* 1–66.

Shiffrin, R. M., & Schneider, W. (1977). Controlled and automatic human information processing. II: Perceptual learning, automatic attending, and a general theory. *Psychological Review, 84,* 127–190.

Smid, H. G. O. M., Mulder, G., & Mulder, L. J. M. (1987). The Continuous Flow Model revisited: Perceptual and motor aspects. In R. Johnson Jr., J. W. Rohrbaugh, & R. Parasuraman (Eds.), *Current trends in event-related brain potential research (pp. 270–278). Electroencephalography and clinical neurophysiology* (Suppl. 40.) Amsterdam: Elsevier.

Smid, H. G. O. M., Mulder, G., & Mulder, L. J. M. (1989). Response competition and the continuous flow conception of information processing: A psychophysiological investigation.

Sternberg, R. J. (1977). *Intelligence, information processing, and analogical reasoning: The componential analysis of human abilities.* Hillsdale, NJ: Lawrence Erlbaum Associates.

Sternberg, S. (1969). The discovery of processing stages. In W. G. Koster (Ed.), *Attention and performance* (Vol. II, pp. 276–315). Amsterdam: North-Holland.

Strayer, D. L. (1987). Personal communication.

Syndulko, K., & Lindsley, D. B. (1977). Motor and sensory determinants of cortical slow potential shifts in man. In J. E. Desmedt (Ed.), *Attention, voluntary contraction, and event-related cerebral potentials* (pp. 97–131). Basel: S. Karger.

Taylor, D. A. (1976). Stage analysis of the reaction process. *Psychological Bulletin, 83,* 161–191.

Turvey, M. T. (1977). Preliminaries to a theory of action with reference to vision. In R. Shaw & J. Bransford (Eds.), *Perceiving, acting, and knowing: Toward an ecological psychology* (pp. 211–265). Hillsdale, NJ: Lawrence Erlbaum Associates.

van Dellen, H. J., Brookhuis, K. A., Mulder, G., Okita, T., & Mulder, L. J. M. (1985). Evoked potential correlates of practice in a visual search task. In D. Papakoustopoulos, S. Butler, & I. Martin (Eds.), *Clinical and experimental neurophysiology* (pp. 32–155). Beckenham: Croom Helm.

Veltman, H., Mulder, G., Mulder, L. J. M., & Wijers, A. A. (in preparation). Resource-specificity of endogenous components in brain evoked potentials and of cardiovascular indices. Unpublished manuscript.

Vicente, K. J., Thornton, D. C., & Moray, N. (1987). Spectral analysis of sinus arrhythmia: A measure of mental effort. *Human Factors, 29,* 171–182.

Wickens, C. D. (1984). Processing resources in attention. In R. Nickerson & R. Pew (Eds.), *Attention and performance VIII* (pp. 63–102). Hillsdale, NJ: Lawrence Erlbaum Associates.

Wijers, A. A., Feenstra, S., Otten, L., & Mulder, G. (in press). Brain potentials during selective attention, memory search, and mental rotation. *Psychophysiology.*

Wijers, A. A., Mulder, G., Okita, T., & Mulder, L. J. M. (in press). An ERP study on memory search and selective attention to letter size and conjunctions of letter size and color. *Psychophysiology.*

Wijers, A. A., Mulder, G., Okita, T., Mulder, L. J. M., & Scheffers, M. K. (1988). Attention to colour: An ERP-analysis of selection, controlled search, and motor activation. *Psychophysiology, 26,* 89–109.

Cognitive–Conative Aptitude Interactions in Learning

Richard E. Snow
Stanford University

As a graduate student in 1961, I decided to devote myself to the study of individual differences and their relation to learning, particularly under instructional conditions. One key influence on that decision was a book J. J. Jenkins and D. G. Paterson (1961) had just published, entitled *Studies in Individual Differences*. Thus, it is a special treat and honor for me that Professor Jenkins is the general discussant for this conference and book.

The Jenkins–Paterson book reprints many classic papers in research on intelligence from Galton, Binet, Spearman, and Thorndike, on down to Cattell, Anastasi, and Guilford, among many others. It is a treasure trove of history that current researchers should not ignore. It is particularly noteworthy that several pieces in the book, especially those from Thurstone (1948), Wechsler (1950), and Gough (1953), point in one way or another to the topic of this conference and book, and to my own concern with cognitive–conative aptitude interactions. Thurstone (1948) argued for erasing the artificial distinction between intelligence and temperament, noting that experimental study of reaction time for different kinds of cognitive responses should reflect both abilities and temperaments. Wechsler (1950) argued against the common conception of intelligence as displayed only in cognitive ability constructs, suggesting that personality characteristics clearly function with abilities during adaptation, adjustment, and achievement in intellectual performance. He identified need for achievement, interests, purposeful consistency, and perseveration as important aspects of this conative side of performance but also noted the weakness of research that relies only on conventional personality questionnaires. Gough (1953) then provided evidence on a questionnaire measure of *intellectual efficiency,* including items pertaining to self-confidence, freedom from fears, effective social adjustment, and wide interests, particularly in intellectual pursuits. In Gough's study, clinical judges also chose adjectives to describe high scorers on this scale as *adaptable, conscientious,, energetic, persistent, responsible,* and *thorough.* The reported correlations between this intellectual efficiency scale and intelligence tests were substantial. Gough thus included the scale in his California Psychological Inventory (CPI).

My reasons for citing these early papers are only partly historical. It *is* worth knowing for the history of the field that in the 1950s these authors, and Jenkins and Paterson, as well as others (Cronbach, 1957), thought that differential psychology was ready to turn to the study of cognitive–conative interactions, and to do so with a marriage of correlational and experimental methods. It is also worth knowing that the old literature contains important leads for modern hypothesizing. But the cognitive information-processing revolution that took center stage from the 1960s on in experimental psychology left motivation waiting in the wings (Norman, 1980) and left the rest of conation out altogether (Snow & Farr, 1987). Still another reason for citing the ideas of Thurstone, Wechsler, and Gough, however, is that I also must rely on the language of personality, temperament, and interest scales as at least potentially indicative of conative aptitude constructs that deserve detailed process analysis in the next stage of research. This chapter includes some evidence relating Wechsler intelligence to conative constructs derived from Gough's CPI and also from the Strong–Campbell Interest Inventory (SCII). Both of these instruments are strongly associated with the University of Minnesota, so evidence about them seems particularly appropriate for this conference.

The history of my own research in this field since 1961 need not be reviewed here (see Snow, 1989). Over this period, some investigators have kept an eye on research on personality and motivational differences in relation to learning. But most have concentrated on building cognitive theories of abilities in learning and problem solving. And there have been many advances. With these advances, research attention has now returned to consider anew how conative and affective characteristics of persons might be brought into the rapidly developing models of cognitive characteristics (see, e.g., Clark & Fiske, 1982; Snow & Farr, 1987; Sorrentino & Higgins, 1986). This initiative is particularly important for research on learning from *instruction,* I believe, because it is unlikely that individual differences in aptitude for learning in educational settings can ever be explained by cognitive theory alone (Snow, 1987, 1989). Unfortunately, however, despite the early papers cited and much other work on personality, the history of differential psychology does not provide a well-organized correlational map of individual difference constructs in the conative and affective domains of personality, and their relation to cognitive abilities, with which to start. As I argue later, the construction of such a map is a critical early step in guiding the needed process analytic research.

Thus, the main purpose of this chapter is to begin the construction of a correlational map of the cognitive–conative aptitude space. In pursuing this purpose, the chapter revisits some of the older aptitude-treatment interaction (ATI) studies and some of the newer analysis of cognitive and conative processes as a base for some speculations about the kind of theoretical map that might bring cognitive and conative aptitude constructs together in research on learning. Some methodological problems and possibilities are also noted.

A GENERAL APPROACH TO APTITUDE ANALYSIS

It should help at first to explain my general approach to the problem, the choice of evidence to attend to, and the emphasis on building correlational maps of an aptitude domain. The approach to be recommended is discussed elsewhere (Snow, 1987, 1989) and exemplified as applied to research on cognitive aptitude for learning (Snow & Lohman, 1984), so the argument and examples can be abstracted here. Fig. 15.1 provides an outline.

Because the catalogue of individual differences constructs and measures produced by differential psychologists over the decades is vast, one has to have

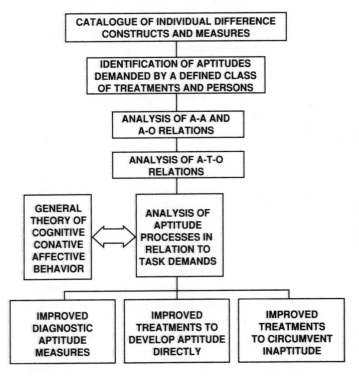

FIG. 15.1.   A general approach to aptitude analysis.

some kind of priority list; the first problem is to decide what individual difference constructs to investigate in relation to learning and how to investigate them with earliest solid payoff. Until recently, differential psychology has not been particularly helpful here, so it is no wonder that experimentalists interested in learning have often thrown up their hands in dismay at the vague admonition to "pay attention to individual differences"; they rightly reply: "Tell us which ones." This is one purpose of constructing an initial map of individual difference constructs that appear correlated with the particular kind of learning of interest. A closely related purpose is to keep track of the correlates while any one construct is investigated; the construct validity of particular interpretations is an ever-present concern.

The first step, then, must be to identify those individual difference constructs in the vast differential catalogue that seem most likely to serve as aptitudes in the defined class of tasks or situations (i.e., treatments) and persons of interest. If we are interested in learning of the sort valued in schools and colleges, it is no wonder that the first aptitude construct chosen for study has been general cognitive ability as reflected in intelligence tests; the situation of interest demands learning from incomplete instruction and there is much evidence that intelligence measures predict learning outcomes (the aptitude-outcome, or A-O relations, in Fig. 15.1) in such situations. Indeed, that is what intelligence measures were designed to do. There are, however, other kinds of learning in other kinds of persons, so scholastic ability might not always be the first aptitude construct of choice; think of psychomotor learning in an industrial or military situation where trainees have been preselected on general ability measures, for example.

A Provisional Map of Cognitive Aptitude-Learning Relations

In research on aptitude for learning from instruction, at any rate, general cognitive abilities are the first choice and the next step is to analyze the A-A relations (that is, the relations among related aptitude constructs and measures), as well as the A-O relations to produce a correlational map of the aptitude-learning domain. In recent decades, this line of correlational research has progressed significantly toward more complete and sharply defined models of ability factor structure through the work of Carroll (1985, in preparation) and Gustafsson (1984), among others. Some of our project work has sought to bring learning tasks into the same structure (Snow, 1980; Snow, Kyllonen, & Marshalek, 1984). The result is a topographic correlational map as shown in Fig. 15.2. This is a radex model (in the style of Guttman, 1970) based on nonmetric multidimensional scaling methods, but it is conformable with the hierarchical factor models of Carroll and Gustafson.

In the Figure, ability tests are indicated by dots; those that typically occur in the same factor are connected by solid lines and labeled with the factor name. We

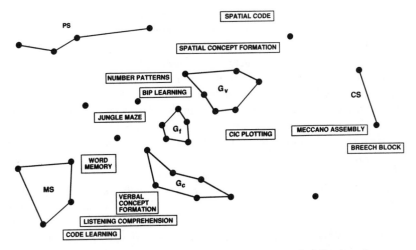

FIG. 15.2. A schematic multidimensional scaling of ability-learning correlations. (G_f = fluid intelligence, G_c = crystallized intelligence, G_v = visualization, MS = memory span, PS = perceptual speed, CS = closure speed)

have produced such scaling solutions based on empirical test correlations in a sample of 241 high school students (the HS sample) and in a sample of 124 Stanford University undergraduates (the SU sample); however, the SU sample, with its restricted range due to academic selection, shows a pinched, somewhat asymmetric pattern. It is noteworthy that both solutions imply a kind of topographic model in which the information-processing complexity apparently required by each test increases as one steps in from the periphery toward the central region. It is also possible to locate various learning tasks in such a radex map, indicated in Fig. 15.2 by labeled squares placed between ability factors. These are drawn in hypothetically, based on correlations between ability factors and learning tasks obtained in other samples (see Snow, Kyllonen, & Marshalek, 1984, regarding the HS sample) or in subsamples (see Snow, Wescourt, & Collins, 1979, regarding the SU sample). The result is a schematic map of ability-learning relations to suggest what proximal ability and learning tasks might be subjected to joint process analyses.

At this point, the next step in our outline (back in Fig. 15.1) brings in existing evidence on aptitude-treatment interactions in predicting learning outcomes (A-T-O relations). In instructional research, there is much evidence that the more general abilities (G_f and G_c) in the center of the radex map often interact with instructional treatment variables reflecting variation in structure and completeness in instruction; these abilities relate strongly to learning in less complete, less structured situations and relate less strongly to learning in more complete, more structured situations (Cronbach & Snow, 1977; Snow, 1977). A schematic representation of this common ATI finding is depicted in Fig. 15.3a. High structure appears to help less able learners but often seems to hurt more able learners, relative to less structured instruction. It is noteworthy that students of high ability placed in a high structure condition, when interviewed, often give evidence of both cognitive and conative problems; they say they experience cognitive interference or motivational turn-off trying to conform to a structured treatment that prevents them from learning in their own way. This completeness or structure contrast is a broadly important treatment variable across many otherwise different instructional and training situations, so it deserves priority attention in further analysis.

The ATI demonstration is a particularly important step because it suggests how the aptitude-learning relation can be experimentally manipulated and thus better understood. We need to know, in other words, which aptitudes are functionally involved in learning and how their relations to learning can be experimentally controlled by what experimental variables. Beyond the simple generalization of Fig. 15.3a, furthermore, experimental manipulation can also suggest how pairs of aptitude variables function interactively in learning. Fig. 15.3b shows an example of ATI effects in a portion of a bivariate aptitude distribution involving prior knowledge and quantitative ability. The experiment contrasted live versus filmed physics demonstrations in a semester-long introductory undergraduate course. The result indicates that performance immediately after demonstrations was superior under live conditions for students high in ability (Q) and low in prior knowledge of physics (K) but superior under film conditions for students low in Q but high in K. The effect persisted on a delayed recall measure. The interpretation was that the live condition permits and requires the exercise of mathematical ability in understanding the demonstrations, particularly their mathematical formulations, which were often done incompletely or hurriedly by the live instructor on an overhead projector. That is, the relatively incomplete and less structured live demonstration demanded more complex and inferential mathematical processing to comprehend, especially if prior knowledge of relevant physics was low. In the films, the mathematics was presented in a complete and simpler, well-structured fashion, well integrated with the physics of the demonstration. This is a particular benefit for the low ability student with good prior physics knowledge, but no benefit for the more mathematically able, less informed student (for details, see Snow, Tiffin, & Seibert, 1965). In short, here is an example of how ATI experiments can be used to dissect functionally different aspects of cognitive aptitude operating in learning from instruction.

These examples also suggest how certain instructional task conditions can be mapped into the radex structure. One could tag certain ability constructs or learning tasks, or pairs, to show the instructional conditions predicted to make relations stronger or weaker. I chose not to clutter Fig. 15.2 this way, but the reader can imagine what would result.

There is no claim that such maps are complete—only that they offer a good summary of evidence so far on cognitive ability and meaningful learning, includ-

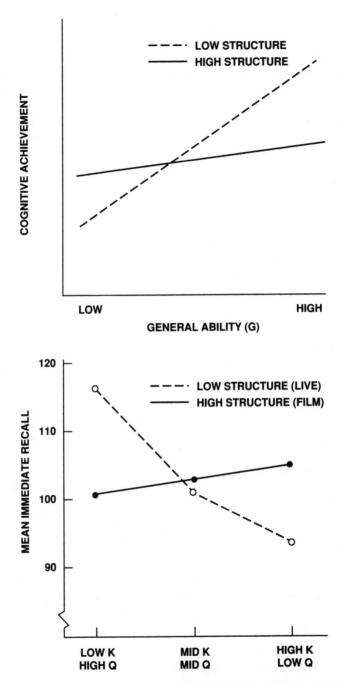

FIG. 15.3. Graphs of cognitive aptitude-treatment interactions when high and low structure instructional treatments are contrasted, showing (a) the typical result with general ability (*G*) as aptitude and (b) an empirical result distinguishing prior knowledge (*K*) and quantitative ability (*Q*) as aptitudes.

ing learning from incomplete instruction. This provides a guide for joint process analysis of cognitive ability and learning constructs. Thurstone (1947) argued long ago for exactly this use of exploratory factor analysis. The topography of ability test and factor correlations first provides a rough map to guide experimental analyses of performance processes in the most important ability tests and learning tasks, and then helps tie the results of these analyses back again into the broader network of ability constructs. Process analysis of particular tasks has now produced models of some of the component processes and strategies associated with particular central ability constructs (Bethell-Fox, Lohman, & Snow, 1984; Kyllonen, Lohman, & Woltz, 1984; Pellegrino & Glaser, 1980; Sternberg, 1985a, 1985b), and has also been extended to examine individual differences in learning—to trace process-level constructs through the stages of skill and knowledge acquisition in particular tasks (Ackerman, 1986, 1987; Snow & Lohman, 1984; Sternberg, 1985a). There are also important advances in the joint measurement of ability and learning differences using so-called dynamic procedures, wherein ability assessment and learning conditions are integrated (Brown & Ferrara, 1985; Campione & Brown, 1987). And, some studies (Kyllonen, Lohman, & Woltz, 1984; Pellegrino, 1984) have begun to show why there appears to be a continuum of information-processing complexity in the radex map, as one moves from simpler tasks in the periphery of the radex to complex tasks in the center. In short, the tests close to the center of the radex are tests that produce high correlation with complex learning under incomplete instruction, and they are also the ones that require adaptive strategy shifting during performance; perhaps, therefore, flexible strategic assembly and adaptation is a common aspect of general ability test performance, and also learning performance when instruction is relatively unstructured and incomplete.

Thus, cognitive psychology has been working back and forth across the arrow connecting the two central boxes back in Fig. 15.1. Detailed analyses of Raven Matrices, letter series, analogies, and other central tasks are now in hand. Guided by the map, the results can be tied back in to produce process models of the G_f, G_c, G_v and other ability constructs and their role in learning from instruction. A theory of cognitive aptitude is thus built up. The final outcome, as suggested at the bottom of Fig. 15.1, will hopefully be the production of improved diagnostic aptitude measures, improved instructional treatments that train the development of learning aptitudes directly, and improved instructional designs that allow circumvention of stubborn inaptitudes that cannot readily be removed by direct training (see Snow, 1982).

A Provisional Model of Cognitive Aptitude-Learning Interactions

At present, a provisional, admittedly vague theory of cognitive aptitude for learning from instruction can be summarized as follows (see Snow & Lohman, 1984, for details). Fig. 15.4 provides a schematic representation to suggest that

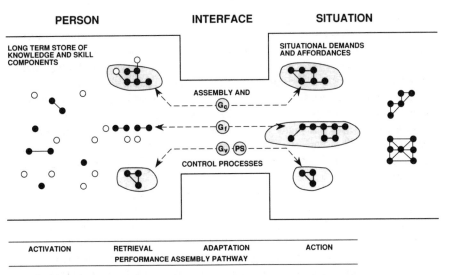

FIG. 15.4. A schematic flowchart of the person–situation interface suggesting phases of a performance assembly pathway and some contrasts between fluid (G_f), crystallized (G_c), and special abilities (G_v and PS), in the face of situational demands and affordances.

persons must assemble their performances in the person–situation interface. Aptitude differences show through in the organizational assembly and control activities learners use to adapt to new instruction. These are the same activities learners use to adapt their performance in complex cognitive ability tests. The individual's cognitive system is considered a very large bank containing bits of experience, components of skills, and chunks of knowledge, from which samples are drawn according to the demands and affordances of particular cognitive and learning tasks, in particular instructional conditions. Persons assemble performance strategies from this bank and adapt them to the task conditions as they unfold. The three major cognitive aptitude constructs can be distinguished in this strategic assembly and control process. Fluid intelligence (G_f) reflects the more flexible assembly and adaptation of strategies for performance in novel unfamiliar tasks. Crystallized intelligence (G_c) reflects more the retrieval and adaptation of old assemblies for familiar tasks. Visualization (G_v) ability reflects a collection of specialized spatial skills that pop in and out of relevance in a variety of tasks that afford their use; other special abilities such as Memory Span (MS), Perceptual Speed (PS) and Closure Speed (CS) can be similarly regarded.

Fig. 15.4 suggests that there is a performance assembly pathway, from *activation* in and *retrieval* from the person's bank of experience, to *adaptation* in the person–situation interface, to *action* in the task or instructional situation. The situation demands or affords certain systems of component processes in action that may or may not already be systematized, or crystallized, in the prior experience bank of the person. To the extent that prior knowledge and skill assemblies can be used with minor or no adaptation in the situation at hand, G_c and the special abilities will reflect the more relevant aptitude differences. To the extent that major adaptation of prior assemblies or the development of entirely new assemblies is required, G_f will show as the more relevant aptitude. Most instructional situations, of course, will require some mixture. But each situation will have a characteristic demand (or affordance) profile. An analysis of this profile with respect to familiarity–novelty, structure–completeness, and the use of special knowledge and skills will provide a picture of its cognitive aptitude requirements.

Although much further research in this direction is still needed, another principal need now is to bring conative aptitudes into this picture, to study their joint role in learning with cognitive aptitudes. We thus need to go again through the steps of Fig. 15.1. We need studies of A-A and A-O relations in these domains. We need to identify the most likely aptitude constructs in relation to instructional treatment variables already known to be broadly important through ATI research. We then need to construct some kind of map of the constructs in this space (which may be quite different from the cognitive ability and learning radex of Fig. 15.2). This map can then guide process analyses of these constructs operating in learning and can help to tie the results of more focused, narrow experiments back together again into theories of cognitive–conative aptitude complexes in learning from complex instruction.

TOWARD A LIST OF CONATIVE APTITUDES

Unfortunately, in the case of conative aptitudes, we do not have a large cache of A-A and A-O relations to rely on for a map, as we did with respect to cognitive abilities. Many correlational studies of personality dimensions have been reported, but they tend to be oriented toward general theory (e.g., Cattell, 1957; Eysenck, 1982; Guilford, 1959) or toward the identification of aptitude or outcome measures relevant to clinical situations; correlations with ability, learning, or instructional situations are spotty (but see Cattell & Butcher, 1968). Furthermore, much of this work has been conducted within the dimensional structure of a particular questionnaire instrument, rather than across instruments, and has routinely imposed linear models on the data. Thus, in the domain of conative aptitudes for learning from instruction, we can only start with some rough taxonomy and what A-A, A-O, and A-T-O evidence we can scrape together to formulate a tentative list of aptitude constructs apparently worth further attention. As the prior evidence mostly rests on questionnaire measures and the linearity assumption, we will need to be particularly sensitive to other possibilities.

Some A-A and A-O Relations

One good place to start is with Wechsler's (1950) list previously noted, because it matches reasonably well with factor analytic studies of school motivation, some of which are based on interview as well as questionnaire data. Table 15.1 lists Wechsler's hypotheses in three, slightly generalized categories called *achievement motivation, interest,* and *volition.*

In the middle three columns of Table 15.1 are shown the results of three lines of factor analytic research on school motivation, conducted by Chiu (1967) in the United States and by Entwistle, Kozeki, and others in Europe (Entwistle, Kozeki, & Balarabe, 1988, bring this work together, and these columns of Table 15.1 are adapted from their Table). In each column, the distinct dimensions from each line of work are listed. The rows imply rough equivalences across some of the factors in each column, within Wechsler's categories. So, for example, the achievement motivation category includes two factors identified by Chiu, one factor from Kozeki and three from Entwistle; but one of these is essentially the same across studies, though described somewhat differently in each. In the last column of Table 15.1, I have tried to reach construct labels that generalize across the row and that hold promise of connecting with other extant theories and measures. Thus, this first row is labeled *need for achievement* (A_n). A second factor common to Chiu and Entwistle seems clearly to identify fear of failure, which is usually taken to be equivalent to *evaluation anxiety* (A_x). These are the two constituent individual difference constructs of the Atkinson and Feather (1966) theory of achievement motivation, so in this first of Wechsler's categories, we also have a strong process theory of aptitude.

Achievement motivation theory has been substantially elaborated in recent years (see Heckhausen, Schmalt, & Schneider, 1985), as have related theories of anxiety (Sarason, 1980) and attributions of success and failure (Weiner, 1986). But the basic theory still predicts that achievement motivation (the resultant of A_n and A_x will show linear relation to learning outcome when measured as cumulative academic performance but curvilinear relation when immediate learning performance is measured. Lens (1983, 1986) has now shown that examination performance at the end of an undergraduate course displays clear curvilinear relation to both A_n and A_x; optimum performance came from those students with middle positions on both scales and trailed off as students displayed high or low positions on either the A_x or A_n scale. For A_n and A_x, then, curvilinearity in relation to immediate cognitive task performance may be expected. The lack of linear relation to cognitive measures for these conative measures is thus not a cause for no conclusion; it is rather a cause for detective work in bivariate scatterplots.

Wechsler's second category in Table 15.1 contains interests, and the school motivation factors seem to reflect this. Yet this category poses a problem. Interests must be multivariate, and are probably best thought of as hierarchically

TABLE 15.1
Conative Aptitude Constructs Based on Factor Analyses of School Motivation

Wechsler Categories	Chiu Factors	Kozeki Factors	Entwistle Factors	Snow Identifications
	Positive orientation to school learning	Competence thru seeking knowledge	Hope for success	A_n
Achievement Motivation	Failure avoidance		Fear of failure	A_x
			Instrumental motivation	
Interests	Curiosity	Interest in schoolwork	Intrinsic motivation	HI etc.; learning task interests
	Conformity	Compliance with authority	Conscientiousness	CR
		Responsibility for own actions		
Volition	Need for social recognition	Independence and self-confidence		IF
		Identification with teachers		
		Cooperation with peers		EA
		Warm relations with parents		

organized with respect to more distal and more proximal personal goals. Furthermore, broad interest factors predict long-range satisfaction but have not been found related to learning or achievement criteria (Cronbach, 1984). Perhaps there is a curvilinearity problem here too. But there are also both theoretical and new empirical reasons for promoting research on interests as conative aptitudes in relation to school learning. At the broadest level, there is Holland's (1966, 1973) theory of person–situation types related to long-range goals as well as to more immediate situational preference and goals. These are measured as six higher-order dimensions derived from the 23 basic interest scales of the SCII, identified hereafter as *Holland Realistic* (HR), *Investigative* (HI), *Artistic* (HA), *Social* (HS), *Enterprising* (HE), and *Conventional* (HC) dimensions. HI would presumably be most generally relevant to higher academic learning, but other scales or combinations might indicate aptitudes for particular instructional situations.

Beneath these there is now research suggesting that basic interests in different school subjects and activities can indeed be related significantly to cognitive abilities and achievements (Gustafsson & Undheim, 1986). And analyses of interests at the paragraph and page level in school text materials is showing especially strong effects on learning and retention—effects that appear to rival ability-learning relations in size (Anderson, Shirey, Wilson, & Fielding, 1987; Schiefele & Krapp, 1988; Schiefele, Krapp, & Winteler, 1988). There is much other new work on interest in relation to motivation and learning, especially in Europe. Thus, interests deserve new attention as conative aptitudes that may predispose curiosity, intrinsic motivation, and related activities in school work. In this row of Table 15.1, therefore, HI and the general notation of "learning task interests" are listed, but there is a range of possible intermediate constructs here.

The third category in Table 15.1 is called volition to include Wechsler's hypotheses about purposeful striving and perseveration. Here, there are several factor distinctions, especially in Kozeki's work. But they can be grouped clearly into three dimensions, termed here *Conformity–Responsibility* (CR), *Independence–Flexibility* (IF), and *Extraversion–Ascendancy* (EA). These labels are chosen because they seem to fit not only Entwistle's summary but also the results of many factor analyses of the CPI (see Megargee, 1972), as well as several A-O and A-T-O results to be described later.

To demonstrate, all three factors were derived from a factor analysis of the CPI administered to the same Stanford student sample used in our ability scaling work. The results are shown in Table 15.2. The first factor has been identified frequently and is usually interpreted as indicating positive adjustment by social conformity, self-control, and responsibility, hence CR for short. The second factor has also been frequently found; it is often interpreted as extraversion, social poise, assertive self-assurance, and social dominance, hence EA. The third factor is called IF to capture the usual interpretation emphasizing adaptive

TABLE 15.2
Rotated Factor Pattern for the Scales of the California Psychological
Inventory (CPI) in a sample of Stanford Undergraduates (N = 121)[a]

CPI Scale		Factor Symbol				
Symbol	Name	CR	EA	IF	CI	MF
Do	Dominance		63			
Cs	Capacity for Status		70			
Sy	Sociability		86			
Sp	Social Presence		75			
Sa	Self-Acceptance		85			
Wb	Sense of Well Being	62	32			−36
Re	Responsibility	55				
So	Socialization	48			62	
Sc	Self-Control	82				
To	Tolerance	52		58		
Gi	Good Impression	92				
Cm	Communality				38	
Ac	Achievement via Conformance	68				
Ai	Achievement via Independence	36		68		
Ie	Intellectual Efficiency			62		
Py	Psychological Mindedness			60		
Fx	Flexibility			70	−44	
Fe	Femininity					67

[a]Decimals omitted. Loadings less than .36 omitted.

autonomy and independence in thought and action. Notice that it includes Gough's (1953) Intellectual Efficiency scale referred to in this chapter's introduction as showing strong correlation with intelligence measures.

The two other factors in Table 15.2 are probably of minor significance judging from past research (Megargee, 1972). They are usually called *Conventional–Inflexible* (CI) and *Masculinity–Femininity* (MF).

There is a growing body of process theory and research also in this volition category. In particular, the recent work of Heckhausen and Kuhl (1985; Kuhl, 1986) not only ties achievement motivation and volition together along an information-processing pathway called the commitment continuum but also seems consistent with my model of cognitive aptitude processes in learning from instruction described earlier. It thus may help to relate the motivational and volitional aptitude constructs identified earlier to cognitive aptitudes in learning and to one another. The theory posits a commitment continuum along which wishes are transformed to wants, then to intentions, and then to actions. The transition from wants to intentions crosses a kind of Rubicon that separates achievement motivation from volition and action control. Particularly in this volitional or intention–action part of the pathway, there are individual differences in action tendencies and in the need or ability to protect one's intention–action tendencies from competing tendencies. The volitional aptitude constructs already identified can be interpreted as individual differences of this sort and different learning or instructional situations can be expected to favor one or another of these tendencies. There is some A-O evidence to suggest this.

The Achievement via Conformance scale of the CPI and a constituent of the CR factor in Table 15.2 has been shown to correlate with academic achievement, particularly in situations where compliance with teacher structure seems to be functional (Rutkowski & Domino, 1975; Snow, 1977). Some of these studies also show the CPI Achievement via Independence scale to predict achievement in relatively unstructured independent learning situations. This scale is a constituent of IF in Table 15.2.

Some data from one of my own project studies suggest further that IF can correlate with learning activities as well as achievement. A sample of 28 of the Stanford undergraduates from my CPI factor analysis learned BASIC computer programing via an adaptive computer-based instructional program called BIP. In BIP, students work on their own, logging on whenever they choose, day or night. BIP adapts the sequence of instructional tasks to fit student skill acquisition, offers an assortment of hints and other aids, and also records many details of student learning activities. A slope measure reflecting individual differences in rate of skill acquisition across an accumulated 15 hours of instruction in BIP, and also an achievement posttest, were strongly predicted by G_f ability factor scores but also by IF factor scores. And IF related also to some indices of each student's learning activities while proceeding through the program. G_f and IF were uncorrelated in this sample (see Snow, 1980). Thus, BIP is identified back in Fig. 15.2 as an instructional treatment related to G_f but it is clearly also related to IF.

A powerful demonstration of the role of some other of these proposed conative constructs also comes from a military training study, which supports the notion of key transition points to be identified along the commitment continuum proposed by Heckhausen and Kuhl. Lambrechts (no date) administered a battery of personality inventories to all volunteers for the Belgian Navy diving school. For a period of 3 years, however, volunteers were accepted without reference to the personality data; only the standard cognitive aptitude and medical examinations governed selection. Final data for the validation study were available from 80 candidates who subsequently succeeded in the training course and 30 candidates who subsequently failed.

Fig. 15.5 displays one of those rare instances in which linear personality differences can be judged by interoccular trauma test. The Figure includes the personality scales available from the most clearly interpretable measures used by Lambrechts, but the results from other instruments not shown are not inconsistent. The scales are here arranged in order to suggest that two of the conative constructs discussed earlier, EA and A_x, may account for the results. However, the correlations among scales that would be needed to test proximity among scales placed together here were not reported by Lambrechts.

It seems clear that successful and unsuccessful diver candidates differ pri-

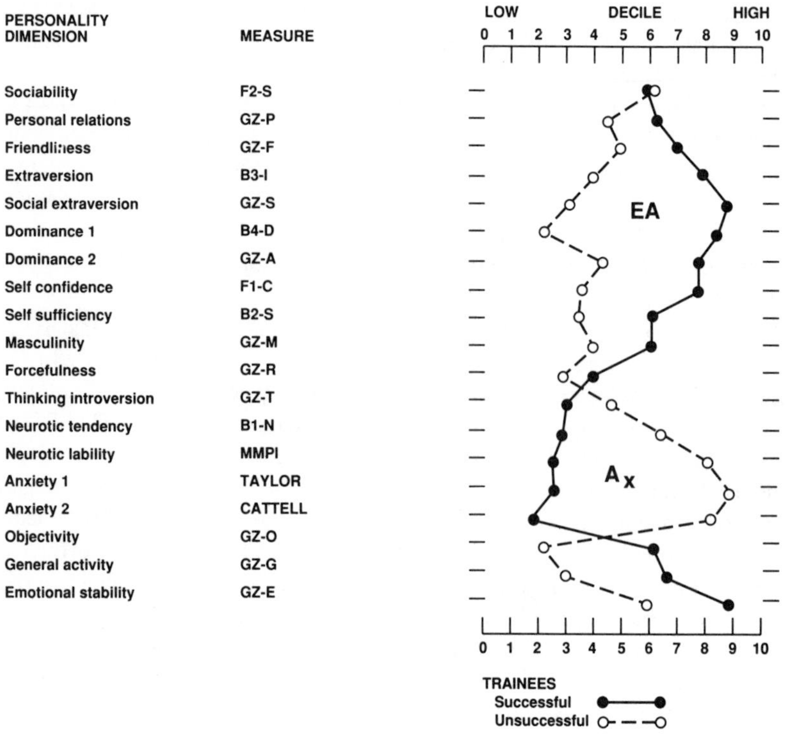

FIG. 15.5. Personality profiles of successful (•) and unsuccessful (○) diver trainees with scales derived from Guilford–Zimmerman (G-Z), Bernreuter (B1 to 4, F1 to 2) and Minnesota Multiphasic (MMPI) inventories (data from Lambrechts, no date).

marily in the two regions identified as EA and A_x, Lambrechts reported that although diver candidates were dropped from, or dropped out of, the training program at various points, a substantial number failed as training moved from pool diving to open-sea conditions. This is consistent with the hypothesis that increase in state anxiety multiplies individual differences in the relevant, conative aptitudes; successful diver candidates appear to be those low enough in A_x and high enough in EA to cope with state anxiety as training progresses. The result is also consistent with the Heckhausen–Kuhl model; the shift from pool to ocean crosses a Rubicon and changes the conative, wish–action pathway. Novice divers whose levels of EA and A_x cannot sustain their original action pathway change their intentions and drop out. A methodological note here is that there may be key points of conative transition in learning or training sequences; conative aptitudes may be critical at these points and not elsewhere in the sequence. Analytic research on any particular learning or training task needs to find and focus on these points.

Some A-T-O Evidence

Let us turn now to some previous instructional ATI studies that included aptitude variables from both cognitive and conative categories, even though in these studies the aptitude constructs may have been analyzed one at a time. Of particular interest here are studies that contrast high structure and completeness with low structure and incompleteness as instructional treatments and that suggest the joint action of cognitive and conative aptitudes in learning.

It is not difficult to find examples showing that both cognitive and conative aptitude measures enter into ATI in instructional experiments. Fig. 15.6 gives some further ATI results from the same study of filmed versus live physics demonstrations cited earlier (see Snow, Tiffin, & Seibert, 1965, for details). In Fig.15.6a and 15.6b, results for the ascendancy and responsibility scales from a forced-choice personality questionnaire called the Gordon Personal Profile (Gordon, 1953) are shown to yield ATI. The results were clear for immediate but not delayed achievement measures. The interpretation was that the film condition can have an adverse effect on learning in some individuals because it removes the active interpersonal character of instructor demonstrations and may foster a passive spectator state of mind; ascendant, self-assertive, more socially dominant personalities and those described as relatively irresponsible are either frustrated by the private nature of the film learning tasks or are allowed to escape mentally from learning in them, respectively. The effect does not show on delayed measures because the intervening instruction allows those who did not get the film messages to recoup their temporary losses. If ascendancy and responsibility as here measured can be interpreted as reflecting EA and CR from our CPI analysis, then these ATI findings tie in with the other work.

Fig. 15.6c involves an aptitude measure reflecting past student use of the Purdue instructional film library, which is an extensive collection, organized to allow private viewing of both instructor-assigned and student-chosen film learning tasks, as well as some entertainment films. The cognitive implication here was that past film library use represents film learning experience—a kind of learning-to-learn from film that has been called film literacy. But it should not be thought of as only cognitive; active pursuit of film learning experience on one's own implies volitional and interest orientations. Perhaps this result hints at a learning task interest factor as aptitude. As shown here, such a film learning interest or set appeared to be particularly valuable for those without substantial prior knowledge of physics. There was some evidence also (not shown) that prior film experience was increasingly valuable as stages of the filmed treatment progressed over the course.

In sum, then, in these studies live learning tasks were best for students described as high in mathematical ability but low in prior physics knowledge *or* ascendant, assertive, self-assured, active, and independent *or* flighty, irresponsible, and unable to stick to tasks that do not interest them *or* unlikely to seek film learning experience on their own. Film learning tasks were best for students

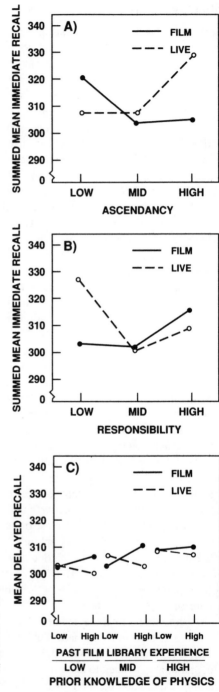

FIG. 15.6. Graphs of conative aptitude-treatment interactions when filmed and live instructional treatments are contrasted, showing empirical results with (a) ascendancy, (b) responsibility, and (c) past experience with instructional film crossed with prior knowledge of physics as aptitudes.

described as low in mathematical ability but high in prior physics knowledge *or* passive observers, lacking in self confidence *or* responsible and conscientious *or* likely to seek film learning experience on their own. A methodological criticism is obvious; these variables should have been studied jointly as aptitude complexes, not as a list of independent descriptors.

A substantial amount of ATI evidence also implicates some of our other constructs in relation to instructional treatment structure—A_x and IF, as well as CR and EA—as conative aptitudes worthy of attention. The two studies summarized here are dissertations by Peterson (1976) and Porteus (1976), but there are other similar results (see Snow 1977, 1987, for details).

Both studies used high school students and both contrasted high versus low structure treatment groups. Peterson used a two-week unit in four social studies classes. Porteus used most of two year-long courses in economics and philosophy. Both included measures of G and A_x as aptitudes but also the achievement via independence (IF) and achievement via conformance (CR) scales from the CPI. Both studies gave striking and similar ATI results. The G × A_x × Treatment Structure interactions suggested that nonanxious learners who lack sufficient ability and able learners who are also highly anxious both need external structure to do well. The less able, less anxious (underaroused) students need to be shown directly and to be externally motivated to do the required things, whereas the more able but anxious (overaroused) students need the certainty that they are doing the required things. Without the external direction and control provided by the high structure treatment, the former students remain lost and apathetic, whereas the latter lose themselves through frantic shifts of attention and effort. This last point is especially consistent with an attentional explanation in which anxiousness in otherwise able learners produces worrisome thoughts, self-doubts, and other intrusions that shift attention to the self and away from the task. External structure in the instructional task should limit such negative intrusions; lack of external structure should allow them.

To use current anxiety theory, both the high G-high A_x and the low G-low A_x students need to reach an optimal level of state anxiety for effective performance. External direction brings the high-high students down to this level; external demand brings the low-low students up to this level. Instruction that provides neither fails both kinds of student. The able nonanxious students, on the other hand, are benefited by the absence of formal structure. They can provide their own structure and work independently, and presumably prefer to do so; they do not need structure imposed by teachers or others. It is not clear, however, why the lack of such structure is beneficial to low G-high A_x students. Again following current theory, perhaps anxiety for these students already serves an optimal activating function so situational demand is unnecessary, even debilitating. Without imposed structure and participation, these students can work inconspicuously.

The other ATI result, which was strong mainly in the Peterson study, can be interpreted as an (IF-CR) × Treatment Structure interaction. It suggests that students scoring relatively higher on IF than on CR are better served by low-structure instruction, whereas those scoring relatively higher on CR than on IF do better under high-structure instruction. One can interpret the difference score between IF and CR as relative orientation toward independence versus conformance. It is important to note that this is a significant ATI on the same sample as the previously discussed G × A_x interaction. The higher-order interaction involving all four aptitude constructs was not tested; this would have exceeded the statistical limits of the study. But there are some modest correlations among the four aptitudes; they are not linearly independent. So we can entertain the possibility that a four-way aptitude space rather than two, two-way aptitude spaces would capture both ATI in the same picture and perhaps suggest aptitude complexes (see Snow, 1987).

Summary

The loose network of constructs here extracted is certainly not exhaustive or definitive as a list of cognitive and conative aptitudes for learning. Each construct can be elaborated, analyzed, and interrelated, and much other evidence not cited here can be brought to bear in this work. Though this list is so far limited to vague personality labels, it need not be viewed theoretically as a list of traits. It is rather a list of provisional categories of readiness for learning in certain types of instructional situations. There is at least some evidence connecting each construct to learning under some kind of instructional or training conditions. And it is noteworthy that the instructional treatment variables that seem to control their relations to learning measures are quite similar. In several instances, evidence suggests that several constructs may operate interactively in aptitude complexes.

TOWARD ANALYSES OF CONATIVE APTITUDES

Analysis of the conative aptitudes and possible aptitude complexes identified previously is the task now before us. And the task includes the study of cognitive-conative process interactions. The strategies and processes that seem to distinguish more and less able cognitive test performers, and presumably more and less able learners, have *both* a conative and a cognitive character. We have really only begun the task of detailing some of the motivational and volitional processes that might operate in learning, and this work has so far not focused on aptitude differences. But the molar conative aptitude constructs identified earlier can be connected to some of the process analysis already in hand. This may suggest how to study individual differences in these processes.

As noted earlier, I favor for this purpose the theory of Heckhausen and Kuhl with its emphasis on the conative commitment continuum. Their questions are:

What is commitment? What processes transform wishes to wants, to intentions, to actions? What keeps some wishes, wants, and intentions from progressing to actions? What regulates the temporal flow of actions and their effects on subsequent actions? Fig. 15.7 shows the detailed continuum model with which Heckhausen and Kuhl are working. It derives from the extensive prior research done by Heckhausen on the expectancy × value theory of achievement motivation and by Kuhl on a theory of volition and action control (see Heckhausen, 1974, 1977, 1980, 1981; Kuhl, 1984, 1985, 1986). Primary attention focuses on approach tendencies related to positively valued goals, but tendencies to avoid negative or aversive events, though they involve other complications, are also considered. In the model, there are four categories of variables operating along the continuum from wishes to actions: values, expectancies, relevance, and activation. There are also three goal levels arranged in hierarchical order: actions, outcomes, and consequences. In Fig. 15.7, only one wish–action pathway is shown, but it is important to recognize that variables in the pathway may differ, and may operate in different ways, when different levels of goals are focused on. I have attached some aptitude constructs to points along the pathway to indicate some hypotheses about aptitude–process connections, and must abbreviate and alter here the description of the Heckhausen–Kuhl theory to concentrate on these hypotheses.

A wish is essentially the undifferentiated value attached to a goal. At any given goal level, these values are the valences or incentives related to an anticipated end state. One can expect also that long-range interests and emotional needs enter here. Expectancies derive from the potency of the goal—the unconditional subjective probability of its attainment. Potency becomes expectancy when the probability of attaining the goal becomes conditioned on a certain action. (Valence and potency are terms used in honor of Lewin, 1935, who first defined them.) Stemming from Lewin, but also from Atkinson and Feather (1966) and especially Heckhausen (1977), there is now substantial theory dealing with the value-expectancy computation that predicts what the preferred goal will be in a given situation. Until this new work by Heckhausen and Kuhl (1985), however, value-expectancy theory has been silent about the wish-action pathway; the relations among goal levels have also not previously been clarified.

One kind of expectancy variable that is important in considering relations among goal levels is the instrumentality of an action outcome for desired or feared consequences. The instrumentality of an outcome is the probability of the occurrence of some consequence given that outcome. At the action level, the end states are the actions themselves; motivation derives from interest, enjoyment, or excitement in performing the act in and of itself. But actions lead to outcomes (the second level) that also have value in themselves, and outcomes have consequences (the third level) also with their own values. Instrumentality connects action, outcome, and consequence.

A wish becomes a want when it becomes endowed with sufficient expectancy

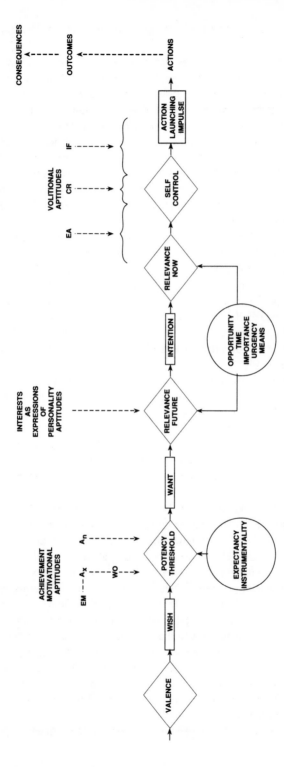

FIG. 15.7. A schematic flowchart of the commitment pathway identifying classes of motivational variables and goal levels (after Heckhausen & Kuhl, 1985). See text for aptitude symbol identifications.

456

and instrumentality (i.e., when it reaches a critical threshold of potency). If a want refers to a higher-order goal level (e.g., a particular consequence of an action outcome), then a complex of other motivational processes are implied; processes at higher levels presuppose or include the processes at lower levels. One can think of borrowed valences from either higher or lower orders, although normally lower-level goals receive their valences from higher-level goals. So, for example, the act of learning from instruction receives valence from the goal of doing well on an upcoming achievement test, which is in turn determined by its instrumentality with respect to the goal of reaching a higher level of education or training. Now consider that at least two aptitudes reflecting past experience in learning differentiate persons' processing in the wish-to-want part of the pathway. They are the two posited by achievement motivation theory, that is, need for achievement (A_n) and fear of failure, or evaluation anxiety (A_x). Recent research has also subdivided the A_x construct into two components: worry (WO) and emotionality (EM). It is the worry component that appears operative in individual differences in learning. As worry is high, attention is diverted from the task and directed toward the self. Doubts and worrisome thoughts disrupt attention to learning. Both A_n and A_x are characteristics of persons that come into play particularly when learning task actions are seen as instrumental to desired (or feared) outcomes and consequences. They also connect to positive or negative expectancies depending on perceived ability in relation to task difficulty. Thus, passing the potency threshold depends on the interaction between A_x, A_n, expectancy and instrumentality connecting to the task, and perceived task difficulty in relation to ability. The effects of A_x and ability in interaction with high versus low structure instruction, as in the Peterson (1976) and Porteus (1976) studies previously mentioned, presumably result because high structure reduces perceived task difficulty and increases expectancy for both high G-high A_x and low G-low A_x students.

Next along the pathway, then, the wish becomes a want. A want must be relevant for the individual in addition to being realistic; relevance variables determine the transformation of wants into intentions. According to the Kuhl–Heckhausen model, the relevance check includes concern for practicality and appropriateness to a particular setting or situation. This check is based on at least five criteria: opportunity, time, importance, urgency, and means. To change a want into an intention requires passing a relevance-future check: Will conditions favor the intended action in the future? Is the intended action relevant to desired outcomes and consequences? Future relevance, especially as connected to higher-level outcome goals and consequences, it would seem, must also be a function of interest patterns. The hierarchy of personal interests may play a role in learning from instruction not only by influencing the value associated with broad goals, and expectancies and instrumentality connecting actions to outcomes to consequences, but also by influencing the future relevance check in particular tasks. Though, there is as yet little evidence to connect individual differences in

broad interest patterns to learning from instruction, past research has been severely limited in focus and methodology.

Finally, for the intention to be transformed into an action, a second, relevance-now check must also be passed: Are conditions favorable at this particular
moment? The same relevance criteria are again applied. A final checkpoint is
self-control to determine if the action program is complete and can be maintained
against competing action tendencies. If these checks are positive, action is then
initiated by an action-launching impulse. This is the region of the pathway I have
labeled volitional aptitudes, and as shown in the Figure, I hypothesize that the
personality factors earlier labeled IF, CR, and EA reflect individual differences
connected to the operation of the relevance-now check, self-control, and action-
launching steps, though they may condition different kinds of wishes, expectancies, and perceived instrumentalities early on as well. Some instructional conditions favor some lines of action and inhibit others. From the examples given
earlier, we can speculate that low structure instructional conditions particularly
favor (and require) the sorts of action programs readily available among persons
represented by high IF—adaptive autonomy, flexibility, and independence in
thought and action during learning. The low structure treatments of Peterson
(1976) and Porteus (1976) fit this description, as does the BIP computerized
program. High structure instructional conditions would frustrate such action
programs but would favor instead those more available in persons represented by
high CR—adjustment by compliance to structure and responsible self-control.
This latter sort of action program fits the sorts of conditions provided by the high
structure Peterson and Porteus treatments and the physics film instruction as
well. But it cannot work in low structure conditions because there is insufficient
structure in this situation to guide conformity by the person. Action programs of
the high EA sort are favored by interpersonal instructional conditions that encourage social self-assertion and ascendancy; the live physics instruction seems
to fit this description.

Fig. 15.8 takes a further schematic step by placing the performance commitment pathway just discussed together with the performance assembly pathway
derived from the earlier analysis of cognitive aptitude. The cognitive and conative aspects of performance must converge in adaptive action during learning
somehow, even though there is no warrant for the simple parallel depicted. The
two pathways surely differ in many process details (see, e.g., Anderson, 1983;
Heckhausen & Kuhl, 1985). Furthermore, they operate on different time scales
and may be organized or lagged differently in different learning situations. But
the parallels between activation and expectation, or retrieval and instrumentality,
or the close association between assembly, control, and the relevance-now check
in adaptation, may at least have heuristic value in designing further research.
And, if the hypothesized placements of different cognitive and conative aptitude
constructs in this scheme make any sense, they do predict certain aptitude relations and interactions rather than others. Indeed, what evidence there is in hand

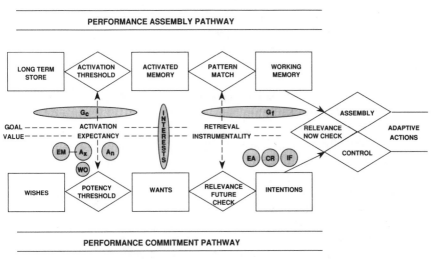

PERFORMANCE ASSEMBLY PATHWAY

PERFORMANCE COMMITMENT PATHWAY

FIG. 15.8.   A schematic flowchart of the joint performance assembly and commitment pathways. See text for aptitude symbol identifications.

does suggest that G_c, A_n, and A_x are somehow proximal—they interact in influencing learning—and G_f and IF at least predict learning in some of the same kinds of situations. The Figure thus helps (at least it helps me) to hypothesize further about aptitude complexes and the processes that might be manipulated in learning experiments to influence their roles.

TOWARD A COGNITIVE–CONATIVE APTITUDE MAP

Although our list of conative aptitude constructs is incomplete and quite tentative, it is not too early to begin exploring relationships among them, and between them and cognitive aptitude constructs. The six Holland theme scores, and indeed all the basic interest scales of the SCII, are available on both the Stanford and the high school samples used to construct Fig. 15.2; these may be related to the six ability factor scores but also to individual test scores. The CPI scales and factors of Table 15.2 are also available on the Stanford sample for this purpose. It is possible also to fashion other scales, such as the anxiety formula score proposed by Leventhal (1966, 1968) for the CPI. Hopefully, exploratory correlational work with this set of variables will suggest a rough map of the terrain, as an extension of that proposed in Fig. 15.2, and may also indicate where new measurement development effort is most needed.

But the methods for exploring this realm are not routine. As noted earlier, the linearity assumption, often blindly accepted in past work, should be questioned here. With personality and interest variables, also, gender differences in correlations as well as means can be expected. So far our work is quite preliminary, so a detailed report is not justified at this time. Only a few hints at possibilities can be given.

A first look at curvilinearity comes from a comparison of Pearson linear correlation coefficients and distribution-free Eta coefficients computed in this matrix of variables. This shows marked divergence from linearity; the HI scale shows sizable linear correlation with G_f, G_c, and G_v measures, but all other Holland scales and the CPI factors show linear correlations with abilities distributed closely around zero, whereas corresponding Eta coefficients are sizable. As one example, for Wechsler IQ $r = .06$ and $.05$ with HR in the high school and Stanford samples respectively, but the respective Eta coefficients are .41 and .65. With HI, $r = .43$ and $.28$ but Eta $= .56$ and $.58$, respectively. In the Stanford sample, Wechsler IQ paired with IF, CR, and EA gives $r = .18$, $-.07$, and $-.03$ but Eta $= .55$, $.60$, and $.55$.

Nonmetric multidimensional scaling has also been applied to both the Eta and the R matrix. In these scalings, two-dimensional solutions typically divide ability and personality variables into two clusters, as expected. But three- and four-dimensional solutions often show additional interesting features of the complex ability–personality relationships. One is that the IF factor and the HI and HR scales appear often more closely associated with ability factors than other dimensions. Another is that the ability factors seem to scale as a simplex suggestive of the complexity continuum of Fig. 15.2, with the personality factors arrayed in parallel.

To examine some of these relations further, we have also produced bivariate (and some trivariate) scatterplots separately by sex and fitted quadratic and cubic trends. Some substantially curvilinear relations between ability and personality variables are displayed, and in some cases these trends differ for males and females. For example, Fig. 15.9 gives bivariate plots in the Stanford sample for one general ability score (G_f) and one special ability score (PS) crossed with CR and IF personality factor scores. For G_f and CR in Fig. 15.9a, the curves are oppositely pitched, suggesting large gender difference on G_f but only among persons above the mean on CR. In Fig. 15.9b, there appears to be a small mean difference on G_f favoring males throughout the IR range; it increases as IR scores increase above its mean, suggesting positive relation between G_f and IR for males but not for females. PS shows substantial mean differences favoring females throughout the range of both CR and IF, in Fig. 15.9c and 15.9d. There is a markedly curvilinear relation between PS and IF; ability is higher at both extremes than at midrange of IF.

As further example, Fig. 15.10 shows bivariate plots in the high school sample for Wechsler IQ scores crossed with the HR, HA, HS, and HC scales, in Fig. 15.10a, 15.10b, 15.10c, and 15.10d, respectively. Mildly curvilinear trends in the same direction for both sexes are seen for HR and HA; a mean ability difference favoring males appears as HA scores are lower. HS gives oppositely pitched curves for the two groups; mean ability differences favoring females appear at both high and low scores levels of HS. HC shows a markedly quadratic trend for both groups; higher ability scores occur in the midrange, and lower ability scores in the extremes of HC.

No substantive generalizations from these data are warranted. There are, however, several methodological observations. One is that the study of ability-personality relations poses difficult new problems requiring nonlinear methods; perhaps an entirely new approach needs to be considered (e.g., see Cronbach, 1988). Another is that the peculiar characteristics of particular samples must be carefully considered. The high school and Stanford samples used here differ in myriad subtle ways that can influence ability-personality relationships. Stanford students are highly selected on variables correlated with both kinds of measures. Both samples are paid volunteers, and the high school plots in Fig. 15.10 suggest that in the low IQ range more females than males volunteer to participate. Finally, it should be clear from both figures that those who make generalizations about sex differences in abilities without considering personality ranges, or vice versa, do so at considerable peril.

FURTHER METHODOLOGICAL NOTES

There is no substantive conclusion to this chapter, because the molar cognitive-conative aptitude hypotheses here presented now need much further correlational and process-analytic research to elaborate our understanding of them before summary statements can be justified. It is better to end with some further points about methodological limitations and possibilities to consider in this future research.

Methodological Limitations

Beyond the earlier discussion, several related methodological limitations attend research on cognitive-conative interactions in learning from instruction.

Most ATI studies investigate only one or two aptitude variables. Even those that include several aptitude constructs often conduct their analyses separately for each one. My own early study exemplifies this weakness and also another: Many investigators block aptitude measures into crude levels instead of treating them as continuous variables. This makes for weak, cumbersome analyses that cannot detect multivariate curvilinearity. The Peterson (1976) and Porteus (1976) experiments tried general linear regression methods to test interactions involving up to four continuous aptitude variables. And the data suggested curvilinear possibilities also, but these could not be studied in detail, given the limited

SU SAMPLE

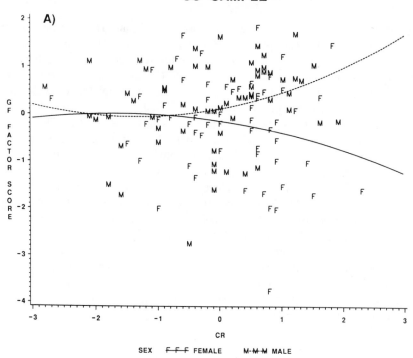

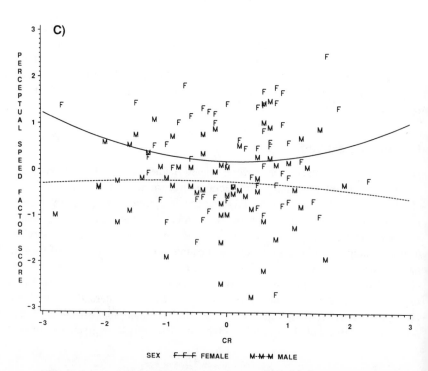

FIG. 15.9. Bivariate scatterplots with quadratic curves fitted separately for males and females in the Stanford sample, showing (a) G_f

SU SAMPLE

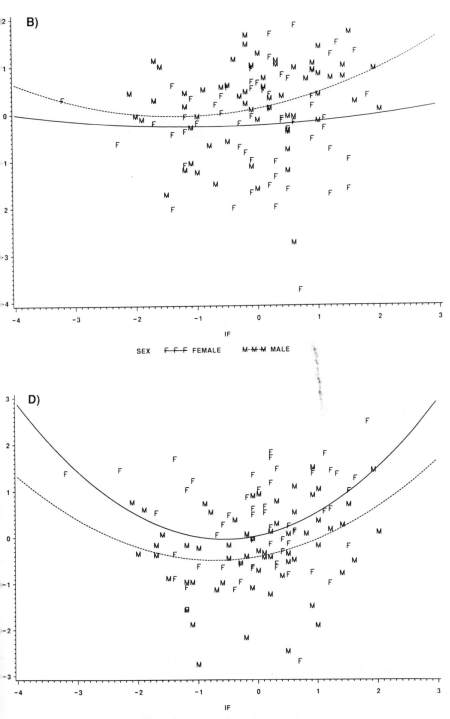

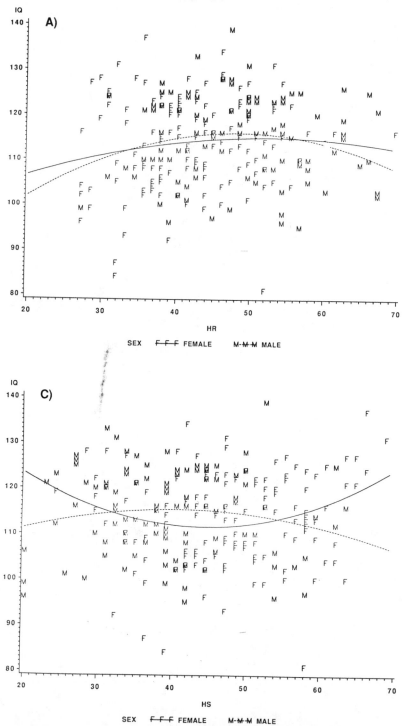

FIG. 15.10. Bivariate scatterplots with quadratic curves fitted separately for males and females in the high school sample, showing IQ

HS SAMPLE

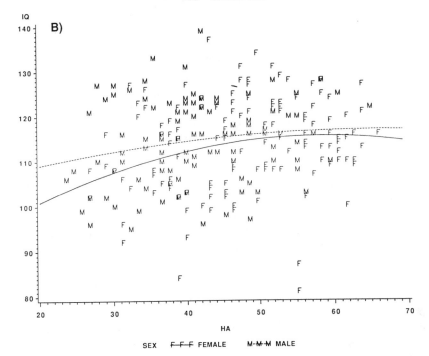

B)

SEX   F-F-F FEMALE   M-M-M MALE

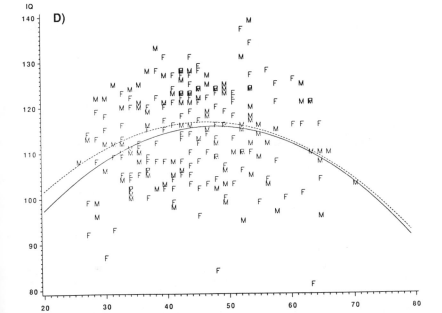

D)

SEX   F-F-F FEMALE   M-M-M MALE

sample sizes available; limited sample sizes are usually all that is available in instructional research. Yet curvilinearity may well be the rule rather than the exception in the study of conative aptitudes, as suggested by theory as well as by empirical results to date. Although there are many other limits in the design and analysis of ATI experiments, most can be overcome with proper planning (see Cronbach & Snow, 1977). But the sample size–curvilinearity problem may often be insurmountable in instructional experiments.

A second limitation derives from the difficulty of obtaining detailed descriptions of learning-related activities, processes, and perceptions of the situation that characterize individuals differing in aptitude during instruction. Though some progress has been made on this front recently, it is obvious that most instructional situations (other than computerized treatments such as BIP) cannot be designed to yield learning activity or process analyses directly. On the other hand, to move instructional experiments into the laboratory to obtain controlled measurements, think-aloud protocols, and the like usually means shortening and weakening the instructional treatment to a point where the most important aptitudes, especially conative aptitudes, may no longer be operative. Thus, new ways are needed to thicken the description of learning activities as learning proceeds in an instructional treatment by capitalizing on whatever the instructional situation allows. Computerized instruction does produce fine-grain description of learning activities, but it is limited to a certain range of treatment situations.

A third major limitation concerns conative aptitude measurement itself. The shortcomings of questionnaire measurement are well known. Projective techniques have their major problems as well. Yet there have been few initiatives taken in recent decades to find new methods of assessing personality for either instructional or process-analytic research purposes. Perhaps as evidence suggests the importance of conative aptitudes in learning, measurement specialists will be increasingly motivated to invest in the basic work needed.

A Possible Approach to Conative Aptitude and Learning Assessment

Part of the personality measurement problem has been the absence of an adequate theory of individual response to personality measures. Some attempts to formulate cognitive processing models of such response have appeared in recent years, focused mainly on the analysis of the subjective meaning structure of inventory items (see, e.g., Cliff, 1977; Cliff, Bradley, & Girard, 1973; de Boeck, 1978, 1981; Rogers, 1974). Now, however, some new results from a different tack may offer a breakthrough; at least they open up an important line for innovative research on the assessment of both conative aptitudes and learning-related actions, thoughts, and perceptions during instruction.

A team of Belgian researchers (Claeys, de Boeck, van den Bosch, Biesmans,

& Bohrer, no date) conducted a series of three studies to investigate a free-response self-description instrument and to compare it with conventional, fixed format personality measures. The free self-report gave the respondent only this instruction: "Describe your personality as completely as possible, using any personal adjectives you choose. Do not say how you want to be, but say how you really are. Try to use words of common usage." The adjectives were then scored for various personality dimensions, using a computerized dictionary of adjectives and system of weights for each of the personality dimensions, based on expert judgments previously obtained. A traditional inventory and a fixed list of adjectives for self-rating were the comparison measures; each represented personality dimensions such as extraversion, agreeableness, conscientiousness, and neuroticism.

In brief, the results suggest that the validity of personality measures may be substantially increased when a free-response self-description instrument is administered first in a battery including other, conventional instruments. The interpretation is that the free-response condition first activates a person's recall of relevant information from personal knowledge structure; in other words, the content of active or working memory is enlarged and intensified in a state of free, self-focused attention. The effect is to improve the validity of the person's responses both to free-format instruments and to the fixed-format inventories that follow. When not preceded by free recall, conventional inventories, rating scales, and questionnaires may appear circumstantial, so response to them may be impulsive, superficial, and hence less valid.

Table 15.3 shows some of the results of two studies with college students and of a third study conducted in a military officer selection context. Predictive validity differences for the two test administration orders are quite clear for the college samples. The military results also show some validity differences, though they are attenuated by several factors that operate in this context and not in the university-based research. Still, it is notable that two personality dimensions in the military study—the achievement motivation and self-confidence scales—showed a validity differential that deserves closer examination in further research.

Deserving of much further research also is the possibility that the personal knowledge structure that individuals bring to bear in self-reports of personality can be activated by free recall to increase the validity of ensuing reports. The rationale of conventional measures is that individuals will reveal their personalities by recognizing themselves as fitting in some degree statements composed by researchers. Such an approach essentially ignores the individuality of personal self-concepts, as well as the possibility that such self-knowledge may not routinely be consciously available. Free response, on the other hand, allows individuality of response and may also provide a more intensive conscious search of stored personal knowledge. The distinction is parallel to the recognition versus recall contrast in memory research, about which a great deal is known in cog-

TABLE 15.3

Correlations of a Combined Behavioral Criterion with Three Self-Report Personality Assessment Methods in Free/Fixed and Fixed/Free Order Conditions

	Trait Dimension	Free/Fixed Order			Fixed/Free Order		
		Free Description	Fixed Inventory	Fixed Rating Scale	Fixed Inventory	Fixed Rating Scale	Free Description
Study 1[a]	Extraversion	.46	.52	.41	.14	.27	.07
	Agreeableness	.52	.46	.49	.25	.32	.15
	Conscientiousness	.54	.52	.41	.33	.23	.25
	Neuroticism	.56	.55	.38	.10	.04	-.13
	Average	.52	.51	.42	.08	.22	.08
Study 2[a]	Average	.41	.41	.34	.25	-.06	.05
Study 3[b,c]	Achievement motivation	.31			.10		
	Facilitating anxiety	.28			.27		
	Debilitating anxiety	.21			.21		
	Social anxiety I	.21			.18		
	Social anxiety II	.31			.28		
	Self-confidence	.39			.30		
	Average	.29			.22		

[a]N = 24 and 19 per order condition in Studies 1 and 2 respectively.
[b]Study 3 used a military selection sample, a different inventory method, no fixed rating scale, and no free description method in the fixed/free condition, so correlations for free description are not shown; negative anxiety scales are reflected to eliminate negative correlations.
[c]N = 256 and 365 in free/fixed and fixed only conditions in Study 3.
Source: Claeys, de Broeck, van den Bosch, Biesmans, & Bohrer, no date.

nitive psychology. It is also to be noted that the free recall form of reporting personal conceptions is akin to the open-ended self-report methods used in cognition research on learner's conceptions of their own learning in particular instructional situations. One can imagine descriptor systems designed along the lines of the Belgian free self-report, but focused on learning-related motivations, interests, perceptions, and action tendencies, as well as learning activities. It might even be possible to collect such scaled descriptions periodically during learning from instruction. The coordination of these lines of research might produce a richer and more integrated view of the cognitive and conative psychology of personal knowledge, as well as practical improvements in aptitude and learning assessment technology.

OPEN DISCUSSION

The discussion began with a question about the findings obtained in the Belgium Navy diving study. Subsequent questions focused on how best to conceptualize the complex relations among abilities, interests, and volition.

> **Overmier:** I would like to go back to the so-called admiral graph [Fig. 15.5] and ask you a question about those data. Presumably, if you were an admiral and took those data to heart, you would give persons some type of anxiety tests early on. You wouldn't admit [for training] those people who scored high on the anxiety scales because those persons tend to fail. But there are things that people do after they have finished, for example, they have dangerous tasks to perform. I guess I wanted to know if we have the same kinds of correlations or assessment of the relationship between these measures and their past performance, for example, their accident proneness, and things of that sort?

> **Snow:** That is a perfectly good question. However, I don't know the answer. This data set doesn't have any other criterion measures. There may be some now, but I have seen no further report on these studies since 1985 when I first learned about this work while visiting in Belgium. Obviously, we need performance criteria down the line. Maybe what you are saying is that I shouldn't show this to an admiral until I have more information.

> **Overmier:** Variables such as extroversion, for example, may also correlate with high accident proneness. Low anxiety persons, for instance, may not see the danger in situations where danger really exists.

> **Snow:** Quite right.

Kyllonen: I have both a comment and a question. The comment is related to Snow's first law of conservation of instructional effectiveness ("No matter how you try to make instruction better for someone, you will make it worse for someone else".) This law may potentially explain one of the controversies in the tutoring system literature; that is, whether intelligent tutoring systems ought to be designed to provide exploratory learning environments or whether such systems ought to be designed to be heavy-handed—to provide guided sorts of environments. John Anderson's computerized tutors, which guide the student very strictly through the process of instruction, tend to be best for low ability students. On the other hand, Valerie Shute and Bob Glaser's economics computerized tutor, which is a wide-open exploratory environment, was quite a success among Carnegie Mellon and University of Pittsburgh students but was much less successful when administered to presumably lower ability Air Force subjects. Shute had to do extensive modifications to get the tutor system to work effectively with the Air Force population. Furthermore, the nature of the modifications that Valerie made had to do with giving students explicit instructional goals. I think this first law (as it pertains to high versus low structure in instruction) nicely explains this distinction.

In addition to my comment, I also want to ask a question. What do you think about the relationship between interests and abilities? I think there are some people who would argue that the reason to ignore variables such as interests is that these variables result primarily from differential patterns of abilities.

Snow: I wouldn't dispute that notion as a hypothesis. However, I don't think there is strong evidence one way or another for which comes first: whether persons develop abilities in areas in which they are interested for some reason or whether interests result from the exercise of abilities in a domain. It is a perfectly good developmental kind of question and there have been few studies on this issue. Jan-Eric's data speak a bit to this question and a study by Cooley also comes to mind. If you are interested in describing individual differences in readiness to profit from instruction at a given point in time, however, then interests (whether they come from abilities or vice versa) are still descriptions of important aptitude differences—if you can demonstrate that they are indeed important.

To reiterate, I think that there is a sort of hierarchy involving strong vocational interest kinds of dimensions; dimensions that Holland would interpret as the result of person–situation interactions across the learning history of the individual. As you go down the hierarchy, I suppose that you get to more and more specific, or topical, interests. Further, these narrower kinds of interests at the lower ends of the hierarchy are probably more likely to result from more immediate learning or ability kinds of functions.

Kuhl: I would like to comment on your relating several personality factors to volition. I would like to emphasize one distinction that I think is important within the category of volitional variables—the distinction between motivational determinants of volition and ability determinants. Volition, as I see it, is at the interface of cognition and motivation. In a way, it is a superimposed level of control, a higher level of control. So you must make the motivation–cognition distinction on that level again. It occurs to me that your CR factors might relate more to the motivational basis for this volitional goal of maintaining whichever goal is active at that time. And Independence and Flexibility might relate more to the ability part of the story. And I think that you would agree that these things do not tell the whole story—that there is more to this ability to maintain than this personality variable. But it does seem similar to this action–state orientation distinction because the core of it might actually be Flexibility versus Independence.

Snow: Yes, your point is well taken. I present these as starting points rather than as explanations. And I am trying to relate them to some sort of conception of what processes are involved.

REFERENCES

Ackerman, P. L. (1986). Individual differences in information processing: An investigation of intellectual abilities and task performance during practice. *Intelligence, 10,* 101–139.
Ackerman, P. L. (1987). Individual differences in skill learning: An integration of psychometric and information processing perspectives. *Psychological Bulletin, 102,* 3–27.
Anderson, J. R. (1983). *The architecture of cognition.* Cambridge, MA: Harvard University Press.
Anderson, R. C., Shirey, L. L., Wilson, P. T., & Fielding, L. G. (1987). Interestingness of children's reading material. In R. E. Snow & M. J. Farr (Eds.), *Aptitude, learning, and instruction, Vol. 3: Conative and affective process analyses* (pp. 287–299). Hillsdale, NJ: Lawrence Erlbaum Associates.
Atkinson, J. W., & Feather, N. T. (1966). *A theory of achievement motivation.* New York: Wiley.
Bethell-Fox, C. E., Lohman, D. F., & Snow, R. E. (1984). Adaptive reasoning: Componential and eye movement analysis of geometry analogy performance. *Intelligence, 8,* 205–238.
Brown, A. L., & Ferrara, R. A. (1985). Diagnosing zones of proximal development. In J. Wertsch (Ed.), *Culture, communication, and cognition: Vygotskian perspectives* (pp. 273–305).New York: Cambridge University Press.
Campione, J. C., & Brown, A. L. (1987). Dynamic assessment: One approach and some initial data (pp. 82–115). In. C. S. Lidz (Ed.), *Dynamic assessment.* New York: Guilford.
Carroll, J. B. (1985, May). *Domains of cognitive ability.* Paper presented at the meeting of American Association for the Advancement of Science, Los Angeles.
Carroll, J. B. (in preparation). *Human cognitive abilities.* New York: Cambridge University Press.
Cattell, R. B. (1957). *Personality and motivation structure and measurement.* New York: World Book Co.
Cattell, R. B., & Butcher, H. J. (1968). *The prediction of achievement and creativity.* Indianapolis: Bobbs-Merrill.

Chiu, L. H. (1967). *A factorial study of academic motivation.* Unpublished doctoral dissertation, Teachers College, Columbia University.

Claeys, W., de Boeck, P., van Den Bosch, W., Biesmans, R., & Bohrer A. (no date). *A comparison of one free format and two fixed format self-report personality assessment methods.* Unpublished manuscript, Department of Psychology, University of Leuven, Belgium.

Clark, M. S., & Fiske, S. T. (Eds.). (1982). *Affect and cognition.* Hillsdale, NJ: Lawrence Erlbaum Associates.

Cliff, N. (1977). Further study of cognitive processing models for inventory response. *Applied Psychological Measurement, 1,* 41–49.

Cliff, N., Bradley, P., & Girard, R. (1973). The investigation of cognitive models for inventory response. *Multivariate Behavioral Research, 8,* 407–425.

Cronbach, L. J. (1957). The two disciplines of scientific psychology. *American Psychologist, 12,* 671–684.

Cronbach, L. J. (1984). *Essentials of psychological testing* (4th ed.). New York: Harper & Row.

Cronbach, L. J. (1988). Playing with chaos. *Educational Researcher, 17,* 46–49.

Cronbach, L. J., & Snow, R. E. (1977). *Aptitudes and instructional methods: A handbook for research on interactions.* New York: Irvington.

de Boeck, P. (1978). Validity of a cognitive processing model for responses to adjective and sentence type inventories. *Applied Psychological Measurement, 2,* 369–376.

de Boeck, P. (1981). Individual differences in the validity of a cognitive processing model for responses to personality inventories. *Applied Psychological Measurement, 5,* 481–492.

Entwistle, N., Kozeki, B., & Balarabe, M. (1988, April). *Motivation, attributions, and approaches to learning in British and Hungarian secondary schools.* Paper presented at the American Educational Research Association, New Orleans.

Eysenck, H. J. (Ed.). (1982). *A model for personality.* New York: Springer-Verlag.

Gordon, L. V. (1953). *Gordon Personal Profile manual.* Yonkers-on-Hudson, NY: World Book.

Gough, H. G. (1953). A nonintellectual intelligence test. *Journal of Consulting Psychology, 17,* 242–246.

Guilford, J. P. (1959). *Personality.* New York: McGraw-Hill.

Gustafsson, J. E. (1984). A unifying model for the structure of intellectual abilities. *Intelligence, 8,* 179–203.

Gustafsson, J. E., & Undheim, J. O. (1986, April). *Individual differences in cognitive development as a function of interests and activities.* Paper presented at the American Educational Research Association, San Francisco.

Guttman, L. (1970). Integration of test design and analysis. *Proceedings of the 1969 Invitational Conference on Testing Problems.* Princeton, NJ: Educational Testing Service.

Heckhausen, H. (1974). *Leistungsmotivation und Chancengleichheit.* Gottingen: Hogrefe.

Heckhausen, H. (1977). Achievement motivation and its constructs: A cognitive model. *Motivation and Emotion, 1,* 283–329.

Heckhausen, H. (1980). *Motivation und Handeln.* Berlin: Springer-Verlag.

Heckhausen, H. (1981). Developmental precursors of success and failure experience. In G. d'Ydewalle & W. Lens, *Cognition in human motivation and learning* (pp. 15–32). Leuven, Belgium & Hillsdale, NJ: Leuven University Press & Lawrence Erlbaum Associates.

Heckhausen, H., & Kuhl, J. (1985). From wishes to action: The dead ends and shortcuts on the long way to action. In M. Frese & J. Sabini (Eds.), *Goal-directed behavior: Psychological theory and research on action* (pp. 134–159). Hillsdale, NJ: Lawrence Erlbaum Associates.

Heckhausen, H., Schmalt, H-D., & Schneider, K. (1985). *Achievement motivation in perspective.* Orlando, FL: Academic Press.

Holland, J. L. (1966). *The psychology of vocational choice.* Waltham, MA: Blaisdell.

Holland, J. L. (1973). *Making vocational choices.* Englewood Cliffs, NJ: Prentice-Hall.

Jenkins, J. J., & Paterson, D. G. (Eds.). (1961). *Studies in individual differences.* New York: Appleton-Century-Crofts.

Kuhl, J. (1984). Volitional aspects of achievement motivation and learned helplessness: Toward a comprehensive theory of action control. In B. A. Maher (Ed.), *Progress in experimental personality research* (Vol. 12, pp. 99–170). New York: Academic Press.

Kuhl, J. (1985). Volitional mediators of cognition-behavior consistency: Self-regulatory processes and action versus state orientation. In J. Kuhl & J. Beckman (Eds.), *Action control: From cognition to behavior* (pp. 101–128). New York: Springer-Verlag.

Kuhl, J. (1986). Motivation and information-processing: A new look at decision-making, dynamic change, and action control. In R. M. Sorrentino & G. T. Higgins (Eds.), *The handbook of motivation and cognition: Foundations of social behavior* (pp. 404–434). New York: Guilford Press.

Kyllonen, P. C., Lohman, D. F. & Woltz, D. J. (1984). Componential modeling of alternative strategies for performing spatial tasks. *Journal of Educational Psychology, 76,* 1325–1345.

Lambrechts, Lt. (no date). *Psychological selection of divers.* Oostende, Belgium: Belgian Navy Hyperbaric Medical Center.

Lens, W. (1983). Achievement motivation, test anxiety, and academic achievement. *University of Leuven Psychological Reports, No. 21.*

Lens, W. (1986, April). *The motivational significance of future time perspective and school results.* Paper presented at the American Educational Research Association, San Francisco.

Leventhal, A. M. (1966). An anxiety scale for the CPI. *Journal of Clinical Psychology, 22,* 459–461.

Leventhal, A. M. (1968). Additional technical data on the CPI anxiety scale. *Journal of Counseling Psychology, 15,* 479–480.

Lewin, K. (1935). *A dynamic theory of personality: Selected papers.* New York: McGraw-Hill.

Megargee, E. I. (1972). *The California Psychological Inventory handbook.* San Francisco: Jossey-Bass.

Norman, D. A. (1980). Twelve issues for cognitive science. *Cognitive Science, 4,* 1–32.

Pellegrino, J. W. (1984, December). *Components of spatial ability.* Paper presented at the NATO Advanced Study Institute on Advances in Measuring Cognition as Motivation, Athens, Greece.

Pellegrino, J. W., & Glaser, R. (1980). Components of inductive reasoning. In R. E. Snow, P. A. Federico, & W. E. Montague (Eds.), *Aptitude, learning, and instruction: Vol. 1. Cognitive process analyses of aptitude* (pp. 177–218). Hillsdale, NJ: Lawrence Erlbaum Associates.

Peterson, P. L. (1976). *Interactive effects of student anxiety, achievement orientation, and teacher behavior on student achievement and attitude.* Unpublished doctoral dissertation, Stanford University.

Porteus, A. (1976). *Teacher-centered vs. student-centered instruction: Interactions with cognitive and motivational aptitudes.* Unpublished doctoral dissertation, Stanford University.

Rogers, T. B. (1974). An analysis of the stages underlying the process of responding to personality items. *Acta Psychologica, 38,* 205–213.

Rutkowski, K., & Domino, G. (1975). Interrelationship of study skills and personality variables in college students. *Journal of Educational Psychology, 67,* 784–789.

Sarason, I. G. (Ed.). (1980). *Test anxiety: Theory, research, and applications.* Hillsdale, NJ: Lawrence Erlbaum Associates.

Schiefele, U., & Krapp, A. (1988, April). *The impact of interest on qualitative and structural indicators of knowledge.* Paper presented at the American Educational Research Association, New Orleans.

Schiefele, U., Krapp, A., & Winteler, A. (1988, April). *Conceptualization and measurement of interest.* Paper presented at the American Educational Research Association, New Orleans.

Snow, R. E. (1977). Research on aptitudes: A progress report. In L. S. Shulman (Ed.), *Review of research in education* (Vol. 4, pp. 50–105). Itasca, IL: Peacock.

Snow, R. E. (1980). Aptitude processes. In R. E. Snow, P. A. Federico, & W. E. Montague (Eds.), *Aptitude, learning, and instruction: Vol. 1. Cognitive process analyses of aptitude* (pp. 27–64). Hillsdale, NJ: Lawrence Erlbaum Associates.

Snow, R. E. (1982). The training of intellectual aptitude. In D. K. Detterman & R. J. Sternberg (Eds.), *How and how much can intelligence be increased?* (pp. 1–37). Norwood, NJ: Ablex.

Snow, R. E. (1987). Aptitude complexes. In R. E. Snow & M. J. Farr (Eds.), *Aptitude, learning, and instruction: Vol. 3 Conative and affective process analysis* (pp. 11–34). Hillsdale, NJ: Lawrence Erlbaum Associates.

Snow, R. E. (1989). Aptitude-treatment interaction as a framework for research on individual differences in learning. In P. L. Ackerman, R. J. Sternberg, & R. Glaser (Eds.), *Learning and individual differences: Advances in theory and research* (pp. 13–59). New York: Freeman.

Snow, R. E. & Farr, M. J. (Eds.). (1987). *Aptitude, learning, and instruction: Vol. 3. Conative and affective process analyses.* Hillsdale, NJ: Lawrence Erlbaum Associates.

Snow, R. E., Kyllonen, P. C., & Marshalek, B. (1984). The topography of ability and learning correlations. In R. J. Sternberg (Ed.), *Advances in the psychology of human intelligence* (Vol. 2, pp. 47–104). Hillsdale, NJ: Lawrence Erlbaum Associates.

Snow, R. E., & Lohman, D. F. (1984). Toward a theory of cognitive aptitude for learning from instruction. *Journal of Educational Psychology, 76,* 347–376.

Snow, R. E., Tiffin, J., Seibert, W. F. (1965). Individual differences and instructional film effects. *Journal of Educational Psychology, 56,* 315–326.

Snow, R. E., Wescourt, K., & Collins, J. (1979). *Individual differences in aptitude and learning from interactive computer-based instruction* (Tech. Rep. No. 10). Stanford, CA: Stanford University, Aptitude Research Project, School of Education.

Sorrentino, R. M., & Higgins, E. T. (Eds.). (1986). *Handbook of motivation and cognition.* New York: Guilford Press.

Sternberg, R. J. (1985a). *Beyond IQ: A triarchic theory of human intelligence.* Cambridge: Cambridge University Press.

Sternberg, R. J. (Ed.). (1985b). *Human abilities: An information processing approach.* New York: Freeman.

Thurstone, L. L. (1947). *Multiple factor analysis.* Chicago: University of Chicago Press.

Thurstone, L. L. (1948). Psychological implications of factor analysis. *American Psychologist, 3,* 402–408.

Wechsler, D. (1950). Cognitive, conative, and non-intellective intelligence. *American Psychologist, 5,* 78–83.

Weiner, B. (1986). *An attributional theory of motivation and emotion.* New York: Springer-Verlag.

16

The More Things Change, the More They Stay the Same: Comments from an Historical Perspective

James J. Jenkins
University of South Florida

When Dr. Kanfer called me before the conference and asked for a title of my talk, I replied that "Closing Remarks" would be appropriate. I supposed that such a title would cover almost anything that I might choose to say. Now, of course, I have been influenced by the many clever titles that we have heard here and I have been inspired by the contents of these papers to reflect on this conference from an historical perspective. Hence the present title.

A PERSPECTIVE ON THE CONFERENCE

How can one discuss something that is so sweeping, so differentiated, so diverse, and so technically demanding? Perhaps the best that a commentator can do is to abandon the task of making specific comments on a paper-by-paper basis and ask instead whether there is some perspective from which we can view the endeavor as a whole. The deepest perspective I could remember came from Binet and Henri, writing in 1895. As Leona Tyler (another Minnesota graduate) put it in her classic work on individual differences:

> Binet and Henri began their article, "We broach here a new subject, difficult and as yet very meagerly explored." They then proposed as the two chief aims of this undertaking: first, the study of the *nature and extent* of individual differences in psychological processes; and second, the discovery of the *interrelationships* of mental processes within the individual so as to arrive at a classification of traits and determine which are the more basic functions. (Tyler, 1956, p. 9)

It appears to me that their brave beginning still captures the heart of the enterprise and still outlines our task, although we can scarcely claim that the subject is new or meagerly explored.

In 1957, 62 years after Binet and Henri, David Lykken and I reviewed the field of individual differences for the *Annual Review of Psychology*. Like Binet and Henri, we tried to say something very general about the nature of the field:

> The study of the "nature and extent of individual differences" begins, as the phase implies, with the identification of the variables which differ, from individual to individual or from time to time, or both. The psychologist cannot write scientific laws without specifying the variables, that is, the traits or the dimensions of individual difference which are related by these laws. (Jenkins & Lykken, 1957, p. 79)

That is a proud, strong statement. Unfortunately, it is not true. Obviously, there *are* a set of laws that can be written about average performances in average situations that simply ignore individual differences. And most experimental psychologists, of course, prefer to do just that.

In the period that we were reviewing back in 1957, there were quite a few traits around. People claimed to be measuring traits such as anxiety, intrapunitiveness, stress tolerance, variability, rigidity, sense of personal adequacy, conscientiousness, castration anxiety, personal complexity, identification with father, humorousness, degree of cortical inhibition, overcompensation, and on and on, seemingly without limit. (This is just a sample of variables that people wrote about 30 years ago. It is noteworthy that we do not seem to be much concerned with some of those traits these days.)

Lykken and I argued at the time that collecting measures of just-any-trait-that-one-could-imagine would not be productive. We hoped that there was a way to tell which variables might be worthwhile.

> To the scientist, the useful variables are those which map the domain of his interest so as to allow a nomological network of minimum complexity. We would regard the proper objective of differential psychology to be the identification, with increasing specificity, and the measurement, with increasing precision, of this kind of variable (Jenkins & Lykken, 1957, pp. 79–80).

Then we talked about "this kind of variable." We pointed out that this kind of variable is attacked in differential psychology largely through factor analysis, and we devoted about half of the review to factor analytic work, discussing the methodology and reviewing what factor analysts were doing. Then we wrote the following incredible paragraphs—remember we were both youngsters, I was 6 years out of my degree, and Lykken had just completed his:

> In looking over the factor analysis yield of the past two years, we find ourselves with mixed feelings. We are impressed with the great energy which has been

expended. We are filled with admiration for a few studies which are either continuing long-term programs or which grew up from very thoughtful research plans. And finally we are appalled by what in some cases seem to be a sheer waste of time and money.

But in all the studies, good and poor, one looks in vain for the next step. Where are the superior scales of factorial purity? Where are the traits manipulated, investigated and observed in nonfactorial settings? Where has the analysis been carried beyond the hypothesis stage? It is our feeling that the "pure" factor analyst can with some justice claim that he is not responsible for the entire job; that he is pointing the way for others. But no one else seems to be doing anything with these promissory notes, and the entire enterprise is suffering in consequence. (Jenkins & Lykken, 1957, p. 88)

Obviously, Lykken and I were young and impulsive and felt strongly about these things. We went on to urge a fusion of differential psychology and experimental psychology, just as we have heard here at this conference, but we also anticipated resistance to such a program. Robert Thorndike (1954) had just published a study of the values of psychologists. He found three bipolar factors. The most shocking factor that emerged involved laboratory values. The correlation of "laboratory values" with the "collection of large data sets" and "psychometrics" was *minus* .80! and the correlation between "laboratory experimentation" and "study of individuals" was *minus* .84! The experimentalists and the psychometrists not only do not see eye to eye; they are diametrically opposed in their values. As reflection shows, that is a real problem for the development of the field. Almost immediately, Cronbach (1957) published his famous paper on "The Two Disciplines of Scientific Psychology," which gave independent corroboration to the existence of this problem.

Ten years later, as we have heard from Adams, there was a conference on learning and individual differences at the University of Pittsburgh, sponsored by the Learning Research and Development Center. That conference had a variety of differential psychologists and educational psychologists (including, for example, John B. Carroll, Robert Glaser, and Robert Gagné) as well as a significant number of experimental psychologists (including for example, Postman, Underwood, and Melton) and some hybrids like myself. We trod much of the same ground and requested much of the same thing that had been requested for the past 10 or 20 years: namely, that the experimentalists and the differential psychologists get together and try to do something in a constructive and integrative fashion. In his summary, Arthur Melton said: "What is necessary is that we frame our hypotheses about individual differences variables in terms of the process constructs of contemporary theories of learning and performance" (Melton, 1967, p. 239).

If that sentence sounds familiar, it is because Jack Adams quoted it with vigorous approval in the opening paper of this conference just two days ago. The basic notion is that the processes about which the experimentalists seek to build their general laws are identical with the dimensions along which we should make the important relevant measures of individual differences. From one point of view, that seems both necessary and ideal. But when one reflects on the underlying assumptions, it is not by any means necessary that this be the case.

At root, this position endorses a particular form of atomistic reductionism. It assumes that the resources of the organism consist of a fixed set of immutable components out of which behavior is constructed in an additive fashion. It further assumes that it is just these components which vary from individual to individual in such a fashion as to be detected in R-type factor analysis. The view further supposes that behavior is context-free, neither interacting with situational circumstances nor with the person's current cognitive knowledge. And it has no room for differing task strategies which would mask the supposed underlying variables. It requires an enormous leap of faith to think that the general program is going to work out. It implies a remarkable coherence or integration concerning the nature of people and the nature of situations and events that happen in their lives.

The encouraging thing about this conference is that investigators present here are asking the appropriate questions and they are pushing along the interface of the fields to ask whether the general plan is feasible. It is an empirical question of course, and it is good to know that we are seeking answers to these important questions.

ARE THE EXPERIMENTALISTS ON THE RIGHT TRACK?

A crucial assumption (with which this conference opened) is that the experimentalists are working with the right processes. But should we gamble on this? At the Pittsburgh conference in 1965, the experimentalists would have bet very heavily on the critical importance of mediating processes (remember mediation theory?) and the dominant principles of human S-R learning as exemplified by paired-associates learning experiments. Who would have thought that the vital concepts of proactive interference, retroactive interference, and a variety of such topics would fade from the current literature on human cognition in the way that they have? Many of the hot topics of the experimental literature of 20 years ago are rarely found in the current journals. Is it not reasonable to suppose that what the experimentalists are doing now is going to look as primitive and limited in 20 years as what we were doing then?

I do not wish to be misunderstood; I would be happy to find that we have discovered the final set of processing variables that we need, but I see little reason to suppose that this is the case. I cannot agree with Adams' opening paper, in which he strongly advises the differential psychologists to take up the experimentalists' variables. For a different appraisal one should read Allen Newell's chapter, "You Can't Play 20 Questions with Nature and Win," in which

Newell points out some of the difficulties with our current approaches. He refers to 59 paradigms of current interest, most of which are exclusively artificial, laboratory tasks and wonders about their viability (Newell, 1973). Or read Paul Meehl's remarks on why it is hard to do soft psychology (Meehl, 1978). Both of these articles express important reservations about what we are doing in the laboratory and about the fragile nature of our theories. There are a number of difficulties here that we have to face.

Adams admits that this program may not work and that it may not be useful for the field to pursue this course at first. But he argues that if the differential psychologists will follow the experimental psychologists, then when the experimentalists finally get the right variables, the differentialists will have achieved a truly powerful analysis. Adams stresses the laboratory variables, not only as the best source of idealized tasks but also as the ones that need to be defended against attack from pragmatists who want useful dimensions. He believes that usefulness is seldom a motivation that drives basic scientists, and finds this an acceptable situation.

I find myself in disagreement with Adams on both counts. I am *not* sure that the field can afford to neglect practical applied problems while we wait for the right variables to be developed, and I think usefulness *is* something that often does drive basic scientists (and should do so). Most of my experience in research is contrary to Adam's position. For example, when research in speech perception first began, our colleagues in auditory psychophysics told us that if we were just patient, they would work their way up to that level of complexity and tell us how speech perception worked. They intended to explain speech perception in terms of basic auditory psychophysics. After 30 years of research on speech itself, the record suggests, rather surprisingly, that speech perception research has had a greater impact on auditory psychophysics than psychophysics has had on speech research. The applied problems coming from the real world of speech phenomena have broadened psychophysics and given it new problems to study. (And psychophysicists have still not explained speech perception). At the same time, enormous progress has been made in understanding speech perception at its own level, as is evident in the applications of speech and voice technology that we see on every hand. Reductionism is not always the best route to follow.

We have often seen these failures of reductionism in our science. Although the following comparison seems pretentious, I must remind you that when Pavlov discovered psychic secretions, his fellow physiologists attempted to discourage him from pursuing the phenomenon. They argued that if one simply continued to do research in traditional physiology, the complex levels of phenomena would eventually explain themselves. To our great benefit, Pavlov did not accept the advice of his colleagues.

It is also noteworthy (and a promising sign) that the information-processing tasks that are popular today are not pure experimental variables that emerged from current psychological theory in the laboratory. Many of the experimental tasks that form the backbone of the information-processing approach originally came from applied situations. Psychologists needed to know more about the cognitive load on control tower operators; they needed to understand the reading process better; they needed to solve a host of human engineering problems; they needed to teach complex skills; and so on. Those problems are real and the interaction with those problems gave the experimental laboratories a set of new problems to work on.

It is interesting that after one takes these tasks to the laboratory, they can appear to be pure processing functions. I fear that this is true only because the experimentalists can isolate the subjects in a booth and seal off the rest of the world (It is then not at all clear that we can transfer our findings back out to the field and its applied problems without a great deal of work on the complexities of the applied situation.) I think the moral is clear: The laboratory profits from the stimulation of the world and real life problems as much as the real life problems profit from the laboratory research.

One of the most common types of report that one finds in the experimental literature today is an experiment about an experiment. The pattern is as follows: A particular kind of experiment is developed (often for some good reason) and has as interesting outcome. That is fine, of course. But then other experimenters start to bend the situation to their particular biases and personal theories and begin changing parameters without external (real world) motivation or justification. One experiment follows another and the rush of experiments about experiments is on. There is no limit to the number of parametric studies that can be conducted or minor modifications one can make in any given experimental situation. Soon the experiment has moved out of contact with the real world and becomes an object in itself, enough so that a theory of the experiment is developed. This process goes on until the field finally tires of the experimental situation and goes on to something else.

Of course it is not necessarily true that the experiments fail to find something interesting, but there is little guarantee in such cases that the experimentalist is working on a good problem. The easiest way to upset some of my colleagues is to focus attention on some classic, established phenomenon (like the Sternberg exhaustive search experiment) and ask, "What does that mean in the real world? That is, what is the situation in the real world to which the Sternberg situation is an analog?" I do not have an answer to that yet. Although the experimental results from the Sternberg paradigm are very pretty (one rarely finds such neat linear functions) and the experiment is highly replicable, there is some sense in which it is not about anything. Now, it is conceivable that when we study such micro units of processing, we are going find some important variables, but that is a statement of faith, not a statement of fact.

For another example, turn back to the good old days of paired-associates learning. A novice might ask why all of the experiments were conducted with a 2-second exposure of the stimulus and a 2-second exposure of the response.

Where did these 2-second intervals come from? They were a product of Arthur Melton's laboratory. In the 1930s, Melton conducted a series of studies of paired-associates learning and examined the resulting learning curves. The 2-second, 2-second combination gave the results that looked most like learning curves were supposed to look. That decided the matter; almost everyone who studied paired associates from that time forward used those intervals and got the right kind of curves because Melton had picked the situation that would get the right kind of curves.

The standardized experiment approach guarantees a certain amount of order in the field but it makes me nervous because it means that the theory was self-fulling. The experimental parameters were selected on the basis of the theory and then the results were used as evidence for the theory. This situation prevailed until other investigators (Estes, 1964, for example) pointed out that the smooth learning curves might be an artifact of any one of a number of variables, some of which were directly contrary to the accepted associative theory.

Real life has things to tell us. Let me give you a brief example. In our laboratory, Dr. Strange and her colleagues tried to tamper with ordinary experience and found some surprising results. Everyone knows, of course, that native speakers of Japanese have trouble pronouncing /r/ and /l/. What is not so well known is that native speakers of Japanese do not *hear* the difference between /r/ and /l/ either. That is, when a speaker of American English says *rock* or *lock*, the Japanese cannot tell you which one was said; in fact, they may not be able to tell the syllables were different from each other. For native speakers of English, this is incredible; how could anyone fail to hear such a clear difference? Yet the fact persists; those speakers do not hear what you and I hear so clearly.

Suppose that we undertake to teach Japanese listeners to hear the differences and to identify these speech sounds. After all, we are supposed to know about learning—but do we know anything about perceptual learning that we can employ here? Strange and her associates have given Japanese subjects thousands of discrimination trials, and thousands of identification trials, but the learning is painfully slow. In this case at least, it is an interesting and unexpectedly difficult problem to get listeners to hear what they do not already hear. None of us were prepared for that outcome (see MacKain, Best, & Strange, 1981; Sheldon & Strange, 1982; Strange & Dittmann, 1984; Strange, Polka, & Dittmann, 1986; Underbakke, Strange, & Polka, 1984).

Janet Werker and her colleagues (e.g., Werker & Tees, 1983) have recently demonstrated that babies at 6 months of age are sensitive to the sound distinctions employed in all the languages on earth, as far as we can tell. With simple instrumental conditioning operations, they have shown that babies differentiate speech sounds from Hindi and Salish (a Canadian Indian language) as well as English speech sounds. This differentiation can still be seen at 8 months but it begins to weaken by 10 months, and by the time the babies are 12 months old, they do not respond differentially to the sounds that are made in the languages that are not spoken around them. This argues that perceptual sensitivities are being shaped rapidly even in the preverbal child; certain sensitivities are maintained and other sensitivities are being suppressed or inhibited. This in turn argues that the Japanese adults with whom we are working have almost an entire lifetime of suppressing, inhibiting, or ignoring the /r/–/l/ difference because it plays no role in their language. What is an appropriate technique to reverse this lifetime of practice?

On the optimistic side of the role of experience, there is some evidence in Werker's studies that people who heard Hindi when they were babies can profit more from a college course in Hindi and have a greater chance of sounding (and hearing) like native speakers than people who were never exposed to Hindi. So, it appears that there may be some useful potential distinctions laid down in the first years of life, even though they are unused for years. But if the distinctions are not laid down in that first year of life, how can the psychologist help to make them available? I think that is a good problem; but it is not a problem that comes out of the standard kinds of experimental paradigms that we are talking about. Yet, surely, these findings indicate something important about how people develop and function. These phenomena point us toward a new understanding of the possible roles of experience through the interaction between early experience and linguistic capacities in later life.

Adams took us through an interesting review of Woodrow's work on capacities for learning. But we must notice that such studies shed no light on issues like perceptual learning. I doubt that g has anything to do with whether or not a particular Japanese ear is going to become sensitive to the difference between /r/ and /l/. Is there any reason to think that this kind of learning is like any other kind of learning? Like motor learning? Like academic learning? If we do not believe that learning is a particular unified entity, then we cannot ask simple questions such as "Is there a relation between general intelligence and learning?" Indeed, we must specify in great detail what we mean by *learning* in each particular instance. It is conceivable that there are only specific tasks to be learned or specific competencies to be required.

PERSISTING PROBLEMS

Because I have neither the time nor the expertise to discuss the individual papers, I simply want to mention some fairly deep problems that either explicitly or implicitly impact on our activities here. These problems are not new or original but they are persistent. I will just remind you of their existence.

Top Down or Bottom Up?

The first deep problem we could call Binet versus Spearman. Binet was what one might call a validist; he was interested in intelligence and he wanted to measure it in any way that he could. It appears that he did not care how; he just wanted a technique that worked. For example, he studied palmistry and phrenology but rejected both of them. He studied lightning calculators to see if he could get some clues. He was dogged in his pursuit of his goal. When he finally decided that intelligence was only to be approached behaviorally and rationally, he defined it as good judgment and good sense and began developing his little tasks to appraise these traits. His tests then led to the scale, complete with the metric of mental age. It is clear that he continually pursued an instrument that would do the hard work of identifying good and poor students. He stayed goal oriented. For all of the debates about the nature of intelligence and the controversies about the uses of testing, it is clear that intelligence testing was and is one of the major successes of applied psychology.

Spearman on the other hand was an engineer and what we might call a reliablist. Where Binet was impulsive and intuitive, Spearman was analytic and mathematical. In 1904, he wrote two classic papers, one on the measurement of correlation (Spearman, 1904b) and one on the measurement of intelligence (Spearman, 1904a). Because he believed that intelligence was made up of the fine-grained lower-order processes, he argued that the appropriate measures should be of that type, e.g., discrimination of shades of gray. His early work is firm in the faith that if one measures enough of these judgments and discriminations, and measures them precisely enough, one can assemble what is needed to appraise intelligence. In many ways, his arguments sound like the arguments of the information processors today.

That battle is still going on. It has been represented in several of the papers that we have heard at this conference—validists, if you like, against reliablists. In sum, the issue is whether one appraises a complex behavior by describing or measuring it at its own level or whether one should try to build it up out of the appropriate elements. In my judgment, that issue is still unresolved.

What Can We Take for Granted?

The second deep problem concerns what we should take as given—the question of a priori statements. My experience is that one should always be skeptical. As we have heard, E. L. Thorndike asserted that if one finds variance increasing with age, it is evidence for genetic determination of a trait, whereas if one finds variance decreasing, it is evidence for environmental determination of the trait. It seems to me that we would be quite reluctant to accept that as so clearly given in these days. But we have other a priori statements. Pellegrino says in his paper that it is obvious that speed is judged as a function of distance divided by time. He uses this given to justify a particular analysis. However, I am not sure about that argument. There are a variety of smart mechanisms that do not follow our simple analytic rules. The speedometer in your car, for example, does not know anything about distance or time and, in fact, does not make use of either of these concepts when it reports speed to the driver. The speedometer is actually an analog device that is run magnetically. It is the speed of the whirling disk that pulls the needle over and the needle is calibrated to read out as if it were the quotient of a fraction (i.e., miles per hour), but that is not the way it actually works. It's a smart device.

Bouchard raised a very general objection of this sort in the discussion period following Jack Carroll's talk. He pointed out that biological organisms frequently have curious evolutionary histories. It is commonplace to observe that organisms have evolved to do a variety of tasks in ways that do not fit our analysis of their activities. As Snow also suggested, there can be smart mechanisms that exist in encapsulated form simply to compute something for us. These mechanisms may not compute it in the way we believe it ought to be computed. We know that engineers can create smart mechanisms, so why not nature?

(The most interesting smart device that I have used is a planimeter. A planimeter is an instrument that is designed to measure the area of an irregular plane figure, say, for example, the area of a lake on a map. One puts the instrument down and traces the outline of the irregular figure. As one traces the outline, the planimeter drags a little wheel along with it. Sometimes the wheel rolls and sometimes it is just dragged along. When one is finished, one just reads the area off the dial on the device. At no time does one see the height and width of the figure, which we human beings would need to compute an area. But the area measure comes out just the same. This mysterious device was invented centuries ago and one can find an explanation of how it works in the encyclopedia.)

Hardware or Software?

The other thing that goes with smart mechanisms, and again, this has been suggested by some speakers, is the possibility that the smart machines may be soft assembled. That is to say that we can become a certain kind of machine for a certain kind of task. This is what must happen if there is an emergence of *integrated* skill, that is, the kind of thing that Pellegrino is studying. If such integration occurs, it is over and above the assembly of simple resources as the body begins coordinating for the task. At this point, it would be fair to talk about a softly assembled machine to perform that given task or family of tasks.

I recently heard a colloquium by Geoffrey Bingham about the process of hefting a rock to determine how far it can be thrown (see Bingham, 1987). Given a set of rocks, subjects are asked to pick out in advance (by hefting) the rock that they can throw farthest. Then, obviously, the experimenter must ask the subjects to throw all of the rocks to see whether the judgment was correct. The surprising thing is that subjects are very good at this selection task and usually pick in advance the rock they can throw farthest. It appears that what is happening is that subjects are flexing the tendons in the lower part of the arm and wrist as they heft the rock; this stretching communicates to the body what it needs to know because those tendons are mostly responsible for the snap that is activated when one throws a small object.

How did the subjects ever learn to do that? How does it really work? Bingham has spent 4 to 5 years trying to figure out how that information from hefting is transmitted from the pull on the tendon to wherever it goes in the nervous system to coordinate the throwing movement. It is clear that there are some really interesting things that are assembled here in smart machinery that (one assumes) gets built out of experience. I seriously doubt that we would find this assembly of machinery if we were looking at factors represented in traditional kinds of motor tests. At this point let me plead along with other speakers that we recognize the importance of smart machines and give more study to how tasks get arranged.

As another example, I noticed in the data for Kleinbeck's dual task that the amount of interference began decreasing with experience on the task. It is as if the organism says, "I've got both these tasks to do, I guess I have to arrange some way in which to do it." We have also talked about making a task automatic, and that is clearly related to the same issue. Something new happens as performance is automated; something new is introduced into the equation and the organism becomes a different kind of machine.

Benchmark Tests and Tasks

Problem number three is the often-repeated question, "Where are the tests?" Almost everyone has complained about the absence of factorially pure tests that we should have available by now. Where are they? Why are they so hard to build? Perhaps our lack is not because of a lack of effort but, rather, that such tests are very difficult to build. It is easy to complain about what is available, but it's much harder to get a good battery of factorially pure tests together. Everybody admits that test scores are messy, everybody admits that there is specific method variance and that there are a variety of facets to consider. And we all confess that there are lots of reasons for covariation besides the latent trait that we are looking for. The basic fact that we do not have these tests may be telling us something important about individual differences psychology.

Laboratory tasks, I must warn you, are similarly contaminated. Many of these tasks consist of very complex processes that are little understood, even though they look simple on the surface. The speed–accuracy trade-off that Lohman is working on, for example, turns out to need a great deal of further analysis. It is not a simple trade-off (as the experimental literature often seems to assume); errors and time are not simply different measures of the same thing—they have different meaning. I think the same thing can be said for Pellegrino's task. Now that he is going on to examine a dynamic task, it appears that this task involves different variables (not just more complexity) than the static visual tasks.

The Need for Skepticism

The fourth problem is that we all believe that some other branch of psychology has a better grip on the truth than we have in our own domain. My advice is that we look with friendly skepticism on our colleagues' findings until we are fully acquainted with them. One thing that disturbs me about Pellegrino's work, for example, is that he is using the task taken from Clark's research. Unfortunately, there are strategies for handling that task which may not have anything to do with syntax as it really occurs in everyday language use.

I cannot speak in detail about the Clark experiment, but I was closely associated with the research of Clifton and Odom (1966) that examined syntactic relationships in laboratory tasks. As their monograph shows, what one finds in terms of psychological relations between linguistic forms depends heavily on the kind of task that one asks the subject to perform. (Generalization of a motor response gives quite different results from ratings of sentence similarity.) Overall, within a particular kind of task, Clifton and Odom found nice relationships between grammatical transformations and measures of psychological similarity. However, the question that must be raised is whether any of their research applies to sentences when they are at work in the world, that is, sentences as communications. Unfortunately, I think there is very little transfer. Their work applies to *sentences as syntactic objects,* and the relationships that hold between sentences as arbitrary syntactic objects (when you do not care about their content) are radically different from the relationships that hold between sentences when you care about their content, that is, when they are really about something. This is just one example of the problems that arise when we move from the laboratory out into the world.

What things look like, even in relationships between laboratory tasks, may not be an indicator of the situation beyond the laboratory. A specific example that illustrates this comes from my early work with Wallace Russell on word association, a venerable tool of both the laboratory and the clinic. (For a general description of this research, see Jenkins, 1963). We examined free association both as an individual differences parameter (the propensity to give popular associations) and as a materials parameter (the popularity of a particular associative pair, e.g., *table–chair*). We found that we could put these variables together and predict performance on free recall tasks involving associative clustering in recall. We went on to ask what it meant for an individual to be high or low in this associative dimension we were measuring. We were pleased to discover that people who are low in free association scores (i.e., those who give unpopular associates) have highly variable interest profiles over time. That is, such subjects may have one interest profile today and a radically different one tomorrow. Similarly, with personality tests, these subjects had one pattern on the Minnesota Multiphasic Personality Inventory today and a different pattern tomorrow.

Encouraged by these results, we set out to explore the consequences of these studies in the real world—and found almost nothing else! We could not find any cognitive task that reflected the major changes that one might suppose to be involved. There was simply no projection from the associative dimension to anything but these verbal-verbal tasks which have no right answers (interest tests and personality tests). Even tasks like naming colors were not predictable from the free association scores. For limited kinds of laboratory tasks, there are some relations between association scores and variables such as unreliability of performance or increased variance in tasks where there are no correct answers. However, as soon as one turns to tasks that have correct answers, the relationships simply vanish. We never found any real tasks out in the world that correlated with popularity scores on the free association test, and we looked a long time (see Jenkins, 1960). As Bob Shaw humorously summarized this research; "Association is what the head does when you turn off the mind."

Are We Making Progress?

Very early in the conference Carroll asked: Is the research process cumulative? Are we really making progress? He concluded that the research was indeed cumulative and that we are in fact making progress. But I believe that we cannot be sanguine about this and must continually ask this question. The evidence against cumulative progress in some fields of psychology is sometimes quite shocking. From time to time, outstanding figures in the field publicly lament the state of the field. What is the case here?

If you survey the results of 60 years of factor analysis, how much do we know? Jack McArdle asked Carroll to choose the studies that he would say were really high quality. You will recall that Carroll went back to Thurstone's work as being of the highest quality. We must ask ourselves why the best studies are not the ones that have just been completed. Are we not at a higher point of the art than ever before? To me, this suggests that we are not cumulative in quite the way we would like to be.

This state of affairs is not unique to factor analysis or to the study of differential psychology. It is true in most fields of psychology (see Jenkins, 1981). We do not have much in the way of cumulative science except in behavioral management (behavioral modification) and in the areas that are close to the physiological interface. Everyone will admit that we know a lot more about the senses than we did 50 years ago. In general, the closer we are to biology and physiology, the more we see our science as cumulative. The farther we are away, the more we seem to be marking time. Tests are not much better than they have been over the last 50 years: They work and they save people money, but they are not noticeably stronger or better. Just as we have not achieved the pure tests that we would like to have, we also have not achieved a markedly higher level of practical tests. So, I think we must have some questions about whether we are working productively or not.

I *hope* that we are truly making progress. When I look at the elaborate analyses presented here and reflect on what we do know, I am encouraged. We really do know more about cognitive structure than we did 20 years ago. However, I think there is little room for complacency. We still must ask that question to keep ourselves aware of the problem of just doing studies to pile up studies.

Whence Factors?

Someone asked the fundamental question that is involved in many of our assumptions: Where do the factors come from? This is obviously another deep problem. Ordinarily, we do not know their origin. No single factor analysis will tell us, and usually we do not attempt to answer the question. There is a surprising absence of developmental research that could contribute to this question. There was only one paper presented here that treats time as a variable. Typically, we look at the cognitive functions at one point in time and try to reach conclusions about structural relations. But we cannot say whether the structure is the result of training or the common culture or the organization of our school system or growing up in families in which certain beliefs become reality through selective experience or whatever. We point to the structure as a description and believe that if we replicate it enough we have a piece of the psychological reality. But we all must realize that we are ignoring the basic question of developmental stages versus developmental continuity and the question of how our subjects move from one organization to another organization. These are still open questions that call for more research.

Individual Versus Group Precision

There is a continuous tension between the style of research on the two forms of quantitative psychology. One relies on large numbers of tests and large populations of subjects while the other relies on large sets of repeated measurements. (This is again related indirectly to the Binet–Spearman issue.) The canonical psychophysicist never publishes anything until there are at least a thousand pieces of data in each point that is plotted. Many a psychophysicist hires a subject at the beginning of the academic year and runs the subject all year long. The faith is, of course, that one visual system is like another visual system or one auditory system is like another auditory system. By and large, we accept that statement of faith, but it may or may not be adequate. How many retinas have actually been explored? I was startled to discover that, until recently, only one retina had ever been actually sliced up and counted carefully. The statements in our textbooks about the number of rods and cones and the like was, for the most part, based on one retina and extrapolated to all mankind. There is a real problem in moving from one kind of precision to the other. They not only rely on different techniques, they involve different philosophies of science.

Micro or Macro Time?

Another problem is the time scale problem. This problem has been laid in front of us quite dramatically. The various investigators here are working on time scales ranging from 10 to the minus 3 seconds up to 10^9 seconds (that is, 0.001 to

1,000,000,000 seconds). Is it at all reasonable to suppose that we are going to find the same kinds of factors at all scales of experience? Brain mapping and laboratory reaction time tasks are working in milliseconds. Crystallized intelligence, on the other hand, may well be on the scale of lifetimes. Fluid intelligence may have roles to play at both scales of temporal experience. Clearly, we really do need to give a great deal of thought to the problem of interrelating the time scales.

Is There a Method of Choice?

I would like to give an entire lecture about *the* method of choice, but I think what we have heard from the presenters during the last 3 days can be summarized by saying there is not single method of choice at this time. When Lykken and I wrote our *Annual Review* chapter, it was clear the method of choice was R-type factor analysis. At that time, we thought that we would see an enormous development of P- and Q-type analyses to fill out and solidify the findings of the R-type. Yet, the papers given at this conference suggest that alternative forms of factor analysis have virtually vanished. Nobody does P and Q analysis anymore. Instead, we have seen a shift to more complex forms of R-type analysis with structural equations and confirmatory factor analysis. Structural models seem to me to be complicated enough (and jerry-rigged enough) that I am not sure whether to trust them or not. When somebody works, as Gustafsson said he did, all day long, making 40 passes through the computer to get the LISREL solution, do we really understand the meaning of the outcome? Is there sleight of hand? Have we made the variable appear because we massaged the data well enough, or is it really there and this is a subtle way of getting it out so that we can all see it readily? I do not think we have enough experience with most of the structural analyses to know yet, and I think there are at least a few instances of blatant misuse.

On the bright side, the papers presented at this conference indicate the use of an enormous variety of methods, from traditional factor analysis through the structural equations, to pattern analyses. We have seen these techniques applied to growth and we have seen them applied to a variety of experimental and applied data. It is apparent that we have a variety of choices available. I do not think that one can talk about a single method of choice any more. One of the things that this conference has to applaud is that the field now has a diversity of techniques, all of which can be utilized. For example, McArdle could say to us; "I did this and this and this to bring this heterogenous material together. I am in a unique position; I can do things differently from the way people have done it before; I can look at problems in a different way."

The constraint is that we must not deceive ourselves about our use of techniques and start (as I have accused the experimentalists) doing experiments about experiments. That is, we should not let the technique carry us off to the point where we are influencing the solution so much through this complex screen that we do not even know how much we have influenced it.

Organism–Environment Interaction

There is finally a global question about all of our work. Snow suggested it and Bouchard mentioned it. The conference participants who are working in connotative and volitional areas see it clearly. I want to call your attention to it once more. The organism and the environment form a coherent system. There is a strong temptation in modern experimental psychology to try to pack the world into the head of the subject. Thus, it is said that one acts on the basis of his representation of the world (instead of on the basis of the world itself). One focuses on the organism and asks what is going on in the organism's head and forgets that the organism is only part of the picture. Experimentalists try to do many kinds of fancy analysis to infer what is going on in the head. But we may only characterize the environment's representation in the head in very restricted ways. In concentrating on the organism, we often forget that we have narrowly selected a special laboratory environment which determines what we see and what we infer, attributing to the head the constraints and dimensions that we may have created in the situation.

In fact, it is necessarily the case that the organism and the environment are a single interacting system, not two independent components. This is not to say that there is not a skin that separates the two, but rather that the skin is not a wall that separates two independent entities. The organism and the environment have shaped and have been shaped by each other. Of course, there is a skin that encloses the one and separates it from the other, but both biologically and psychologically the two are interdependent. We are the kinds of beings that we are because we live in the kind of world in which we do. And the world is the kind of world that it is because we have shaped and changed it for our own purposes. We must think about presenting more of the environment and considering more of the environment rather than being content with the narrow circumstances that we ordinarily examine.

A number of speakers have said we must be thoughtful; we cannot examine the organism–environment interaction if we only analyze traditional situations. Part of being thoughtful is trying to think about *the organism in the world* and asking whether what we are saying about the organism makes any sense in the global context. At this conference, I see a lot of hopeful signs that investigators are being thoughtful, and I see many lines of research coming together to try to do realistic psychology. Nevertheless, I think it is important that we hold the interactionist view ever before us as an understanding goal toward which we must work.

I hope that in 20 years when this group meets again, we will have really important things to say about psychological structures of organism-in-the-real-world. That will truly be a test of the success of this whole endeavor.

REFERENCES

Binet, A., & Henri, V. (1895). La psychologie individuelle. *Année psychologie, 2,* 411–465.

Bingham, G. P. (1987). *Smart mechanisms and the kinematic specification of dynamics: Hefting for maximum distance throws.* Paper presented at Psykologiska Institutionen, Uppsala Universitet, Uppsala, Sweden.

Clifton, C. E., Jr., & Odom, P. B. (1966). Similarity relations among certain English sentence constructions. *Psychological Monographs, 80* (Whole No. 613).

Cronbach, L. J. (1957). The two disciplines of scientific psychology. *American Psychologist, 12,* 671–684.

Estes, W. K. (1964). All-or-none processes in learning and retention. *American Psychologist, 19,* 16–25.

Jenkins, J. J. (1960). Commonality of association as an indicator of more general patterns of verbal behavior. In T. A. Sebeok (Ed.), *Style in language* (pp. 307–329). New York: Wiley.

Jenkins, J. J. (1963). Mediated associations: Paradigms and situations. In C. N. Cofer & B. S. Musgrave (Eds.), *Verbal behavior and learning* (pp. 210–245). New York: McGraw-Hill.

Jenkins, J. J. (1981). Can we have a fruitful cognitive psychology? In H. E. Howe, Jr. & J. H. Flowers (Eds.), *Cognitive processes: Nebraska symposium on motivation, 1980* (pp. 211–238). Lincoln: University of Nebraska Press.

Jenkins, J. J., & Lykken, D. T. (1957). Individual differences. In P. R. Farnsworth (Ed.), *Annual review of psychology* (Vol. 8, pp. 79–112). Palo Alto, CA: Annual Reviews.

MacKain, K. S., Best, C. T., & Strange, W. (1981). Categorical perception of /r/ and /l/ by Japanese bilinguals. *Applied Psycholinguistics, 2,* 369–390.

Meehl, P. E. (1978). Theoretical risks and tabular asterisks: Sir Karl, Sir Ronald, and the slow progress of soft psychology. *Journal of Consulting and Clinical Psychology 46,* 806–834.

Melton, A. W. (1967). Individual differences and theoretical process variables: General comments on the conference. In R. M. Gagné (Ed.), *Learning and individual differences* (pp. 238–252). Columbus, OH: Charles Merrill.

Newell, A. (1973). You can't play 20 questions with nature and win: Projective comments on the papers of this symposium. In W. G. Chase (Ed.), *Visual information processing* (pp. 283–308). New York: Academic Press.

Sheldon, A., & Strange, W. (1982). The acquisition of /r/ and /l/ by Japanese learners of English: Evidence that speech production can precede perception. *Applied Psycholinguistics, 3,* 243–261.

Spearman, C. (1904a). "General intelligence" objectively determined and measured. *American Journal of Psychology, 15,* 201–292.

Spearman, C. (1904b). The proof and measurement of association between two things. *American Journal of Psychology, 15,* 72–101.

Strange, W., & Dittmann, S. (1984). Effects of discrimination training on the perception of /r-l/ by Japanese adults learning English. *Perception and Psychophysics, 36,* 131–145.

Strange, W., Polka, L., & Dittmann, S. (1986). Training intraphonemic discrimination of /r/–/l/. *Bulletin of the Psychonomic Society, 24,* 419–422.

Thorndike, R. L. (1954). The psychological value systems of psychologists. *American Psychologist, 9,* 787–789.

Tyler, L. E. (1956). *The psychology of human differences.* 2nd ed. New York: Appleton-Century-Crofts.

Underbakke, M., Strange, W., & Polka, L. (1984). Trading relations in the perception of /r/–/l/ by Japanese learners of English. *Journal of the Acoustical Society of America, Suppl. 1, 76,* S27.

Werker, J. F., & Tees, R. C. (1983). Developmental changes across childhood in the perception of nonnative speech sounds. *Canadian Journal of Psychology, 37,* 278–286.

Conference Program

Thursday, April 14, 1988

SESSION I 8:30 a.m.–12:30 p.m.
                    Chairperson: J. Bruce Overmier

    Welcoming Remarks: J. Bruce Overmier
                                 William E. Montague

    Jack A. Adams
      "Historical Background of Research on Individual Differences in Learning"

    Uwe Kleinbeck
      "Volitional Effects on Performance—Conceptual Considerations and Results from Dual-Task Studies"

    John B. Carroll
      "Factor Analysis Since Spearman: Where Do We Stand? What Do We Know?

SESSION II 2:00 p.m.–5:00 p.m.

    J. J. McArdle
      "Structural Modeling of Multiple Growth Functions"

David F. Lohman
"Estimating Individual Differences in Information Processing Using Speed-Accuracy Models"

Robert Cudeck
Discussant: "Simple Solutions and Complex Problems"

Friday, April 15, 1988

SESSION III 8:30 a.m.–12:30 p.m.

James W. Pellegrino
"Assessing and Modeling Information Coordination Ability"

Jan-Eric Gustafsson
"Broad and Narrow Abilities in Research on Learning and Instruction"

Patrick C. Kyllonen
"Role of Working Memory in Acquisition of Cognitive Skill"

Phillip L. Ackerman
Discussant: "Abilities, Elementary Information Processes, and Other Sights to See at the Zoo"

SESSION IV 2:00 p.m.–5:00 p.m.

William Revelle
"Personality, Motivation, and Cognitive Performance"

Julius Kuhl
"Motivational and Volitional Determinants of Learning and Performance"

Ruth Kanfer
Discussant: "Connecting the Dots between Distal and Proximal Motivational Processes"

Saturday, April 16, 1988

SESSION V 9:00 a.m.–12:00 noon.

Gijsbertus Mulder
"Computational and Energetical Mechanisms in Human Performance: Physiological Analysis"

Richard E. Snow
  "Cognitive-Conative Aptitude Interactions in Learning"

James J. Jenkins
  Closing Remarks

Additional Discussion Participants

Thomas J. Bouchard, Jr.
Department of Psychology
University of Minnesota

Charles R. Fletcher
Department of Psychology
University of Minnesota

Miguel Kazén-Saad
Department of Psychology
University of Osnabrück

Herbert L. Pick, Jr.
Institute of Child Development
University of Minnesota

Matthew K. McGue
Department of Psychology
University of Minnesota

Christopher E. Sager
Department of Psychology
University of Minnesota

Auke Tellegen
Department of Psychology
University of Minnesota

Paul van den Broek
Department of Educational
Psychology
University of Minnesota

Name Index

Page numbers for references are in italics

Spence, K. W., 14, *21*, 306, 317, 329, *341*
Spencer, H., 11, *21*
Spiker, V. A., 394, *432*
Stake, R. E., 7, *21*, 252, *279*
Stamm, J. S., 353, *374*
Stankov, L., 110, 115, *117*
Stephens, D., 258, 259, 260, 262, 268, *279*
Sternberg, R. J., 15, *21*, 47, 48, 57, *67*, 126, 127, 141, 143, 152, *163*, 207, *232*, 240, *279*, 281, *293*, 392, *434*, 442, *474*
Sternberg, S., 129, *163*, 319, *341*, 391, 406, *434*, 480
Stevenson, M. K., 376, *387*
Strange, W., 481, *491*
Strayer, D. L., 412, *434*
Strelau, J., 299, *341*
Stroop, 431
Suddick, D. E., 110, *117*
Sullivan, A. M., 286, *293*
Sutton, S., 336
Sverko, B., 177, *202*
Swets, J. A., 124, *163*
Syndulko, K., 414, *434*

T

Takemoto-Chock, N. K., 298, *337*
Tapley, S. M., 133, *163*
Tate, M. W., 121, *163*
Tate, R., 308, *341*
Taylor, D. A., 393, *434*
Tees, R. C., 481, *491*
Tellegen, A., 371, 372
Terman, L. M., 135, *163*, 203, *232*
Tessler, R. C., 74, *115*
Thackray, R. I., 304, *341*
Thayer, R., 335
Thissen, D., 167, 171
Thomas, J. E., 215, *231*
Thomson, G., 284, *293*
Thorndike, E. L., 4, 5, *21*, 281, 282, *293*, 435, 483
Thorndike, R. M., 121, *163*, 204, *232*, 477, *491*
Thornton, D. C., 404, *434*
Thurstone, L. L., 8, 12, *21*, 44, 45, 58, 59, 120, 130, *163*, 203, 205, 207, *232*, 252, 261, *280*, 281, 282, *293*, 435, 436, 442, *474*, 487
Thurstone, T. G., 58, 59, 261, *280*

Tiffin, J., 440, 451, *474*
Tilton, J. W., 7, *21*
Tirre, W. C., 248, 249, 250, 251, 252, 263, *279*, *280*
Tisak, J., 76, 90, 91, 113, *117*, 167, 172
Tolman, E. C., 297, 325, *341*
Toth, J., 304, *336*
Touchstone, R. M., 304, *341*
Travers, R. M. W., 4, *21*, 22
Tucker, L. R., 76, 89, 96, 113, *117*
Tukey, 139
Tulving, E., 23, *42*
Tupes, E. C., 299, *341*
Turriff, S., 312, 313, *340*
Turvey, M. T., 417, *434*
Tyler, L. E., 475, *491*

U

Underbakke, M., 481, *491*
Underwood, B. J., 248, 263, *280*, 281, *293*, 304, *341*, 477
Undheim, J. O., 205, 206, 209, *232*, 447, *472*

V

Vale, C. D., 169, *172*
van Arkel, A. E., 395, *433*
van Dellen, H. J., 395, 397, 398, 399, 408, 409, 410, 412, 415, 417, 418, 419, 421, *432*, *433*, *434*
van den Bosch, W., 466, 468, *472*
van den Broek, 274
van der Meere, J. J., 395, 398, 399, 409, *432*
Veltman, H., 404, *434*
Vernon, P. E., 205, 206, 207, *232*, 282, *293*
Vicente, K. J., 404, *434*
Vroom, V. H., 384, *388*

W

Walker, E. L., 308, *341*
Wang, A. Y., 249, *280*
Wechsler, D., 435, 436, 445, 446, 447, 460, *474*
Weiner, B., 317, *341*, 375, 376, *388*, 445, *474*
Weinert, F. E., 343, *374*

Subject Index